True to Yahweh Series **BOO**

GW01271740

GENERAL

The Story of Kalev
Son of Hezron

By Dr. Paul Christopher Woodward, PhDTh

TRILOGY
PROFESSIONAL PUBLISHING MEETS POWERFUL PROMOTION
A wholly owned subsidiary of TBN

General

Trilogy Christian Publishers A Wholly Owned Subsidiary of Trinity Broadcasting Network

2442 Michelle Drive Tustin, CA 92780

Cover design by: JP Staggs

For information about special discounts for bulk purchases, please contackt Trilogy Christian Publishing.

10 9 8 7 6 5 4 3 2 1

Library of Congress Cataloging-in-Publication Data is available.

ISBN: 979-8-89041-023-8

E-ISBN: 979-8-89041-024-5

AUTHOR'S NOTE

The names in this book are transliterations from ancient Hebrew into English. The Bible figures are the same, and actual Scripture is the framework. This is the raw adventure in the lives of *Kalev* (Caleb), *Hoshe'a* (Joshua), *Moshe* (Moses), and those closest to them.

This *is* a Bible-based historical novel. An attempt to "put skin on" the biblical people we inaccurately tend to idolize. This was the greatest supernatural rescue mission in history. These leaders were normal men and women like you and me. Many were obviously type A personalities. Some likely had ADHD and/or dark bouts of depression. Moshe was himself a hot head. He had serious explosive anger and self-control issues. Which probably added to the reasons his wife left him. Yes, the leaders in the Bible had faults like the rest of us. And like the true leaders of today, they flatly refused the job the first time it was offered. Elohim never chooses to use the most "spiritual" or even the ones with their "act together." See 1 Corinthians 1:26–27. Thank Elohim for that!

The Hebrew "captives" in Egypt ate, slept, bathed, and even went to the bathroom. The life of a Hebrew was dominated by pain, deep heartache, loneliness, betrayal, abandonment, etc. (Wouldn't yours be?) They were normal people in extraordinary circumstances, rescued by the same Yeshua we expect to rescue us today.

The Hebrew slaves in Egypt survived on what they could grow and barter. Egyptian beer was not like the cold, clear drink we see on TV. It was an unfiltered, fermented soup of yeast, wheat, barley, and well water. The dross, the grainy scum that naturally bubbles to the top, was mixed back in. Hebrew *emas* (mothers) gave it to their children because it was filling and kept them healthy. Today we know that unfiltered mixture contains protein, vitamin B, iron, niacin, riboflavin, and magnesium.

A quick note about Elohim. The names of Elohim, Yeshua, Yehovah, Yahweh, Elohim…are used according to their applied attribute. This author has studied, loved, talked to, yelled at, cried, and laughed with the King of kings for fifty-plus years. The Torah (Elohim's revealed teaching or guidance for humankind) is the first five books in both the modern Christian Bible and the Tanakh or Hebrew Bible. Yes, the Elohim of the Bible/Tanakh *is* all-powerful, loving, merciful, graceful, patient, kind, just, and quite funny if you care to listen. Yet, Yeshua's Word also portrays Him, at times, as a violent Elohim of war, defending the weak and helpless against evil forces, the quintessential "Mother Bear." We have *Elohim's* personality traits, *not the other way around.* Selah. (Stop and think about that.)

He's the same selfless Yeshua today as the I Am that I Am who created and breathed (caused to breathe out) man into existence. The Hebrew race has and will always be His chosen people. They are the original *main* "vine" the Gentiles, through belief in our Yeshua, are grafted onto. Elohim's acceptance of the Gentiles is evident in the minority of non-Hebrew who were among the children of Yisrael leaving Egypt. Through circumcision, following the visual Holy Spirit of Yehovah, and eventually obeying His Torah, they became Yahweh's chosen. Kalev (Caleb) was not a Hebrew by blood. Yet he ended up the prince of Judah. Neither was Rahab, and she was in the line of Christ.

The triune King of kings is timeless. He speaks from that point of view. His Word is past, present, and future, all at the same time. The most exciting account of Yahweh's Holy Spirit in the Bible is the pillar of fire.

> The [Yehovah] went before them by day in a pillar of cloud, to lead them on their way, and by night in a pillar of fire, to give them light, that they might go by day and by night: the pillar of cloud by day, and the pillar of fire by night, didn't depart from before the people.
>
> **Exodus 13:21–22 (HNV)**

King David used the same historical proof of Yahweh's Holy Spirit. "Reveal your light and your faithfulness! They will lead me, they will escort me back to your holy hill [Jerusalem], and to the place where you live." "Your word is a lamp to walk by, and a light to illumine my path" (Psalm 43:3, 119:105, NET). This same ever-present Spirit of Yehovah is available to us today.

Our Elohim is absolutely not politically correct, *woke*, or *approving* of every lifestyle. Nor does He change to fit a *socially acceptable* theology. See the fourth book of Moses, Numbers 23:19, Malachi 3:6, Paul's epistle to the Hebrews 13:8. We, Jews and Gentiles, are to adapt to *Him* and *His* purposes.

That said, my eternal Yahweh-Rohi adores the damaged one who comes to Him with nothing but a need for His life-giving rescue. He hates the sin yet died and rose out of the grave for sinners like me. The *Yəhôšûaʿ I* know loves to laugh and tease and even has a dry sense of humor. My "Warrior King" is the quintessential Abba. His no means *no*, but His yes means *yes*. He cries when I cry and patiently listens when I yell at Him. Sometimes His wise answers come in faint whispers, and at other times they're like putting your ear next to a blaring car horn. But for this author, His inspired wisdom usually comes in the moment or the last place I'd expect. He knows and provides for my needs and even a lot of my wants. He relishes our time together and excitedly awaits our next conversation. Don't mistake His patient kindness for passive weakness. Our Warrior King is ferocious when His kids are threatened or harmed by His *adversary* (Satan) and its minions. Which includes the demonically duped human hosts. Yehovah's corrections hurt as much as they need to. And sometimes His silence is infuriating.

To this author, Yehovah's existence and love are a given. It's like breathing. If we stop and overanalyze our next breath, we start to hyperventilate. Typically, we just take another breath, and another, and another... Our bodies have a silent confidence that the air is there, so it just breathes. So, too, is Elohim's presence. This is summed up in one of my favorite truths from the movie *City of Angels*. Nicholas Cage, portrayed as an angel, tells Meg Ryan's character, "Some things are true whether you believe in them or not."

My prayer is that Yeshua, the Warrior King's presence, is evident as you enjoy this first novel, *General*.

The NET and HNV translations were used when quoting scriptures throughout the book.

PROLOGUE

Now these are the names of the sons of Yisra'el, who came into Mitzrayim (every man and his household came with Ya'akov): Re'uven, Shim'on, Levi, and Yehudah, [Egypt] Yissakhar, Zevulun, and Binyamin, Dan and Naftali, Gad and Asher. All the souls who came out of the Ya'akov's body were seventy souls, and Yosef was in Mitzrayim already. Yosef died, as did all his brothers, and all that generation. The children of Yisra'el were fruitful, and increased abundantly, and multiplied, and grew exceedingly mighty; and the land was filled with them. Now there arose a new king over Mitzrayim, who didn't know Yosef. He said to his people, "Behold, the people of the children of Yisra'el are more and mightier than we. Come, let us deal wisely with them, lest they multiply, and it happen that when any war breaks out, they also join themselves to our enemies, and fight against us, and escape out of the land." Therefore they set taskmasters over them to afflict them with their burdens. They built storage cities for Par'oh: Pitom and Ra'meses. But the more they afflicted them, the more they multiplied and the more they spread out. They were grieved because of the children of Yisra'el. The Mitzrim ruthlessly made the children of Yisra'el serve, and they made their lives bitter with hard service, in mortar and in brick, and in all manner of service in the field, all their service, in which they ruthlessly made them serve.

Exodus 1:1–14 (HNV)

1

The heated winds lifted the fine red dirt and viciously flung it at the lone man struggling up the dune. The stinging grit burrowed into every pore and gash on his swollen and bleeding face. His parched throat and swollen tongue made it hard to breathe the dust-filled air. Too many places on his wounded body were still agonizingly open and oozing.

"They didn't hurt me. I hate, I hate, I—they didn't hurt me; they will never hurt me. Just keep climbing, just a few more steps," he hissed through his painfully clenched and chipped teeth.

At the same moment he crested the dune, the wind mysteriously ceased. Except for the dull ringing in his ears, there was silence, a consoling and familiar stillness. The sand, baked by the scorching Egyptian sun, was still too hot. He turned to face the river, and with the stiffness of a man twice his age, he tried to ease his hard-muscled frame to the sand. But he lost his balance and plopped down hard on his welted and bleeding backside. He gasped as a feeling of fire streaked from the back of his beaten legs.

But this was *his* hill, and he refused to let the pain or any diseased thought of Egypt invade this sanctuary. "Victory Peak." He exhaled in a long, ragged sigh of relief.

He might be a prisoner, but he refused to acknowledge that he was a slave, yet he owned this pile of sand and dirt as much as any Hebrew could really own anything in this miserable place. This mound was home, not where he slept or ate but his place of refuge. Here he experienced the only sliver of peace he could find.

Kalev hefted the large goatskin he'd pulled up the dune. He took a long pull of the heated water his body had longed for. This was his only reward for surviving another hate-filled day. Once, he'd tried to explain his reasons for the daily expedition up this hill. Still, Hoshe'a, his only brother/only friend, just couldn't or, rather, refused to understand his routine. Yet, to this bruised and bleeding, proud son of Hezron, the daily quest to the top of this sandy hill was as much a need for him as surviving. No—he reasoned—this was *how* he survived. Here he would try to relax and allow the physical wounds to start mending. Up here, there were no whips, no screams of pain, no one demanding he work faster. Best of all, sitting here on his sandy throne, there was no Hotep, his most hated enemy. Just the idea of that pompous Egyptian made his wounds ache even more. Equally important to Kalev, the top of this dune was where he would take his tormented thoughts and compartmentalize them. He'd cram most of his pained feelings into his imaginary clay urn and slam the lid shut. But Kalev would always ruminate on a couple of the more traumatic memories of the day. Decades ago, he'd convinced himself pure loathing was the secret, the fuel igniting his startling strength and self-control. This enabled him to conquer yet another day in a living netherworld. He'd taught himself to ignore the flaming sensation of the leather whips slicing into his sweat-slick skin. The Egyptian overlords seemed to gain a type of evil energy from the brokenness they created in others. "Never let them see you cringe. And absolutely no cries of pain, ever. Those Egyptian beasts hate that," he mused with a painful smile. Kalev harbored a defiant pride in denying the swine with whips their cruel pleasures. But this stubborn son of Hezron had a natural gift for bringing out the violent hatred in his captors. "Your defiance will cost you, slave," they'd scream as they beat him.

Staying unseen is the wise way to survive and avoid the leather of his oppressors. With that philosophy in mind, he'd always *tried* to forget about the screams of the other prisoners. "Act like they don't really matter," he'd futilely repeat to himself. But their pitiable screams remained a constant source of grief and hatred. For this son of Hezron, it was an instinctual impulse to protect the vulnerable, old, and weak.

This morning he'd, once again, failed to stop himself. When he heard her scream, he ran and bent over the old woman on the ground. "Son, stop," she'd pleaded too late. Kalev's defiant help resulted in the lashes meant for the woman and then much more.

Now, as Kalev balanced on the top of the dune, his throbbing head made him dizzy and nauseated. His recall of this morning's torture was hazy. He did remember Hotep screeching his sadistic laugh. With his twisted, evil grin, that excuse for a human called over three other taskmasters. They excitedly beat, whipped, and kicked him toward unconsciousness and, he'd hoped, death. Kalev mumbled to himself, "Those sadistic Egyptian fools never realized that for a Hebrew captive, death is a welcomed gift." Oddly, just before pain sent him into a familiar oblivion, he thought he heard Hoshe'a's voice. Then, like a cool breeze on a scorching day, the blissful darkness enveloped him, and he let go of his tortured reality.

Much later, covered in blood-caked mud, he was shocked into consciousness with an uncontrollable panic; he was drowning. He opened his eyes and realized that only the right side of his throbbing head lay in the mud with his right cheek in the slimy liquid. A few drops of the rancid water had leaked through his swollen and broken lips. Fortunately, he hadn't been breathing deep enough to inhale the muddy liquid. His primal instincts were to sit up. He began to lift his head out of the water; the searing pain in his neck brought back the vivid memory of this latest beating, and he froze. With his swollen right cheek barely above the water's surface, he forced the rest of his body to relax. Kalev had learned the hard way that if Hotep believed him to have passed out from the pain, the beating eventually ceased.

The solution was to remain lifeless as if he were still unconscious. So here, at the edge of the Nile River, probably next to the mud pits, he lay very still and listened for any sound that gave away Hotep's location. After what seemed like hours to his pounding head, the soft sound of the water lapping at his neck was all he could distinguish. He took his time, moving his head and shoulders very slowly, trying to ignore the ringing in his ears.

When he looked up, he realized the sun was low on the horizon. *I've been out for hours*, he thought. He turned his head as far as his bruised and strained neck would allow. To his relief, he was lying on the shore at the base of his sand dune. "How did I get here?" he hissed through cracked lips. With much pain and wooziness, he sat up. Everything he looked at seemed to have a ring of fog around it. To his left he could barely make out the two lines and hoof prints of a chariot in the wet sand. "I was probably dumped here before the river level rose," he guessed. A couple of feet up the bank, he saw the goatskin water bag. It took him several tries to stand on his wobbly legs. Then the dizziness overtook his will, and he fell back to his hands and knees and retched globs of dark red blood. When he caught his breath, he tied the waterskin to his belt and started the painful trek up his hill.

With his vision blurring, he fought to remain vertical. Every joint and muscle was burning with another day's misery. He willed his mind to think of anything but the ache. For now, he would allow the peaceful sight of the setting sun to dull his physical misery and inner torment. Kalev's dark purple right eye had swollen shut. Through his left eye, he watched as a pair of small fishing feluccas (single-sail wooden skiffs) slipped silently past on the perfectly calm river. Normally, he would enjoy the scent of the slow-moving water and the lush vegetation that lined the opposite bank. But tonight he couldn't breathe through his swollen and blood-filled nose. Still, Kalev found some relief in all the good memories in this place. After his ema died, Hoshe'a's ema, Carni, took the nine-year-old Kalev into her home as her second son. Kalev and Hoshe'a grew up like brothers.

He squinted at the shore below where he'd lain most of today. As boys, they'd played on that same muddy river bank. Back then, before the pain of the first whip, this dune looked like the top touched the sky. On that same shoreline, he and Hoshe'a had fought countless make-believe battles against the Nubian, Ethiopian, and Assyrian armies. But their greatest nemesis was Pharaoh Thutmose the First's army. Armed with sticks for swords, he and Hoshe'a had bravely advanced on the fierce hordes and had conquered them all. Kalev winced in pain when the memory made him smile. The likelihood of "great victories" had certainly been in their favor. Their opposing forces were made up of small bushes and young palm trees. The plants were eventually thrashed to death, leaving "their river bank" bare.

Hoshe'a was always the "battle planner." Before the day's combat began, He'd use his sword to draw his complicated attack plans in the wet mud. But as children, Hoshe'a's detailed planning seemed to take forever. Always restless, the boy Kalev just wanted to fight. Finally, after minutes that seemed like hours, Kalev, or "General," as Hoshe'a had nicknamed him, would disregard all of his brother's careful planning. Kalev, the boy warrior, would explode with frustration and run headlong into the fight. Hoshe'a usually tried to catch up, breathlessly yelling something about overwatch, flanking, or some such army term. This fight-to-the-death attitude made Kalev the natural leader of their ferocious Hebrew Army.

Hoshe'a grew up to become one of the few slaves allowed to assist in designing some of the huge granite carvings and underground treasure rooms of Ramses II. Kalev groaned. His own *fate* would brutally force him into manual labor in the mud pits.

Trying to clear the mental cobwebs, Kalev shook his head. This only served to increase the nausea. He violently vomited the blood-tinged hot water and groaned. He always saw pain as a physical weakness to be mastered.

But today seemed different. He wanted to give in to the unbearable agony. Kalev's vision began to darken, and he exhaled a long ragged breath. His limp body slumped to the side with his cheek plowing into the scorching sand. *Please, let me die*, was his last conscious thought.

As Hoshe'a climbed the dune to check on his friend, he abruptly stopped and just stood there. Silently he began to sob as he stared at all the open wounds, the bleeding welts, and the darkening bruises that completely covered his little brother. *I should have yelled sooner*, he thought.

Hoshe'a had always secretly admired his "brotha from another ema." But today, He helplessly watched his six-foot-one, 300-pound best friend take a beating that would have killed any other man. "Yahweh, please," he groaned loudly as he frantically ran, then knelt in front of the still body. "Yahweh, please," Hoshe'a screamed again at the cloudless sky. Kalev's left eye was swollen shut and partially buried in the sand. It only flinched as the right eye slowly opened.

"Where was *your* Yahweh today?" The slurred whisper shocked the frightened Hoshe'a. "What," Hoshe'a stammered. Kalev moaned. Though slurred, his words carried the usual venom when he talked about Yahweh. "I said, where was *your* Yahweh today when they were trying to kill your best friend?" For the first time, Hoshe'a took the words personally. It sliced into his heart like a hot knife. His eyes filled with tears of both relief and guilt.

Hoshe'a had brought a large basket filled with strips of cloth, vinegar, turmeric paste, *qaneh bosem* (marijuana) oil, and clean, cool water. He wanted to try and put his injured brother back together again. Hoshe'a spent the next hour and a half in tears, cleaning his friend's wounds and trying to force watery turmeric and *qaneh bosem* paste down Kalev's throat.

"That's all I know to do. Ema will have to take it from here." Hoshe'a helped him to a sitting position and gave him some more water. Kalev painfully coughed, then hissed, "Thank you." Hoshe'a knelt so he was face to face. Through barely controlled sobs, he blurted out, "Kalev, I'm sorry. I'm so sorry." Kalev tried to focus his one open eye as Hoshe'a struggled to steady his voice.

"I saw you today in the mud pit." For a moment Kalev stiffened and locked his good eye with Hoshe'a's. Because of the cuts and bruises, Hoshe'a couldn't see his friend's face turning a dark crimson with embarrassment. Kalev hated his own weaknesses but was powerless to stop the beating. He felt humiliated that Hoshe'a witnessed his lack of control. Kalev didn't know what to say, so he just looked down at the sand.

Hoshe'a could just make out the rare expression of sadness on his friend's face and started to choke up again. "When I realized that it was you they were stomping, I couldn't—I didn't," Hoshe'a stammered as the new sobs gushed out. "I am so very sorry, Kalev." Kalev looked up at his best friend and saw the torment in his eyes. Though his jaw felt sprained and his lips were deeply cracked, he whispered, "I'm the one that's sorry. I'm sorry you had to see that." After a long pause, Kalev slurred a grated hiss, "Why were you there?"

Hoshe'a took a minute to gather himself. "Panhs, the Pharaoh Ramesses' chief architect and my master, had me follow him to the number four brick furnace. It's the one on the hill just above your mud pit. Panhs was regaling the furnace manager with the story of Pharaoh's many praises of appreciation for Panhs' hard work on Pharaoh's latest statue." Hoshe'a shook his head in disgust. "I'm sure that's exactly how that diluted little sycophant remembered it. They were my designs, but whatever. That's when I heard the uproar from below the hill. I slowly backed away from Pahns' small audience and ventured a glance over the edge of the hill. At first, I didn't understand what I saw. Four mud-splattered Egyptians were cussing at and feverishly kicking a fallen ox that was covered with the watery clay. That's when I recognized the sound of your groan. I, um, I just stood there. I didn't know what to do. When I realized my little brother was being savagely beaten to death, I yelled at the four possessed Egyptians. I told them the ox they were trying to kill probably did the work of ten slaves. I asked them what they'd do when their output of bricks shrunk because of their childish cruelty."

From below, the four mud-streaked faces had glowered at the figure standing on the hill above. Hoshe'a was wearing robes befitting an assistant to the "great Panhs." The four slave drivers mistook Hoshe'a for a higher-ranking Egyptian official. With his hands on his hips, Hoshe'a glared back. Panhs, furious at Hoshe'a for interrupting his self-praise, stormed over to demand an apology. At the sight of the pompous Panhs appearing next to Hoshe'a, the four Egyptians quickly retreated from the pit. But before Panhs could start his rant, Hoshe'a turned and profusely apologized for his outburst, a tactic that always seemed to pacify his master.

Then Hoshe'a grew silent. He couldn't take his eyes from his lifeless little brother. He barely acknowledged Panhs' order to wait at the furnace for a new sample of brick. Panhs stomped back to his chariot and disappeared in a cloud of dust.

Hoshe'a stood there frozen with fear. Eventually, he realized he'd been holding his breath, silently willing his friend to breathe. Still trembling, Hoshe'a purposefully exhaled, then ran back to his own chariot and raced down the hill.

The large crowd of slaves, including the old woman for whom Kalev took the beating, stood in a circle around him. Kalev had tried to come to the rescue of each one of them numerous times. They had desperately wanted to come to Kalev's aid but were sure their help would invite further whippings.

When the helpless slaves saw Hoshe'a's chariot tearing down the hill, they quickly pretended to ignore and work around their fallen protector.

The chariot was still moving when Hoshe'a vaulted out and ran to Kalev. With tears streaming down his cheeks, Hoshe'a knelt in the mud and held his unmoving brother's head and shoulders in his arms. He rocked back and forth as he pleaded with Kalev, "I'm sorry; I'm so sorry. I didn't stop them—please, don't die, please…" The old woman forgot about Hotep when she recognized Carni's son. She sloshed through the mud and placed her hands on Hoshe'a's trembling shoulders. She spoke softly into his ear, "It's okay, my son; he's still breathing. Let's get him out of here before Hotep returns." As only a Hebrew *savta* (grandmother) could do, she ordered a couple of the other slaves to help Hoshe'a put Kalev in the deck of the chariot. She then took Hoshe'a's face in her hands and sternly told him to take and hide Kalev someplace safe and do it now.

Hoshe'a had mounted the chariot and frantically whipped his horse. With no idea where he was going, he just followed the river. About a mile up a familiar tributary, Hoshe'a realized Kalev's feet were dragging in the wet sand. He roughly reined in the frothing horse and slid sideways to a stop at the bottom of Victory Peak. He'd accidentally taken his friend to the safest place he and Kalev had ever known.

Kalev was slightly shorter yet twice as wide at the shoulders. His little brother's huge, hard-muscled body easily outweighed Hoshe'a by a good 150 pounds. As children, Kalev's mass had been a constant source of both admiration and intimidation to Hoshe'a. Now he stared at his broken and bloody friend partially curled up on the chariot deck. Kalev's breaths came in shallow gasps and painful moans. For the first time in Hoshe'a's life, his brother looked small and vulnerable. It broke his heart.

Hoshe'a knew he had to get back to the brick furnace before Panhs sent someone to look for him. He tried in vain to carefully lift his friend from the unstable chariot deck. Hoshe'a could only tug and roll Kalev's bulkiness off the back step. Kalev barely moved when he plopped in a heap on the hard-packed mud near the water's edge. Hoshe'a left his own goatskin of water next to Kalev. Through tears of shame, he climbed back onto his chariot and drove off.

Now, atop Victory Peak, Kalev slurred through his broken lips, "You brought me here?" Without looking up Hoshe'a just nodded. "Brother, you saved my life. Hotep would have come back and finished the job." "Hoshe'a, thank you."

When Hoshe'a heard his friend slur the words "thank you," he smiled. It wasn't the words as much as how they sounded. Hoshe'a started his typical inappropriately timed chuckle. And, as usual for Hoshe'a, he couldn't control the increasingly loud belly laugh that gushed out.

Kalev was stunned at first but quickly realized his slurring speech was causing Hoshe'a's laughter. He reached over, pretended to throttle his friend, and began his own odd-sounding chuckle. It hurt to smile, and his wheezing laughter only widened the bleeding cracks in his lips. The laughter felt like a soothing medicine. "Brother, you've a talent for making me laugh at the wrong times." Hoshe'a sat on the hot sand. "Kalev, my friend, we're, um, captives in Egypt; it's always the right time for a Hebrew, uh, prisoner to laugh." This carefully worded statement only served to fuel more laughter. Eventually the two men relaxed, and, with a rare sense of peaceful contentment, they silently watched the sun go down on the far side of the river.

Though Kalev tried to help, it took Hoshe'a three attempts to get his brother to a semi-standing position. With his arm around Kalev's waist, Hoshe'a strained as they staggered their way home. At one point Hoshe'a had teased, "You realize if you fall on me, I'm dead and Ema will be furious."

When they entered the small courtyard, Hoshe'a eased Kalev down to a flat rock next to the freshly dug well. Kalev leaned over and dry heaved. Without warning, Hoshe'a reached behind the well, lifted a large clay jar of cool water, and poured it over Kalev's head. The shock of the water on his wounds caused him to suck in a watery breath renewing the feeling of drowning. Amidst the resulting gasps, Kalev loudly coughed out a few Egyptian expletives. He tried to stand on his shaky legs but awkwardly plopped back onto the rock. Before Kalev could refocus his eye, he heard Hoshe'a start his usual dim-witted laugh.

The loud chaos brought Carni out of the house with a broom in her hand. In the bright torch lite, Carni immediately figured out what was happening. Kalev was obviously bleeding from multiple wounds, barely able to keep from falling over. His wet face was distorted with pain. And next to him was her son, sounding like a braying donkey, doubled over with laughter.

That her sons were both thirty-nine years old was beside the point. Carni was "the ema." Her maternal instincts took over. In six quick strides, she was standing between her two sons. In a blur of movement, she head slapped Hoshe'a's neck and turned to care for Kalev.

Hoshe'a, howling with laughter, hadn't seen or heard his furious little ema bearing down on them. His first clue was the not-so-gentle slap on the back of his shaved head. But Kalev had seen her fly off the porch. He always enjoyed watching her practiced "attitude adjustment" of Hoshe'a.

Carni knelt in the mud in front of Kalev. She looked at his darkly bruised eyes. She didn't need to ask the obvious questions; the glazed look in Kalev's left eye told her more than she wanted to know. Her own eyes started to tear. "Oh, little one"—the name she'd playfully given him as a child.

Carni cleared her throat. She quickly reminded herself that now was not the time for pity; it was the time for an ema's decisive action. Without looking at Hoshe'a, Carni barked her rhetorical question in a tone any military officer would have admired. "Would you help me get him into the house?" Still rubbing the back of his stinging head, Hoshe'a recognized that too-familiar pitch in his ema's voice. She wasn't asking!

Together, ema and son struggled to help Kalev into the house. They took him to a deck-level couch in the dining area. They both tried to ease him to the cushions, but between his wet skin, the slippery blood, and Kalev's substantial bulk, they could only guide his fall backward onto the pillows. He hit the cushions on his side, exhaled a high-pitched moan, and passed out. In the lamplight Carni knelt beside Kalev. The tears flowed freely. "Oh, little one, what have they done to you?" In the brighter torchlight, Carni saw many more bruises, a large lacerated bump over his left ear, and discolored swelling over his ribs. Hoshe'a had rarely seen his ema look this panicked. "Hoshe'a, get some water, my herb basket, some honey, and tear more cloth bandage strips *now*!"

2

Kalev remained unconscious, yet he vividly saw his memories play out in front of him. He watched himself and Hoshe'a as children. He could see them playing at the base of the dune. Their unscarred backs were darkened by the sun. It was barely sun up. The gray mist over the river cooled the early morning air. They had just started their pre-battle ritual when little Kalev noticed something in the mud closer to the water. Both boys instantly forgot about the "raging Egyptian army" closing on their position. The boys stared at the claw and wavy tail prints left in the mud by a rather large crocodile. Still bent at the waist, Kalev pointed. "I think he came out here and went back in over there. It couldn't have been more than an hour ago." Hoshe'a, himself still bent over, pointed at some ripples in the water and whispered, "He's right there, just waiting for us to take one step closer." Without another word, both boys started backing up the steep bank. Suddenly, Hoshe'a screamed, "Look out—there he is." At that same instant, Hoshe'a leaned back into the hill. And with both feet, he shoved Kalev in the back, sending him up and out over the water. Hoshe'a meant to quickly climb to the top of the dune and proclaim his victory. But, as usual, he made a costly mistake. He started to snicker, and then he couldn't stop laughing. This resulted in his slow zigzag up the sandy dune.

The shove in the back caught General Kalev so off guard, it seemed that time had stopped for the little warrior. He'd been catapulted almost six feet out over the water toward the imagined danger. His short frame tumbled through the morning air before his face slapped the water. As his head was going under, he heard Hoshe'a's screeches of laughter.

Hoshe'a, still laughing, heard the graceless splatter of his closest friend hitting the water. His second mistake was to slow his climb to look at the splash. For a brief moment, he felt real pride in having actually launched his friend out that far. Only then did he remember how General reacted to this type of prank. His pride instantly transformed into a rush of urgency to get to the top or anywhere else but there. He'd just turned uphill when he heard his much stronger friend breach the surface of the green froth. The eruption of churning water and the primal wail of his new foe signaled *Hoshe'a's* imminent danger.

General's graceless flop/dive into the shallow water forced his head into the soft silt. More than the need for air, his focus was on the rising emotion of sheer horror. He was convinced he was about to be eaten by a large, hungry crocodile.

In one fluid motion, he removed his head from the vacuum of the mud, sprang to his feet, and began to run as if the mud and water didn't exist. He couldn't remember taking a breath, only the high-pitched sound of terror exploding from his throat. In three rapid lunges, he landed on dry ground. He saw Hoshe'a laughing and stumbling uphill toward Victory Peak.

The General's screams of pure terror morphed into his battle cry, at least the best version he could manage. Propelled by revenge, the General only needed a few quick steps and a leap to cover the distance between the hunter and his prey. He violently slammed into Hoshe'a's back, driving his friend face-first into the sand and forcing the air out of his lungs.

Smiling at the memory, Kalev saw himself flipping Hoshe'a onto his back, moving to his head, and gripping Hoshe'a's neck in a headlock before his vanquished foe could take another breath. As the boy general slowly squeezed the neck and throat of his wheezing friend, Hoshe'a, with a look of fear growing on his sand-covered mug, squinted up at his conqueror's muddy face and croaked, "Do you give up yet?" The General's face went blank. Then the boys began to snicker, then laugh and howl.

By the end of the little warriors' day, they'd forgotten about the prank and celebrated numerous hard-fought triumphs by racing up to Victory Peak. Breathless, with their "blood-soaked" weapons held high, they would scream their battle cry in triumph. No matter how hard they tried to stay ferocious, the somewhat higher pitch of the young boys' screams would cause them both to start laughing again.

Finally, out of breath and their sides aching from laughter, the sweat-streaked boys would collapse to the sand. Strangely for the two friends, their celebration would give way to a sense of hushed calm. As the sky became dark orange, Kalev and Hoshe'a spoke in muted whispers until the two little warriors grew silent. A feat their parents would have sworn to be impossible. They laid on their sun-darkened bellies, heads in hands, and watched the hazy sunset. Or, as the General repeated every evening, "That's the great sun Elohim Ra sliding into his watery grave."

The adult Kalev's pleasant dreams morphed into the usual nightmares followed by black emptiness. At times, he could hear familiar voices, but they seemed far away like he was floating up and away from them.

It was the morning after the Nile turned red. Hotep wasn't aware that all of Egypt's water supplies had turned to blood. Because of that sycophant Panhs, he and his men started drinking earlier than usual. His powerful wine was laced with powdered mushroom, *qaneh bosem* poppy tar. Now he was suffering his customary terrible morning-after headache.

During the previous Pharaoh's reign, Hotep had been one of the highest-ranking generals in Pharaoh's army. He was the general over Ramses the First's chariot corps. Hotep and his men were battle-tested and experts at their deadly craft. After one of the Egyptian Army's more protracted victories, the pharaoh had publicly awarded Hotep, his "most violent general," a gold-plated Khopesh sword. It had the royal seal and the falling star symbol etched on the ornate hilt. The handle was silver, inlaid with rare clear-glass pieces and jewels. The sword was forged from "the metal of *shamayim*." Stars/rocks that had fallen from the sky, beaten into beads, and blended into mined iron ore. Its scabbard was made of thick albino lion cub skin. It was General Hotep's prized possession, and he was rarely seen without it.

It was even rumored the old fool slept with his *sheathed idol.*

Eight years ago, Pharaoh Ramses I, conqueror of worlds, was found dead in his bed. Hotep had always suspected Pharaoh's illegitimate son, the product of the pharaoh's indiscretion with one of his countless palace [illegible] chamber maids. The murdering prince took the throne that night. Ramses II knew the army was loyal to his abba, Ramses I. So, as his first order of business, the paranoid young viper immediately demoted all of the higher-ranking officers and ordered them to the pits, mines, and quarries as taskmasters over the loathsome slave labor. Hotep's shameful demotion and banishment would always haunt him. He hated the current [illegible] pharaoh but took out his usual drug-fuelled rage on the slaves, especially the Ox. One day in the pits, in one of his more vicious moods, Hotep used his priceless sword to carve his name, petoh, in the Ox's back.

When Hotep first saw "the Ox," his disdain-filled name for Kalev, he'd despised that [illegible] slave from the start. Hotep saw too much of his rebellious younger self in Kalev. Every time he thought he'd beaten that iron-willed, [illegible] bull into submission, the animal would be back the next day as stiff-necked as ever. Oddly, Hotep had never heard the [illegible] beast speak or cry out in pain. Yet the bitter ex-general always sensed the slave's underlying bull-headed defiance. It fueled Hotep's preternatural, white-hot resentment. Especially yesterday.

Hotep was too acquainted with death and the moans of the dying. He knew he and his men had stomped the life out of that [illegible] slave. Regrettably, it was the same day that [illegible] Ramses II had doubled the production output requirement. "[illegible]," Hotep painfully moaned to himself. But this morning Hotep didn't care about any of it. He'd let his eager subordinate slave driver control the pit today.

The bleary-eyed ex-general dipped his hands into his water basin, closed his eyes, and splashed it in his face. The taste, smell, and the burning in his eyes partly startled him out of his stupor. He took his dirty towel and wiped the fetid water out of his eyes. He looked down and was amazed to see his towel and the front of his robe completely covered in old, thick blood. "Not the first time," he slurred with a smirk. Hotep knew his personal slave wouldn't dare pull a stunt like this. It had to be that [illegible] Captain Narmer, Hotep's previous army second-in-command. That [illegible] Narmer thought Hotep's violent tirades were hilarious and tried to goad him into one as often as possible.

Hotep's head was throbbing. He groaned, drank the remaining dregs of the bitter wine mixture, dropped onto his pallet, and slipped into his wonderfully drug-induced dream world.

3

Kalev began to wake up. The room looked vaguely the same as just before he'd "passed out." He assumed that he'd been unconscious for an hour or so. Kalev saw a hazy image of Hoshe'a walking in. When Hoshe'a saw that Kalev was waking up, he yelled much too loudly for Kalev's throbbing head for their ema to come quickly.

When Carni ran into the room, she had tears in her eyes. She reached over and hugged Hoshe'a, who, Kalev saw, had tears in his own weary eyes.

Kalev parted his cracked lips to speak. His tongue felt like wood in his dry mouth, and when he attempted to ask a question, his parched throat seemed to close, and all he could do was cough. This only increased the pain level in his ribs, forcing him to try to sit up. However, he could only muster enough energy to raise up on one elbow. Before the coughing spell was over, Hoshe'a had put a cup of water in his hand. Hoshe'a and his ema tried to support Kalev's back with one hand and stack a couple of his sweaty pillows behind him with the other.

Breathing hurt, but coughing felt like fire blasting through his chest. He tried to drink more water, but this started another coughing fit, spraying water all over himself.

When his coughing finally quieted down and he was able to drink, he once again saw the exhausted Hoshe'a and Carni just standing there staring at him. "What?" he asked. "I guess I fell asleep."

Carni asked, "Little one, what do you remember?" Kalev looked at them both, a little puzzled at the question, but wheezed, "Well, I remember that this morning Hotep and his fellow jackals beat me into emptiness; my brother here saved my life and then tried to drown me." Hoshe'a began to protest and then caught sight of Kalev's split-lipped smile. "I guess my attempt failed," Hoshe'a chided and started to laugh. His laughter caught in his throat when he glanced over and caught *the look* from Carni. Kalev tried to laugh but only coughed.

Carni stepped closer, knelt beside Kalev, took his hand, and in a trembling whisper, said, "Little one, all of that happened ten days ago. We thought you were dying; you wouldn't…" Her tears began to flow freely. Hoshe'a knelt beside his trembling ema, put his arm around her shoulder, and added softly, "Kalev, she never left you alone." Carni whispered hoarsely, "And when your brother came home from the palace, he would care for you until he left the next day." Kalev was astonished. "Thank you both," he croaked. These words seemed hollow considering their self-sacrifice, but the dizziness was mixing up his thoughts again. The last time he'd felt cared for, his ema was still alive. This was his last thought before he collapsed into a fitful night's sleep.

It was two days later before Kalev could sit up and eat something solid. Carni's turmeric and herb paste did relieve *some* of the pain in his chest. The gashes on his face and back were starting to dry up, and against Carni's advice, Kalev devoured four loaves of her fresh bread. The next evening he was sitting out on the front portico when Hoshe'a walked through the front gate. When he saw Kalev leaning back against the front porch wall, a look of fear crossed his face. Hoshe'a sprinted to his friend, grabbed his arm, and swung him through the front entryway into the house.

"What the [illegible] are you doing," Hoshe'a yelled. Kalev weakly jerked his arm away. "It's okay; I'm feeling stronger. Ema…" Hoshe'a cut him off. "No, *you're* dead, you [illegible] ox." Kalev just stared at Hoshe'a with a confused look. "It's time we talked. Sit! Now, where's Ema?" he whispered. Kalev cautiously answered, "She went to the marketplace." Hoshe'a quickly dragged a chair next to Kalev's. "Our ema wouldn't *appreciate* me telling you this. She thinks it's too soon to burden you with the news about the recent chaos. However, you need to know the danger you're in." Kalev didn't respond, but he was keenly aware of the growing concern in Hoshe'a's voice.

"Kalev, yesterday I rode to the furnace to get another sample of Panh's bricks. I overheard Hotep as he was walking down to the Pit. Kalev, he was asking another taskmaster to send him four more slaves to replace the one he *killed* a couple of weeks ago. *Brother, you're dead.* Most of our people in the village believe you never recovered."

Unknown to Hoshe'a and Kalev, Carni had just returned from the marketplace. When she heard their voices, she waited outside a couple of feet left of the doorway. She wasn't spying on them per se. *After all, it's a Hebrew ema's responsibility to know all that's going on in her house.*

Kalev smirked. "Have you told anyone you tried to drown me and then left me for alligator food?" Hoshe'a didn't smile or acknowledge the sarcastic jab. "Kalev, I'm serious. You didn't see the countless tears our ema cried when you wouldn't wake up. I will *not* allow you to do that to her again. So stay out of sight at least during the day. Do you understand me, General?" Kalev accepted the verbal chastening as he stared at the deck. Kalev's voice sounded shaky. "I do understand. Hoshe'a, I wanted to thank you again for all you and ema sacrificed for me. I, um…" Kalev looked up at Hoshe'a and thought he saw tears forming in his eyes. Hoshe'a shook his head. "Brother, I may be Ema's flesh and blood, but I swear you've always been her favorite." Kalev dryly replied, "And that's as it should be." Without warning Kalev reached over and landed a solid punch to the center of Hoshe'a's chest, almost knocking him out of his chair. Kalev just laughed as he watched Hoshe'a doubled over trying to catch his breath. Carni, hearing the dull thud, knew exactly what Kalev had done to Hoshe'a. She started to move to the door when she heard Hoshe'a's raspy voice. She froze and continued performing her "responsibility." When Hoshe'a finally caught his breath, he smirked. "Don't forget, little brother. I know where you sleep." Kalev smiled but noticed Hoshe'a's hesitant expression. "Hoshe'a, you're terrible at keeping a secret. What else?" Hoshe'a glanced at the door and then exhaled a groan.

"Kalev, on the day you were beaten, did you notice the color of the river, the smell?" Kalev thought for a moment. "When I woke up drowning, thank you very much, I couldn't see very well, but I do remember it tasted like metal." "Little brother, after unloading you at the water's edge, not in it, I went back to the number four furnace. From that hill, I could see this dark red water flowing *upriver*." Now Hoshe'a had Kalev's full attention. "Upriver?" asked Kalev. "Yes, it was so bizarre that I rode down to the water on my way back to the palace. Brother, even before I bent down to touch it, I could smell death. Kalev, it was blood, not red water. The Nile had become a river of blood. Pharaoh's palace had the same sickening smell. Even the water pots, filled from the royal wells, were overflowing with blood." Hoshe'a abruptly stopped his update. He hesitated, and Kalev knew his brother was holding something back. "Hoshe'a, it's okay; you can tell me." He took a deep breath, checked the door, and groaned again. "Okay, Kalev, two weeks ago, Panhs arrogantly warned us servants that the day before, a shepherd had stormed into the palace and *demanded* an immediate audience with Pharaoh. This sheepherder was yelling at the palace guards to let him into the great hall. 'They should have cut off his head,' Panhs had added. The Great Pharaoh heard the upsetting chaos and commanded the guards to let the dirty Bedouin enter. Brother, the shepherd, uh"—Hoshe'a nervously cleared his throat—"Panhs said the shepherd loudly stuttered that he was the son of Hatshepsut—his name, it was…" "Hoshe'a!" Carni screamed. Both men jumped in their chairs.

Though Carni was four foot eleven on a good day, her ominous presence seemed to fill the doorway where she stood. She respected her two sons as men of this household. However, it was an ema's duty to determine what was harmful for her sons. Both men knew that tone, and there it was, "the look." As they had done for almost thirty years now, Kalev just smiled, and Hoshe'a cringed, as both knew what was coming. "Hoshe'a, out here *now*, please!" Kalev started feeling lightheaded and growled, despising his weakness. He reluctantly headed back to his pallet to lie down. As his bald head hit the pillow, he clearly heard the infamous, unanswerable question all emas yell at their kids, "What were you thinking?"

4

About a week later, in the evening, as Hoshe'a walked through the front courtyard gate, he noticed Kalev standing by the far corner of the house. The huge man silently motioned for Hoshe'a to follow him back to his barn. Kalev led him into his stall and shut the door. He sat on his cot and pointed at his chair. "Sit. You wanted to tell me something important last week before Ema stopped you." Hoshe'a grimaced and nervously glanced at the door. "Listen, Kalev, I was wrong to bring it up. So instead, um, let's talk about how, since you're dead, you can stop shaving your head. You can finally let real hair cover up some of those dents in that melon head of yours." Hoshe'a nervously chuckled. Kalev silently glared at his fidgeting big brother. "Kalev, please, it's too dangerous, or, um, I promised Ema…" "Hoshe'a!" Kalev boomed in the small space.

Hoshe'a's little brother took a long, slow breath to calm himself. Kalev used to really enjoy spending time with Hoshe'a. But for the last year it had seemed like Hotep had robbed him of this small pleasure too. Now he felt like the least frustration would send him into a raging tirade. He hated feeling like this—so angry all the time.

"Hoshe'a, brother, our big scary ema's not here." Then Kalev's eyes narrowed as he carefully studied his brother's expression. "Brother, you're my best friend…" Hoshe'a interrupted in a useless attempt to lighten the mood. "I'm your only friend." Kalev *forced* an appeasing grin. "That's a fact, but what is so terrible that it scares you!" Hoshe'a groaned and rubbed his face. "My day just went from bad to worse! [illegible]. Okay, but please stay calm. And don't act like your typically explosive self. It will probably hurt, but pretend you're a rational, clear-thinking adult." Kalev growled menacingly. "Brother, if you don't tell me right now, you'll see firsthand how 'explosive' this rational, clear-thinking adult has become. Now speak!" Hoshe'a's shoulders slumped in defeat. He took his own deep breath, and the words surged out so fast that they were almost incoherent.

"Remember I told you about the shepherd demanding an audience with Pharaoh? And that the shepherd stuttered his name? Kalev, that shepherd's name was, um, Prince Moshe." Hoshe'a reflexively sucked in a breath and screwed his eyes shut. He wordlessly chided himself, *Once again, you bonehead, you've said way too much.* So Hoshe'a regretfully forced himself to sit there, face in hands, and weather the inevitable *haboob* (violent dust storm) that was about to hit. But there was only a terrifying silence. After moments that seemed like hours, Hoshe'a developed enough courage to glance through his fingers at his best friend. Kalev's face had morphed into a horrific mask of insane rage. Hoshe'a inadvertently shivered. *That look would even cause Hotep to tremble*, he thought.

For Kalev, hearing the name of the man he held responsible for his abba's murder seemed to suck the air out of his lungs. He froze in place as his hands began to shake. It'd been over thirty years, but in his mind's eye, he was watching it play out in real time. Yet, as his memories became his immediate reality, time seemed to stop. He thought he could actually smell his ema's fresh barley bread.

He saw his beautiful ema ask his seven-year-old self to take a meal to his abba at the royal baker's house. Kalev watched his short but stocky frame sprint down that hard, dusty road. The little boy darted around the rear corner of the royal baker's huge house and almost fell through the bushes as he skidded to a stop. Next to him were four adults cowering behind the same hedge. What the boy saw terrified him to the core.

His bleeding abba was lying on the ground in front of a long row of ovens. The little boy's kind yet strong hero futilely tried to shield his face from the baker's whip tearing into his skin. Kalev remembered the *shed* (evil spirit) like hatred in the baker's eyes. It was the only time he remembered hearing his abba cry out in pain, and it was terrifying.

The numbed seven-year-old boy opened his mouth to scream stop, but he was interrupted by an ear-piercing adult war cry. Then a third man streaked into the boy's view from his right. In one fluid motion, the white-robed man's left hand ripped the whip out of the baker's hand while simultaneously driving his big right fist deep into the surprised tormentor's face. There was a sickening cracking sound.

The wide-eyed little boy watched as the lifeless baker crumpled face-down in a quickly growing dirty puddle of blood and brain fluid. The faceless but muscled third man had caved in the baker's face with one blow. Kalev didn't watch the stranger drag the baker out of sight.

The adult Kalev relived the intense nausea as a terror-filled wave of complete powerlessness tried to drown the little boy. The adult Kalev watched again as his severely wounded abba dragged himself through the fetid puddle to the closest palm tree. Then the boy's tender heart imploded. He saw his abba's silent tears mix with blood, then stream down his cheeks. With supernatural courage, his beaten and bloody abba painfully propped himself against the thorny tree. This was Kalev's hero, the strongest man he'd ever known. A proud man respected and adored by his friends, workers, family, and even Queen Hatshepsut.

The boy sobbed. Kalev's little self splashed through the dark red puddle. He could still smell the acrid stench of the thickening bloody ooze. The boy yelled through shuddering sobs, "Yahweh, please help," as he sprinted to his abba. The groaning Hezron pulled his young son down to eye level. The boy howled through his tears, "I should have stopped him, Abba, but I'm not big and strong enough. Abba, how can I make it better? I have to help you. I gotta be stronger..."

Hezron gently cupped the boy's face in his trembling hands. "Son, I love you so much. Kalev, you *will* be stronger, and you *will* help others in need of that strength. Son, I'll be okay; I just need some water to clean up. But, Kalev, promise me you'll never tell your ema what you just saw." The boy wordlessly nodded. He never did tell his ema or anyone else.

The young Kalev fearlessly ran into the baker's house and drug out a sloshing water jar taller than himself. The frantic boy had to raise up on his tiptoes to ladle out the cool well water, one cup at a time. He poured it on every one of his abba's wounds. Hezron smiled through the pain. He knew his crying little son was desperate to "make it better." To the adult Kalev, the rest of the day was a blur.

Yet the memory of the subsequent evening's violent attack was seared into every fiber of his mind, will, and emotions. He clearly remembered his ema sitting next to the boy as his abba Hezron sat in his usual place at the head of the table. They'd just finished a meal and were repeating a prayer of thankfulness to Yehovah.

The adult Kalev resented the memory of his foolish, childish feelings of closeness he thought he'd felt for his parent's impotent Yahweh. Kalev felt acid rise in his throat as he recalled how his parents incessantly prayed to their deaf Elohim. They'd pray for help, protection, and deliverance from this putrid existence of pain and great loss. And where was their Yahweh *that* night?

Kalev watched as the little boy's semi-safe life was ruthlessly destroyed. They all jumped when their front door exploded inward. To the boy Kalev, the sound was like a nearby thunderclap. Screaming Egyptian guards filled the room. He wouldn't learn the Egyptian language until he was forced into the mud pit. But the Egyptian pigs' screams were obviously laced with foul curses. "How dare they swear at my abba," the boy growled under his breath. Even as a child, Kalev had always had a big attitude. He saw himself grab the bread knife and leap onto his chair. No one was going to hurt his abba again if *he* could help it. Had it not been for his ema grabbing his arm and forcing him back down, he would have lunged toward the first sneering soldier. But the huge armor-clad Egyptian pigs never even looked his way. Then, as the helpless child watched, the Egyptian soldiers violently dragged his silent abba into the street. They stomped the life out of his hero, his abba. That night, the boy ran to Victory Peak and screamed his oath to the stars, "*I will* be stronger! *I will* kill every one of those L\(|||)✝ɘ9 Egyptian butchers." That was the first time he'd ever cussed. It was also the beginning of a lifetime powered by deep-seated hate. Which, in turn, caused a misguided refusal to cry for his abba.

A year later, his ema explained that the guards had accused his abba of killing the royal baker and hiding him in the sand. But Kalev knew the truth. Eventually, Kalev discovered that the real murderer, "the third man," was called "Prince Moshe."

Kalev snapped out of the flash of memory and growled, "Prince Moshe." Hoshe'a flinched again. With his eyes still closed, Hoshe'a thought he heard a faint scratching on the deck in front of him. Kalev had bent down and reached under his cot to retrieve his abba's recently sharpened Khopesh sword. He leaped to his feet and then burst out of his door with a blood-curdling roar. The sword felt very light—the grip seemed perfectly molded for his hand, and he knew it was forged and purposed for this exact moment in time.

The proud son of Hezron was usually very fast for a man his size. But the rage appeared to cause his muscled legs to churn twice as fast. Conversely, to his mind, time had slowed by half. His surroundings blurred by, but he was mentally too busy to notice. Kalev's conscious mind wasn't even aware that his mental picture of Moshe was really the taunting face of Hotep. But in his hate-filled rush to get out, he'd forgotten to ask Hoshe'a where Moshe stayed at night.

Kalev shot through the back gate to the courtyard, rounded the front corner of the house, and picked up speed as he sprinted toward the front gate. He was feverishly calculating the exact amount of level sword ark, neck placement, and depth it would take to remove this Moshe's head.

Suddenly, out of nowhere, Carni appeared five yards in front of him with one hand on her hip. And with the other, she pointed her bony finger at his face like a straight, double-edged sword. "*Stop*!" she screamed. It took all he had to slide to a stop and not plow through her. Her unmoving finger ended up about an inch from his nose. Kalev slowly growled in an ominous voice that sent a shiver down Carni's spine. "*Move*!" The tiny but fierce ema ignored the fear and defiantly stiffened. Carni matched his growl. "I told you to *stop*!" She took a deep breath as heart-pounding tears leaked down her cheeks. "Kalev, your ema was my best friend. On her deathbed, she warned me this day would come. She made me promise to keep you from killing that man. Son, it wasn't his fault; he was trying to save your abba." If Kalev's mind hadn't been so flooded with hate, he'd have asked how *she* knew his abba's killer's intentions. It took a full twenty-five seconds for Kalev to order his thoughts enough to calm down a little. Carni, acting much bolder than she felt, never took her eyes from his. She instinctively knew that he'd found out about Moshe being close by. And Hoshe'a would pay dearly for that.

With hundreds of conflicting emotions clouding his thoughts, Kalev pleaded in a voice that sounded like a scared little child. "My ema said that?" Carni's motherly heart broke. She nodded as her tears flowed. Pushing her advantage, she bravely reached across to remove the sword from his pulsating right hand. So shocked by the last ninety seconds, he'd unconsciously tightened his death grip on the sword, and his numb hand refused to let go. Kalev stiffened his resolve and slowly shook his head. He looked down for a split second to see her hand on his white knuckles. He argued to himself, *She doesn't understand. I* have *to kill that man; I* have *to avenge him for Abba's murder*. He opened his mouth to object, but Carni beat him to it. With her scowling eyes still locked on his, she screamed at the top of her lungs, "*Noooo*!" He took a deep breath. "Ema, he…" But her scream cut him off again. "Little one, let go *now*!" They glared at each other for an eternal thirty seconds.

Suddenly, thirty-plus years of emotions, the ones he'd thought he'd sealed in a large mental urn and hidden in a dark place, exploded from his eyes. The towering man's booming voice broke, "But he was my abba…"

The ever-present memories, years of excruciating torture, the sudden interruption of his life's mission, and decades of pent-up black bitterness surged from his gut. Kalev stood there shaking.

Blushing from a self-conscious humiliation, he feebly tried to object. "I couldn't help Abba then, but now I can make it right. I have to…" Then he sensed something deep inside break. And for the first time since he was seven years old, tears of grief began to pour from his eyes. He mourned his abba's and ema's untimely deaths, his stolen innocence, and the stinging reality of his imprisonment in this land of the *sha'dim* (evil spirits).

Still trembling, Kalev dropped to his knees, held Carni tight, and sobbed uncontrollably, all the while loathing himself for this public display of weakness. But he couldn't stop it either. The fifty-eight-year-old little Hebrew ema was about a third of the size of her mountain-of-a-man son. Yet she reached up and pulled his sweaty head down to her shoulder. She whispered through her own tears, "I know, my little one. I know."

Carni was still trembling from the emotions dump. Two minutes ago, she'd put on her bravest "ema" front and cringed at the blind hatred in Kalev's eyes. She wasn't even sure he'd see her in time to stop. But she knew her boys. She knew that once Kalev committed that misguided, rage-fuelled murder, his soul would never survive. Her "little one," Carni's endearing nickname for Kalev, would be lost to the darkness and never return. Carni knew she was the only person on earth who dared to stand up to her giant son. But she'd kept her promise to her best friend. She'd protected their son from himself. She sighed to herself, *A true ema's job is never done*. So she stood in the middle of that courtyard, her hand gently stroking her son's hair, and quietly cried with him. She gladly held him until he was ready to let go.

Hoshe'a had known better than to follow his howling best friend. He didn't *want* to know what was about to happen. He was content to silently sit there in blissful ignorance. That was until he heard the oddly loud and commanding voice of his ema scream, "Stop!"

Kalev's older-by-two-months brother jumped out of his chair, afraid of what Kalev might have done in his frantic state of mind. Not sure what to do, Hoshe'a ran around to the front of the house and hid behind a pillar. Eventually he peered around the column. There stood his very big friend casting a shadow over their ema. He winced when his ema boldly reached for Kalev's sword. Hoshe'a began to step from around the pillar when he heard his little ema roar, "Little one, let go now!" Hoshe'a stopped in place. He knew Kalev had glanced his way and saw him stupidly motionless near the pillar. He was sadly fascinated to see this huge man break down into tears and fall to his knees. He quickly turned away and headed back inside. He remembered Ari's abba, Adir, saying, "It's not shameful for a warrior to cry, but it's a very private matter."

The sun was setting as Kalev, now absolutely exhausted, let go of Carni and wiped the snot and tears from his face. He looked into her bloodshot eyes as she whispered, "Breaking the seal on that jar will serve you well in the days to come." Kalev just nodded. *How did* she *know about my mental jar?* he wondered.

That night they all sat down at the evening meal. The afternoon's chaos in the courtyard was never discussed nor spoken of again. If Kalev hadn't been so emotionally spent, he would've enjoyed the foreboding silence between Carni and Hoshe'a.

5

Yehudah, the son of Abraham, and his family had settled in Egypt 400 years prior. They'd taken possession and worked a large portion of eastern Goshen between the cities of Tanis and Ramses (Avirus). This part of Goshen was handed down from generation to generation until it was bequeathed to Kalev's abba, Hezron. So Kalev's family *was once* quite wealthy.

Hezron was well known and respected as an honest seller of wheat, barley, corn, melons, alfalfa, grapes, dates, lemons, and spicy peppers. He'd sell his produce to his workers at half price. Then to the other Hebrews in Goshen. But the greatest quantities were sold to the Egyptians and foreigners visiting Egypt. Hezron was especially honored by Queen Hatshepsut. She found his ongoing dealings with the royal palace to be very honest (a rare trait in any society) and always paid him double what he'd asked.

Kalev's family originally owned about 3000 acres; their smallest parcel bordered Hoshe'a's ancestral land. Kalev's abba had many people working for him, and he paid them very well. After his abba was murdered, Kalev's ema, with a grieving heart, had to begin selling the land just to survive. Over the years, acre after fertile acre was sold off. Their original 3000 acres had dwindled down to Kalev's current forty-eight usable acres. They were directly beside and behind Hoshe'a's home. Attached to the back wall of Hoshe'a's house was "Kalev's stall," as Hoshe'a often teased him.

It was little more than a four-stall barn. Three of the stalls had open fronts facing the acreage. In the first stall was Ox, Kalev's long-time bovine friend. He kept Ox well hidden behind a tall false wall of hay bales. As far as Kalev knew, Ox was the only living creature in Goshen more powerful than himself. The Egyptian priest's guards had pillaged all of the other oxen and cattle in Goshen over two years prior.

In the second stall was a family heirloom. Kalev's *saba* (*grandabba*) had handcrafted an unusually large and well-built six-wheeled wagon. His abba had used it to carry large quantities of wheat to the marketplace. The third stall was where they kept two ox yokes, four heavy metal plows, and multiple scythes. Hezron had collected various planting and harvesting tools from all over the known world.

The fourth stall was his. It was completely enclosed—sort of—and contained a simple cot next to a cooking fire pit. In addition to a large animal trough, Kalev had a single chair. When he didn't bathe in the canal, Carni would fill the trough with turmeric-and-Harmal-laced water. He'd bathe in the trough at the end of the more traumatic days. Which so happened to be every day for the last four years.

Hezron, though gone for thirty-some years, had very loyal workers and friends. Now, those same good and proud men were either kidnapped, beaten to death, or reduced to Egyptian slave labor. Out of pure loyalty to their abba's friend Hezron and his son, Kalev, the worker's sons worked Kalev's remaining forty-eight acres. The boys had decided amongst themselves that in the planting season, they would harness Ox, usually next to the smallest boy, and plow, plant, and harvest. But for Ox's sake, they'd only work after sunset. On the moonless nights, oil lamps were placed on both sides of the row they intended to plow, and then they'd aim Ox between the lamps.

One night, as a practical joke, Hoshe'a had informed the boys of Kalev's long-time nickname. Due to his massive bulk and commanding presence, the title stuck, and no matter how much Kalev objected, they insisted on calling him "General."

Kalev had always been a light sleeper. Since his teens, he'd wrestle with reoccurring nightmares. Many of the bad dreams were reliving the more painful days of torture. And then there was the endless parade of the lifeless, muddy faces, the countless corpses he was forced to carry to the "death wagon." They were someone's ema or abba or savta or *saba*.

But the dreams that tormented his unconscious mind the most, the ones he refused to think about in the light of day, were the memories of the thousands of lifeless little broken bodies of children. Some no more than five or six years old. They were usually injured castoffs from the pharaoh's mines at Wadi Hammamat. Already half dead, they were thrown into the mud pits. Because of the fetid, strength-sucking mud and blistering heat, most of the little ones didn't last more than a day. Then one of the many Egyptian pigs would whip Kalev again until he pulled the small lifeless bodies out of the mud and put them on the wagon. Some days the number grew to over a hundred, and it felt like that was his only job. Body after body, face after face. Then, as he awoke to another pain-filled day, the night terrors would evolve into nonstop self-accusations. *Why didn't you help them, Kalev? Aren't you strong enough yet? You could have done so much more...*

Since his last brush with death, in addition to the other nightmares, Kalev's mind replayed a very specific dream almost every night. First, he saw Hotep's face glowing with fire, screaming at him with his usual unintelligible drunken profanities. Then the scene would change to the pale, surprised face of his tormentor, sightlessly staring at him as it sank into darkness. No matter how many times he told himself it was pure weakness to be scared, he continued to wake up drenched in sweat, promising himself he'd kill Hotep before he'd allow that [illegible] pig another chance to whip him.

Just before dawn, in the middle of one of the more violent dreams, he was startled awake. He heard voices or, rather, a voice. It sounded like military orders being yelled at soldiers. "Hotep," the barely conscious Kalev growled. He sprang from his cot and cautiously tried to peer between the door slats. He couldn't see anything in the semidarkness. *How has he found me? It doesn't matter, Kalev. Kill him or die trying*, his fuzzy mind commanded. Kalev quickly stumbled back to his cot, reached underneath, and pulled out his abba's sword. With a polished Khopesh sword in one hand and the scabbard in the other, the half-asleep son of Hezron crashed through his door. All of that black oozing hatred for Hotep came screaming out in what would later be known as "the General's war cry." After the first couple of unsighted strides forward, the howl of rage stuck in his throat as it all came into focus.

There, only fifteen yards beyond his stall, stood eighty-three wide-eyed little boys. It took Kalev a few seconds for his mind to process the scene. He must have looked like an idiot to these boys, splintering his stall door and screaming like a madman, "Arghh."

Feeling like a total fool, Kalev sheathed the sword and sheepishly continued walking forward. He self-consciously whispered to the familiar-looking leader of this group. "Hi, um, Ari (Lion), is it? Um, I'm sorry about that little show of insanity. Um, you gave your orders with the authority of an Egyptian captain. I was ready to tear your head off." The teen proudly grinned at the comparison. "Thank you, General, Sir." Instantly, eighty-three pairs of little heels slapped together, and eighty-three high-pitched voices yelled in unison, "General, Sir." Now Kalev *really* felt like an idiot. "I'm sorry to interrupt your, um, maneuvers, is it?" The teenager nodded. "Yes, Sir." "Well, um, please continue." Kalev flinched when the teen yelled in his face, "Yes, Sir!"

Once Kalev felt the embarrassment ebb, he became curiously impressed. The boys were assembled in perfect ranks and columns. Three separate groups, or companies, as "Captain" Ari later explained. All three companies had one boy standing in front. Captain Ari had three lieutenants standing behind him, each in line with their company. Following Kalev's *assumed order* to continue, the captain turned to his lieutenants, whispered some instructions, and told them, "Get your people moving." Ari proudly watched as his "men" carried out his orders. The lieutenants relayed their orders to the company leaders (First Sergeants). They, in turn, yelled to their platoons their specific orders. Kalev smiled when he heard the new recruit company's First Sergeant scream, "All right, you wannabes, we'll complete our mission from last night, then clean up, eat, and get some sleep. Move it, you pukes!"

As each First Sergeant marched their companies in different directions, all four officers walked over to Kalev and stood at attention. Okay, he felt like an idiot *again*.

Kalev couldn't have known that the sight of him smashing through his door with his sword drawn had made a lifelong impression on every boy there. The "troops" would be talking about that first morning for decades to come. The boys agreed they would rather be following than see that scary face coming at them. Honor and respect for their "warrior general" were now carved in stone.

Kalev was embarrassed. These boys had mistaken him for a real soldier. The four officers stared at him as if waiting for an order. Kalev shrugged as he quickly thought back to his make-believe army days with Hoshe'a. He remembered some of the jargon. "Um, stand at ease." Ari smiled. "Sir, why don't we go to the TOC, um, our tactical operations center, and have some bread and beer? We're all a little tired."

As they walked through part of Kalev's field, he noticed that one of the platoons had started to pull up the remaining dry cabbage leaves. He knew they'd store them and then add them to Ox's feed. He turned to Ari. "You know, those cabbage leaves give Ox terrible gas. I woke up one night, and my nose was burning from the stench." The boys laughed.

"But seriously, I really appreciate all the work you've put in to keep these fields producing. This sword and these fields are all I have left from my abba." Ari nodded. "My abba always spoke very highly of your abba, Hezron. He told us about how he and your ema helped our family and so many others. So, it was a given that when I got old enough, I'd gladly help in your fields." Kalev nodded his thanks, then said, "I wish I could have helped more. But up to a couple of weeks ago, I was, um, a little occupied." They all laughed. "Oh, and I'm sure my big-mouth brother told you of my death. So, since I'm a ghost, I have all the time I need to do more work around here." They smiled politely, but all four of them shook their heads. Ari spoke for the group. "Thank you, Sir, but that won't be necessary. When our people aren't drilling, they work in the fields. It has the added benefit of teaching them responsibility for something bigger than themselves. We teach them that a good work ethic builds a strong character, and it's a person's character that determines their destiny. It's part of the core values we try to drill into their heads." Kalev was silently amazed. *Character, core values? Who is this kid? He sounds more adult than* I *do*. Not knowing what else to do, he nodded his approval. "Well, um, Ari, what's your rank?" The fit teen smiled. "I'm a captain, Sir." They all stopped walking so Ari could introduce them. "These are my best friends and lieutenants, Akiba (Jacob), Yadin (Yah will enact Justice), and Yadin (Power)." Not knowing what else to do, Kalev shook each of their hands in turn. "Well, um, officers, I'm impressed. My ema had a hard time just keeping two boys in line. From what little I've seen, you guys are doing an incredible job with these boys." All four teens beamed with pride. "What's your secret?"

They slowly walked toward the dense grove of neglected date palms. The ones that marked the southern border of Kalev's fields. Ari explained, "My abba, once a farmer, was forced into metalworking for the pharaoh's infantry. As a boy, I used to watch the soldiers form up, drill, and perfect their fighting skills. A couple of the soldiers were kind to my abba and me. They taught and drilled me on multiple sword, knife, bow, and hand-to-hand fighting techniques. I secretly trained with those two soldiers on their off-duty days until I was fourteen. That's when a sergeant saw them teaching a Hebrew slave how to slice a throat. The lessons ended immediately. In fact, the next morning that same sergeant came to my abba's shop looking to *forcefully*, um, *invite me* to go to work in the quarry. I'd been working in your fields the night before, so I wasn't home yet. That morning, my abba and I agreed I needed to… disappear during the day." Kalev smiled. "Smart plan." Ari motioned behind them. "As Yadin, Yadin, and Akiba became 'mud pit age,' they, too, needed to disappear." The weary-looking eighteen-year-old captain shook his head. "Somehow, parents from all over Goshen found out what we were doing and started sending their boys for us to 'disappear' them too. At first, it was only a couple at a time. Then, well, you just saw what our numbers are up to. It was obvious from the start that the only way we were going to keep that many boys from absolute chaos and being found out by the Egyptians was to require military discipline from every one of them. Surprisingly, the parents have told us they are thrilled with what they've seen." Kalev was intrigued with these kids' forward thinking. "How do you keep them motivated to follow orders?" Kalev asked. Yadin spoke up, "Simple, it's obey our orders or head to the mud pits. Or worse, head home and tell your ema you *didn't want* to follow our instructions. Every boy in this army dreads their ema's fury." Kalev smiled knowingly.

They stopped in front of the dense stand of old date palms. They'd never been cultivated, so the dead palm fronds covered the entire tree all the way to the ground. The trees had grown so close together, they looked like a solid wall. Kalev started to suggest they go to the right if they were headed to the river. But stopped when Ari removed a rope hidden in the branches of the tree to his left and then pulled down. The branches on the tree right in front of Kalev swung upward. It looked like a gaping mouth ready to swallow them whole. Kalev smiled and followed the four boys into the mouth, which quietly closed behind them. They walked forward about five yards down a perfectly trimmed arched passageway through the old growth to a small stack of logs they used as steps.

The steps led up to a solidly built platform. The large deck was made of similar-sized logs, expertly lashed and nailed together, then covered with evenly gapped aromatic cedar planking. Kalev guessed it measured around ten by twenty yards. The surrounding six-foot walls were made of tightly woven palm fronds. A very large linen covering formed a peaked roof and hung about ten feet above a huge table in the center of the area. Kalev let out a low whistle. "This wasn't here when I was a kid." Ari laughed. "Well, actually, Sir, when we started clearing out this area, we found a hollowed-out space and two woven mats a couple of kids had left here decades ago." Kalev smiled. He'd completely forgotten about this place. Ari nodded at Yadin, then continued. "I'm told it was called their…" "Outpost," Kalev interrupted. Ari smiled and glanced at Yadin. He handed Kalev the old wooden sign Hoshe'a had carved when they were nine years old. Kalev smiled at the memory. Ari continued, "When we finished building, we naturally named it 'the Outpost' to honor our chief architect and builder, Captain Hoshe'a." Kalev's eyebrows shot up. *Captain Hoshe'a?* he silently wondered to himself.

There were four separate sleeping stalls along one wall. Kalev pointed. "Do you sleep here?" Yadin nodded. "Yes, Sir, almost from the beginning we realized that it wasn't safe for us or our families to sleep at home, even at night. As you know, Sir, the Egyptians are not shy about breaking in and taking whatever or whomever they want." This caught Kalev off guard, and he became overly defensive. "What did Hoshe'a tell you about me?" Yadin hurriedly apologized, "I'm sorry, Sir. I didn't mean to offend you. Both of my parents and little brother were taken in the night about six months ago. I was here at the time." Kalev nodded. The humiliating torrent of emotions a couple of days prior had left him on edge more than usual. He sincerely apologized, "No, *I'm* sorry. That kind of wound never seems to completely heal. And I'm sorry for your loss." The boy scowled at his feet. "Thank you, Sir." Ari quickly changed the subject. "In the last couple of years, your brother and your ema have told us a lot about you. It wasn't gossip; they're both extremely proud and protective of you.

"Once, Captain Hoshe'a told us about how you saved a dying little boy by hiding him underneath the death wagon. He said you brought him home and your ema took care of him. He said you were a lifesaving hero." Kalev's cheeks flushed with embarrassment. He hated being singled out and praised for what came naturally. And he certainly was *not* a hero. Kalev silently stood there and fidgeted, feeling ineptly self-conscious.

Ari quickly broke the awkward silence. "Um, let's eat." All four of them attacked a large pile of fresh bread that had suddenly appeared in the center of the large table. Kalev didn't remember seeing anyone else on the platform, and the bread wasn't there when they first climbed up. He let it go but kept an eye out for the little food *malakhs* (angels).

Ari took a drink of the pungent beer. "Many of our troops were orphaned at a young age. 'The Outpost' is the only real home they've ever known." Kalev was curious. "If they're orphans and this is a secret, how did they get here?" Yadin laughed. "Your ema finds them and brings them here." He grinned at Ari. "Sometimes the orphans make better troops than the rest of us. They immediately appreciate what we provide them—food, clothes, and a bed."

Yadin chimed in, "Most of them consider us their family. Last week, a squad leader in our new recruit training platoon, Corporal Abraham, overheard one of the recruits grumbling about his parents *forcing* him to join and that he didn't like working in the fields. But before the corporal could, um, *adjust the troop's attitude*, one of the smaller orphan troops walked up and slapped the complainer hard on the back of his head. Then he began to verbally tear into the taller kid. He told him he was a pampered little [illegible]. Then the little warrior started jabbing his finger into the whining recruit's chest. He said the [illegible] should appreciate what they have here or leave. That they were living like pharaohs compared to living on the streets, eating what they could steal from the markets and sleeping in cattle stalls or worse. Our impressed corporal Abraham finally had to intervene when the orphan troop drew his sword and told the grumbler to get out of his [illegible] AO before he [illegible] skewered his [illegible] like a roast pig. The other troop shut up, and the corporal promoted the orphan troop on the spot." They all laughed.

Ari added, "More importantly, we instill purpose beyond just survival. They learn to trust and be trusted, to be a valuable part of a team, a true brother to the other troops." Kalev was astounded. "Ari, you make *me* want to join. I *am* kind of an orphan," he chuckled.

Ari glanced at his lieutenants, then soberly nodded. "The rest of us see our parents occasionally, but always after dark. Some of the parents bring food and even clothes at night." Ari grabbed another loaf. "Sergeant Carni recruited eleven of our troops' emas to bake bread every day and deliver it to Ox's stall in the evening. After sundown, we secure it and bring it here." Akiba handed Kalev another loaf of fresh bread and refilled his cup. Kalev noticed the beautifully carved and padded dark wood chairs and the massive table in front of him. "Was this carved from a single piece of wood?" Yadin nodded. "According to Captain Hoshe'a, Pharaoh had ordered the chief royal carpenter to send a large contingent of his 'woodworking minions' to cut and carry a giant blackwood tree out of the Nubian jungle. They sailed it up the western coast of the Red Sea to the port at al-Jarf. The chief carpenter knew the tree was too big to haul across the desert. So he was at the port when the tree arrived. It took the man a month to carve out these chairs and table. It was supposed to go to the home of the pharaoh's favorite [illegible], I mean, chambermaid. But we, um, found it and brought it here." Kalev didn't feel he had the right to know the specifics of how they "found" it. It was obvious that this whole operation had taken a lot of work and planning, and he was an outsider.

Kalev looked at the teens. "I'm curious—how do you recognize a sergeant versus a private or whatever?" As the other's mouths were full, Ari untied a leather string from around his neck. It had a brightly polished round piece of thick gold hanging from the center. He handed it to Kalev. It was expertly inscribed with the words, "Captain, Battalion Commanding officer." Kalev appreciated the expert engraving. Ari swallowed and then spoke up. "My abba works with another, um, captive prisoner." Kalev nodded his thanks to Ari respectfully using the huge former slave's own terminology. "The man's name is actually Dan, son of Dan from the tribe of Dan." Ari chuckled. "He's the chief engraver for the Egyptian Army. Dan said that every one of the thousands of Egyptian soldiers wants their swords and knives engraved with one self-exalting accolade or another." Akiba chimed in with a mouth full of bread. "Three of Dan's younger sons are sergeants in Heh Company. The three older ones are each a company's First Sergeant." Ari nodded. "They've been with us from the beginning. So Dan refused any payment for his work. He told me it was easy to, um, forage some of the gold used in the palace. He said that to the Egyptians, gold is as common as sand. He said, 'Of course, to those [illegible] Egyptian pigs, the thousands of slaves that die in those gold mines every year was a trivial issue.' Dan said that it would always be a privilege to create these designation medallions."

Yadin had come up with the idea of small, easily identifiable rank, company, and battalion insignias etched on a small oblong silver medallion. Each new recruit, as part of his graduation out of the advanced fighting skills company, was issued his initial insignia. The officers had started their own tradition of adding their names to theirs. This small token had become a source of amazing pride for every troop. Each time a soldier was promoted, he would formally hand down his old rank to the next in line. For every single troop, the pride in *their* army would swell with every promotion.

But he was intrigued with this table. Long ago, his abba had instilled in the boy Kalev an appreciation for wood, metal, and stone carving craftsmanship.

Someone had carved into the tabletop a detailed relief map of his and Hoshe'a's property. The map covered the whole six-by-fourteen-foot table surface and was coated with a glistening clear resin. He noted that the contours of the peninsula, his forty-eight acres, and Hoshe'a's ten acres of farmland were carved in precisely scaled detail. He saw the old-growth palms. But they looked undeveloped. *Smart*, he thought. There was a miniature of Carni's house. His attached barn even had Ox's head sticking out from under the roof. At the southwestern edge of his land was his dune. A little handwritten sign stuck out of the top of his hill. "This is the General's *private* dune. Stay away or die." Kalev smiled. "This is incredible craftsmanship." Ari nodded. "One of our troop's abba volunteered to carve out our AO, um, our area of operations. He's that same royal carpenter's slave and carved this out of spite for his arrogant master."

Ari read Kalev's quizzical expression. He instinctively knew the huge man wasn't going to ask about their foraging missions, so he hesitantly volunteered the confidential info. "We send out at least one platoon of, um, foragers almost every night. They usually *find* what we need, and we store the, um, *surplus*." As if on cue, Kalev heard three low growls. "Are those camels?" Yadin scowled and shook his head. "Absolutely not, Sir, that was the sound of our 'surplus' from last night's foraging mission." Kalev really liked this guy.

Ari glanced at the other three, who soberly nodded in unison. "Sir, um, we understand that she's your ema, but we'd prefer this information not to get back to Sergeant Carni. Captain Hoshe'a thought it was wise to keep these missions on a need-to-know basis. The captain said our foraging missions have, um, *troubled* quite a few people in the palace, especially the pharaoh and his temple priests. So, for security reasons, mission-critical personnel are forbidden from talking about these operations to anyone, including family members or other civilians. Captain Hoshe'a specifically stated that your ema doesn't have a need to know." Ari smiled. "Speaking off the record, Sir, I think the captain is worried your ema would accuse and *correct* him for being a bad influence on us. Her *corrections* can be, um…" Kalev chuckled, "Yeah, I know. And that's exactly what she'd do."

Yadin smiled. "But she really appreciated the large crates of foreign herbs, spices, and bolts of linen for bandages we gave her last week. She didn't even ask where they came from." Akiba frowned and shook his head. "She's a Hebrew ema. She already knew or at least suspected." Kalev nodded. "She always knows."

He looked around the TOC again. Kalev was amazed at the deceptive construction. "Has she ever seen this place?" Yadin spoke up. "Sir, she's also in charge of our evening meal prep and service. She's been here from the beginning." The boy's eyebrows knit as he concentrated, then corrected himself. "She's officially been a part of this army for the last eleven months and five days.

"Additionally, Captain Hoshe'a has been an integral part of this army's development for the last year and two days. The 'foraging' missions were *his* idea. Without his foresight, I suspect most of us would've been dead by now." Ari smirked. "No disrespect intended, Sir, but your brother is smarter than he looks." Kalev chuckled. "Yeah, he hides it so well that I've never noticed." They all laughed.

Ari grew serious and nervously cleared his throat. "Your brother, um, Captain Hoshe'a, sort of tells us which one of the pharaoh's minions is expecting a shipment of, um, different things. Every evening he delivers a map, designating when and where a caravan might be spending the next night. We never forage anything that would normally make its way to our people." Ari smirked. "Captain Hoshe'a, um, well, he said that Pharaoh owes our people 400 years of back wages and we're only collecting a fraction of that sum." Kalev chuckled. "Foraging—I like that term." The relieved boys exhaled.

Kalev cleared his throat and half-heartedly forced a tone of seriousness into his next words. Yet, they sounded more severe than he intended. "I'm very impressed, *but* I have two questions." The boys stopped chewing, and their pleased smiles faded. "First, why am I the only one in Goshen who didn't know about all of this? And secondly, does my brother really outrank my ema?" Kalev took a drink to hide his smile while the other three stared at Ari. To his credit, the captain responded confidently, "Sir, we were told not to tell you about our overall operations. We were, um, *strongly instructed* that you didn't need the added burden." Kalev chuckled to himself. *Strongly instructed. That's a very careful way to label Carni's ultimatums.* "And yes, Sir, officially, your brother outranks your ema. But Sergeant Carni was our unofficial medicinal sergeant from the start. There isn't a troop here she hasn't repaired with her herbs and bandages at least once. That said, um, as you can probably guess...as the army's head ema, she *unofficially* outranks everyone." The other three nodded. "Sergeant Carni deserves to be an officer, but we weren't sure how we'd train her on the military aspects at this point." Kalev was downing his second cup of the nasty beer when Yadin spoke, "Plus, Sir, teaching your ema how to use a knife could be detrimental to Captain Hoshe'a's future as an abba." Kalev gagged, and beer shot out of both nostrils. All four teens were on the deck howling with laughter while Kalev belly laughed between coughs.

Eventually, they all retook their seats, and Ari continued, "Captain Hoshe'a helped to write our first training manual. And like I said, he designed and oversaw the building of this outpost. He even had the foresight to build our sleeping area and drill deck large enough to accommodate 1800 troops." Ari unconsciously lowered his voice and shook his head in wonder. "Sir, from the outside, day or night, you can't tell this outpost even exists. Captain Hoshe'a designed that concealed door we went through. There are three others on the north side and three on the riverside. There's even a gate large enough to get our fishing skiffs in and out. We actually had an Egyptian patrol walk on the small beach between the river and here. We had a fire going in the sunken fire pit, and they still walked by." Ari pointed out the tallest trees. "Those Egyptian pigs never knew how close they'd come to an instant death. Sixteen overwatch archers would have turned the kill order into a competition to see who the best bowman was.

Ari pointed at a parchment hanging next to the entrance they'd walked through. "The number of enemy kills is listed next to each troop's name on the official kills parchment. The two troops with the highest kill counts are promoted." Kalev looked at Ari wide-eyed. The teen captain shrugged. "So far, we've only had two serious skirmishes. But we train our troops to fight, and we fight to kill, to survive."

Kalev sat there stunned. He could tell this boy wasn't talking from a hypothetical point of view but from firsthand experience. He wanted to ask for details, but again, Kalev felt he didn't deserve to know. He wasn't an officer or even a soldier. He knew in his gut he was *way* out of his depth. General was just a stupid boyhood nickname. Kalev silently chided himself, *You're absolutely not a leader. You can't even control your own temper*. Then he remembered something Hoshe'a had read to him when they were boys, "Brother, if you think you're a leader, but no one's following you, you're just going for a walk."

Ari yawned. "So far, we haven't lost a troop." He paused to look at each of his lieutenants. "But my abba said we needed to prepare ourselves to lose troops in every battle. Because if it hasn't happened yet, it absolutely will." The overburdened young captain looked at Kalev with pleading eyes. "Sir, I've thought a lot about what my abba said, but how do we *prepare* to lose somebody we're responsible for?"

The boys saw Kalev's eyes glaze over like he was reliving a memory. He spoke in a quiet, sad tone. "Boys, I can only speak from my own experience. To the Egyptian pigs, a Hebrew's life is worth less than dirt. We're only a means to an end. And death is an ever-present expectation. Maybe even a welcomed probability. I *always* felt responsible for every person in my mud pit. I was *never* prepared for any one of them to die. I tried so many times to protect them, to trade places with them. But it was never enough. Too many of my people were whipped or tortured to death right in front of me." Kalev's voice dropped to a whisper. "I wasn't strong enough to save them. They were my people; it was my job to protect them, but…" No one spoke. "I can still see every one of their faces…thousands of faces."

Kalev forced himself to blink the memories away when he realized three of the wide-eyed teens were staring at him. He was instantly embarrassed at showing his weakness. He wiped the snotty tears from his chin. "I guess that was my overly dramatic way of saying you can't prepare for that gut-ripping sense of loss when one of your people dies. You can only train to fight with your entire being…still, from what I've seen, the end results are really out of our control." Those last words made his stomach churn and left a very bitter taste in his mouth.

Kalev heard a scratching sound that distracted him from his dark thoughts. Yadin was feverishly recording Kalev's insights on a large parchment. He intentionally whispered the final words as he wrote, "…are really out of our control. In summary, according to the General, life's hard, then we die—deal with it." The seventeen-going-on-thirty-year-old scribe looked up from his notes knowing everyone had heard his whispers. The proud son of Hezron scowled at the kid. *Is this puny boy making fun of me?* he wondered. As if the teen could read his mind, Yadin shot the General a barely noticeable sly grin and winked. The deliberately sarcastic life lesson obviously surprised Kalev, and they all started belly laughing again. Kalev liked this kid's brilliantly dry sense of humor.

As the morning wore on, Kalev became more and more at ease and fascinated with Ari and his lieutenants. After eating every loaf in sight, Ari instructed the other three to get some sleep. The three lieutenants pushed their chairs back and stood in unison. He didn't know why, but their actions caused Kalev to automatically stand and face them. The three teens shook Kalev's hand and welcomed him. Again, Kalev didn't know how to respond, so he self-consciously nodded and thanked them back. Ari watched the exchanges and quietly sighed his relief. "And so it begins. Thank You, Yahweh!"

6

"Sir, would you like to see the rest of the Outpost?" Kalev smiled. "Lead on, Captain."

They walked to the TOC's expertly woven eastern wall. Kalev was surprised when Ari pushed on a hidden seam in the middle. Two wide gates silently swung outward, and they started down the four cedar log steps.

Ari spoke so quietly, Kalev had to lean in as they walked. "As you know, Sir, the Outpost is surrounded by dense and very tall old-growth trees. Captain Hoshe'a measured it at approximately thirteen acres. This open area is about seventy-five yards wide and runs the length of the grove." When Kalev stepped through the double doors, he saw what looked like an enclosed village. Numerous boat sails covered with dried palm branches were used as awnings. They covered the majority of the area. In the center of this little town was a very large, mud-brick-lined fire pit. Like the raised TOC, this entire area's deck was built on side-by-side half logs flattened on one side. Along the dense outer tree walls were many one-pallet stalls, each one looking slightly different from the next. Kalev could tell the stalls at the far end of the "Outpost" were occupied and silent. "That's Aleph Company down there; they're sleeping now. Heh and Bet Companies are due in shortly," Ari whispered. "Sunup silence is strictly enforced for both security and the physical need for continuous sleep."

Ari continued his tour. Kalev asked in a barely audible whisper, "The large open area at the far end?" Ari nodded. "That platform is our weapons training, conditioning, and assembly area." Kalev shook his head. "It's huge." Ari nodded. "Captain Hoshe'a said it measures out to 9600 square yards. Like I said, he designed it to hold the weight of 1800 troops.

"Though we all have metal swords, we train with weighted wooden ones to keep the noise down at night." For a while Kalev took in the enormity of the Outpost and the projected growth for this boy army. Ari stepped away and quietly conferred with a younger teen. *Probably a platoon sergeant*, Kalev guessed. He was watching the tired but confident young captain when a heavy wave of emotions threatened to drown his mind. It was the *too*-familiar weight of being responsible for others. He was unexpectedly empathizing with the teen captain. Somehow, Kalev realized that this eighteen-year-old felt responsible for every kid here. That he constantly worried about his troops' protection, whether there was going to be enough food for their next meal, if their training was sufficient, and on and on and on.

Ari walked back and looked more deflated than ever. "Sergeant Lamech just informed me that seven Hebrew children barely made it to your ema's house last night. They all collapsed in her courtyard from exhaustion and hunger. He said they'd walked from Hierakonpolis and they hadn't eaten in days. [illegible]. That has to be over a hundred miles from here. I mean—we've had boys make it here from

Tanis. But never from that far away. The sergeant said they told your ema that their parents had given them a rough idea of where to go. They said that as far up the Nile as Aswan, Hebrew emas are talking about a child refuge in Goshen. Arghh." Kalev experienced another surge of compassion well up in his gut. He hated all these *emotions*. Kalev suddenly experienced a gut-level fire that surged into his throat. Advice that sounded foreign—like it was someone else's idea, gushed out.

"Son, you *can't* do this alone, even with your three lieutenants. Find the other true leaders in this army and promote them. Delegate those responsibilities that are threatening to swallow your mind whole. Some people are better suited to cooking or fishing in addition to fighting. Have your officers and sergeants categorize and capitalize on each troop's strength. Each company needs more of one category of troops than another, depending on the individual platoon's primary missions. As your numbers increase, your natural tendency to control every detail needs to be conquered. Sometimes our worst enemy is ourselves. Captain, force yourself to trust your subordinates to get the job done." Following his verbal explosion, Kalev was left feeling like he'd way overstepped. "Whoa, where did that come from?" he mistakenly thought out loud. The slack-jawed, wide-eyed Ari stood there slowly shaking his head. "I don't know, Sir, but it's exactly what I needed to hear. That was very wise advice. Thank you." Ari looked like he'd finally found some relief. "Sir, our daily muster is just after sundown. We eat afterward. It would be an honor if you attended this evening's troop muster (assembly)." Still trying to figure out the source of his impromptu outburst, Kalev self-consciously shrugged. *Okay*.

Once they were back in the TOC, Kalev whispered, "Captain Ari, I can see you're exhausted. I only have one more question." "Of course, Sir." "You said there's a kill list, and you've had two *skirmishes*. Are those metaphors for intense training or something?" Ari glanced at his sleeping lieutenants and then at the door to the passageway they'd originally used. He silently motioned for Kalev to follow him. Kalev noticed the large parchment hanging on the wall next to the entrance. "Sir, officially, we only train to keep the troops in a military mindset. That's what we tell any parent who asks." He yawned, then continued to whisper. "Unofficially, we've *used* our training two times with lethal success." The serious look on Ari's face answered Kalev's next question.

"One night, a squad of our perimeter guards was patrolling the northern border of your fields. In the distance they saw eleven black-robed thieves ride up and start loading their horses and camels with the bags of wheat stacked next to your threshing deck. The platoon in charge of the harvest was scything, baling, and loading the wagon at the other end of the field. Our perimeter squad leader sent a runner while he and his squad flanked the robbers and then hid in the closest unharvested portion of the field. We'd recently adopted a standing order to be armed every time you left the Outpost." Ari continued, "Akiba and I ordered Heh Company to silently surround the threshing deck and hide. Yadin and I followed." Ari shrugged. "The two of us walked up to the *Egyptian-speaking* thieves and told them to put the wheat down. And, of course, the eleven fools raised their swords and ran toward us. It was only our intention to disarm them, yet when they swung those large scimitars"—Ari pointed at a very large sword hanging on the wall beside Akiba's stall— "our hundreds of hours of training took over. When we finished, three of our soldiers were injured and bleeding badly, so their squad leaders took them to your ema's." Ari paused. Kalev's eyebrows raised. "And?" Ari yawned again. "Let's just say that part of your fields will have very fertilized crops for a long time to come. We brought the horses and camels back here. Each scimitar was awarded to the troop who dealt its owner the final death blow. They were promoted, and this 'kills list' was created."

"The second skirmish happened the night the Nubian raiders stole Ox." This really surprised Kalev. "They did what?" Ari smirked. "That you didn't even know Ox was missing is a compliment to these troops.

"About a month ago—in fact it was during the nights you were really sick and your ema was taking care of you in the main house. That night I'd gone out with Aleph Company; we had just started our night's work when Yadin came running and told us Ox wasn't in his stall. I ordered the platoon to fan out and find him. It wasn't long before Aleph's now First Sergeant reported that he'd seen at least five Nubians floating Ox across the river on a large raft. As far as we were concerned, they'd broken into our house and taken one of our family members." *That's exactly how* I *would feel*, thought Kalev. "All three companies assembled on the training platform. We decided that Heh would scout ahead. They'd use the fifteen three-man boats to quietly cross. The rest of us would use the secured rope to swim across. On the other side, Heh Company used mud to cover their faces. It was a full moon, and the mud didn't reflect light. As we all watched, the whole company just vanished. They'd trained to use the landscape to disappear. It took about fifteen minutes before a muddy figure rose out of the water right in front of me. Akiba's runner reported that it looked like the Nubians were preparing Ox for a ritual sacrifice. He added offhand, 'Oh, and the Nubians outnumber us two to one.'

"Once our other two companies crossed, we decided to split up and flank them on all sides. The good news was that it appeared the majority of them were drinking some kind of strong wine by the bucket full. The bad news was that every one of them had a spear or dagger. Our plan was to cause them to chase Aleph Company south while Heh Company fell in behind and attacked them from the rear. When they turned back to fight Heh Company, Bet would rotate in and attack them from the rear again. Three of the newest privates from a platoon in Aleph Company were tasked to secure Ox and use the same raft to float him back across the river.

"The battle lasted for a while. The enemies with the daggers were the first to fall, as their daggers were the same size as our training weapons. But the arrows were another story. When a platoon ran away, the Nubians would chase and shoot their arrows. This would've been lethal had it been daytime and they'd been halfway sober. Each time our troops reversed course to attack from the rear, they'd retrieve the spent arrows and use them as secondary weapons.

"A couple of weeks later, we were told by one of the parents that this particular horde of Nubians was responsible for killing several Hebrew families in northeastern Goshen. They'd sacrifice an animal, bathe in its blood, and then raid and pillage the closest farm or settlement. Which, that night, would have been your ema's home. We piled the bodies onto their remaining six large raiding rafts. Aleph guided them down the river until it was straight enough to send the death rafts on their own way. Yahweh was with us that night. We ended up with one broken arm, a broken finger, and thirty-two troops a little sliced up and needing bandages. But Ox and your ema were safe." At the mention of Yahweh, Ari heard Kalev suck in a breath. Out of the corner of his eye, the teen saw the big man had stiffened, and his clenched fists were beginning to shake. But the captain wisely ignored the General's reactions. As the eighteen-year-old warrior finished his account, Kalev blew out a long breath. "I'll have to thank your troops personally."

Kalev left the TOC so Ari could sleep. He promised to return for the sundown muster. Kalev headed to the main house.

He and Carni spent the rest of the morning talking about the army of boys they had living on their property. At about noon he went back to his barn and saw that Ox already had food and his trough was full. Kalev went to his stall and unsuccessfully tried to calm his mind enough to sleep.

That evening, Kalev showed up just before sundown. He found Ari beside the drill platform. Kalev chuckled at how relieved Ari looked when he saw him. Ari smiled. "They're finishing up their personal time. That's the daily allotted period they use to clean their teeth, shave each other's head, etc."

The muster took about twenty minutes. It covered the night's abbreviated mission assignments and the introduction of advanced training evolutions. Then Ari gave instructions on proper military bearing and included protocols for their new salute. He stressed, "People, salutes are only for inside our perimeter. A simple salute could tip off the enemy and paint a target on your officer's back. Roger that?" Eighty-three higher-pitched voices screamed in unison, "Roger that, Sir." Ari and two of his lieutenants winced at the same time. Reflexively, all three scanned the Outpost's walls and prayed there wasn't a patrol nearby. Ari rebuked himself for not making sure the entire AO was scouted before every muster. "Add that to the list," he sighed. Ari caught Akiba's attention. The commanding lieutenant of Heh Company smiled and mouthed the words, "Already done, as always."

The muster was quickly followed by a meal of fresh bread, fish, leeks, wine for the officers, and thick Egyptian beer. Kalev was amazed at the number of loaves passed out. The teen captain walked over and handed Kalev an overflowing plate and a large cup of wine. Ari retrieved his plate and sat on the edge of the drill deck with his general and three lieutenants. Kalev asked, "So that's a muster?" Ari nodded, but Yadin snickered. "That was a *cleaned-up version* of a muster." Ari smirked. "We kind of informed our sergeants that they wouldn't be using *this* muster to dress down their troops." Yadin nodded. "Yeah, it can get a little, um, boisterous." All four officers chuckled.

Kalev ate and watched the ninety-plus troops below. They ate, laughed, and went back for seconds. After a while Kalev leaned sideways and whispered to Ari, "This whole afternoon I couldn't stop thinking about you and your troops being battle-tested. Ari, I'm not trained. I haven't fought in any battles. [illegible]—I didn't even know what a muster was until this morning. Son, I'm not a leader, and I'm definitely not a general, but I'd like to…" Ari held up his hand to interrupt. He stood tall on the edge of the stage until the troops went silent. Kalev glanced at Akiba, who shrugged.

Ari's voice boomed in the silence. "Troops. I want to officially introduce you to our General Kalev." Hoshe'a and Carni watched from behind a corner as Kalev's face turned to a deep crimson with embarrassment. Hoshe'a started to snicker, but a rib shot from his ema's elbow stifled his need to laugh at Kalev.

Ari thundered even louder, "This warrior of warriors. He repeatedly took on himself the taskmaster's lashes meant for my savta and…" When Ari finished, Yadin stood. And Kalev quietly groaned to himself. "In *our* home his name is honored for his sacrifices. Every day, the General would do double the work, so my ema and savta could sneak short rests." Yadin looked down with tears in his eyes at the mortified Kalev. "General, thank you." Akiba, followed by Yadin, stood and declared their families' thanks for one of Kalev's selfless acts or another. They were followed by sixty-eight other troops in succession. This continued for eighty heart-rending minutes.

At the end of the testimonies, Ari stood and tied a bright gold medallion around Kalev's thick neck. Then Ari roared, "Troops, I present to you our hero and Supreme Commanding General!" The Outpost erupted in cheers and applause.

Kalev was mortified. He never deserved any kind of praise. Since his abba's murder, he'd always known there was more to prove. To this son of Hezron, compliments sounded hollow, like he was being told to settle for less than his best. He'd never stopped to ask himself what was left for him to prove.

So he hated being singled out like this, especially in front of a crowd. He looked down and saw the front of his tunic was soaked from tears. He chided himself, *What is wrong with you? Before this week, you hadn't cried in over thirty years. Now you've bawled like a baby twice. Pull it together, man!* Kalev wiped his face on his short sleeve and then stood. He self-consciously raised his cup and had to clear his throat twice before he could speak.

"I, uh, I want to thank all those who defended my ema's home and rescued Ox…" Then, without warning, that same feeling of fire rushed from his gut into his throat. Unknowingly, Kalev's next declaration was prophetic. It would set in motion an eternal purpose for an entire generation of child warriors. He held his cup high and yelled, "To the *invincible Army of Yisrael*."

7

About a week later, a very tired Hoshe'a walked through the gate to the courtyard. He saw his little brother and the rabbi's stunning daughter, Raisa. They were sitting and talking by the well. Or rather, she was enthusiastically talking, and he was staring at the ground, barely nodding. Hoshe'a shook his head; she'd always been interested in the big dumb ox. The older brother grew a sly grin as he casually strolled over. "Hi, Raisa." Out of the corner of his eye, Hoshe'a caught Kalev's withering glare before his scared little brother looked back down at his feet.

Since his early teens, Kalev had vowed he'd never marry in this hate-filled place. So he prevented himself from getting close to any girl. Later, in the mud pits, he knew he'd made the right decision. Hotep would have used anyone as leverage against him. The side effect of his self-imposed isolation was his clumsiness around Raisa.

Raisa smiled back. "Hi, Hoshe'a. How's *the great Panhs'* favorite minion this evening?" Still looking at the dirt, Kalev laughed. Hoshe'a let out a groan. But in typical Hoshe'a form, he plowed on. "You'll have to excuse my little brother. Though he *really* likes you, he's afraid of women. I think my ema has scared…" Whap! Kalev looked up to see Hoshe'a's head bob forward and Carni standing there looking apologetically at Raisa.

The huge man was painfully shy and confused around this beautiful woman, but now he was also completely embarrassed. First by what his *stupid* brother had blurted out, then by his ema slamming Hoshe'a in the back of the head. Kalev stole a glance at Raisa and then quickly looked down. *She's grinning at Hoshe'a. Wow, we think alike, so why are you so tongue-tied around her?* he wondered.

Then, much to Kalev's horror, Carni walked over and put her arm through Raisa's. "My dear Raisa, we need to talk." Kalev cringed as he watched his too-talkative ema guide the girl into the house. Kalev stood and started to follow. Still rubbing the back of his head, Hoshe'a smirked. "Um, little brother, I promise, you *don't* want to hear what Ema is telling your, um, bride-to-be." Hoshe'a started his idiotic laugh but abruptly stopped when Kalev slapped the back of Hoshe'a's head so hard, he dropped to his knees seeing stars.

For the next two hours, a very dejected Kalev sat next to the door and listened to his ema tell Raisa his entire embarrassing history. "…and now they call him their Supreme Commanding General and…" Over Raisa's shoulder, Carni saw a broad shadow completely filling the doorway. She ignored her son's ominous glare and continued. "…and now they call him their Supreme Commanding General…" "Ema," Kalev roared, "Stop…" Then he saw Raisa's amazing smile and the words stuck in his throat mid-sentence. His mouth silently moved like a freshly caught fish gasping to breathe. His eyes desperately darted between Carni and Raisa, trying to think of something, anything to say. Finally, angry and very confused, he just turned on his heel and, with a loud arghhh, stomped away.

Kalev paced the length of the TOC stomping and grumbling. Thankfully, as far as he knew, Ari, the other officers, and most of the troops were out on their nightly missions, so there was no one around to experience his foul attitude. You're not scared of anything…but her. And Ema, she told her about this entire operation…and that Yahweh …arghh!

Finally, feeling defeated by his foolish feelings, he sat, put his forehead on the edge of the table, and stared at his feet.

Kalev didn't hear the little private step into the TOC. The troop noiselessly lit all the torches in the "Officer Country" (the enlisted troop's name for the operations center). When the little guy set down Kalev's plate and cup, Kalev was startled out of his gloomy thoughts. "Whoa, I didn't even hear you come in." The boy's expressions bounced between fear and pride. "I'm sorry, Sir." Then the boy remembered. He quickly stood at attention and saluted his general. "I, um, we're told to be silent and deadly, Sir!" Kalev barely stifled a laugh. "Well, private, I'd say you're becoming an expert at the silent part." The beaming boy quickly saluted again and then ran out of the TOC before Kalev could get his name.

The big man took a deep breath and sighed, "I guess Hoshe'a was right. I *am* scared of…" Hoshe'a interrupted, "Of course, I'm right. I'm always right." Kalev looked up and frowned at his smug big brother leaning against the wall. "What do *you* want?" Hoshe'a smirked, walked over, and sat across from Kalev. "Well, Ema won't let me back in the house, and I'm hungry." Instantly the double doors flew open, and the same little soldier walked up to the TOC platform balancing two cups and two plates on his skinny arms. Ari was right behind him and caught one of the plates as it slid off the small troop's arm. Kalev sighed and gave up on his self-pity party. He scowled at Hoshe'a and then smiled at Ari. "So, Captain Ari, how is the training going? I'm sorry I missed the evening muster…" "No problem, Sir. I'm sure you had important business elsewhere." With his mouth full of bread, Hoshe'a snorted but kept eating.

As Hoshe'a and Ari talked, Kalev inhaled his evening meal of fish and fresh bread with minced garlic. The wine was from his own vineyard. It reminded him that they needed to clean out the vineyard channels and open the water gate. He quickly wrote that into the next evening's orders. When Ari finished, he, too, started eating like a starving man.

But Hoshe'a looked dazed. He cleared his throat. "Last night I dreamed about this army. But it was much larger. I saw Ari, you, and many other boys I have never met. I, um, saw you all in battle…" Hoshe'a spoke as if Kalev wasn't there. "Ari, Yahweh has decreed that this army is *His* hand of protection for *His* chosen people. He trusts you to train and help supervise every troop here. That said, it's *His* burden to carry. If you ask, He'll continue to give you His wisdom. It's simpler than trying to figure it out for yourself. Ask and He'll answer. You'll find relief in trusting Him." Hoshe'a nodded toward the fuming Kalev. "He's already sent you an ox to help carry the load."

The awed teen nodded his thanks, then grimaced when he saw Kalev white-knuckling the table. Ari and Hoshe'a both twitched as the Supreme Commanding General of Yisrael's Army abruptly stood. He'd shoved his chair back so hard it tumbled into the wall. His eyes bore into Hoshe'a's, then Kalev growled to Ari, "I'll be back," then stormed out of the Outpost.

With his mouth still full of unchewed bread, Ari curiously looked at Hoshe'a. The army's chief architect shrugged and then blurted out, "He hates Yahweh…"

Kalev walked his field's perimeter for over an hour. Eventually he calmed down and returned to the TOC. He was greeted with wide-eyed stares from the two captains. "Captain Ari, I apologize for my outburst. I, um…well, I'm sorry." "Uh, yes, Sir," was all Ari could think to say as Hoshe'a quickly excused himself and practically ran to the closest gate.

The defeated-looking Kalev plopped into a chair. The same little private, still beaming with pride, came into the TOC, grabbed the evening meal plates, and silently left. Ari and Kalev sat on opposite sides of the planning table, both silent, both lost in thought.

Kalev was the first to snap out of it. "Ari, I'm not sure where this idea came from, but you need at least three troops to work as your personal staff. They can function as your liaisons to your officers in the field and complete other 'off mission' assignments. This will free you up for planning and officer overwatch. You also need a skilled squad to watch your back. It may not seem important now, but it will soon." Kalev shook his head. "I don't understand where these ideas are coming from, but it's certainly not me." Ari wisely shrugged in a knowing silence.

8

Kalev and Ari spent the next night creating two new support companies and outlining a new sergeant's training manual. As the sun rose, the lieutenants returned to the TOC. Kalev stood to leave, and another compulsion welled up inside him. [illegible], he groaned to himself. No matter what these boys called him, he really felt like a fish out of water. It didn't feel right to instruct this kid…but before he could speak, Ari stood and motioned him to the passageway out. Before they opened the gate, the teen whispered, "Sir, I know this has all been a little overwhelming, but I wanted to thank you for your help. The morning you, um, attacked us, I was ready to quit. I'd planned to promote Akiba and demote myself. I felt like I was drowning in the pressure of it all. I couldn't eat or sleep. And then you literally stormed into the picture. I can't, or rather won't explain why, but your war cry brought a sense of relief. So thank you, Sir." Kalev rubbed his eyes and groaned louder than he intended. "[illegible], Ari, I, um, I'm not a trained soldier." Ari chuckled, "It's funny you mention that. My abba, Adir, was an expert with the sword before I was born. He even corrected some of the techniques the Egyptian soldiers taught me. He can throw a knife or a sword and hit a watermelon at fifty yards. He can shoot with deadly accuracy at *150 yards*.

"I saw him yesterday. We were talking about the next grape harvest, then out of nowhere he, um, volunteered to secretly train you. I told him I'd discuss it with you." Kalev felt oddly humbled. "He's willing to train *me*?" Ari cringed. "Yes, Sir, and um, arghh, my abba was, um, not really volunteering. His offer was more like a decisive order. He said he'll meet you in front of your stall an hour before sundown, um, today." Kalev watched Ari's face flush with embarrassment. He put his hand on the boy's muscled shoulder. "Ari, please tell your abba I'd be honored to be trained by one of *my* abba's most trusted friends." Ari exhaled. "I will, Sir. And Sir, for some reason, he asked about your ema Carni. I guess they knew each other a long time ago." Kalev shrugged. "Okay, I'll let her know he said hi." The huge man was instantly surprised when he heard himself blurt out, "Ari, you need to be promoted to colonel and your lieutenants to majors. This will allow you to promote junior officers and delegate more responsibilities. And it needs to happen right away." Much to Kalev's relief, Ari smiled. "Yes, Sir. Thank you, Sir." Kalev quickly left before he could vomit any more embarrassing outbursts.

Instead of heading back to his stall, he walked around the western edge of the Outpost to the river bank. The previous night's perimeter patrol was walking his way as they finished their shift. The last troop in the squad was one of the youngest boys Kalev had seen yet. The General smiled when he saw that the little one was so small, his sword tip stuck out of the bottom of the scabbard and was dragging a line in the sand.

Kalev suggested to the squad leader that he make a back scabbard for the little troop. That's when the little guy screamed something unintelligible and pointed at the river. Kalev turned to look. He watched in amazement as swells, about two feet high, rolled downriver. The sun was coming up behind the waves; its light gave an ominous glow to the sparkling water. By this time most of the battalion, awakened by the little troop's scream, was on the beach watching the odd site.

As the first swell flowed past him, Kalev moved closer to the water. The swells didn't crest nor dissipate like normal waves. And the sun was reflecting off thousands of bright green… *Fish*, he wondered. Then the little troop screamed, "Froooogs," and started to run past Kalev. At the last second, Kalev stuck his arm straight out to stop the boy from reaching the water. The little guy's head bounced off the solid arm and slammed backward into the sand. Kalev was surprised when he saw the little soldier flat on his back with tears welling up in his scared eyes. The mountain of a man knelt, reached down, and stood the boy in front of him. Unbeknownst Kalev didn't realize the entire battalion was watching his every move. He placed his heavy hands on the little one's scrawny shoulders.

"Little warrior, I didn't want you in that water. Those, um, frogs could be swimming ahead of a float of hungry crocodiles. I don't want those crocs to mistake you as a huge 'little frog.'" This elicited a few snickers from the others. But the little troop wiped his eyes, smiled, and squared his shoulders with pride. From somewhere deep inside this small boy came an enormous "RRRRRRRRRRRRRRRRRRib iiiiiiiiiiiiiiiiiiiiit."

The Supreme Commanding General of Yisrael's Army was so surprised by this little boy's verbal explosion, he began to belly laugh. The laughing was contagious, and soon the entire battalion was in pain from laughing so hard. Then, as this tight-knit group of boys was apt to do, a chant started, "Little Frog, Little Frog, Little Frog…" Kalev looked at the proud young troop. The boy couldn't grin any bigger if he wanted to. Ari dismissed the squad back to the Outpost. The squad leader hoisted the beaming little boy to his shoulders. And the young troops proudly marched through the gate to the thrumming cheer, "Little Frog, Little Frog…"

Ari waited until the squad disappeared through the gate. He walked over to Kalev at the water's edge. "He's one of your ema's orphans. He'd been sleeping in the palace cattle barn and survived by catching frogs and cooking them on the cattlemen's abandoned fire pits late at night. Your ema, um, *'asked'* me to *personally* take responsibility for that one. She didn't know his name. And we couldn't understand his speech. Your ema surmised that the boy was brutally molested by the priests at the temple of Hatshepsut. Truthfully, Sir, that was the first understandable word we've heard from him." Kalev grinned as the chant inside the outpost grew louder. "Well, I guess he has a name *now*." Ari rolled his eyes. "Sir, I think we all need to get some sleep. I'd better go squelch that noise before the whole Egyptian army heads our way."

After a fitful day's sleep, Kalev met Adir on the north side of his stall. He was grateful to see they were out of sight from the Outpost. He held out his hand. "Sir, you probably don't remember me. I'm Kalev—a real pleasure to meet you." The bronzed skin and iron-muscled Adir firmly shook his hand. "Son, of course I remember you. I remember when you and Hoshe'a would hide in the back of the wagon and ate so much watermelon you both would puke." Kalev winced at the memory. "You two were always a handful for your emas, but you were also a welcomed comical relief after a hard day's work." Then the man grew a serious expression and locked eyes with Kalev. "But you've grown into an honorable man your abba would be proud of." Kalev was both embarrassed and deeply moved by Adir's compliment. As if the man could read his mind, Adir continued. "Your name is honored in my home. You rescued my ema from that pig Hotep's whip many times. She talks about how you took the lashings for others too. She speaks of your kindness and your gift for infuriating the slave masters." Kalev was looking at his feet in embarrassment. "And now I hear you're protecting my son." Kalev started to protest, but Adir held up his hand. "Ari told me that just before you stormed his troops, he was making plans to turn boys away. This would have resulted in the secret getting out, the boys killed, or worse. The Egyptian pigs would have accused them of trying to raise a revolt, then hung their bodies on the city wall. They've done it before.

"According to Ari, you've taken a huge load off his shoulders. He said they all see you as their protector, their General. Kalev, your abba and I were friends, and I really miss him. He was the strongest and kindest man I've ever known. You have his big attitude." Adir stared at the sunset. "Hezron introduced me to Carni…" Kalev was too lost in his own thoughts about his abba to notice Adir's semi-inappropriate statement.

Kalev tried to gather his thoughts. "Um, you should be very proud of your son. He's the *real* general. Every boy in that fortress respects him, and so do I." Adir nodded. "I *am* very proud of my Ari. Now what can I do for you, General Kalev, son of Hezron?"

Kalev was hesitant. He felt like he was imposing on this man. "I, um, I need to know how to fight. I'll gladly pay you for your time." Adir scowled. "Son of Hezron, I'll not take your money." Kalev returned the scowl. "I value your expertise. Would you have refused this offer if it had come from my abba?" Adir's scowl deepened. "Yes, I would have told him I wanted double my usual wage." He laughed. "Then I would have refused his money too." Kalev nodded his appreciation. "I need your discretion and skilled training. How can I return the favor?" "Kalev, you already have. My son and ema's protection and encouragement is worth more than I could ever repay. Besides, Ari's savta would skin me alive if I took anything from you. Now, let's get to work."

Following the evenings' muster and officer promotions, Ari, Kalev, and Hoshe'a sat on the edge of the training platform and ate. After swallowing a mouthful of beef steak, Ari chuckled. "One of the daytime lookouts reported that the waves of frogs continued until around noon. Your brother here just told me the frogs had invaded the palace. They covered the deck of every hallway and bedroom and were even swimming in the pharaoh's *hashirutim* (toilet)." Hoshe'a, through his usual snickering, reported that Pharaoh squished several frogs when he plopped onto his royal throne.

9

Kalev was impressed with Ari's attention to detail. Ari and his majors saw every mission as important to the army's survival. The planning of the training mission on how to kill silently received the same respect as the operations for planting the fields or fishing.

One evening while the others planned, Kalev read one of Yadin's older mission briefs detailing how to fish from their feluccas (skiffs). They'd "foraged" a thick ocean sailing ship's anchor rope and secured it to trees on both sides of the river. The fishing troops would use the large rope to pull their six three-boy feluccas to the middle of the river. Then they'd tie the feluccas bow rope to the larger rope and glide while remaining stationary. Kalev read that in each small felucca, two troops would fish. And when they weren't hunting crocs for food, the third boy's job was to watch the water and to protect their "battle buddies" from the larger crocs looking for an easy meal. The fishing troops had to catch as many fish as their felucca could carry. They'd usually fish every other night.

That night, Kalev was walking across his fields when he heard very faint screams coming from the river side of the Outpost. He rushed through one of the hidden doors to the training area. He was amazed to see a nine-boy squad straining to pull an enormous croc tale through a too-narrow riverside hatch. Kalev ran to help. Eventually, they tugged the eighteen-foot croc into the eating area. It was the largest croc Kalev had ever seen. On its lifeless back sat a boy that was even smaller than Little Frog. He straddled the neck of the enormous croc, tightly gripping the handle of a sword that was stuck straight down through the croc's brain. The little private was completely soaked, yet he refused to let go of the sword, and no one could have wiped that smile of pride off his face. Every troop in the army lined up to pat his little back and comment on his bravery. Later, Kalev would read the "daily after-action report."

The newly recruited seven-year-old orphan was incorrectly assigned overwatch for his boat crew. But when they tied off in the center of the river, the boy realized he'd forgotten his spear. Unfortunately, he was in the small felucca with two teen sergeants. When one of the sergeants saw that the terrified recruit had forgotten his spear, he "sarcastically" warned the little private that if he saw a croc, he had better use his sword and kill it. Even if he had to jump on its back and stab it in the brain, or he would be swimming the thirty yards back to shore. This had terrified the little private, as he didn't know how to swim. They had just started fishing when they netted two large perch. The two sergeants struggled to pull the full net into the boat. Suddenly, the enormous tooth-filled jaws of a giant croc rose out of the water and clamped down on the two fish, net and all.

But to the little private, the massive croc was attacking his sergeants. Terrified of being forced to try and swim ashore, he screamed and leaped out of the boat onto the croc's thrashing neck. He buried his sword to the hilt just behind the croc's eyes. This may have killed the monster, but it still went into a death roll. The sergeants reported that the croc rolled three times before it stopped face up. The little private rode the croc through every roll, never letting go of his sword. The sergeants floated the beast to the shore. The young recruit rode on its back and never let go of the sword.

When he finished reading the report, Kalev ordered that all of the croc's teeth be collected and given to Major Akiba. Then he asked Akiba to make a necklace out of the biggest teeth and embed the rest into a long wooden sword.

At the next evening's assembly in front of the entire army, they tied a leather string with seven of the largest crocodile teeth around the little private's skinny neck. Ari awarded the newly promoted private first class the "croc sword of valor." Then Major Akiba stepped forward and yelled, "All hail Little Croc." Everyone cheered, and the predictable chant began to build. "Little Croc, Little Croc, Little Croc…" This went on for about five minutes.

As the squad leaders began to quiet the troops, Kalev looked over and noticed that the little private was crying. Ari walked over and whispered to Kalev, "He was orphaned when he was two. This is the only home he's ever known. Your ema thinks he's about six or seven now. She said we were his family now, but the boy never knew his name." Kalev grinned. "I guess it's officially now 'Little Croc.'" Following the muster, Little Croc proudly sat with the officers and had a hefty meal of crocodile meat, fresh bread, and beer. The kid never stopped smiling.

The next day, after a lengthy and loud dressing down, Major Yadin ordered the two infamous sergeants from Little Croc's boat to tan the alligator skin. They were to formally present the perfectly tanned skin to Little Croc, along with their sincere thanks for saving their lives. Little Croc became a living legend. The story of his bravery was told to every new group of recruits.

About a week later, Hoshe'a walked into the TOC and sat across from his brother. It was obviously mealtime, but he wasn't hungry. He waited until Kalev finished talking to one of the food servers. Kalev saw him and joked, "Like the food here that much, or did Ema kick you out again?" Hoshe'a distractedly smirked. Kalev could tell something was on his brother's mind. He stood, forgetting that this simple act caused everyone in the TOC to stop eating and stand. He waved them back to their seats. "Captain Hoshe'a and I need to inspect the vineyard." Ari cleared his throat. "Uh, Sir, Captain Hoshe'a was promoted to Major last night." Kalev smirked and rolled his eyes at Hoshe'a. "Okay, *Major*, walk with me."

Kalev grabbed two large loaves of bread, and they headed out to the field. When they were alone and out of earshot, Kalev sat on the log they used as a channel dam for the vineyard. But Hoshe'a began to nervously pace. With his mouth full of bread, Kalev smirked. "What's going on in that small brain of yours, big brother?"

Hoshe'a looked around nervously. "Kalev, I need to know that I can trust you to stay calm." Kalev frowned. "Uh, that didn't work out so well last time. Maybe I shouldn't know." "Yeah, well, I've been debating that with myself for the last four weeks." The new major/brother groaned. "Kalev, I'd like to speak to this army's Commanding General now." Kalev stopped chewing and scowled. He didn't like the sound of that. "Brother, um, this is serious. We really need your help!" Oddly, Kalev started to panic. "Has something happened to Ox or Ema?" Hoshe'a scowled. "Ema will be pleased to know that your concern for her ranked behind an animal. No, they're fine." Kalev looked at Hoshe'a. He saw that his pacing brother's hands were trembling. Now he *really* didn't like where this was going. Kalev yelled, "Hoshe'a!"

Hoshe'a said a quick, silent prayer, then sighed. "Kalev, the story starts with a baby who was born a Hebrew. At that time the pharaoh became afraid of the Hebrews because they'd become too numerous. So he ordered his army to destroy all children two years old and younger. Those were horrible days; every Hebrew family knew a fresh torment, whether directly or indirectly. Yet the ema of that specific baby hid him until he couldn't be concealed any longer. She took a basket and lined it with pitch and slime so it was watertight. She placed the three-month-old in the basket and set it adrift in the river just below our Victory Peak." Hoshe'a glanced at Kalev to make sure he was following. His little brother had started eating again with a smile on his face. "The current took it down the river until it lodged in the reeds near where the pharaoh's daughter, Hatshepsut, would go to bathe. She found the baby and kept him as her own. This child lived the favored life of Egyptian royalty. As he became older, his ema had plans to make him the next pharaoh.

Somehow, forty years later he found out that he was a Hebrew. He began to see the Hebrew slaves in a new light." Kalev stood, and they started walking toward the north end of the field. But Hoshe'a stopped and paused his story long enough to get Kalev's full attention. The older-by-six-months brother began to speak rapidly. "One day this, um, prince saw a, um, person whipping a Hebrew slave. But out of pure emotion, he took it upon himself to free the slave. He killed the, um, person, and though he hid the body, he couldn't hide the publicly obvious act."

Kalev kept walking a few more steps before he turned around. In the bright moonlight, Hoshe'a saw the stiff, flat effect and the fiery stare. So Hoshe'a talked even faster. "Confused and fearing for his life, he fled to Midian. For forty years, he herded sheep for a Midianite priest who believes in Yahweh." Hoshe'a cringed but forced himself to keep going. "About two months ago, he returned to Egypt. He's obediently following Yahweh's directives. The Nile turning to blood, then the frogs, that was him. Twice now he's gone before Pharaoh and demanded the release of the Hebrew people. Now he's threatened Pharaoh again with a plague of gnats. Of course, Pharaoh laughed him out of the throne room. Pharaoh Ramses II had always hated Moshe, but now, with these past two 'inconveniences,' as Pharaoh jokingly calls them, the hatred has intensified. And we're scared for Moshe's life. But Moshe has refused any physical protection for himself." Hoshe'a almost whispered the last sentence.

He forced himself to glance over at Kalev. The Supreme Commanding General of Yisrael's Army was sitting on the edge of an irrigation ditch. With his elbows on his knees and his face in his trembling hands, he rocked back and forth. Though it was a cool evening, Hoshe'a saw that his brother was sweating profusely.

Hoshe'a didn't say another word. He plopped down on the same side of the ditch but made sure he was out of Kalev's reach. It was some time before Kalev surprised Hoshe'a with a whispered question. "What did Ema say when you told her?" Hoshe'a was shocked. "She said you would know the right thing to do." Kalev smirked. "She said it with *the look*, didn't she?" "Yes, she did." Kalev roared so loud that Hoshe'a knew they could hear it from the Outpost a quarter mile back. "Arghhhh."

Kalev stood and paced, or rather stomped around, for the next fifteen minutes. At one point, Hoshe'a thought he heard Kalev mumble, "Never let your emotions control your actions, never let your emotions control your actions, never let your emotions control your actions…" Kalev said this with a quiet rage that made Hoshe'a cringe. Eventually, the huge man plopped down next to Hoshe'a, making the older brother wince. Then, just as quickly, Kalev jumped back up.

He and Hoshe'a argued for the next two hours. Kalev continued to pace for most of that time. "Arghh, he was responsible for my abba's death, that [illegible] deserves to die, even if he had 'good intentions.'"

Hoshe'a was silent for a while but knew this had to happen. Surprising himself, he stood, pointed a shaky finger in Kalev's scowling face, and croaked out, "General, this is an army; armies have spies. Send two spies just to watch him or rather watch his back." Kalev grew eerily quiet. Hoshe'a saw a battle raging in his little brother's eyes.

Finally, without a word, Kalev turned and silently walked toward his stall. Hoshe'a didn't follow. He knew it could go either way. About ten yards later, Kalev whirled around and pointed a finger at Hoshe'a. "No promises."

After a sleepless day, Kalev sat at the TOC table as they had their first designated "command and staff" briefing. Eventually he forced himself to stop brooding and listened to Major Yadin as he finished his latest troop strength report. "In the last two weeks, eighty-one new recruits have started their basic training." Ari groaned. "So, in the last *three* weeks, we've more than doubled in size?" Yadin read his accounting sheet again. "Yes, Sir. Our troop strength is now 273. Not including the seventeen that wandered into Sergeant Carni's courtyard this evening. But like most of our new recruits, it'll take them at least three days of food, sleep, and medical care before they can start their basic training." Ari nodded. "Major Yadin, I assume we have enough supplies to support this troop increase." Yadin nodded. "We can handle the influx of almost 150 new troops a week. In fact, our biggest concern now is the need for more storage space." Ari smiled. "Major Hoshe'a and I are working on that. For the next two weeks, all troops not already assigned to other missions will be clearing ten more acres of trees to the east. We'll hollow out the inner groves like we did here. Anything else before the General speaks?" No one spoke up, and Ari nodded to Kalev. "Sir?"

Kalev reluctantly addressed the four teenage officers and Hoshe'a. "Gentlemen, we need to detach two squads for a special assignment." Kalev swore under his breath. "These troops need to be or look like a typical Egyptian boy. They must be intelligent; that means they can be trusted to keep their mission a secret. They must be experts in all weaponry and concealment techniques. Up to this point, the troops have functioned as companies or in squads. But these soldiers must be able to function independently or in pairs. They need to complete their daily mission without the target knowing they were there. Their mission is to be Prince Moshe's shadow troops. They'll follow him into the city, then back to his tent." He glared at Hoshe'a again. "Per the *major* here, these 'spies' can't be seen carrying any weapons. They'll need to look like street children. Of course, they'll be wearing full robes over their hidden knives and daggers. Yadin, make sure their robes have a slit on both sides for easy access to their weapons." Kalev groaned to himself and then glared at Hoshe'a. "This mission is extremely dangerous. Failure or capture could have a devastating impact on the future of this army." Kalev rubbed his tired eyes. In unison all four teens glanced at each other. Kalev slowly nodded. "Yeah, I really hate this, but Major Hoshe'a and Sergeant Carni think this is the right thing to do. That said, I'm asking for a unanimous go or no-go." Kalev hoped for one objection. Which would let him off the hook with ema. But all four of them answered at the same time, "Go, Sir."

To Kalev, that response sounded rehearsed. He scowled at Hoshe'a. The new major sheepishly shrugged, and Kalev growled under his breath. "Okay. They'll report directly to me before the nightly muster. Once again, people, this is a highly classified mission. Major Akiba, I'll leave it to your discretion whether these specialized troops need to be an isolated group at night or not. Major Yadin, how long do you need for background checks and train…?" Kalev stopped mid-sentence when Yadin slid his detailed train-up time frame across the table.

Ari cleared his throat. "Sir. Um, we've been working on this plan for over a month. But we didn't consider the troops' nationalities or skill levels. And concealing the weapons is a great idea."

Ari really didn't like Major Hoshe'a forcing him to keep his general in the dark, so he subtly threw Major Hoshe'a under the chariot, so to speak. "Sir, um, Major Hoshe'a told us he would inform you and get your approval before we executed the mission training. Apparently he felt we needed more time to plan." The TOC went silent, and everyone stared, first at their audacious teen colonel, then at the squirming Hoshe'a. With surprising restraint, Kalev hissed at Hoshe'a. "Do you have anything else to add… *Major*?" Hoshe'a opened his mouth to defend himself, but Kalev's ominous tone and terrible glare kept him silent. He simply shook his head and whispered, “No, and thank you.” Then Kalev’s older brother quickly left.

Kalev took a long drink from the cup of wine that had magically appeared in front of him. He turned to Akiba. “I’m assuming that the most skilled fighters are in Heh Company.” Akiba proudly grinned, “Yes, Sir.” “Good. Within the hour, get Major Yadin twelve names for six two-troop teams. They *will* meet the criteria for this shadow mission. They need to start transitioning to day operations starting tomorrow morning. Kalev glanced at Yadin and held up his large parchment. “Is this a hard or projected train-up schedule?” Yadin walked around the table and studied his parchment. “Sir. Assuming Major Akiba’s troops have already been trained to meet the mission parameters”—he glanced over at Akiba, who soberly nodded—“they should be operational in four days from tomorrow morning. But, Sir, I’m not sure where we can train in daylight.” Kalev opened his mouth to make suggestions but stopped. He needed to heed his own advice to Ari. The General grew a sly grin. “Just make it happen, Major.” He turned to Ari. “Colonel, why don’t we leave the details to the majors? We need to discuss other business. Let’s take a felucca ride.”

10

The two weary senior officers crossed the river, walked about two hundred and fifty yards east into the desert, and perched on a couple of flat boulders facing each other. The teen lay back and stared at the blanket of stars. A huge full moon was just rising from the southeastern horizon. For a while they sat in silence, lost in their own heavy thoughts.

Finally, Ari whispered, "I forgot what it was like to just sit and enjoy the quiet. I didn't know this army thing would grow so large. I mean, 295 young boys? Seriously? It seems like everyone wants to ask me a question or hand me a report. And lately my days are filled with running from one crisis to another. I feel like I'm choking inside, like I can't breathe." Kalev didn't know how to respond. Besides, the kid sounded like he was just thinking out loud.

Suddenly a strong northerly breeze picked up. While Ari talked to the stars, Kalev watched a slow swirling dust cloud pass between their two boulders. A deep but quiet voice seemed to whisper as the cloud blew by. "Uneasy lies the head that wears the crown." Kalev turned and watched the cloud pass to the south. But in its wake he thought he heard—was that laughter? Then the breeze completely stopped, and the desert went silent again. Hotep's ex-prisoner shook his head to clear his jumbled thoughts. It wasn't the first time his past injuries had scrambled his thinking.

But when Kalev turned back, he saw Ari sitting up and staring right at him. The boy had a sly, knowing grin. "Sir, what did you just say?" Kalev shrugged. "I didn't say anything; it was probably just the wind blowing through those bushes over there." They both knew that wasn't the case, but they let it go.

Ari shook the thought out of his head and cleared his throat. "Sir, you said you had some business to discuss." Kalev nodded. "Yeah, um, Ari, I've been training with your abba for a couple of weeks now." Kalev unconsciously rubbed his sore shoulder. Ari chuckled, "Yes, Sir, that can be a little painful." Kalev winced. "In addition to my daily ego-crushing weapons training, he's teaching me to have a forward-thinking mindset. To predict and always have contingencies for every type of attack." Kalev rubbed his shoulder again. But before he could recite Adir's mantra, Ari blurted it out, sounding just like his abba. "Improvise, adapt, and overcome. Improvise, adapt, and overcome. Improvise, adapt, and overcome!" They both laughed. "First of all, that was a great impression of your abba, right down to the spitting." Ari chuckled, "I've had those words drilled into me since I picked up my first wooden sword." Kalev nodded. "Your abba's theme needs to permeate every mission plan. But that's the type of military foresight that starts at the top. And that's you and me, I guess."

Kalev shook his head. "Ari, just between us, I'm still not sure I'm the right man for the job. But it is what it is, and whether we like it or not, *we're* in charge. You and I need to model your abba's mantra as this army expands. We need to remind each other that growth brings new *opportunities* to delegate those mind-crushing responsibilities. Son, truthfully, I don't know where these ideas are coming from, but they make sense." Ari smiled. He knew exactly where they were coming from, but he kept that to himself.

"That said, we need to restructure Heh Company. It will become this army's primary fighting force. These twelve shadow troops are only the beginning. The other two companies are critical, but ultimately, their missions are in support of Heh Company. So, if you don't mind, I'm promoting you to an aleph-grade general effective immediately." Ari's mouth fell open.

"I want you to start working yourself out of overseeing the entire battalion. In three days, you will be the new commanding officer of Heh Company." Kalev held up his hand before the crushed-looking teen could object. But he had to pause when he felt that same verbal explosion begin to build in his gut. "Son, this is a multi-level promotion. At this stage, your undivided attention will help grow Heh Company into a lethal fighting force that will be revered for decades to come. All your pain-filled training and attention to detail has prepared you for this specific mission at this precise time. And it begins tonight."

Kalev paused, stunned by his own arrogance. *How dare you walk in and take over this kid's creation*, he chided himself. But Ari knew his general's words to be a prophetic command directly from Yahweh. The burdened teen's mind knew this was the right tactical move, but his heart felt like he'd just been divorced from his own family. Suddenly, as if in confirmation, he heard Yahweh's voice boom in his gut.

"'My appointed General Ari, I know the plans I have for you,' declares your Yehovah, 'plans for your good and not for evil. Obedience to My directives will give you a future and a hope. Ari, son, know that every time you pray, I hear you. The I AM that I AM is *always* with you! I will free My chosen; I will gather *My* people and bring them home. And Ari, son of Adir, you have an integral part to play in this epoch adventure. Trust in your Yahweh, and I will give you a peace your mind won't understand, but your heart will relish. General Ari, breathe in My *yesh*'" (presence).

Yahweh softly exhaled His Spirit into the teen's lungs. Ari felt a life-giving fire streak through his body. He ravenously gulped another breath and held it. This caused the Creator of the universe to laugh. The breath of wind and the sound of Yahweh's laughter exhilarated Ari's mind, will, and emotions. With every ensuing breath, the earlier heaviness grew lighter. He felt like he was floating in an almost painful joy. It felt like time had stopped, but that was okay with the teen general; he was enjoying every swallow of the crisp eternal air. "Oh, and Ari, don't worry about the big guy and Me. I've got your General right where I want him!" Then the I AM that I AM laughed again. After a short while, Ari realized he'd slid off the rock and was kneeling with his smiling face in the dirt. He looked up, but the General was gone.

Kalev had heard the same voice and watched Ari's limp body slide to the sand. Before he could ask the kid about what was going on, a nauseating wave of fear and loathing threatened to drown him. He knew he had to get out of there. Kalev practically ran back to the felucca. He refused to think about the voice or his reaction. He half-heartedly tried to justify his escape as being necessary. He had more important things to worry about than a hallucination in the desert. Still…

When Ari returned to the felucca, Kalev saw that the boy's face was almost glowing. The General ashamedly offered a lame excuse for his gutless exit. Ari graciously nodded. "No worries, General, you have things to do. I, um, I just needed some alone time to think. So thank you for the privacy." Now Kalev was *really* embarrassed. This eighteen-year-old kid was more mature than Kalev thought he'd ever become.

As they pulled the felucca across the river, Kalev quietly continued their previous conversation. "The twelve shadow troops, and eventually all of Heh Company, need to train in secret. Probably out where we just were. As far as Heh Company's command and logistics needs are concerned, I'll leave that in your more capable hands. I think even Heh will grow a need for an even more specialized platoon. Akiba seems built for that. But I trust you, Ari. Take it and make it your own." When they reached the door into the outpost, Ari turned. "Sir, um, I'm not going to press this sensitive issue. But I think you already know that voice we both heard was not a breeze blowing through bushes. It was the voice of Yahweh." Without another word Ari quickly saluted and disappeared inside, leaving Kalev trembling with resentful rage.

11

Immediately after Ari's idiotic statement about his impotent Yahweh's supposed voice, Kalev ran to his stall and slammed the door. He spent the next five hours cussing, yelling, and cussing some more into his pillow. At dawn, he sheepishly looked out of his stall door, desperately hoping no one heard his endless tirade. He was both exhausted and starving. He made his way around to the front of the house, hoping his ema had some extra bread.

As the half-asleep Hoshe'a hurried out the front door, he gracelessly bounced off his brick wall of a brother headed in the opposite direction. He fell back into the house and landed on a chair. Kalev grinned as he reached passed Hoshe'a for the remaining two loaves on the table. He grinned at his brother's complaints and insults. Kalev swallowed a mouth full of bread and sneered at his brother. "Aside from your extreme clumsiness. Are you satisfied with the shadow mission?" Kalev really didn't care about Hoshe'a's answer. He was sending children to protect a man he loathed. Hoshe'a calmed down. "Yes, Kalev, tha…" Kalev's hand shot up. "Stop, don't thank me. Hoshe'a, you don't know how close I've come to tracking that coward down, killing him, then hiding *his* body in a shallow grave! Now *that* would be poetic justice. And I still may!" Hoshe'a, seeing the hate-fueled fire in his brother's tired, red eyes, cringed. "I understand," he croaked quietly.

Kalev shook his head. "Hoshe'a, why are you so invested in this fool's safety?" Hoshe'a locked eyes with Kalev and then looked down to the table. He didn't say a word. Kalev instantly understood that Hoshe'a's silence meant his reasons had something to do with *his* non-existent Yahweh. "Never mind, I don't want to know."

Kalev waited until Hoshe'a looked up again, then locked eyes. He threateningly growled. "Now *you* owe me. Or rather, you owe those boys who're about to risk their lives for that coward." Hoshe'a mutely nodded. Kalev spoke matter-of-factly, "You are going to design and build a base of operations on the other side of the river. East into the desert. It needs large training, eating, and sleeping areas. It will eventually house over five hundred boys and be soundproof and independent from the Outpost. It will have its own ovens, wells, etc. It can't be visible day or night. I want to stand right next to it and not know it's there. Do you understand?" Hoshe'a scowled at his defiant little brother. "Let's see. You want me to do the impossible on flat open desert. And I get the feeling this isn't a request. You really are Ema's son." "Hoshe'a!" Kalev roared. "[illegible] *yes*, don't get your loin cloth in a wad. I'll start working on it tonight. Phans is leaving for a trip up the coast. He'll be gone for a couple of weeks, so I'll have a lot more time here. I'll get it done." Kalev nodded. He took a calming breath. "Thanks." Then the iron-fisted man playfully punched Hoshe'a in the chest, knocking the wind out of him. "The idiot's shadow troops should be operational in four days. I'll let you know."

Kalev stood and headed to the kitchen for more bread. Hoshe'a rubbed his chest and gulped air. "Oww, you big [illegible] ox." He watched his brother foolishly rummage around in their ema's kitchen. Hoshe'a smirked. He knew that somehow his ema would know Kalev had breached her inner sanctum, and he hoped he was here to see that rare encounter. "Ya know, for a Supreme Commanding General of Yisrael's Army, it's pretty stupid to be rooting around in Ema's kitch…" But Hoshe'a never got to finish his warning. From the front door, Carni screamed, "Kalev, what are you *thinking*!"

Kalev and Hoshe'a flinched in unison. But this time Hoshe'a was smart enough to keep his mouth shut. And for once it was *his* turn to watch their ema's wrath descend on someone else. In three strides Carni stood beside her guilty-looking son. She slapped the back of his bald head so hard Kalev spit out a glob of bread. Hoshe'a darted out the door and was halfway to the front gate before he exploded with laughter. Carni grabbed her broom, and the forty-year-old, iron-muscled man cringed like a little kid about to be broom-whipped. The chastised Kalev watched his fierce little ema sweep the wet glob of bread into the garbage pot. But she wasn't done with her tongue-lashing. "Kalev, you know better. No one touches anything in *my* kitchen, *ever*!" Kalev was startled to see three little girls awkwardly peek around the corner. The tallest one loudly whispered to the other two. "Even *I* knew that." The Commanding General glanced back at Carni. "Who're they?" "Little one, don't change the subject. I haven't seen you in days; then I come home to find you nosing around in *my* kitchen." Kalev responded like he had for decades. He walked over, gently picked Carni up, held her in a bear hug, and whispered. "I missed you, Ema!" She feebly protested but hugged his neck anyway. Then she growled in his ear. "Get. Out. Of *my*. Kitchen. Now!"

Kalev put her down and walked out of *her* AO. Carni yelled at his back like a drill sergeant. "Sit down, young man, you're going to eat. Arghh, look at you, your skin and bones." The little girls watched as Carni flew into action. Then the littlest one walked over and held up her arms to Kalev. He stared at her. Before the boys showed up at his stall door that fateful morning, sort of, his only interaction with little kids was in the mud pits. And that was mostly when he carried their lifeless little bodies to the death wagon. His stomach turned at the horrific memory. He didn't move, so the little girl took it upon herself to crawl up in his lap, stand on his thighs, and touch his nose with her little finger. The noise in the kitchen went silent. Kalev's eyes crossed as he watched her touch his nose. The tiny girl thought that was hilarious and started a high-pitched giggle. Then she spoke so fast, Kalev had a hard time understanding.

"I'm Evee I'm new here we just walked here last week 'cause we were living in Tanis but the people there were mean and their breath stinks and they tried to hurt us but they did hurt Abana in her private parts but they tried to hurt me and Rachael so we ran and hid under a table like this one but it was smaller than this one Abana and all of us ran and walked at night but Abana carried me 'cause I was sleepy and we don't know our emas like your ema is Sergeant Carni but none of us has an ema or abba or anyone so we went to the market near here 'cause we were very hungry and Abana's robe was torn by that very bad man who had stinky breath too but he touched her down there and we hid under another table again but it was bigger than this one and sergeant Carni said we could come home with her then…"

Kalev's head began to hurt. He seriously doubted this little one had taken a single breath. Kalev glanced up to see the other two little girls staring wide-eyed at him. Carni stood behind them smiling through her tears. While little Evee continued her breathless, one-sided conversation, the huge Commanding General's eyebrows shot up in a silent plea for his ema to intervene. Carni wiped her eyes and mouthed the words, "Suck it up, General."

Without missing a beat, Evee touched his nose again to get his attention. "…and Sergeant Carni who's your ema said you were a real general and your army is hiding in the trees like we were hiding under those tables but not this one 'cause we don't need to hide under tables anymore 'cause Sergeant Carni said but maybe we could hide in the trees with the boys if they're not mean to Abana or they aren't mean to Rachael and me 'cause Sergeant Carni is your ema but she said you are a nice general and you're not mean to little girls can we hide in the trees too?"

It took Kalev a couple of seconds for his brain to catch up. Still mesmerized, he continued to watch the formidable little girl's smiling face. "*Ema*!" he yelled. The fearless little one giggled again, climbed down, and rejoined the other two.

Carni walked in with an overflowing plate of rare dried beef and cooked cabbage. In her other hand, she held his favorite tall cup filled to the brim with the deep purple wine from last year's harvest. She went back to *her* kitchen and pulled out a stack of sweetbread she'd previously hidden. On her way back to the table, she gave the girls a loaf and told them to take it out on the porch to eat it.

Kalev hadn't touched his plate, and his self-justified scowl tracked Carni back to the table. Seething, he remained silently motionless. It took Carni a while before she looked his way and met his fiery stare. Only then did Kalev point to the door and growl. "What. Are. *They.* Doing here! *Their girls!*" It sounded more like an accusation than a question. She gave him *the look* to no avail. "Did you honestly think all orphans were boys?" She'd matched his biting tone. But Kalev ignored the question. "And you told them about the *Outpost*?" Kalev felt anger churn into his throat. "What were *you* thinking, Ema? Who else have you told? ծରରծψᛦ, maybe we should just send a written invitation to the whole Egyptian army. Yeah, let's see if they could drop by for the evening meal, you know, the one following our guerrilla army's evening muster."

Oops… He knew he'd gone too far. But, ψծծծରରծψᛦ, it was *his* job now to protect those boys… Carni matched Kalev's glare, slowly stood, and leaned across the table. The foreboding in his little ema's low and slow growl made the hard-muscled giant clinch. "*I* was hiding those boys *long* before *you* were in the picture, *General*!" She pointed in the direction of the Outpost. "I've fed and bandaged every single one of those boys. My robe dripped with the blood of those survivors after their Nubian skirmish. It took me a week to scrub the blood stains off this deck." Carni leaned so close their noses bumped as she hissed. Kalev's decades of "ema experience" had taught him to stay silent, not move, and don't look away. "It's been weeks since I've slept a whole night. Do half-dead refugee children show up at *your* door in the middle of the night? And another thing. Your brother spent countless, sleepless hours building that Outpost. He made sure those boys had a place to secretly live and thrive. Tell me, oh high and mighty Supreme Commander, what have *you done* for them? *Talk*?" Her scolding took on a life all its own.

"And as far as those traumatized little girls are concerned, I'll let you know when it becomes *your* business. Until then, you'd better make room for them because these are only the first of hundreds. Like it or not, little one, you've become the abba to hundreds and soon-to-be thousands of orphaned children. So Supreme Commanding little one, as a, um, very close friend used to say: improvise, adapt, and overcome!" Kalev's mind was so preoccupied, he'd missed Carni's loaded statement connecting her to his trainer, Adir.

The sound of children's laughter drifted in from outside, temporarily interrupting her tirade. Kalev opened his mouth to respond, but his ema wasn't finished. She pointed to the door again. "Those two boys worship the ground you walk on. They remind me of you and Hoshe'a. Treat them well or else!" She let the ominous warning hang in the air.

Carni grabbed the front of his tunic and pulled. Now their noses were smashed together. She hissed. "And don't you *ever* use that tone with me again. I'm your ema, and you will *always* respect me! Do you understand me, *General*?" They both heard five little gasps coming from the porch. Kalev sensed the three girls standing in the doorway and heard two more pairs of little feet scurrying away.

He quickly turned his face enough to kiss his fuming ema's cheek, then whispered, "I'll always respect you, Ema. I promise. And I ask that you show *me* respect in front of my troops." Carni cupped his face in her hands, kissed his forehead, and whispered back, "I agree. Now eat your food." She pinched his cheek and quietly sighed, "Look at you. You look like one of those starving orphans I found in the courtyard this morning."

Glancing over Kalev's shoulder, she saw the wide-eyed little girls at the front door. Sergeant Carni stiffened to attention and loudly declared, "Yes, Sir, General, Sir, right away, Sir. I'll take care of them and train them while the new medical billets are built, *Sir*!" Carni threw a perfect salute. Kalev smiled at her subtle *order*. *Great*, he thought, *girls, arghh*. But with his back to the door, Kalev gave her a slight nod, cleared his throat, and roughly replied, "Very well, First Sergeant, you're doing a fine job. Carry on." It wasn't lost on Carni her son had just unilaterally promoted her. She winked. "Thank you, Sir. *Now eat*, um, *please* eat, Sir."

12

Adir removed his foot from the back of the General's neck. Kalev slowly got to his feet. And for the eighth time this afternoon, Kalev spat the dirt from his mouth. "Kalev, you're too hesitant, and when you *do* move in, you lean your head in the direction of your next move. I can read you like a map. Surprise me, son! But remember, never give your opponent time to recover—strike and keep striking until he stops breathing. Whether from a quick 180-degree twisting snap or a hard stomp when he's down, necks break easily."

Kalev was using muscles he never knew he had, and they were all on fire. Adir's bored smile was infuriating. But what was worse, the man only had a single drop of sweat on his forehead. "I'm proud of you, son; you're almost there, but it's getting late, and I know you have things to do." Kalev barely had the strength to sheath his abba's nicked sword. Then he grew a sly grin. "So let me see if I've got this straight—you're quitting when I have you right where I want you." They both belly laughed, causing Kalev to wince from another muscle strain in his side.

"Sir, at tonight's muster, Ari is being promoted to general. I think you should be the one to tie on his new medallion." Adir smiled. "I'd be honored. It'd be good to see him; it's been a couple of weeks." Kalev opened his mouth to explain, but Adir put his hand on Kalev's sore shoulder and interrupted. "Kalev, I don't need to know why. I trust you both enough to assume your OPSEC (Operational Security) protocols have kept him away. Kalev nodded. "Yes, Sir. And thank you, Sir. He'll really be glad to see you tonight. Oh, and I was wondering if you could bring some of his clothes with you. My ema said your son is looking a little ragged these days." Adir grinned and shook his head. "I remember when he was a boy, the kid refused to wear any clothes at all. Ari would complain to his ema that they itched and kept him from fighting his enemies faster. He swore that clothes were for the other boys 'who aren't as fast a fighter as me.' He'd run around the whole day with nothing but his scabbard belt and wooden sword. This was a daily feud between him and his ema. I always thought it was hilarious, so I rarely stepped in. The boy would leave the house clean and dressed in a 'not-itchy' tunic. Then he'd show up for the evening meal wearing only a thick coat of dirt and his 'sword belt.' His ema would scream, grab his arm, drag him to the well, and wash him off. It was great entertainment. One time Ari accused her of trying to drown him. Following that particular attitude adjustment, he would silently let her scrub him from head to foot from then on." Adir chuckled, "Then his ema would march him to our 'hiding tree,' make him pull out his 'itchy' tunic, and watch as he reluctantly put it on. Only then was he allowed back in the house." Kalev laughed. "Hoshe'a ran around like that till he was eighteen, but let's keep that our little secret."

Adir was still laughing when he climbed onto his wagon. He pointed to the bulging tarp in the wagon bed. "As you know, I'm a blacksmith for the Egyptian infantry. But only when the army is in garrison. Last week the entire army left to go to war with the Assyrians. They took nine other blacksmiths with them. They'll be away for months. In the last five years, I've hidden away over fifty scimitars and about 150 Khopesh swords." With a sly grin, he pulled back the tarp covering the large pile of gleaming weapons. "They're all yours if you need them. I also, um, found a large pile of very rare iron sword blanks. I hid them behind my house. If you'd like, I can bring these to the Outpost tonight." Kalev was pleasantly surprised. "That's amazing, Sir. We need every sword you can spare. But *I am* paying you for these, the blanks, and any future weapons." Adir knew he'd have to bribe a few people and set up a covert supply chain to continually smuggle more metal out of the city. And it wouldn't be cheap. So he agreed to receive the money. "The bows are made quickly, and the metal arrow tips can be forged in a couple of hours. But a proper folded iron sword takes time, and the process can't be rushed."

Adir thought for a moment. "I guess we could build you a forge, and I could show a couple of the boys how to work the metal. I'd gladly take on four boys as apprentices. They need to be strong and used to hard work." Kalev was both humbled and grateful. "Thank you, Sir. We'll get started on clearing out a space for the new forge. And I'll have Colonel Yadin find the right boys for the job." Kalev paused. "Sir, I'd like to introduce you to the boys as a major. And it's time you're read in on our more sensitive operations. I could use your input." Adir self-consciously nodded. "It'd be an honor, General." Then Adir paused for a second and locked eyes with the taller man.

"Kalev, if Hezron was here, he'd be as proud of you as I am. His boy has become a true leader of men." Kalev's sight blurred, and his eyes dropped to the ground as tears began to stream to his nose. He couldn't trust his voice not to tremble, so he whispered, "Thank you, Sir. That means a lot to me. I miss him every day." Adir nodded. "Me too, son; me too." Adir turned in his seat and reached for the oxen reigns. Right then, Carni came around the back of the house and froze.

A couple of days prior, she was herding the three girls home from the Outpost. They each balanced large bundles of torn tunics in need of mending. Carni insisted that sewing was a skill every *good* woman should learn. Yet, for their imposed medical training, it was a requirement to practice the same stitching. "Eventually, it *will* be needed to close a boy's wound."

Halfway across Kalev's acreage, Adir reined in his horse right in front of the burdened women struggling across the field. Because of the teetering large bale of clothes Carni carried on her head, she didn't see the horse, ran into its hind quarter, and dropped all three bundles. Frustrated at the rider's rudeness, she glanced up to reprimand whomever. Carni inadvertently sucked in a sharp breath. She gawked at the same tall man with the boyish grin she'd always had a crush on. Even after her abba promised her to her deceased husband, Nun, she secretly wished she'd married Adir.

"Carni, I thought that was you." The fifty-three-year-old woman froze, and her mouth fell open. She tried to say something halfway intelligent, but all that came out was, "Um, yes. It's me." The three girls giggled. Carni looked over, loudly snapped her fingers, and pointed. "Take them into the house, then go play by the river. Move it."

As the girls stumbled toward the house, Carni looked up at Adir apologetically. He chuckled, "Even after forty years, some things haven't changed. You're the same bossy girl I loved as a teen." Now Carni was stunned. She instinctively croaked. "You loved me too?" Adir laughed as he dismounted. "Yes, you and I *both* loved you." She playfully slugged his shoulder as he bent down to retrieve her bundles.

Carni mistook Adir's movement, thoughtlessly leaned over, grabbed his head with both hands, and passionately kissed her long-lost boyfriend. Pleasantly surprised, Adir gladly returned the long kiss. It'd been a long time since his wife died. And he'd never kissed another woman until now. And this one was a tiger. His mind suddenly locked on movement in the top of the palm tree, sixty yards away.

They were still kissing when Adir slowly pulled his head back enough to see Carni's tear-stained face. He stood to his full six feet height and glared over her head. "We're being watched." It took a few seconds for her dazed mind to register his words. She'd forgotten about the Outpost lookouts. But the boys in the top of the trees were the furthest thing from her mind. Surprised at her own *observed* brazenness, the ema of two forty-year-old boys smiled through her joy-filled tears. Carni took a half-step back and slowly shook her head in amazement. She felt like an excited thirteen-year-old girl again. As he continued to count the lookouts in the trees, she deliberately surveyed Adir's broad shoulders and bared rock-hard arms. His tunic was taut over his muscled chest, flat stomach, and his delicious upper thighs. Something stirred in her "lower stomach."

Still staring at his abs, she reluctantly recovered her faculties and cleared her dry throat. "You, um, your beautiful skin…I mean, I'm—you look hungry; I mean, we're both really, *really* hungry. Let's, um, go to my house, and I'll fix you something, um, mouthwatering—I mean food; I mean something to eat." For the next eight wonderful hours, they'd been too busy to eat. By the time Adir reluctantly left for Kalev's training session, Carni was too exhausted to cook, so she let herself fall asleep smiling.

But now, standing here behind her house, her cheeks flushed; her mouth started to water, and her heart pounded in her chest. Adir saw Carni, glanced down at Kalev, then back at her, and smiled. Carni gasped. Instinctively she mouthed, "Does he know?" Adir cleared his throat to cover a laugh. He shook his head. "Kalev, I'll see you tonight." Lost in his memories, Kalev wordlessly nodded. Adir smiled, winked at Carni, and then rode away without looking back.

Kalev mindlessly watched as Adir rode away. The noise of the weapons clanging together in the back of the wagon masked the sound of Carni's footsteps as she walked up behind her huge son. Lost in her own luscious memories, Carni distractedly touched a deep, grit-filled cut on the back of Kalev's left arm. When her surprised little one tensed, Carni instantly realized she'd made a mistake. The jolt of fiery pain caused an immediate primal reaction in the distracted General. In a blur, Kalev spun as he drew his abba's sword. The weapon sliced through, barely stopping two inches from the side of his little ema's neck. Kalev's eyes went wide; he dropped the sword and pulled her to him. He started shaking and began to sob. "Ema, I'm so sorry…please, forgive me, please…"

Oddly, as she watched the sword speed toward her head, her only thought was, *Who's going to feed Hoshe'a when he gets home?* Carni took a deep breath as the panic subsided. "Little one, it's okay; it was my fault. I shouldn't have touched…" Kalev pushed her away and held her at arm's length interrupting her apology. "How can you say that? I almost cut your head off." Carni gave him *the look* and said, "Then I guess it's a *lesson learned* for both of us."

13

The drained general and Major Yadin sat on a pile of freshly cut palm logs. They were out of sight from the Outpost. Kalev liked briefing out here instead of in the TOC for two reasons. First, there weren't the usual well-meaning interruptions. Secondly, when he was even close to the Outpost, the skin on the back of his neck itched. He was sure he had at least six sets of eyes on him at all times. Even in the TOC he could just make out the watchmen in the tops of the surrounding palm trees.

He and Yadin were finishing up their individual nightly briefing. "Yes, Sir. According to Major Hoshe'a, the gnats in the palace are so thick, no one, including the pharaoh, can eat or sleep. Even with their keffiyehs (a square cloth traditionally worn as an Arab headdress and face scarf for protection from the sun and sandstorms) over their mouths, they keep choking and coughing up globs of the tiny flies. It's just as thick outside the palace as it is inside. Major Hoshe'a joked that their god, Khepri *junior* must really be mad at the temple priests." They both laughed.

Yadin glanced at his precise and extensive accounting report and smiled. He loved working with numbers. "It's been a logistical challenge to stay ahead of the exponential influx of new recruits. As of this morning, our numbers total…555. Two hundred two of those troops have come in the last three days." Kalev let out a low whistle. "So far we've been able to supply their first issue, clothes, cots, blankets, and training swords, etc., and have plenty to spare." The teen genius slowly shook his head. "The sheer volume of goods the foragers are bringing in every night is more than adequate to meet our current needs. But, if our numbers keep growing at this rate, we'll need all the supplies the foraging troops can find.

"Tonight, my company will finish clearing two more acres to hide our dry stores and our current surplus of camels and horses. Do *you* know how to ride, General? And do you need a horse?" Kalev remembered his abba's riding lessons when he was barely old enough to stay in the saddle. He enjoyed that comforting memory. "I do know how to ride. But make sure Heh Company gets all the horses they need first. Oh, and please keep in mind we will *eventually* need a separate living area for a platoon of, um, medical troops. Yadin brilliantly deduced the underlying meaning. "Girls, Sir! In the Outpost!" Kalev groaned and unconvincingly repeated Carni's question. "Did you honestly think all orphans were boys?" Yadin grinned. He knew this wasn't the General's idea, but he wouldn't dare disagree with the General's ema. "No, Sir. I'll get Major Hoshe'a's input, and we'll get to work on it tonight." Kalev nodded his thanks.

"Is that all, *Colonel*?" Yadin scanned his list again and began to roll it up. The teen nodded. "That's it, Sir." Without missing a beat, he added, "Respectfully, Sir, I'm a major." The General smiled and shook his head. “At tonight’s muster, you, Ofek, and Akiba will be promoted to colonel. Ari will be promoted to aleph-grade general.” Kalev locked eyes with the new colonel.

“Colonel Yadin, I’m proud of you! And I’m so grateful for that amazing brain of yours. Thank you for all your hard work. I imagine it’s been overwhelming.” Yadin nodded self-consciously. “Um… you’re welcome, Sir. But honestly, Sir, in these last few weeks, I’ve had a lot of fun with these challenges. It’s certainly not work for me.” Kalev chuckled. “Well then, Colonel, please send Colonel Ofek over before you go and *play* some more.”

When Yadin left, Kalev started to stretch out on the log. He ached all over. That afternoon’s training evolution began with Adir announcing that Kalev needed to shorten his hand-to-hand reaction time. This resulted in faster and more frequent faceplants in the dirt. The man’s superhuman speed/dexterity was both painful and awe-inspiring.

Suddenly, the back of Kalev’s neck started to itch. He quickly sat up and silently scanned in a complete circle. But all he heard was the hot wind blowing through the tops of the closest date palms.

Ofek walked up, yawned, and sat across from Kalev on another log. “Major Ofek, I’ve already met with Yadin, so now I’d like to know how *you’re* doing. Can I help with anything?” Ofek frowned, then looked down at his haphazardly scribbled notes. “Well, Sir, truthfully, I think these boys are getting bored with the training. Most of them haven’t been able to use what they’ve learned. And the ones who are already blooded looked lost or bored or both. Kalev considered this. “A new recruit graduates from basic training, then what?” “Then they’re assigned to a company based on the army’s immediate need. Kalev paused. “I’ve carefully watched their basic weapons training. Major, given your battle experience, how do you think the troops, just out of basic, would do against an armed platoon of experienced Egyptian soldiers?” Ofek quickly opened his mouth to respond. But to his credit, he wisely shut it and thought about his general’s loaded question. “Truthfully, Sir, against trained soldiers, we’d probably lose 60 percent.” Kalev grimaced. “Would you agree that loss percentage is unacceptable?” “Yes, Sir, but…” Kalev held up his hand. “Don’t get me wrong, I, too, still have a lot to learn. But 60 percent?” Ofek’s shoulders slumped.

Kalev nodded thoughtfully. “After this evening’s muster, find and ask Ari’s abba if he has any time to help you develop an advanced combat skills program.” Kalev unconsciously rubbed his neck. “The man is an expert, and we’d be fortunate to have his input. Ask him about a schedule for each weapon and hand-to-hand evolution. And that includes a rigorous skills testing. Then, I’d like to see a detailed training outline for the added weapons training evolutions. We’ll also need the previously graduated troops to undergo the same advanced weaponry skills exercises.

Ofek barely acknowledged the General’s directive. Kalev saw the boy’s confused and distracted expression as he tried to make sense of his own scribbled notes.

Kalev noticed Ofek's knee was nervously bouncing like it had a mind of its own. The General chuckled when he realized his own knee was keeping pace. "Colonel, it looks like we write our ideas in the same chicken scratch. Mine has degraded to the point where I can't even read my own writing. Ask *Colonel* Yadin for help drawing up the advanced framework." Ofek sheepishly nodded. "Yes, Sir. I, uh, never really had the patience to learn to read or write well." Kalev knowingly nodded. "Then, *Colonel*, report to my ema tonight after speaking with Adir. When *she's* done 'instructing' you, you'll be writing perfectly." *Or die trying*, Kalev silently thought. "So, *Colonel*, do you understand tonight's two important missions?" Ofek was still scowling, lost in thought as he slowly stood. "Yes, Sir, thank you, Sir." Kalev grinned. "Then make it happen, *Colonel*." He deliberately drew out the boy's new rank. But the preoccupied teen simply saluted and walked away. Kalev grinned to himself. "Wait for it…" But, to the General's surprise, the scatter-brained teen never turned around.

Kalev chuckled as he stood and began to walk toward the Outpost. His neck started itching again, so he slowed his pace but didn't turn around as he slowly reached for the knife. He stopped when he heard two young boys obliviously start to argue. "Oww, stop it." "I told you to be quiet, but you didn't. And the Supreme Commanding General of Yisrael's Army almost saw you. We're ordered to be silent and deadly, but you didn't do the order. And you're not even deadly." "I'm deadlier than you!" "Oww, you are not; you're a [illegible] head." "You're a [illegible] head." The loudly whispered argument degraded into a familiar-sounding knock-down boy fight. Including the requisite angry screams and cussing. The dead fronds on the closest palm tree rattled. Kalev grinned as he walked away. "Wow, they really do sound like Hoshe'a and me."

The sun was setting when Kalev and his officers pounded the platform's steps. They stiffly marched to the rear of the assembled troops. This was their first "official" inspection of the entire army. Kalev noticed that the teen officers were beaming with pride. Their handpicked First Sergeants had grown into their role, and they ruled their troops with a restrained Iron fist. The obvious results were commendable.

However, just before this evening's muster, Ofek alerted them to a serious security breach. "Yesterday, a platoon of basic trainees was given a half-day leave to go home and see their families. One of the trainees was observed by his squad leader talking to a large group of the recruit's family and friends. They had gathered on the road in front of his house. The kid was mindlessly spewing details about the Outpost and their training. That's when his squad leader, visiting his *own* parents next door, intervened. He apologized to the recruit's family and said the recruit was needed for an important assignment elsewhere. He marched the basic trainee back to his company and informed his drill sergeant."

So now, they all knew the army's OPSEC had just reached a critical tipping point as they dutifully marched behind their loudly grumbling General. They slowly moved through each rank, inspecting each troop in the company. They made sure the troop was properly clothed, knew how to salute, where to position his scabbard, and how to stand at attention with eyes front. The inspection started with Aleph Company. As expected, Heh Company was squared away, and the line of officers never had to stop to correct any infraction.

Eventually, they reached the rear of the basic training company. It was easily twice the size of the other two. But before they inspected the rear rank, Kalev abruptly stopped. Every trainee visibly stiffened. The General loudly cleared his throat and then erupted in an earsplitting roar. Following a long, mixed string of Hebrew and Egyptian expletives, he yelled, "I've seen enough." This had the calculated effect of causing a panicked tension throughout the ranks. Kalev's subsequent [illegible] tirade would be carefully chronicled by Yadin and retold around every survivor's campfire for decades to come.

Kalev, Ari, and the three other teen officers mounted the newly erected four-foot-high platform at the front of the drill deck. The red-faced general walked to the front edge and glared at almost 600 boy warriors.

The Commanding General of Yisrael's Army loudly cleared his throat again, made a show of rubbing his temples, and then silently glared at each rank of wide-eyed troops. No one dared to fidget, let alone breathe a word.

After a very long pause, Kalev let loose his practiced opening roar. "Do you hear that?" No one spoke. "That's what [illegible] OPSEC sounds like, you bunch of loose-lipped [illegible] [illegible] wannabe troops. *Silence*!"

Then, to everyone's surprise, the Commanding General leaped off the stage, sidestepped a wide-eyed first lieutenant, and bent down nose to nose with the basic training platoon's First Sergeant. Kalev instinctively knew this warrior got things done. Ari and the other three briefly traded concerned glances but kept their superior military bearing.

Kalev's almost inhuman glare scared the fourteen-year-old sergeant, but to the boy's credit, he took the spit-drenching "reprimand" like a pro. Kalev howled at the teen's face. "If I hear of any more troops talking to any civilians, including their parents, about this Outpost or any part of our operations, they will pack up and head home or back to the [illegible] streets.

"If the [illegible] kid is [illegible] lucky, he'll have a couple of days before the [illegible] Egyptian soldiers chain his [illegible] [illegible] and give the [illegible] wannabe a one-way trip to the [illegible] Wadi Hammamat mines, or the [illegible] mud pits. But first, the [illegible] little ingrate and his squad leader will explain to his ema why her [illegible] son *refused* to follow orders and keep his [illegible] mouth shut and his [illegible] disgraceful expulsion from this [illegible] amazing army." This threat caused the purposed, collectively terrified gasp from the kids fortunate enough to have a family. No one wanted to tell their emas they were removed from the army's protection because of their own stupidity.

The towering general's eyes remained locked on the First Sergeant. But the five-foot-one teen appropriately stared right through Kalev's sneering face like he wasn't even there. Though his face gleamed with Kalev's spit, the kid hadn't flinched, and Kalev was really impressed.

The mountain-of-a-man general wasn't finished and continued to roar. "It only takes one [illegible] to run off his [illegible] mouth in front of the wrong [illegible] person and we're all dead or worse." Kalev stiffened to attention. Glancing down, the General sneered at the top of the First Sergeant's head and quietly hissed. "No more trainee leaves will be granted until graduation. And First Sergeant, I hold you *personally responsible* for making sure your drill sergeants pound this order into every [illegible] trainee's head from day one!"

Not wanting or waiting for a reaction, the huge general did a perfect about-face and leaped onto the stage. He glared at all three companies. "That's right. I hold each one of you First Sergeants personally responsible for making sure this order is *severely* reinforced!"

Kalev paused. He wanted to give them a reason in addition to the fear of disobeying this order. Then that uncomfortable fire rose in his throat again. He yelled even louder, "This army is a living brotherhood, a family. It's *our* family. *No one, and I mean no one,* threatens the security of MY family, no one!"

Kalev was stunned by the *supposedly* terrified troops' response. Despite the profane tongue-lashing, screeching war cries began erupting through the ranks. He turned to look at his subordinates. Their surprised smiles must have mirrored his own. He turned around and glared again. As he'd hoped, the cheering converted into a unifying chant. "We are a brotherhood, a brotherhood, a brotherhood…"

Kalev gladly let the cheering die on its own. "Army of Yisrael, are we clear about OPSEC?" A mass of hoarse voices screamed an ear-splitting "*Yes, Sir*," and then the tense, deafening silence returned. Kalev expressly sneered down at the basic training company's First Sergeant again and loudly growled. "*We'll see!*" Only then did Kalev remember that this was the oldest son of Dan, the army's magnanimous *volunteer* medallion engraver. Kalev winked and nodded approvingly at the First Sergeant.

The General lifted his practiced scowl to the rest of the boy army. "There are troops—some may even be your friends—who can't talk about their specific missions. That is inter-army OPSEC. Do not talk to them about that; is that clear?" "*Yes, Sir!*"

"Troops, our numbers are obviously growing. Expect every aspect of your daily life and missions to change. Let your superior's orders be your expected new normal. Embrace the suck, and we'll all be better warriors for it.

"This army's new motto is, '*Improvise, adjust, and overcome*'!" Then Kalev yelled at the top of his lungs, "Repeat that!" The army thundered, "Improvise, adjust, and overcome, Sir!" The still sneering general nodded his approval. "Army of Yisrael, our only easy day was yesterday, so suck it up and drive on. *Roger* (received and understood) *that*?" "Roger that, Sir!"

Kalev paused, took six steps to the left, and then formally thundered into the silence. "Colonel Ari, Majors Yadin, Akiba, and Ofek, report!" The four teens took three steps forward and faced the troops. Each of their company's first lieutenants mounted the stage and stood behind their commanding officer. Kalev moved behind Ari and received Ari's updated medallion from Yadin's first lieutenant.

Right then He caught sight of a beaming Adir and a blushing Carni. It never registered in Kalev's mind that Adir had his arm across Carni's shoulders from the front as his ema leaned back against his trainer's chest. Carni instantly blushed at the realization that Kalev had caught them being not-so-subtle "*very* close friends."

"For the selfless courage it took to maintain this growing and thriving army. For demonstrating the 'lead from the front' attitude in battle. These commendable officers have brought honor upon themselves both individually and Yisrael's Army as a whole. Thus, Major Yadin, Major Akiba, and Major Ofek are hereby promoted to the rank of Colonel." The first lieutenants replaced their company commanders' medallions with their new rank.

Kalev nodded at Adir, who was now standing alone. The man proudly grinned as he walked up and took Kalev's place behind Ari. He leaned forward and whispered, "I've always been proud of you, son, but especially tonight." Kalev handed Ari's slightly larger medallion to a tearing Adir and stepped back. The Commanding General read the citation and roared.

"This army exists because of this selfless man's inspired, heartfelt vision and tireless labor. He leads from the front. He is a *true* man among men. This model leader's integrity and courage *will* be reproduced by every troop here. Colonel Ari has brought great honor upon himself, his family, and the Army of Yisrael. And so, it is my privilege to promote Colonel Ari to the rank of 'aleph-grade general." Kalev winced inwardly as he wondered if the subsequent cheers and applause could be heard all the way to the palace. He had to yell, "*General* Ari, take over."

14

Following the muster. Hoshe'a plopped down next to Kalev on the edge of the platform. As usual, the officers were required to let the enlisted troops go through the chow line first. Hoshe'a cracked a vibrating fart, and Kalev's stomach loudly growled at the same time. They looked at each other and belly laughed. They both wondered if there would be any food left after 580-plus growing boys had gone through the line.

When the last officers left the serving table, Kalev and Hoshe'a started to stand. Suddenly, out of nowhere, Carni appeared, grabbed Kalev's arm, and forcefully pulled him aside. Hoshe'a sat back down close enough to overhear the impending *discussion*. He knew the obvious warning signs. From as far back as he could remember, their ema gave off a weird energy force when an attitude adjustment was on the horizon. "Better him than me," he chuckled.

After thirty-plus years, Carni's ema undertone was obvious to Kalev, but to Carni, she spoke with due respect as she nervously glanced around. "General Kalev, um, tonight I had to make a last-minute, uh, First Sergeant command decision." She spoke faster, "The three girls have done an excellent job, but, um, I needed more food prep and serving support. The boys assigned to *help* me just weren't cutting it. They were constantly complaining about doing girls' work." She sighed, "Somethings never change." Kalev scowled and began to tell her he'd *personally* take care of the troops' attitude adjustments. But his ema interrupted.

"Do you remember what happened the one time I let you and Hoshe'a into my kitchen to help?" Kalev grinned. "I remember that for no reason at all. Hoshe'a threw your flour and olive oil at me." Carni scowled at the memory. "*Wrong*! I'd gone to the well for some water. By the time I got back, your everyday arguing had escalated into an all-out yelling food fight in *my kitchen*!" Kalev's eyebrows shot up in a futile attempt to look surprised and hurt at the accusation. But he knew better than to disagree with his ema's supernatural memory. "I knew then I was fighting a losing battle, so you were forever banished from *my kitchen*." Kalev smiled to himself. "The staged food fight was Hoshe'a's brilliant idea." Ema never asked them to do *her work* again. Carni activated her best inner-ema chutzpah and declared, "So I ordered the boys back to, um, Colonel Ofek for reassignment and recruited ten additional new girl recruits to help tonight." "*You what?*" Kalev roared louder than he meant to.

Hoshe'a watched his family in stunned silence. Kalev and Ema were actually sparring with "*the look*." His huge little brother had *always* managed to avoid 99 percent of their ema's targeted wrath. But now, in front of the troops, his little brother was actually going toe to toe with ema. And Hoshe'a was loving it. Kalev lowered his gravelly growl. "After what we talked about, you went ahead and unilaterally decided to breach our security protocols and bring in more civilians? Seriously? Didn't you hear me *politely* ask you to clear all future girl recruitment with me first?" Even as a forty-year-old man, Hoshe'a was ecstatic to see his little ema stiffen, swiftly grab Kalev's neck, and pull his giant brother's head down. She ominously leaned closer to Kalev's reddening face. "You didn't say that. And that's another thing. We are going to discuss your vulgar verbal attack on these boys later. But for now, I needed help; I got it, end of story! Besides, little one, *you've* asked for civilian help. Adir, Dan, etc." Kalev used every ounce of mental energy he had left to control himself. Then he unconsciously looked around. From somewhere in his jumbled thoughts, he blurted out, "Where *is* Adir?" Carni gasped, and her wide-eyed face went beet red. She hesitated. "I, uh, I don't know!" Then, without another word, Carni just walked away, leaving her enraged son/General swearing under his breath.

Kalev was still grumbling when he rejoined his big brother. As usual, Hoshe'a just *had* to add an ill-timed comment. "Well, that went well. You really told her." Hoshe'a started laughing as Kalev began a new round of swearwords at the serving table.

When Kalev had finally calmed down enough, Hoshe'a cleared his throat to get his brooding brother's attention. He motioned for Kalev to look back. Kalev turned to see Little Croc standing behind him with a well-used empty plate. Little Croc's cheeks gleamed in the bright torchlight. Grease dripped like sweat from the boy's smiling face onto the big crocodile tooth necklace, then down the front of his filthy tunic. Kalev uselessly tried to stifle a laugh. This only caused Little Croc to smile even bigger. Little Croc's company's First Sergeant, Achaz, ran over and apologized to the General and major. As the First Sergeant began to herd the reluctant little boy back to his company area, Kalev leaned over and whispered to Achaz, "Why don't you go ahead and line up your company for a second round?" Little Croc overheard this and quickly ran back to his place behind Hoshe'a. Hoshe'a then leaned over to Kalev and whispered, "I like this little guy's attitude; he reminds me of someone a lot bigger." Kalev reached over and playfully punched his brother in the shoulder. This knocked Hoshe'a out of line and back about three steps, almost tripping over Little Croc.

The boy saw this, and his little mind reasoned that the General had pushed the major aside to make room for his favorite shadow troop. Little Croc marched two steps forward to stand beside his favorite General. This produced a high-pitched snort from Carni. At the sight of Little Croc taking his *rightful* place in line, she respectfully asked Kalev, "Was *that* one of *your* unilateral command decisions?" Kalev scowled at his infuriating ema. The distracted General held his plate out to be served and looked up at the server. His jaw dropped. "Hello, Kalev." Raisa's smile caused his brain to stop.

And, of course, Hoshe'a started snickering. In a practiced blur, Carni raced over and dug her fingernails into Hoshe'a's skinny arm. Aware of the gathering boys' stares, Carni politely growled, "Major, I need you to inspect the new oven." Then expertly jerked him away.

The innocently blushing Kalev croaked, "Um," then quickly looked down. His mumbling was barely audible. But to the ever-patient Raisa, this huge man's shyness made him even more loveable. "Raisa, you're beautifully here. I didn't see you. Uh, I mean—I didn't know you were here tonight. Uh, I'm glad your pretty smile is here tonight; I mean, thank you for serving the food, um, tonight. I wasn't told you were coming in here to help here…arghhhh."

Kalev didn't realize the entire Outpost had grown silent and was intently watching their general's encounter with "that girl." Somehow, Hoshe'a had escaped his ema's life-threatening grasp and suddenly returned to stand behind his fumbling brother. Hoshe'a loudly whispered, "Don't hurt yourself, General." He poked his head out from behind Kalev. With his stupid grin, he chuckled, "I think what my brain-damaged little brother is trying to say is he's *really* glad you're here. He thinks you're breathtaking and he *really* likes you a lot. And…" But Hoshe'a's next embarrassing statements were violently expelled from his lungs.

Kalev barely noticed his arm automatically jerk backward. His sledgehammer-sized elbow slammed into Hoshe'a's bird chest. Everyone, including a semi-approving Carni, watched in amazement as Major Hoshe'a flew up and off the stage. Kalev's older brother soared five yards before he bounced off a pile of new bedding and finally landed with a groaning thud next to the fire pit.

The big man, still staring at his full plate, apologetically shrugged. Thoroughly enjoying her gentle giant's astonishing display of power, Raisa smiled approvingly. "I saw your ema in the market today. She and the girls were carrying large bundles of onions and garlic. Carni seemed more than pleased to accept my help. That's when she asked for my support tonight. I knew she had an ulterior motive, but I agreed because I'd hoped to see you."

Raisa slowly reached across the table and gently lifted his chin to stare into his eyes. Her touch caused Kalev to unconsciously suck in a breath and hold it. "Kalev, I understand and greatly admire what you're doing here. I even enjoyed your, um, colorful speech. Sweetheart, I give you my word I will never, um, breach your, um, OPSEC."

Kalev was so lost in her shining blue eyes; a whole thirty seconds passed before he could respond. Even then it took a nudge from the impatiently hungry Little Croc to remind him to say something. The towering general sheepishly croaked, "Um, thank you? And, um, I'd better eat this, and, um, thank you." Raisa smiled and graciously nodded to give him an out. Kalev groaned. Still unaware of his massive, silent audience, the dazed Supreme Commanding General of Yisrael's Army left the platform, slumped against a wall, and slid to the deck.

Heh Company's First Sergeant deliberately shattered the embarrassing silence with barked orders. "If you're done eating, report to your duty stations…Heh Company, grab your shovels and assemble on me…Aleph, report to the eastern grove…"

Carni and Raisa served the remaining troops, but their empathetic stares always returned to the defeated-looking Kalev. Carni leaned in to whisper, "I've never seen him so tongue-tied. You're perfect for each other. Your children will be a beautiful handful." Now it was Raisa's turn to blush and look down.

Hoshe'a was still rubbing his bruised chest when he leaned against the woven palm frond wall and slid down next to his *brutal* little brother. He opened his mouth to complain, insult, and/or cuss at Kalev. But stopped when he saw his best friend's tortured expression. Hoshe'a grumbled to himself for a while, then shrugged it off. Kalev pounded his fist into his forehead. "Stupid, stupid, stupid…" Hoshe'a smiled through his own pain. "Brother, you're not the first general in history to be conquered by a woman." Kalev groaned.

Ari balanced a plate stacked with seven loaves in one hand and two very large cups of wine in the other. He handed his brooding general a cup before he sat on Hoshe'a's other side. "I thought you might need a drink, Sir." Kalev distractedly nodded his thanks.

For the next twenty minutes, the General remained silently lost in his own thoughts. So Hoshe'a and Ari talked in low tones knowing the big man wasn't listening. Hoshe'a nodded. "Wow, that was a lot faster than I'd planned for!" Ari smiled, "Yeah, it's amazing how much digging 400-plus restless boys can do in a couple of weeks. Your idea about using the wagons has saved us at least 180 hours and hundreds of walking miles.

"According to your schematics and timeline, the main deck's excavation, including the added 175-yard extension to the southern end of the main deck, will be finished two days ahead of schedule. The three enclosed tunnels and the four wells with the attached wooden water channels *should* be finished within the week." Hoshe'a let out a low whistle. "Oh, and remember we'll eventually need a lot of that excavated hard-packed dirt for the final building phase." Ari nodded. "We've already noted that on your construction plans." Ari took a long drink of the sweet wine. "To date, Yadin's foragers have stockpiled enough think cedar planks, Zebra wood beams, nails, and pegs to completely enclose 'the Pit' twice over."

Hoshe'a chuckled, "So you *did* name it the Pit?" "Yeah, Akiba and I thought that sounded better than the troop's unofficial title, 'the [illegible] Pit.' So far, we've cleared out 131 black, red, and Egyptian cobra nests. And, of course, the competition for the longest cobra killed is ongoing. So far, the record is just under fifteen feet. The thing weighed in at 276 pounds. The tanners said a fourteen-plus-foot skin can be made into a full tunic, double sword back-scabbard, two knife sheaths, two pairs of sandals, and a wide belt. Those items and an updated snake-shaped medallion will be awarded to the winner at our first company muster following the Pit's completion. The larger sand viper skins will be stitched together to make company banners. We'll have plenty of skins leftover to make a type of large, two-troop camouflaged shield. I've seen the first one. It's a perfect screen." Hoshe'a packed his cheeks with bread while Ari continued. “Sir, I still don’t understand your ramp idea, but that’s okay…” Hoshe’a started to explain the geometry and pulley system. Ari held up his hand to interrupt his chief architect. “Whoa, I’ll leave the engineering mechanics up to you and Yadin. Just tell me when and where you need my people. Do you think the deck and elevated drill deck can be operational before the final phase starts? I’d like to start training again.” Hoshe’a did the calculations in his head. “That shouldn’t be a problem. The final phase is built in four sections. We’ll start on the north end next week. That’ll leave the southern drill deck open and clear to train for about two weeks. So, for now, I think it’d be wise to shorten your daily training schedule. We need to complete all construction as soon as possible. I’m hoping we can finish before the haboob season starts in about three weeks.”

“Roger that, Sir. Do you think we can add two forges to your deck plans? I’d like Heh Company to be as self-sufficient as possible.” Hoshe’a took a long drink, belched, and then nodded. “The forges and the additional 180 two-level stalls shouldn’t take more than five days.” Hoshe’a scowled at his cup. “Usually, obtaining skilled manpower and proper materials are the greatest time challenge to any building project.” Hoshe’a glanced at Kalev to make sure his little brother wasn’t listening. He lowered his voice anyway. “It seems that Yahweh has more than blessed us.” Kalev instantly tuned into their conversation and growled , under his breath. Hoshe’a and Ari both cringed. Thankfully, Akiba walked up to the three and handed both generals and Major Hoshe’a the list of trained and operational shadow troops.

“Sirs, the top three will deploy tomorrow morning. General, would you like to brief them before they head out?” Kalev read and reread the list. Then silently glared at the colonel. Akiba nervously glanced at Ari, who gave him a slight nod.

The colonel hesitated. “Sir, uh, I’m sure you’ve noticed both Little Croc and Little Frog look like full-blooded Egyptians. Sir, as you suggested, we’ve replaced Little Frog’s sword with a long dagger. First Sergeant Carni designed a tunic for him so he could wear an easily accessible back scabbard under his robe. He’s become lethal with both his dagger and the throwing stick (boomerang). I’ve watched both boys relentlessly spar and train. Their skills are even more surprising because of their small size. They’ll soon be a couple of our best fighters. They are our best shot for completing this mission undetected.” Kalev shook his head. “If they can stop arguing long enough to stay covert!”

Akiba nodded. “Yes, Sir, along that line, we’ve asked Sergeant Abraham to, um, *stress*, to those two in particular the absolute need for strict OPSEC.” Ari shook his head dubiously. “So are they sufficiently terrified of the need for Abraham’s additional *corrective actions*?” Akiba shrugged. “Truthfully, Sirs, that’s up to them. They’ve been trained, so we’ll see, but…” Kalev looked up from the list; the teen was scowling. “But what, Colonel?” “Permission to speak freely, Sir?” Kalev warily nodded. “Sir, up to now, our goal was to hide and train our troops. But now, we’re tasking them to hide in plain sight of the enemy and do it without any rear defense force. There are too many unknowns about this mission. I don't like it!"

Kalev silently agreed but only glowered at Hoshe'a. "Colonel Akiba. You've instructed them to remember and trust their training." Still worried, Akiba nodded. "Son, I have my own questions, but ultimately, a leader must trust that their troop's training is sufficient to complete their mission. Believe me, I'd trade places with them in a heartbeat. But I certainly couldn't hide in plain sight. And a fighting-age male in the marketplace would set off all kinds of alarms." Kalev glanced at Hoshe'a and growled. "I'd probably end up killing the target instead of protecting him anyway…no, I hate this plan, but tasking the little kids is a wise choice. I guess this is where *we* officers need to suck it up and drive on."

Kalev turned to Ari. "That said, why were Little Croc and Frog following me today?" Ari shook his head. "Sir, for the last three days, their shadow task has also served as a skills test for this particular mission." Kalev picked up on the indirect answer but purposefully let his silence do its work. Ari stared at Hoshe'a, hoping for a little support. Finally, the teen general shrugged and let out a frustrated growl. "Arghh. Sir, your ema, uh, *asked* us to covertly watch your back. She wanted to make sure your death was kept secret." "My *ema*, when?" "Um." Ari cringed, then glared at Hoshe'a again. The major was unsuccessfully trying to evade all three of their stares. "When you were unconscious from the beating."

"At first, myself, Akiba, and Yadin took turns. But after that first morning you, um, attacked us, every troop present volunteered for the covert overwatch mission. Those two were on the additional twelve-hour shadow mission for today."

Akiba cleared his throat and scowled knowingly. "Sir, am I to understand that they were discoverable?" Kalev grinned. "Their fight over who was more secret and deadly got a little loud." Akiba groaned, then looked at Ari. "I'm sorry, Sir. And as far as Prince Moshe's shadow mission is concerned, I'll separate and assign [illegible] a different day. I'll also bring Sergeant Abraham up to date on the sda[illegible] latest breach of protocol." Ari scowled. "Make it happen, Colonel. Tell him to use the boy's alternate days for their, um, additional *remedial* training." Akiba grew a sly grin. "Absolutely, Sir!"

15

Kalev had forgotten about his morning briefing and had fallen asleep about an hour prior to daybreak. Just as the hazy sun peeked over the eastern horizon, three sleepy-eyed boys pounded on the General's stall door, then wisely took four steps backward. The loud knocking caused Kalev to automatically leap out of bed. He still couldn't control this visceral reaction. Half asleep, the towering general roared and then busted through his newly repaired stall door again. With his sword raised, he looked like he was ready to kill. The three little boys were surprised but instantly recovered. All three quickly saluted, and Little Croc spoke up. "General, Sir, we were ordered to report to you for our before-mission talk." Kalev rubbed his eyes and took a deep breath. The three boys finally came into focus. He was suddenly embarrassed again. "I'm sorry about that." He cautiously looked around and then pointed to the stall next to Ox.

The brave little boys gently sat on the row of hay bales at the back of Ox's stall. Kalev smiled; he could tell they were well-armed. The General scowled to cover his uncertainty. "Out of this entire army, you three were chosen for this dangerous mission." All three boys smiled at each other, then proudly sat a little straighter.

"As you know, your mission is to find the man Moshe and guard his flanks. Your primary mission is overwatch. Do not let him see you. Do you understand?" "Yes, Sir," they shouted a little too loudly. "You need to look and act like common street orphans. If you have to communicate with each other, you'll only speak Egyptian. If you're not fluent in the language, remain silent. Blend into your surroundings, observe, and, as a last resort, protect him. You will follow him until he returns to his camp. Then quickly report back to Colonel Akiba. Any questions?" "No, Sir," they yelled in unison.

"If the target notices you, you'll break off from the detail and immediately report back to your colonel. You three are the first of many. A full platoon is being trained up for this mission. But you are the first, our best!" Little Croc's hand shot up. Kalev stifled a grin and nodded. "Sir, can we eat while we're at the market?" Kalev shrugged. "I guess so." The General put his finger to his lips and whispered. "But always remember mission success is measured by your expert ability to remain *deadly silent*. Do you understand?" "Yes, Sir," they forcefully whispered back. "Stay safe, troops." Kalev stiffened and saluted. The three oblivious and brave boys saluted and ran away.

Suddenly, Kalev felt sick. He walked over and plopped down on a hay bale. He put his face in his hands. "Great leadership, Kalev. You've just sent them on a suicide mission. All it would take is one curious soldier, and all of this is lost. What have you done?"

Kalev looked up to see Carni. "I heard those boys yelling. And yes, they look exactly like the Egyptian street orphans they *used* to be." She saw Kalev's worried look and smiled sympathetically. "Worrying over children. Well, little one, welcome to parenthood."

Kalev stood to go back to his stall, but Carni reached up and put a hand on his arm. "Son, I needed to talk with you about two other things." Kalev sat back down and exhaustedly nodded for her to continue. "I was at the market yesterday. And Adina pulled me aside and said she'd always be in your debt for taking her son. But now she's scared for her four daughters. They've become old enough to work as servants or, worse, in the palace. She wants you to take and train her girls too. Kalev, I already have fourteen girls living in the house. There's no more room. Plus, last night after the evening meal at the outpost, Yadin, Raisa, and I did a food store inventory. We have the resources to make bread, beer, and wine. And, of course, there is plenty of fish and/or croc meat. But last night was the last lamb or goat meat in this part of Goshen. Families have sacrificed to give us their remaining stores of vegetables, goat, and lamb."

Carni read her son's expression and winced. She'd just inadvertently added to the problem. Kalev's desire to protect the young and weak was overwhelming his rational thinking. It added another layer to his too heavy burden. "I'm sorry, little one. I'll figure it out." Still staring at his feet, Kalev shook his head. "Ema, I don't know what to…" But she'd already walked away.

Following the next evening's muster, Kalev watched as stacks of loaves were placed into eight huge baskets. The General followed the loaves, Ari, and Akiba out to the riverbank. The sun had already set, and the dusty burnt orange sky was darkening to a deep blue. Ari watched as Akiba distributed the loaves to the boat crews first, then to each squad leader before they shuttled across the river. Kalev watched the silent and expertly orchestrated operation. Ari's worried expression embodied how Kalev felt. Kalev whispered, "Ari, I know how you feel. I assume they haven't reported in." "Not yet, Sir." Kalev didn't have to read the boy's face. He knew they were both feeling the same nauseating dread. "Ari, it's my burden to carry, not yours." Ari looked at Kalev without a word.

As if on cue, the three Egyptian-looking boys came swaggering down the shoreline. Kalev grinned, then quietly commented, "Our spies seem pleased with themselves." Ari grumbled something under his breath as the boys stood tall, saluted, and Little Croc declared, "Mission accomplished, Sir."

Ari, sounding more on edge than a commanding officer should, growled. "That's not up to you, Private. We'll contact our sources. *They'll* decide if you've accomplished your mission." Kalev knew the teen was trying to hide his tortured relief, so the General stepped forward and demanded, "Report." Little Croc started to speak, but Kalev cut him off. "Who is this squad's leader?" The tallest boy saluted. "Sir, I am, Sir." Kalev looked at the boy's medallion. "Very well, Corporal, report."

"Sir, we marked our target and his brother on the road to the marketplace near the palace. We thought we should split up and follow from different directions. My size makes me look a lot younger than I am." Kalev had to cough to cover a laugh. Ari just looked away and pretended to be watching the last of Heh loading onto the feluccas. The ten-year-old continued, "So I ran right past them and watched from behind the first stall at the market. The one with the fresh bread. I started to sit, but I almost sat on my axe blade." Ari couldn't take it any longer, so he covered his mouth, pretended to cough, and just walked away. "We took up positions behind and to each side of the target. We slowly rotated through each position like we were trained. The target and his brother stopped in the center of the market. When they stopped"—he pointed at Little Croc—"he was paying more attention to the apples than the target. He almost ran into the back of the target's brother." Little Croc's eyes fell to the dirt. He sniffed and quietly whispered, "I was hungry, but I'm sorry, Sir." Kalev let the boy think about his mistake. Then growled, "Lesson learned?" Little Frog looked at his general with sad eyes and nodded. Kalev nodded to the corporal. "Continue." "General, Sir, you know that place where there are five steps up to the place where they display slaves?" Kalev nodded. "The target's brother stood at the top of those steps. The target would whisper something to his brother—then his brother would yell at everyone. He yelled about the history of the Hebrews, how they came to Egypt, and how it was time to leave. Then he'd point at the target and say he was the one Yahweh had chosen to lead us out of Egypt. Sir, sometimes the target would turn toward the palace, point his finger, and stutter his demand for Pharaoh to let the Hebrews go back to the land Yahweh promised to their abba, Abraham." Kalev subconsciously stiffened. "Sir, the target sat at the feet of his brother the whole day. Just before sunset we followed them back to their camp on the city side of the canal. Then we came straight here." Kalev nodded. "Give Colonel Akiba this same report. Tell him I think at least two of our shadow troops need to be hidden at the market ahead of the target." The other private, Menachem, spoke for the first time, "Sir, on the way out of the city, I heard the target tell his brother that Yahweh had spoken to him and that they'd head to Pharaoh's throne room first thing tomorrow." The corporal added, "I was thinking, if there is going to be an attack on the target, the palace would be the perfect place." "I agree. We need to keep eyes on the target, even in the palace." "Sir, how do we…?" Kalev cut him off. "Corporal, that's a question for your colonel." "Yes, Sir." Kalev nodded. "Now go get some food. Please bathe and get some sleep. And well done." The three boys beamed with pride, saluted, and left. Kalev turned toward the river and looked for Ari, but he and his troops were gone. Even the guide rope was already submerged. The familiar peace of the quiet river returned, and Kalev closed his eyes and soaked it in as if it was life itself.

In time, Kalev returned to the nearly empty Outpost. He sat by the fire pit and wearily watched the tall flames dance upward. Carni saw him and brought over two plates of food. They both ate in silence until Kalev loudly belched, "Good meal, Ema." Carni slapped the back of his bald head. "Manners, General. I taught you better than that. I…" Kalev grinned, pulled her close, and whispered. "Have I told you how much I've missed you lately?" Carni grinned and pretended to push him away.

Kalev yawned. “I didn’t sleep much today. I’ve been thinking about what you said.” Carni started to apologize for adding to his burden, but Kalev interrupted, “Ema, I’m not sure what to do about the food we need. But I *can* see two necessary missions for the girls.

“First, you’ll need to train a support platoon of troops to help with the food acquisitions, storage, and prep. Ema, you know what this child army needs now: food, medical supplies, etc.” Kalev rubbed his temples. “Yadin is a genius when it comes to accounting and organization. But this army needs your powerful ema skills to plan and train for our future needs. For instance, I know we’ll need a butcher to train at least two squads of troops. They’ll learn how to dress out a lamb or goat or whatever. But that is the extent of my foresight. This logistics thing makes my head hurt.

“Secondly, according to Adir, every platoon of soldiers needs at least one qualified medical troop. He referred to these troops as medics. The medics will work and train with their assigned platoons. That means they’ll have to go through the exact same basic and advanced training as the boys.” Kalev held up his hand to stave off her objection. “The military training is non-negotiable. And *if* they graduate, they can go through your food, logistics, and/or medical training evolutions.

Once your primary platoon of girl recruits has graduated, *you’ll* be promoted to the rank of captain. Yadin will be your superior officer. But you will be the commanding officer over both the food support and medical platoons. Watch their basic training classes. Make a list of the girls you’ll want as your two lieutenants and First Sergeants. Then submit that list to Yadin for his approval.” Carni hadn’t thought that far ahead, and now she felt trapped. “Wait a minute, little one. I’ll probably have close to twenty little girls running around here by week’s end. And probably a lot more in the next couple of weeks. Kalev, I’m not a soldier and *definitely not* an officer. I’m not qualified, nor do I want to be responsible for that many girls.” Kalev smiled and whispered, “Suck it up, Captain, and, oh, welcome to *my* world.”

The Commanding General and his ema walked back to the house in silence. Hundreds of worries bombarded their minds, and talking seemed to take too much effort. Kalev was able to catch Hoshe’a just before he went to sleep. “Hoshe’a, I need to talk to you *outside*.” Hoshe’a complained all the way into the courtyard. Kalev got right to the point, “How did my spies do today?” “Kalev, I don’t know. I work in the palace; though I heard Aharon shouting in the marketplace, I didn’t see him or the boys.” Kalev grabbed the front of Hoshe’a’s robe and pulled him close. The intensity in his stare was unnerving. “Listen carefully, Hoshe’a, I’m ordering these little boys into the viper pit of a merciless enemy. They could easily be picked up and used or sold as slaves.” Kalev took a deep breath and then hissed. “The *least* you can do is observe and report back daily. You know how I feel about *him*…and believe me, I will not sacrifice one of those boys’ lives for that jackal.” Hoshe’a cleared his dry throat. “Kalev, I would never ask you…” Kalev cut him off, “No report, no protection!” Hoshe’a nodded. “I’ll figure something out. Thank you for watching his back. Oh, I heard that Moshe and Aharon will be appearing before Pharaoh tomorrow morning." Kalev scowled, "Then I expect you to keep an even closer eye on the boys." "Wait, you mean *in* the palace? How…?" "I don't know—just observe and report," Kalev ordered. Wisely, Hoshe'a silently nodded. Kalev grumbled something under his breath, turned, and headed for his stall.

Kalev had decided that until Heh's outpost was completed, the command and staff meetings would remain on an as-needed basis. Except for the foraging missions and minor emergencies, Kalev had plenty of extra time to train with Adir.

After a couple more painful weeks, Adir assured the General that their private sparring had exceeded his expectation and they needed to move Kalev's personal weapons and tactical planning evolutions to the Outpost's drill deck.

Initially, Kalev was glad he wouldn't have to eat any more dirt. But his relief was rudely interrupted the first time he face-planted into the hardwood deck. He bit his cheek, split his bottom lip, and smashed his crooked nose. Kalev wasn't sure which tasted worse: the dirt or his own blood.

Early on, Ari and Hoshe'a decided that Heh's outpost needed to go underground—literally. General Ari and Colonel Yadin's 250-plus available troops dug out and then hauled the hard-packed dirt and sand into the desert. Every other night Yadin's 380-plus basic training troops joined in the digging. Altogether, it took them three and a half weeks to excavate the massive three-acre area. "The Pit" was twenty-five yards deep, seventy-five yards wide, and 385 yards long.

The Commanding General told Ari that he didn't want to know any details concerning the building of Heh's outpost. Kalev wanted to see if he could "overhear" any information from the troops involved.

One morning, just before sunrise, he'd purposely met the first troops returning from the other side of the river. Four of the newest basic training recruits were shocked to see the army's Commanding General materialize on the beach in front of them. In unison, all four panicked troops glanced back at the other shore. Their drill sergeant stood on the beach with his hands on his hips and glared at them. Their expressions morphed into all-out terror. Kalev gruffly asked the tallest one, "So, Private, what was your mission tonight?" The wide-eyed boy glanced between his battle buddies and their sergeant. To the eleven-year-old boy, the sound of the General impatiently clearing his throat made him nauseated with dread. Their drill sergeant was the meanest [illegible] he'd ever met. But this fire-breathing demigod was Sergeant Abraham's boss's boss's boss. And he'd just asked a direct question. "Sir, General, Sir, um, uh, we were over there following orders, um, General, Sir." The other three frightened boys didn't know what else to do, so they stood at attention, saluted, and repeated, "We were over there following orders, General, Sir." Their furious drill sergeant instantly dove into the river and swam toward his [illegible] recruits. Kalev was astonished that this sergeant could both swim and breathlessly swear a continuous string of Egyptian and Hebrew expletives at the same time. But before the belligerent drill sergeant could reach the beach, Kalev scowled at each boy, growled something foul under his breath then nodded. “Very well, troops, carry on.” The four quickly saluted, lifted their skiff to their shoulders, and escaped through the closet Outpost entrance. But Kalev knew the was no escaping a drill sergeant’s wrath. There was an ingenious method to the basic training madness. Every troop was mentally broken down, stripped of any individualism, and then built into a cohesively lethal unit of warriors.

Kalev waited for the still-swearing Sergeant Abraham to reach the beach, stand at attention, and begin to apologize for those  recruits. Kalev held up his hand, and the teen stopped yelling. “Sergeant Abraham. From what I’ve heard from your superiors and what I’ve just witnessed, you are an asset, a true force multiplier for this army. Keep up the great work.” Kalev didn’t wait for a reply from the astonished teen. They wordlessly traded salutes, and Kalev walked away. He counted exactly ten seconds before the drill sergeant resumed his explosive “corrective admonishments.”

16

It was around two in the morning on a moonless night when an ominous wraith slowly rose out of the river mist. It climbed the bank southwest of where Heh Company was supposed to be training. His robe was black. His dark keffiyeh was pulled low over his head, with the tail covering the lower half of a mud-smeared face. Only his darting eyes seemed human. He walked like an Egyptian crane. Bent over, he'd pause mid-stride, look, then carefully place each silent step. But, as far as the specter could see, there was only scattered brush, flat, hard-packed sand, and scattered boulders on this side of the river.

Ten minutes into the desert, the dark figure saw a dim glow coming from the other side of what he mistook as a solitary boulder. Low crawling, he slithered around the rock and peered over the edge of a huge, brightly lit trench. Scattered bushes, boulders, and low dunes surrounded the trench's rim. The deck area was set up like the original Outpost. But these decks and walls were lined with a beautifully finished tongue-and-groove cedar planking. Hundreds of six-foot-wide by twelve-inch-high loft-over animal stalls lined both walls the entire length of the deck. The man in black saw an entire company of silent boys sitting on a raised platform listening to an older teen's instructions. Based on the faint echo, he guessed the stage was over 300 yards away. "...using the edge of the shield, swing it sideways, aiming between the chin and chest..."

Suddenly, the watcher felt a severe sting on the back of his neck. It burned like a camel spider bite, so he reached up to sweep it off, but the pain intensified. The watcher instinctively realized it was a sword, knife, or spear tip. He froze in place. The young teen bent down to the stranger's ear and hissed, "Without a word, you'll obey my orders *exactly*. Nod if you understand me, da[illegible]?" The ominous stranger smiled but complied.

The perimeter guard used his spear to goad the supposed "Egyptian marauder" down a recessed ladder. It was obvious that the wide-eyed little troop waiting at the bottom was unsure what to do next. The belligerent squad leader loudly whispered down to his counterpart. "I have to make sure he was alone. Take him to the General; if he doesn't comply, [illegible]." The small sentry marched the towering phantom at spear point down the length of the amazing structure to the training area. The dark stranger kept his hooded head bowed in apparent submission. The little troop would intermittently jab the big man in the back, but this only served to "poke the bear."

By the time the pair stopped in front of the platform, the entire Heh Company had stood and crowded to the edge of the stage. The sentry's irritating spear tip jabbed the black-robbed man again as he began to officially present the intruder to his superior. But before the troop could speak, the stranger spun. In a blur of practiced movement, the spear was jerked out of the shocked boy's grasp and rotated in the air as the watcher drew his own sword. The stunned boy tripped and fell backward, knocking the air from his lungs. The dark man stood over the dazed guard with his sword and the sentry's spear tips barely an inch from the little boy's tearing eyes.

The outsider heard 200-plus swords drawn from their sheaths. But it was the distinct sound of multiple bow strings stretching that froze the man in place. General Ari grinned to himself at the scene below but silently waited to see what would happen next. Still glaring at the cowering little guard, the stranger growled in Egyptian, "That was [illegible] foolish. *Never ever* move that close to your captive; now you're vulnerable and unarmed."

To his credit, the little guy with a big attitude returned the sneer and surprisingly growled back in the same language. "Maybe, but you're outnumbered 253 to one, so who's the [illegible] fool now, you [illegible] Egyptian pig?"

With his mud-caked face still hidden behind the keffiyeh, the stranger grinned up at the oldest teen on the stage. "General Ari, debrief now." Ari sheathed his own sword, cleared his throat, and stiffened to attention. "Yes, Sir, General Kalev, Sir." At the mention of his name, the entire battalion sheathed their swords and stiffened to attention. Kalev looked down. "Lesson learned?" Slightly embarrassed, the still defiant private nodded. "Yes, Sir." Kalev helped the boy up, flipped the spear around, and handed it to the troop.

General Ari turned the training evolution over to Colonel Akiba and jumped off the platform. Ari and his general started toward the other end of the inverted outpost. As they walked away, Kalev heard Akiba yelling orders. "Sergeant, I want four two-man teams evenly spaced around the upper perimeter. He should have been stopped at the river. Set up warning noisemakers near all possible access points. Everyone else is to complete this evolution before we begin the ten-mile run." "Yes, Sir," came the loud reply.

Kalev shook his head and chuckled. "General, I didn't know you'd trained a flight of archers." Ari grinned. "Sir. Everyone in Heh Company is an expert marksman." "Excellent job, General Ari. I'm proud of you, son." "Thank you, Sir." "And did the latest protection team return tonight?" Ari grinned nervously. "Yes, Sir."

"Sir, as you know, two weeks ago our spies couldn't figure out how to follow the target into the palace. But yesterday, Little Croc, Little Frog, and two other privates were assigned to the target's overwatch." Kalev abruptly stopped walking and scowled at his adjutant. "Wait, they shadowed the target at the same time?" Ari shrugged apologetically. "Sir, every day we have to adjust the number of troops on each of the five shadow missions. Keeping track of each troop's place in the variable rotation is mind-numbing. Colonel Akiba's lieutenant forgot to assign Croc and Frog to separate missions. It was an accident. But they did very well." Kalev silently waited. He could tell Ari felt overwhelmed again.

"Honestly, Sir, Colonel Akiba and I still hate the dangerous unknowns. And so far, the target hasn't shared his schedule with us." Kalev smiled at the boy's attempt at humor.

"Yesterday, the target and his brother bypassed the marketplace and walked straight to the palace. The four troops split into two pairs. Privates Little Croc and Little Frog followed the target to the palace, while Privates Amun and Hapi waited just inside the city wall. They wisely figured that if anything happened to the other two, they would find Major Hoshe'a, and hopefully he could do something about it." Kalev nodded. "Smart move." Ari looked relieved. "Privates Little Croc and Little Frog saw a line of water jars beside the palace entrance. They quickly hid and watched as numerous servants their own age carried the tall urns inside. So the two audaciously brave boys each picked up a water jar and followed the others."

Kalev's jaw dropped, and he stared at Ari wide-eyed. The teen general shook his head. "It seems those two have a rare character flaw or strength, depending on the circumstance. Those two are wilfully oblivious to danger. I guess after being abandoned as young children and having to survive on the streets, everything else is easy. And because of their justified fear of Sergeant Abraham, they blindly obeyed the order to improvise, adapt, and overcome.

"So, once they were in the main hallway to the throne room, they could easily see and even hear the target and his brother. Windows lined the east side of the corridor. In front of each window was a potted date palm tree. The boys broke off from the others and started watering each palm, working their way toward the throne room. At one point, they saw Major Hoshe'a following his master. They were walking right toward the two troops. Our boys stuck their heads in the palms and tried to look like they were testing the soil. Panhs and your brother walked right by without even turning their heads. Then they heard the target's voice echo down the hall. The boys reported that the target fearlessly threatened the pharaoh. Moshe, or rather the target, said that if Pharaoh didn't let the Hebrews go to worship the one true Yahweh, Yahweh would send a massive swarm of flies, the likes of which has never been seen. And, of course, Pharaoh cursed the target and his brother, then had the guards remove them from the throne room. When the two brave little troops saw that Moshe and Arron were heading their way. They simply turned their backs, put the empty water jars on their shoulders, and quickly walked in front of the cussing target and his brother, right toward the main entrance. When the boys exited the palace foyer, they turned to the side, placed the empty water jars down, and bent over to pick up full ones. Our two brave troops linked up with the other two and followed the targets out of the city and back to his encampment. They ran back here to report."

Ari groaned, "Sir, I'm really proud of them. They improvised and adapted flawlessly. But...arghh. Sir, personally speaking, that knowledge only adds to my dread about future missions. I'd prefer to go myself. I hate this waiting and watching. I'm not built that way." Kalev nodded. "Me either."

Then a thought hit Kalev, and he chuckled. "Ari, my ema would say you sound like an abba. You worry about your kids like any caring parent does." They both unconsciously sighed in unison.

After they'd walked about a hundred yards in burdened silence, Ari glanced at his brooding commander and grew a sarcastic smile. "Sir, we're too young to have 900 children. At least *I* am." They both laughed.

"Sir, with your permission, Colonel Akiba and I agree that the two privates should be promoted at the first muster after the Pit is completed. And that the boys' report should be written into the basic training manual." Kalev smiled. "You're calling this amazing refuge the Pit?" Ari smiled. "Yes, Sir, Colonel Akiba and I thought that sounded better than the troop's unofficial title: the L⟍Ш✛ᘓ Snake Pit. Great idea, General, make it so."

"General Ari, how many days in a row have our troops been protecting the target?" Ari smirked. "It's been seventeen days straight, Sir." Kalev nodded. "And how long before this *Pit* is self-contained?" Ari looked around. "Major Hoshe'a's plans have us fully operational in ten days."

"Very well. I think we all could use some downtime. These boys need to be boys. Ten nights from now, all training evolutions, foraging missions, and further building projects will be suspended for forty-eight hours. Following that evening's muster and promotion ceremony, all troops will have the night off. During the meal, Little Croc will give a summary of this latest mission to the whole battalion. Then I'd like a pair of your best-trained troops, and maybe even your abba, to demonstrate some of the new advanced fighting techniques." Ari smiled with pride. "Absolutely, General." Kalev thought out loud, "It's been a long time. Somehow, I'm going to find some beef for that evening's meal. This whole army has earned it.

"The next evening we'll conduct inter-army competitions right here. We'll set up targets for the longest bow shot, knife and sword throws, hand-to-hand matches, trick riding, etc." Ari smiled his approval. "Great idea, Sir. We should probably have the enlisted troops and officers compete separately. I'll ask my abba to put on a couple of additional advanced fighting skills demonstrations." Ari grew a sly grin. "He'll need a sparring partner." Kalev winced. "I agree, and I think you're the perfect candidate, General Ari." Finally reaching the far end of the main deck, the two generals sat at the newly built officer's dining table. They watched little Evee run toward their table with two sloshing cups of beer. She slammed them down on the table, almost spilling the rest of the pungent beer on the two generals. When she ran back to the new ovens to get some sweetbread, Kalev smiled. "So the girls have invaded Heh Company too?" Ari rolled his eyes and groaned. "Your ema didn't ask for approval; the girls just showed up one night." Kalev shook his head. "The First Sergeant will receive additional instruction on how to use the chain of command."

Right then, Hoshe'a plopped onto the bench across the table. "Can I be there for Ema's browbeating?" Kalev shook his head. "Of course. In fact, I order you to perform the perilous attitude adjustment yourself." Hoshe'a's eyes went wide as he tried to think of an excuse. But eventually the major glanced at Ari, then softly stammered, "Uh, um, okay."

Kalev looked up at the bright stars and full moon. Then he took in the magnitude of the new outpost. "By the way Major Big Brother, I really like what you've done with the place." Both generals laughed. "But seriously, Hoshe'a, I never knew this kind of thing was even possible. I'm really impressed. Thank you." Hoshe'a smirked. "General, your worshipful awe for me is almost thanks enough. But I'd really feel appreciated if *you*, um, let me watch *you* give ema the educational attitude adjustment." Ari smiled knowingly. "So, Major Hoshe'a, I'm sure I didn't just hear you refuse your Supreme Commanding General's direct order."

Kalev smiled. "General Ari, one more thing." "Yes, Sir?" "When any of our soldiers are threatened, don't hesitate to remove the threat. The moment you saw me grab his spear, your sword should have been at my neck." Ari was smiling. "Sir, the second you stepped onto the main deck, I knew it was you." Kalev looked doubtful. "Your shoulders stretched that robe too tight, the size of your feet, and the way you pound the deck instead of just walking. But mostly the way your, um, full-sized head made that keffiyeh look small. Hoshe'a cleared his throat to hopefully hide a laugh. The 'hesitation' you saw was my test to see if any of my troops acted outside of my directions. I was halfway hoping someone would. I wanted to see you put my abba's training into action."

Kalev put his hand on the teen's shoulder. "So, General Ari, did you just call your Supreme Commanding General a fathead?" Ari's eyes went wide, and he started to stutter. Kalev and Hoshe'a belly laughed. "Relax, son. I'm just kidding. But seriously, do you really think this robe makes me look fat?" Ari smiled. "Yes, Sir, um, with all due respect." Hoshe'a was drinking the thick beer when he started to laugh. Beer shot out of both nostrils, causing Ari and Kalev to laugh themselves to tears. They ate, drank, belched, and teased each other for a while.

Eventually, they got back to business. "Ari, take some time to visit with your abba. He said he misses you. Did the initial load of Khopesh swords reach Heh Company first?" "No, Sir. Ofek, Akiba, and I agreed that the majority should be used for advanced weapons training. The rest will be engraved and issued as a formal reward for achievements above and beyond."

Kalev cringed and then stared at Ari. Reading his thoughts, the teen general chuckled. "Sir, do you agree that the two boys' actions in the palace embodied the above-and-beyond attitude?" Kalev couldn't argue with that. "But how in the world will Little Frog be able to carry a full-size Khopesh? He can barely keep that long dagger out of the dirt." Ari laughed. "My abba is already working on a scaled-down version for the two boys." Captain Dan from the Dan tribe will engrave them and update the four troops' medallions next week.

"By the way, Sir. With your permission, I think it's appropriate to offer Dan a commission as a captain. He appreciates the army's OPSEC. Plus he's grateful for his sons' protection. He's already memorized the basic training manual. He said that if we ever offered basic training to adult recruits, he'd be the first in line."

Kalev thoughtfully nodded his approval. "Sir, per your suggestion, all three of his oldest sons, our company's First Sergeants, have been offered and refused a commission. They all three independently said they'd rather work for a living." Kalev laughed. "I get that."

17

As the rising sun began to lighten the dark blue horizon, Kalev tiredly plodded north next to the canal. This tributary divided the Hebrew farms and hamlets from the Egyptian fields. "[illegible], not *one animal* in all of Goshen," he grumbled aloud, then returned to his oblivious funk.

The skin-crawling irritation on the back of his neck broke his dark musings. The General stopped, dropped into a combat crouch, drew his sword, and scanned in a practiced 360-degree spin.

That was when he felt a barely perceptible vibration in the air. As the buzzing got louder, he watched an odd haze rapidly approach from the south. In less than a minute, the haze had darkened the morning sky. He watched as a thick greyish blanket of very large biting horse flies rained down to about four feet over the canal. The wave surged toward the city. *And hopefully into Hotep's tent*, Kalev mused. After a couple of minutes, the massive layer of insects stopped in unison and settled to the ground. As far as Kalev could see, every square acre of the Egyptian fields was blanketed with Egypt's beloved symbol of military prowess. Kalev smirked. "Who's the conqueror now, you [illegible] Egyptian pigs?" Kalev studied the flies and then mockingly yelled at the empty sky. "Nice trick. But I needed cattle, not flies, you useless [illegible] Yahweh!" Kalev spat in the dirt, shook his head in disgust, and continued his walk up "complaining lane."

Lost in his sour brooding, Kalev had unconsciously walked half a mile past his house. He was still lost in thought when he tripped over something and toppled to the dirt. Kalev sat up as a lamb limped over, climbed into his lap, and nibbled at his tunic. He held the very wet and smelly lamb at arm's length and stood. He was instantly swarmed by a huge flock of wet and muddy sheep. "Where did you come from?" he wondered aloud.

That's when he saw that a wide swath of the bank on both sides of the canal had collapsed. There were hundreds of hoof prints in the mud. Kalev tracked the prints to his right. Large segregated herds of animals were eating the tall Goshen grass. Kalev thought aloud, "They must have fled from the horse flies. Wait, it just happened. How did they know the flies were coming?"

Kalev saw a brief glimpse of an intriguing white horse's head. It raised up, looked right at him, then dropped down. But it was on the far side of a herd of giant cattle. He started weaving his way through the sheep and a goat herd in that direction.

When Kalev was a boy, his abba tried to describe the size of auroch cattle to his young son. "They're bigger than Ox and could eat you and Hoshe'a both in one bite." Now, the mighty Commanding General nervously crept past the largest animal he'd ever seen. This bull was easily six foot six at the shoulder and twice the weight of Ox. The animal stopped chewing and stared at Kalev with unblinking eyes. *Is he smiling at me?* Kalev wondered. Suddenly, loud laughter erupted from somewhere in the herd. Kalev's sword materialized in his hand. Knowing he couldn't see over the tall bull, he dropped to a knee and used his other hand on the bull's underside to steady himself. He quickly scanned for any humans amongst the forest of animal legs.

That was the exact moment the bull decided to *energetically* empty his bladder. The full force of the large gushing stream hit the side of Kalev's face and open mouth. The General jerked his head back, fell off balance, and plopped on his backside under the cow behind him. Not only did the bull keep going on Kalev's bare legs, but the rest of the herd joined in. All of a sudden, Kalev was sitting in a rapidly growing puddle of cow pee and watery dung. He hastily scrambled to his feet while trying to spit out the rancid taste from the bull. Kalev used his drenched tunic to try to wipe the bull's stinging body fluid out of his eyes and mouth, but it only made it worse. More laughter exploded from somewhere. Kalev yelled in frustration. "Shut [illegible] up!" The laughter faded to a booming chuckle.

In time, Kalev was able to blink away the salty sting and focus his tearing eyes. Once again, the Commanding General stood nose to nose with the gigantic bull. "That wasn't funny, you [illegible] cow." As if the bull understood Hebrew, the massive beast raised his nose and loudly snorted, spraying globs of bull snot onto the General's chest. Kalev looked down, shook his head, swore, and then wisely made his way out of the stinking mass of cattle.

On the far side of the aurochs stood a herd of sixty-five beautiful Egyptian stallions and mares. They all grazed on the grassy field, but every one of them tracked Kalev with their eyes. He slowly approached the tallest one. The pure white stallion held his tail high and stopped chewing when Kalev gently patted his neck. That was when the General realized that every horse was already saddled and ready to ride. Every piece of each horse's tack (padded saddle, saddle blanket, cinch, reins, bridle, bit, etc.) sparkled. Every two inches of the beautifully softened leather was festooned with polished gold, silver, glistening pieces of blown glass, and jewels.

Kalev reached up, scratched the horse's forehead, and whispered, "What are you doing here, boy? Did those flies scare you? Don't worry, they'll be gone soon, and you can go home." In response, the horse bent his neck around, looked Kalev square in the eyes, and snorted twice. For some odd reason, Kalev wondered what the horse was thinking. The previously laughing voice spoke up, startling Kalev.

"Um, you don't want to know what he's really thinking. My understanding of horse is a little rusty, but his sarcastic snorting had something to do with a horse's, um, hind quarter, Yahweh, and a gift horse's mouth or something like that. Oh, and I won't *even* repeat what the bull said, so don't ask!" The voice started laughing again. Kalev drew his sword again and spun. He franticly searched for the voice's owner but only saw animals. The laughter seemed to come from all directions. Kalev shook his head. "I'm tired. I need to sleep."

The Commanding General sheathed his sword, patted the amazing horse's neck, and then skirted around the cattle back to the road. That's when his exhausted mind acknowledged the absolute silence for the first time. The animals weren't making a sound. Plus, every single creature was staring right at him. Kalev awkwardly looked around to make sure no human was in earshot, then yelled, "Well, um, goodbye." Kalev laughed, yawned, and headed for home. It wasn't long before his mind slipped back into his usual oblivious brooding. "Come on, Kalev, concentrate. Where can you get some meat for those boys?"

About twenty yards from the house, Kalev heard rapid panting. He looked down and saw a healthy Egyptian wolf pup prancing beside him. Just then, Hoshe'a walked up with an enormous smile. Kalev teased him, "Hey, big brother, what're you doing home? Won't Panhs miss your, um, *insights*?" Hoshe'a didn't even reply. He simply took Kalev's chin and turned his head around. A silent, single-file line of hundreds of animals was following him. Kalev and Hoshe'a started to belly laugh. The entire animal parade stopped in unison until Kalev began walking again.

That's when Hoshe'a sniffed the air and then wrinkled his nose. "What is that *stink!* It's burning my nose!" Kalev looked away when Hoshe'a leaned closer, sniffed, and winced again. "I think they're attracted to your body odor. I always knew you and Ox had too much in common." Kalev moved to punch his brother in the arm, but this time Hoshe'a deftly spun away. Kalev smiled. "Nice move."

A few steps later, Kalev scratched his neck again, then stopped and turned to yell at the animals in frustration. "*Stop looking at me* and *go home*." But the silent creatures didn't move a muscle; they just stared at Kalev. It took every ounce of self-control for Hoshe'a to steady his voice. "Maybe you should give your order in Egyptian." When they finished laughing, Hoshe'a pointed behind them. "I'm pretty sure you just became the most wealthy Hebrew rancher in Egypt." Kalev stopped and naively stared at Hoshe'a. "What?" And then it hit him. "But those aren't my animals." Hoshe'a grinned. "You're right. Why don't you take them back to Hotep? They're probably his and his fellow torturers anyway." Kalev paused, grew a sly grin, and cleared his throat. "Hmm. Now that this general has had time to re-evaluate all possible contingencies, I've determined that this army needs a first-class BBQ."

The laughing brothers were almost to the courtyard gate when Kalev stopped and grabbed Hoshe'a's sleeve. With a wide-eyed, panicked expression, Kalev yelled, "*Arrgh, Hoshe'a,* find the hammer. I forgot to build an ark." They both laughed so hard that they couldn't breathe.

Carni was in the house teaching eighteen of her newest girl recruits. She stopped mid-sentence when she heard her two boys laughing. *No*, she thought, *they're screaming like a couple of little girls.* The fierce little ema, followed by her newest foundlings, headed to the front door. As they watched in surprise, the entire courtyard began to overflow with groups of animals. No herdsman, no ropes—and still they came through the gate one at a time. Every animal seemed to be watching Kalev's every move.

Miraculously, even the large flock of goats was silent. In fact, the only sound echoing off the courtyard walls was her two embarrassing sons. The Commanding General of Yisrael's Army and his major big brother were bent at the waist, snot dripping from their noses, wheezing with laughter. The littlest girl squealed at the sight of the cute little wolf pup jumping up and trying to lick the two funny men's faces. Carni groaned aloud and rolled her eyes. She grabbed her porch broom and shooed her way through the crowded courtyard.

Kalev was the first to see her coming and straightened up. He leaned over to Hoshe'a, who was trying to catch his breath, and pointed. "Have you ever noticed that our Hebrew ema always seems to be armed for battle?" This started a whole new round of laughter.

Carni marched up waving the broom like a sword. "Kalev, you're a mess. Get cleaned up. And get these stinking beasts out of my courtyard; I don't want *any* of their little gifts left here either." Kalev got a serious look on his face. "But, Ema, Hoshe'a is too heavy to carry, and you, of all people, should know he leaves his little gifts everywhere." Carni considered swinging the broom handle at these two hyenas but didn't want to break her broom. "Arghh," she screamed, then turned and stormed off. A wide-eyed Kalev glanced at Hoshe'a, and the two started howling again. They ended up on the ground with the puppy licking their tear-stained faces.

Kalev, still sitting on the ground, noticed seven pairs of feet near the gate. The General wiped his face and stood. He made his way to the gate. "Gentlemen." They stiffened to attention. "Find Colonel Yadin. Tell him that the General needs Bet Company and all the rope they can find. Then report back here immediately." "Yes, Sir." The boys took off in a cloud of dust.

Hoshe'a, dutifully followed by the little wolf, pushed aside some sheep to get to the well. He cleaned up and gave the puppy some water. At the gate, Kalev brushed himself off and purposefully made his way to the house. He didn't even notice that the animals had actually parted, giving him a straight shot to the front porch. The General stepped inside and saw the wide-eyed girls and his furious ema. He didn't realize the acrid stench from his auroch encounter had instantly begun to pollute the inside air. Kalev stood tall and squared his shoulders. Generating his best authoritative voice, he said, "Major Carni, outside, please." Both Kalev and the girls saw Carni's glaring "*look*" as she stormed passed him out the door.

Kalev intuitively grabbed his little ema and hugged her. "My lovely ema, have I told you lately how much I've missed you?" Carni started gagging from the stench. Sensing his approach had missed the mark, Kalev spoke faster. "First of all, I'm sorry for acting so foolish in front of your troops. But, Ema, I'm in charge of protecting and the feeding of hundreds of children and teens." He pointed at the crowded courtyard. "That laugh really felt good, and I needed it." Kalev noticed that Carni had taken two steps backward, and her glare had weakened a little. "These animals followed *me* home. I saw them in old Rabbi Issachar's empty field. I guess that massive swarm of biting horse flies had scared them to our side of the canal." From the doorway a timid but strong little voice interrupted. "Um, can we pet the goats?" Carni rolled her eyes and shook her head. Kalev continued. "I need you to..."

The little four-foot-eleven ema let her giant little one talk as she examined his face. Over the last couple of decades, Carni helplessly watched her little one slip away piece by piece. Day after tortuous day, her huge son would return home with a little more Kalev beaten out of him. But the little one who'd disappeared decades ago was coming back. He looked tired, but there was something else. *That's it*. She subtly gasped in pleasant surprise. There were fewer hate lines on his face. She'd noticed lately, as any good ema would, that though her son was weighed down with worry, he'd begun to look younger at the same time. She loved him as her own. *Now*, she thought with a scowl on her face, *it's my job to get this boy married.*

"*Ema,* you haven't heard a word I've said, have you!" Carni snapped out of it. "I have. You want me to take these goats, hide them in the outpost, feed them, milk them, and make cheese." Kalev asked, "Well?" Carni thought for a moment. "No, I won't." Carni turned and looked at the eighteen sets of eyes peeking from around the doorframe. "But I know who will." Kalev smiled. "Then I'll leave you to your lessons." Carni stepped closer, held her nose and quietly growled. "Don't you ever enter my house smelling like that again, or I'll strip you naked and use my scrub brush from head to toe. Do you understand *me*, General?" Kalev nodded, glanced at the girls, then stiffened to attention. "Yes, First Sergeant Carni. I agree. I think they'll be excellent troops. You're doing a fine job; keep it up."

Kalev watched a weary but wide-eyed Yadin weave his way through the crowded gate. In all the chaos, Kalev had forgotten most of the army was asleep. He smiled when he saw Bet Company trying to form up on the road in front of the gate, but a herd of camels kept harassing them. Kalev shook his head. *Where did all those camels come from?* he wondered.

Yadin and his first lieutenant finally joined Kalev and Hoshe'a on the front porch. Kalev smiled apologetically. "Colonel, I regret interrupting your sleep. But this wasn't *my* idea." Yadin looked back at the still-growing herds. "Well, Sir, it looks like you've won this month's 'best forager' competition grand prize." He turned to his lieutenant. "Jacob, tell the General what he's won." "General, Sir. You've just won. Wait for *iiiit...a new camel*! That's right, this energetic beast of burden comes with a customized embroidered double canopy, perfect for a pharaoh and his queen's night out on the riverfront. No more embarrassing saddle sores for you, Sir. No, this baby has a double-padded, thick-velvet-covered, high-back saddle. You'll ride in style with a newly upgraded set of calf leather bridles decorated with cute little silver bells. We've even added two additional waterskin holders for those long romantic excursions into the desert. It comes with an optional set of steps at no additional charge. Egyptian tax and Hebrew service fees are excluded, as it was, um, acquired from a caravan headed to Ra's temple in Thebes. Congratulations, Sir!"

Kalev stared at the boy blankly. "Um, thank you?" Hoshe'a was laughing so hard that he had to walk away. Yadin grinned. "We'll keep it in the new stall area till you're ready to take it out for a trot." He turned to his subordinate and spoke with authority. "Lieutenant Jacob. Make a list."

The younger teen sat on the edge of the porch. He retrieved a scroll, reed pen, and ink from his shoulder satchel. "First, find the troops that grew up with animals and let them take the lead. For now, harness that ram over there and lead it to the new pins. The sheep *should* follow. Then move the goats the same way. We'll need Heh Company to ride herd and cut the aurochs evenly between the Outpost and the Pit. Find the two abbas who volunteered to butcher for us. Ask them for their help dressing out, um…" Kalev smiled as the boy scowled in furious concentration. "We'd better make it five aurochs and eight of the larger ewes. Make sure they're not pregnant. We'll need to immediately reinforce the cattle pins. Get two squads started on building the proper-sized corral for those giant things. Ask General Ari if he needs any more horses and…" Kalev interrupted. "Colonel, if it's not needed elsewhere, I'd like that onery pure white stallion for myself." Yadin nodded. "Lieutenant, make sure the General's horse is housed in the number one stall in the Pit. Assign a troop to care for the General's horse. Once you've delegated all that, get some sleep, then get back here after sundown. Ask Major Carni to look over our inventory and see what else we need for the Pit party." Yadin glanced at his frowning general and shrugged. "That's what Major Hoshe'a called it, Sir." Yadin looked back to his lieutenant, who was obviously distracted by a very cute teenage girl petting a goat. Yadin yelled impressively, "Lieutenant!" The kid leaped to his feet and stood at attention in front of Yadin. "I want all these animals out of sight, watered, fed, and bedded down within the hour. Make it happen. Now!"

The boy quickly stowed his scroll, ink, and pen in his shoulder satchel and then leaped off the porch. He smiled at the girl as he hurried by. At that moment, the largest ram goat decided the distracted lieutenant was attacking his does. So the goat naturally chased Lieutenant Jacob. The animal butted the unsuspecting lieutenant's behind so hard that the teen actually launched out the gate and into the side of an unflinching aurochs bull. The bull seemed to accusingly glare at Kalev like it was his fault. Kalev scratched his own neck and shrugged. "Hey, it wasn't my fault," he mused. The lieutenant stood on shaky legs and brushed himself off. When he looked up, he was staring straight into the bull's dripping and flaring nostrils. The boy wisely ducked and then cleared the area.

The colonel laughed and accidentally stepped closer to his general. The teen colonel jumped back like he'd been slugged in the chest. "Whoa, that's a powerful, um, musk you're exuding there, General." Kalev groaned. "Yes, that bull and I had our *own* encounter earlier." Yadin chuckled. "Yeah, it smells like he dominated that encounter and marked his territory all over you, um, Sir." Kalev couldn't argue with that summary, so he joined Yadin in a good laugh.

Yadin followed Kalev to the well. "Sir, we completed the Pit last night. General Ari has the muster planned for three nights from tonight. He wanted to make sure Heh's newly qualified privates were trained up before the Pit party and competition." While Kalev poured buckets of water over his head, Yadin leaned against the well and started a mental accounting sheet in his head.

Right then the seventeen-year-old new girl recruit walked up to get some water for First Sergeant Carni. She smiled at the concentrating Yadin. "In case you were wondering. There're fifty-two auroch cattle. Including one very happy bull, twenty-six cows ready to calve, and seven yearlings. The sheep numbered eighty-seven ewes, eighteen lambs, and two rams. It looks like half the ewes are ready to lamb. There are exactly seventy-seven doe goats, forty nannies, twenty-one kids, and three rams. Those horses are beautiful. There are eight stallions, fifty-seven mares, including twenty-four, no, maybe twenty-five that are ready to foal any day now. I counted five colts, but there may be more; they kept running around. So far, I've counted seventeen camels, but it looks like there's a steady influx. According to my calculations, and I'm just estimating, that herd has grown two point five camels per minute. Are you finished with the well, Sir? I need to get back." The girl quickly filled her bucket, smiled at the oblivious Yadin, then hurried back into the house.

Kalev yawned, then quietly disappeared to his stall. He'd feel guilty about leaving them with all the work—later. The second his head hit the pillow, he closed his eyes. As he dropped off to sleep, he could have sworn he heard that same disembodied voice playfully singing in his head. "Hey, it's okay, okay; you're welcome…"

18

An hour before sunset, Kalev flew out of bed terrified. The horrifying dream had started with the usual mosaic of Hotep's contemptuous sneer in different contexts. As usual, it faded into silent blackness. A welcomed contentment followed as he floated into a dark and deeper sleep.

After a while, the peaceful rest was shattered by the glare of a blinding sun. Kalev saw himself alone on a vast expanse of empty desert. No hills, gullies, or scrub brush, just a flat plain from horizon to horizon. That was when the fear-filled dread started. Instantly, the sky turned black, completely eclipsing the sun. Kalev watched himself draw both his father's and a large golden Khopesh sword. He instinctively knew that specific Khopesh was the blade Hotep had used to carve his name in Kalev's back. As the trembling Kalev watched from above, millions of winged creatures flew in a circle forming a vortex over his head. A screeching darkness filled the center of the massive tornado. Then they began to land in an ever-widening circle around him. Except for a six-foot buffer zone, the entire desert was filled with the distorted, red-eyed beings. Some were man-sized; others were deformed giants. But none of them spoke. They stood there wheezing and glaring at Kalev with an oozing hatred that took his breath away. In the dream, the violent stench of a million rotting bodies caused Kalev's physical stomach to want to dry heave. Still asleep, Kalev's loud groaning could be heard outside his stall. Without warning the sha'dim (demons) attacked from every side. Kalev watched as the beings instantly formed a lethal mountain over him. It was over before he had a chance to swing his sword. Then a massive hole opened beneath the roiling mountain of seething sha'dim, and the whole scene began to fall into the palpable black void…

Partially awake and completely naked, Kalev stood trembling in the center of his stall. He was gasping for air and drenched in sweat. He didn't trust his shaky legs, so he froze in place and waited for his full senses to return. Someone, probably his ema, had placed two large buckets of cool well water next to his trough. He dumped each one over his head. Now he felt like himself. He dressed in his only other loincloth and tunic. In the last few weeks, his painfully strenuous training with Adir had caused his muscles to grow and harden even larger. His thickly woven tunic ripped under the arms and down the sleeves. Kalev didn't mind. Combined with the various little cuts and slices, courtesy of Adir, his tunic felt nice and airy. Suddenly, a chill of panic shot down his spine, and Kalev's neck began to itch again. That's when he heard the soft flapping noises on the other side of his door. The General shook his head to make sure he was awake. Somehow his sword had materialized in his hand. He didn't even remember retrieving it from under his cot. Then he heard the little wolf pup bark and two little kids laughing. He saw the kids, through his stall's dilapidated slats, in the stall next to his. Little Frog wrestled with the pup while Carni's littlest recruit watched and clapped. Kalev took a deep breath and relaxed. He tightened his sheath belt and headed out the door.

Not six feet beyond his door stood a perfectly straight line of birds. Kalev had never seen this type of bird before. He bent at the waist to look at the fowl's long, skinny legs. That was when he heard Little Frog gasp and yell, "Look, the General made a bird army." The little girl gasped, and Frog kept going. "He made them do a muster. Do you think he's cussing at them too? He cussed at us, but Private Menachem deserved it because he breached…" At the same time, Hoshe'a rounded the corner and immediately broke into his high-pitched, braying laugh. And, of course, that was when his mentor rode up and joined in the laughter. Kalev smiled. He had to admit it was one of the strangest things he'd ever seen.

Adir walked over to Kalev and shook his head. "The Egyptians call them Fayoumis (chicken). And, of course, they worship the things. One of the garrisoned soldiers told me you prepare them just like quail or ibis. I'll tell Carni. They produce eggs every day. You can fry or boil the eggs. I see two roosters, so you can breed what you don't eat." Kalev shook his head. "I lost count." Hoshe'a walked up with a smirk. "Don't hurt your damaged brain, little brother; there are 101." Kalev let out a low whistle. The bird in front made a clucking noise, and the one with the red-skinned beard let out a high-pitched call. "Hoshe'a, that sounds like your laugh." Kalev didn't feel Hoshe'a slug his arm. He was transfixed on the birds' eyes. "Why does each eye move independently?" Adir chuckled. "I guess it's so they can watch for predators attacking from all directions. And on that note…" Adir barely moved, but his sword was suddenly at Kalev's throat.

After an hour of grueling sparring and archery practice, Kalev and Adir headed to the well to wash off. Or at least the filthy and bloodied Kalev did. Adir hadn't even broken a sweat. They'd just reached the gate to the front of the house when two squads of boys and twenty-two teen girls jumped from the barn's roof and landed in puffs of dust. They all started laughing. The single-file line of Fayoumis was marching behind the General around the corner of the house. Kalev heard the laughter and turned to look back around the corner, almost squishing the first two Fayoumis. "Arghhhh!" He hopped over the chaotic line of birds and then stormed back around the corner. He scowled at the closest squad leader. "Where did you come from, Sergeant?" The teen stiffened to attention and pointed. "Sir, we were observing from up there." Kalev looked up. "On top of the barn? Who gave you permission to be up there?" By now they were all standing at attention. The young sergeant cleared his throat. "Sir. Per General Ari, it was our two squads' turn to observe your advanced training techniques." Kalev was mortified. These troops had just witnessed five severe faceplants and two hard back slaps from the flat of Adir's sword. "You watch our sparring sessions? Since when?" The sergeant saw General Ari materialize right behind the Commanding General. "Yes, Sir, well, for the last two months, we…" From the roof of the barn, Ari interrupted, "Sir, I'm sorry, but my abba and I, well…" Adir walked up behind Kalev and put his huge, calloused hand on his shoulder. "Son, it was my idea. These kids needed to see how a true warrior can get knocked down and repeatedly get back up." Little Croc's voice rose from behind the crowd of teens. "Commanding General, Sir. Your first day you fell down thirty-one times. But today it was only five. Me and Frog are always watching you fight, but he forgot to bring food to watch with today 'cause he saw your bird army—then he was playing with Shomer and that girl, so he forgot." Little Frog came out of the closest barn stall. "Shomer is a warrior recruit same as all the girls. Besides, you always eat it any way you…" "Enough!" Kalev roared. Ari jumped down. "I'm sorry. Sir, I'll take care of it. Sergeant, get these weird-looking birds back to the Outpost and build them some temporary cages so they don't run off. And you, girls, report to Sergeant Abraham for your initial basic training briefing. *Move it, people!*" That was when the real show began. Fourteen boys began chasing 101 birds that were determined to stay in line behind Kalev. Dust and pin feathers choked the air. Kalev shook his head and groaned. He and Ari went through the gate and quickly shut it. Ari sat beside the well while the General washed up.

Waves of familiar laughter wafted from the house. Ari shook his head in disgust and grumbled under his breath. "Arghhhh. My abba's acting like a teenager. Could they be more obvious?"

Beside the well, Carni had washed and left three of her kitchen aprons drying in the sun. Kalev used one to dry his face, another to daub the blood from a few scratches and cuts, and the third to get the remaining dirt and water out of his ears and armpits. "I'm sorry—what did you say?" Ari shook his head. "Nothing, Sir."

Ari and the General grinned at the sound of the yelling, cussing, and squawking coming from the other side of the gate. "Sir, from the sound of it, I think it would be easier if you let those birds follow you back to the Outpost. By the way, when did you become an animal whisperer?" Kalev shrugged. "I guess it's my cheerfully magnetic personality." They both laughed, pushed the gate open, and stepped back into the dusty chaos.

The troops were sent ahead to secure a space for the  birds. The Fayoumis quickly fell in line behind Kalev. He and Ari took their time getting back to the Outpost. It was rare that they had time just to talk. Kalev noticed his second in command's sly grin.

"Seriously, Sir. How is it that the exact animals we needed showed up in that field at that time and followed you home? And these birds. I didn't even know they were edible or even existed." Kalev knew where this conversation was headed. He knew he could explain away some of it, but these birds… Kalev shrugged. "Truthfully, I don't know." Kalev turned to look back and stopped. "Ari. Why does that line look twice as long as it did at the house?" Right then Yadin rode up on one of the new stallions. "Sir, where did you find so many Fayoumis? I bet you've just cornered the market." Yadin paused to count. Kalev and Ari hadn't stopped walking, and the stallion instinctively began to back up. "Sir, there are 387 so far." Kalev looked up at the boy. "I think you need to double the troops you have assigned to assist the butchers." Yadin nodded. "Already done, sir." Yadin looked up, shook his head, and smiled. "Sir, it looks like a flock of twenty more are running to get in line. At this rate we'll be eating well for months to come." Yadin stopped the horses' prancing backward. "I need to bring First Sergeant Carni up to date." He looked up again and smiled. As the teen turned his horse toward the house, he shook his head and, without thinking, blurted out, "Yahweh's timing is impeccable." Yadin immediately recognized his mistake, glanced apologetically at his glaring General, then quickly road away. "[illegible] Yahweh," Kalev grumbled. Ari wisely kept his mouth shut. Kalev entered the gate to the birds' temporary area. The boys had masterfully used the previously downed palm logs to build a walled circle fifteen yards across and six feet high. The General marched the birds in circles, shrinking the circumference on every lap. When the last Fayoumis entered, Kalev quickly staggered his way back to the closed gate, trying to keep the mass from following him out. But no one accounted for the fourteen roosters that flew up and sat on the top log. Kalev didn't know what else to do, so he put up his hand and yelled, "*Stay*!" And they did.

Hundreds of troops watched in awe as their General made the animals march and obey his orders. The Outpost erupted in applause, cheering, and peals of good-natured laughter. Much to Kalev's annoyance but completely out of his control, the boys started a too-loud chant that would be added to the mighty warrior's legacy. "Our Supreme Commanding General rules man and beast! Our supreme…" Kalev's face reddened, and he motioned for Ari to follow him out.

Kalev didn't understand this whole [illegible] animal parade thing. That they needed the self-sustaining food was a given. He really *was* grateful for the one less worry. But his real frustration was the implication that there really *was* a Yahweh, and *He* was the force behind it all. Again Ari, sensing his general's inner debate, wisely kept his mouth shut.

Twenty yards upriver, five pairs of close-set, unblinking eyes watched the two men on the beach. Meanwhile, out of frustration, Kalev didn't wait for the skiff to be loaded in the river for their crossing. The huge man abruptly dove in and began to swim across.

Ari cringed. Previously, by Carni's well, Ari had slyly handed off Kalev's sword to his father before Adir had gone into the house. The General was so preoccupied with the birds that he didn't realize he was unarmed. Additionally, this morning, the fishing troops reported that they'd seen several large crocs last night. They'd speared two, but at least four more had gotten away. Ari frantically looked upriver, but the hungry eyes had already submerged. Ari drew his knife, carefully clamped it between his teeth, and dove in. He couldn't remember a time when he'd swam that fast.

The two men had just made it to the beach and begun to stand when a long chorus of soft whistles followed by loud, hollow thumps echoed just behind them. Both men turned. Only then did Kalev realize he'd foolishly left his sword by the well. To both men's relieved surprise, seven male and four female crocs, averaging thirteen feet in length, lay dying on the beach right in front of them. Thick patches of arrows completely blanketed the huge beasts. Kalev looked up and saw the Outpost's high overwatch troops nocking more arrows. Four more squads of archers crowded the opposite bank. Several five-man skiffs were already loaded and heading across. Ari's finger circled above his head as he yelled, "Excellent shots, warriors. That was a difficult angle for many of you. So thank you for not killing your two generals." Ari's ear-piercing war cry was joined by all the others. Kalev turned to see a double line of hundreds of troops from Heh Company lining the ledge above them. They were brandishing odd-looking longbows. The General looked back down at the dead crocs. When the cheering and chanting died down, he yelled, "Every archer is to receive one of the teeth on a leather lanyard." More cheers and chanting echoed off the water.

19

Kalev and Ari climbed the steep riverbank and headed for the Pit. For a while they walked in silence. Yet both of them were wordlessly debating the same question. Finally, Ari asked it out loud, "Sir, were those crocs following you too?" Kalev groaned—then his semi-pent-up frustration exploded in a yell. "I don't know, Ari!"

Suddenly, a calming, cool breeze swirled around them. Then a faint yet powerful voice whispered, "Yes, you do, son. You've known your Yahweh-Rohi's plan for you all along. Kalev, just like your Yeshua, you have the same self-sacrificing heart of the I AM. Before you were born, He instilled in you the divine compulsion to care for and protect the weak and vulnerable.

"Listen to Me, Kalev, son—stop being a stubborn bonehead like your abba was! Adapt, adjust, and expect your Yahweh-Jireh's amazing provision. Yahweh is compelled to protect *you*, empower *you*, and show *you* His miraculous wonders. The size of your needs and desires is irrelevant. They're always dwarfed by the magnitude of My provision. Ask *big*, then expect *bigger*! Kalev, I'm offering *you* a most precious gift. An all-expense-paid personal relationship with the King of kings and Lord of lords, tax and shipping included." The voice chuckled. "But wait, there's more!"

"Son, Yahweh is always available to you. With Me, you can do anything. But if you insist on going it alone, these children, *your* children, Kalev, will pay dearly for your self-justified arrogance."

"Kalev, son of Hezron, today I call heaven and earth to bear witness. I have set before you reviving life and violent death. Liberal blessings of prosperity, protection, and undeserved favor or a cursed existence that will suck out any remaining life from your decaying soul. As always, the choice is yours alone. Yet Kalev, know this: whatever you choose, it will affect these thousands of young ones and the millions more to come. General, let's take this journey together. So choose life so that you, Raisa, and your offspring may live. Oops, I got a little ahead of Myself. Disregard that last reason.

"That said, son, it's time for you to suck it up, put on your spiritual big-boy tunic, make it right with Yahweh, and lead these boys home! You were built to be a general for this exact time and place. Now make it happen. Oh, and I AM Yahweh, and I approve this message!" The voice's laughter faded as the swirling breeze stopped.

Though Ari had automatically recognized the soothing voice of Yahweh, the message to his general was private, so he reluctantly forced himself to stop listening. "That's the thing with Yahweh"—Ari smirked—"He always gives you the choice to listen or opt out."

Kalev's reaction was the complete opposite. When Kalev heard the breeze's first words, he'd sucked in a sharp breath. It felt like he'd been punched in the chest. Even in the darkening sunset, Ari saw that the General's wide-eyed expression was contorted in panic. When the voice blew away, Kalev dropped to his knees and began to silently weep.

Ari's keen eye searched their surroundings for any nearby perimeter guard or shadow troop. He wanted to make sure no one saw the General like this. The teen general personally appreciated this intimidating man's kind and genuine heart. The General had suffered and survived fifty lifetimes worth of tortured pain. His memories alone would cripple anyone else. He deserved to fall apart once in a while.

But these young refugees/warriors needed to see their Commanding General as larger than life, a conquering warrior bent on conquest, a demigod. Additionally, it was imperative that these boys and girls knew *their* general to be a rock, impervious to pain, fear, or defeat. And no matter what happened, General Kalev would see them through to victory.

Ari looked around again, then silently sat in the dirt next to his sobbing friend. The teenage general reached up, put his hand on the huge warrior's trembling shoulder, and waited.

After a short while, Kalev sniffed and wiped the tears from his cheeks. Still staring at the dirt in front of him, he whispered, "You heard that voice?" Ari fidgeted, then took a deep breath. "Yes, Sir, I did, um—it was Yahweh. I've heard it many times before." Kalev glanced at Ari. "I heard it too. But the voice *I* heard, um, was my abba's. He said that…" Ari interrupted. "Sir, as always, I'll listen if you need a sounding board, but I suspect most, if not all, of that message was only meant for your ears." Kalev nodded, and both men stood. They unconsciously looked around for any nearby troops.

The two generals walked another hundred yards when Kalev thought he'd recognized a boulder near the rim of the Pit. Ari turned south, and they weaved through boulders, scrub brush, and finally along a dry creek bed. Three hundred yards south of the river, Ari abruptly stopped.

For Kalev, hearing his father's voice instructing him to choose life, whatever that meant, or else, had shaken the huge warrior to the core. Plus, it was getting dark, and this aimless wandering in the desert was really annoying. "General Ari, are you lost, or did you move the Pit without telling me?"

Ari smiled and leaned against a boulder that easily slid to one side. Kalev walked over and looked down. A brightly lit, perfectly round, cedar-lined shaft dropped straight down. Ari went down the perfectly carved ladder first. Kalev's head had barely dropped below the surface when the boulder slid back in place over his head.

Kalev dropped the last few feet and froze to the spot. The entire area was now underground. The Pit looked huge before, but now it seemed twice as large. The ceiling overhead was a maze of interlocking triangles and beams. And above it all was a patchwork of exotic wood boards.

Before the Outpost, Kalev had never seen any form of construction. His family's and Carni's homes had been built and then enlarged long before he was alive. In the mud pits, Kalev had molded millions of bricks. Yet he'd never seen one of them used to build anything.

He was still staring at the ceiling when Hoshe'a walked up. "So, little brother, was this what you had in mind?" Still staring up, Kalev slowly shook his head. "I didn't know this was even possible. Hoshe'a, I…" Hoshe'a smirked. "I guess I did glean a few things from Panhs' bloviated lectures on how *he created* symmetrical architecture. You should see the pharaoh's underground treasuries—talk about complex. The man traps put in place in case of thieves took over a year to develop."

Kalev finally looked at his brother. "Did *we* forage all this?" Hoshe'a grinned. "Pharaoh's priests have a habit of building and rebuilding their homes larger every year. They have full access to the temple/Pharaoh's treasury and its unlimited funds. There has always been a steady stream of caravans transporting cedar, cypress, and pine lumber.

"Initially, we alternatingly scavenged boards from one caravan or another. They usually came in from Sumeria, Phoenicia, and Lebanon. When the Outpost was completed and we had enough extra, we stopped; we didn't think we needed any more wood. It wasn't worth the security risk for just surplus.

"Lately, large ships and caravans are arriving from places like Karkamesh, Tarse, Ur, Babylon, etc. But on the same evening you *ordered* me to build this, one of Moshe's shadow troops reported seeing huge, unguarded piles of wood stacked outside of the city walls. The priests had stockpiled so much wood they had nowhere else to store it. Most of what you see came in from merchant ships.

"Kalev, there were 3872 two-inch-by-ten-inch-by-ten-foot finished planks. Plus, the priest had *graciously supplied* us with twenty-one flatbed, high-sided, and preloaded wagons. The rest of the lumber was neatly stacked in piles against the city wall. On one wagon, we *found* eight large crates of woodworking tools, planers, chisels, saws, hammers, hand drills, awls, etc.

"The entire army used every horse, donkey, and camel we had. We foraged every single board nail and length of rope we could find. By sunup there wasn't one useable board left." Ari smirked. "On a remaining piece of splintered board, Little Frog had his squad leader carve a short, um, thank-you message in Egyptian." Ari grinned. "It read, 'Thank you for the wood and wagons. Ra isn't real; you're not silent and dangerous, and you're a stupid Egyptian 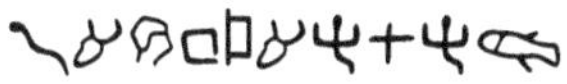 pig.' They propped the sign against the wall on top of a small pile of camel dung." Kalev laughed. Ari added, "I'm sure the priests didn't raise too much of an alarm, as they were probably looting thousands of pounds of gold and silver from the royal treasuries, then hoarding the more exotic wood. All without the pharaoh's knowledge." Hoshe'a's stomach loudly growled. Ari smirked. "I guess it's time to eat."

The three men started toward the dining tables at the far end of the Pit over three hundred yards away. As they walked, Kalev noted the hundreds of unoccupied stalls on both sides of the main deck.

Kalev glanced at Hoshe'a. "Have we established a separate area in the Outpost for Ema's support company?" Hoshe'a slowly shook his head and then nodded toward Ari. The teen pointed toward the kitchen at the far end. "Um, well, Sir. It was decided that the girls will be occupying the Pit's north-end stalls." Kalev stopped walking. "Wait, they're moving in here? That wasn't what I told my, um, the First Sergeant. This is Heh Company's base. I thought you wanted to remain autonomous." Ari scowled, then shrugged. Hoshe'a started to speak, but Ari interrupted, "Sir, um, First Sergeant Carni, uh, *requested* the girls to be quartered in the Pit. She said it was the safest place for them." Kalev knew exactly what Carni's *requests* sounded like. He'd talk to Carni ASAP. She was blatantly disrespecting the chain of command protocol. He bit his tongue and then growled. "This is your AO, General Ari. You alone have the final word." Ari wordlessly nodded, and they started walking again.

Eventually, Ari broke the very tense silence. "Initially, I thought it was a good idea to have two platoons of support girls on-site. The double-level stalls are divided by walls on each side; they're large enough for two girl troops each. They can even curtain off the front of the stalls if they want to. So I guess the semiprivacy isn't an issue. Plus, on both the western and eastern walls, there's a four-stall tack storage area between the girls' stalls and the first squad of boys. The northernmost stalls are closer to the kitchen area, so I guess for now, it's okay. This is only a stopgap until the new fortress is built. I was waiting for your go-ahead to bring the girls in, Sir." Kalev hesitated.

"How *are* the first squads of girls adapting to the basic training regimen?" Ari didn't answer right away, then nervously cleared his throat. "Sir, um, they've excelled at many of the basic training evolutions, especially weapons and fighting techniques. But, um…well, according to our two best drill sergeants, the girls are having a hard time adapting to our military protocols. Especially when it comes to obeying orders from a boy their same age. They lack the respect and fear of disobeying an order. Those are two critical foundation stones this army is built on. And what's worse, the boys in the other basic training squads are watching it all." Kalev stopped walking again. Hoshe'a knew what was coming, so he didn't stop. "That is not acceptable! Has First Sergeant Carni been informed about this?" Ari shook his head. "No, Sir, we weren't sure she'd understand/or approve of our strenuous basic training methods." Kalev growled under his breath. "General Ari, please send a runner to find the First Sergeant." "I'll take care of this whole thing right now." "Yes, Sir."

Ari let out a loud staccato set of whistles, and four distant troops sprinted toward them. Hoshe'a waited for the other two to catch up. He'd heard his brothers growl and tried hard to semi-stifle a laugh and sound official. He cleared his throat and stood at attention. "General Kalev, I believe it to be necessary for the furtherance of my understanding of military procedures that I should be present for your transfer of information to the First Sergeant." Kalev scowled. "You mean you want to watch me dress down Ema." Hoshe'a sounded like a little kid. "Please, I promise I won't say a word." Kalev rolled his eyes.

They'd only made it halfway to the dining area when the two sergeants ran up and saluted. Ari scowled. "Split up, find First Sergeant Carni, and tell her she needs to report to General Kalev in the Pit's

TOC *immediately*." "Yes, Sir." All four troops ran for separate ladders.

Kalev watched them quickly ascend. That was when he noticed the evenly spaced holes in the ceiling. Hoshe'a spoke up. "Those are air intakes. There are added intakes in the wall at the rear of each upper sleeping area. We built multiple larger exhaust vent holes above the kitchen and forge areas. The heat from the forges and ovens naturally rises, which draws in the air from these intakes and is eventually vented to the outside. The whole process causes a continuous cool airflow toward the kitchen vents. The smoke from the torches and the normal animal smells, boy and beast, are vented in the same way." Ari smiled and pointed up. "Those bushes and boulders we walked around up there hide the intake vents and the two-man perimeter-guard spider holes." Kalev was surprised. "Really. I almost relieved myself on one of those bushes." Ari grinned. "That would have been a good test of their commitment to stay covert." All three laughed. "Two days ago, four herders and a large herd of goats walked right over the top of us. In fact, they followed that dry creek bed the entire length of the Pit's roof. They never knew they had forty-four sets of eyes tracking them the whole way." Kalev nodded. "Impressive."

The General noticed a taller stall he assumed was designed for a camel. He heard a curious gurgling and walked to the back of the stall. "Is that running water?" Kalev bent down, smelled it, then took a drink. "It's well water." Ari smiled. "We were digging near that far ladder we came down when we uncovered an underground spring. Our brilliant chief architect quickly designed a primary aqueduct system to slowly flow through each stall's animal trough on both sides of the Pit. The secondary channel flows through a series of enclosed wooden gutters and then diverts to flow to the kitchen, the senior officer quarters, the troop's washing troughs, and then the toilets before it empties into the river. All excess water and sewage is channeled into the river through a submerged culvert, seventy-five yards downstream from where we fish." Kalev turned. "Hoshe'a, this really is incredible. Thank you." Hoshe'a didn't know how to respond to his little brother's heartfelt sincerity. So he circled back to his request. "Um, you're welcome…so can I watch?" They both laughed, and Kalev agreed. "But no laughing, or I'll give that bird chest of yours a new bruise."

Eventually they reached the north end. Ari pointed to a passageway. "Sir, if you'd follow me." Ari smiled. "I wanted to show you our new TOC. We added it after the roof was completed and camouflaged." Hoshe'a smirked. "It's kind of a dual-purpose area." Ari continued, "While the troops were finishing the roof, the battalion officers unanimously wanted to build a specific addition." Kalev followed Ari down the brightly lit, cedar-lined passageway.

Halfway to the end of the hallway, Ari stopped in front of a pair of dark-wood double doors. Above the door was a large, expertly engraved, silver-and-gold sign that read, "Kalev, son of Hezron, Supreme Commanding General of Yisrael's Army." Below it was a simple wooden sign: "Tactical Operations Center."

Kalev was embarrassed. "Ari, this is *your* TOC. Your name should be up there." Ari smiled, opened the door, and stepped aside. Hoshe'a nudged Kalev into a large, thirty-by-sixty-foot, brightly lit room. The ceiling looked to be fifteen feet high. The walls and ceiling were lined with tongue and groove planks of bleached white wood. In the center of the room was the original one-piece map table. "Is that the same table?" Ari grinned. "Yes, Sir." "How did you…?" Hoshe'a pretended to scowl. "Yeah, it wasn't easy getting this beast down that small ladder shaft." Ari and Hoshe'a laughed, then traded knowing glances. Kalev scanned the square holes in the ceiling above the torches and the one three-by-three-foot intake vent above the center of the table. "Hoshe'a, this place…this TOC…it's brilliant." Kalev really was astonished at the genius it took to build this massive structure. But at the same time, his praise of Hoshe'a made them both feel awkward.

In one of her conversations with Raisa, Carni mentioned that "brothers will *always* be brothers, and boys will *always* be nine-year-old boys." Her forty-year-old sons were proof.

Kalev smirked. "Hoshe'a, has Ema seen this place? Maybe she'd change her opinion of you." Kalev smiled. "And no matter what I've heard her say, *I* never thought you were a lost cause, never." Ari laughed. Hoshe'a shook his head and grew a sly grin. "Yeah, well, from what I've heard, she's already arranged for you to marry the rabbi's daughter within the next two months." Kalev's mouth fell open. Hoshe'a laughed, "Gotcha…maybe!" Kalev scowled and exhaled.

Hoshe'a pointed Kalev toward the far end of the room. He hadn't been here since Ari and the other officers added the addition. The three men headed that way. Ari beamed. "Sir, every troop in the army has helped to build the Pit. But the officers wanted to build this for you specifically. We agreed it wasn't right for this army's top General to sleep in a dilapidated animal stall." Kalev shot Ari a semiserious warning glance. Ari backpedaled. "Though it *is* the finest dilapidated animal stall I've ever seen." Kalev had to laugh at that one.

They stopped in front of an unusually wide, deck-to-ceiling, heavy-looking door. The ruby-encrusted handle shaped like a life-sized cobra was made of four-inch-thick gleaming silver. Ari nodded. "We're not really sure what this door was built for. This one and three others, along with the bed, table, the two couches, the four chairs, and clothes' closet, came in by ship. They left them all crated but unguarded on the dock overnight. We only took the furniture, twelve crates of gold torch holders, and this door. And though we *were* grateful, we didn't leave a thank-you note that time. We found the low table, blankets, and pillows another night." Kalev looked a little lost. Hoshe'a grinned and stepped closer to examine the intricate carvings on the door. "Oh, that's where this went. This door was meant for one of the pharaoh's four hidden treasure vaults. We had to move on to another project while this one's replacement was built."

Hoshe'a turned to Kalev and Ari and inadvertently switched into his big-brother-lecture mode. "It's made from a single slab of Sumerian Halub wood. It's only grown in one place, and I'm guessing the bed was meant for the pharaoh and his latest imported horde of foreign harlots. I'm sure it, too, was carved from a single tree trunk. The cost of the Sumerian's expert craftsmanship is staggering. This door alone probably cost its weight in gold and silver. But I'm sure the bed was imported from Lebanon, north of Phoenicia. The pharaoh brings in the largest cedar trees I've ever seen. Some of their diameters are as large as…" Hoshe'a saw Kalev's eyes glazing over. "Oh, that's right. I forgot to explain in 'Kalev language.' Okay, how's this? Ugg, big door, pull open before walking forward. Then pull closed." Hoshe'a quickly turned to Ari and whispered like a patient parent. "We've been working on that one for years. He's almost got it." Then he put his hand on Kalev's shoulder. "Only use head to open or close big door one time a day. Two times makes big Kalev more stupid. Bed good, hopefully not break. Bath in animal trough when stinky, like right now. Clean clothes good; change loin cloth every ten sunrises whether you need it or not! Try again to remember: don't put old loin cloth on head…that is bad—makes people run away. Ugg, now, Kalev repeats after big brother, 'When Kalev pays visit, he uses toilet, not bathing trough.'" Then Hoshe'a repeated it very slowly, "Come on, you can do it, 'Toiiiiilet, nooooot trooooough…!'" Ari bit his tongue so hard that he could taste blood.

Kalev reached over and easily yanked the big door open, semi-playfully trying to smash Hoshe'a behind it. Inside, the room was brightly lit and much larger than his whole barn. Wide, fragrant cedar planks lined the three visible walls, ceiling, and deck. The intensely bright wall torches reflected off of the polished gold holders and large oblong disks behind each one. There was a comfortable-looking bed on the adjacent wall. Kalev guessed it would easily sleep six people his size. Next to it was a solid-looking table and four high-backed chairs that looked like lesser thrones. Kalev pointed. "I guess Ema *has* been here. That's obviously one of her not-so-subtle hints." The table was set with two large gold plates and utensils on opposite sides. The other two settings were smaller, kid-sized. Hoshe'a laughed, "If you only knew…" Kalev ignored his brother, thinking it was another joke.

Halfway to the other end of the room, two high-backed couches faced each other. Between them was a long, oblong-shaped table. It looked to be made from a single piece of exotic wood, just like the AO map table in the other room. But this tabletop was a gold inlaid map of what Ari rightly assumed was the known world and trade routes. While his brother kept walking toward the wash area, Hoshe'a warily glanced at Kalev's back and then motioned for Ari to sit.

Hoshe'a pointed and cautiously spoke in low tones. "This is a Phoenician map. Do you see Egypt's northeastern border here?" Ari nodded. "From that border up to here and inland to here is the land Yahweh promised Father Abraham. This map claims the majority of the land is Phoenician. I've seen two other Canaanite maps that claim the same area as Canaanite." They both subconsciously glanced at Kalev's back. "If I understand Moshe correctly, neither the Phoenicians, Canaanites, and/or Syrians will welcome us with open arms. We'll be fighting for every acre of fertile land."

Ari sucked in a breath. Oddly, this news was very sobering. He whispered, "I've always thought this was just a way to hide and defend them. But this just got very real!" Hoshe'a saw the concern in the boy's eyes. "Ari, ultimately, it's *Yahweh's* responsibility to deliver on His promise, not *ours* to make it happen." Hoshe'a pointed at the ceiling and smiled. "We *will* be free, we *will* fight, and we *will* conquer because we have the biggest and *baddest* Yahweh in the land!"

At the far end of the forty-yard-long chamber, Kalev had opened a door and stood there staring. The smaller fourteen-by-fourteen-foot space was also lined with the dark red cedar paneling. There was a torch on each wall with the usual exhaust vents above each one. A larger intake vent was in the center of the ceiling. The trough from his stall was full and sat against one wall. But sitting on the deck, in the center of the room, was a three-by-three-by-three-foot solid gold cube with an oblong hole in the top. Kalev thought he heard the sound of a small rushing creek coming from the hole. At the same time, he stepped in and bent close to listen to the hole. Hoshe'a and Ari appeared at the door. They physically strained not to laugh. But Hoshe'a couldn't pass this one up. "Arghh, not again. Kalev, how many times have I told you? Sit on it, not stick your head in it." Ari fell to the deck howling in laughter.

Kalev smirked. But instead of giving Hoshe'a the satisfaction of successfully humiliating his little brother again, Kalev stood, turned around, lifted his tunic, sat, and loudly relieved himself. Hoshe'a's eyes went wide, and his face flushed from the awkwardness. "You [illegible] pig." He slammed the door shut and quickly marched away swearing. This whole scene only intensified Ari's cramping laughter. He never had a brother. So this ongoing outrageous competition between his General and the major was both shocking and hilarious.

Kalev sat there laughing. That's when he noticed the words carefully carved into the back of the door. "General Kalev, when you sit on the golden hole, imagine Hotep looking up at yours. Enjoy!" Every officer's name was elaborately inscribed. But at the very bottom of the door, barely legible words were scratched into the smooth surface. "'[illegible] on Hotep heads that [illegible] Egypt pig,' says Little Croc and Little Frog, best silent and deadly Yahweh's army warriors."

Eventually, the relieved and freshly bathed Kalev followed the very sore but smiling Ari toward the chamber exit. Kalev stopped at the intriguing-looking bed. The side rail was easily three and a half feet off the deck, with the poofy blanket another foot higher. "I've never slept on a padded bed before." Ari turned and watched as Kalev sat on the edge of the bed, then clumsily fell backward. The sight of the mountain of a man floundering in the fluffy blankets and deep mattress caused Ari to break out in another round of painful laughter.

Following a long string of Hebrew and Egyptian expletives, Kalev was able to extricate himself out of the "fluff pit from Sha'al." He quickly stood, gasping like he'd almost drowned. The Commanding

General of Yisrael's Army scowled at Ari, then pointed at the jumbled pile of blankets and pillows. The teen was still sitting on the deck, wheezing with laughter, when Kalev roared. "What is that L∿ɯ✝ϱϱ thing? It tried to eat me!" Ari futilely tried to answer, but the whole thing was too funny. Kalev had to admit the scene with his brother followed by the attacking bed *was* probably pretty comical to watch. He sighed, then smiled. Kalev looked around the room again. He spotted a single rope hanging from the ceiling, but he'd let Ari gather himself before he asked about it.

He hadn't noticed the dark opposite wall when he'd first walked through to the other end. The forty-yard-long shadow-box-type wall was paneled in the blackest wood Kalev had ever seen. It was covered with different types of swords, spears, shields, throwing knives, axes, bows, arrows, strange-looking helmets, body armor, and/or chest protectors. Kalev appreciated that every piece of wood, ivory, bone, tooth, falling-star iron, gold, silver, and glass was meticulously polished to a mirror-like finish. He'd have to ask Adir to show him how to use most of this lethal collection.

After decades of agony and death in the fetid mud pits, Kalev knew how to deal with hardship and pain. He expected and/or accepted the incessant mental and physical abuse. He was even comfortable living in a sparse animal stall that was one stiff wind away from disintegrating. But being offered gifts like this barn-sized sleeping chamber, the golden commode, and the worldwide weapons collection almost physically hurt. A confusing sense of unworthiness churned in his stomach, and he didn't know how to deal with it. He quietly commented to himself, "This place…I don't deserve this."

And if this embarrassing feeling wasn't confusing enough, he heard his abba's voice in his head again. Only this time it sounded different, like it was timeless yet still very familiar. "My *nehh* (undeserved favor and protection) has always surrounded you, proud son of Hezron. Kalev, your supposed *weakness* is really your strength. For only in *your* humbled weakness will My miraculous, explosive power be unleashed in your sight. Show My children and your own how to readily accept My gifts and then use them to give to others."

The following rumble of the voice's deep laugh shook Kalev's already jumbled insides. "Remember you will, my padawan. Protect My followers; never remove your helmet; *this is the way*!" Kalev had no idea what these confusing words meant. He felt like he was losing his mind. In the last few years, the General had wondered when the results of Hotep's numerous kicks to the head would take their toll. Kalev sighed, "Well, you had a good run while it lasted. Maybe you should just let the bed eat you and be done with it."

Kalev shook his head to consciously dismiss his and the other voice's ramblings. They were simply the result of an overtired mind. Kalev gritted his teeth. "Ari, I've never…um, this isn't right. I mean, um, I don't think I can, um, arghh…thank you."

Ari saw this huge man's awkward yet genuine vulnerability. And, as any superior subordinate would do, the teen general artfully gave his general a face-saving out. "Sir, you have over 2000 boys who potentially have nothing to do. This Pit and the Fortress we're building on the Outpost's side of the river helps to bolster a sense of ownership and purpose. You should have seen the faces of the boys bringing back the boards they knew belonged to the temple priests. They all had a part in the foraging. And especially that door. This went doubly for the officers who built you this room. If you have to, think of this room as the end result of a leadership, team-building evolution." Ari was now beaming like a new father. He stood and motioned Kalev to the large door.

The backside of the large wooden slab had been planed and sanded smooth. At the top were the words, "In honor of our Supreme Commanding General Kalev. A true *gi-bor* (hero). Emulate his **courage and self-sacrifice. He is a man among men, a morally excellent warrior.**" Two thousand one hundred seven names were carved in very small Hebrew, Egyptian, and other indecipherable letters. Kalev didn't know what to say. After a long pause and afraid that his voice would crack, he whispered, "I'll thank them all at the muster."

Ashamed that his eyes were becoming blurry, the huge general quickly turned around, almost knocking his ema off her feet. She watched her little one wipe his eyes—then his awkwardness morphed into a menacing glare. Switching into her typical defiant mode, Carni shot Kalev *the look*. But the little four-foot-eleven Hebrew mother instantly realized she'd just stepped onto a completely unfamiliar battlefield.

Without breaking eye contact with his warily confused ema, the General growled. "General Ari, would you please excuse us and close the door behind you?" Kalev appropriately waited for Ari to quickly leave the TOC. When the door closed, Kalev pointed at the closest chair. "First Sergeant Carni, sit."

For one of a very few times in her life, Carni felt out of control. She sat as ordered. Kalev took a breath. All the recent emotional drama threatened to spill out of his mouth, but he willfully ordered his thoughts. "First Sergeant Carni. Before the next muster, you are to gather up your little girl platoon and make other arrangements for their provision and protection. They will not become a part of this army…"

For the next ninety grueling minutes, the battalion's Supreme Commanding General and the honorary First Sergeant had the most explosively heated argument in their thirty-one years as a family. This resulted in Carni's unequivocal surrender and agreement, both with Kalev's reasoning and his unyielding requirements. "General Kalev, you are this army's commander. The girls and I *will* comply with all army protocols before dawn." Kalev was very familiar with his ema's tone and determined glare. He almost felt sorry for those little girls…almost. The General nodded. "I hope so."

The exhausted Kalev almost tripped when he tried to sit on the stupid-looking padded chair at the head of the table. Someone had actually put it on an eight-inch-high platform. Kalev shook his head and swore under his breath. Out of nowhere Carni smiled. "All that said, little one, I am so proud of you.

You're going to be an excellent husband and father." In less than a heartbeat, Carni knew she'd said too much. Kalev stiffened, and everything Hoshe'a had said came flooding back. After another verbal battle, Carni stiffly stood up, saluted, and quickly stormed out.

20

An hour later, they were about to finish the evening's muster at the Outpost. Kalev stepped to the front of the stage and pointed toward the river. Kalev's voice shook the drill deck. "Army of Yisrael, you have accomplished your mission to create the Pit. And you did it with a proficiency I have grown to expect from this battalion. I'm proud of you all—well done!"

Eventually, the war cries, followed by the usual cheers and chants, subsided. The General had to clear his throat a couple of times before he could speak again. "And I wanted to specifically thank every officer for my room. It's, um…" Kalev quickly glanced back at Ari with a lost look on his face. True to form, the teen general took over as the red-faced Kalev stepped back a couple of steps.

Ari boomed, "Battalion, let the Pit, and eventually the Fortress, serve as a source of pride. They're an example of what this army can accomplish when we follow orders and work together. Honor your sergeants and officers with your obedience and determination. Constantly lead, follow, or get out of the way because this army of brave warriors is destined to *always* conquer any challenge." While the troops enjoyed more raucous war cries. Ari looked toward the northern wall and nodded. Majors Dan and Adir, followed by the newly promoted First Sergeant Abraham, Little Frog, and Little Croc, mounted the stage.

Ari continued, "When I was your age, my abba taught me a valuable lesson. In warfare, a true *gi-bor* is not driven by self-preservation. But is a soldier who strives to defeat his greatest fears to the point where his own safety becomes irrelevant. Then, his sole mission is the survival of his fellow troops. He always endeavors to do better for others and help the helpless. The *gi-bor* boldly runs into battle and decimates any threat to that end. Our Supreme Commanding General symbolizes this *gi-bor ethos*. Long before this army was formed, this brave leader was daily disregarding his own welfare to protect his fellow Hebrews. This *gi-bo*r spirit continues to this day as he leads this growing army of lethal warriors." Ari held up his hand to stem the usual cheering. "Follow his lead! Become the *gi-bor* our Commanding General personifies."

Ari turned and respectfully nodded for the mortified Kalev to step forward. Yadin handed Ari an elaborately written scroll. The teen general unrolled the parchment and thundered. "For demonstrating outstanding leadership, tireless self-sacrifice, and complete dedication to duty. Our Supreme Commanding General Kalev has brought great honor and respect upon himself, this brave army of warriors, and the Hebrew race. In keeping with the highest traditions of this battalion, we award this army's *gi-bor* with the weapons befitting a leader among leaders."

The other officers took a step forward as Dan began strapping a thick two-sword back scabbard to the big man's rock-hard shoulders. Ari explained to Kalev in a low tone, "Major Dan created this personalized back scabbard and ankle knife sheath." While Dan bent down and tied the ankle sheath, Ari nodded toward his grinning abba. Adir stepped forward, slowly unwrapped Kalev's father's sword, and presented it to Hezron's son. Kalev's jaw dropped. The iron sword gleamed in the torchlight. He didn't know the "falling star" (meteorite) iron could be polished to a mirror-like finish. Somehow, all the small nicks in the blade were gone and it looked lethally sharp. Kalev unconsciously sucked in a breath when he saw the simple inscription at the base of the blade. Kalev's mouth went dry. "General Hezron, a Mighty Leader, Man among Men, Loving Husband, and Very Proud Father." Kalev ran his finger over the words and a spasm of grief squeezed his throat. He quickly felt behind his shoulder for the first slanted opening and carefully sheathed the heirloom. With tears streaming down his cheeks, Kalev turned to Dan and Adir and croaked, "Thank you both." They smiled and nodded.

Ari motioned to the First Sergeant. Abraham stiffly marched forward and presented his general with the iron Khopesh sword. The General grabbed the translucent white rhino horn handle and held the two-foot-long sword vertically. His eyes immediately went to the lettering and arrow pointing down to the inside of the hooked blade. It read, "*knsymn*" (enemy's neck). Kalev scowled in a brave attempt to stifle his laugh. Ari smiled. "It's a trophy from our encounter with the Bedouin raiders. Yadin, Akiba, and I asked my abba to customize it." Before they all lost their military bearing, Ari quickly turned to the troops. "The Pit is set up for tonight's competition. The first event will start in two hours. Eat well and fight hard. Company captains, take over."

To everyone but the General, the smell of the evening meal was mouthwatering, and as usual, Kalev was the last to eat. He stepped up to the serving line intending to ask for small portions. Still lost in thought, he received two plates and a large cup. The General distractedly thanked the little girl server and headed out the Outpost's riverside door.

Both Carni and Raisa tracked Kalev's exit. After they had a chance to sit and eat, Carni started her typically blunt ema-daughter conversation. "So are you ready to marry my son?" Raisa looked toward the door and smiled. "I've been ready to marry that man since I was a child. But…" Carni patiently waited for the thirty-five-year-old woman to gather her thoughts. "I, um, I'm not so sure he's ready to marry *me*."

Carni shook her head and stared into the middle distance between them. "That boy has survived decades of horrendous mental and physical cruelty. Except for his visceral hatred of Yahweh and Moshe, I watched my tenderhearted little one slip into a protective state of emotional numbness. The Kalev I knew and helped to raise vanished. Kalev is thirty-nine years old. He's not taken a wife because he refused to marry and give his taskmaster Hotep another target for his rage at Kalev. It broke my heart. I realized both the hatred, the numbness, and the self-imposed isolation was the only way he could cope with his brutalized enslavement. Still…" Carni sniffed and wiped her eyes. "I thought I'd lost him for good.

"That said, when he tries to talk to you, I see a spark of the little one I once knew and still love. Nevertheless, when it comes to the matters of the heart, my Kalev is still an obliviously innocent nine-year-old boy. Raisa, he needs you; you both deserve to be happy. He can barely breathe, let alone speak, when he sees you. An ema knows when her son is in love. But he still sees his feelings as a vulnerability, a weakness he can't afford. Sweetheart, the mighty Commanding General of Yisrael's Army won't be ready to marry until you *tell* him he's ready. I'll take care of the details, but it's time for you to step up and take control of this situation. Remember, no matter the age, in the hands of a subtle and loving wife, a husband is like clay. He can be molded into a tender and vulnerable, loving man. This goes double for my little one.

"Daughter, these days life is too short and unpredictable to wait for happiness, for love." Carni looked up and saw Raisa's tears glistening in the moonlight. "However, my son may be the Supreme Commanding General of Yisrael's Army, but in our hands, he's clay to be molded. Now when you…" Hoshe'a was doing a little spying of his own. He listened as the two women talked, or rather conspired, for two more hours. Hoshe'a grinned. "Oh, little brother, you're in trouble…"

21

Kalev climbed his dune and sat. He was grateful for the temporary solitude; he needed to think. Only then did he look down at his plates. The huge man was surprised to see them piled high with beef, mutton, fish, and bread. He groaned. For the first time in decades, he wasn't hungry. Kalev set the plates in the sand and emptied his cup in one long pull.

Hearing his abba's voice earlier made his head spin and his guts clinch. He repeated the words in his head. "Son, Yahweh is always available to you. With Him, you can do anything. But if you insist on going it alone, these children, *your* children, Kalev, will pay dearly for your self-justified arrogance." Kalev looked at the star-filled sky and whispered, "But he…arghh."

When Hoshe'a caught up with him, Kalev was obliviously staring at the water. The older brother plopped down next to him. "Now what are you brooding about? I swear, Kalev, lately you seem to worry about everything." Hoshe'a looked at Kalev's plates. "Are you going to eat that?" Only then did Kalev realize that Hoshe'a was sitting next to him. "What?" Hoshe'a laughed and pointed. "I said, 'Are you going to eat that?'" Kalev unconsciously shook his head. Hoshe'a grabbed the closest plate and began shoveling the amazing beef into his mouth.

Still staring at the water, Kalev asked, "Hoshe'a, can I talk to you? Can you keep from making a joke? This is serious." Hoshe'a stupidly grinned, then mumbled with a full mouth, "I'll try to be serious, but I can't make any promises." Out of the corner of his eye, Kalev saw Carni materialize behind his unsuspecting brother. Kalev glanced at Hoshe'a, who had started another one of his dimwitted laughs. True to form, Hoshe'a's laugh was cut short when his head jolted forward, and a lump of bread shot out of his mouth. At the same time, Kalev heard the oddly satisfying sound of Carni's head slap. "Hoshe'aaa, your brother carries the responsibility of thousands of children on his shoulders. All he asked you to do was to have a serious discussion without your usual ox's hind-end attitude. Arghh, you're so infuriating. I don't know how I'm going to find *you* a wife. Why can't you be more like Kalev!" Hoshe'a looked at Kalev and whispered too loudly. "Where did she come from?" Kalev's smile broadened, and he pointed toward the sky.

Hoshe'a groaned and stood and defiantly faced his fuming little Hebrew ema. "Ema, I'm a grown man; you can't keep head slapping me like I was a child. I'll laugh when I want to. And another thing, Kalev should know that you and Raisa…" To Kalev, Carni's arm seemed to move faster than any sword strike he'd ever seen. Before Hoshe'a even registered his ema's blur of movement, Carni had raised onto her toes, reached behind Hoshe'a's neck, and slapped his already stinging bald head again. Kalev was impressed with her speed. The loud *whap* sound seemed to echo off the water. Hoshe'a roared, "Ema, stop! That hurts." Carni ominously growled, "Good. Stop disrespecting your ema, apologize to your brother, then go help the girls pour the water from the boiling pot!"

Hoshe'a glanced at his wide-eyed brother, then quickly moved out of his ema's reach. Still rubbing the back of his neck, Carni's forty-year-old boy turned to walk away. He stopped only long enough to snatch both plates off the sand, then headed down the dune. When he reached the bottom, he yelled back up, "I'm sorry, Kalev; we'll talk later. And, Ema, I *am* a man now, and you have to respect me." Carni took one step forward causing Hoshe'a to head toward the Outpost a little faster than normal.

Kalev knew his ema was still coiled up, ready to strike like a cobra. So he shouldn't, or rather, he couldn't laugh. In a huff, Carni sat beside her younger son. Out of self-preservation, Kalev resumed his thousand-yard stare at the water. Carni knew she needed to switch into her advisory-parent mode, so she took a couple of deep breaths and waited for him to take the lead.

Kalev was quiet for a long while. Then he shook his head. "We were sitting at the table the night my abba was murdered. He was reciting the old stories of Abraham, Isaac, and Jacob. He spoke of how Yahweh protected Abraham on his journey from Ur of the Chaldeans, southwest to the land Yahweh had promised him." Carni saw her little one subconsciously sneer every time he said the name Yahweh, but she silently allowed him to continue. "My abba told us that Yahweh even protected Isaac when Abraham had purposed to kill him on an altar." Kalev paused, then sniffed and groaned again. "Abba was talking about how Yahweh prepared the way for Joseph to come to this cursed land and prosper. That was when the Egyptian pigs broke in and dragged my abba into the street." Kalev's eyes went blurry, and he shook his head in self-disgust. *What are you doing, Kalev? Crying is weakness*, he inwardly chided himself.

Even sitting, the big man towered over Carni. But she saw his heart, and somehow she knew he was headed in the right direction. She heard Yahweh's voice snicker. "Yep, I've got 'em right where I want 'em." Kalev sneered at her. "Why couldn't *your* 'all-powerful' Yahweh protect my abba and the rest of his 'chosen people'? If *your* Yahweh *could* protect him and the rest of us but didn't, then He's a cruel and merciless shadow. If your Yahweh even exists, and He *couldn't* save my abba, then He's feeble, and I despise His dishonorable weakness. He's no different than the Egyptian's gods, and I'll hate Him, too, for the rest of my life." Kalev spewed these words with such forceful bitterness, it briefly caused Carni to shrink back. But she still remained silent. Kalev whispered. "Ema, I don't mean to offend your beliefs; I just don't understand…"

Though it broke her heart to see him struggle like this, she knew he'd carried this black oozing hatred for too many years, and it was time he let it go. *With a little help from his ema, of course*, she thought.

Then a supernatural unction welled up inside her, and she blurted out, "Little one, for 400 years the Hebrews have lived in this land. We had great blessing but then bitter agony and death. Yet this whole time we, including your abba, hoped and prayed that Yahweh would bring us back to Abraham's promised land. Though we've only heard His silence so far, we *have* to believe He chose the Hebrew race for a greater purpose than this. Otherwise, I agree with you; what's the point!" Carni took a deep breath and plowed ahead. "No, little one, Yahweh *has* promised that we'll leave this vile place. I can't tell you when or how, but I think it's soon." Kalev sat there shaking his head. "How can you say that? Ema, like you said, it's been 400 years, and our people, not to mention the thousands of little children, are still dying under the Egyptian pigs' whips. I'm too old and too scarred up to believe that ignorant Yahweh myth."

Carni felt a righteous indignation take over. She stood. Barely tall enough to stare eye to eye with her still seated and scowling son. The defiant little Hebrew ema put her hands on her hips, leaned in, and loudly cut loose. "So, according to you, your abba was an ignorant fool to believe in Yahweh!" Kalev sucked in a sharp breath, and his hands began to shake. His voice ominously rumbled, "Careful, Ema."

Carni was suddenly unsure this was the right tactic. But her love for this man forced her to continue. "Kalev, you saw your father being whipped. But do you honestly think that was the first or only time? I learned how to heal wounds by watching my best friend Rachael cry as she repaired her husband almost every day for years. Still, Hezron believed and taught you that Yahweh the Yeshua was powerful, good, and His promises to save were true.

"Plus, oh high and mighty judge of the universe, ask yourself: Why aren't the last three plagues that are decimating the Egyptian crops and vexing *their* people *not* spilling over into Goshen? And why *haven't* the Egyptians discovered over 2000 children traveling to, then hiding right over there, so close to the city? And tell me, Supreme Commanding General, what happened when you inadvertently challenged Yahweh to provide for those same children? Oh, that's right, whole herds of cattle, horses, sheep, goats, chickens, and even a cute little wolf pup found *you* and followed *you* home."

Carni shuddered. "Open your eyes, son; after that last beating, you should be dead. Your recovery was supernaturally beyond my ability to heal you. Kalev, whether you like it or not, you are a walking, thriving example of Yeshua's love and saving grace. And if that isn't enough, He's even brought you a gorgeous and loving wife, who, for some reason I can't understand, refuses to let your fears and obvious hatred of Yahweh scare her away.

"Son, I say this in love. Wake up and deal with this hatred before it eats you alive and everything you care about is taken from you." Carni pointed at the closest palm tree. "Even those two little boys are wondering why you hate Yahweh so much. After what *they've* survived, they deserve a better abba!" *I'm not their abba*, Kalev thought, but he wisely let it go.

Then the unction inside of her morphed into something even more powerful, and it scared her. "Son, you've known your Yahweh-Rohi's plan for you all along. Kalev, just like your Yeshua, you have the same self-sacrificing heart of the I AM. Before you were born, He instilled in you the divine compulsion to care for and protect the weak and vulnerable…" Kalev gasped. Carni had just repeated his abba's words exactly. *Even Ari didn't know those details*, he mentally argued. Stunned, Kalev didn't see his little ema's wide-eyed expression as she quickly covered her mouth, turned, and hurried away.

22

For a long while, Kalev continued staring at the black river, uselessly hoping for an obvious solution. He debated with himself about what his ema and his *abba* said. A small yet growing part of him knew they were right. But that only intensified the battle raging in his mind. Eventually, Kalev shook it off when he remembered he needed to get to the war games.

The General descended the dune and was almost to the remaining boat when Raisa left the Outpost and walked right past him to the river's edge. She pretended not to notice him as she bent down to wash out her pans. Kalev smiled. *She's the same size as Ema*, he mused. He cleared his throat and then went silent, not knowing what to say. Raisa still playfully ignored him and continued washing the pans. Eventually, she got tired of waiting for him to say something, anything. The breathtaking little woman grinned. "Do you like what you're staring at? Is my robe too tight? Does it make my, um—does it make me look fat?" The powerful general was immediately disarmed and stammered, "Um, uh, yes, I mean, no. I mean, you're beautiful, and I like you this size. I mean, that tight—I mean…arghh."

Raisa laughed as she gathered the cleaned pots, turned, and walked up the bank. She stopped close in front of him. Her proximity made his heart pound, and sweat broke out on his upper lip. He'd unconsciously been holding his breath. Now he felt lightheaded. Wordlessly, Raisa put the pans down, reached up, and gently pulled Kalev's head down to her eye level. Even though it was a moonless night, Kalev could still see that her brilliantly blue eyes shone with a mischievous gleam. She leaned in nose to nose and impishly whispered. "I like you this size too. But you need new clothes; this tunic is so tattered, you're practically naked." Then she slowly kissed his cheek, winked at his wide eyes, retrieved her pots, and disappeared into the Outpost. For a short while, Kalev remained bent over with his eyes shut. He savored the moment and didn't want it to end.

Then, hidden behind some dead palm branches, a too-loudly-whispered argument broke his reverie. "Ewww, she kissed the General. Now he's gonna be sick or something. Isaac said girls have a sickness they can give to boys." "Shhh, he'll hear you. See, I said I was more silent than you." "No, you're not, and you smell bad; you need a bath." "No, *you* need a bath; you smell like a dead fish!" "Well, you smell like…" Without looking back Kalev roared, "You both need to bathe; get in the river *now*!"

Walking in the desert on a moonless night was a little tricky. Kalev almost tripped on the uneven ground a couple of times. Eventually he made it to the familiar-looking boulder. That's when he heard the very faint sound of thousands of war cries. Out of habit, the General quickly spun in a circle, naturally afraid a garrisoned squad of Egyptian soldiers could have heard the same thing. Kalev growled to himself, "This can't happen again."

That's when he sensed movement right near his ankle. He quickly stepped back, thinking it might be a sand viper or worse. But in the faint starlight, he couldn't make out any further movement. He remembered what Ari told him about the Pit's perimeter guards. Kalev stood to his full height and quietly growled. "Never move when a threat is near. It could cost you and your battle buddy your lives. Do you understand?" After a few seconds of silence, a very young voice whispered, "Yes, Sir. We're sorry, Sir." Kalev smiled. He was very glad Hoshe'a didn't see him talking to a rock. "Still, you're doing a fine job. I've mistaken you for a real rock twice now." "Thank you, Sir," another voice said. Kalev chuckled. "I assume this boulder is covering some kind of access into the Pit." The boulder slid aside, and the two boys jumped to attention. The slightly taller one saluted. He pointed to a wooded hatch in the ground. "Yes, Sir, um, maybe, um, Sir." Both boys looked unsure. "We're here to guard that door, but Sergeant Ezekiel said we can't ever open it, but we did once, but it was too scary. The sergeant said it's a ladder down to *Sha'al* (the unknown place). But we think he doesn't even know." Kalev lifted the heavy hatch open. Knowing Hoshe'a, this had to be a useable access point. He felt for the first ladder rung.

The General started down the ladder. He smiled at the worried-looking boys. "It's okay. I'm the Commanding General of Yisrael's Army; nothing scares me. But don't follow me." Both boys cautiously peered over the edge, looked at each other, and warily nodded. Kalev pulled the door closed over him.

23

The General had counted thirty-six rungs as he descended into the pitch-black shaft. There was no breeze, and though the walls were paneled in wood, the air was starting to smell stale, like damp dirt. He began to wonder if this was simply an extra vent for something else. Then his foot touched solid wood. Thinking it was the deck to a hidden passageway, he stepped down and began to feel the walls for another opening. His hand found a piece of rope sticking out of the wall. Kalev had barely touched it when the deck gave way. The six-foot-four, 285-pound muscleman yelped as he awkwardly tumbled down another ladder. His feet landed on something soft, but his head bounced off the deck, and stars shot across his vision.

After clearing his head, the first thing he saw was the ladder slowly folding itself back up to the trap door. The large door then raised and seamlessly disappeared into the ceiling of his brightly lit bed chamber. Only a long piece of swinging rope remained.

Kalev did a quick bone and body check. His hard head and arms took the brunt of the fall. He bled from a few different cuts, but he'd survived much worse. Kalev slowly made it to his feet and felt a little dizzy. He sat down and looked around. Except for the bed, he really appreciated this amazing room. But once again, the confusing feelings of humility and vulnerability plagued his mind.

The disembodied voice suddenly rattled around in his gut like a live animal. "For only in *your* humbled weakness will My miraculous, explosive power be unleashed in your sight..."

Earlier that evening, Kalev had convinced himself that this voice was simply the addled thoughts of a man who had been kicked and hit in the head countless times. So Kalev simply replied, "I heard You the first time, but I still don't like it."

The voice boomed louder. It seemed to come from everywhere. "Soon it will be written of you, son of Hezron. But My servant (a leader who serves others) Kalev, because he has a humble and obedient spirit and has followed Me unequivocally, him, the I AM that I AM will bring into the land I promised his abbas; he and his seed shall drive out their enemies and enjoy the land. And I will prosper them. Kalev, son, *I am* Yahweh. *I am* slow to anger, and I have an unfathomable amount of undeserved kindness. Your Yeshua has already forgiven your misguided faults and disobedience...but boy, sometimes you *really* try My patience..."

After a pause, a comforting, silent breeze blew into the General's face. It smelled like...jasmine, like his ema, Rachael. The huge man took in a ragged lungful of the scent and held it as tears freely streamed down his face. Kalev's abba had always brought his ema jasmine oil perfume from the city. He'd requested it to be part of the payment for the produce he sold to Queen Hatshepsut.

Suddenly a spasm of grief and loss overwhelmed Rachael's son. For ten grueling minutes, the General sobbed into a couch pillow. After a while he sat up, embarrassed by his woman-like show of emotions. He quickly stood. When he craned his neck to wipe his tear-stained face, his ragged tunic disintegrated and fell off his shoulders in two pieces. Kalev smiled. "I guess Raisa was right." The big man stood their completely naked in the brightly lit room. "Now what?" he asked no one. That was when he remembered the tall rectangular box at the far end of the room next to the table with the large wooden bowl. Its shelves were loaded with folded things.

He plodded over to the box. The top shelves were filled with different sizes of gold-embellished towels, six more man-eating pillows, and six shiny loincloths embroidered with pictures of flowers and scantily clad, dancing women. The center shelf had two stacks of tunics and robes. The bottom shelf held a collection of decorated reed sandals no *real* man would ever wear.

Kalev tied one of the oddly shaped loincloths under and around him. He promised himself to keep it hidden from everyone. Yet he had to admit the slippery feeling cloth felt cool and airy. The big man quickly donned a too-tight-fitting tunic, then started for his large door. The powerful general had unintentionally shied away from the demon bed.

Kalev started to push on the door when it flew open. Hoshe'a, Ari, Yadin, Ofek, and Akiba stared at him wide-eyed, then started laughing. The contrast between his bloody face and arms and the elegantly small tunic he was wearing looked hilarious. Kalev leaned against the door frame and smiled. He wasn't really sure what they were laughing at. The big man self-consciously checked his crooked nose for the usual post-trauma bloody boogers. But it was clean.

When they finally calmed down, Ari hooked a thumb back toward the double doors. The wide-eyed Little Frog and Little Croc stood there completely soaked, dripping river water. Next to them were the two stunned-looking boulder guards.

Ari spoke quietly. "After you closed the upper door, those two perimeter troops, Little Frog and Little Crock, heard you yell. They panicked and opened the exit hatch. The four boys only saw the 'dark hole.' They were terrified you'd fallen into Sha'al."

The General looked at the doors and yelled a little too sternly, "Sha'al has been conquered." Kalev slowly drew his two swords. All four gasped and glanced at each other. "Now get back to your assigned areas." The boys shot out of the room.

Ari smiled. "We never thought about you entering the shaft from that direction. Plus, you're supposed to light the torch on the shaft wall before you climb up." Akiba nodded. "It was built for escaping or ambushing an enemy." "That's smart," said Kalev. Yadin pointed at Hoshe'a. "We copied this major's precise and brilliant plans. He built one over each of our rooms, this TOC, and at the end of each passageway. He even built one into the ramp. He really *is* a genius." To Kalev, his red-faced brother may be an immature loud mouth who couldn't stay serious to save his life. But he, too, hated being singled out and praised.

Ari addressed Kalev while scowling at the fidgeting Akiba. "General, we need to get back to the war games before they try to kill each other again. By the time we got back here after the meal, four squads from Aleph and Heh were already in a bloody brawl over who killed the melon-head target first. It's escalated into a rivalry between platoons. Absolute pride and bragging rights have become their only focus. The infighting is reaching a boiling point."

Kalev approved of the competitive attitude, but Ari looked worried. "I thought we agreed this was supposed to be a demonstration of individual battle skills, not war games." Ari nodded toward the embarrassed Akiba, who shrugged and explained. "Arghh. Before the competition started, my captain and I were 'privately' designating which troops should compete in each event. All I said was that there should be a prize for the best overall platoon. I never thought he'd…" Ari interrupted, "*And*, as usual, this 'private' conversation was repeated to every other company captain, then first lieutenant, and so on down the chain." Yadin added, "Now we have to make sure they're pointing their arrows in the right direction." Kalev nodded. "I'll take care of this—lead on."

They were almost to the double doors when Hoshe'a pulled Kalev back and let the others leave. Hoshe'a stood in front of Kalev, obviously struggling to keep his semi-stern expression. When the older brother cleared his throat, it sounded like he was choking, "Uh, General…" But couldn't finish. He pointed a trembling finger at Kalev's chest, then stepped back. Kalev expected another prank but looked down anyway. The mountain of a man hadn't noticed all the gold needlework on the front of his tunic. And if that wasn't bad enough, the depictions were of trees, bunnies, and deer. "[illegible]!" Hoshe'a coughed. "Oh, I think it's pretty. But the *best* pictures are on your back. There're two cute little dancing ponies on top of a chorus line of dancing oxen." Hoshe'a started laughing so hard that he thought he'd puke. Kalev pleadingly looked at his howling brother. "Hoshe'a, seriously, it's all I have to wear; do you think anyone will notice?" The laughing older brother couldn't breathe, but he vigorously shook his head no. "Good," said Kalev. So he left his howling brother on the deck of the TOC.

The General knew rumors of his "conquering Sha'al" probably raced through the battalion like lightening. *I can use that*, he thought. Halfway down the hall, he stopped, bent down, and scooped up a hand full of torch ash. The General smeared it on his bloody face, arms, and his "pretty" tunic. He ripped off his embroidered sleeves and tore the tunic in a couple of places. The General drew his swords and wrapped the sleeves around both of his sword handles. He held the sword tips over the closest large torch flame.

It took a while before the sword blades began to smoke, then both tips started to glow red. Then the huge general deliberately stomped his way out to the drill deck. He held the swords out from his sides and stopped halfway between the ready-to-loose archers and their targets.

In a heartbeat, the raucous, angry crowd of 2000 boys and girls all gasped in unison. With his smoking swords held at the ready, the blood, ash, and sweat-smeared vanquisher of Sha'al silently glowered at each group of stunned troops.

The Commanding General of Yisrael's Army sneered and pointed his swords at the deck in front of him. His violent war cry split the silence like thunder. He expected the troops to follow his lead, but they all stayed silent and stunned at the sight. Kalev halfheartedly scowled at the thousands of shocked faces that crowded the walls and dining area. The General prematurely sheathed his superheated swords in his thick leather back scabbard. Now the leather began to smolder. Even Ari had to admit the rising smoke behind the sneering general's bloody head looked ominous. "We are a single army," Kalev bellowed. "A brotherhood of warriors to the death. Sha'al has been violently warned that *no one* threatens me or *my* troops and lives to talk about it. So hear me—except for drill instructors, I will personally end anyone who tries to fracture this army's protective unity." He swiftly drew his swords again. "Sha'al was only a warm-up for me. If *you* doubt my resolve to safeguard this army, this family, present yourself and fight me." Kalev allowed the ensuing heavy silence to linger for fifteen seconds. The terrified troops glanced at each other without moving a muscle. "Remember this warning. Honor, protect, and defend each other with your life. The Army of Yisrael is one living corps. Act like it! Colonel Yadin, let this warning be written and posted!"

Kalev didn't realize this simple speech would be repeated word for word by every drill instructor to every new recruit for generations. It also added to both the General's mythical demigod status and his lengthy fact-based legacy.

Without another word, the towering general sheathed his swords and pounded his way toward the kitchen. As he neared the officer's dining tables, the fear-filled, silent crowd of armed troops quickly parted like an ax through palmwood. Kalev smiled to himself as he sat, loudly pounded the table, and thundered, "*Compete*!" But no one moved.

Eventually, the expected chants were faint and unsure at first. Kalev grimaced. *That wasn't what I meant*, he thought. *Still, if they reach the same unifying objective, you'll just have to suck it up and drive on*. The chants quickly built to a rumbling crescendo. "General Kalev conquered Sha'al. General Kalev conquered Sha'al. General Kalev…" The chants turned to cheers, and the fierce competition continued. But this time there was only friendly teasing and loyal encouragement.

At the opposite end of the Pit, two black-clad men, with keffiyehs covering their faces, stood half-hidden behind the drill deck's platform. Ari had pre-arranged for the perimeter guards to escort these two leaders onto the drill deck and set them up behind the stage. They'd brought out two chairs and a table before the "war games" began.

After the wild-looking general's speech, the competition resumed. The two men dropped down behind the platform and plopped into the extravagantly padded thrones. The taller one was much older yet retained the same lean-muscular build he had in his twenties. The other man was short and pudgy but carried himself as a chief rabbi/prince should.

They spoke in hushed tones. The older man smirked as he studied the Phoenician letters engraved into the solid gold chair's arms. "If I were to guess, these thrones were meant for two of Ramses's sycophants. I assume the pharaoh didn't 'donate' them to a bunch of gold-mine-aged refugees." The rabbi smirked and shook his head. "No, these gaudy thrones, more furniture, every piece of building material, camels, food, etc., was, um, how did Hoshe'a put it? Oh yes, they were 'foraged' from caravans and docked cargo ships headed up the Nile to the city. Hoshe'a said their foraging was justified. It was a mere fraction of the 400 years of back pay the Egyptian pharaohs owed Yahweh's people." The older man smiled. "He's exactly right. But how..." The rabbi grinned and shook his bushy head. "Hoshe'a said something about drunk camel herders, but it was best not to ask too many questions." They both laughed. The taller one raised up just enough to peer over the stage again. He sat back down, rubbed his eyes, and tiredly sighed like he carried the world on his shoulders. "So he's the one..." The rabbi solemnly nodded.

"Arghh, of course he is. It couldn't be some wimpy little guy afraid of his own shadow. It had to be a Nephilim-sized granite mountain." He sighed again. "I hate it, but as usual, I guess I just have to suck it up, trust Yahweh, and drive on." The rabbi chuckled. "That mountain of a man is both Yahweh's choice for my Raisa and to lead this underground army. That said, I know that if he doesn't kill you, you'll eventually become best friends." The rabbi quietly laughed. But the older general/shepherd/prophet only groaned, then offered up a few silent pleas to Yahweh. In time, the old warrior gave in to the familiar peace that came from releasing his heart-crushing worries to his powerfully caring Yeshua.

He reached for one of the pitchers of the fabulous wine and filled the deep, jeweled goblets General Ari had provided. The rabbi chuckled. "At least he makes the best wine I've ever tasted." The tall leader nodded as he leaned back and marveled at the support beams almost eighty feet overhead. "This place is incredible. No pharaoh or king in history has ever had this kind of fortress. Not to mention the beginnings of an absolutely obedient and devoted army..." He paused, then slowly shook his head. "What I could have accomplished with an army like this... This General's subordinate officers also seem very squared away."

The Egyptian general's trained eyes automatically sighted six very well-hidden and very armed sentries above. But in actuality, twenty-one sets of eyes had locked onto the two suspicious-looking men the moment their feet touched the drill floor. The tall man continued. "General Kalev's OPSEC is extraordinary. And you say he's *not* prior military?" He took a long drink.

Rabbi Nachshon shook his head and scowled. "No, but he survived twenty-five-plus years in the mud pits. He was beaten and/or tortured daily by one of the most sadistic taskmasters in Egypt. I think the sha'dim-possessed man's name is Hotep." The tall man spluttered and coughed. "You mean General Hotep?" "I guess so. Do you recall him?" The older man nodded with disgust. "I remember his opium-fueled rages."

Then he stood and peered over the edge of the stage again as he continued the quiet conversation. "Hotep was a brutal soldier and a terrible leader. His men hated and never trusted him. I can't imagine what that General Kalev had to endure." Nachshon nodded.

"But he *is* combat trained by Ari's father. Adir is one of the Egyptian army's most trusted armorers." "Really?" the surprised ex-general asked. "An armorer is a crucial part of any successful army. Plus, the man who forges military weaponry has to be an expert in the battle techniques used for each type of weapon. Otherwise, his product is worthless on the battlefield. Oh [illegible], and that's the man who wants to end me." Nachshon smirked. "Look at the bright side. Yahweh's called you both to lead together. The King of kings and pharaohs *probably* knew what would happen when you two bulls were placed in the same pasture. Speaking of bulls, I'm hungry." The other man shook his head. "T [illegible]."

Even though he was almost 300 yards away, they both made sure Kalev's back was still turned. The suspicious-looking men quickly made their way to the ladder and swiftly climbed. Or rather the tall man swiftly climbed to the high exit. By the time the red-faced and wheezing Nachshon had climbed out of the Pit, he only wanted to lie in the dirt, cough, and die. The tall man was lost in thought as he waited and slowly paced nearby. It took almost ten minutes for Nachshon to return from "death's door." "Moshe, help me up."

As they walked back to the prophet's tent, Moshe deliberated out loud, "I know this boy army is quickly evolving into the most feared fighting force the Canaanites will have ever seen. And I do see the beginnings of a purpose-filled greatness in Hoshe'a." Nachshon concurred and added. "In spite of his ema's opinion, Hoshe'a will *eventually* get his act together and become one of this nation's greatest leaders." The tall prophet distractedly nodded, and they wordlessly walked for a while.

Halfway to his tent, an indignant Moshe broke the silence. "But this General Kalev…it's his choice to move *toward* Yahweh or his persistent, self-justified *revolt against* the I AM that will determine *his* future."

However, it was Kalev's future with his precious Raisa that worried Nachshon. Still, the rabbi was honored to be a drinking buddy and sounding board for El-Gibhor's (the Lord is mighty to save) mouthpiece. Moshe let out a deep breath. "Either way, I've submitted my future existence to Yahweh-Rohi. Besides, where I'm going when I die is paradise compared to this [illegible] life here."

"Nachshon, I'm tired of this whole debacle. I actually *told* Yahweh that choosing me was probably

His first and biggest mistake." The rabbi stopped walking, and his eyebrows shot up. "And?" Moshe growled. "He laughed! I tell you, Nachshon, sometimes He is so infuriating. Did I tell you that on top of everything else, two days ago, Yahweh tells me to circumcise my six- and seven-year-old sons? I uselessly debated with Him for a whole day. I told Yahweh they're too old for a briss and too young to understand. But, as usual, Yahweh overruled my objections, and I did it. T [illegible]. It was a [illegible] screaming bloody mess. Then, last night, Zipporah actually gave me a scroll of divorce. *She* divorced *me*. I didn't even know that was possible. She said she couldn't live with a man who'd mutilate his own children. Rabbi, she took my two resentful boys back to Midian! I'll probably never see my family again…[illegible], at what point does Yahweh stop taking from me?" He paused. "I guess that's *Kalev's* point, isn't it?"

24

Back in the Pit, the cheers and chants got louder as the competition's semifinals heated up. Kalev had *already* devoured an entire loaf of hot sweetbread and drank two cups of wine before the others even sat down. But his bottomless stomach was still growling.

Carni remembered Hoshe'a stealing Kalev's evening meal. So the quintessential Hebrew ema just knew her little one was "starving to death." As always, the Commanding General was very appreciative when his Major Ema set the platter in front of him. The heavy, solid gold tray was piled with four plate-sized, two-inch-thick steaks, three fish filets, three ears of freshly picked corn on the cob, and two loaves of hot yeast bread. But before he dug in, he pulled her close, and they began their decades-old ritual. "Ema, thank you! You're the best ema ever. How did you know I was starving to death?" "It's my job to know. Now eat up. You're nothing but skin and bones." They both smiled.

Based on Hoshe'a's previous comments and his own thirty-one years of experience, Kalev guessed that his ema was the instigator of any conversation about marriage. His mouth was full, but his growl was low and intimidating. At least it was to everyone else. But this four-foot-eleven typically meddlesome ema was fearlessly formidable in her own right. Kalev swallowed. "Ema, before I forget—we *will* talk about your *advice* to Raisa later." Carni stiffened, which only confirmed Kalev's suspicion. "Emaaaa, it's not your place to…"

Assuming Kalev was too distracted to see, Hoshe'a slowly reached across the table to sneak a steak off Kalev's plate. Without looking away from Carni, Kalev's hand blurred as he drew his ankle dagger and carefully rammed the tip through the web between Hoshe'a's two middle fingers into the tabletop. His "big" brother screamed like a little girl and jerked his *barely* bleeding hand back. The astonished teens began belly laughing, but Carni gasped. She started to head slap Kalev but noticed the growing crowd of children watching, so she let it go.

Carni looked up and shook her head at her oldest. *Will he* ever *learn?* she wondered for the 1000th time. The fierce little ema shot the wounded and groaning Hoshe'a her best "I'm very disappointed in you" look. Still shaking her head, Carni leaned close to Kalev's ear. "Little one, he probably deserved that. But, son, as I've told you countless times, *do not* permanently deform your brother. It's gonna be hard enough to find him a wife as it is."

When Kalev and Hoshe'a were eight years old, they became obsessed with lighting different things on fire. They learned the hard way not to stand behind Ox and try to light the tip of his tail. Then one day, the curious little arsonists discovered that dried corn stocks would burn bright and smoke like a chimney.

However, the clueless boys had started their experiment right in the *middle* of their neighbor's congested field. They watched in awe as the growing column of smoke rose high in the darkening sky, then fell back and spread out toward their house. Meanwhile, the blaze was rapidly encircling the two oblivious firebugs.

Kalev was the first to realize their mistake. He grabbed his brother and easily lifted him over his head, then threw Hoshe'a over the flames toward safety. *And once again, the little brother saves the life of the older one*. Or so he thought.

But Hoshe'a had landed short and rolled through the still-burning corn stocks. Kalev vaulted through the flames and rolled a few feet away. The two boys looked at each other's smoking eyebrows, hair, and tunics, then started laughing as they stood.

Like a raging sha'dim rising out of Sha'al, an ominous image appeared out of the thickening smoke cloud. Behind the ghostly shadow, the setting sun had turned the smoke orange. Reflecting the flames, a pair of otherworldly eyes glared down at them.

Even then, all the innocent-looking Kalev had to do was point at his coughing brother. Before Hoshe'a could stop gagging and protest, Carni had rushed over and pulled Hoshe'a's burning tunic up over his head and threw it aside. She grabbed his ear and began dragging the naked and screaming Hoshe'a back to the house. She growled at Hoshe'a's smiling best friend. "Kalev, please, don't ever light Hoshe'a on fire again." The last thing Kalev saw was a pair of fiery eyes shooting him *the look*.

The adult Kalev chuckled at the memory. "I'll try, Ema, but he makes it so hard to resist." "Arghh," she growled, "I swear, you two are forty going on nine years old." By then the astonished teens had exploded into fits of laughter.

Carni looked down at her little one's new linen shirt. "I see you've destroyed another clean tunic." Kalev smiled. "Yeah, but it was too tight and girly. I just customized it a little." Carni chuckled. "I'll see what I can do about the size. Oh, and I forgot to bring the foraged large loincloths from the storage room. They'll be next to the tunics when you get back to your room tonight."

Kalev's eyes went wide, and he froze midchew. He quickly pulled Carni closer and described the "loincloth" he had on. His ema coughed into her sleeve until she could control her laughter. "Those are the pharaoh's couch pillow covers. And their silk, so little one, if they haven't fallen off already, they probably will before you get back to your room, so be careful."

While Carni was whispering to Kalev, the fifty-six-year-old woman hungrily stared at Adir. Kalev groaned, then frantically whispered back, "Ema, I know you. Please don't tell anyone, especially Raisa!" Carni distractedly nodded and then smiled at her son. "Little one, if it falls off, I won't have to tell *anyone*." Kalev slyly grinned, then teased his ema. "Then I guess it's time to go *kushi* (commando, without undergarments). It feels so airy, so liberating!"

Carni's face flushed with embarrassment. She desperately wanted to head slap her disrespectful son.

Instead, she paused and grew a playfully dark grin. Everyone at the table watched as Major Carni whispered something into the General's ear, then swiftly walked away. Kalev's eyes went wide. He dropped his face into his greasy hands and loudly groaned. "[illegible]!"

Hoshe'a had curiously observed his ema and Kalev's whispering. He saw her hug her "favorite" son's neck, then walk away, making sure she brushed Adir's back with her hip. Hoshe'a rolled his eyes. Carni's "birth son" didn't know what they'd whispered about. However, he thoroughly enjoyed Kalev's embarrassed expressions. And when Ema finally walked away, his ox of a brother suddenly stopped chewing his cud.

Before he put his face in his hands, Kalev's terrified expression made his blood-caked appearance look even more chilling. Hoshe'a guessed that behind that ash and blood mask, all color had drained from his little brother's face. Hoshe'a let out a loud snort and playfully harassed Kalev. "Oops, I guess I *wasn't* kidding about, um, having to marry you-know-who you-know-when."

Kalev groaned again, looked up, and shoved his empty-greasy-platter hard across the table. As he intended, the serving dish silenced and knocked the air out of his teasing brother. Right then Kalev caught sight of a scowling Carni, followed by Raisa, headed his way. "[illegible]."

The Sha'al-conquering general shot to his feet, hoping to escape another embarrassing encounter. That was when his silky loin cloth decided to drop to his ankles. The fierce yet very humiliated general quickly sat and buried his dirty crimson face in his hands and softly groaned, "[illegible]."

Carni and Raisa walked up behind the still bleeding and wheezing Hoshe'a. "Ema, I'm fine. I just need a…" Ignoring her son's protest, Carni forcefully grabbed his hand and inspected the cut. She placed a bowl of her special mixture on the table in front of him. "Don't eat this." With his face still in his hands, Kalev snickered. The nasty-looking paste was a combination of beef grease, honey, turmeric, and concentrated *qannabbos* (cannabis) oil. Raisa held a small urn of clean water, and a long strip of cloth bandage was looped over her arm. Hoshe'a started the same whining protest he'd repeated since childhood. Carni leaned in and whispered to Hoshe'a, "In all the times you've seen your battered brother's blood pooling on my floor, did you ever see him crying about it? Stop whining, Major, and hold still."

Carni glanced at the teens. "Boys, come over here and watch. My medics may not be able to get to you right away. So you might have to take care of your own wounds before they get worse or begin to fester. It could be the difference between losing a limb or worse." The teens looked at Ari, who quickly stood and walked to the other end of the table. The others crowded around. The little ema switched into her ema teacher mode. "First, if possible, clean the wound…"

With his face still buried in his hands, the mortified Kalev ventured a look through his splayed fingers. Raisa was smiling right at him. The man she'd loved since childhood would never know that Carni had told her in graphic detail about Kalev's use of the silk pillow cover. Which, at the moment, was acting like shackles around Kalev's ankles, destroying any hope of escaping this embarrassing Sha'al with any semblance of dignity. But like a young boy in trouble, Kalev quickly closed his fingers and moaned, "That's just great, just [illegible] great." He laid his forehead on the table and groaned again…

To anyone else the scene would've been hilarious and a subject of numerous future ribbings. But not to Raisa. The shy innocence of her future husband only made her love him more. Carni scowled at her forthcoming daughter-in-law. "Raisa, are you paying attention?" Soon, Carni finished cleaning and bandaging her son's wound. Raisa flashed the unknowing Kalev a smile as they walked back to the kitchen.

Eventually, Kalev looked up and drained his freshly filled cup. The grinning Adir leaned sideways and talked louder than normal. "Nicely done, General. But I don't remember training you in the art of sha'dim killing, let alone how to single-handedly conquer Sha'al." Kalev smirked. "I guess it came naturally." They both laughed.

"Adir, Sir, it's good to see you. Where've you been this week? I want to show you my new room and toys." The skilled warrior averted his eyes and cleared his throat a couple of times. He hated lying to his protégé, but he'd promised Carni to let her tell Kalev about their "close friendship." "I, uh, I've been busy at the forge. I just bought another 150 of the smuggled Khopesh sword blanks."

Kalev nodded, then leaned forward and got Yadin's attention. "Make sure Major Adir leaves with enough gold coins to cover the cost of 800 smuggled swords. And double his pay for our troops' forge training and his expenses. Oh, and use the rest of *my* coins to pay him for my combat training." Yadin nodded. "Yes, Sir, right away."

Adir angrily whispered to Kalev, "I told you I will *not* accept any pay for my *volunteered* time." Kalev shook his head. "Carni told me that my abba constantly insisted that one should always pay a man what he's worth. Otherwise, you judge him and his work to be worthless… Was my abba wrong? *Are* you and your time worthless? It's just good business to pay you!"

Adir smiled and shook his head. "I swear, Kalev, you're just like him: strong-willed and stubborn as an ox." Kalev's abba's best friend paused, and his voice trembled. "You look and sound just like him. I truly admired your abba. He also taught *me* that integrity and loyalty always preceded a good business decision." Adir paused and stared into the middle distance.

"One time Hezron was so sick, your ema actually sat on his chest to keep him from taking the harvest to the city." Kalev smiled. "I guess I got my stubbornness from both parents then." Adir nodded. "Your father was the most successful farmer in all of Goshen and most of Egypt. He was respected by everyone, especially your ema.

"That said…your ema was an autonomous force. Your abba once told me that 'Yahweh made man to be the head of the family, period. Yet even the King of kings knows that the woman is the neck that turns that head any way she wants.' Believe me, your abba knew it and stayed in his own lane.

"So when Hezron became ill, your ema found me in the field and 'suggested' I go into the house and 'volunteer' to deliver the wagon of oranges for him. I foolishly told her I'd never done it before, so she should probably find someone else… That was my first big mistake of the day! Rachael stood there with her hands on her hips and gave me that Hebrew ema glare. You know, the look that feels like it's boring a hole into your brain." Every head at the table nodded. They'd all experienced the malevolent force of the *look*. Kalev looked around cautiously, then lowered his voice.

"Sir, I hate to interrupt your story, but I have to know. Are all women *taught* how to give that *look*, or are they born with it?" Adir smiled. "I believe it may be both. They're born with the ability and taught how to enhance it by their savtas and emas."

From the other side of the table, Hoshe'a yelped and slapped the table. "Adir, you're exactly right! See, I have this theory." Kalev rolled his eyes. "That evil look originated in the garden of Eden. It was passed from the sha'dim-filled serpent to Eve, then she passed it down to *her* daughters, and so on down the generations to *our* ema. And ema has perfected it and wields its evil power. Kalev, we never stood a chance…I wish you *had* conquered Sha'al and destroyed the *look*'s evil power over all men."

Thirty years of painful experience had taught Hoshe'a that anytime they talked about their ema, he should watch his brother's eyes. Kalev always seemed to see their ema's sneak attack before it happened. The General knew this and decided it was *his* turn to play a practical joke. He locked eyes with Hoshe'a and grew a practiced smile. Then he made a show of quickly glancing over his brother's shoulder and gave a half nod.

Hoshe'a violently jerked his head down, hoping to dodge his ema's imagined attack. In the rush to duck, Hoshe'a's head hit, then bounced off the table, and he fell backward onto the floor. He lay there bandaged and moaning as everyone at the officer's table belly laughed themselves to tears.

Eventually, Adir wiped his eyes and continued his true story. "Needless to say, your ema quickly changed my mind, and I escaped into the house. Rachael ominously stood overwatch as I offered to deliver the oranges to the city. Hezron saw your ema's look, then weakly smiled. He said he knew it wasn't my idea, but since I was still alive, He believed I'd *chosen* wisely." Kalev smiled.

"Hezron told me I was to deliver the load to the temple priest's manager. He gave me the signed contract scroll, *just in case*. He warned me that this specific treasurer always tried to get the produce cheaper than the agreed price. Then he'd turn around, inflate the price, sell the majority of the produce on his own black market, and keep the difference for himself. So by the time I got to the temple, I already had a chip on my shoulder.

"The lavishly overdressed manager haughtily sneered when he saw this young kid drive up with the oranges. I told him I was sent by Hezron and showed him the contract the high priest had already signed.

But the vulture snickered, licked his lips, and sneered. He said he was a very important and busy man. And because I'd made him wait for a whole five minutes, I'd broken the contract and had to accept half the price. The pig grinned like a self-important champion, then slowly turned to walk toward the temple unloading area. This guy was a real [illegible], so I…"

Adir paused for effect and ate a piece of bread. Kalev grinned. He never knew his mentor was such a good storyteller. Yadin anxiously asked, "So what did you do?" Adir took another swallow of wine and continued.

"The [illegible] thief fully expected me to gratefully accept his lowballed offer, then dutifully follow him to the temple's unloading area. As he walked away, I knew he was still watching me over his shoulder. So I shrugged at the pig's back, mounted the wagon, turned the oxen in the opposite direction, and headed toward the Hebrew marketplace…"

Yadin's eyes went wide. His jaw dropped, causing the others to start laughing. "The manager ran and tried to keep up with the wagon. He yelled that he'd honor the contracted price. I ignored the guy and goaded the oxen to pick up the pace." The other teens knowingly watched Yadin and tried not to laugh. Their genius friend was predictably fascinated with this tale of "audacious bookkeeping peril."

"I guess the arrogant minion was warned not to return without the only fruit left in the area. The wheezing manager caught up again and offered a couple of coins more than Hezron's price. I stopped the wagon and politely reminded him that it was late in the season, and these were the most prized and *only* oranges for sale in upper Egypt. The pig furiously asked what I wanted for the load…"

Adir paused again to drink some wine. Yadin, being the accounting genius, smirked. "I would have demanded 15 percent more than the agreed price." Adir smiled and slowly shook his head. "No, I told him what I'd accept. The man went apoplectic and swore for about five minutes. But when I turned in my seat to ride away, he finally agreed to *my* higher price.

"I drove *past* the space he'd told me to park the wagon and followed him right into the temple's sacred courtyard. I told the offended-looking manager I didn't trust him. So he'd better hurry and unload because I intended to sit right there and count each piece of gold before I left. To hedge my inexperienced ultimatum, I reminded the evil little pig that Queen Hatshepsut would hear about it if he harmed me or my oxen or cheated her favorite supplier. And to add a little *incentive* for him to hurry, I got down, walked to the rear of the wagon, and relieved myself on their sacred glazed bricks. The man went nuts.

"I didn't know that in two hours, every priest in Egypt would descend on that courtyard. They were to offer up their yearly human sacrifices to Ra. But this 'unclean' Hebrew teen had just defiled this most sacred place. And if that wasn't offensive enough, my team of very Hebrew oxen were relieving *themselves* right on cue.

"The little pig exploded. He screamed for his abused servant boys to hurry. While they unloaded the fruit, I sat in the shade of their 'Mighty Ra' statue and ate two of the largest *Hebrew* oranges. I tore up the peals and evenly distributed them between the enormous statue's toes. Just another reminder that a non-Egyptian had breached the walls of their holy place." They all laughed at Adir's audacity.

"When they'd emptied the wagon, I mounted the seat and waited for the manager. After two minutes in the hot sun, I got mad and started singing a praise song to Yahweh…in Egyptian, of course. I liked the way my voice echoed off their sacred walls and tiles, so I sang louder.

"The temple door slowly opened, and the scared-looking manager/pig ran to the wagon with three small chests. He told me to stop my sacrilegious singing, then placed the little chests on the floorboards at my feet. I started to argue, thinking he was trying to cheat me. The treasurer nervously looked around again, then loudly whispered that the chests were my *bonus* for leaving right away. I shook my head and hissed back. I said the three little chests weren't nearly enough. In addition, I was an important and busy man, and he'd taken too long to return. So now it was time to empty my bowels.

"At the same time I started to get down again, I saw the rat angrily wave at another door. Eight young boys emerged, sliding two five-foot-long coffins across the slick tiles. The panicky manager grabbed four long boards and fashioned a ramp up to the wagon bed. I still don't know how they pushed those things up and into the wagon. I guess the wheezing sycophant saw my dubious look, so he reached up and flipped open both lids. The sarcophagi were filled to the top with sparkling gold ingots. The little pig seemed to grow taller and hissed like a cobra. He called me a dirty [illegible] Hebrew and told me to get out before I became their next human sacrifice."

Knowing he was being watched, Adir paused for effect and slowly drained his cup. Kalev glanced at the agitated-looking Yadin and chuckled. Adir smacked his lips and continued. "It took ten of us to heft the gold-filled coffins into Hezron's front room. We opened the lids of the coffins and chests." He turned to Kalev and chuckled. "Your abba bolted upright, started laughing, then promptly puked.

"Your ema had cleaned up the mess, politely scolded your abba, then stayed in the kitchen pretending not to hear the counting. But when we told your abba the final tally, she raced out of the kitchen and sweetly demanded that Hezron give me the three little chests.

"But before your abba could speak, I thanked them both for the generous offer, but I flatly refused to take the 435 gold and silver coins. I avoided your ema's intensifying glare. Then I quickly walked out before she could *respectfully* force me to take them." Adir shook his head and frowned at the memory.

"Hezron had always overpaid me, so my family had all we needed anyway. Plus, two years prior, I lost my saba. During his burial, Hezron had three large, plain-looking urns put into her kitchen. All three were filled to the top with gold coins. After the funeral, Hezron invented a story about my *saba* investing in his farm and that the proceeds were waiting for her at home.

"But she *and* my abba died that same year. So I inherited the three urns. I remember feeling guilty about keeping so much of *Hezron's* money. I didn't know what to do, so I put them in our barn, covered them with blankets and hay, then promptly forgot about them. At least until your parents offered me those chests.

"As I walked home, the guilt about the urns came flooding back. It just wasn't right to keep my generous mentor's money. So I went to the barn, loaded the urns into our wagon, and took them back to Hezron… That was my second big mistake of the day!

"Your abba was leaning against the front doorpost, glaring at me when I pulled up. I never knew how he'd found out I intended to return the urns. But it was obvious he knew. It was one of the few times I ever saw him that livid. He told me to get down and face him. Before he started tearing into me. I quickly told him that it was *his* money, and I felt guilty keeping it, and besides that, he paid me enough and… but your sick abba verbally exploded. He yelled that I was insulting him and trying to steal Yahweh's financial blessing over *his* family. He pointed at the urns and said that gold was a gift to my savta. And a gift is as much a blessing to the giver and *his* generations as it is to the receiver. Hezron said it was foolish and shortsighted of me to *try* to give *my* inheritance to him."

Adir smiled. "I didn't know your um, determined, ema had taken the little chests out the back door and made her way around to the rear of my wagon. I was too busy listening to your abba thundering about how I needed to grow up and think about my future family." Adir locked eyes with his son but kept talking to Kalev.

"Hezron lowered his voice, put his hand on my shoulder and said, 'Yahweh has given us the power to design our own legacy. Adir, that gold can't speak lasting truths or love your family. It's simply a tool you can use for a short period of time.' He assured me that when we reached our 'promised homeland,' I'd need the money to get started on my own family farm.

"Then Hezron paused and locked eyes with me. He asked the wisest question I've ever heard. 'In a hundred years, how will *you* be remembered, if at all? This gold will eventually end up in the coffers of some already rich king or pharaoh. That's a historical fact.' Hezron shook his head, then continued in a fatherly voice. He said, 'Son, an exemplary life that personifies truth, honor, respect, personal integrity, mercy, and grace is the only *true* legacy that will last.'

"Then Hezron clapped his hands once and declared that the matter of the urns was closed, never to be spoken of again. He playfully added that I was interrupting his evening meal. Without another word he turned around and went back into the house. After all that *schooling*, I actually felt relieved and much wiser than your *average* seventeen-year-old general." Adir playfully slugged Ari's shoulder, then took another drink.

All eyes shifted to the red-faced Yadin. But Adir didn't have to look. He'd known Ari's friend for most of the frustrated kid's life. He knew numbers and totals were everything to the boy. That's why he'd playfully left the key sums out of the story.

Over the lip of his wine cup, Adir winked at Kalev. The General cleared his throat and forced a straight face. He asked Yadin's obvious question. "So, Major Adir, I was wondering. How much did you get for the oranges?" Adir pretended to concentrate. "I don't remember." Kalev, Ari, Akiba, and Ofek burst out laughing. But Yadin exploded into a long stream of multilingual expletives. Adir smiled at Kalev. "Did I just hear that boy swear in Sumerian?" Kalev shrugged. "Probably."

When Yadin took a breath, Adir yelled, "Oh, I remember now!" Yadin went silent. "I made up a price for each orange and told him I could get double that at the marketplace." Yadin's jaw dropped. "But Hezron's produce never made it to our marketplace, right? I thought the palace or the priests always bought it all." Adir had taken a bite of the sweetbread, so he just nodded. Yadin was confused. "So how did you know what each orange was worth?"

Adir shrugged and swallowed. "I took Hezron's contracted price for the whole load, multiplied that by thirty, then divided that number by 3000 and added 10 percent. I gave the little thief that price for each of the 3000 oranges. I told him if he hurried, I'd knock off 10 percent from the total. I doubt the little rat ever counted the oranges or the gold." Yadin's mind went into full accounting mode. Then he looked up stunned. "That comes out to eleven-point-five-ounce gold ingots per orange." Adir smiled. "Plus, the bonus!"

25

Once the teens and Hoshe'a left to watch the competition finals, Adir swallowed hard and spoke to Kalev in a caring tone. "Son, you know me. I only want the best for you and your ema—I mean your whole family." Kalev nodded as he chomped into another loaf of fresh bread. "So I say this because I care. Besides, I know I can filet your hide in any sword fight, so you can be mad at me, but you'll never intimidate me." Kalev knew this to be true and warily nodded. Adir took a deep breath and boldly plowed on.

"Kalev, your abba's life will always be the supreme example of an honorable man. And *he* honored his, and our, Yahweh the King over all kings and pharaohs. Even in his violent death, he believed in Yahweh-Ghmolah (the Elohim of Recompense). He hoped *his son* would experience Yahweh's deliverance and see with his own eyes the defeat of these vile Egyptians.

"So Kalev, stop dishonoring your abba with your self-defeating hatred toward our Yeshua (Elohim our Deliverer). Yahweh didn't torment our people for 400 years; the Egyptians did. *They* chose to enslave us, *not* Yeshua. Did Yahweh hold the whip that lashed your back? *No*, it was that psychopath Hotep.

"Son, your abba knew that his El-Shaddai-Rohi (Invincible Elohim) *is* the Ultimate Conqueror. Yet out of Yahweh's love for us, His greatest creation, He limited Himself and all His created *malakhs* (angels and demons) in the use of that power. Elohim will not allow man's free-will choices to be overruled. And that includes men's cruelty toward other men.

"It's only because of Yahweh's unmerited favor and loving-kindness that we escape the result of *our* wrong choices. Kalev, whether you decide to believe it or not, that same limitless mercy is the only reason *you're* still alive."

Adir felt the powerful wind of the Elohim rise from his gut. "Kalev, son of Hezron. If you're not *strong enough* to accept that Yahweh is our loving Savior yet refuses to overrule any man's free will, you're not the man your abba hoped you'd become. The conquering deliverer he wanted you to be." Without another word, Major Adir drained his tall mug of wine, excused himself, and headed toward the kitchen.

The raging battle in Kalev's mind, coupled with the gallon of wine he'd gulp down, made him feel dizzy and nauseous.

He tried to order his thoughts. *Adir* did *know and love Abba like a brother*, Kalev mused. *Plus, he* was *correct. Abba never blamed Yahweh for the Hebrews' agonizing 400-year captivity, including his own torture. And Adir* does *care for me and my family. So why is this Yahweh thing so hard for me to accept...? Argh.*

The sun was rising when the troops' cheering reached a fevered pitch. But Kalev, "going *kushi*," had already run to his room, heaved his meal into the golden toilet, and then let his bed swallow him whole. He'd wrongly hoped a long day's sleep would help calm his mind.

But it didn't take long for the tormenting dreams to return. He saw himself back in the mud pits. The searing heat of the Egyptian sun and the foul smell of the gray mud made him dizzy. He looked down and saw his legs were encased in dry mud up to his calves. He couldn't move. *How did I get back here…?* But before he could finish the thought, Kalev heard one, then three, then hundreds of blood-curdling screams. He looked up to see a monstrous Hotep swinging a scimitar the size of a date palm, back and forth like a harvesting sickle. With each swing he scythed multiple bodies in two. Hundreds of men, women, and children were just standing there screaming as if waiting in line for their turn to be cut down. Instantly the countless shrieks merged into one hideous question. "Kalev, where are you? Why won't you help us?" Kalev looked down again. Now the sunbaked mud was enveloping the lower half of his body; it felt like he was becoming a brick. He wildly struggled to get free. The screams were reaching an earsplitting climax. "Kalev, where are you? Why won't you help us?" "I'm trying…I can't…!" he screamed in sheer terror. Then he saw the gigantic eyes of Hotep glaring at him as if they were on fire. Screaming Egyptian curses, the monster lunged toward Kalev and swung its gleaming gold sword, slicing Kalev's body in half. "Noooo! I'll kill you, you piece of [illegible]," Kalev yelled, then bolted upright in his bed.

Someone had mistakenly doused all five torches in Kalev's room. So now, the filthy, sweat-soaked general couldn't tell if he was still asleep, still in his nightly battle with Hotep. Kalev had never slept in total darkness before. In his barn stall, even on moonless nights, he could still see the stars through the slats in the roof.

He was standing, or rather trying to balance, on the too-soft bed. His mind raced as he tried to understand what was happening. "Where am I? Is this Sha'al? I knew it had to happen sometime…" He shook his aching head and started to remember the previous evening. "Okay, deep breath, deeeeep breath."

It took the huge man some effort to stumble then swim his way to the edge of "the bed from Sha'al." Kalev finally reached the side then just fell off. But before he could stand, he felt a rumbling in the deck. As he stood next to the quivering bed, he heard a faint roar. "What the…" He quickly moved toward what he hoped was the door. He kicked something hard and stumbled, crashing into a wall. Whatever he'd kicked, crunched his pinky toe. "[illegible]," he howled.

With swords drawn, Ari, Little Frog, and Little Croc flung open the heavy door and rushed in. They fanned out and scanned the room for invaders. But when he saw their embarrassed general sitting on the edge of the bed holding his foot, Ari promptly dismissed the boys.

When they were alone, Kalev shook his head. "Someone extinguished all the torches in here. So I couldn't see, and that stupid chair…" He pointed toward the pile of broken wood, ripped padding, and still-swirling duck feathers near the door.

Ari cleared his throat a couple of times but failed to keep a straight face. "Sir, in this army, that is not acceptable. I'll see to it that *another* chair is severely disciplined for that one's insubordination." Kalev chuckled through the pain. Then he felt the rumbling again. "Ari, what is that noise?" "I'll show you." "Okay, but give me a minute to clean up."

Kalev scrubbed his face and hands, then checked twice before he donned the very large, very humiliating embroidered loin cloth and tunic. That's when the deck started vibrating again. A barefoot Kalev limped and smirked as he followed Ari down the hall. "You know, out of the three of you bedroom assaulters, Little Frog looked the fiercest."

Ari shook his head. "He and Little Croc have taken your protection personally. Last week Akiba caught Little Frog 'warning' one of your other shadow troops. He'd drawn his sword and told the other troop to stop acting stupid, keep his eyes on his target, or he'd kill him and take his place. The much larger *sergeant* playfully drew his own sword and chuckled. At least until he realized Little Frog's sword was pricking his throat. Akiba ran up in time to hear Little Frog threaten to take the other troop's head off and feed it to the crocs. Akiba ordered Little Frog to run laps around the drill floor until they puked." Kalev shook his head. "It sounds like he needs some remedial 'chain of command' training." Ari grimaced. "Already done, Sir. Little Frog and *Drill Sergeant* Abraham spent three punishing days and nights together. The troop won't make that mistake again."

They walked out onto the main drill floor. That was when Kalev noticed for the first time that his new stallion's corral was right by the hallway entrance. He saw Little Croc sitting cross-legged on the horse's back, while he brushed the sweaty stallion. The boy was using a shiny, jewel encrusted gold hairbrush, probably meant for one of Pharaoh's concubines, to brush the horse. He smiled and gave the fearless troop an approving nod. "I guess I should give him a name."

Ari chuckled. Little Croc swiveled around and stood on the horse's hind quarters. But the horse didn't seem to notice. "His name is Boaz 'cause he's the fastest winner." Kalev scowled, "How do you know he's fast?" Little Croc panicked. He knew he wasn't supposed to ride the General's giant horse. But it was fun to race the other troops, plus, he reasoned, Boaz liked it. The guilty-looking boy slid off the horse and then tried to backtrack. "I meant Boaz looks fast. I mean, his name means he's fast 'cause he is—I mean…"

Carni walked up behind her son and scowled at the little troop trying to hide under the horse's belly. "He sounds and hides just like you and Hoshe'a." Kalev turned. "You mean he sounds like me and Hoshe'a *used to*." Carni condescendingly patted her son's shoulder. "Of course, General, whatever helps you sleep at night." Ari started laughing and the deck started rumbling again. Kalev shot his subordinate a concerned look. The teen general pointed at the far end of the drill floor. "Watch this." The rumbling grew louder as an ever-widening sliver of the setting sun's orange light streamed in. It looked like a portion of the Pit's ceiling was collapsing.

The amazed General Kalev, General Ari, and Major Carni started walking toward the other end of the Pit. Kalev watched as a huge section of the desert lowered to form a ramp up to the surface. Even with the steep grade, the boulders and small dunes that lined the edges didn't move. He even recognized the meandering dry creek bed they'd followed to the access ladder. Ari smirked. "According to Major Hoshe'a, the last twenty-five yards of the Pit's roof are lowered by a series of massive ropes and pullies." The slack-jawed general just stared.

A massive herd of saddled horses suddenly appeared at the top of the ramp and quickly raced down to the main deck. They were followed, but not herded, by a platoon of troops on horseback. When the 200-plus horses reached the main deck, they curiously stopped and crowded around the officer's platform. The mounted riders joined another hundred troops and encircled the restless herd. Each troop chose a horse and led it to a stall. It was all over in a couple of minutes. The mounted riders were followed by a single man. The moment he reached the main deck, the ramp began to rise to its original position in the ceiling.

Even from a distance, Kalev recognized his brother's plodding gait. The General silently ran up behind him as Hoshe'a continued to talk to one of the dismounted troops. "…Sergeant, I don't know how to ride, but I think I need to learn." The teen sergeant saw the General sneaking up behind his brother and smiled. "Yes, Major, I can help with that. Choose a horse, and we can get you started after the evening meal."

Kalev quickly put his surprised brother in a headlock. Through his gasps, Hoshe'a squeaked out, "Now you've done it. You. Will. See. My. *Wraaaaaath*." Kalev and the sergeant started laughing. He let go of his coughing brother and put his arm around Hoshe'a's shoulder. "Let's get some wine."

They all walked back toward the dining tables. Kalev sincerely thanked Hoshe'a again. Knowing this would embarrass his older brother was only a bonus. "Hoshe'a, I never knew that ramp thing was even possible." Hoshe'a cleared his throat and shrugged. "Yeah, about that. I actually stole the plans from the generous and mighty Pahns." They all laughed.

Kalev grew silent as he limped next to his brother. Hoshe'a looked down with raised eyebrows. Kalev grumbled. "My room was pitch black when they put out all the torches." Hoshe'a grinned. "I can fix that."

As they got closer to the tables, the mouthwatering smell of hot bread made Hoshe'a and Kalev's stomachs growl at the same time. Their ema heard the loud rumbling, turned, and rolled her eyes. "You two…"

All the senior ranking officers gathered at the table. Kalev poured Hoshe'a a cup of beer and praised him again in front of the others. Hoshe'a tried to laugh off his awkward feeling. He looked at Kalev. "I thought you detested Egyptian beer." Kalev shrugged. "I'm hungry." Hoshe'a proudly took in the ongoing development of the Pit. The new two-tiered stalls now ran the entire length of both walls, but less than half were occupied.

Major Hoshe'a grew sullen. "I'm amazed at the lengths this pharaoh will go to create the greatest treasuries and burial chambers ever. Two weeks ago, I helped Pahns make a map of all the complex traps and secret passageways under the whole city. He said Ramses is worried that he'll have to escape the palace for one reason or another. Now we're building hidden underground corridors from the palace to the stables, the river, and the treasuries. This pharaoh is suspicious of everyone, especially his inner circle."

Kalev looked concerned. "You know too much, big brother." Hoshe'a sadly looked down and nodded. "Yeah, I know…because of the constant turnover, cave-ins are happening almost daily." He looked toward the kitchen and lowered his voice. "Brother, you can't tell ema." Kalev nodded suspiciously. "Yesterday, a secondary tunnel to the river collapsed. I was the only one to make it out. But on the bright side, Pahns disappeared four days ago." Hoshe'a's smile faded. "Kalev, your supposed death and my near miss gave me an idea. As far as Pahns knows, I died in that cave. So I guess I'm already dead." Kalev smiled. "Good. I'm sure ema could use your 'full-time' help around here." The teens tried to look like busy eating, but all four of them laughed anyway. "Hey, about my bedroom torchlight…"

Kalev tried not to scowl as he watched their ema quietly walk up behind Hoshe'a. His oblivious brother shrugged and grinned. "I don't know, General; the thought of making my little brother sleep in a dark hole kind of gives me a warm, tingly feeling inside." Kalev inadvertently winced. Hoshe'a groaned. "She's right behind me, isn't she?" Kalev half nodded. And true to form, Major Hoshe'a quickly ducked and hit his forehead on the table *again*. Carni hadn't moved. But Kalev sensed a new type of attitude adjustment headed Hoshe'a's way.

Half in defense of his brother and half in anger, the huge General shot to his feet. "Major Carni, I need to speak with you in the TOC *now*." She scowled but dutifully followed. Kalev slammed the huge doors behind them. "Now, about Raisa…"

For the next fifteen minutes, ema and son yelled and argued. When the heated discussion ended, Kalev was sitting at the head of the table. He rubbed his tired-looking eyes and groaned. Carni saw the look of both resignation and sheer terror on his face. She got up and sat beside her son. "Ema, I know I couldn't ask for a better wife. But I can barely talk to her, let alone ask her to marry me. Besides, I'm way too busy with all of this and…" She took his huge, scarred hand in hers. "Little one, did you know that Raisa is the one your ema chose for you just before she died?" Kalev sat back, stunned. "She made me promise that when the time was right, I'd make the match. Son, you need Raisa. She'll keep you out of that dark, lonely place your thoughts and dreams take you."

Then Carni grew a sly grin. "Besides, after what you two boys have put your ema through, you *owe me* grandchildren." Kalev winced, then grew his own mischievous grin. "Well, Raisa is beautiful and is probably great in…" The forty-year-old man never saw his ema's other hand race up to slap the back of his head hard. "Don't you ever disrespect me or Raisa again!" He chuckled and pulled Carni close. "Ema, have I told you how much I've missed you lately?" She kissed the top of his head.

Kalev saw the regret in her eyes. "I'm sorry, son; after what that evil pig did to you, I know you *probably* can't have children. So I guess your brother will have to carry on the family name. Yahweh help us all."

Eventually, Kalev took a deep breath, sighed dramatically, and tried to look sad. "Ema, um, about Hoshe'a…" Kalev paused for effect. Carni slowly sat back in her chair and growled at her son. "What do you know!" Kalev cleared his throat and wished he could have produced tears. "Ema, I'm pretty sure Hoshe'a won't be giving you grandbabies either." He paused and sighed again. "Hoshe'a just told me he's so lonely, he's planning to fake his own death and disappear. I tried to talk him out of it, but…" Carni shot to her feet. "He what!" Kalev waited until she'd stormed down the hall before he broke out laughing. "That was way too easy."

Kalev was halfway down the hall when he passed the fuming Carni headed the other way. She was pulling his scowling brother by the arm toward the TOC. "Kalev, what did you…?" Now it was Ema's turn to slam the doors. Kalev grinned. "I wonder who he'll have to marry."

26

Three weeks later, Kalev had fallen asleep with his head on the table. Heh's troops had silently extinguished all but one torch in the TOC. Between the all-night foraging raids, the combat riding lessons, weapons training, and working with Hoshe'a on the final plans for the Fortress, he was beyond exhausted. The sleepless nights didn't help either.

He just couldn't shut his brain off. The bouts of indecision concerning Raisa and the ongoing mental battle over the reality of a just Yahweh had reached a tipping point. He knew he was quickly losing his mind.

Kalev had been asleep for two hours. He was reliving the same terrifying dreams when there was a loud pounding on the TOC doors. More asleep than not, the giant man raced to the doors and threw them open. Before he could stop himself, he'd lunged at Ari. A group of boys watched in disbelief as their general grabbed the stunned Ari's tunic and threw him into the opposite wall.

The teenage general's gasp and wide-eyed look brought Kalev to his full senses. The General looked down in horror. Kalev's long, jagged dagger had reflexively materialized in his other shaking hand and was dangerously close to Ari's stomach. He quickly sheathed it and walked back into the TOC. General Ari quickly recovered and growled to the stunned and confused shadow troops. "Remember it's dangerous to wake a sleeping leopard, let alone a 320-pound one!" Then the wise kid straightened his tunic and walked into the TOC like nothing had happened.

After he shut the door, Ari subtly chose a chair out of the General's arms' reach. "I'm sorry to wake you, Sir." Kalev's hand was shaking as he quickly tried to swipe the tears off his cheeks. He shook his head in embarrassed self-disgust. "Son, I am so sorry. I don't know why I do that. Maybe the dreams…I know it's a weakness I *have* to control… Please, Ari, you know I'd never try to hurt you…*like I just did*, 𐤀𐤀𐤀𐤀𐤓𐤓𐤀𐤔𐤕!"

Ari stared at his General—his mentor's pained expression. Two days ago, Adir told his son some of the lesser-known, insidious details of the various tortures this man had survived. Ari glanced at the scars from multiple stabbings halfway between Kalev's shoulders and neck. His abba said, "According to one of the more wicked Egyptian soldiers, to be tortured in these specific places was some of the most excruciating pain any man could experience. If they survived, it drove most men to insanity." Ari's abba was amazed that Kalev had survived as long as he did.

But the mental pain and regret bleeding from this big man's eyes made Ari's face flush with anger. The teenage general hated that Egyptian pig Hotep. He hated what the Egyptian people put this man, his own father, and the rest of the Hebrew race through. 𐤀𐤓𐤓𐤀𐤔𐤕, he thought, *I hate Egypt too.* Which was odd, as this was the only home he'd ever known. Ari felt his hand going numb. That was when he realized he was white-knuckling the grip of his sword.

The mortified general took a deep, shuddering breath and willed himself out of his too-familiar self-loathing. "Again, Ari, I am so sorry…"

"Um, did you need me for something?" Ari had to will his own demons away before he could speak. "Sir, just after our last command and staff meeting, the target's shadow troops returned with a lot more than information from the palace." Kalev yawned. "Let's get the others back in here."

In two minutes, most of the senior officer corps and the more experienced majors and captains sat around the TOC's map table. Every lieutenant in the army lined the walls. The three Egyptian-looking shadow troops stood at the far end. Two older troops flanked a much smaller one. But only the top of the littlest one's keffiyeh showed above the table's edge.

When the doors were shut, Kalev nodded. "Report, Corporal." The skinny twelve-year-old nervously looked around the table and cleared his dry throat twice. "Um, Sirs, the three of us followed targets aleph and bet, using the bounding overwatch technique, through the marketplace and into the palace. We picked up the two large and one small watering jars as usual. The targets were tracked down the 2347-step hallway to Pharaoh's throne room. We pretended to water every other one of the 117 potted date palms along the way…"

Ari, Akiba, and Yadin naturally glanced at their friend. Yadin was smiling ear to ear. Then he not so subtly leaned toward Ari and whispered, "If it's possible, I *need* this corporal assigned to my company. [illegible], I'll promote him to lieutenant. He reminds me of—of *me*." Ari tried to mask his laugh with a cough, but it sounded more like he was gagging. All he could do was nod at his ecstatic lifelong friend.

"When targets aleph and bet entered the throne room, we hid behind the big gold doors. We heard the, um, loud discussion between our targets and the pharaoh. Sir, the next plague that's probably already happening is supposed to make all the Egyptian livestock sick and die. The animals on the Egyptian side of the canal will all be dead by this time tomorrow." The corporal stared at the ceiling. "I estimate there are still 4786 cattle on the Egyptian side of…"

To the same degree Yadin was enjoying the exciting accounting action, Kalev's overloaded mind was starting to wander. Sensing this, Ari cleared his throat impatiently. The boy snapped out of his mental calculations and stiffened. "Um, sorry, Sir. We followed the targets out of the palace, through the marketplace, and out of the city. Per our mission parameters, halfway to the target's encampment, we transferred overwatch to the camp's sergeant of the guard, then headed home. We'd just crossed the canal bridge when we heard hundreds of aurochs and sheep splashing into the canal…"

As curious five-year-old boys are apt to do, the smallest shadow troop kept trying to raise up on his tip toes to *barely* see over the table. The little bobbing keffiyeh interrupted his squad leader. "Sir," he excitedly yelled, "we didn't know sheeps could swim, Sir. But they caaaan! I seen it; they can swim, Sir, even the baby sheeps…!" The embarrassed squad leader quickly put his hand on the boy's shoulder to keep him from bobbing up and down. Then he growled and scowled the little troop into silence. Now the top of the keffiyeh was nervously swaying from side to side.

Most of the officers, Kalev included, started coughing into their sleeves to cover their laughter. Ari leaned close to the General and whispered, "You should see what happens when that one, Little Frog, and Little Croc get together." Kalev smiled and nodded. "My ema said I need to laugh more…but not now."

The perturbed corporal glared at the little one as he continued his report. "The herds swam across, ran up the near bank, and silently stopped on the road." The twelve-year-old shook his head. "Sir, they formed four straight lines approximately one point twenty-five miles long. First the aurochs, then the sheep. We…"

The little keffiyeh couldn't help himself. He raised on his tiptoes and leaned his head back. From his point of view, the only thing Kalev could see above the table was a pair of lips. The big man was afraid he'd bite his tongue off to keep from laughing.

The lips quickly exploded in one breathless statement. "They didn't say one Egyptian word Sir wouldn't they moo in Egyptian Sir I don't know Hebrew very well, but I know they didn't say any Hebrew words 'cause they're Egyptian cows and sheeps but I know enough Egyptian words, and they didn't say one Egyptian moo word or baaaa word they just stood there staring at us Sir like they…" The squad leader and his subordinate must have both swept the legs out from under the little troop, as the lips suddenly disappeared.

Yelling to be heard over the chorus of loud coughing, Ari quickly dismissed the three. The two *visible* shadow troops were followed by a limping keffiyeh out the closing doors. Kalev joked, "That was the best L⟍(|||)ᛉღ AAR yet."

Eventually the belly laughing subsided. Yadin cleared his throat, looked at his accounting sheet, then reported. "Sir, the herds followed those three back to the Outpost. There are 551 cows, 16 happy bulls"—Kalev and the others chuckled—"144 calves. 327 sheep, 77 happy rams, and 200 lambs. And they're all in the field behind Major Carni's house."

Kalev noticed Yadin was scowling at his notes. The General nodded for the teenage colonel to continue. "Sir, just like the other outbreaks, this animal disease will only last a few days." The brilliant Yadin shook his head in disgust. "But the real problem…arghh."

"You see, four days after the Nile and their wells were polluted with blood, Mo…I mean, the target caused the blood in the Nile to disappear. But for whatever reason, our wells remained polluted."

Kalev nodded and inadvertently interrupted Yadin's story. "I remember sort of—I kind of slept through that week." Nervous chuckles rumbled through the room. Kalev smiled. "And I forgot to thank you all for digging my ema's new well. I swear the cool water tastes sweeter." Hoshe'a laughed. "It should; we had to dig that one fifty feet deeper." Ari scowled at Hoshe'a with raised eyebrows, then tilted his head toward the others around the room. Hoshe'a smiled. "I mean, I only managed the digging and shoring. These men tirelessly worked from dusk to dawn for three nights; you should be proud of them, General!" Ari nodded his thanks. And Kalev sincerely addressed the others. "I *am* very proud and humbled by all my troops' generosity and self-sacrifice. And please convey my appreciation to the other troops." Hoshe'a added, "Since then, we've dug two more deeper wells to supply the Fortress. I think we actually hit a huge cistern on the eastern one."

The frustrated Yadin cleared his throat. He truly hated his precisely ordered concepts being interrupted. It seemed to take so much energy to get his thoughts back on track. He scowled at his accounting sheet again. Columns of numbers and sums always seemed to calm his racing thoughts and frustrations.

But he continued, "In order to avoid another *attack* on their water sources, the shortsighted pharaoh ordered his garrisoned soldiers to dam up the farmers' field canals and reroute the water to flow into pools at the city center. As is human nature, most of the people in Ramses thought it far more politically beneficial to have their slaves draw the water from the pools and boil it than to dig new wells and possibly offend the pharaoh's delicate sensibilities. But the smart Egyptians who *did* have their slaves dig new wells had to tunnel two times deeper than we did just to gain a trickle of water." Hoshe'a snorted. " to be Egyptian these days." Everyone but Yadin chuckled.

The teen quickly continued, "As you know, Sir, the twenty-seven most productive Egyptian farmers live outside the city walls. And most of them have ten slaves or less. They all *initially* tried to water their combined 4522 acres of wheat and corn by hand."

Now he was speaking *Kalev's* language. The son of Hezron, just like his father, easily did wheat and corn seed versus gallons of water ratio in his head. Then declared, "This is the hot season. Plus, they delayed their corn planting. It's impossible to reach the necessary yield watering by hand. They're idiots to try." Yadin nodded. "Yes, Sir, so they collectively agreed to reduce their viable crop size by half." Kalev let out a low whistle. "I would hate to be a farmer on that side of our canal."

Yadin cringed but nodded. His friends could tell he'd almost reached his maximum level of self-control. His voice sounded strained when he resumed. "Sir, half of the land around the city is covered in shriveled grape vines, dead or dying orange trees, and dried-up immature vegetable plants. For the last three months, we've foraged most of the fruit, vegetables, flowers, and oil before it reaches the city." He pointed at the ceiling. "So those herds will be the only meat and mutton left in Egypt." He paused to let that sink in around the table.

"We've stopped the foraging missions for now. Sir, as our targets left the palace, a large contingent of the Egyptian Army's wounded, escorted by two full companies of soldiers, returned to their barracks. As soon as they figure out the only remaining livestock crossed the canal…" Kalev finished the statement. "The army will be hunting for them on this side of the canal." Yadin nodded. "Yes, Sir, they will." The TOC went deathly silent.

The room remained soundless as their General scowled at the ceiling in thought. Without a word, Kalev stood, walked out the doors, down the passageway, and stopped in the center of the Pit's immense drill floor. Everyone in the TOC, including the three-shadow-troop comedy show, silently followed the General but respectfully halted a few steps to the rear. Hoshe'a walked up beside Kalev, saw his brother counting out loud, and smirked, then whispered, "You're going to hurt your brain doing that."

The scowling general surveyed the empty stalls and shook his head. "Not enough. Where are we on the Fortress?" Hoshe'a smiled proudly. "Two weeks ago, we completed the reinforced roof. Even Pahns would be astonished at my new style of interlocking trusses. They…" And once again, Hoshe'a saw Kalev's eyes begin to glaze over.

So the General's older brother quickly switched into his "building-a-hidden-fortress-for-dummies" dialect. Standing behind the brothers, Akiba knew what was coming. He leaned over to Yadin and quietly chuckled. "Wait for iiiiiiiit."

Hoshe'a cleared his throat. "Ugg, made big wood over deep hole. When big orange light in sky went away, we spread lots of dug-up dirt over big wood over hole. Then, when big orange light in sky went away again, we made long not wavy lines in dug-up dirt. When big orange light in sky went away again, we spread stinky cow [illegible] on the little hills between not-wavy lines in dug-up dirt. When big orange light in the sky went away again, we pushed little seeds into the hills between the not-wavy lines in the dug-up dirt."

Except for the attentive little drooping keffiyeh troop, the group strained not to laugh. In a blur, Kalev balled his fist and faked a punch toward Hoshe'a's chest. The six-month-older brother threw up his hands and jumped back in a feeble attempt to block the supposed hammer blow. "Okay, okay, I'm sorry." Kalev scowled but let Hoshe'a continue.

"I couldn't figure out a way to grow crops on the ramp. So we actually moved your entire field thirty yards north to widen the wagon track between your field and the Outpost. It made it easier to hide the unplanted ramp. In three weeks, the Fortress's roof will be sprouting barley." Kalev shook his head and mouthed the words to Hoshe'a. "Ema was dead wrong about you."

Hoshe'a quickly checked behind them, then nodded. "She usually is… So the ramp, rooms, ovens, and forges were completed two nights ago. The Fortress is an improved version of the Pit. It's almost 60 percent longer and 30 percent wider. We built into the east wall twenty-one evenly spaced, 10-foot-high-by-45-foot-wide-by-150-foot-deep, inset animal corrals and/or pens. Nine hundred horse stalls fill in the gaps between the corrals. I don't remember the exact number of the western wall's two-tiered horse stalls. But I think it's 810." Standing behind the major and General, the frustrated Yadin exploded with his "official accounting totals." He hated incorrect or estimated sums. "*Actually*"—Kalev glanced at the smirking Hoshe'a, and they both turned around—"the Fortress has a cumulative total of 3124 ten-foot-wide-by-twelve-foot-long, two-tiered horse stalls. There are currently *902* interspersed on the east wall and 2222 on the western wall. There is room for an additional two large ox corrals on each side of the ramp."

Both brothers smiled when they saw the twelve-year-old shadow troop over Yadin's shoulder. The kid rapidly shook his head, opened his mouth, then wisely shut it. Hoshe'a nodded his thanks to Yadin then continued.

"Okay, what he said. At present the Fortress can easily hold more than 4500 head of cattle, sheep, and goats. There's even enough room for your growing flock of crazy chickens." Yadin opened his mouth to correct the major again, but Ari touched his arm, and the frustrated accounting savant shut his mouth.

The Commanding General turned to Ari. "Have any of our original Outpost troops moved into the Fortress yet?" Ari shook his head. "No, Sir, we were waiting for your inspection." "Okay, two more things, then we'll head over there."

The towering General turned to the three young shadow troops and took a knee. As any good leader would, Kalev enjoyed receiving input from the lowest-ranking troops. This always reminded him that every army decision affected hundreds of lives and seemed to keep everything in perspective.

"Gentlemen, how much time do you give us before the palace guards start looking for those cattle?" The three boys were astonished that their opinion mattered. "Sir," the older of the three spoke up, "from what we heard, the disease will last for four more days and nights. I figure they'll start looking at sunrise on the fifth day. Their priests have nothing to sacrifice, so they'll send out *their* guards and slaves also." Kalev nodded. "Gentlemen, I'm especially proud of you three. You completed your mission and saved us all from being discovered and possibly killed. Well done! Now go get some food and sleep." The three smiling boys puffed out their bird chests and proudly traded salutes with their Commanding General. All three started sprinting toward the dining area.

Kalev turned to the three colonels. "I want those herds underground within the next hour. They all need to be fed and watered. Plus, have your people erase all hoof and footprints, starting fifty yards back from the canal on their side. As soon as the cattle are underground, no more riding for the next week. Colonel Yadin, ask Sergeant Abraham if he could set up a rotating detail of recruits to keep disappearing all footprints on both sides of the river. Then the three of you meet us in the Fortress for the inspection. Afterward we start having the muster in the Fortress." The three colonels saluted and then headed toward the dining area.

Kalev paused, then looked concerned. "Ari, if we have enough actual bedrooms, let's ask the chief rabbi and his, um, family if they'd agree to stay in the Fortress for the next week. I'd feel better if she… 𐤀𐤀𐤀𐤓𐤓𐤀Ψ↓, if *they* had an active overwatch." Ari tried not to smile. "…Oh and give your abba the same invitation. That said, by my order, Major Carni is to pack up and report to the Fortress within the next two hours. She too will be our '*guest*' for the next week. That is nonnegotiable!"

Hoshe'a cleared his throat and tried to scowl. "Um, General Ari, permission to be present when you order Major Carni to pack up and move into the Fortress for seven days. I think it will be very educational for my advancement as a battlefield commander." Ari glanced at Kalev who half nodded. Hoshe'a punched Kalev in the shoulder. "Thank you, oh mighty one." Then he, too, headed toward the aroma of fresh sweetbread.

That was when Kalev saw the littlest shadow troop running back. The out-of-breath little boy stood at attention in front of the two generals. He looked lost and very confused. "Sir, um, General, Sir, could you give me…? I mean, you gave Little Frog and Little Croc their names, but…"

Though the boy remained at attention, tears streamed down his face, and he couldn't seem to continue. Kalev glanced at Ari curiously. General Ari barked, "At ease, troop," then smiled at Kalev. Ari did a crisp about-face so the boy couldn't hear their conversation. He leaned close to Kalev and whispered, "Do you remember we told you about foraging all the priest's unguarded lumber?" Kalev nodded. "That night, beside the city wall entrance into the temple of Ra, Little Frog kicked what he thought was a pile of soiled rags. But the pile whimpered. The kid looked like he hadn't eaten in days and had collapsed in a puddle of his own blood, pee, and Ψ𐤀𐤓𐤓𐤀Ψ↓.

"Major Carni said that it was seven days before this one could speak. And even then it was obvious he didn't know any Hebrew. Eventually, Sergeant Menes was able to understand this boy's story.

"This little guy doesn't remember anything before 'the dark place.' In fact, the night we found him was the first time he could remember being outside. Yadin did the math; the kid is actually five years old.

"That day, all of the thirty-one temple priests had ritually abused him. They called it his fifth annual blessing. The only reason they'd thrown him outside was because he looked dead or at least dying. Your ema said that this one was abused in ways she'd never heard of. She said the kid was incontinent and couldn't control his bowels for the first four days. He couldn't even hold down broth for the first three. It took another ten days before we gave him a loft in the Pit. And before you ask, I agreed it was the best place for him.

"He picked up our language very quickly. About three weeks later, he asked Akiba if he could be 'a soldier like his new friend Little Frog was an army soldier troop.' When I was sure he could handle it, he was handed off to Sergeant Abraham for basic training. The kid sailed through basic. I guess after his short lifetime in that temple Sha'al, even Sergeant Abraham's training methods were a welcomed relief.

You've seen the end result." Ari shook his head. "As far as I know, this fearless little survivor doesn't have a name. I think he's asking for you to give him one."

For some reason, Kalev's chest felt tight, and his eyesight was blurry. The giant General got down on one knee in front of the trembling little troop. "Son, I am very proud that you are such a brave warrior. You are a survivor just like me."

Kalev kept his eyes locked on the little boy's. "General Ari, from now on, this troop's name is…" He meant to say Little Keffiyeh, but what came out was "…Yoshiyah" (Yahweh is my healer). The little boy instantly wrapped his scrawny arms halfway around the shocked general's tree trunk of a neck, buried his face in Kalev's shoulder, and loudly sobbed his thanks.

Eventually, Kalev looked at Ari and Hoshe'a imploringly. They both wiped their tear-stained faces, and Ari cleared his throat. "Private Yoshiyah, attention."

The little troop stiffened to attention in front of his new hero. The boy's face was smeared with dirt, snot, and tears. But the smile on Little Yoshiyah's face made all three adults grin. Ari futilely tried to scowl. "Private Yoshiyah, rejoin your squad. You are dismissed." The lopsided keffiyeh finally fell off when Kalev's new "little one" proudly saluted and raced off. Kalev watched as Little Frog and Little Croc met him halfway, and the little squad raced toward the dining area. "Now there's three of them."

Kalev stood and wiped his cheeks. He turned to see Hoshe'a grinning and Ari with his hand over his mouth. Hoshe'a cleared his throat and grew sarcastically serious. "Sooooo, Yoshiyah?"

27

Kalev, Ari, Hoshe'a, and the colonels had just finished inspecting the new Fortress. They were about a hundred yards from the ramp when the massive thing opened. Kalev turned to Hoshe'a and just shook his head in amazement.

When the ramp thumped onto the deck, 1375 cattle and sheep rushed down the decline. A full company of mounted troops lazily followed. Most of the army watched as the thundering dust cloud rolled toward their general and his five subordinates like a monstrous pointed haboob. Kalev's jaw dropped when the mass of animals reached the bottom of the ramp, fanned out into a V shape, and raced right toward them.

Two months prior, the huge general remembered he'd been impressed when he saw his first adult aurochs bull. "Okay," he now admitted, "maybe I was a little more intimidated than impressed." The thick, very sharp horns spanned almost six feet tip to tip. The bulls' shoulders were above his six-foot eye level. But what made Kalev really anxious at the moment was that he knew the average weight of just *one* of these sixteen even larger bulls was well over 2500 pounds. The soon-to-be-trampled Commanding General grimly smirked. "Those will make a lot of huge beef steaks. That really  for me; I won't get any!"

The thundering hoof beats caused streamers of dust to fall from the ceiling. The whole life-threatening scene was ominous. "Arghh," he roared, "*seriously*, *again*? First Hotep and the other Egyptian pigs and now Egyptian cattle. *Seriously?* He groaned, "I'm starting to think everything in Egypt wants me dead."

Kalev looked at the others. Instead of seeing their panicked expressions, everyone else had their eyes closed and lips moving. He looked back at the wave of cattle and smirked. "And of course, the largest bull's on point!" And it was aiming right at him. Kalev sighed, closed his eyes, and resignedly started walking forward. He hoped he'd die quickly.

The choking cloud wafted over him like a blanket, but the deafening sound just stopped. He wondered if he was already dead from the violent impact with the lead bull. And time seemed to stop.

But in the crushing silence, he sensed the "voice" in his gut again. "Ah yes, just like the feel of your favorite loincloth—nice embroidery by the way—you can always count on death and taxes. But today, that's up to you, son of Hezron!" The ex-Egyptian "captive" heard a loud cracking as the ground began to violently shake. He knew his eyes were still closed, but when he looked down, he saw he was spanning a widening rift in the splintered wooden deck and red dirt below. Then a violent wind blew straight down from overhead, making it hard to breathe. It sounded like thousands of tormented screams as it blew past him. That was when he saw himself in two ongoing scenarios, one on either side of the chasm he was straddling.

On the left side, he saw the entire Egyptian Army's chariot corps racing down the Fortress's ramp. And, of course, Hotep was leading the charge. An armed yet small-looking Kalev stood alone and helpless at the bottom. It was over in a couple of seconds. Then he saw Hotep maniacally laughing as he lifted Kalev's mutilated yet still-writhing body over his head like a trophy. Amidst a chorus of underworldly chants, Hotep walked over and threw Kalev into the black-sucking shaft to Sha'al. And for a split second, Kalev locked eyes with himself. Unbridled terror morphed into a pleading stare as the flailing body silently plummeted into the darkness. Then the scene began to repeat but in real time.

At the same moment, on the right side of the black abyss, Kalev saw himself smiling from ear to ear. His hair was long and wavy, and his close-cropped beard almost covered the faded scars on his cheeks and chin. Raisa stood beside him beaming. She'd never looked more breathtaking. Little Frog, Little Croc, and three little girls flanked them both. Yet, in his rock-hard arms, he saw a squirming little baby. And somehow he knew it was *his* baby girl. *But that's not even possible*, he mentally argued. The voice that interrupted his thoughts made the huge warrior cringe in fear.

"Son of Abraham, son of Hezron, today Ha-kadosh (the triune Elohim) invokes *samayim* (the *shamayim*) and the entire *eretz* (the earth) as a witness against you. See that I have set before you both a never-ending life filled with hope and purpose and one that only leads to an endless death and excruciating torment. Blessing or curse, your choice! Therefore, choose life so that you and your descendants may live!"

The voice changed to the fatherly tone that sounded more like his own abba's. "Son, love Yahweh, your Elohim, wholeheartedly, unequivocally! Embrace Him. Decide to show this army what explicit allegiance to the I AM looks like. They're watching your example either way! Then, let His life-giving favor be *your* legacy to this and your future generations." He paused again.

"Son, El-Gibhor (Elohim mighty to save) is your ever-present rescuer! I alone will give you the *supernatural* ability and strength to conquer your enemies and remain in the land I promised to your abbas Abraham, Isaac, and Jacob. Once again, proud son of Hezron, Yahweh has set before you life and death, blessing and curse. Kalev, you're running out of time, so choose wisely." Then He paused, yet this silence was oddly comforting.

When He spoke again, His tone was the epitome of grief. It seemed to encapsulate billions of hopeless voices, screaming in panicked resignation. The horrendous sound was oddly familiar to Kalev. "I remembered you, son of Hezron. When I forced myself to remain on that cross, I experienced the same mind-numbing torment *you* survived almost every day. Unbearable physical pain and a heart filled with sorrow became My world. At one point, I couldn't even see my abba standing right in front of Me. But through that pain-filled fog, I saw your scarred and bloodied face. I wept for you, Kalev, and FYI, I've already forgiven you. Now I offer you My loving wisdom and hope you'll make the right decision.

"By the way, nice act earlier. If I hadn't already accomplished the task, I would have believed *you* were the one who annihilated Hasatan (Satan/Lucifer) and his deceived sha'dim. But we'll have to talk about '*your*' heroic spiritual exploits later. Yet, for now, know this. I've already conquered death. And in eternity, *you've* been chosen to lead in this critical period of time. So please accept your Yeshua's loving offer of salvation." Then the voice morphed into the most dreadful thunderclaps Kalev would ever experience.

"Do not doubt Me, oh mighty General Kalev. When the sun rises, two mornings from now, I *will* have your decision, and you will experience *Mine*. That choice will set in motion your natural and eternal future..."

The whole experience seemed like it'd taken hours to unfold. Yet in actuality, only a few seconds had elapsed. In the instant before Kalev opened his eyes, he felt something drip onto the front of his tunic. He hoped the foreboding encounter had not caused some kind of mortifying feminine reaction like tears or a runny nose. The embarrassed General instantly started to raise his hand to check his nose and cheeks. But halfway to his face, his iron hammer of a fist slammed into something even more unyielding. Kalev's eyes flew open just in time to see the massive bull raise his head back and snort a fresh, hot stream of snot into Kalev's open mouth.

Over a thousand sets of eyes had watched their general force the raging herd to slide to a stop in front of him. Then they were awed at the sight of their hero slugging the largest bull because of the animal's snorting disrespect.

The stunned silence was instantly shattered by Kalev's dry heaving, Hoshe'a and the four teens screaming laughter, and over a thousand cheers, chants, and war cries. Akiba handed his gagging general a small skin of water as Yadin's first lieutenant yelled into his colonel's ear.

While Kalev tried to wash the salty, oyster-like gook out of his mouth, he noticed that the entire silent herd had turned to stare at him like they were waiting for orders. That was when the grinning Yadin walked up. "Sir, uh, Sergeant Abraham was wondering if you'd teach him how to turn '[illegible]-[illegible]' animals into '[illegible]' troops." This only fueled more screaming laughter from his senior officers, but Kalev ignored the question and glared at the huge brown eyes in front of him.

The General loudly barked, "Colonel Yadin, do we have enough additional feed?" The quirky genius wiped his eyes and pulled out one of his ever-present accounting scrolls. "Yes, Sir. Two weeks ago, we foraged two massive shiploads of bailed grass feed. We used ninety-one wagons, and it still took us most of the night."

Yadin playfully poked Akiba. "This one had dressed up like he was the pharaoh's 'admiral of the fleet.' As it was starting to get dark, he boldly rode onto the dock like he owned the place. He used one of our most gaudy-covered wagons, drawn by six beautiful stallions we'd already broken in. The audacious [illegible] slowly descended onto the dock and shook hands with both of the two Phoenician ships' captains."

Akiba chimed in, "Those were the largest cargo ships any of us had ever seen." Yadin nodded. "Both heavily armed crews lined their respective ships' rails and suspiciously stared at the arrogant, too-young-looking admiral. They quickly forgot about the intruder when Akiba threw off the canvas cover. The huge bed was filled with a large pile of wooden cups and eight of our largest hog skins. Each skin held just under 130 gallons. Four of the bloated skins were filled with fermented goats' milk, two with our oldest beer, and two with that four-year-old batch of wine. We mixed into each skin five pounds of grounded gray poppy seeds foraged three nights prior.

"We'd planned for 'the admiral' to just give the captains the skins." Yadin pointed at Akiba. "But this one actually traded them for sixty coils of rope, fifty round Phoenician brass war shields, and 800 square feet of gold-fringed sail cloth." They all laughed. Akiba stiffened and pompously nodded. "No one out-negotiates the admiral!" Following another round of laughter, Yadin continued his animated storytelling.

"Both cheering crews leaped onto the dock. I guess Major Hoshe'a's goat's milk concoction was pretty powerful. It only took about ninety minutes for the 147 crew and officers to drink and eventually pass out. They didn't even finish four of the skins. We left the partially used ones as a parting gift. We didn't want to waste the others, so we brought back the four unused skins. They're great to use as bait for our next foraging mission."

Yadin snickered. "But we did leave each captain a small pile of the obviously Egyptian coins. You know, the new ones with Ramses' ugly face stamped on one side. I left a very grateful thank-you note addressed to each captain and 'signed by the pharaoh.' Oh, and we also left one sword, one shield, and a spear… After all, there's no reason for the *magnanimous* Son of Ra to be greedy." They all laughed.

Yadin cleared his throat; the others glanced at each other, then playfully bowed to their friend and stepped aside. The preoccupied Yadin ignored his friends' sarcasm. "Sir, we completely emptied the ships' massive holds. The combined total foraged that night is 2892 bales of both barley and grass hay. Eighty barrels of dried corn, eighteen ox calves, twenty-nine auroch calves, and sixty-five sheep. Plus, we 'found' both captains' trunks of gold and clothes. They also unwittingly donated all their nautical star charts, two large trunks of various medical instruments, salves, and bandages, and an assortment of different-sized brass and iron swords and spears. So, Sir, to answer your question, yes—we have the additional feed."

Kalev, still a little bewildered by his worrying vision, nodded. “Okay, let’s get ’em corralled before the muster.” Yadin had barely stepped to the side when he raised his hand. He used his index finger to make a circle over his head while cutting loose with a series of ear-splitting whistles.

28

Later that night, Kalev addressed the troops. "As you've heard, the priests, palace guards, and probably the royal butchers will be looking for any livestock that survived the latest animal plague. Our spies and I believe that the Egyptians will come hunting for these new herds of cattle and sheep as early as four mornings from now." Kalev stepped down from the elevated platform and began to walk between the ranks. His voice was no less stern and commanding. "Yisrael's Army, listen clearly. We've trained to fight in many ways with different weapons. You're trained to kill quickly and silently, up close and from a long distance." Then Kalev shouted, "And you're ferocious." As Kalev stood in the middle, the entire battalion erupted in one combined war cry.

While he waited for the cheers and chanting to die down, he remounted the stage and addressed his senior officers, "Have the latest promotions been issued?" Ari nodded.

"Tonight, I will add to your lethal quiver a most treacherous tool that for some"—he glared down at Little Croc and company in Heh's second rank—"will be the most difficult to master. It's not enough to know how to fight, even excellently; you must know *when not to fight*. It's the job of your officers, your First Sergeants, and your sergeants to relay correct timing in battle. Your job is to *wait* for, then execute your orders. Do you understand me?" The entire battalion thundered as one voice, "Yes, Sir." "Timing can be the difference between life and death—yours, your battle buddies, and this battalion. Starting tonight Yisrael's Army is at full alert. Soldiers, we own the night. But for now, they own the day. If you encounter an enemy while hidden, you won't move a muscle. If you're stepped on, peed on, or maybe even spat on, you don't move or make a sound until ordered to do so. We have worked too hard and too long for our home to be discovered and destroyed. And I, for one, am *not* going back to the mud pits." Kalev yelled this with all the accumulated resentment he had inside. "Battalion, prepare for inspection." All but the first ranks took one step backward. The scowling General and his senior officers left the stage.

Starting at the rear, they circulated through the companies. When they'd reached Heh Company's second rank, Kalev stopped in front of the little trio of boys. Kalev made a show of instantly standing straighter, drew his shoulders back, and stiffened to attention. The three small boys quickly mimicked their General. But for some reason, all three thought it was imperative to stand on their tiptoes. As one, the trio started to fall backward. To retain a semblance of military bearing, Kalev coughed and had to quickly turn and march to the front of the battalion.

The officers remounted the stage. After a brief discussion, heads nodded, and the Army of Yisrael's senior officers drew their weapons and held them in front of their face as a weapons-ready salute. This had the desired effect. Over two thousand swords were drawn and followed suit.

Ari stepped forward and boomed, "Close ranks." The ground shook as thousands of troops took one pounding step forward. "Attention to orders…until further notice, no soldier, whether above or below ground, will talk out loud. If you must speak to anyone, you *will* whisper quietly or use hand signals."

Ari motioned toward the others on stage. "Yisrael's Army, I hope you know that we would die defending you, and I know you'd do the same for your fellow soldiers, your sergeants, and your officers." Ari lowered his tone. "The order is: silent and ready!" Kalev and his staff quietly slapped their heels together, sheathed their swords, and silently saluted. Ari lowered his voice enough so only the companies' officers could hear. "Company commanders, you have your orders."

Following the oddly quiet evening meal, Kalev met with most all the officers in the Fortress' much larger TOC. Unlike the planning table in the Pit's TOC, this one was oval and sat thirty officers at one time. The walls were lined with chairs for the junior officers.

"And do light checks around vent and lookout positions. Are the smoke stacks from the ovens and forges out of sight?" A captain from Aleph Company spoke up, "Yes, Sir, we extended them to release the smoke gradually, each through various tree tops. So no sparks and only a little smoke makes it out."

That was when a newly promoted sergeant sheepishly opened the double doors, walked in, and unsuccessfully tried to hide in the back. All the officers in the TOC glared at the twelve-year-old kid. Kalev cleared his throat and scowled. "Sergeant, do you have something to add to our *command and staff* meeting?" The kid looked terrified and began to loudly whisper, "I'm sorry, Sirs, but I thought you'd want to know right away." Kalev sensed the urgency and nodded.

"Sirs, I'm in charge of Mosh—I mean the target's camp overwatch. About two hours ago, the target's sister and some Egyptian servants began to strike the target's tents. They loaded up five camels and two large ox wagons. The entire caravan headed south. They've camped behind Major Carni's house." Kalev glanced at Hoshe'a, and his scowl deepened. Hoshe'a guiltily nodded. He knew his new priority was to keep Moshe away from his avenging brother.

Kalev nodded for Ari to take over. "Sergeant, when they've finished setting up camp, and you're absolutely sure they're asleep, silently dig in and re-establish the overwatch rotation." "Yes, Sir," the kid whispered, saluted, and raced out of what the enlisted troops unofficially called "The Lion's Den." Kalev finished the briefing and dismissed the junior officers. He turned to his yawning staff. "I'm starving!"

On the way to the eerily quiet dining area, Kalev stopped and turned to the others. He reminded himself to whisper. "There will probably be two groups of Egyptians coming our way. At daylight, the civilians, mostly servants, slaves, and a few armed Egyptian taskmasters, will make up the search parties. But just before sundown, the palace guards and garrisoned soldiers will start their systematic patrols. This scenario will repeat until they either find something or give up. So, following the plague, let's let them find a few cattle and sheep scattered around that five-acre meadow two miles north of here."

He eyed the others but spoke to Ari. "General Ari, I want you to use the next three days to transition to day shift. The entire battalion's daytime operations are yours to command." Kalev tapped the boy's chiseled chest with his finger. "Besides, you need to stop slacking off. It's time you pulled your weight around here!" The others started to laugh out loud, but Kalev's glare stopped them cold. Ari mirthlessly smirked. "I *was* getting bored."

At sunrise, Kalev fell asleep on the blankets beside his bed. He slept at least twelve hours. At sundown he'd opened his bedroom door, and a new plate of hot food was waiting for him on the TOC's map table.

Following his meal, he hung a large blank parchment on the wall next to the map of Egypt. From memory he started a poorly drawn battalion chain of command tree. Soon, it branched out so far, he couldn't remember the names. He knew they needed to divide the army into two battalions.

But when Kalev stepped back and saw his name at the top, the too-familiar sense of extreme incompetence threatened to swallow him whole. He slowly shook his head. "Boy, what are you doing? How do you expect to protect so many lives? Plus, someone's gonna figure out you're barely winging this. You're just a poser with a general's medallion."

A voice thundered behind him. "General Kalev, son of Hezron, you were born to be their leader!" Startled, Kalev's hand instinctively drew his sword as he whirled around in a combat crouch.

There, standing where the table had been, was a huge man. Kalev instinctively recognized him as a battle-hardened warrior, his enormous, scarred hand on the handle of his drawn sword. The massively muscular man's smile was comforting yet sent cold shivers down Kalev's spine. He was dressed in a pure white robe extending down to his feet and wrists. He wore a wide golden belt around his chest. His hair looked like bleached wool. His feet were like polished bronze. His face shone like the Egyptian sun at noon. But it was his eyes that Kalev locked on. A powerful severity burned in those eyes, like a white-hot flame that seemed to shoot bolts of multicolored light through Kalev's chest into the drawing behind him. Kalev was still dubious about his supposed "life or death" choice concerning the existence of a Yahweh. And for a fleeting moment, he wondered if this was his promised end.

For some reason, he began shaking in terror. An unseen fog of fear seemed to consume his entire body. The Warrior's voice thundered, "General Kalev, I've felt every whip that lashed the backs of My chosen…I've heard every scream…"

Kalev dropped his swords and fell flat with his face to the deck. He felt powerless to raise his head but interrupted the Warrior anyway. From deep in his core, a sarcastically angry laugh gushed out, "And still, You did *nothing*!" For nearly fifteen seconds, there was a looming silence.

Kalev resignedly sighed when he recognized the sound of a sword being drawn from its metal sheath. But he was completely surprised when a hand gently touched the back of his head. A soothing warmth flooded his whole body as he breathed it in.

The voice changed. It kind of sounded like his abba's, but it penetrated then vibrated every fiber of his being. "Son, as I told you, We will *not* overrule man's free will. But that same free will can choose to love, protect others, and do the will of My Abba. The impulse to defend the weaker of My chosen people is a choice you *and* My son Moshe make instinctively."

Kalev unconsciously stiffened at the mention of Moshe. "Kalev, son of Hezron, Moshe's choice to kill that baker was birthed from a misguided desire to *defend* your abba." The Giant Warrior let that sink in before He continued, "The unseen battle between the deceived forces that influence Ramses and his army and My forces that protect those who have chosen to follow Me has grown to a fevered pitch. The torment you've seen with your natural eyes is only a minute result, an echo of the battles that rage in the spiritual realm. General Kalev, stop and open your eyes." Time stood still, or rather, it ceased to exist here.

Kalev saw himself on a trackless, barren plain. He was ankle-deep in a foul-smelling black sludge. Like out of a river fog, a battle between light and dark forces came into focus. Hundreds of thousands were locked in a seemingly endless, chaotic fight to the death. The clang of massive swords, the screams of wounded horses, and the horrific unnatural screeches of the dying grew deafening. The stench of war was overwhelming. Large black deformities darkened the sky as they flew overhead. They shrieked in rage just before they were cleaved in half and then melted into the deepening ooze. And in the middle of all the confusion stood this same huge Warrior. Kalev didn't question how he knew; he simply understood that this Warrior was also a King. This Fighter's long white curly hair and massive arms were glistening with sweat, splatters of black ooze, and even His own blood that trickled from numerous shallow cuts and scratches. His muscled arms were bared. On His right forearm were bright-glowing letters, like a branding lit from within. Kalev mouthed the word "salvation." The Mighty Warrior's white robe was stained with black splatters of the creatures' blood. His enormous gleaming sword easily separated the grotesque heads from deformed dark bodies. His movements *appeared* to be both effortless and too fast to see. But very similar to Adir, each purposeful movement was a demonstration of a beautifully choreographed lesson in sword fighting. Kalev unconsciously admired the Warrior King's awe-inspiring grace and ferocity.

At one point in the battle, Kalev and the Great Warrior King briefly locked eyes. In that instant, the son of Hezron saw his father's eyes smiling back at him. The huge El Shaddai (Elohim of Power), Supreme Commander of Yahweh's bright forces, broke eye contact and continued the battle. Yet somehow, Kalev was able to interpret the myriad expressions that raced across the Great King's face. Most severe was the pained look of tremendous sadness. He instinctively knew he'd contributed to this Warrior King's fathomless burden and was deeply ashamed. This moment of extreme clarity was too intense for

Kalev, and he looked away.

Intuitively, Kalev knew the bright forces *should be* winning this offensive without much effort. But that wasn't the case. The Warrior King's bright troops were being severely wounded, though not dying, at the same rate as the opposing dark forces were being killed.

Thankfully, out of the corner of his eye, Kalev glimpsed the Warrior King's giant sword spinning through the air right at him. It felt oddly familiar. Just like Adir had painfully drilled into him, he deftly timed it to grab the handle but allowed it to complete its half spin over his right shoulder. "Just in case you're flanked," Adir had warned. Still, Kalev was surprised when the sword abruptly stopped rotating and he heard a wet thud. The Warrior King had expertly thrown his sword and cleaved the skull of an enormous, winged creature that had landed just behind Kalev.

For only the second time in his life, Kalev felt too small to "help." The son of Hezron was only tall enough to stand face to face with the deformed creature's oddly grinning mouth. The hate-filled thing let out a screech that would haunt Kalev's dreams for the next year.

But it was the hideous sha'dim's venomous breath that seemed to suck all the air from Kalev's lungs. As the thing fell and began to melt into the nauseating ooze beside him, he watched himself splash to his hands and knees. He took a deep, ragged breath and projectile vomited. The same dark-looking bilious ooze gushed from his mouth.

Before Kalev had a chance to puke again, he was instantly back on his feet. He watched as he smoothly swung the Warrior King's double-edged, five-foot sword back and forth in huge swaths. It reminded him of scything wheat.

Kalev couldn't tell how long he'd endured the life-threatening chaos. Eventually, his sector of the battlefield became eerily quiet. He saw the battle continue miles away, but he was too fatigued to move in that direction. His gasps were ragged as he leaned hard on the great sword like a crutch. That was when he saw what he somehow knew to be the sword's name. The two words glowed white-hot like a bellowed forge. He silently mouthed, "*The Word*." Kalev unexpectedly sensed shrieks of nauseating terror race through his feeble body.

The weakened general bled from multiple wounds. Blood stung his eyes as it trickled down from his forehead. He felt like he was dying from the exhaustion alone. The huge man started to crumple like a burnt piece of parchment ash in the wind. But two powerful hands caught him under the arms and gently brought him to his feet.

Now the son of Hezron was face to face with a smile that shot daggers of warm, rejuvenating light through his body. Yet, instead of basking in the tremendous pleasure, Kalev's legs wobbled. He splashed to his hands and knees again then puked. Now, every time he exhaled a black cloud formed in front of the General's face. Decades of hate, resentment, and unbearable sorrow billowed from his mouth and stung his eyes. Kalev groaned. He felt the familiar, welcoming sensation of death pulling him downward. The son of Hezron cried out, "Sir, please go away—just let me die. I am a wicked man. You know I've hated You for most of my life. I don't deserve this…"

Even though Yahweh knew this remorseful attitude bode well for this humbled soldier, The Mighty Yeshua's tears flowed freely down His own scarred cheeks. Each crystalline tear reflected a different facet of Kalev's heartrending grief.

Elohim pointed down at the top of Kalev's head. Drops of the Warrior King's blood trickled from His scraped knuckles, down His index finger, and splashed on Kalev's blood-streaked and sweaty head.

Instantly, the General shuddered. At the same time, excruciating heat and almost painful joy coursed through his core. Still, overwhelming sobs erupted from Kalev's gut. He hoarsely exhaled a lifetime of sadness… Eventually, Kalev's wails calmed to a whimper.

The humbled general previously noticed the countless scars on the Warrior's bruised and blood-streaked hands. *They kind of look like mine*, he thought. But it was the sight of the odd-looking indentation in the center of the King's palm that caused Kalev's nausea to return. "Please, Sir, I don't…"
"General Kalev," the familiar voice boomed, "son of Hezron, before We created this earth, before you were born, I knew you. Son, I. Know. You!" Oddly, it was those last three words that caused him to vomit another impossible amount of the thick, dark bile from somewhere deep in his core. As if He hadn't noticed, the Great Warrior King stood Kalev up again.

"General Kalev, I ask you for the last time. Do you acknowledge that I, the Victorious Son of the Most High Yahweh, the Supreme Commander of the Angel Armies, exist?" The Warrior King's eyes bore deep into Kalev's core. As if it was the most natural thing in the world, Kalev stiffened to attention and roared, "Yes, Sir. I unequivocally acknowledge that You exist, Sir." "Do you agree that I am for you and not against you?" "Yes. Sir," Kalev screamed even louder.

The Elohim held out His hand, palm up. Kalev saw the oddly square indentation. "Touch the scar, Kalev." The tentative son of Hezron reached out, and his finger gently touched the old wound. What his mind saw in that instant would take him decades to unpack. This time the sobbing Kalev remained on his feet. "Yahweh, I'm sorry! Please…!" But instead of tears, black streams of ooze ran down is nicked and bleeding cheeks.

The Greatest King held the spent general by both shoulders. The Warrior King's blindingly joy-filled smile returned. As the terrorizing shrieks faded away. Kalev felt completely restored, inside and out. Even the residual taste of the thick black puke was gone. He felt like a little kid again. And just like he had with his own father, Kalev vaulted into the waiting arms of the grinning Warrior King. The Truly Supreme Warring Yahweh leaned down and kissed the top of Kalev's head just like his abba always had. Then the same voice that created the earth boomed.

"Kalev, son of Hezron, by the blood of the Lamb and the word of *your* testimony, your Yeshua proclaims this day that you are forgiven, you are called, and you are set apart as 'faithful to Yahweh.' Do you accept these, My hard-won mercies?" Luxuriating in the Warrior King's enveloping embrace, Kalev's muffled yell was no less emphatic. "Yes, Sir. I gratefully accept!"

Suddenly, Kalev simultaneously felt the heat from a white-hot flash of fire and the searing burn on his upper left chest. But when his eyes shot open, he was back in the TOC on the deck between the map table and the wall.

29

The silence in the room left him feeling very small, very alone, and completely empty. He longed for that life-giving hug to envelope him again. The General lay on the hard deck, too physically and emotionally spent to move.

Kalev was startled awake by the subtle sound of one of the double doors slowly opening. He watched from under the table as small feet walked by on the opposite side. He thought about quietly lying there until the troop left the room. But something made him slowly get to his knees and peer over the edge of the table.

Raisa was replacing Kalev's previous evening meal plate and mug with full ones. That was when she saw the top of a shaved head start to rise over the opposite side of the table. She bit her lip hard, trying not to laugh. But when she saw Kalev's child-like wide-eyes peer over the edge, the gorgeous little woman couldn't help herself. Her laughter filled him with the same warmth he'd experienced in the Warrior King's embrace.

The mountain of a man awkwardly stood, and his scowling face flushed with embarrassment. Once again, the words tumbled from his lips before he knew how they'd sound. "Raisa, how are you so amazingly beautiful?" She blushed and giggled like a little girl.

Kalev walked around the table and nervously sat on a chair facing her. Then he saw the food, and with a lopsided smile, he thanked her and dug in like he hadn't eaten in weeks. Raisa pulled out one of the overstuffed side chairs and watched her "*future* husband" devour his food. Kalev paused and swallowed. "Hey, I thought I just ate. What time is it?" Raisa smiled. "Well, according to these *evening* meal plates, it's just after sundown." Kalev stopped chewing and swallowed. "Wait, I've been sleeping for almost twenty-four hours?" Raisa smiled. "By the looks of that wood plank outline on your cheek, I'd say that was about right." Kalev sucked in a breath and looked around the TOC with a panicked expression. Raisa smiled. "No, my love, the sun still rose in the sky without you. Apparently, your officers in the Pit thought you were sleeping in the Fortress and vice versa. Are you surprised they can be trusted to run the place without you?" Kalev smiled and shrugged. Raisa proudly grinned. "You taught them well, General Kalev." Kalev blushed and shrugged again but stayed silent. As usual, Raisa seamlessly filled Kalev's awkward silence. "I was just about to knock on your door when I realized you were staring at my legs from under the table." Kalev's face flushed an even deeper red. His jaw dropped, and his mouth silently moved like a fish out of water. In the end, all he could do was vigorously shake his head. Rasia started laughing again.

Eventually, Kalev regained a scrap of composure. He took a long pull of wine then unconsciously smirked. "I think that was the first complete day off since I died." Kalev chuckled, but for the first time, Raisa slugged his arm hard. And by her expression, it would probably be the last time. "Oww. Kalev, please don't talk like that. I prefer you alive." Kalev smiled. "Okay." Raisa stood to leave, but Kalev asked her to stay while he ate.

Between bites, he tentatively replayed to her both the threatening vision/warning he had in front of the bull and what he'd just experienced. Raisa silently listened and watched the increasing intensity burning in his eyes. In addition to the growing hollow feeling in her lower stomach, her love for him was exponentially growing by the minute.

Finally, she thought. Kalev finished his narrative, "…and then I was back here." He glanced at her for some reaction, then quickly looked down at his empty plate. Honestly, he expected her to derisively laugh at his silly story.

Then, once again, he spoke before he thought it through, "And I wasn't staring at your beautiful legs. Uh, I mean, I wasn't looking at your legs. I mean, okay, I was looking, and they *are very* beautiful, but I wasn't…*arghhh!*" Kalev dropped his face into his hands. He didn't know what else to say, so he waited in embarrassed silence, hoping she'd just walk away.

But Raisa remained quiet for about thirty seconds more. When Kalev looked back up, they were almost nose to nose. Her scowl was impressive, and he couldn't keep from smiling. "Kalev, you *do* realize that Warrior King is also Yahweh, right?" Kalev self-consciously nodded. "He told you that you were set apart and marked as true to Yahweh, right?" Kalev nodded again. Only this time the slight movement made him obviously wince from a dull burning on his chest. Raisa slowly reached over and pulled the collar of his tunic to the right, exposing the upper part of his rock-hard chest. Kalev watched as her eyes grew wide. Her finger slowly traced, and she quietly mouthed the still-red, perfectly formed letters from right to left. Her voice grew in intensity with each consecutive letter.

"Peh, aleph, tav, heh, peh, lamed, tav, ayin, yud, aleph, mem." Even though the fresh burns stung, her touch took his breath away. His mouth hung open as he watched her wide, deep blue eyes move to each letter.

Then with admirable resolve, Raisa declared, "*My* Kalev is true to Yahweh…and that settles it!" She firmly cupped his face in her hands and kissed *her* naïve and wide-eyed groom. She'd dreamed about this day since she was a little girl. Raisa's kiss was soft at first, then both her breathing and her kiss rapidly grew in intensity.

In his ignorant innocence, Kalev didn't know he was supposed to close his eyes and enjoy the kiss, so he saw it when her eyes flew open. Her pupils were dilated, and she looked both surprised and embarrassed. The radiant four-foot-eleven fireball quickly stepped back.

Though his first real kiss ever *was* staggering, he truthfully wasn't sure what to say. The surprised general paused a beat, then opened his mouth to express his thanks. Yet for some inappropriate reason, Kalev remembered how Hoshe'a's mouth was always getting him in trouble with their ema. So, for the first time, Kalev clamped his jaws shut before he said something really stupid to his beautiful friend. Which was fine, as it looked like his "kissing girlfriend" was about to pick up the slack.

Raisa nervously straightened the back of her robe and stammered, "Kalev, I, um…we, um…" She stood straighter, cleared her throat, and forced herself to settle down. With her hands on her hips and in an impressive commanding voice, she proclaimed, "Kalev, son of Hezron, true to Yahweh…now it's time—you *will* marry me." Her eyes went wide again, and she slightly hesitated before she whispered in a less demanding voice. "In two weeks!" Then she sucked in a sharp breath. Raisa looked as stunned as Kalev felt. She stepped forward again, only this time Kalev stuck out his lips to receive another kiss.

Yet instead, Raisa awkwardly tapped his forehead four times as she quietly declared, "Let. It. Be. Written!" The daughter of the prince/chief rabbi of the Judah tribe turned and ran out of the room.

Kalev's jaw dropped and he gawked at the double doors booming shut. He wasn't sure, but he didn't think that was the way it was supposed to go. He slumped back into his throne, terrified and confused. In the silence he croaked at the ceiling, "What…just…happened? Seriously, what…just….happened!" Then, seemingly from every direction, he heard the Warrior King chuckling. Kalev shook his head. In a small voice he asked himself, *And why did she just pet my head like I was a puppy or something?* The voice of the King of kings and pharaohs exploded in an ear-piercing laughter. Kalev scowled, "It's not *that* funny." Then it sounded like the Warrior King was laughing so hard hat He couldn't catch His breath.

30

For a man who hated any sign of emotion, except for laughter or angry fury, this was a day to forget and/or remember—he wasn't sure. To Kalev, complicated mental chaos almost physically hurt, and he saw this as a personal weakness. So he grabbed the closest parchment and began making a list in the hope of ordering his jumbled thoughts. *Okay, Kalev, take a deep breath. You can do this…I hope.*

(1) Almost trampled by a herd of disgusting beef steaks. (2) Choice, painful death, and ending up in Sha'al. (3) Choice, growing long hair, a beard, and having a family. (4) Experiencing an unseen war, then puking the black sludge. (5) Agreeing that Yahweh exists in real time and He is good. Plus, getting branded because I agreed. (6) My first kiss followed by the order to marry. (8, 9, 10) Feeling very confused, elated, terrified, oddly content, exhausted, and last but not least, being the butt of Yahweh's laughter… "Is that it?" he wondered out loud.

Instantly, the Warrior King spoke up. "Uh, you missed one." Kalev groaned. "Don't forget the army functioned just fine while *you* slept a whole day away." Kalev thumped his forehead on the table. "Thanks for that."

Yahweh's subsequent laughter was so intense that even Kalev chuckled. Then he sarcastically tested his new relationship with the King of kings and pharaohs. "Don't you have something better to do, like giving Hotep some flesh-eating disease that liquefies his brain or something?"

Yahweh abruptly stopped laughing and Kalev cringed at the silence. Had he just crossed some eternally damning line? But Yehovah playfully remained silent, just for the effect. Then He roared, "You know…that's a great idea. I never thought of that one. Wait a minute. I gotta put that on *My* list…liquefy brain…" They both laughed.

Then the Warrior King's voice grew serious. "Son of Hezron, that designation on your chest was meant as an outward proof, a reminder of your total commitment to Yahweh. In every generation, I have a faithful remnant. Usually too few in number, yet their trust in Me is explicit. They, and now you, Kalev, are *My* legacy so to speak. That mark may not be a medallion, yet it *is* something to be humbly proud of. But…if you want, I will gladly remove it." Kalev groaned, "Sir, please stop with the choices. Can I choose later?" "Sure, son… Hey, I don't want to add to your brain storm, but I noticed you keep wearing tunics with pictures of cute bunnies. If you want, I could burn a permanent cute bunny onto your back."

Laughter echoed off the walls. But for the Commanding General, the room began to spin. Kalev felt nauseous and started gagging. Somehow he got to his feet and staggered into his room without puking. He mistakenly fell face-first onto the too-soft bed. He was out before he realized he'd been swallowed whole by his inanimate archenemy. And for one of a very few times in decades, he enjoyed a dreamless sleep.

31

Two evenings later, Kalev sat on his shortened throne in the Fortress's TOC. Following the usual command and staff updates, the General turned to Colonel Ofek, commander of the basic and advanced training company, thought it through, and then looked at Ofek. "Colonel Ofek, have our numbers in the training company leveled off?" "No, Sir. We still have ten to fifteen more coming in every few days.

"The newest group stated it took them ten nights to get here from the upper Nile regions. They bring stories of hundreds of children being taken from their homes and marched in shackles to Thebes or Ramses to labor in the quarries or worse. They said that at least fifty-one of their group either inexplicably disappeared or were caught and killed on their way here."

The frustrated Yadin took over. He glanced down at his parchment with a worried look on his face. "Sir, our numbers have reached 3387. And that doesn't include the twenty-five scarecrows that collapsed in Major Carni's courtyard before sun up today. As far as we know, there haven't been any security leaks about our mission or specific location…yet! But the odds of this operation remaining secret are increasing against us. Plus, I think it would be a grave error to underestimate the Egyptians' ability to find us." Kalev was too familiar with that line of thinking. He nodded his head. "Honestly, Colonel, I agree."

Kalev turned to address the entire officer corps. "I've lost a lot of sleep over that same fear…but let me ask all of you something. Why *haven't* we been discovered yet?" The Commanding General of Yisrael's Army let the question linger in the dead silence.

Kalev inadvertently adjusted his tunic. It still irritated the healing burns on his chest. Ari's eyes grew wide when he noticed the red top of one of the perfectly branded letters. Kalev saw Ari's expression, cleared his throat, and whispered, "I'll explain later."

Following the briefing, Kalev asked Ari, the colonels, and even Hoshe'a to stay behind. Unexpectedly, Raisa and six little girls brought in the evening meal. Mounded plates and frothy mugs placed in front of the men.

Kalev hadn't realized his mouth was hanging open until the girls closed the door behind them. Ari leaned over and loudly whispered, "Sir, I think you can close your mouth now." The others chuckled as they dug in. Kalev cleared his throat. Without another word, the ripped giant stood and threw off his tunic. Everyone stopped midchew and gawked at the letters on his chest. He began his wild story. With as much detail as he could remember. He started with the huge, snotty bull. Twenty minutes later, he accidentally ended his narration with Raisa's order to marry her.

The embarrassed son of Hezron quickly donned his "cute bunny" tunic, plopped down on his throne, and shoved still full plate away. For at least a full minute, the room remained strangely silent. Yet they never took their eyes off him. Then, a thunderclap of voices exploded in the room. Everyone was asking their questions at the same time. Kalev laid his forehead on the table and groaned.

It took another thirty minutes to answer their questions and concerns as best he could. But it was Ari's final question that silenced the others. "Sir, *how* did He fight…? I mean, what techniques did the Creator of the earth use to defeat the sha'dim?" Kalev thought about that for a long while. The teens intently watched their Commanding General in silence. Without a word, Kalev got up and walked over to the map wall and hung a large blank parchment.

In the past Kalev always let Hoshe'a do the illustrating, then he'd promptly ignore it. But this was different. He knew he was the only one who could draw this. Kalev just stood there staring at the blank sheet, wondering how to start.

Then he heard Yahweh's voice softly whisper, "Close your eyes." Kalev obeyed. Instantly, he saw himself back in the battle again. Only this time he was standing right next to the lethal Warrior King. Kalev carefully watched as the chaotic scene around them began to slow down.

At first, El Shaddai's sword thrusts and parries appeared as random defensive blurs of motion. Yet, slowly, they took on a precisely designed style of flawless, smooth movements. His wrist barely twitched as Yahweh rotated His wrist under, then over, twisting the swinging blade. He would duck and then weave just out of reach of the enemy's sword.

Kalev stood there and watched in admiration as the Warrior King jumped high into the air, flipped over the head of the creature, and dragged His lethally sharp sword through the deformed skull. Again, time became irrelevant. The slow-motion battle continued around them, but the Warrior King sheathed His sword and smiled at Kalev. "Lesson learned?"

Kalev's body twitched and his eyes flew open. He was back in the TOC facing the parchment. He raised his hand to start drawing what he'd seen when he realized the four-by-five-foot parchment was already filled. Small, complex step-by-step diagrams surrounded a perfectly drawn picture of the Warrior King's sword and its inscription.

Kalev, still staring at the intricate instructions, quickly concealed his own surprise by asking, "Any questions?" He turned when the room remained silent.

All four wide-eyed boys and Hoshe'a just stared at him. Ari, still stunned by his General's intricate diagrams, cleared his throat. "Um, Sir, we were waiting for you to finish. General, Sir, I think my abba should see this." Kalev nodded. "I agree—get him down here as soon as possible. Colonel, get with Major Adir and implement these advanced techniques immediately."

The General looked back at the diagrams and shook his head in amazement. "Colonel Yadin, let's get your people in here to make copies. Gentlemen, make your copies!" "Yes, Sir," they all replied.

Eventually Ari turned. "Sir, these are not independent moves. They're sequential." Hoshe'a nodded.

"Brother, how did you, of all people, create this? It's flawless. See the spaces? That means each diagram can be isolated and taught separately. This is amazing; each swing or step or leap is built on the previous one." Hoshe'a slowly shook his head, then grew a sly smile. "Ema was wrong about you too!"

Yadin stepped back from making his copy. He unconsciously blurted out, "Your Warrior King is smart!" Kalev watched as the surprised teen slowly realized what he'd just said, and his face flushed in embarrassment. "I mean, uh, of course He's smart. He's Yahweh; it's His job to be…" Kalev smiled to himself. "So that's what *I* look like to Raisa." The General heard the Warrior King's booming laugh and joined in.

32

Every time he *saw* the Warrior King or experienced one of His otherworldly visions, it left the son of Hezron mentally exhausted. This morning, the always-hungry General was too tired to eat. He felt like he could sleep another twenty-four hours.

As the sun began to rise, a bone-tired Kalev headed up the ladder at the far end of the Fortress. At the top, a little private manned the spider hole that guarded the southernmost hidden entrance. The little guy watched his massive GENERAL fill the access shaft as he climbed toward him. The boy wasn't sure if he was supposed to warn the General about the waiting Egyptian. *He's General Kalev, 'the conqueror of Sha'al'; he already knows that guy is out there*, the little troop reasoned. *The General's going out there to kill the pig...* he hoped. So the eight-year-old troop kept his mouth shut. Near the top of the ladder, Kalev silently nodded at the abnormally worried-looking private. When the little guy simply nodded back, the General understood that to mean it was okay to proceed.

Kalev took a deep breath of the cool morning air. He intended to take a shortcut through the Outpost to the river. The Commanding General took one step and then froze in place. The back of his neck began to tingle. He'd grown accustomed to the presence of his shadow troops and the high overwatch troops, but this was different, a lot different.

Kalev rapidly crouched and did a quick scan of his flanks. Fifty yards away, he caught sight of a dark-robed figure with a black keffiyeh covering most of his face. The single man, most likely an Egyptian priest, stood defiantly at the edge of the field. He supported himself with a long staff that Kalev mistook as a spear. "[illegible]," Kalev hissed. "After all your warnings, *you* are the one that caused the army's downfall…arghh," he hissed. "And so it begins."

Hidden in the tops of five palms, ten pairs of eyes had tracked the Egyptian since he appeared on the road next to the canal. Now eight well-hidden shadow troops, including the three boys, watched as General Kalev crouched and then drew his swords. Now all the hidden troops silently drew their own swords or bows and waited for the General's order. With a roar that would've made any mother bear on earth proud, Kalev raced toward the priest.

Still running, Kalev was about five yards away when he yelled, "Not on my watch, you piece of…" He dropped and slid on his knees, intending to slice the man's legs out from under him. Instead, the General hit an invisible wall, which was actually Yahweh's hand, and crumpled in a heap at the Egyptian's feet. Kalev's swords flew out of his hands and landed almost ten yards away.

The dark-eyed man reached down, tapped Kalev's forehead four times, and said, "Son of Hezron, receive the Holy Spirit of Yahweh!" Behind the pair, the squad leader in charge of Kalev's shadow troops signaled the high overwatch to stand down, whispered to his squad, and they all faded back into the trees.

Kalev was instantly face to face with the Warrior King again. Only this time, Yahweh forcefully blew His sweet breath into Kalev's nostrils and open mouth. After fifteen minutes with his hands in the air and strange words flowing from his inner being, Kalev became aware of a deep, gravelly voice in the distance.

Reluctantly, Kalev forced himself back into time. He shook his head and saw the man's penetrating gaze. "Who are…" The dark robed man interrupted the huge warrior by clearing his throat. He spoke in flawless Hebrew, "Now you will…" but the man abruptly stopped. He cautiously reached down and pulled Kalev's collar aside. At the sight of the letters on Kalev's chest, the obviously stunned man sucked in a sharp breath. "So I wasn't dreaming," he whispered.

The short and slightly pudgy man untied his face scarf revealing a gleaming smile. "Apparently, Kalev, son of Hezron, son of Pharez, son of Yehudah, Yahweh has deemed you faithful. And has destined you to lead as both a tribal prince and this army's warring general." Kalev had no idea what the guy was talking about. And then it hit him. *This man is a priest. He's Nachshon, the prince of the Yehudah tribe, and more importantly*—Kalev's face flushed with embarrassment—*this is Raisa's abba. Great first impression, bonehead*, he chided himself. Nachshon's smile grew. This mountain of a man's expressions were too easy to read.

Nachshon continued, "I see now that it was a wise decision to entrust my only son into your care…" This caught Kalev by surprise; he didn't remember Raisa having a brother. But he wasn't about to tell his future abba he didn't know Raisa's brother was in the army. So he just nodded. "…And now, I'm told you wish to wed my only daughter?" Wide-eyed Kalev innocently shrugged. "Well, um, truthfully, Sir, she, um…" Nachshon started laughing. "Let me guess. My strong-willed Raisa *told* you to marry her. And I bet she even gave you a specific time frame." Kalev was mortified. He opened his mouth, then shut it, and nodded in defeat." Nachshon slapped Kalev on the shoulder. "Welcome to Raisa's world, son. My children's narratives have not done justice to the warrior I just witnessed. Which is good 'cause my Raisa has a way of, um, intimidating most men." "Yeah, about that…" "Don't worry—you'll learn. Plus, she loves you, and that *might* help!" Nachshon laughed. "Hey, do you think there's any of that wonderful bread left?"

Kalev and Nachshon took their time surveying the Fortress' livestock corrals and pens. The General wanted to give the changing shifts enough time to eat and clear out before they sat down. They made their way to Kalev's favorite table. It was the closest one to the kitchen, thus closer to the food, and had the bonus of a better view of Raisa.

Kalev watched intently as she ruthlessly pounded another large mound of dough. Raisa distractedly looked up and saw Kalev sitting next to her abba. Both men continued to talk as they stared at her. Raisa awkwardly moved to sidestep the table and head their way. At the same time, the daughter of the prince of the Yehudah tribe distractedly raised her apron to her face to wipe off any smudges. That was when the very large clay jar of flour mysteriously decided to "jump" off the edge of the table.

The resulting white cloud stuck to everything. She mistakenly grabbed a wet rag and quickly swiped at her face. But that only smeared the flour into pretty swirls across her face and forehead. Kalev didn't even notice the white mess. To him it was like seeing her beautiful face for the first time.

Without looking, Nachshon whispered, "Kalev, breathe." The chief rabbi's subsequent laugh mistakenly caused Raisa to stop short. She touched her crusty cheeks, gasped, then ran back to the table and tried to clean her face again, using the same gooey rag.

Nachshon cleared his throat to break Kalev's wide-eyed stare at his daughter. The man's glare instantly sobered Kalev. Nachshon quietly growled. "Kalev, son of Hezron, swear to me that you will prize her as I always have." Kalev earnestly nodded, absentmindedly saluted, and then, once again, he spoke too soon, "I will cherish her more than my swords, Sir." Kalev sucked in a sharp panicked breath. *Please tell me I didn't just say that,* please, he wordlessly pleaded in his mind. He quickly averted his eyes and groaned.

Nachshon's head snapped around like he'd just been slapped. He was about to unleash his own brand of ferocity when he heard Yahweh's smiling voice. "Easy there, killer. Look at his heart." The chief rabbi of the Yehudah tribe obediently blinked.

Through the years, Nachshon's ema had repeated a couple of stories about Kalev's fearless exploits in the mud pits. But in a few seconds, Yahweh flashed this brave man's entire life before his eyes. The horrendously vivid details, including Kalev having to carry the countless children's bodies and the daily torture, made him nauseous. Yet this was all tempered by the realization that through all of it, Yahweh had protected the important part of this man's childlike innocence. Now he realized what both Raisa and Yahweh saw in this man. So with a playful slug in Kalev's shoulder, the last one he'd ever attempt, he painfully smiled. "So let me see those cherished swords of yours." With a young boy's gleam in his eyes, Kalev drew both swords and his dagger and proudly displayed them on the table in front of his future abba. The rabbi was genuinely impressed by the mirror-like sheen on all three weapons. He nodded. "Very well. We'll discuss the mohar in seven days!" Kalev looked up and naively blurted out, "What?" The old man continued to laugh as he stood and walked away.

Because of the isolation order, the evening's command and staff meeting was thankfully short. The General had just finished his meal when someone loudly knocked on the double doors. Akiba stopped eating and went to the door. Kalev continued to speak as he watched Akiba rush out without looking back.

Kalev cleared his throat to get the other's attention. "General Ari, It's time we split the army into two battalions. The new battalion should have the same number of companies. The new companies will initially use the preexisting the designations and mission goals. You'll have to align the missions in each battalion.

"For the next few days, the current circumstances are forcing us to keep our heads down anyway. Use the time to create two new chains of command. Promote as needed. But keep reminding the troops to only whisper. The promotion celebrations will have to wait."

Kalev watched Ari's shoulders briefly slump then straighten again. As the others stood and moved to the wall to chart the logistics, Ari remained seated. Kalev smiled. "Aleph Battalion will remain in the Fortress. I assume you'll designate the new battalion as Heh." Ari distractedly nodded. "Um, yes, Sir." "Okay. Heh Battalion will be based in the Pit."

Kalev loudly cleared his throat. The others turned. "The new battalion is now designated as Heh and will be based in the Pit." The others nodded like they already knew. Yadin respectfully nodded. "Yes, Sir. What about the original battalion?" Kalev thought for a second, then smiled. "It *is* the battalion that blazed the way, so it will be designated Aleph Battalion." Ofek and Yadin smiled proudly.

Both always-vigilant generals turned at the soft sound of the double doors slowly opening. Raisa's gorgeous face appeared around the edge. Her eyes locked with her husband's, or rather soon-to-be husband's. "I'm sorry to interrupt."

She waited for a response, but Kalev was frozen in place. The others glanced between their stunned-looking General, Raisa, and Ari. The Bet (second) grade general stepped in. "Yes, mam, what can we do for you?" Raisa's smile grew wider at the mam reference, which served to cause their Sha'al-conquering general to involuntarily gasp. "Would anyone like some hot sweet and date bread?" Except for Kalev, they all cheered. But Kalev remained silently lost in her smile. Hoshe'a glanced between his glassy-eyed brother and the rabbi's gorgeous daughter.

The older and, to Raisa, the very annoying brother started laughing. Then he yelled, "Raisa, you better get in here before our illustrious general stops breathing and soils his beautifully embroidered loin cloth. He may even…"

The large, full cup of the pungent beer slammed into Hoshe'a's temple with a loud thud. Kalev's instantly unconscious brother bounced off the solid wood map table and then the wall before he lay in a crumpled, bleeding mess under one of the thrones. The two wide-eyed colonels were impressed by their General's silent and lightning-fast accuracy. They were 99 percent sure the major wasn't dead; besides, he deserved it for his flagrant disrespect. Yadin quickly took his seat, and the bread was served. Yadin checked to confirm that Major Hoshe'a was just "sleeping" and then joined the others.

The army's senior staff carried immense loads of responsibility twenty-four seven. Yet, they all, including Kalev, tended to act like excited little kids when it came to hot sweetbread. As she placed her specially made bread in front of Kalev, Raisa's lips deliberately brushed his ear. Kalev involuntarily shivered with an unusual excitement. Raisa whispered, "General, it's now less than thirteen days." She grew a sly grin. "Oh, and I told my abba to expect a large *mohar*. After all, I'm worth it!"

The awestruck general's future wife motioned toward Hoshe'a's recently vacated chair. "Will your [symbols] brother be needing any bread anytime soon?" Kalev shook his head and put a finger to his lips. Raisa giggled as she hustled the little girls out of the room.

All three teenage boys futilely tried to ignore the look of sheer confused terror on their General's face. When Yadin and Ofek resumed their loud "discussion" over the distribution of livestock assets between the two battalions, Kalev looked at Ari and yelled in frustration, "What [symbols] is a mohar?"

The typically Hebrew arguing abruptly ceased, and the two colonels curiously stared at the two generals. Ari grinned. "Sir, according to my savta, a mohar is the price you give to the abba for your future bride (*kallah*). A *Mattan* is the gift you give to the bride." Yadin smirked. "You can buy a wife?" The boys chuckled. Then Ari continued, "Yes, and she eventually brings something of value, cattle, a deed for land, etc., from her abba's house as a gift for the groom." Ari started to grin at Kalev, then saw the panic in his eyes. Kalev turned toward the other boisterous teens. "Ari, she deserves a better man than me. What if I say something stupid…*again*? I don't want to hurt her…and I don't know anything about…arghhhh." Kalev hoped the Warrior King would step in with some wise advice. *A little help here, please*, the General mentally pleaded. Before Ari could reply, the double doors flew open. And in an instant, the entire senior staff's semi-safe world violently crashed down around them.

33

They'd just run out onto the main deck when Kalev saw Akiba on his knees in front of one of the youngest troops. The boy was covered with ash and reeked of smoke. His face was blackened except for the streaks of snot and tears. Carni raced by and hit her knees. She held the trembling kid. To his credit, when the little guy saw Ari over Carni's shoulder, he sniffed and tried to stand at attention. "Then Akim and me hid for a long time while they took stuff out of the houses…the soldiers burned it all. Akim ran to fight them, but I was too scared. I didn't know what to do." The boy practically screamed between sobs, "General Ari's"—sob—"abba and…"—sob—"they burned, then the thunder and the white rocks…" The boy finally broke down and cried uncontrollably.

By the time Carni picked up the boy and turned around, she only saw the backs of the small force racing to mount up. Ari was the first one up the ramp. Kalev and the colonels rode as fast as their horses could run in the dusty air. Soon the smell of smoke and the orange glow of the burning houses came into view.

Even before they entered the village, they all cringed at the smell of burnt flesh. Kalev and the colonels dismounted at the head of the dirt path, which served as the main road down the center of the small village. Yadin immediately puked. Kalev heard a couple of the troops behind them start to heave.

Ari started screaming and collapsed in front of what looked to Kalev like a large smoking pile of blackened rubble. But as Kalev walked up behind his friend, he was stunned to see that the smoldering pile was really a stack of blackened and contorted bodies and parts of bodies.

The crushed son of Adir pulled one of the burnt corpses out of the pile and held it as he rocked back and forth, continuing to wail. Kalev instantly turned around and heaved. The inconsolable teen was cradling the upper torso of his abba's charred and severed body. Handfuls of burnt flesh sluffed off into the boy's lap. Kalev's tears blurred his vision. He didn't know what to do, so he sat in the dirt behind the screaming boy, gently put his huge hand on Ari's shoulder, and silently wept.

Akiba's tears streaked his own face. He walked toward his best friend and the General, not sure what to do. Like their souls, the sky had blackened. A very bright flash, coupled with an earsplitting crack of thunder, drew his attention to the far end of the village.

Three squads of Heh's elite and heavily armed troops rode up, dismounted, and his most experienced captain whispered into his ear. Akiba resignedly nodded. He quickly glanced back through his burning tears, mounted up, and led the squads back toward the other end of the still-burning village.

At the edge of the full canal, Colonel Akiba dismounted and was immediately awed by the loud cracks of thunder and huge chunks of bluish-white rocks streaking out of a black cloud. But the chaotic scene was only on the Egyptian side of the canal. The glowing rocks were as big as a man's head and probably twice as heavy. He noticed that when they hit the hard-packed ground, they didn't bounce. The fiery ice impacted the ground at such a high rate of speed that they exploded from steaming craters. Yahweh's streaking fingers of retribution collectively fell in such numbers; it formed a single, bright white curtain along the entire west side of the canal.

The commander of Heh Company pointed at the Egyptian side of the little hamlet's makeshift bridge. His lieutenant confirmed they were staring at the remains of at least twenty black-clad Egyptian soldiers, their horses, and even two splintered chariots. The obviously dead and flattened bodies moved each time they were pummeled by the bright ice rocks. In addition to the rumbling ground, Yadin felt a strong breeze blowing from behind him. The ice-rock storm seemed to be breathing in the putrid, smoke-filled air.

A rapidly growing rank of Heh's troops soon lined the canal in both directions. Yadin couldn't blame them. Yahweh's unnatural show of lethal power not five yards away was mesmerizing.

Eventually, Akiba motioned for his captain, their three lieutenants, and four First Sergeants to follow him. Even though they were a good fifteen yards from the canal, Yadin had to shout to be heard. "I want four squads. One squad on each side of this main road and one down the rear of both rows of houses. They'll go house to house and look for survivors. They're to use their horse blankets to cover the dead. If they find any water jars, have the older troops try and dowse the house fires without getting too close. The remaining troops will meet me back at General Ari's house." Akiba sighed. "We have a lot of graves to dig."

Once the AO was clear, Heh's commanding colonel started a slow, silently sobbing walk back to Ari's house. In all the chaos, he'd forgotten his horse. Which really didn't matter because the expertly trained horse was dutifully following a few steps behind his rider.

The dirt road was littered with broken pottery, charred clothing, splintered furniture, and charred body parts. A row of too-small arms was laid out on the top of a low wall in front of a burning house. For some reason, Akiba's unconscious mind counted eleven right arms and fifteen left. That sight and the stench of burning flesh caused him to retch twice before he made it back to Ari's house.

By then, most of the army had either ridden or driven wagons to the horrific scene. Out of respect for Ari, they were all ordered to dismount, form up, and silently stand at ease. Every troop was individually threatened against puking.

Kalev noticed the defeated-looking Akiba, followed by his horse, walking his way. Ari continued rocking the upper half of his abba. The big man lightly squeezed the sobbing boy's shoulders and whispered, "Keep holding him. I'll be right back."

The General stood, wiped his eyes, cleared his throat, and met Akiba a few yards away. The glassy-eyed boy looked pale and shaking. The boy's face mirrored how Kalev felt. The ex-slave's mind had inadvertently fallen back into its decade-long failsafe detachment. Only this time, overwhelming personal grief and loss battled against the deadness.

With a severe compassion, he honestly didn't feel he barked, "Colonel Akiba, report!" The thunder of hundreds of heals slapping together as the army came to attention was lost on the focused general.

As expected, the incongruent command startled the colonel out of his dazed stare. Akiba snapped to attention. "Uh, yes, Sir, um, I have troops searching the village for survivors, but…" He didn't have to finish. Kalev nodded for him to continue. The teen glanced at Ari, then pointed over his shoulder at the road to the canal. "Uh, I don't know how to describe what's happening over there…but I'm pretty sure the Egyptian pigs that did this are dead."

Yadin and Ofek joined the pair. They wordlessly watched as their friend began to slide into a glazed stare. All three colonels jumped when the Commanding General snapped his fingers in front of Akiba's face. "Colonel!" The boy stiffened again. "Yes, Sir, sorry, Sir. My people are in the process of trying to put out the fires, collect the, um"—the teenage colonel swallowed hard to keep himself from puking again—"body parts and wrap them for burial." Kalev refused to imagine the cadaverous sights the village still held.

The General issued a long string of clipped orders. "…and…" He turned and glanced at Ari and the still smoking pile in front of the hoarsely sobbing teen. "Um, send enough troops back to fill three large wagons with sheets, blankets, towels, a long coil of rope, shovels, ten eight-foot-by-one-inch-by-ten-inch planks, saws, and several large urns of water. And grab a ram's horn. I think the Rabbi will need it at one point in the sacrament. When they return, *within the next twenty minutes*, I want a line of thirty evenly-spaced, deep graves. Start the line over there."

Then the Warrior King prompted Kalev, and he automatically repeated Yahweh's words. "The foot of each grave should always point in the direction of Yahweh's promised land. At least their bodies can face toward freedom." The three colonels quickly glanced at each other. Their general's spiritual transformation would take some getting used to.

Kalev continued, but now his voice sounded detached. "Use the back of one of the wagons as a staging platform. The oldest and/or hardest troops will individually wash and wrap every body or part. Yadin, I want *you* to carve the names into the markers. At least one of our troops knows everyone who lived here. And make sure there are enough stones for each troop to show his respect at each grave. This is probably the first burial most of them have ever experienced. And I'm sure it won't be the last. Let's show them the right way to do it."

Akiba cleared his throat a couple of times, and the others patiently waited for him to speak. "Um, Sir, from the little I saw in the village, I think we need seventy-five graves to start with. Plus…" He paused, then pointed back and the little hamlet's main path. "We're, um, missing a troop. I'm told he was visiting his ema." Kalev winced, then slowly nodded his understanding. "I assume your people are searching for him." The teen nodded, but they all knew the kid was probably part of the carnage. "Okay, keep looking." Kalev turned to the other two colonels. "I want all remains to be respectfully buried within the next two hours. Then the rabbi can pray over each filled-in grave."

In spite of his nausea, the Commanding General stiffened to attention and did a crisp about-face and raised his gravelly voice. "Now is *not* the time for you to wallow in your own feelings. It's time to show respect for a fallen soldier and the rest of this village. So ruck up, troops, and get the job done."

Kalev did another about-face, lowered his voice, and tilted his head toward Ari. "Gentlemen, I know you want to help our friend, but at this point, Ari needs some mental space. It's okay to *silently* sit with him. Your caring presence is enough for now, but let him be the first one to speak…I want this funeral done right. So get on it!"

The General never acknowledged their salute. Out of the corner of his eye, he'd seen the battered Hoshe'a on horseback. Beside him, Raisa, her abba, and Carni raced a horse-drawn wagon. They'd all disappeared around the back corner of the closest burning house.

Kalev glanced back at Ari, who'd stopped rocking but continued to sob and hold Adir's upper torso. He, too, wanted to comfort the boy, but… "Not now," he growled to himself. "There'll be time later."

Kalev saw an abnormally frantic Hoshe'a running at full speed. He'd rounded the back corner of the closest house and headed toward his younger brother. Kalev tried to ignore the egg-sized lumps on Hoshe'a's forehead and temple. The wheezing and still woozy Hoshe'a coughed as a cloud of acrid smoke blew past them. Suddenly, a terrible thought hit Kalev. He sucked in a ragged breath and roared, "Where's Raisa?"

Hoshe'a slid to a stop, bent over, and put his hands on his knees. He shook his head. "Raisa's fine, sort of. But her abba ran into his burning house and still hasn't come out. Ema is with Raisa, but they're both starting to panic. And Kalev, Ema still doesn't know about Adir." Hoshe'a took another wheezing breath and then looked up. Kalev was gone.

The General skidded to a stop in front of his Raisa and ema. Carni's arm was around the sobbing bride-to-be, and they both sat in the ash-covered dirt. In front of them was a small pile of charred rags. Kalev relaxed a little. *Good...* he thought. *No body parts in that one.*

Carni looked up and nodded toward the house. Black smoke billowed from the three windows and doorway. Twenty minutes ago, the still-burning door was a thick and brightly painted slab of blackwood. Now it hung like a large fire-breathing mouth, half-open and ready to fall off its clay frame. From inside the house, Kalev heard the faint sound of a crash, a yelp, and high-pitched coughing. The big man groaned, "Okay, I'll get him." Then the proud son of Hezron ran head first into the ominous smoking maw.

Behind him, Carni cringed as she watched her little one selflessly leap past the burning door and vanish inside. "Yahweh, please protect him *again*," she pleaded under her breath. Raisa had screamed at her dangerously stubborn abba when he'd jumped off the wagon and ran into the burning house. Now she watched in numbed horror as her husband-to-be jumped past the flames. Up to then, she'd just loudly wept. Now her disjointed thoughts gushed out between panicked sobs. "Kalev…Abba…are they…gonna die?" Carni hugged the trembling little woman tighter and whispered, "Raisa, Yahweh is protecting them both. I know He still has plans for them," Carni silently hoped. Raisa, still sobbing, nodded. Then she pointed at the smoking pile in front of them, "That…was my…wedding dress and…everything…I own…what am I…gonna do?"

Glowing ashes fell from the flaming beams overhead. Through the dark, smokey fog, Kalev quickly realized the entrance to the front room was almost blocked. Blackened and glowing boards had collapsed from the ceiling. Closest to Kalev, the jumbled stack of panels was still on fire, and the heat was intense. The Commanding General ignored his watery eyes and his own wheezing cough. Kalev tried to rush past the small flames and accidentally burnt his right shoulder. In the main room, an upturned table and four chairs were still blazing. The rabbi was too close to the flames roaring behind him. With bare hands, Nachshon moved aside smoking ceiling boards. Then the prince of the Judah tribe grabbed something from under the pile then collapsed to his knees in a coughing pit. Kalev knew he had to get the man out of there. He jumped over a stack of flaming palm fronds that had fallen through the still-collapsing roof. Kalev put his hand on Nachshon's shoulder and croaked, "We have to leave. *Now*!" The rabbi weakly nodded and then gagged.

Kalev easily picked up the small man and cradled him in his arms. But because of the rubble and smoke, Kalev stumbled backward, crushing the flaming table between his back and the wall. He ignored the hot, searing pain, adjusted his load, and worked his way toward the back door. They made it about ten yards from the house before Kalev threw the unconscious man forward and collapsed onto all fours. He alternatingly puked between his own uncontrollable hacking.

Hoshe'a was instantly by his brother's side. He dumped a large jar of water over Kalev's head, back, and legs. But to the General, the cool water felt like a thousand white-hot knives. Kalev clinched his teeth and loudly growled between intermittent, ragged breaths. His smoke and now water-induced coughing renewed the panicked feeling of drowning. Hoshe'a smiled. "You can thank me later." Carni had watched in disbelief as her ignorantly careless oldest son poured an entire twenty-gallon urn onto her youngest's smoking back. Her scream mixed with Kalev's loud groan. "Hoshe'a!"

The older brother pointed at Kalev's charred tunic, innocently shrugged, and inappropriately smiled. "What was I supposed to do? He was on fire; the prancing ponies and cute bunnies were burning!" His furious ema was cradling the unconscious rabbi's head in her lap, or she would have already taken charge of the situation.

As she helplessly watched her Kalev's pained expression, Raisa numbly ran over to Carni with a wet rag and cup of water. The army's chief medical officer/ema started washing the unconscious rabbi's face. Instantly, the man's eyes flew open; he bolted upright and started another round of ragged coughing. Carni forced the protesting Nachshon to take some water. Raisa knelt beside her wheezing abba and sobbed. "You crazy old man, you almost cost me my abba *and a husband*." Then she wrapped her arms around his trembling neck and sobbed.

Once Kalev got his wheezing under control, he sat up. Hoshe'a handed him a small skin of watered-down wine. Akiba and one of his sergeants walked up. The colonel and Hoshe'a spoke in whispers as they both stared at Kalev. The sergeant leaned over, looked at the General's back, and winced. "Thank you for saving my abba." Kalev barely heard the thank you, but his brain never registered the rest of the statement. He simply half nodded at the sergeant. The embarrassed General finally stood and downed the rest of the skin. He and Akiba watched as Raisa, the sergeant, and Carni helped the rabbi into the back of the wagon.

Kalev's bloodshot eyes locked with Akiba's. Already knowing the answer, the big man had to ask. "Did you find the missing troop?" Akiba looked at the ground and shook his head. "Yes, Sir, his name is Akim. We found him with his sword in his hand and…" The tall boy/colonel started sobbing. Kalev put his hand on his shoulder. Eventually, Akiba croaked, "…his, um, detached head was sitting upright on his chest." Akiba fell to all fours and violently vomited. Kalev stood there with his hand on the boy's trembling back and silently wept his own bitter tears. Eventually, Kalev motioned for the sergeant. Then too gruffly whispered, "Get him some water." When the colonel finally stood, Kalev gave him a waterskin and put his hand on the teen's shoulder. "There will be a time to grieve, but not yet." Akiba nodded, then quietly whispered, "Yes, Sir. Later…"

Yadin and Ofek walked up from behind the General and their burdened-looking friend. The wide-eyed teens gaped at the back of Kalev's head and legs and the oddly shaped pattern burned into his back.

The General turned, and the two averted their stares. "Good, Colonel Yadin, I suppose there are four rooms in the Pit and/or the Fortress that can be converted into bedrooms with running water, vents, etc.?" Yadin nodded. "Yes, Sir." "And do we have enough surplus beds, pillows, linens, and furniture to furnish those rooms?" "Yes, Sir."

Kalev quickly turned to glance at Raisa. When he turned back, Yadin already had his scroll out and was using the irritated-looking Yadin's back to write his list. Kalev asked, "I assume we have a surplus of men's and women's clothing too." Yadin paused, looked away for a few seconds, then nodded.

"Sir, we have exactly 231 keffiyehs in five different colors, 900 male and 435 female robes. One thousand five hundred one pairs of sandals, not including the twenty-five pairs that have the diamonds and rubies on the thongs. We also have forty-seven highly polished mirrors, thirty-two gold, hand-held, and fifteen full length. We also have…" Kalev interrupted the accountant when he cleared his throat. "Very good, Colonel. Find one of the older medic girls and let her pick out seven changes of women's clothing, sandals, hair brushes, mirrors, and whatever girl stuff she thinks Raisa will need. Stage it all in the largest of the four rooms. Stage the second room with clothes for the rabbi. Then I want the majority of Major Carni's house moved into the third room. Move Major Hoshe'a's bed and clothes into the smallest room." The others looked at each other but didn't laugh. "Yes, Sir." "Okay. As soon as the burial is completed, get your people over there and make it happen." "Yes, Sir."

Kalev and the three colonels walked back to the wagon. He cleared his throat and spoke in his commanding General voice. "Following the burial, Major Carni, Major Hoshe'a, miss Raisa, and Rabbi Nachshon, you will be moving into the Pit and/or the Fortress." He looked at Carni, who'd already opened her mouth to object. Kalev roared at her. "That, Major, is an order. Period!"

As he watched Ema give his brother *the look*, Hoshe'a grew a large smile and started his usual poorly timed chuckling. Out of the corner of his eye, Kalev saw the growing crowd of wide-eyed boys surrounding the wagon. Carni saw them too. She cleared her throat a couple of times in an attempt to control her defiant protest. The little Hebrew ema shot Kalev her best *look*, saluted, then turned toward the rear of the wagon. Without breaking stride, she reared back and slapped the back of the unsuspecting Hoshe'a's head. "Boys or no boys," she quietly growled. "He desperately needed that."

As Raisa fell in beside Carni, she shot Kalev a sad but grateful smile. A stern-faced Kalev glanced at Hoshe'a. His brother was rubbing his neck but still had a huge smile. At any other time, Kalev would have started laughing. But not today.

Instead, the General asked his brother, "Have you been buried alive yet?" Hoshe'a continued to smile and pointed to the canal. "After that, I don't think anyone will be asking about me ever again." Kalev nodded, then grew a sly grin. "Good, no loss."

Following a report on the burial's progress, Kalev walked back toward Adir's house. Two of Carni's medicine girls were standing behind Ari, whispering to each other. When they saw the General, they took a few steps back. Kalev walked around in front of Ari and sat in the dirt. The horrendous stench from Adir's charred upper torso caused a burning bile to instantly rise in his throat. Kalev swallowed hard to keep it down. The oldest boys from Heh Company were gingerly removing all the bodies and parts from the pile behind him.

Ari looked over Kalev's shoulder and spoke in a flat tone. "Sergeant Othniel, that one is my savta; be gentle with her." Othniel nodded. "Of course, Sir, like she was my own." Kalev stood and whispered to two of the burial troops. They grabbed a blanket and positioned it behind the dazed Ari. Kalev tiredly knelt in front of his shattered friend. He looked into the boy's vacant-looking eyes, then slowly reached across to take the body out of the boy's lap.

Ari instantly shot Kalev a fierce look and clamped down harder on his abba's arm, causing a horrible squishing sound. Kalev swallowed hard and sat back. He didn't know what to say. Then, from deep in his roiling gut, the words gushed out, "Ari, if he could, what would your abba say to you right now right now?"

Slowly, the boy's expression started to change. With tears and snot streaking his ash-smeared face, he rasped between heart-rending sobs. "He'd say…that Savta and he…were very proud of me. That he'd always love me…" He paused, sniffed, and futilely wiped his face. "He'd say I still…needed to work on my false-edge backswing." Kalev half-smiled, then unconsciously rubbed his shoulder. "One of *my* most painful lessons. I thought he'd broken my shoulder."

"Ari, look at his face." Kalev paused. Ari looked down for a long while. But consciously forced himself to not look. He didn't want to remember his mentor like this.

After a while, Ari looked up. The pain in his eyes made Kalev want to puke again. The teen looked decades older. "Son, is that the powerful and fearless abba you remember?" Ari slowly shook his head. Kalev put a hand on the trembling boy's shoulder. "Son, that's only the empty shell that covered the real him. Right now, my friend Adir is standing safe and strong by Warrior King's side."

Kalev had no clue where his consoling words were coming from. Up to a few weeks ago, Kalev had never allowed himself to grieve. Or, rather, he couldn't. He would have killed himself decades ago. So his words sounded foreign and almost hurt.

Fresh tears ran down the boy's face. "Son, it's time to let go…we need to honor the memory of this great warrior." Ari half nodded. Kalev signaled for the blanket. Then slowly reached over, wrapped the blanket around the remains, and lifted it out of Ari's lap. Kalev walked to the first grave, and with lengths of rope, they slowly lowered his friend and mentor into the dark hole.

A shrill scream erupted behind Kalev. He quickly turned to see his ema on her knees at the head of Adir's grave. To Kalev her wailing sobs, though appropriate at this time, seemed almost too much. Hoshe'a walked up behind her, knelt, and put his hand on her back. Raisa suddenly appeared at her confused Kalev's side. She took his hand and pulled him down to her level. To be heard above the wailing, Raisa had to talk louder into his ear. "Kalev, your ema knew him." Kalev looked at her, confused. His future wife half-smiled at the muscled man's innocence. "She. *Knew*. Him." She watched his eyes. Then it clicked. "But—but they weren't married!" Raisa slowly shook her head. "But she really loved him." Slack-jawed, Kalev glanced between his ema, Adir's grave, then back to Raisa. "Did Hoshe'a know?" Raisa smiled. "My love, everyone but you knew."

34

Two hours later, Raisa's much-weaker abba, flanked by that same sergeant and Raisa, began the burial ceremony. Among the dead were the brave little warrior Akim; Ari's abba, Adir; his savta; and fifty-one others. Most of the dead's relatives stood or knelt and wailed at the head of each marked grave. Though for too many, their loved one's remains were buried in multiple graves. Nachshon acknowledged them all by name. The entire battalion had assembled and remained at attention with swords drawn.

From the rear corner of Adir's smoldering house, a cloaked Moshe watched and wept. Before this morning, this whole "mess" was kind of academic. Yes, he saw the devastation, and yes, the too-heavy burden was a constant. But he'd always felt detached, like he was watching it all happen to someone else.

Then, as he was having his usual before-dawn argument with Yahweh, the King of kings and pharaohs went silent. Instantly, millions of timeless screams, Hebrew screams, hit his gut like a violent wave. As his sister watched, "Yahweh's mouthpiece" ran out of his tent and puked several times.

As Moshe watched the burial, the pleading screams of the tortured and dying, the lethal warnings to Ramses, and the realization of Yahweh's infinite purposes all coalesced. It just became *very* personal. The shaking eighty-year-old prophet gasped for air and fell to his knees. He just wanted to die. *I don't deserve it*, he thought. *But maybe I could be buried with these innocent victims. Then, Yahweh would have to find someone else.*

Kalev stood at the head of Adir and his ema's graves. Kalev supported Ari with his arm around the trembling teen's shoulders. A pretty teenage girl hugged the dazed eighteen-year-old general's other arm. Kalev saw that Nachshon was holding a charred, leather-bound book. The General shook his head. *So* that's *what the old fool almost died for*, he thought. Then, for some reason, Kalev shivered.

With a strong voice that belied his frailty, the weak rabbi sang the Mourner's Kaddish. "Exalted and hallowed be Yahweh's Great Name in the world which He created, according to Their plan. May Yahweh's majesty and saving strength be revealed powerfully and immediately. To which we say *Emunah* (let this be so)." Everyone repeated, "*Emunah.*"

"Blessed be Yahweh's great name to all eternity. Blessed, praised, honored, exalted, extolled, glorified, adored, and lauded be the name of the Holy Blessed One, beyond all earthly words and songs of blessing, praise, and comfort. To which we say *Emunah*..."

"May there be abundant peace from heaven, and life, for all your chosen people. To which we say *Emunah*..."

As Nachshon and the others were reciting the Kaddish, Ari, staring at his savta's grave, weakly whispered to Kalev, "Do you know what she called *you*?" Kalev followed Ari's gaze to the grave. "I deeply cared for your savta." Ari went on, not really hearing Kalev's reply. "She called you her deliverer. In fact, every one of these people lying here called you their hero. Even Raisa's ema." Kalev's head snapped up. "Her ema?" Ari barely nodded as Nachshon continued. "…May the One who creates harmony on high, bring peace and deliver us all. To which we say *Emunah…*"

The prince of the Yehudah tribe paused and visibly trembled. Kalev was startled to hear the Warrior King's voice thunder from the rabbi's mouth. "Let it be written! Sons of Abraham, do not fear! Stand firm and see the Yeshua (salvation) of your Yehovah that even now is unfolding before your eyes. I will restore the years that were taken. For your tormentors, these life-devouring locusts you will never ever see again. Soon, you will have plenty to eat. Your hunger will be fully satisfied. Then you will praise the name of the Yehovah, your Elohim, who has acted wondrously in your behalf. My people will never again be put to shame. You will be convinced that I AM is in the midst of Yisrael. I AM the Yehovah, your Elohim; there is no other. I will pour out My *Ruah* (spirit, wind, breath) on all kinds of people. Your sons and daughters will prophesy. Your elderly will have dreams and visions; your young men will proclaim prophetic revelations. Even on male and female servants, I will pour out My Spirit in those days…I AM, the Yehovah, your Elohim, hears *your* pleading cries for justice. And We. Will. Answer!"

The entire battalion watched as Raisa's spent father wordlessly crumpled to the ground. Kalev, still distracted, had Akiba call the battalion to at ease. The General knew he had to take charge of the whole situation. He boomed in a voice that pierced the dusty, smoke-filled air and silenced the loudly howling civilians.

"This army exists because of the training and weapons forged by this mighty warrior Adir and his son. Major Adir is now and will always be my friend and mentor. Never forget these victims died at the hands of our enemies. Sear this memory into your brain. And when it's time, take it with you into battle. Remember this day when you feel you can't swing your sword one more time. *No mercy* to your enemies. Yahweh has already judged the Egyptian platoon that did this. They are dead.

"Battalion, attention…we salute this hero and these chosen ones of the Warrior King." Kalev turned to his colonels and quietly ordered. "Gentlemen, if we're done here, let's get people back, clean up, eat, and continue their usual missions or sleep. In respect for these fallen, I want 'the Pit's' and 'the Fortress's' troops silent until sunup tomorrow."

As the battalion was dismissed to leave, Hoshe'a pulled his oddly trembling brother aside. He needed to get his little brother back to the Pit and care for the extensive burns on his back. "Kalev, listen, your back…" But Kalev motioned toward the girl with her hand on Ari's shaking back and interrupted Hoshe'a, "I assume she knows Ari." Hoshe'a exhaled, then nodded. "She's *his* Raisa. Her name is Deborah…" Right then the girl stood and tried to help the exhausted Ari to his feet. They both stumbled and almost fell onto the grave. The two men rushed over to help. Kalev looked into the teen's vacant eyes. "Son, Ari, can you ride?" Ari looked at Kalev and exhaustedly whispered. "Sir, my abba died." Kalev grimaced.

Kalev looked at Hoshe'a. "Get him on that wagon and back to the Pit." Then, in a forced, commanding voice, he addressed the weeping female troop. "Deborah, is it? Get him cleaned up and have Major Carni take care of his hands. I know he hasn't eaten in a while. And get him some wine, a lot of wine. Stay with him. I'll check in as soon as I get back." The girl sniffed, stiffened to attention, and saluted. "Yes, Sir, right away!"

Kalev glanced at his softly sobbing ema on the wagon's seat, then whispered to Hoshe'a. "Brother, by the time you get there, Ema's room in the Pit should already be set up. Tell her that Ari needs her help. That should be enough distraction to get her there." Hoshe'a nodded. Eventually, everyone else had raced back to the Pit, and the huge man was left alone. Kalev stood there and began to shiver.

35

The General had stayed behind intending to double-check the smoldering houses for any remains. But the familiar, detached numbness took over as he mindlessly walked down the little village's main path toward the canal.

The roaring fire ice storm was still pummeling the Egyptian side. Any normal person would be afraid of the lethal destruction only steps away. But the son of Hezron wasn't normal. He'd experienced way too much death, too much personal pain and suffering to be "normal." No, Kalev's type of fearless, "deadened status quo" was the only way he'd survived, especially this morning. *Though, after today,* he'd thought, *what's the point of surviving?*

At the edge of the canal, his detached mind warred with the feelings of soul-crushing grief. This, coupled with the sight of the falling curtain of glowing ice, made him feel nauseous. He dropped onto all fours and forcefully retched into a clump of bushes.

The dazed Commanding General crawled to the edge of the canal and sat with his feet almost touching the green water. Kalev distractedly watched the violence only ten yards away, then looked up at the roiling black clouds. He wanted to scream, "Where were *You*?" but he already knew the answer. "It was the Egyptian pigs' choice to obey their [illegible] sha'dim masters' orders," he growled.

Then a chorus of invisible, high-pitched voices screeched from somewhere overhead. The sound was deafening. "And once again, you useless pile of [illegible], you weren't strong enough to help! Why don't you just kill yourself? It *will* stop the pain." At the same time, a sickening cloud of smoke from the village enveloped him. Akiba had reported that one of the house's flames had kept them from recovering the five bodies inside. So the smoke still reeked of burning flesh.

Instantly, Kalev had a bird's eye view of a treeless, 370.6581-acre field. In his dealings with the Warrior King, he's stopped wondering how he knew details and just went with it. It would have driven Yadin crazier. The white, ice-covered fields had hundreds of long-row houses. Some were two-tiered brick; the others were single-story and made of wood. They were all lined up like the narrow columns on Yadin's accounting scroll. Three strange, narrow, numerous, tall, odd-looking, double-rowed fences evenly divided the massive area. The view of the same place changed. Though it was night, Kalev was able to see the glowing top of fifty-two chimneys. Ash fell like snow, but the smell was the same stench currently blowing from Adir's hamlet behind him.

In the beams of odd-looking, intense lights, Kalev saw thousands of people shivering in the freezing night air. They were all similarly bald, and gray-striped clothes hung from their gaunt yet familiar-looking frames. And once again, somehow he knew nine out of ten were Hebrews. It was always dark when the thousands of scarecrow like people were formed into long lines. The lines were evenly divided then each disappeared into four different 5000-plus-square-foot death rooms. Each room had enough space for almost 6000 captives at a time. Two of the huge rooms were above, and two below the buildings with the smoking chimneys. At first, the scene would repeat every three days. But after a couple of years, the lines would go in, and as he watched, thousands of naked bodies were wheeled out, stacked in massive piles, and burned.

Kalev's view changed, and he recognized the unseen, dark-winged sha'dim forces that he'd fought against beside the Warrior King. They flew in thick choking flocks just over the gray-striped captive Hebrews' heads as they disappeared into the four buildings. The ear-piercing, evil laughter made the General's head throb with rage. He knew this was a dream or, rather, a nightmare, yet he wanted to do something, anything to help. The dream took him to hundreds more places in myriad different periods of time. The same burning flesh smells and swirling flocks of sha'dim plagued every new scene.

Suddenly, he saw himself from the same overhead point of view, and the sun was well past noon. Kalev vaguely remembered that long day in the mud pits. He'd completely filled the death wagon with just over sixty bodies, mostly the used-up children from the mines. He watched Hotep whip him and four others, then point uphill toward the four large brick ovens. That's where his memory broke off.

Kalev saw himself drive the wagon up the hill while the others trailed behind. Five of Hotep's drunken minions net them at the huge furnaces. The pigs laughed, whipped, and yelled at them to hurry. Kalev powerlessly tried to stop the scene; he didn't want to see anymore. Yet he couldn't distract his mind's eye from the horrifying sight of himself and the other men throwing five of the little limp bodies into each of the blazing ovens. Then they carefully stacked the others nearby, like a chord of wood. Kalev watched the other men stay behind as his vacant-eyed self drove the wagon back down the hill. The same nauseating stench followed him back to the pits. He parked the wagon, hobbled, watered, and fed the oxen, then walked away. Just another day in the mud pits.

The combined scenes of countless Hebrew deaths climaxed in a wave of hopelessness that threatened to violently suck the air from his lungs. Kalev knew this nightmare was a glimpse of the future. He also realized it had come from Yahweh, but it would be years before he really understood why.

Then, in a brilliant flash of light, the timeless commanding voice of the Warrior King ripped Kalev's dark thoughts into a million pieces. "And it will be written of Me. I, your Yahweh, will make your oppressors eat their own flesh; they will get drunk on their own blood as if it were wine. Then all humankind will recognize that I AM the Yehovah, your Yeshua, your protector, the powerful ruler of Jacob... All things have been handed over to Me, your Yeshua, by My Abba, Yahweh. No one knows the Son except for His Abba, and no one knows the Abba except the Son and anyone to whom the Son, your Elohim, decides to reveal Him. So come to me, all you who are weary and burdened, and I will give you rest. Take My yoke on you and learn from Me, because I AM gentle and humble in heart, and you will find rest for your souls. For My yoke is easy to bear, and My load is not hard to carry."[1] Then the voice softened. "Son of Hezron. I have marked you as faithful to My Abba. He is the All-Powerful Yahweh. His words created the *shamayim* and the *eretz*. No mere flesh could see His glorious face and live.

"Yet, Kalev, I speak to you as a faithful friend. I desire a relationship that is both personally vulnerable and fiercely proactive. So I ask you again, General Kalev. Do you trust that I am good?" Kalev nodded. "Do you believe that the Creator of laughter can laugh and tease like a friend?" Kalev warily nodded. He really didn't feel like being the butt of a joke right now.

Then just as quickly, he was back on the edge of the canal. Kalev opened his eyes and blinked because of the glaring bright sun. What seemed to last hundreds of lifetimes was actually over in three heartrending minutes. Now, the clash of opposing thoughts that raced through his brain made him dizzier than before. The dry heaves seemed to last forever.

From the lowest window of the closest burned-out house, the three boys wept as their hero sat by the canal rocking back and forth and loudly groaned. General Kalev was the only abba figure they'd ever known, and he retched violently. All three felt an overpowering sense of helplessness, and it both scared and infuriated them. Little Frog whispered, "We need to watch his back better 'cause we're too far away. But Yoshiyah, you're not silent and deadly enough like Croc and me, so stay here." As usual, the littlest of their small trio remained silent. Then followed them anyway.

The three small warriors low crawled out the back door and hid behind some scorched brush halfway between the canal and the house. That was when the storm ceased and the angry clouds disappeared. Soon, the warm sun dried their tears. The young boys had been up all night, and now it was close to noon. Without checking, each one assumed the other two would keep watch while they dozed off. In unison, all three shadow troops fell into an exhausted sleep.

Kalev slowly got to his feet, and the shivering intensified. Something soft nudged him forward, and he almost fell into the canal. He turned to see Boaz. As with the three boys, Boaz acted like a devoted shadow when untethered. "I don't feel so well, boy." It took Kalev one more dry heave and three tries before he barely made it into the saddle. He reluctantly closed his eyes and never remembered the rest. Ten minutes later, the perimeter guards relayed the warning that Boaz was carrying the dead-looking general across the sand bar and was headed from the Pit's ramp.

The ramp lowered, and Boaz slowly walked down to the main deck. The huge horse carefully walked fifty yards further, then stopped. Unprompted, the horse slowly knelt on all fours but remained upright.

When the grieving Carni was alerted, she knew Kalev's extensive burn injuries had caught up to him. Today the fierce little ema lost her soul mate in the worst possible way, experienced the results of an evil she'd never wanted to imagine, and grieved with the families who lost a loved one. But now this was her own, her little one, and she *would not* lose him too!

The commanding officer of the growing medical platoons wiped her tear-stained face, grabbed a blanket and a few of her supplies, then ran for the wagon. At the same time, she yelled a breathless stream of orders. This unleashed her very well-trained teams of medics, and they flew into action.

The General's ferocious-looking ema jumped back onto the wagon seat, turned the four-horse-drawn wagon around, and aimed it toward the ramp almost 300 yards away. Raisa, Hoshe'a, and the three colonels had to run to jump into the wagon bed. Carni fiercely snapped the reins, and the beautiful Arabian stallions shot forward.

The senior medical captain and her two First Sergeants immediately took control. The major had relentlessly drilled into them that every medical emergency was unique and required educated, on-the-fly decision-making. They were used to prepping a medical wagon, but they expertly adapted to this emergent situation. Fifty-five seconds later, the General's large bedroom erupted into a previously choreographed, controlled chaos. They removed the blankets, pillows, and feather beds. Then the captain found and "sweetly asked" a squad of hormone-fueled, older boys for help.

The overzealous male troops had raced to the dining area, violently knocked the legs off two of the heavy, five-by-eight-foot table tops, then staged them horizontally across the General's sturdy bed frame. The medics spread one of the puffy duck-down blankets over the wood, then covered that with a section of rougher sail canvas. The layered wraps were tucked under the boards transforming the General's "man-eating" bed into a perfectly firm treatment platform. They weren't told what the extent of the General's injuries was, so they prepped for everything.

The nearby table was pulled to the bedside and stocked with all the salves, oils, and every different-sized bandage they could get their hands on. Major Carni's unopened box of medical instruments was the table's centerpiece. They even staged different lengths of paired-splint sticks against the wall.

The captain spoke to the eager squad leader, and four four-feet tall urns were rushed in and filled with cool water. Another ornate table was moved to the opposite side of the bed. Making sure to flex their glistening manly muscles, the helpful squad of boys wrestled two very large solid-gold and diamond-rimmed basins onto the table. They, too, were filled to the sparkling brim. In the torchlight, the diamonds and the watery gold colors brightly danced across the dark red ceiling.

Once those were filled, the senior squad of teenage medics whispered to each other. Still giggling and in unison, each medic walked over and kissed a surprised boy's cheek. After the pretty captain gave the sweaty squad leader a peck on the cheek, she shooed the whole slack-jawed squad out of the room.

Even at thirty-seven vibrating miles per hour and from a hundred-plus yards away, Carni recognized Kalev's too-familiar slumped form on the back of the kneeling horse. She knowingly groaned to herself. "Ooooh, little one."

Ten short yards from Boaz, the four-foot-eleven ema stood, reined the horses to the left, and then immediately pulled the reins back as hard as she could. The wagon bed violently swung sideways stopping right in front of the horse. Of course, the high-speed maneuver had violently thrown the surprised passengers from the wagon bed. All five landed in a yelling, jumbled heap.

Carni ignored them and leaped off the wagon. Before the others could untangle themselves, Carni started shouting orders in the silent stronghold. The major medic quickly threw a blanket over Kalev's limp shoulders. With the help of the three colonels and Hoshe'a, they lowered the smaller-looking but still heavy general to the rolled-out blanket on the deck. As Raisa watched and wept, she felt like her world was disintegrating before her eyes.

But to her credit, the beautiful five-foot, future General's wife scowled, rebuked herself, wiped the tears off her face, and scrambled onto the wagon seat. Carni ordered the men to roll the sides of the thick blanket inward. This created a type of stretcher they could lift.

Once the almost 300-pound man was loaded into the back, Carni jumped in beside Kalev and began her examination. And again, the other four had to sprint to jump into the wagon. Once they drew near to the TOC's hallway, Raisa expertly turned and backed the wagon up to the hallway entrance.

The same squad of boys volunteered to carry the General to his room. Though there were eight of them, they strained to keep the stretcher from bouncing and off the ground. The massive prostrate General was carefully lowered to the padded treatment platform. Carni immediately ordered all the troops out. Raisa smiled and whispered her thanks as she shut the heavy door. Or at least she thought she'd closed it.

Except for the patches that stuck to his skin, Kalev's tunic and even the back of his loincloth practically fell off. Carni couldn't stop the involuntary guttural groan. From the back of his neck to his heels, the bright torchlight revealed the full extent of the oozing trauma. The multiple patterns of darker, scorched scar tissue accentuated the charred and bright red bubbled flesh. It looked like blackened wood splinters were embedded into his back and upper legs. Carni reasoned that the deadened scar tissue was the only reason the otherwise crippling pain hadn't kept him from making it back. "Yahweh, please," she groaned as she climbed up on the wide table, sat beside him, and began to care for her little one.

Raisa had rushed from the door and started lighting all the additional torches on the opposite wall. When she heard Carni's groan, she turned and reflexively shrieked. Carni had told her about the numerous times Kalev was beaten and bloodied. But her imagination didn't come close to the reality that was this mass of old scars and new seeping burns. That decimated back and lifeless pale face belonged to her lifelong love. The rabbi's daughter felt the bile rise in her throat. Out of the corner of her eye, Carni saw Raisa race past and head toward Kalev's golden toilet. The little Hebrew ema heard her son's future bride vomit several times.

After washing her face, Raisa sheepishly returned to Carni's side of the bed. The fiery little ema softened her voice. "He'll be okay…eventually." Raisa's voice cracked. "How can you do this over and over? I couldn't…I can't…" She began to sob.

Carni abruptly stopped tweezing the charred splinters out of Kalev's leg. Then she slowly put the crude forceps down on the clean towel covering her son's bare buttocks and sighed. She crawled over to the side table and wiped her hands on a wet towel. Still on the platform, Carni raised up on her knees and towered over Raisa. With a glare that would have intimidated a lethal army, she pointed a long, skinny finger down at Raisa's nose. She growled in a menacing voice, "If you want to marry my son, you'd better pull it together, little girl. This man is a hero. It's in his blood to sacrifice his mind and body so others, like *your abba*, can live. It's what makes Kalev, Kalev." Carni sighed again. "And too often, that heroic attitude comes at a heavy price…I guarantee this won't be the last time…"

Carni purposely let that hang in the still, putrid-smelling air. She picked up the forceps and went back to work. Without looking up, the army's chief ema/medic continued the conversation. "Raisa, did you know his ema chose you?" This surprised Raisa—she'd always thought it was her own idea. "She was my best friend. On her deathbed, she made me promise to make the match. Your ema and I agreed long before your abba was involved. This man, this defender of the weak, needs you to be just as strong and fearless when *he's* weak and defenseless.

"Daughter, trust me, I feel like falling apart every time. But I can't, *and neither can you.* This is our job. We place the well-being of those we love above our own emotions. In a small way, it's what makes us heroes to the hero." Raisa dried her eyes. "Yes, mam, I'll suck it up and be strong for him." Carni nodded. "Then, after you've done all you can, you go into another room, ask Yahweh to spare his life, and completely fall apart in private…but for now, get up there on the other side and carefully help me.

It took two grueling hours and, for Raisa, two more nauseated trips to the "golden box with a hole in it" before they'd completely debrided the burns and coated every inch in a honey and turmeric paste.

Both women wearily crawled off the platform and straightened their stiff legs. Carni wiped her hands and tried to blow the acrid stench out of her nose. "Well, that's all we can do. It's in Yahweh's hands now. I think we should…" A couple of loud sniffs came from under the bed interrupting her thought. She locked eyes with Raisa, winked, and motioned for her to come to Carni's side of the bed. Kalev's Major Ema pulled Raisa close and whispered, "You'll birth your own children, but like it or not, those three are your first."

The major stiffened to attention. She used the voice that always accompanied *the look.* "You three, report now." At first nothing happened. Raisa had to bite her tongue when she heard a loud whisper. "Ow, stop it, Croc. I knew I was more silent and deadly than you. No, you weren't…" Carni cleared her throat and boomed, "I. Said. *Now*!" The three little boys scurried from under the bed and raced to attention in front of the General's Major Ema. She saw the tear streaks down the trio's blackened faces. She knew they loved Kalev like an abba, and they'd been crying. "Your general will be okay." All three glanced over at the bed and then sniffed in unison. Carni and Raisa turned around to hide their smiles. Raisa coughed in a futile attempt to choke down her own laughter.

Carni winked. "Major Raisa!" Raisa blinked. She didn't know she had a rank, but she stiffened to a version of attention anyway. "Yes, mam!" "Cover the General with a single linen cloth. Keep it off the more severe burns. A medic needs to be with him at all times. Because of the wounds weeping, we'll need to reapply the paste every day for a while. He's lost a lot of water. We'll need to force him to drink a lot of water as soon as possible. Do you understand, Major?"

From behind the women, Little Frog loudly whispered, "She's not really a major 'cause the General didn't say she was a major; she's just a pretty lady he likes a lot." Little Croc kicked Little Frog in the shin, and Little Yoshiyah silently smiled at them both. Little Frog scowled at the smaller boy, "Shut up, Yoshiyah; it's not funny!"

Knowing that the newest addition to the trio rarely spoke, Carni whirled around and pointed at the two older boys' faces. "Did I tell you to speak?" All three wide-eyed boys shook their heads. "She does and will always outrank you. You will show her the same respect you show every superior officer. Do you understand me!" Frog and Yoshiyah vigorously nodded, but Croc yelled, "Yes, Sir, um, mam, um, yes, Sir, Major Ema, mam." This time Raisa had to turn and walk back to the basin at the far end of the room. The boys watched her cough the whole way. Carni snapped her finger in their distracted faces, and the trio jumped in unison. "Grab that stack of dirty towels and follow me." Because of the hours in the burnt flesh-smelling air, Carni really couldn't smell a thing. But after decades of experience, she acted on an educated guess. "You three smell like you rolled in ox dung." Croc shook his head, pointed at Frog, who shook his head, then pointed at Yoshiyah. Carni growled, then pointed at the door. As they were leaving, Carni caught sight of Raisa walking back, grinning and wiping tears from her cheeks. "Um. If it's all right, Major Ema, I will take the first medic watch." Carni smiled and nodded.

36

Kalev was unconscious for three long days. Raisa had spent at least twenty hours a day caring for him. When Kalev finally woke up, the deep ache reminded him he was still alive. He saw that he was in his room, but he didn't remember how he got here. In fact, he barely recalled the mass funeral.

More torches were added to the walls, and the room was so bright that it hurt his eyes. He stiffly moved to the side of his hardened bed, climbed down, walked to the golden toilet, and relieved himself. From there he walked to the basin, drank two large pitchers of water, splashed some on his face, rubbed his bleary eyes, and headed back to his bed. Halfway across the room, he froze. Three thoughts instantly flooded his mind. First, except for the stiff blanket that had become one with his back, he was standing there completely naked. Secondly, a wide-eyed, exhausted-looking Raisa was sitting on the far side of the bed. She'd just opened her eyes and was staring right at him. But instead of a look of horrified embarrassment, she wore a strange-looking smile. Third, his ema was sitting in the chair on the near side of the bed, and she was giving him *the look.*

Kalev was instantly mortified and groaned. He stiffly backpeddled to his closet. There were no loincloths, and he knew that without one, the tunic wouldn't completely cover his private parts. Still, he had to do something. Kalev quickly pulled the new, too-tight tunic over his head and down. *Big* mistake. As the gritty tunic scraped downward, it peeled off the blanket/bandage. This caused a cascade of fiery pain as the blanket was ripped away. He almost passed out from the pain and crumpled to his knees.

Raisa, Carni, and the three boys were instantly at his side. Though he allowed them to help him back to the side of his bed, Kalev knew that if he passed out again, he'd crush them all. On their way back to the bed, Raisa shot a mischievous smile at Carni. "Has your son always walked around the house naked?" The boys started giggling, and Carni laughed. "Not since he was eighteen." Kalev groaned.

They sat him down in the chair next to the bed. And, of course, this resulted in further exposing him to the world. The boys started belly laughing. The major loudly cleared her throat, pointed at the big door, and shot them her best *look.* The boys, remembering the agonizing bath they endured just three short days ago, abruptly stopped laughing and quickly raced out the door.

Carni pulled off the stained-down blanket, replaced it with three others, and added a soft pillow. Then Kalev's ema reached across the side table and grabbed the mixing bowl of very bitter turmeric, *shemshemet* (cannabis) herb, and crushed poppy seed paste. Without warning, she ladled a too large glob into Kalev's mouth. Before his brain had a chance to recognize the disgusting concoction, Carni forced him to gulp another pitcher of water.

The two small women could only guide the huge man to the side of the bed. Stiff with the deep aching pain, Kalev crawled to his pillow and laid on his stomach, unaware that he was completely exposing his back side.

Then, just when he thought this whole embarrassing debacle couldn't get any worse, Carni told Raisa where she could find a stack of *extra-large* loincloths. "He needs the support; these tunics just aren't long enough." Then Carni winked at Raisa. Kalev's eyes were closed in an attempt to stop the room from spinning. Still, he groaned, "Ema, stop."

Kalev didn't see the *very* pleased Raisa leave the room. So, when Carni crawled onto the softer bed and lifted the bottom edge of his tunic, Kalev growled even louder. "*Emaaaa*!" She crawled back to the side table and grabbed a very sharp knife. As she began to cut the tunic up the back, she growled, "Oh, suck it up, General. Raisa's seen you completely naked countless times in the last three days." Kalev roared even louder, "*Emaaaa*!" Then his head started spinning out of control, and his world went black.

Carni examined Kalev's wide-muscled back again. The darker wounds didn't seem to be healing. In fact, they were oozing even more milky fluid. Her son's burns were taking a greater toll on his body than she first thought. And for the hundredth time in three days, she started to both get mad and cry. Then the fiery ema in her took over, and she jumped to her feet and stood on the bed. The momma bear in her glared *the look* at the ceiling.

With one hand on her hip, she pointed up and screamed, "I don't know what else to do! *Fix him*!" Carni flinched at the immediate, thunderous reply. "Yes, mam! Right away, mam! Anything else, Major Ema, mam?"

Carni's mouth hung open in the ensuing silence. Then she dropped her arm to her side, adjusted her robe, and cleared her throat. She started to say no. But instead, the typically audacious Hebrew ema went for broke. "Yes, there *is* one more thing. Find Hoshe'a a wife. I'm out of options."

And for another terrifying heartbeat, there was total silence. Carni grimaced. Now she knew she'd crossed the line. Then, the Yeshua, the Creator of everything, the bringer of terrible plagues, actually cleared His throat. "Hmmm, that's a hard one, even for Me. But I'll work on it." The deafening laughter seemed to boom from everywhere. Carni decided to not push her luck. So as the laughter continued, she finished removing the tunic.

The next morning, Carni opened one eye to check on her son. But all she saw was Raisa fitfully sleeping in the chair on the opposite side. She leaped to her feet and scanned the room. Afraid he'd passed out again, Carni ran to the toilet room, but it was empty. She yelled to Raisa. "Where is he?"

Kalev was very thirsty and extremely hungry. He realized the morning meal was served over an hour ago, so he headed to the kitchen to see if there were any left overs. The teenage girl pounding a lump of dough looked up in surprise. "Sir, you're alive—I mean, I heard you were almost; I mean, I heard you were really sick." The Commanding General smiled. "Well, I didn't die. I'm feeling a lot better, and I'm starving!" The girl nodded. "Yes, Sir, we have fresh loaves of barley, sweet and date bread almost ready to come out of the ovens. I'll bring them over as soon as possible." Kalev smiled. "Thank you."

He turned just in time to see a very small pair of legs disappear under a table. Kalev turned back to the girl, pointed over his shoulder, and whispered. "Could you bring twice as many loaves and three additional plates?" She knowingly smiled. "Of course, Sir. And, Sir, um, I wanted to thank you for treating my uncle's body with so much respect. It means a lot to our whole family." The big man swallowed hard. "You're, uh, welcome? I wish I could have protected them…" The girl's stare was oddly piercing. "Sir, he and the rest of them are with Yahweh. And respectfully, Sir, your job is to get us all out of Egypt as soon as possible!" The wide-eyed girl gasped at her own audacity. Without another word, then turned and ran to the ovens.

Kalev was dumbfounded. Her words cut into his core like a knife. And yet, in a way, they sounded like a commission, like a direct order from the Warrior King. *Your job is to get us all out of Egypt as soon as possible*, he repeated in his head.

He was sitting at his usual table, brooding over the girl's statement when she and two others sat the five mounded plates and three deep mugs of beer in front of him. The young prophetess grew a guilty frown. Kalev wished he could remember her name. "Sir, I didn't mean to overstep—I mean, um…" Kalev smiled. "I want you to know, uh… My name is Arella, Sir." Kalev knowingly nodded. *Well, that figures…* he mused. *Her name means messenger*. That's when he saw her medallion. "Well, First Sergeant Arella, I heard what you said, and I think you're right. So please, if you have any more thoughts like that, I'd like to hear them. I can use all the help I can get." She smiled with relief. Kalev looked down at all the food, then back up at her quizzically. Arella shrugged and smiled. "Sir, you did say you were starving." Then she pointed down at the table. The girls hurried away giggling.

Kalev pushed one plate to the other side of the table, then moved one to each side. He pulled the other two close and tore into the loaves. He inhaled the first two loaves, then with his mouth still full, he loudly mumbled, "There's too much sweetbread here. I can't eat it all; what a waste." The General purposely didn't look up from his food when the three boys appeared behind their plates.

He ate in silence for another couple of minutes. Then, for some unknown reason, he mumbled the word "mohar." Kalev stopped chewing and actually pushed his plates to the center of the table. He'd just lost his appetite. The General rested his chin on his hand and thought out loud, "I can't marry her without a mohar. I have no more money. I only own a few acres and ox…" His voice slowed as his mind feverishly tried to find a solution. "I have no money. I own fourteen acres and one ox…"

Kalev was so lost in thought that he didn't see the boys push *their* plates away and strike the same thoughtful pose. Right then, the panicked Carni and Raisa came barreling out of the hall onto the main deck. Carni grabbed Raisa's arm and pulled her to an abrupt stop. Raisa rounded on her future mother with a scowl. The little ema was grinning when she reached up and gently turned Raisa's chin toward the dining area. Raisa's tired eyes began to tear up. "Just when I thought I couldn't love him more, I see him with those boys and…" Her voice trailed off. Carni nodded. "Daughter, cherish him and protect that tender heart like a mother bear." Rasia hugged Carni. "I will. I promise."

"…I have no money. I own fourteen acres…" Little Frog slapped the table and yelled, "I got it!" Kalev tried to act surprised. "Whoa, where did you three secret and dangerous troops come from? I thought I was alone." Little Yoshiyah smiled. "That is our mission, Sir. We're supposed to be secret and dangerous. Sergeant Abraham said so."

Kalev had to clear his throat a couple of times to keep from laughing. Little Croc quickly stood on the bench and jabbed his finger in front of Kalev's face at Little Frog. "But he made you see us." The little boy looked at his hands and sniffed. "I'm sorry, Sir. I didn't stay secret." Then he looked up at Croc with a defiant glare. "But I'm still more dangerous than you."

Before Kalev could tell them not to, the two boys drew their scimitars. Little Frog's sword came so close to Kalev's ear that he felt the wind whistle by. Kalev grimaced then growled. "You're both very dangerous. Now put those away." Kalev heard muffled laughing coming from across the table. Little Yoshiyah had resumed eating and was really enjoying the show.

As usual, by the time Croc and Frog sat back down and resumed eating, they'd forgotten all about the fight. Kalev watched all three boys pack the bread into their mouths. *They'd give Hoshe'a a run for his money*, he thought. "So, Little Frog, you have a solution for my mohar dilemma?" The little guy stared up at his general like the giant was speaking another language. Kalev laughed. "…I have no money…I own fourteen acres…and one ox…" The boy slapped the table again. "I got it, Sir." Then he smiled at Little Croc and continued eating. Kalev glanced across the table at the smiling Little Yoshiyah. The boy sipped his beer, belched, shrugged, then stated, "He gots it, Sir." Kalev growled, "Little Frog, what do you *got*?" The boy smiled. "You have a treasure room, Sir." "Oh yeah," yelled Little Croc, "his treasure room. That has lots of mohars in it!" Kalev chuckled as he stood. He told the boys he needed to check on the rabbi and General Ari. Then they could show him the "treasure room."

When Kalev looked in on Nachshon, the still-wheezing man was sleeping. He assumed the girl sitting at the small side table was one of Carni's medics. The older girl quietly stood at attention. The General whispered, "At ease. How is he?" She nodded. "He's fine, Sir. He was up and walking around today, but he tires out pretty quickly. I was the first one to treat his burns and get him cleaned up. I sort of got used to the peace and quiet in here. Plus, Major Raisa appreciates my staying with him. It gives me time to write my stories too." *So now* she's *a major*, he thought. Kalev smiled. "Well, keep up the good work, uh…" She reached into her robe and pulled out the medallion hanging around her neck. "I'm *Morasha* (legacy), First Sergeant." He smiled. "Well, thank you, First Sergeant."

Kalev almost left, but then he remembered that in one-on-one situations like this he needed to slow down. "So what are your stories about?" She beamed. "They're about you, Sir." Kalev blushed. "Me?"

Kalev was reluctantly learning from his ema that the typical young girl was usually overly dramatic and emotionally volatile. They tended to talk too fast and seemingly in one breath. This girl was no different. Kalev let out a long breath and prepared for the verbal onslaught. Sergeant Morasha got excited and very animated.

"Yes, Sir, I'm writing down all the *sabas'* and savtas' stories about why you are a hero, then I'm chronicling all the first-hand accounts about the first day you became our general and almost killed General Ari and how you named Little Frog, Little Croc, and Little Yoshi and how you saved Little Frog from being eaten by the giant crocs chasing the frogs and how you created the animal army, and then you went to Sha'al and killed all the sha'dims, and three days ago you ran into a raging fire and rescued my rabbi like a real hero. I guess I'm the right girl for the job since I was an orphan and I never had a name until I met Major Raisa and her brother, Sergeant Othniel, and the Rabbi about seven years ago; that's when Rabbi Nachshon here named me Morasha and said that one day I would chronicle the legacy of a great man who was marked as true to Yahweh and he and his brother would lead a great army and kill all the people who stole our land, so I'm writing about your legacy and stuff like that, Sir."

Kalev had to consciously remember to close his mouth. *How did she do that?* he wondered. *And how did the rabbi know seven years ago about the army? And that I'd decide that Yahweh was real and He was good. Not to mention the branding.*

Except for putting on his Commanding General persona, he hated being the center of attention. He was anything but a hero. Yet that girl's proud smile kept him from objecting. The huge man awkwardly shrugged and stammered, "Uh, um…okay, um, good work, carry on." He moved to shut the door, then had a thought. "Have you met Colonel Yadin?" The girl's face flushed, and she started a nervous giggle. General quickly shut the door and then self-consciously headed toward Ari's room.

Kalev took a minute to collect his racing thoughts, then knocked on Ari's door. When he didn't hear a reply, he slowly opened it. "Ari?" "Yes, Sir, come in," replied a very raspy voice. It was the first time he'd been in Ari's room. Kalev lit another torch. The boy looked fifty years older. Dark circles ringed his sunken eyes, and he looked gaunt. "Son, when was the last time you ate?" Ari shrugged. "I'm not hungry, Sir." Kalev grabbed a chair and took it to the boy's bedside. He used his foot to push the filthy pile of clothes away. He knew they probably reeked of burnt flesh, but at the moment, his nose wasn't working very well.

Kalev stared into his friend's vacant eyes. "You know, your father was my mentor. We spent hours talking tactics, strategies, and war mindsets…but, Ari, his eyes would always light up when we talked about you. You were his reason for living. The thought of you got him through some pretty tough times…" Kalev paused, then realized the boy was actively listening. "Ari, he made me promise, or, rather, he forcefully 'asked' me to watch over you if anything happened to him. And we both know that when Adir 'asks' like that, there is only one right answer." This made Ari smile. "He can be rather, um, influential." Kalev chuckled. "And then there was your savta. Did you know she saved my life?" Ari's eyebrows shot up. "Yep, she was the one who orchestrated my final escape from the pits. I would be dead without her. And yes, at times, her unlimited stories about you and your childhood adventures made me want to whip *myself* senseless." Ari laughed for the first time in days. "The funny thing is, Sir, she was always repeating those same stories to me, too, and I was there." They both laughed. After a short pause, Kalev said, "Ari, the truth is this pain will never go away. It will dull with time, but you'll always yearn to see them again." Ari nodded. "It really hurts, Sir." Kalev squeezed the boy's hand. "I know, son. I really know." Kalev's eyes started to water.

Then he had a distracting thought and stood up. "Hey, I was wondering if you'd stand with me and Hoshe'a at my wedding." Kalev conspiratorially looked around the room and then whispered, "I'd like to go and get my bride in six days." Ari smiled. "It'd be an honor, Sir." Kalev pretended to wrinkle his nose. "Son, you'll have to bathe first—at least a couple of times between now and then." Ari self-consciously smelled his armpit, then grimaced. Kalev nodded. "Yeah, I'm pretty sure Ox would be offended." The teen laughed even harder. Kalev stood and lit four more torches around the room.

Ari swung his legs over the side of the bed. "Um, Sir, if you don't mind me asking, what have you decided to give the rabbi for the mohar?" Kalev sat down again. "Yeah, about that. I, um, I don't really own anything except my swords, some land, and Ox. Ari smirked. "So you don't have Raisa's *Mattan* either?" Kalev scowled at his hands and shook his head. "I ran out of money a while ago, and…" Ari reached over and put a hand on his General's rock-hard shoulder. "Sir, you have a treasure room!" Kalev doubtfully smirked. "Yeah, the boys said something about that." "Give me a minute to clean up, and I'll show you." Kalev playfully wrinkled his nose again. "Ari, son, please take five minutes." They both laughed again.

37

When Ari disappeared into his toilet/tub room, Kalev stuck his head out the door. Five wide-eyed girls abruptly stopped trying to console their sobbing friend. They all stiffened to attention, saluted, and just stared at him. The General swallowed his smile and barked. "General Ari is cleaning up. He needs food, wine, and water. Light the other torches in here, change his sheets and blankets, and burn that pile of clothes…" The girls glanced a Deborah. Then Kalev barked even louder. "Now!" He stepped into the hall and three of the girls rushed past him into the room. The other two sprinted toward the kitchen.

Kalev let his smile bleed through his stern expression. He sensed this disheveled-looking girl had barely left Ari's side. "At ease, uh…" He couldn't see her rank. The exhausted Deborah, with tears and snot running down her face, smiled, then reached into her robe and uncovered the medallion hanging around her neck. "Deborah, Sir. Captain."

She wiped her face on her sleeve. But before Kalev could continue, the girl exploded with another round of crying. The General sighed. *And so it starts*, he thought. Once again, he could barely understand the rushed words as she mumbled through her tears. "I couldn't…two straight days and nights…smelled so bad…I didn't know…love him…else to do!" Then, too exhausted to care about decorum, the female captain raced forward, hugged her stunned Commanding General, and sobbed even louder.

The shocked Kalev just stood there with his hands at his sides. He didn't know what to do. The only female emotions he grew up with were either Ema's anger or her laughter. Those were easy because they were the only two reactions he allowed himself… *Until the breathtaking Raisa stepped into your world*, he thought. So this "emotional mess" was way out of his AO. Not sure what to do, he hesitantly reached down and squeezed her shoulder, hoping this was a sign he cared.

Unfortunately, he forgot about his iron grip. The girl yelped and pushed away. "Owww," she screamed. Kalev tripped over his tongue, awkwardly trying to apologize. Then the embarrassed Commanding General unconsciously reached over, slapped the back of his own hand, and scowled at it. "Stupid, stupid hand!" The surprised girl started laughing. Regrettably, she leaned forward and hugged him again. "I never knew my abba. I mean, you're like our abba—I mean, thank you for caring, Sir, and uh, thank you for helping Ari. I mean, *General* Ari…"

From the end of the hall, a familiar voice angrily cleared her throat. Kalev turned to see the two most important women in his life. They were both standing there, hands on hips, giving *him the look*. Kalev groaned inwardly. *Raisa shouldn't be giving me* the look *too!* Then, for some unknown reason, the memory of Ema catching him putting a freshly squished mouse under Hoshe'a's pillow flashed through his mind. Thus, his rapid-fire explanation sounded more like a nine-year-old's "You just got caught, and

Hoshe'a's not around to blame" excuse.

"Um, Ari's up and bathing; he needs to eat, and they're changing his sheets, and Deborah started crying—then I didn't know what to do, so I squeezed her shoulder to help her stop, but I squeezed it too tight, so then she squealed, and I slapped my stupid hand, and she started laughing and hugging again and…" Kalev suddenly realized how idiotic he sounded and abruptly stopped.

To Raisa, her "husband" had never looked more innocently cuter than he did at that very moment. The few seconds of silence made Kalev want to repeat the explanation using his "adult words."

Then Carni scowled at Raisa, and they both started laughing. Seeing the puzzled look on her huge little man's face, Raisa mindlessly squealed like a little girl, sprinted, and leaped into his arms. Then, before her brain could catch up, she kissed him hard.

The forty-year-old man's ema understood her son. She knew this whole experience was new and exciting for Kalev. She also knew from her own recently heartbreaking romance with Adir that this could get out of hand in two minutes or less. And what was worse—they had a growing audience.

Major Carni snapped her fingers and forcefully pointed toward the kitchen. Sensing the approaching storm and anxious to learn how to kiss a boy, Deborah and her five friends had already ducked inside of Ari's room. Six pairs of eyes silently watched the romantic display through a crack in the door. Though they kept looking back and quietly giggled, the forty-seven other girls raced for the kitchen. The ensuing discussion and unofficial stream of gossip lasted for a week and filtered through the population of teenage troops.

The trio of boys finished eating both theirs and the rest of the General's bread. Seeing the growing crowd of "stupid" girls crowding the hallway, the boys decided to show Little Yoshi the "secret door" to the very dark, opposite end of General Ari's passageway. Now they were watching the whole "stupid girl crying and kissing show" in complete disgust.

About thirty seconds into the increasingly passionate kiss, Carni walked up and tapped Kalev's arm. The son of Hezron was *really* enjoying the kiss, but he still didn't know to close his eyes. So, when Carni tapped his arm, he continued kissing Raisa but shifted his gaze to Carni. That one little eye movement, observed by the six gawking girls, became a source of laughter for the next five decades. And it quickly made its way into Sergeant Morasha's stories.

Raisa's beautiful blue eyes fluttered open, and a pleasantly shocked expression raced across her flushed face. As Kalev reluctantly put her down, he innocently grew his crooked smile and shrugged at Carni. "What?"

Major Carni stiffened her back, pointed her finger in his face, and yelled, "Not until you're married!" Kalev shrugged, and before he could stop himself, he blurted out, "So until we're married, we should only act like *close friends*?" Carni's eyes went wide, then just as quickly narrowed into the meanest *look*

Kalev could remember. "Hoshe'aaaa," she growled. Kalev strained to look disappointed, then somberly nodded.

Hoshe'a's younger brother knew it was childish. But since the first time he'd convinced Ema that it was Hoshe'a's fault the barn almost burned down, he just couldn't help himself. It was irrelevant that Hoshe'a was actually a quarter mile away fishing when that fire started. Shifting the blame became a source of enjoyment that always warmed his hard heart. It was just a close-brother thing!

So the adult brother stood there slowly shaking his head. "Ema, don't blame Hoshe'a; it's not really his fault. Lately he's been so lonely that he's not thinking straight." Kalev felt Raisa try to pinch the back of his arm again, which only made it harder not to smile. Carni growled. "Arghh. I told Yahweh to find him a wife, so He'd better step it up."

Kalev wasn't sure if anyone else could hear, but the Warrior King's voice boomed around him. "Wow, she *is* intimidating, isn't she! I guess I'd better *step it up* and find that boy a wife!" The booming laughter was so intense, Kalev had to put his face in his hands just to hide his smile. But to Carni it looked like Kalev was trying not to cry.

The always protective ema put her hand on his arm. "It's okay, little one." It took a second before Kalev realized he could push this childish advantage a lot further. Keeping his face in his hands, he slowly shook his head. "No, Ema, it's all my fault; Hoshe'a even said so." Kalev barely split his fingers to check Carni's expression. Yep, he was headed in the right direction.

Carni's despondent looking younger son dropped his hands and sighed. "In fact, last week, in front of my whole senior staff, he lost it. He stood on the table and got in my face. He actually screamed that it wasn't fair and I shouldn't get married before him. Then he took my knife and held it to his throat and swore that if I went through with the marriage, he'd kill himself." Kalev paused for effect, raised his hands to his face again, and shook his head. "Oh Ema…I don't know what to do; I just don't know…"

Then to seal Hoshe'a's fate, Kalev's head snapped up. He resolutely squared his shoulders like he'd made a decision. Kalev slightly turned so he could address Ema and Raisa at the same time. "I'm sorry, Raisa; we can't get married if it will kill my big brother." A soft chorus of gasps came from the cracked door. Thankfully no one heard.

Both women's jaws dropped. Carni was the first to recover. She pointed at Kalev. "You two wait right here. There *will* be a wedding. Wait right here. *Don't move*!"

Carni ran screaming a long string of uninterrupted garbled words as she ran, then climbed the closest ladder. The only words Kalev could decipher were "Hoshe'a…cut it off." Kalev waited until his raging ema was halfway up the ladder before he busted out laughing. He looked down at Raisa; she looked like she was about to cry.

"Were you serious about not getting married?" Kalev grinned. "Of course not!" They didn't hear the soft relieved sigh coming from the door. Kalev picked his soon-to-be bride up in his arms. But she put her hands on his chest and leaned back. “Wait, does she fall for that every time?” Kalev grinned. “Let’s see. I was five, and now I’m forty…yep, so far!” They’d just started kissing again when they heard Ari inside his room, “Hey, great bread, and why are you peeking through my door?”

38

The *very* frustrated General reluctantly put Raisa down when the six guilty-looking girls and Ari filed into the hall. The teenage general had a loaf in each hand; his mouth was full, but he wasn't chewing. He was staring at Deborah with that lost-little-boy look. But the six girls were excitedly smiling at Raisa. Kalev cleared his throat. "Um, *Major* Raisa…" She winked at the other girls, then smiled up at *her* man. He leaned down and quietly whispered, "So who made you a major?"

The breathtaking, short woman raised up on her toes, and for the other girls' benefit, Raisa made a show of slowly kissing his ear. Kalev shivered as the wonderful sensation sped from his earlobe south… too far south. Raisa breathily whispered, "Your ema…" The shivering instantly ceased. Kalev growled something colorful under his breath, then mentally tabled the "major" issue for another time.

To the eighteen-year-old Ari, Deborah was the most beautiful fourteen-year-old woman on earth. Halfheartedly, the newly orphaned general forced himself out of his wonderful daydreaming. He swallowed the bite of bread and got back to business. "Excuse me, General, Sir!" I believe we have a senior staff meet…" But before he could finish, Raisa spun around, tapped Kalev's abs four times, and then the seven screaming and laughing females raced for the kitchen. They were met by even louder screaming and laughing. Ari quizzically smiled at Kalev but remained silent. Kalev winked. "General Ari, as your commanding officer, I highly recommend kissing!" Kalev glanced at his stomach. "But I still don't get this petting me like a puppy thing."

Instantly, a sequence of loud little-boy critiques echoed from the darkness at the far end of the hall. "Yuk…girls are stupid…is that what a kiss looks like…yuk…he should wash his lips off…Ox doesn't even kiss the girl *oxes*; he just…" When Kalev snapped his fingers in the narrow passageway, the deafening sound scared the boys into silence. The boys would later *swear* to Sergeant Morasha that when they'd come running, the glaring general's eyes actually burnt holes in their tunics.

Halfway across the drill floor, they stopped as they were joined by the three colonels and a wary-looking Hoshe'a. While the trio of little boys argued over who had to kiss a girl first, the others gave Ari manly hugs and briefly brought him up to speed on the latest reports. The worried-looking Hoshe'a pulled Kalev aside a few steps. He kept looking around as he spoke, "I heard Ema was hunting for me, and I mean *hunting*!" Then he locked suspicious eyes with Kalev. "What did you tell her?" Kalev innocently shrugged. "All I said is that I wouldn't get married without my big brother's approval, and you'd be hurt if I didn't ask." Hoshe'a looked confused. "Why would that make her so angry?" Kalev shrugged again. "You know Ema; she always thinks *her* approval is all that matters." That seemed to make sense to his big brother. "Yeah, she's been ranting about giving up on trying to find me a wife. Like I need her help."

They both laughed, but for different reasons. “Yeah, I told her I’d rather slit my throat than get stuck with a nagging shrew.”

Kalev’s eyes went wide. “Wow, that was, um, brave. How did that go over?” Hoshe’a shrugged. “I’ll let you know. I said it just before I escaped into the desert. I’ve been dodging her for the last three days.” Kalev smiled. “I’m sure that’s the reason she’s mad. So, big brother, *will* you stand with me at my wedding ceremony?” Hoshe’a smiled. “Of course I will. We’ve always been there for each other. It’d be an honor.” They hugged and Kalev started laughing again.

As they all started walking toward the TOC, Hoshe’a glanced over his shoulder at the smiling teens and quickly deduced what was happening. He started chuckling. “So, General, have you figured out your mohar and *Mattan* dilemma yet?” Kalev scowled. “I spent all the money I had left on battle lessons. So I’m left with my swords and/or Ox. Other than that…” He shook his head in disgust. “I should have planned ahead and saved something. But I never thought—I mean, she just told…arghh!” Everybody else laughed.

Kalev started to enter the TOC when his senior officers and the boys sprinted past the double doors. The loud echoes of slapping sandals ceased as they slid to a stop at the far dead-end. The unsuspecting Little Yoshi kept running, then just disappeared. Kalev stared at the slyly grinning teens, then wordlessly scowled at his brother. “So was I supposed to walk down there and disappear into a secret hole in the floor or something?” Hoshe’a laughed. “As a security measure, I redesigned this side of the Pit after I realized that if the paneling and hall torches were set at the right angle, the passageway would appear to dead-end. And in the Fortress, I upgraded the same hallways to look like they were slanting up and shrinking before they stopped.” “Wow, that’s amazing—one of your inventions really worked.” Kalev playfully punched Hoshe’a’s arm, sending his 150-pound brother into the wall. “Oww, Kalev, stop it.” As they started down the passageway, Hoshe’a grew a mischievous grin. “Oh, did I mention I may have installed a few of my latest man trap ‘inventions’? Just for extra security, of course.” Kalev froze, and laughter erupted from the far end of the hall.

Ever since they were kids, Hoshe’a had really enjoyed tricking Kalev into trying out his new inventions/practical jokes. Which usually didn’t end so well. *Okay*, he thought, *they were always a disaster*. And a few, *allegedly*, almost got Kalev killed. But the real downside was that Ema always seemed to know, and he was always getting blamed for it. Still, to this day, it gave him a warm feeling when he completely surprised, disgusted, or scared his little brother. Hoshe’a had always assumed “it was just a close-brother thing!”

When they reached the far end of the hall, Kalev was astonished to see that what looked like a dead end was actually a T intersection. The wide-eyed general stared to his immediate right then left. Hoshe’a proudly started his too-technical description. “This horizontal hallway runs for exactly a hundred yards in both directions. I experimented with this type of vaulted ceiling, then later incorporated the design into the…" Kalev was really impressed, so he let his brother jabber on. "…can see, it's eighteen feet taller and wider than the hallway behind us. At the time, I was thinking these rooms could be used as barracks for the senior enlisted troops and/or different-sized animal stalls. In the Fortress, we extended the southern running passage an additional 175 yards…" Hoshe'a smiled at Yadin and nodded. The fidgeting kid looked like his head was ready to burst. Ari and the other two colonels strained not to laugh when their friend exploded with a string of rapid-fire details.

"The Fortress' northern running hallway has two levels of different-sized rooms on both sides of the passage. The southern passage has the same two levels of rooms running the entire length. However, the southern running wing includes 340 rooms. Each room is a uniform eight-foot high by fifteen-foot wide by twenty-foot deep. They all have their own sinks with running water. One hundred of the ground-level rooms, fifty on each side, are either occupied or reserved for junior-grade officers. The senior enlisted occupy the rest. Specific toilet and bathing trough rooms are evenly spaced between every sixth senior enlisted room. The…" Kalev held up his hand. "Colonel Yadin." The kid's face went red. "I truly appreciate your amazingly precise details. You and Major Hoshe'a…"

Kalev turned to include his brother. But he was gone. He looked at Ari, who shrugged. Akiba started laughing. "I guess Major Carni really has him spooked. Sir, would she really hurt him, or is he just, um, different around her?" Kalev winked at Yadin to let him know he hadn't forgotten him. Then the General forced a serious expression. "Honestly, Colonel Akiba, I believe that question has a twofold answer. First, Major Carni is a force of nature. And when she's in her 'attitude adjustment' mode… well, let's just say that fire ice storm was minor in comparison." The trio of serious little boys nodded their confirmation. Everyone else laughed. Kalev turned back to Yadin. "Now…" Ari interrupted. "I'm sorry, Sir—what was the second half of your answer?" Kalev innocently shrugged. "From the bits of information I've been able to piece together over the years and from my extensive observation. I have determined that when Major Hoshe'a was a baby, Major Carni may or may not have dropped him on his head…more than once." The teens glanced at each other, wondering if it was true, then back at their smiling general. At the same time, Little Yoshi punched Little Frog in the arm. "Told ya!" The entire Pit probably heard the peals of screaming laughter.

Once Kalev and the teens could catch their breath, the General motioned for Yadin to follow him. They walked halfway back to the TOC. Kalev smiled apologetically, then whispered, "Colonel, I'd like to tell you something in confidence." He waited for the seventeen-year-old genius to nod. "Son, maybe it's because I've literally been kicked in the head to many times. Or maybe it's because I wasn't very smart in the first place. I mean, okay, when it comes to farming, from the amount of wheat seed needed per acre to how early to plant corn to get the greatest yield etc., I can keep up." Kalev cocked his head toward the others. “But honestly, we’ll *never* be able to reach your level of intelligence. And frankly you intimidate the rest of us. You’ve been blessed with a gift, son. I might make fun of him, but my brother is the only other person I’ve ever met that could even come close to your multilevel thinking. This army needs that brain of yours. It won’t survive without you. So the next time you have a report, or you’re just answering a question, please remember to dumb down your answers and keep them short for the rest of us intellectually insecure people…does that make sense?” Yadin somberly nodded, then grew a pained expression. “I thought I was already doing that.” If Kalev hadn’t seen the boy’s confused expression, he’d already be laughing.

The General paused and looked at the ground. “Okay, think of it this way. How many unnatural instructions do you think Ox can respond to?” Yadin actually looked at the ceiling and started mumbling some kind of calculations. Kalev bit his tongue so hard that his eyes started to water. The General cleared his throat. “Let me help you. He can only respond to two. And remember, you have to think like an ox.” Yadin scowled and then nodded. Kalev was surprised when the boy actually pulled a quill and ink jar from his pocket and began writing on the wall.

“(1) The first direction an ox understands is when the goad slaps your hind quarter, you move forward until the nose ring is pulled back. (2) When the nose ring is pulled, it hurts your nose, so you follow the nose ring in the direction it’s pulled until your nose stops hurting and/or the goad slaps your hind quarter again. And that’s it.” Yadin actually glanced back and hooked his thumb toward his friends. “Well, that explains a lot.” Kalev chuckled. “Try not to sound *too* patronizing when you talk to us oxen…Oh, and when you are discussing things with my brother, consider this. He may smell like a jackass and bray like a jackass, but he understands like an expertly trained stallion.” Kalev was on a roll. “So to summarize, when speaking to the common man, simplify to a livestock level of intelligence. That is until you meet your match. And since I know you’ll remember, store this additional little piece of life-changing ox wisdom in your reference list. (1) If you meet that special girl, she may or may not be your intellectual equal, but she is always right. (2) Even if she’s not correct, she’s right and should not, under any circumstances, be told she’s wrong. (3) When in doubt, default to 1 and 2.”

Kalev’s eyes were tired, so he hadn’t tried to read Yadin’s smaller writing until the boy finished. Kalev squinted. The title read, “Animal Wisdom for the Human Ox. According to General Kalev, Supreme Commanding General of Yisrael’s Army.”

Kalev knew most people would probably be offended. But he was kind of proud. Yadin turned, read the General’s face, and smiled. “Would you like to sign it, Sir?” Kalev grinned. “Sure.” The colonel bent down, wrote two more statements, then drew a line at the bottom. “Sign on top of that line, Sir.” The son of Hezron dipped the quill and signed his name, then read the final two statements above his signature. “I am Kalev, the Supreme Commanding General of Yisrael’s Army. And I approved this message!”

When they rejoined the others at the hallway intersection, Kalev smiled. "So I assume we're here because there's some surplus I could scrounge to use for my mohar." They all laughed. The General figured there were a couple more tunics and a sword blank he could grind and engrave for Nachshon. And maybe he could dig out some fabric for Raisa to sew a dress.

Once the others had finished laughing, the embarrassed Kalev shrugged. "I'm not sure when, but I'll pay for whatever I can find." Oddly, they started laughing again. Ari motioned to the trios of eager younger and older boys. "Men, open the doors and light the torches." Kalev started to walk forward, but Ari stopped him. "Sir, let's allow them to light it up first." He pointed down the hall in the other direction. They walked that way, then stopped next to the first closed door.

"This is our southwestern wing. We're using those first five larger rooms on the left side for food storage. They were built with ramps down to spaces ten feet below this level. Major Hoshe'a said it's consistently cooler down there. These first two rooms on the right store the initial clothing and bedding issue for each new recruit."

Kalev noticed bright torchlight glowing from the furthest rooms on each side. Ari nodded. "The last room on the left is our 'meat room.' Yadin and Major Hoshe'a built it large enough to butcher seven aurochs or sixteen sheep at a time. I think Yadin said the room is eighteen feet high by forty-five feet wide by sixty feet deep. In the rear, it has a wide gated and curvy passageway out to the main corral. That's the one closest to the ramp. The cattle and sheep are funneled into the butcher's area one at a time. They're killed, hung, bled, skinned, and cut up. We use the unusable parts of the remains as croc bait. We started catching so many crocs every night, we had nowhere to store the excess meat. Besides, the meat doesn't keep well. So we've limited the nearby baiting to once every week. Otherwise we float the carcasses into the main part of the river before we dump them in the water. I swear every croc in Egypt must have gotten the word there was free food in Goshen.

"Anyway, the majority of the butchered beef is brought out that door and either put in the short-term, cooled storage room or cut into thin twelve-inch strips, salted, then dried on those long racks behind the ovens. When we have enough dried strips, we seal the dried beef or mutton strips into urns or old wine barrels. Most of the time, the beef steaks or lamb are wheeled straight to the kitchen. At this point, three abbas periodically butcher for us when they can. They trained four squads from Aleph Company. And those troops have done an excellent job. As an incentive to excel and recruit others, once a week, at the end of their shifts, the 'meat room butcher squads' are allowed to cut any size of choice steak and take it to the kitchen to be cooked. And just to make the point, it's usually on the night everyone else is eating fish or croc. The Fortress has kind of the same setup. But they prepare all the fish and/or croc meat and produce. Major Carni and a couple of her girls determine what food is distributed to which outpost.

"The room next to the 'beef room' is where the hooves, horns, and untanned hides are kept until they can be worked. It's fascinating to watch the whole process *if* you have the time." Kalev distractedly smirked, and Ari nodded. "Yeah, me either."

The too-thin-looking teen general looked over his shoulder. "They're almost ready for us." Then he continued his visual tour. "We're using two of the larger rooms on the right to make and store the beer. Those rooms have larger air intake and exhaust vents. Yadin's production lines are incredible. The 'brew squads' mix the beer, cook, cool, and allow it to ferment two weeks before it's used. And, of course, Yadin has calculated how much they need to increase production according to the number of troops added every week. That includes enough extra to fill five five-foot-tall urns every ten days. Those are sealed and stored with the wineskins and urns. Sir, as you know, we had our annual grape harvest and celebration three months ago." Kalev nodded. "Did you also know that those same fifteen-year-old vines yielded seven times more this year than ever before?" Kalev didn't know that. "Seven times?" Kalev did the "farm math" in his head. "After crushing and straining, that would produce over 7700 gallons." Ari looked surprised. "Yes, Sir, Yadin said we ended up with 7707 gallons. It's the best wine *I've* ever tasted."

Ari laughed. "Yadin wanted to see what would happen if he added a cake of yeast to one of the largest urns of wine. The problem was one of his troops sealed the jar and stored it in the beer room close enough to the brewing fire to keep it warm. At the time you were still sleeping in that stall. We figure it had fermented five days before the subsequent explosion. It shook the whole Pit so hard we thought the roof would cave in. Luckily it was during the evening meal, so no one was killed. It took three straight days to clean up the mess. If you look, the pockmarked walls were stained a deep purple. But since then, your brother, I mean, Major Hoshe'a, designed and built a well-ventilated 'wine vault.' He and Yadin are the only ones allowed in there. They ferment the viper wine for three weeks. Yadin keeps the jars covered with the heavy sail cloth and punches holes in it." "How's that going?" Kalev asked. Ari wrinkled his nose and shrugged. "Major Hoshe'a tasted the first batch and coughed so hard that we thought he was going to puke right there. On the spot he ordered the production of the 'viper wine,' as he named it, to be doubled and limited its use for eighteen-year-olds and over. Personally, I don't like the smell or the taste. It burns the inside of my nose and all the way down my throat." Kalev smiled. "I'll have to try some. Maybe when I meet the rabbi, I can get him looped enough to accept my meager mohar." They both laughed. But for different reasons.

Ari pointed to the last room on the right. "That's the largest side area in the Pit. It's where Major Carni teaches and houses her medics, the cooks, the serving staff, and her *assault troops*." Kalev's eyebrows shot up. Ari shrugged. "We should probably talk about that one later. Plus, Sir, we need to talk about forming Aleph and Bet into their own battalions." Kalev nodded. "I like that idea. Please bring it up at the next command and staff."

Kalev anxiously looked over his shoulder. He needed to get scrounging as soon as possible. But Ari grew serious and cleared his throat. "Uh, Sir. First of all, I've felt guilty about not giving you the 'behind the scenes' details about the army's logistics and support functions. It wasn't my idea to keep it from you. My abba said we shouldn't add to your already full plate." Kalev was surprised. "Adir said that?" Ari nodded. Kalev thought about it. "Your abba is one of the wisest men I've ever met. If he said that, I accept his judgment, and *you* have nothing to feel guilty about." Ari looked relieved. "Sir, the main reason Major Hoshe'a, the colonels, and I wanted you to know this now is to preface what you're about to see." Now Kalev was intrigued.

"Sir, this army still exists because you sacrificed yourself for us and our families. Every troop here knows and trusts that their general will always be there and fight for them. In fact, most of them believe that was your main motivation for your preemptive attack on all of Sha'al." They both laughed as they started walking back toward the now brightly lit northeast passage.

"Sir, that said, we wanted you to understand that the Warrior King has and is providing everything we could ever need or even want." Kalev smirked at his friend. "I guess when you say 'everything,' you've included that girl Deborah." At the same time Ari's face turned bright red, the little boy trio heard Kalev's last question and yelled "yuk" in perfect unison.

The General stopped at the intersection and spoke to the boys in a dubious tone. "So, you three silent and very dangerous warriors, which one of these rooms is my treasure room?" Kalev chuckled. Little Croc quickly stepped in front of the other two. "General, Sir, all these rooms and all the stuff is yours. The room at the end is your treasure room. We all decided, so it's all yours. And you can't say no like Little Yoshi said you'd say 'cause we all decided, and it's all yours." Little Yoshi nudged him. Little Croc growled in disgust.

"And if you have to, you can share a little with that lady Raisa, but you didn't say she was a major, so she's just your friend, and Frog and me don't think we should salute her 'cause she's just your friend and only a pretty lady and not a major." Kalev glanced at Ari, who shrugged. "Again, it wasn't our decision. But he is right. Every troop in the army had a say in the decision to assign the surplus in those rooms for your use only. Your senior staff, Majors Hoshe'a and Carni, agreed you should use the contents of that farthest room for your mohar."

For the next half hour, Kalev became increasingly embarrassed as they progressed through each of the twelve storage rooms. Most were the size of the TOC or larger. The first two were filled to the ceiling with Persian rugs, hanging lamps, rigid camel canopies, horse tack and saddles, and wagon tack for the oxen.

One of the two largest rooms was crowded with unique-looking weapons. He recognized many of them from the ones hanging on his display wall. Ari and the colonels waited in the hall while the General and the boys went inside the foraged weapons room. The senior officers quietly discussed a few things then Yadin hurried away.

The General was inside admiring one of the Minoan iron shields when he felt a puff of air pass between his raised arm and his side. A twelve-inch dart with black feather fletchings buried its tip into the hard cedar wall in front of him. Kalev spun to see all three boys holding what looked like hollowed-out reeds that were taller than they were. Little Croc hit Frog in the arm. "I told you you'd miss the shield." "So I'm better with the bow." "No, you're not!" Kalev rolled his eyes, then leaned forward and wiggled the dart out of the wall. He held it up to reprimand the boys when he noticed a foul smell coming from the tip. It was dried human excrement. Kalev quickly jerked it away. He remembered Adir saying something about this type of weapon used by the Nubians.

The General glared down, then cringed when he saw that all three boys were wearing broad leather belts filled with the small, poisoned darts. And what was worse—the dart tips were exposed. "We're sorry, Sir," Little Yoshi whispered. "Don't move," Kalev warned. He walked over and carefully removed the leather belt from each boy. He grabbed the reeds, quickly walked to the back of the room, picked up a wide Persian carpet, and carefully rolled it all into a tight bundle. He bound the bundle with a long leather sword belt. Then he hung it on the highest display hook in the room.

The huge general glared down at the tearing boys and loudly roared, "Those darts are tipped with [illegible]. That makes them as poisonous as viper venom. You almost killed me." All three gasped, and the tears flowed in earnest. "Those will only be used after a specialized weapons training evolution. Do you understand me?" All three guilty-looking boys vigorously nodded. Then started pointing fingers and accusing each other of almost killing the General. And, as usual, that quickly devolved into a screaming fistfight. But Kalev had already left the room.

While a very loud Yadin got the melee under control and out of the area, Ari showed Kalev another room. It was filled to the ceiling with open trunks of exotic-looking female robes, tunics, face veils, sashes, an assortment of jeweled sandals, and other girl things he didn't recognize. Kalev stared at all the "girl clothes" and panicked.

Thankfully, that was when Carni walked in and put her arm in his. She knew that look too well and smiled. Kalev groaned. "I found Nachshon a few tunics and a coat…but Raisa's *Mattan*, um, Ema, I can't. I mean, I don't even know where to start…"

The little ema's smile broadened, and she tried to squeeze his rock-solid arm. "Don't worry, little one. I can help. It's what I do!" She looked over her shoulder. "General Ari, if you don't mind, could you find Captain Deborah and ask her to come and help me?" Ari's eyes went wide, and he wordlessly sprinted away.

Carni chuckled as she went back to her task. "Unless Yahweh can do one of His miracles for your brother, your General Ari is next on my list to get married." Kalev smirked. "You have a list?" Carni shot her youngest a sideways glance. "Son, I've always had a list. And lately, it's gotten so long that I had to ask Miriam for help." "Who's Miriam?" Carni shrugged. "A friend…"

Kalev wasn't sure if he was supposed to wait and approve the clothes or something, so he just sat on a tall stack of puffy, shiny blankets. He fiddled with a short bunch of folded cloths that were tied together at both ends.

"Kalev, do you recall seeing Raisa and I sitting in the dirt in front of a smoking pile of rags? I'm sure you remember that. It was just before my youngest son *stupidly* ran into that burning house to save Nachshon." Kalev nodded at Carni's back. "That pile of burnt rags was all that was left of her clothes, including her wedding dress. It was her ema's." Kalev groaned, "I didn't know that." "While you were healing—oh, I want to check your back later—Raisa told me she was scared that you wouldn't accept her because she didn't have the proper wedding dress." Kalev groaned again.

"That's stupid. I'd accept her naked." Carni whipped around and glared. Kalev tried to backtrack, "I mean, especially if she was naked. I mean, even if she didn't wear a dress, which I wouldn't mind—I think; I mean…arghh." Out in the hallway, Ari made the mistake of leaning over to Akiba and quietly whispering, "Our general needs to quit while he's behind or, rather, while he still *has* one." Both boys bit their tongues, sprinted into the next room, and slammed the door before they started laughing.

Carni turned back around before she smiled. Kalev scowled as he thought about it. He mindlessly picked up another bunch of bound rags and started slapping them against his cheeks trying to make different sounds. "Ema, listen, I meant that I want her to have the most beautiful dress you can find. And all the girl's clothes you can pack into three of those large trunks. Ari said there are three other storerooms you can search." "I'll be glad to, little one.

"By the way, have you seen your  brother?" Kalev was surprised and playfully gasped. "Ema, language." Carni stopped what she was doing, slowly turned, and gave him *the look*. "I'm sorry, but those were the kindest words that came to mind."

Her piercing glare intensified. "Now, have…you…seen…your brother?" Kalev knew his fiery little ema possessed special powers, and somehow she knew he had. "Yes, mam. I did see him." Carni turned back to her searching. "And!" He paused for a second, then grew his usual sly smile. "Well, if I remember right, before I told him you were looking for him, he did say he'd be honored to stand with me and Ari at the wedding. Then he started mumbling something about *not* needing your help to find a wife and that he'd rather kill himself than spend the rest of his life with another nagging, um, something. I really don't remember the rest."

As the grinning Commanding General watched, his ema white-knuckled the rim of the trunk in front of her, and her scrawny arms started shaking. Kalev smiled as he contentedly resumed slapping his cheeks with the little bundles.

Once Carni was able to calm herself, she looked over at her son. The little ema rolled her eyes and quickly walked over to her clueless little one. As Deborah walked in the door, she froze at the sight of Raisa's husband hitting himself in the face with the bound rags. Carni viciously grabbed the bundles out of his hands and leaned in. Deborah watched Carni whisper into the General's ear. The Commanding General of Yisrael's Army's face lost all color. The huge man was out of the room in two very fast steps.

Ari and Akiba opened the door and saw their general squatting against the wall and vigorously rubbing his cheeks. "Are you okay, Sir?" Kalev was mortified and quickly changed the subject. "So what's in that room?"

The high-ceilinged room contained a collection of forty large folds of colorful material and carved poles. Each one was bound in multiple coils of gold and silver braided rope. Ari smirked. "Little Croc said they were rich-man tents."

They finally made it to the thick door at the furthest end of the hall. But Kalev turned around, pointed, and addressed the two remaining teens. "Gentlemen, thank you for the gesture. But I can't possibly accept…"

Ari held up his hand. "I'm sorry to interrupt, Sir. But I'm not about to stand up at the next muster and tell all those troops you didn't agree with their *selfless* decision and you refused their *gift*." Kalev clinched his jaw and thought, *I hate it when he does that; he sounds too much like ema.* The General blew out a long breath. "Okay, I accept it all. I'll thank everyone at the next muster." Then he paused. "Since it's mine now, I want my senior staff to each have a tent, some clothes, and the weapons of their choice. We'll issue the rest as needed. And this isn't up for debate. Besides, from what I just heard…"

That's when Yadin slid a long flatbed cart sideways around the corner, bounced it off the wall, then rushed their way. Yadin ran behind, laughing at his friend. Once the other two arrived, Kalev smirked and then continued his gotcha moment. "As I was saying, based on Major Carni's latest unofficial report, you four better start thinking ahead about your *own* mohar and *Mattan*. You're all on 'Ema the *shadchan*'s' (matchmaker's) priority list." The General's senior staff's jaws dropped in unison. Kalev smiled. "Quite the *dilemma*, isn't it, boys?"

He was still laughing when he turned around and read the polished silver sign on the door. "General Kalev's Treasure Room." The subtitle read, "Keep out or silently die and be jackal food." Kalev laughed again. He wondered what the little boys had collected and called treasure. The General pulled the oversized door open, and his laughter caught in his throat. "Ohhh [illegible]." Yadin smirked. "Yes, Sir. Quite the dilemma indeed."

39

Kalev and the prince of the tribe of Yehudah sat at Kalev's favorite table. Each of them had a large cup of the incredibly strong wine. The rabbi greedily drank as they watched Raisa. She pounded the large lump of dough like she was trying to kill it. Kalev's open-mouthed stare made Nachshon smile. He could tell this man was respectfully scared of his daughter. The old rabbi leaned over and whispered, "I'd certainly be careful, but to me, ahh, son, to me, she's my priceless songbird." Nachshon reached over and lifted Kalev's chin to close his mouth. Only then did the captivated general respond to Nachshon's statement. "I agree, Sir…priceless…"

Kalev grinned as he raised his hand and held up three fingers. At the same time, both men jumped when they heard a loud crash and a long stream of Hebrew expletives echo from the kitchen.

Raisa, obviously frustrated about something, had pounded the dough so hard, a large urn of flour fell off the edge of the table. The resulting cloud of flour stuck to everything, including her sweaty face and dress. Her black hair was now a light gray.

But Kalev didn't see the mess; he only saw his very soon-to-be wife. His mind was so lost in her fiery blue eyes, he didn't even hear the high-pitched, not-so-ladylike expletives continue to cascade from her beautiful mouth. Apparently, the other girls knew exactly why she was in such a foul mood and wisely stayed away.

Eventually, the beautifully whitened Raisa resumed thrashing the persecuted lump of dough. The old man chuckled to himself. "Okay. Sometimes she's more like an angry bird of prey." Raisa finally placed the dough into the hot oven. She picked up two water jars and headed for the closest underground well.

The General had the increasingly tipsy rabbi turn around on his bench. The fully armed senior staff, followed by three bruised and bloodied boys whose weapons *shouldn't* have been unsheathed, formally marched the flatbed cart in front of Kalev and Nachshon. The teens and boys formed a single rank behind the cart, saluted, then marched a few tables down the line, sat, and watched the show.

A beaming Kalev caught sight of his ema, Raisa, Deborah, and that same sergeant peeking around the edge of a tall bread-cooling rack. They saw the proud General's one raised eyebrow and ducked out of sight. Still beaming, Kalev glanced down at the rabbi and literally stopped breathing. The instantly sobered prince of the Yehudah tribe was staring back with a horrified expression. He pointed a trembling finger at the cart.

"Who…are…they! And *why* are they here? Is this some kind of sick joke?" It took Kalev a couple of seconds to understand the question. Then the son of Hezron burst out laughing. He kind of had the same initial reaction.

A month ago, the boys had somehow convinced their new and much stronger squad leader to secure a donkey and cart so they could go on a "special, secret foraging mission." While they were out on their unsanctioned operation, they *found* four seven-foot sarcophaguses. The two boys and their squad leader somehow stacked the coffins onto the rickety cart and brought them back. Neither the boys nor their ex-squad leader thought to look inside and make sure they were empty. One wasn't. Yadin said he'd turned his back to reprimand the squad leader. When he turned back around, the five-pound, obviously female mummy and the two boys were gone. Yadin said he'd caught up with them at the river bank, but they'd already heaved the mummy into the water. As he retold the story, the colonel shook his head in amazement. "The two boneheads thought it would sink to the bottom and nobody would know. But, true to form, it didn't sink out of sight. In fact the thing floated upright halfway out of the water. It slowly danced up and down and spun around as it floated down stream. The colonel reported that he wanted to tear the pair a new one—he really did. Instead, the three of them silently watched the girl mummy dance away in the bright moonlight reflecting off the black water. It kind of looked alive, and it was having fun!" When it finally disappeared, Little Frog softly sang, "Goodbyyyye, ugly girl mummyyyy, goodbye tonight…"

The two boys were immediately assigned to "remedial" tanning duty. Kalev didn't realize the process included soaking and continuously stomping the skins in a bath of watery dung, cow urine, crushed acacia leaves, and bark. Each skin took three days. Though every new recruit was assigned the week-long Sha'alish duty, it served as a "less lethal" deterrent or punishment. It was the worst job in the army.

Eventually, Little Frog and Little Croc finished their two weeks of disciplinary hide-tanning duties. Sometime during their punishment, the pair decided that the General needed a treasure room.

The other troops in the company liked the idea. It only took them three nights of northern trade route foraging to completely fill the twenty-five-by-forty-five-feet room with the treasure trunks and crates, floor to ceiling.

Then, one day, unbeknownst to Colonel Yadin, the boys and eight younger troops dumped out all the solid gold and silver coins, jewelry, ingots, bars, and statues. The trunks and crates were chopped into pieces and piled in a corner. The two self-appointed "keepers of the treasures" told Yadin that "one big sparkly dune looks richer than a bunch of dirty crates." At the top of the twelve-foot-high mound, they positioned five miniature solid gold sarcophaguses in a circle. And finally, as a way to "scare away Egyptian pigs/robbers," the boys stood their four "mummy boxes" facing the back of the door to the treasure room. It was the first thing Kalev saw when he opened the door.

In hindsight, Kalev thought, *I probably should have used a couple of emptied clothes trunks…too late now*. Kalev apologetically shrugged. "I'm sorry, Sir; these were the largest containers I had at the moment. Kalev walked behind the cart, and with rapid flourishes, he flipped the top off the four sarcophaguses. They were so full of coins, they spilled down the sides in streams of glistening gold. "Rabbi Nachshon, I formally ask to marry your daughter and present this as the mohar!" Kalev was pretty pleased with himself until he read the man's expression. The rabbi stood. To Kalev the man's emotionless face scared him to the core. *Oh [illegible], what have I done?*

By then the three boys had already climbed on top of the table to get a better view. Little Frog whispered so loudly that Kalev could hear him, "Maybe Major Raisa's abba is mad 'cause we put too many coins in the ugly girl mummy's box, and they spilled out and made a mess on the cart. General Ari, do you think he's ma…?" When Kalev looked over to glare at the boys, all he saw was the three colonels stuffing three pairs of howling legs under the table.

The unnervingly scowling Nachshon slowly examined each gold-and-silver-filled case. Kalev thought the statues would be offensive; the rabbi didn't need the jewelry, and the bars were too heavy. So the cases were only filled with coins. Once Nachshon finished digging his hand to the bottom of the fourth sarcophagus, he examined the tunics, keffiyehs, and even three of the shiny, embroidered loincloths. Which, under the current circumstances, Kalev was really regretting. Raisa's abba lifted the masterfully crafted, white leopard skin long coat, then abruptly made a show of throwing it on the pile of coins.

The old man coughed, spit on the deck, then glared up at the sweating General. "Is this all my daughter is worth to you?" Four loud gasps echoed from somewhere in the kitchen. Kalev's mouth hung open. Then, in a mindless panic, he blurted out, "Uh, no, Sir, she, um, your sweetly singing bird of prey is worth much more gold and more of that wine and more clothes and swords and, and, you can have Ox." The rabbi shook his head in mock disgust. "What am I going to do with an ox?" Again, Kalev's mouth was miles ahead of his brain. "I can find a wagon for him. I mean, a wagon for both of you; I mean, you can pull or, um, he can pull you in the wagon—I mean…arghhh!"

Kalev flopped down to the edge of the cart, dropped his face in his hands, and groaned to himself a little louder than he intended. "It was Raisa's idea. I'm just following her orders, though I like her orders, and I especially like how she…" The rabbi lost it.

The old man's laughter seemed to comingle with the thunderous laughter of the Warrior King. Soon everyone in earshot was rolling on the floor screaming with laughter. Everyone except Kalev. He'd just survived the most terrifying experience in his life. And he needed a drink.

While the walls echoed with laughter, both man's and Yahweh's, the scowling Kalev stood, walked back to the table, poured his deep golden mug full of Yadin's disgusting yeast-fermented wine, plopped onto the bench, and downed it in five huge gulps.

Eventually the rabbi caught his breath enough to pull himself off the floor and climb up the table's bench. As the tear-stained face of the rabbi peered over the edge of the table, Kalev's confused and brooding eyes locked onto him. “So, Sir, I’ve been thinking about it. I’d really like to keep Ox and my swords. So, given that, do you accept this mohar or not?” The head slowly dropped out of sight and a whole new round of screaming laughter boomed off the walls. Kalev, still confused, filled his cup again and drank it down in another five gulps.

40

As Hoshe'a had dreaded, his ema finally found him. He was sitting on Kalev's dune watching a fishing felucca float by when his ema attacked. She hit the back of his head so hard that he fell forward and tumbled halfway down the dune. The little Hebrew was standing over his sprawled body in a second. "What do you mean you'd kill yourself before you'd let your brother marry before you?" She quickly glared at the pale blue sky. "Like that's going to happen any time soon." Hoshe'a started to protest, then remembered when Ema was this mad, it was better to keep his mouth shut and take it. *She really doesn't want answers to her questions anyway*, he reasoned. After a solid twenty minutes of screaming, she stormed up the hill and disappeared.

Now, in the Fortress' noisy dining area, the raucous and slightly tipsy teens were joined by the weary-looking Major Hoshe'a. The clearly defined, red, and swollen handprint on the back of his neck was instantly a source for a new wave of overly loud laughter. The sullen Hoshe'a, who'd brought his now-half-full urn of viper wine, sat mumbling under his breath and seemed to ignore the playful insults.

Apparently, the officers were kind of celebrating the General's successful transaction. But Kalev was noticeably absent. Ari told Hoshe'a, "The General's still in his room, sleeping off his, um, morning ordeal." He respectfully failed to mention that though it had ended well, the two gallons of the nasty wine had taken its toll.

Halfway through their impromptu betrothal celebration, Akiba joined the senior officers and reported his latest sitrep (situation report). The serious look on his face quelled the mood. "Sir, Gemmell Squad from our perimeter platoon just reported in." Ari sighed, then automatically glanced at Yadin, who, in turn, reluctantly pulled a blank parchment, quill, and small-sealed jar from one of his stained pockets.

"They were late to their patrol jump-off point. It's that furthest northwestern marker of our AO." Ari was picturing their patrol map in his head. "The boulder-lined bend in the road from the trade route to General Kalev's road?" Ari asked. Akiba nodded. "Yes, Sir."

Then Hoshe'a, keeping his eyes shut against the glare of everything, interrupted. "General Kalev has his own road?" The others laughed. "Yes, Sir, well, it's what the original company of troops named the road that curves right in front of the General's stall. That road was where they first encountered their conqueror of Sha'al." Hoshe'a groaned. Ari smirked, then nodded for Akiba to continue.

The colonel sneered. "The squad was late on station, so the sun was already up. That *ex*-squad leader won't make that mistake again. But he reported that they'd just split the squad, flanked the road, and headed this way. That's when, he stated, 'the chariots came out of nowhere.' The cabbage plants in those fields bordering the road are ready to harvest, but the troops knew there wasn't enough cover to hide.

So they were caught out in the open with nowhere to run. At least the squad leader was still thinking at that point. He ordered the squad to toss their weapons into the fields." Ari nodded approvingly. "That was smart." Akiba smirked and shook his head. "Yeah, but that's where his 'tactical intelligence' ended.

"According to the rest of his squad, their 'experienced' leader looked terrified. He just stood there without another word. Then, as the first frothing horse began to make the turn toward them, the newest private assigned to their squad pulled a little parchment ball out of his pocket, held it up so the others could see, and then kicked it across the road. The other troops instantly caught on. They made sure the lead chariot driver saw them kicking the ball to each other before they held it and let the twelve chariots pass.

"After the trailing chariot driver, a lower-ranking sergeant according to our squad's oldest troop, pulled past them, they started kicking the ball again. But that sergeant reined in and stopped a few yards down the road. They said that he glared back at them, and they all agreed that his eyes looked like they were on fire. The '[illegible]' had just started to turn around when our troops heard someone ahead of him let out three loud whistles. The pig continued to glare at our people, spit in the dirt, then swore he'd be right back to 'play his version of Hebrew-baby kickball.' They watched the pigs disappear around that wide turn south. Our people quickly retrieved their weapons and then ran for those nearby dunes in the northern fields. They're the ones closest to that same bend in front of General's barn.

"They hid in what they called 'the sand bowl.'" Yadin perked up. "Wait. I always thought it was a single dune." "Yeah, so did I. But the squad leader described it as a circle of tall dunes surrounding a green floor." Hoshe'a lifted his head off the table. "I don't remember any sand bowl. But that's where my abba had a small barn and ox corral. And it did have a freshwater spring. That's where I taught Kalev how to swim, sort of."

Akiba glanced at Ari, who was glaring at the major. Akiba quickly continued, "Apparently, over the years, the sand piled up around those structures, then covered them completely.

"Our squad climbed the dune on a slant so the sand would slide down and cover their tracks." Yadin made sure that information got back to Yadin's basic training platoons. "They'd just hidden on the inside of the dune when they saw three of those same chariots thunder past the base of the dune and then abruptly stop. From there it's easy to see up the road to where they last saw our squad. The squad leader reported that the chariots turned into the field and made a complete circle around the dune. I guess they didn't feel like climbing a sand dune to check the top. So they rode off toward the city. Our people let them cross the canal before they headed back here and reported." Ari nodded, then paused.

"Okay. First of all, I know those boulders hide the road up to that bend. But that's no excuse for relaxed situational awareness. They had to have heard something!" Akiba let out an exasperated breath. "Again I've rectified that problem." "Good. Secondly, we need to enlarge that patrol sector to include the road *before* it enters the boulder field." Then Ari's voice grew angry. "I'm positive that section was the initial ingress point for that L⟍⋓⫯ϱ९ᘏ♆+ʍ squad of Egyptian pigs who destroyed my father's village and…" Ari fell silent and just glanced at his second-in-command.

Akiba nodded. "Yes, Sir, it was. That night after the burial, we went back to the village to do a final body recovery. We, um, found another eight people. Seven were the Aleph Squad's leader Dam's family. He thought they'd ran to another village where his savta lives. But they were only two doors down at their friend's house when *it* started. Once we buried those bodies, we searched the remains of the Egyptian murder squad. They had definitely just returned from their most northern outpost. We retrieved a few Canaanite and Minoan swords. So we think this latest company of chariots came from that same forward operations base." Ari snapped out of the black grieving thoughts that threatened to devour him again. "Okay. Thirdly, set up a permanent forward overwatch for that section of the road. I'm curious about that circle of dunes. We may be able to use it for another overwatch." Akiba smiled. "I just got back from there.

"It's perfect for us. The dunes are at least thirty feet high. I stepped off the grassy deck at the bottom. I estimate it's just over thirty-five wide by forty-five yards long. And it *does* have a bubbling spring at the western end. It's perfect for watching up that road, and we can use the inside floor to train the new recruits in archery and knife throwing. And because of the steepness of the face of the dunes. I'm pretty sure you won't be able to see any torchlight from the inside of the bowl." But Akiba cut his report short when he realized First Sergeant Carni had been standing behind Major Hoshe'a for most of the report. Her oldest son's forehead was still on the table, and his eyes were still closed. All four smiling teens watched as the grinning First Sergeant Ema leaned close to the unsuspecting Major Hoshe'a's ear and politely *yelled* at Akiba. "Colonel Akiba, I'd like to see that sand bowl. I think General Kalev may need it for a while." Hoshe'a bolted upright. And amidst peals of laughter, the Commanding General's brother sprinted for the closest horse stall and unceremoniously heaved his guts out.

41

The next morning, Kalev, post mohar ceremony, sat at the subdued officer's table. Hoshe'a, the night before, had "sampled" too much of their newest batch of even older viper wine. The pale-faced and wreaking idiot whimpered to no one in particular, "I'm never gonna drink again."

The General, on the other hand, had wisely gulped three large chalices of water when he'd first come round. Now his headache was *almost* gone.

He sat with his senior staff at their dining table. Akiba was filling him in on the latest encounter with the Egyptian pigs. Kalev growled. "It sounds like, except for the squad leader's brainfart, that squad had performed admirably. Especially the new private. His quick thinking probably saved all their lives. What's his name? He should receive a promotion or at least a commendation." Akiba smiled at Ari, who volunteered, "After Little Frog's, um, outburst during your mohar negotiation. All three were split up and assigned to different duties. That squad's newly assigned private was Little Yoshi. And yes, I personally promoted him to corporal in front of his whole platoon. I was sure to describe his quick thinking as an example to follow." Kalev smiled. "Good job. I wish I'd been there when Little Frog and Croc found out their quiet little friend outranks them now." Akiba chuckled. "Actually, the little guy pushed his advantage a little too far. I had to break up the brawl. Then I *did* tear the two *privates* a new one."

Kalev was on his fifth cup of water when he saw his ema walk up behind the groaning Hoshe'a. Her disgusted glare at the back of his brother's slightly drooping head clearly conveyed her intentions. She knew Hoshe'a's head was throbbing with yet another hangover. The General caught her attention and shook his head. Normally, he'd just sit and enjoy the show. But his brother's pathetic look had sucked all the fun out of it.

So, just as his defiant ema raised her hand to line up her shot, Kalev leaped to his full height and loudly snapped his finger. He pointed at the startled Carni and roared, "First Sergeant, in the TOC, now!" Without waiting for the stunned Carni, Kalev turned and marched toward the TOC and the overdue showdown.

Inadvertently, the snap of Kalev's fingers, followed by his thunderous order, caused the unsuspecting Major Hoshe'a to groan and cover his ears. It also resulted in a onetime, unheard-of miracle. Every one of the 1998 children in the Fortress instantly went silent. Every troop present watched in awe as their general herded his Major Ema into the TOC and slammed the huge double doors. It seemed like the entire Fortress' deck vibrated, and Hoshe'a winced when he saw a large puff of sandy dust fall from the rafters.

Ari quickly averted his own stare and began shouting orders for the junior officers to start the next evolutions. As the others quickly dispersed, Hoshe'a greedily drank two cups of water, belched, and then forced himself to his feet. Hoshe'a stood and slowly made his way toward the TOC. Even with his head threatening to painfully explode, he couldn't resist eavesdropping on this momentous encounter.

The Commanding General of Yisrael's Army was livid. Initially, Carni tried to put on her "defiant Hebrew ema" expression. But she knew her son cared about these kids and only wanted the best for them. Soon her shoulders slumped, and she just nodded as Kalev roared on.

"And I mean no one gets promoted without General Ari's and/or my prior approval. In this area of operation, you're an *honorary* First Sergeant, not my ema. Do you understand me?" Straining to sound respectful, the Major Ema nodded. "General, Sir, I'm sorry, and you're right. I was only trying to find a way to promote respect for your future wife. It won't happen again." Though the very rare apology surprised him, the General continued his loud growl. On the other side of the double doors, Hoshe'a's fist shot into the air in victory. "Yes!" Then just as quickly he grabbed the sides of his head and slid to the floor groaning.

"Now about these girl *assault* troops. Again you…" Fifteen long and loud minutes later, the General slumped into his chair at the head of the table. He'd suddenly run out of steam and dropped his face into his hands. "Every time you pull one of these unilateral stunts, it undermines our authority. The chain of command is the basis for this entire orphan army. Confidence in that hierarchy and, especially, their immediate superiors gives these kids a sense of security and directed purpose. And for the majority of them, it's the first time in their lives they've been able to relax and enjoy those luxuries. Plus, Ema, stop head slapping Hoshe'a in front of the troops! He deserves it *more than you know*. But not in front of the troops!" Carni clenched her jaw, then relented. "Son, you're right…but what do you mean more than I know?" "*Ema*!" She stood, walked over, put her arms around his neck, and whispered into his ear, "Have I told you lately how much I've missed you?"

At the same time, Kalev stood intending to hug her back. But he froze as his Raisa's breathtaking smile came through the double doors. She held a plate of hot bread and another cup of water. But Kalev only registered her glowing face, and his mouth dropped open.

Carni used the distraction to grab the back hem of his tunic. In a flash, she whipped it up to his neck. Raisa was appreciatively surprised when the top of her future husband's rippling muscled thighs, rock-hard abs, and thankfully too-tight loincloth was exposed. She knew she should look away, but…

"Emaaaa!" the mortified Kalev yelled as he spun and tried to reach behind him to knock her hand away. This revealed his V-shaped, hard-muscled back to his leering bride. Both women gasped but for *totally* different reasons. Kalev glared down at his stunned-looking ema, yet *she* was staring at Raisa. "Did you see that?" Kalev's grinning bride was startled from a rather exciting daydream. Raisa cleared her throat and slowly nodded. "Yeaaaah, I did! I saw his back too." Carni snickered.

"Son, your back looks completely normal…" "Better than normal," Raisa huskily whispered under her breath. "In fact"—Carni continued—"um, I *think* the scars from when that pig Hotep carved his name into your back are gone, I think."

Kalev's eyes went wide. "Ema, really? Check again." Without thinking, he whipped his tunic off and craned his neck to look back at his ema. Carni smiled and motioned for Raisa to leave. Which she did…eventually.

Once Raisa had finally left and shut the doors, Carni smiled at Kalev's back and mumbled under her breath, "Wow, her hungry leopard stare reminds me of me." "What did you just say? Ema, is it gone or not!" "Yes, son, it's completely gone." She ran her hand over another place on his back. She immediately sucked in a sharp breath, and her eyes began to tear up. "And so is the largest dark purple scar."

Carni sheepishly looked up at the ceiling. "Yahweh, um, I'm sorry for my attitude. I was, um, scared, and, well…thank You for healing my son so quickly. Oh, and I'm sorry about my *order* to find Hoshe'a a bride…" Kalev spun around. "Wait. You *ordered* the Warrior King, the King of kings and pharaohs, to find Hoshe'a a bride?" Kalev glanced at the ceiling, then back at his guilty-looking ema. "First Sergeant, once again, you have a lot to learn about proper procedure and respecting your superiors." Carni looked up and mouthed at the ceiling, "I'm sorry."

The General brought the plate and cup back to his seat. Then his ema transformed into *her* supreme commanding ema's voice. "I assume, after he accepted the mohar, Nachshon instructed you on the *proper procedure* for approaching your betrothed, then bringing her to the wedding feast." Kalev took a drink, then without looking he slowly shook his head. "No, he was still literally under the table laughing and drinking when I ran into my room, threw up, then fell asleep next to the golden toilet.

"I wasn't even sure he'd accepted the mohar until Ari told me this morning. He said Nachshon grabbed the clothes, filled the leopard skin coat's two pockets with coins, then told Ari to take the rest back. So I assume that means he accepted. No, he didn't tell me anything. But that's okay because Adir and I had already discussed the wedding procedures. In fact, he got excited when we talked about him and you…" Kalev wisely shut up. Which was fine with the still-grieving Carni; she didn't want to hear the end of that statement. It took some effort, but the determined ema continued her questioning.

"So, after the blessing, what's next?" Kalev swallowed hard. "Well, according to Adir, the husband is supposed to lead the horse his new wife is riding back to the home he's built for them. Then, um, he never told me what happened after that. He just smiled, then swung his sword at my neck again."

Still eating, Kalev pointed over his shoulder. "So I guess I bring her back to my room here. It does have a table and chairs. Plus it's close enough to not need a horse to…" The head slap actually caught him off guard, and he faceplanted into a loaf of bread. Before he could even complain, his scary little ema had grabbed his ear and viciously twisted it as she pulled it close to her mouth. Carni roared at the top of her lungs, "Don't you even *think* about bringing that beautiful bride back to this hole in the ground. That girl has waited for you for the last eighteen years. She deserves better. And she's going to get it, or I'll make sure *you* die trying. Now, do *you* understand *me*, General, *Sir*!" Kalev rubbed his ear. "But, Ema, I didn't build a house." His childlike statement made her smile. "That's already taken care of, little one. Your senior staff is already on it. Now, when are you going to come for your bride?" Kalev turned and scowled at Carni. "That protocol I know about, and, Ema, the timing is none of your business." Carni shrugged. "You're right. But you may want to know, just like last night, she's probably on her way back to the house. She sits in that upstairs window watching for her groom to come through the gate. After that little scene a minute ago, it's pretty obvious she wants you to retrieve her as soon as possible." Kalev froze midchew. He was instantly on his feet and roared. "So you two were in that house last night and this morning?" Carni innocently nodded. "Yes, little one, it's okay. We were just…" Kalev raced to the door, threw it open, and boomed down the hall. "Colonel Akiba, report." In less than thirty seconds, the General had filled Akiba in, who, in turn, yelled for the First Sergeant in charge of the shadow troops to report. Carni wisely stayed at the other end of the table. The General was panicked, but he thought it through and realized he personally couldn't crash that courtyard gate and bring Raisa back here.

Then the same familiar sergeant sped through the double doors. Kalev and Akiba stood. "Sir, this is First Sergeant Othniel." The teen saluted, but Kalev didn't return the salute. "Who is guarding my ema's house?" The teen shook his head. "Why would we…?" Kalev cut him off. "Apparently, my ema and Major Raisa decided on their own they'd stay there before the marriage feast. I want a double perimeter dug in and hidden. I'll be there to inspect in thirty minutes." The blood drained from the sergeant's face. "But I thought they were here…" Without waiting for further orders, he turned and ran.

Kalev glared at Carni, but before he could yell, Ari and the other three came running in. Ari immediately saw the brewing storm. "Sir, what happened?" Kalev turned to Carni and repeated the Akiba's earlier report. "Ema, they rode right in front of your house! Best case, they would have killed you both. I'm surprised the house is still standing." "But we were already here…" she weakly protested. Ari expected a much larger explosion from his general. But to his credit, the General clamped his muscular jaw shut and glanced at his second-in-command. Then hurried out.

Forty-five minutes later, a wearily relieved Commanding General came back through the double doors. "I'm sorry it took so long. I had to make sure she made it here…" Their General froze in place, and his jaw dropped. In unison his senior officers and rabbi Nachshon groaned, "Oh [illegible]-[illegible]!"

The shocked son of Hezron was staring at a much older yet clearly recognizable face. This was the man who was directly responsible for his abba's death. It felt like he was that boy again, watching his father's brutal murder happen for the first time. Kalev clearly heard and ignored the Warrior King's warning, "Kalev, just breathe."

At the same time, a perturbed Raisa walked into the TOC right behind her man. In a half second, the rabbi's daughter deduced the situation and lunged for Kalev's already-moving arm. "Kalev no," she screamed at her oblivious husband's flexing back.

He'd spent thirty-one cruel years hoping for this chance to avenge his abba's death. And for the first time, he *was* strong enough. "Now I *can* help!"

As he abandoned all reason, a grief-filled, primal war cry rose in his throat. His swords instantly materialized in his trembling fists. As if he was observing the whole thing from the other side of the table, Kalev, the only son of his ema and murdered abba, watched himself begin to sprint the thirty feet down the side of the table toward his lifelong enemy.

To everyone present, the next five chaotic seconds seemed to unravel in slow motion. The former Egyptian prince/general had practiced this encounter in his mind for days. He'd run through every conceivable move and their outcome. But this was very real and happening at twice the speed he'd rehearsed in his mind.

At the same instant Kalev took his first step, the obviously unarmed Moshe leaped from his chair, vaulted over the corner of the table, and landed on all fours in front of the howling haboob, racing to end his life. He bowed his face to the deck. Moshe surprised himself. He was actually grinning as a peaceful wave of relief washed over him. *Finally. This unbearable burden will be someone else's problem*, he mused. The birth son of Jochebed, the Hebrew raised by the Egyptian Queen Hatshepsut, sighed, closed his bloodshot eyes, and patiently waited for his swift end.

Ari and his three wild-eyed friends shot to their feet, instinctively drew their own swords, and then just stood there motionless and stared at their terrifying General. The rabbi had remained seated. He hopelessly glanced between his screaming daughter, her lethal husband, and Yahweh's prophet flying over the end of the table. The old man closed his own eyes, rested his forehead on the table, and groaned, "Ohhh Yahweh!"

Kalev's eyesight tunneled and focused. All sound, including his rage-filled wail, ceased. His entire world became the exposed neck of his lifelong enemy. Specifically, the small area on that neck where his swords would land. Ten feet in front of his target, the General simultaneously raised both swords above his head and leaped.

The jumping tactic was designed to deliver the maximum amount of lethal downforce on the target. Adir had relentlessly drilled into him the need for both swords to be held two inches apart and swung to reach maximum downward speed as they hit the target just before his feet hit the ground. Adir was relentless. Kalev had practiced sixteen straight hours and wasted 132 melons to perfect this maneuver.

The instant his right foot left the ground, time and motion completely stopped. Again, as if watching from the other side of the table, he saw himself in the air with his swords beginning their downward arc. Only this time, he was motionless, frozen in midair. From the other side of the room, he looked like a hieroglyph painted on the opposite wall. Then the Warrior King's voice calmly reverberated in his ears.

"Proud son of Hezron, I will ask you four questions. If you honestly answer no to any of the four, you may complete your kill shot. However, if your answers are all yes, you will cease and listen to my servant Moshe. Oh, and by the way, this contract is nonnegotiable. Do you agree?" Kalev saw his painted silhouette nod.

Without pausing, the Warrior King's deafening voice boomed. "First. Have you ever failed yourself or others, resulting in deep, dark regret?" The timeless voice stopped. Every self-centered, painfully embarrassing word he'd ever spoken began screaming in his ears. These were immediately followed by his countless stupid reactions made in haste, anger, or both. The words marched through his mind like they were on display for everyone to see. A crushing wave of guilt crashed over him. Then he remembered the taste of the black ooze he'd vomited after that battle against the dark forces. He vividly understood the aftertaste's tang was from these same hate-filled regrets. Seemingly, from the other side of the room, Kalev watched tears stream down the one-dimensional picture's cheeks. Then the hieroglyph nodded.

Eventually, the voice broke the silence again. But it was different, softer. "Second question. Son of Hezron, do you affirm that the I AM who created the *shamayim* and the *eretz* is your Yahweh? That your Warrior King has and will continue to show you His boundless loving-kindness and unearned favor?"

Kalev instantly saw his breathtaking Raisa. He stared at her glistening black hair that delicately framed her glowing face. Her deep blue eyes seemed to see right into his core. And that smile, her lips, and… Then he saw the glyph of himself smile and nod again.

The voice boomed again. "Third question. Are you the Supreme Commanding General, the future prince of the tribe of Yehudah, the true leader of thousands We've called you to be?" This caught Kalev off guard. He wanted to scream no. Then every person he'd ever helped, every troop in this army, and, most importantly, his Raisa, all yelled with one voice, "Yes, you *are*!" His silhouette on the opposite wall hesitantly nodded and whispered, "I hope I am, but please help me overcome my unbelief."

The Warrior King's voice softened even further, and His words seemed to blow through and swirl around him. "General Kalev, you who are designated as true to Yahweh, based on what you've just seen and heard…will you pardon and show My same unmerited favor to My servant Moshe?"

Instantly, he experienced another picture. A huge black oozing wave of the same regrets and so many more, past, present, and future. The monstrous swell of putrid sludge violently surged upward. It'd grown so large that it completely blotted out the picture of his puny self. It finally crested, curled forward, and crashed in a violent spray.

In a flash of understanding, he realized that the fathomless black wave filled with painful self-doubt and self-loathing regrets wasn't his. The picture and the black ooze were owned by the man kneeling below him.

Fresh tears of empathy gushed from his glyph's eyes. They streamed in a steady flow down to the TOC's actual deck. Then he heard the Warrior King's voice choke up as it rasped, "You who are without sin may cast the first stone…"

For what seemed like hours, Kalev grieved and wept for this man. Then he saw himself straighten and declare, "I've been forgiven of much, so I will forgive this man." The Warrior King's war cry crashed through Kalev's suspended picture like a violent concentrated wind.

Instantly, all of his own burdened memories, his hate-filled thoughts of revenge, shattered into millions of pieces. As the violent war cry wind continued, the pieces rapidly swirled in an ever-shrinking circle. Then the vortex of small black oozing pieces imploded in a clap of thunder.

In the subsequent silence, Kalev watched as his picture seemed to float increasingly higher every time he repeated the words, "I forgive him…I forgive him…I really forgive him…" Yahweh's final words boomed so loud and shook him so deep, he'd never forget. "Kalev, son of Hezron, true to Yahweh, listen to my servant Moshe's heart. Just like *yours*, son, his beats in time with Mine." As with his other adventures with Yahweh, the whole encounter had transpired in a single blink.

Instantly, he was on the other side of the table, flying through the air. The sights and sounds around him hit his chest, much like the Warrior King's violent war cry. In the same moment, Kalev heard Raisa's screaming, and he saw the four motionless teens' confused expressions and the rabbi with his head on the table.

Then he was suddenly horrified as he felt himself racing toward the ground as his swords flashed by his face in their downward arc. He hopelessly willed the swords to spread apart and closed his eyes. Then there was a sickening thud and twang. His muscle memory kicked in and he felt his knees slightly flex to absorb his weight as he landed. Kalev's heart sank.

Without opening his eyes, he stood. He didn't want to look. Then from below him, he heard a raspy voice complain, "[illegible], *you missed*! Arghhhh!" Like a little kid, Kalev forced one eye barely open and peaked down.

Lying there, sprawled between his feet, was the older version of Prince Moshe. Astonishingly, Kalev's swords *had* separated just enough to pierce each sleeve of the old man's tunic, pinning him face down to the deck. Moshe struggled to get up. He awkwardly ripped off both sleeves. His arm brushed against the razor-sharp Khopesh sword blade, and a small trickle of blood began to run down his taut, muscled arm.

Moshe sat up. With his long white hair hanging in his face, he glanced first at his arm, then at the still vibrating swords firmly embedded in the deck, and finally up at Kalev. Surprisingly, Moshe quickly returned his face to the deck and moaned. "Son of Hezron, I don't deserve it, but I plead for your forgiveness. I was a foolish idiot. I regret…" Kalev cut him off. "I've already forgiven you. Ask the Warrior King. But"—Kalev smirked—"you really should talk to someone about all your oozing regrets; they really do smell."

At first Moshe looked surprised, then he nodded, and his face flushed with embarrassment. "You saw it too. The wave—I mean, my wave." Kalev knowingly grinned and shrugged. "What wave?" Kalev reached down to help the man up. But the sound of loud puking made them both look under the table. Still bent over, Hoshe'a gave them a weak wave, smiled, and then violently dry heaved again. Kalev grinned, plopped onto the ground, and the two men sighed at the same time, then started laughing. The two warriors instantly realized they both had the same stupid-looking lopsided smile and their laughs were identical. In perfect unison, the two generals abruptly stopped laughing and warily sized the other up.

The Warrior King chuckled. "See? It's fun to play nice." Then Yahweh broke out in a howling belly laugh. Both men shook their heads and smirked the same way. They both heard Yahweh chuckling. Moshe grinned. "Finally, someone I can grumble about Yahweh with." Yahweh's laughter abruptly ceased and both wide eyed men started laughing. Moshe examined his torn sleeve on his only tunic. "Yeah, I heard you slayed every sha'dim Sha'al. That's quite a feat. I'm really surprised you missed me." Kalev tapped the bleeding wound Moshe's other arm. "I never miss." Moshe liked this guy. He reached over and wiggled one of Kalev's swords, then shook his head. "Yeah, the wooded deck has been slain with astonishing accuracy!" They both started laughing again.

42

Originally, according to Raisa's ultimatum, the General and his bride were to receive the marriage blessing tomorrow evening fifteen minutes before sunset. His ema had reminded him about the exact time almost every day since the proclamation. But Kalev knew that tradition really mattered to Raisa's abba, so ultimately, a set time and date was out of the question. Last week, after a long sleepless day, he'd decided that tonight, at sundown, would be the *go time* for his covert marriage mission to begin.

Carni's son made a point of not discussing his decision with anyone. He hadn't even alerted Sergeant Othniel or his double layer of *experienced* perimeter troops stationed around the house. They'd find out when the stealthy general suddenly appeared out of the darkness. He needed to test their readiness anyway and figured he'd kill two birds with one stone.

The massive son of Hezron emerged from his cold bathing trough and toweled off. "Tonight, even Ema will be surprised." He smirked. Kalev was pretty pleased with himself. The General opened the door of his bathing trough room, took one step toward his clothes shelf, and tripped. The towel flew one way, and he tumbled the other. He never heard the three little girls' gasps from the other end of the room. Nor did he hear his bedroom door boom shut as his head bounced off the deck for the second time. Kalev angrily shot to his feet and howled at the ceiling. He didn't even know the meaning of a couple of *Hotep's* expletives that gushed from his throat. The Commanding General looked back. Someone had placed one of the padded chairs right in front of his trough room door. Now it was a pile of splintered wood and torn fabric. Kalev abruptly stopped complaining. A small cloud of padding feathers had poofed into the air. Hoshe'a had always teased his little brother about being easily distracted by the strangest things. Now the stark-naked, 310-pound, muscle-ripened man stood in the middle of his room wordlessly intrigued. Kalev watched the countless pinfeathers twirl around. Each feather spun in a different direction, each gently falling in a different way.

Once he'd forced himself to stop watching the captivating show, he automatically resumed his grumbling and turned toward his clothing shelves. His completely *empty* clothing shelves. Even his favorite loincloth was gone. The naked general quickly spun to make sure he was alone, then screamed, "*Hoshe'aaaa*!"

After another stream of colorful language, Kalev closed his eyes and took four four-count tactical breaths. He walked over and leaned down to reclaim his towel. That was when he saw the last tiny white feather softly descend into a too-shiny jumble of bright white material. "[illegible]," he screamed. The son of Hezron's brilliantly planned covert bride-retrieval mission was completely blown.

Kalev's towel fell off when he lifted the disgustingly effeminate-looking tunic to the torchlight. The *almost* long enough shirt was made of the same shiny white material as the stupid loincloth and gold-embroidered keffiyeh piled at his feet. "That's right, General Kalev"—he sarcastically announced at the ceiling—"you've just won a *shiny, new girl tunic*. And look…it has the pretty prancing ponies and happily frolicking bunnies *you've* grown to adore…but wait, that's not all…not only is it big enough for Ox, but it has the added bonus of…*wait for iiiit*…yes, you guessed it! It's completely *see-through*… That's right! Now the whole army can see your business as you lightly flit around the AO! Congratulations!" Instantly, loud, invisible peals of Yahweh's applause and cheering exploded from every direction. Kalev scowled at the ceiling. He threw the tunic into the pile and fiercely kicked the whole shimmering mess into the corner. Then he glared at the ceiling. "Not in *my* lifetime!" And, true to Yahweh's sense of humor, the invisible audience sadly sighed, "Ahhhhhh…"

He grabbed his *barely*-long-enough towel and tied it around his waist. The Commanding General stormed out of his room and threw the double doors open so hard, they bounced off the adjoining walls and then boomed shut behind him as he raced past. He stomped down the hall, around the corner, and viciously yanked on the first storeroom's handle. His towel fell off, but the thick door didn't move. The frantic General pulled again with all his strength, and it still didn't open. He yanked on all of the other doors, even his treasure rooms, but none of them moved. His thunderous voiced echoed down the oddly quiet hallway. "*Hoshe'aaaa*!"

Kalev ran back down the hall, grabbed the towel, tied it around his waist again, then furiously raced out onto the drill floor. The scene was surreal. Somehow, in the short thirty minutes he'd been in his room, the usual number of torches that lined the Pit's drill floor walls was tripled. A small platform stood near the dining tables, and the larger senior officer's platform at the far end had a shiny blue backdrop. But what surprised him the most was the complete quiet.

The Pit had never been silent. Both fortresses operated on Yadin's complicated yet expertly choreographed twelve-on-twelve-off rotation. There was always something happening, either on the drill deck, in the stalls, at the dining tables, or in the kitchen. But he'd never seen it so empty. The army's Commanding General unconsciously lost his towel for the third time. Only now, he had an audience. Boaz and every other animal in the place stopped chewing, turned their heads, and stared at the funny human's naked body. At the same time, another misplaced round of Yahweh-induced cheering and applause erupted through the Pit.

Thirty minutes later, a humiliated Kalev and Raisa's previously saddled and decorated mare stood at the base of the silent Pit's ramp. Kalev watched as the weakening last rays of the setting sun turned a few high clouds dark orange. A thin layer of ground fog from the river began to drift down the ramp toward him. Ari suddenly materialized beside his obviously sweating general. "Nice tunic. I thought I was alone. I was sent down to make sure you followed through…" Kalev rounded on his second-in-command. "How did you…how did anyone know…?" Ari supportively smiled. Kalev roared, startling the horse. "Arghh, *Eeeeeeeemaaaaaa*!"

The nervously sweating yet defeated-looking General, the mare, and his grinning assistant had just started up the ramp when the darkening soft mist at the top began to mysteriously swirl. Sixty of Carni's younger troops ran to form a well-rehearsed and evenly spaced line across the top of the ramp. Kalev heard Ari suck in a sharp breath. The men and beast stopped walking.

At the top, Deborah appeared from the far right. To Ari, it looked like she was being carried by misty angels. Her face glowed in the light of the single candle she held with both hands. As Captain Deborah started down the line of girls, each of their palm-sized oil lamps began to glow a soft orange. Kalev reached over and closed his friend's mouth for him. "You might think about breathing."

In unison, sixty little girls loudly gasped and pointed toward their two Commanding Generals. Kalev and Ari quickly glanced at each other, then down at Kalev's shimmering tunic. Before Ari could make another teasing comment, Little Yoshi, since he had a "more better rank," followed by Little Frog and Little Croc, strutted past their generals and took up a position in front of them. The trio wore oversized gold-flecked turbans, each with huge ostrich feathers. Little Yoshi's, of course, was wider and longer since he had a "more better rank." All three boys wore matching gold-and-blue vests over brilliantly white flowing shirts. Their too-large pants billowed in the misty ground fog as they walked. At the moment, no one could see the curled-up, pointy-toed shoes that threatened to trip them with every step. The whole incongruent scene was hilarious.

Kalev smiled. He was grateful that the boys were drawing all the attention away from his transparent tunic. The General leaned forward and whispered loudly, "You three look like kings." Still looking forward, Little Frog nodded. "We know, Sir; your ema already told us." Little Yoshi did a quick about-face. But because of the ramp's steep-down angle, he stumbled into the two others, who roughly shoved him backward. The other two started grumbling at their "superior." Instead of pushing the turban up, the littlest guy leaned his head back to see. "Are you ready to follow us, Sir? 'Cause First Sergeant said if we're late, she'll make us kiss all those girls up there, and we don't even know how, or we even don't want to." Kalev and Ari glanced at each other, then coughed in unison to stifle their laughs. "Yes, Corporal, please lead the way."

Suddenly, Boaz, saddled and gaudily decorated, cut in front of the two generals. The beautiful white stallion, without any lead rope, dutifully followed the trio. After a few steps, the proud animal craned his neck around to look at Kalev, snort, then vigorously shake his head. The garishly large lotus decorations attached to his neck and thin, shiny saddle cover fell off and disappeared into the ground fog. Kalev looked at his tunic as he whispered to Ari, "I wish I could lose all *my* decorations like that." Ari didn't even glance at his friend when he whispered back, "Sir, it's probably wiser to wait for a much smaller audience before you shed those pretty horsies and bunnies. On the other hand, there's very little left to the imagination, so whatever you want to do, Sir. It's *your* party!"

The little girls gasped, giggled, and whispered to each other as "Kings Yoshi, Frog, and Croc" strutted to the top of the ramp. When the General's small group emerged into the cool evening, they were immediately surrounded by the little girls with little lights. Boaz looked back, shook his head, and snorted again, then kept walking. Kalev groaned under his breath, "Me too, boy, me too…"

That was when Kalev noticed that his horse carried a large gold-embossed saddle built for a camel. Hoshe'a told Kalev later that Carni had to forcefully order the reluctant Little Croc to remove the attached canopy and frame. The giggling horde of sixty little girls was soon joined and organized by the rest of Carni's growing girl company.

Ari glanced at his panicked-looking General and whispered, "Sir, we've pushed the interlocking layer of perimeter guards out a half mile in every direction. They have orders to attack all intruding forces up to twelve in number. Otherwise we'll have at least a five- to nine-minute heads-up. The wary General looked around. "Good thinking, General. I've been a little distracted lately." Ari smiled. "As always, Sir, I've got your back." Kalev reached over and squeezed his friend's shoulder in unspoken thanks. And as always, Ari refused to flinch under his general's iron grip.

They crossed the river in silence, and then Ari heard Kalev complain to himself again when he saw the entire pathway between the General's dune and the Outpost to the house was lined on both sides with older girls holding oil lamps. Somehow, his ema's entire company was wearing identical shiny white robes. *But theirs aren't see-through*, Kalev groused to himself. He still couldn't figure out how his ema could possibly have known, but he promised himself he *would* find out.

When they neared the courtyard, the older girls herded the younger ones to either side of the gate. Ari moved forward and led Boaz to the side, allowing his anxious friend to pass. But before Deborah and two other officers could grab the trio's sleeves, the three little kings, accompanied by another round of little girls blowing kisses their way, strutted right past the older girls into the courtyard like they owned the place. Kalev walked through the gate and stopped. "*Emaaaa*," he growled under his breath, not for the last time that night.

The entire courtyard shone like it was the middle of the day. Dozens of extra torches lined the walls and portico. Fragrant lotus blossoms were strung between the pillars and surrounded the brightly lit entryway. Two rows of lamps lined the blossom-covered pathway to the front step. Each window glowed with three larger oil lamps. Raisa's horse followed Kalev, who followed the trio to the first stair up to the porch. Kalev started to move to the head of the procession when Little Frog yelled, "Mrs. General, we are here!"

Kalev's mouth went dry, and he froze in place when he saw the front door open. She wore a single lotus blossom in her shining black hair. Her simple white robe was strikingly elegant. Raisa looked down at the two boys. "Which one of you is my beloved?" All three boys grimaced and shook their heads. Then Little Yoshi, because he had a "more better rank," proudly proclaimed, "We know we look like dangerous kings, but you're a girl, and me and my men refuse to kiss…" Kalev darted forward and stepped in front of the boys. Behind his back he quickly signaled the boys to *silently* break off and wait outside of the gate.

Kalev's mouth hung open. Raisa's deep blue eyes were ringed in black like Egyptian royalty. *I could stare into those eyes forever*, he thought. For a moment he was speechless. She smiled. But after fifteen long seconds of awed silence, her eyebrows shot up, and she cleared her throat. It actually took the completely disarmed man two attempts before he could croak, "I, um…" Kalev swallowed hard, squared his shoulders, and loudly declared, "I am Kalev, the son of Hezron, the Commanding General of Yisrael's Army. I am your beloved, and I have come for my wife!" Then in a weak, childlike voice, he added, "If you'll have me."

Raisa smiled as tears began to freely run down her cheeks. "And I am Raisa, the daughter of Nachshon. I am and always will be your beloved, your wife. If you'll have me." Without thinking, Raisa took one step, leaped off the porch, and landed in Kalev's arms. They kissed until Kalev's translucent loin cloth started tightening. The embarrassed General quickly pulled his head back to disengage. He stared into her eyes. She smelled like flowers. And tight loincloth or not, Kalev leaned in to kiss her again, but a very loud and too-familiar voice boomed from the porch. "Not only do you have an audience, but you're late. Get moving, General." The strained loincloth instantly deflated.

Without putting her down, Kalev whirled around and softly set his very blushing bride onto her saddle. Ignoring his ema's *look*, he grabbed Boaz's lead rope and started out of the courtyard. Suddenly, a very "late to the party" memory shot across his thoughts. He remembered Adir saying that traditionally, the moment the bride's abba accepted the mohar, the bride became the husband's wife, and they would go and complete the marriage. Kalev still didn't know what "complete the marriage" meant. But Nachshon had warned him, "Yahweh has declared a better way. You're not to show any affection until after the marriage blessing." *Apparently*—he smiled to himself—*Raisa didn't get the same warning.*

Led by seven of Raisa's closest friends, Kalev guided her horse and its precious rider out of the gate and down the even brighter path toward the river. As they passed through the gate, all the girls began to sing a song, obviously written by her abba.

"You're the most handsome of all men! You command your army in an impressive and fitting manner! For this reason, Yahweh grants you continual blessings. Hone your swords, O warrior! Appear in your majestic splendor! For you *are* victorious! Go forth for the sake of what is right on behalf of your people! Then your right hand will accomplish mighty acts! For Yahweh is a man of war. Yahweh is His name. Your swords are sharp and penetrate the hearts of Yahweh's enemies. Nations will fall at your feet. You love justice and hate the chief sha'dim. Your bride will stand and fight at your right hand. For this reason, Yahweh, your Elohim, has anointed you this night with the oil of joy.

"And you, O daughter of Yehudah, observe and pay attention! This warrior chosen by Yahweh is now your shield. Submit to Him. Honor and respect Him always. From today forward, He is your husband, your master! Your children will carry on the reign of your ancestors; they will be rulers throughout the land Yahweh promised to us.

"We are your maidens of honor. We are filled with joy as we follow you. We walk with abundant joy as we follow this mighty son and beautiful daughter of Yahweh…"

Little Yoshi, Frog, and Croc walked behind Raisa's horse. Ten of the little oil lamp girls jostled each other for the chance to hold the boys' unwilling hands. Halfway to the Fortress, Little Frog stopped and loudly ordered the girls, "Stay behind us 'cause we know we look like kings 'cause First Sergeant said we do, and you look like girls, and we're dangerous, and we will never kiss a girl, so stay back 'cause we don't want to hold you *girls'* hands."

They'd crossed the sand bar and were almost to the Pit's ramp before Kalev realized he hadn't said a word the whole trip. He always second-guessed himself, but tonight, the rapid-fire thoughts of inadequacy made him feel dizzy. He willed himself not to turn and stare into Raisa's eyes again, even though he knew those beautiful eyes seemed to calm his inner chaos.

Just before they reached the brightly lit ramp, another thought hit him like a sled of mud bricks. *So, oh mighty battle planner, where are you spending your wedding night?* The memory of Carni's ear-wrenching words screamed in his head. "Don't you even think about bringing that beautiful bride back to this hole in the ground." The added panic made him tremble. The drenching sweat stung his eyes and blurred his vision. He almost stumbled over the little girl in front of him. "Arghh," he groaned again. Then the Warrior King's laughter boomed in his head, "Son of Hezron, relax; you'll survive—and you may even enjoy yourself. I promise!"

The marriage procession descended through the whisps of ground fog flowing down the ramp. In the glow of the bright torchlight, it looked like a stream of soft white cotton. The eerily beautiful singing began to echo off the Fortress' walls, sounding like a legion of angels. The girls split off and flanked the flower-strewn platform at the bottom of the ramp. Kalev led Raisa's Horse beside the stage and handed the reins to the strutting Little Yoshi.

As Kalev moved to lift Raisa off the saddle, he accidentally looked up, and their eyes met. Kalev noisily inhaled and froze. With his mouth hanging open, he stared at her smile. His world went silent. It was wonderfully terrifying how beautiful she was. He didn't want to lose that moment of awe. But eventually, Kalev closed his mouth, shook his head, and whispered to himself, "Why me? You deserve so much better." Raisa mistook his expression and words. Her smile grew into a sly grin, and she whispered, "If you run, your ema, my brother, and I will hunt you down and…" She didn't finish—just smiled and giggled. Kalev looked confused but let it go. A heavily armed Othniel stood next to the rabbi and beamed at his sister. The Chief Rabbi of Yehudah was proudly wearing the white leopard skin coat. He was flanked by a stupidly smiling Hoshe'a and Ari.

Kalev easily lifted his bride up to the platform. Then, out of pure habit, he purposefully strode to the front of the stage and up the stairs. The trio proudly trailed their general, but this time, it was a ferocious, glaring Akiba that barred their way. He quietly growled. "Form up with your squad. And take those ᒪ৲Ш✢ᘓ hats off." The trio's shoulders slumped in unison, but they reluctantly complied.

As Kalev's right foot touched the top stair, Ari yelled out, "Army of Yisrael, attention." The thunder of 3891 swords drawn and heels slapping together shook the ground. The General was on mental and emotional overload. *What are you thinking? You don't deserve her. If she hasn't yet, she'll see right through that façade. You're just a beat-up forty-year-old kid playing soldier. A wannabe leader who's clueless about being a husband, let alone one she deserves. You can't even give her children. What are you thinking! Oh, that's right—you're not thinking* as usual. *Just turn around and walk away, at least for her sa…* And then he locked eyes with the reason his entire world had changed. Those eyes, that smile, they seemed to quiet those self-destructive doubts and second-guessing. Her glowing face had a way of focusing his mind and confusing it at the same time. The General never felt himself move, but before he knew it, he was standing beside her and feeling very dizzy.

The pale and sweaty Nachshon smiled at his lost-looking son-in-law. He discreetly leaned toward Kalev and whispered, "Kalev, breathe." The General exhaled in a loud, contented sigh, causing chuckles from everyone in earshot. Raisa took Kalev's sweaty hand, leaned toward him, and whispered, "Kalev, son of Rachael and Hezron. It's *you* I've saved my whole being for. I have always loved only you." She grabbed the front of his flimsy tunic. "Kalev, I do see the *real you*." She looked at his chest. "In fact, we all can see you very clearly." Except Kalev and Nachshon, the others started coughing to cover their laugh. Then she looked up at Kalev's embarrassed expression. She smiled as fresh tears began to fall. "I want to spend the rest of my life with the gentle man I see right now…oh, and his 3000 kids too."

Nachshon loudly cleared his throat and stifled a cough. Raisa took it as a reprimand for her "very improper" statements. Kalev saw Raisa shoot her father *the look*. She was already an expert. Kalev smiled at Hoshe'a and Ari, then whispered, "Yeah, they're born with it." The three of them *inappropriately* laughed.

The General couldn't help but look down at his Raisa's fiery blue eyes. The mountain of a man mindlessly blurted out, "Mrs. General, how are you more pretty than the last time I looked at you?" Kalev's eyebrows shot up. "ძᏍᏍძ♆✢, you just sounded like Little Frog," he reprimanded himself…*aloud.*

The rabbi firmly placed his trembling hands on the couple's heads and ordered them to kneel with their faces to the ground. Without any prompting, the Army of Yisrael quickly sheathed their swords and knelt with *their* faces to the fog-covered deck. At the very back of the assembly, Moshe, his brother, and his sister did the same.

The head of the tribe of Yehudah closed his eyes and opened his mouth, and at first, nothing came out. Then, in a voice that to Kalev sounded just like the Warrior King, the old rabbi sang. "Shema, Yisrael, Adonai, Eloheinu. Adonai, Echad, Adonai Echad, Adonai Echad Baruch Shem Kevod Malchuto Le Olam Va'ed, Le Olam Va'ed, Le Olam Va'ed: Hear, O Yisrael, the Yehovah, our Elohim—the Yehovah is one. Praise be His name forever. Your kingdom will reign forever. We know Your kingdom will reign forever."

Nachshon paused. With tears streaming down his gaunt, gray-stubbled cheeks, he took a ragged breath and then continued.

"Blessed are You, Yehovah, our Elohim, Ruler of the universe, who creates the fruit of the vine.

"Blessed are You, Yehovah, our Elohim, Ruler of the universe, who created everything for His glory.

"Blessed are You, Yehovah, our Elohim, Ruler of the universe, who created humanity. May the barren one, the land You promised to our abba Abraham, rejoice greatly and delight in the ingathering of her children within her in joy.

"Blessed are You, Yehovah, who causes us, Your chosen people, to rejoice in our promised inheritance.

"Blessed are You, Yehovah, our Elohim, Ruler of the universe, who created humanity in His image, in the image of the likeness of His form, and made for them an everlasting establishment.

"Blessed are You, Yehovah, our Elohim, Ruler of the universe, who created joy and gladness, groom and bride, mirth, song, delight and rejoicing, love, harmony, peace, and companionship. Soon, Yeshua, Yehovah, our Elohim, may there ever be heard throughout the tribe of Yehudah and from all the sons of Abraham voices of joy and gladness, voices of groom and bride, the jubilant voices of those joined in this 'taking of a wife,' the voices of young people feasting and singing.

"Blessed are You; I AM that I AM, our Savior, our deliverer, who causes the groom to rejoice with His bride, *Emunah*."

Nachshon ordered them to rise to an upright kneeling position. Behind them, in unison, the troops silently rose to stand at attention. Hoshe'a handed the smiling yet sick-looking old Rabbi the quart-sized, jewel-encrusted golden goblet. It was filled to the brim with last season's deep purple wine. Nachshon took a sip and then quickly handed it to Kalev before he started hacking. Kalev shot a withering glance and growled at his wide-eyed brother. He'd seriously hurt Hoshe'a if this was the viper wine. But Hoshe'a vigorously shook his head. The dazed groom grabbed the heavy cup with both hands and drained it. Ari was laughing as he took the empty chalice. Kalev helped his bride to stand. They turned around and faced the huge audience. Nachshon took another wet breath and yelled, "The marriage contract is complete." And that was it. They were married.

At once, the silence shattered with almost two thousand war cries echoing through the massive fortress. Even the Warrior King let loose with His own deafening war cry. This, in turn, started a hilarious chorus of animal bleating, snorting, and bellowing. Kalev didn't hear any of it. He lifted his little Raisa off the ground into his massive arms. With tears streaming down their cheeks, they kissed in front of the massive, wildly cheering crowd. At the rear of the battalion, two companies of troops began blowing *shofars* (Ram's horns). Carni's well-practiced troops held up their tambourines and began singing and dancing around the platform. Back near the dining area, Carni had arranged for a group of musicians to set up on the smaller stage. They began to play every kind of instrument. There were harps, three- and ten-stringed lyres, lutes, cymbals, bells, castanets, hand-held drums, flutes, trumpets, *shofar*, and double pipes. The troops were brought to attention and then loudly dismissed. And the feasting began. Kalev was in his own little world with his wife in his arms. They dreamily locked eyes and repeatedly kissed.

Nachshon backed up to the blue backdrop, bent over, and started coughing. He'd been coughing sporadically since the fire. But two days ago it became constant and really hurt. Then yesterday he started coughing up blood, a lot of blood. He'd thought he'd kept it a secret. But the old rabbi *would not* be denied giving his daughter's wedding blessing.

Knowing Nachshon's condition, Ari kept an eye on the ill-looking prince of the Yehudah tribe. Thus, he was the only one who saw Nachshon's knees start to buckle. Othniel had already left the stage, so Ari quickly elbowed Hoshe'a, and they caught the quivering man under the arms and kept him from collapsing to the deck. They gently moved the wheezing rabbi behind the shiny curtains and sat him down on the rear edge of the stage. Major Hoshe'a and General Ari stood behind the wheezing and coughing old man to keep the newlyweds from seeing what was happening. Right then Deborah was dancing by and instantly saw the concern on her "future husband's" face. She walked to the stage, and Ari bent down and filled her in. She grabbed six of her junior officers before they danced past. Ari and Hoshe'a gently lifted the semi-conscious rabbi off the stage. The men put Nachshon's limp and sweaty arms around their necks and grabbed the back of his sash. Deborah and her officers quickly surrounded the three men and pretended to be dancing in a circle. By the time the men got Nachshon to his room, he was completely unconscious, with a small trickle of blood dripping into his beard. Carni rushed in the door and started shouting orders.

43

The trio proudly marched in front of the untethered Boaz and stopped at the stage's bottom stair. Without putting her down, Kalev carried his Raisa toward the stairs. Little Frog quickly did an about-face, looked up, and yelled something at the horse's nose. Raisa and Kalev started laughing when the large stallion lowered to its knees.

The General smiled and nodded his thanks to the beaming little guy. Then the new husband gently lowered his new wife to the saddle. He climbed on behind her, and Boaz rose to his full height. Her towering man leaned forward, put his arms around her, and took the reins. His hot breath on the back of her sweaty neck made her shiver.

Without any prodding, the horse followed the parading trio around the stage and up the ramp. The little girls were already in their assigned positions. They formed a lit path for the bridal procession, eagerly waved at the marching trio, and then quickly fell in behind as Boaz passed. At the top of the ramp, a new path curved right and then north. The oblivious Kalev dropped the needless reins and reveled in the smell of Raisa's long black hair. The feel of her small yet amazingly voluptuous body leaning back against his chest caused his loincloth to squeeze him harder than ever.

Ten ranks of the littlest "yucky oil lamp girls" preceded the trio of little kings. The five girls in the rear rank kept turning around and blowing kisses at the little stern-faced sultans. All three of them kept loudly whispering at the girls to stop it. The remaining three hundred girls marched in perfect step behind the new couple. Kalev hadn't noticed and really wouldn't have cared that they'd bypassed Carni's house and his brightly lit barn, with a flower-strewn Ox looking very annoyed. The glowing footpath entered the tall cornfields. The small hand-held oil lamps barely lit the previously prepared road through the corn stalks. Whisps of ground fog swirled up and then vanished as the parade marched down the quiet path.

The girl's soft singing seemed to ebb and flow as they got deeper into the beautifully green field. "Shema, Yisrael, Adonai, Eloheinu, Adonai, Echad…" They repeated the same song the entire journey.

Above the stalks, a canopy of stars surrounded a very bright full moon. Five wordless minutes into the field, Raisa felt the rock-hard chest behind her start trembling. Kalev choked back tears and whispered into Raisa's ear, "I never thought this was possible for me. I, um, I hope that someday I can be the husband you deserve." Raisa smiled through her own tears of joy, leaned back even harder, and softly replied, "My love, you're the only one I've ever wanted. So I guess Yahweh has already established that we deserve each other." She turned her head and kissed his solid arm.

Kalev wanted to ride with her in his arms forever. But too soon, Boaz slowed as their path intersected with the main road and stopped. Kalev instinctively grabbed the reins. The surprised couple watched as Little Frog quickly did another about-face. He pulled on Boaz's halter until they were eye to eye, then silently pointed at the dune across the road. The boy did another about-face. On Little Yoshi's screaming command, the girls and the trio parted, and Boaz automatically shot forward, almost tossing Kalev backward off his hindquarters. When Kalev realized what was coming, he quickly leaned a little too hard forward causing Raisa to grind her chest into the saddle horn. Boaz raced almost vertically up a dune.

All the girls gasped in unison as the sight of the tall white stallion and its surprised riders began to glow as they reached the top of the shadowed dune.

Then, just as abruptly, Boaz stopped at the top, almost sending his riders over his head. Kalev was about to reprimand the horse when Raisa gasped. After spending the last ten minutes in the moonlight and the soft glow of the palm-sized oil lamps, Kalev's eyes took a couple of seconds to adjust to the bright glare.

Thirty feet below, hundreds of tall torches surrounded a large oval of dark green grass. On the right side of the stark green carpet was the most dazzling tent either of them had ever seen. In the bright flickering torchlight, the life-sized, embroidered-gold lions and horses that covered the roof and the sides seemed to move and dance on the deep blue background. At the far end of the basin was a large, raised bathing pool. The reflection of the torches off the bubbling spring water shot pinpoints of gold dancing across the dune behind it. They both were speechless as Kalev jumped down and lifted Raisa off the saddle. She quickly glanced back down the dark side of the dune to wave her thanks. But the trio of strutting sultans and the company of girls had vanished.

Kalev was still amazed at how light and fragile Raisa felt in his massive arms. He leaned toward Boaz the Lightening Horse and whispered, "Thank you." As if the steed could understand, he bobbed his head, snorted, and then raced down the dark side of the dune. Kalev watched him go, then grinned; he knew this paradise was surrounded by staggered double rings of armed troops in a spider hole. The General really couldn't tell where they were, and surprisingly, he liked that. He knew the troops were painfully aware that First Sergeant would become their mortal enemy if they came within ten yards of the base of the dune.

Kalev lifted his Raisa and swung her around to his back, then quickly plodded down the dune. He put Raisa down in front of the lions guarding the entrance to the tent. Raisa started giggling and pointed. "I'm pretty sure your ema didn't see that." Kalev scowled. Just to the right of the tall entrance hung a large papyrus, obviously drawn by the trio and probably their squad leader. They had to use their imagination to interpret some of the poorly drawn pictographs. Kalev read it aloud, "This is the General's and Mrs. General's rich man's tent. Keep out or die 'cause Corpal Little Yoshi and Privit Frog and Privat Croc are sileent and dedly! And well killing all Egypt pegs ded." At the bottom were three stick figures holding swords with red paint dripping off and pooling at the figures' feet. Kalev chuckled.

"Every word is misspelled." Then he sighed. *Our personal comedians*... Kalev thought. Raisa laughed. "Did I say that aloud? I must really be tired." Raisa stopped laughing and grew a sly grin. "I can fix that...later! But now, my husband, it's time to complete our marriage." "Yeah, what does that me...?" But before the man with the see-through tunic and loincloth could finish his sentence, he was yanked inside the tent.

44

An hour before sunup, two days after the all-night wedding feast, Yahweh woke Moshe out of a troubled sleep. He hadn't slept well since Ziporah "divorced him," took the boys, and went back to Midian. The exhausted eighty-year-old sat up and growled, "What now?" Yahweh laughed. "You need to see this. Get dressed and put on your sword." Moshe was instantly awake. "Well, that's a first." Yahweh had never told him to arm himself.

Moshe followed Yahweh's directions into the cornfield. Goaded by Yahweh's booming voice, the reluctant Moshe expertly wove his way through the rough corn stalks without moving a single one. He stopped and quietly knelt on the damp ground within sight of a road. They were about a half mile north of Kalev's forbidden sand bowl. As soon as his knees hit the rich black soil, he heard the hoofbeats of eleven horses coming up the road in his direction. Moshe drew his sword, expertly crawled to the edge of the road, and prepared to lunge into the road. The moon was still bright, and the second he could make out the lead horse, he heard the distinct sound of multiple arrows piercing bodies, combined with the high-pitched squeal of the wounded and dying horses.

Moshe's leaped onto the road. He quickly moved to the first rider and used his sword tip to pull aside the bottom of the man's black robe. He recognized the grooved, hooked blade of Egyptian army's standard-issue Khopesh sword.

Two squads of archers silently emerged out of the stocks. Moshe recognized Akiba. "Bedouin raiders?" he quietly asked. Moshe shook his head, bent down, and retrieved the sword. Akiba took the sword and looked at the blade. Moshe nodded. "Yeah, it's pretty nicked up. They were probably relieved after a battle and didn't take the time to have them sharpened. They just wanted to get home." Moshe shrugged. "I did the same thing once or twice." Akiba nodded. "But why the black robes and keffiyehs?" Moshe noticed the wounded horse at his feet blink. He drove his own sword deep into its heart. "Since Yahweh's been decimating Egypt for the last eight months, I'd wager they haven't been paid in at least eight. They've probably raided every caravan and village between here and the Megiddo valley." Moshe knowingly smirked. At least the ones you boys haven't "foraged" first. Akiba and the other teens snickered.

Moshe stood aside and was very amazed. Two squads swiftly pulled most of the bodies from the horses and lined them up side by side. Then they proceeded to remove most of the arrows from each body and strip it of any personal item that may identify who they are. Another two squads swooped in and collected all the tac and most of the saddles. The saddle bags were methodically searched for anything of worth. Then the saddles were also lined up on the edge of the road. Twelve large horse drawn wagons raced up the road and reined in in front of Moshe. He recognized the heavily armed lead driver from General Kalev's wedding feast.

Standing in the middle of the carnage, Akiba used a series of growls to signal for Captain Deborah to report. She splashed her way back through the black-looking blood and excrement. The impressed Moshe heard the fierce-looking Deborah use a series of ibis calls to signal her orders to the drivers behind her. The evenly spaced horses and wagons trampled a wide path through the corn stalks on each side of the road. As the first two wagons drew even with the last dead horse. Deborah blew three staccato whistles. The wagons slowly turned into the fields. They let the horses weave their way through the stocks, then stopped about ten yards from the road. A single faint made it to the front of the line, and the girls expertly backed the wagons back toward the road. Each wagon was perfectly aligned with each dead horse.

The wagons tail gates were lowered in unison. Then each girl stood beside their wagon smiling at each other. A platoon of teen-boy troops crashed through the stocks from the south. They all quickly dismounted and started unloading the wagons. Long coils of rope and sturdy four-by-eight-inch boards were unloaded from each wagon. As Moshe watched in astonishment, odd-looking pulleys were attached to rings bolted to the boards at the front end of the wagon bed. The ropes were fed through, and then both ends were pulled out of the wagon bed. At the end of each of the six, the tongue and grooved boards were slid together then laid into brackets at the rear end of the bed. This formed a gradually sloping ramp, down to the dirt fright in front of the dead horse. The horses' hooves were tied together and then attached to one end of the rope. With four older boys on each rope, the dead horse looked like it simply floated up the ramp. One of the bodies was placed into the wagon bed. The girls kissed the boys on the cheek, mounted the wagon seat, and waited. After the horses were removed, the remaining bodies and saddles were taken care of. The saddles, tack, weapons and personal items were loaded into the twelfth wagon. The squads assembled and then melded into the cornfield. The entire operation from the attack to a vacant road took less than twenty minutes. And the only sounds that carried where the initial screams and the whistles. Otherwise the maneuver was performed with wordless hand signals.

When Akiba finished directing his four platoon sergeants, Moshe walked up shaking his head. "That was a work of art. I assume this happens frequently." Akiba smiled. "Well, truthfully, Sir, we've only done this twice before. We used our AARs as a tool to develop, fine-tune, and train our people for contingencies just like this." "Colonel, I can tell you for a fact that I have never seen such precision in my life. If they can fight with this same kind of expertise, Yahweh's chosen people are in great hands." Akiba grinned. "Funny you should mention that. We…"

Akiba was interrupted by eight young but very loud voices coming from the stocks five yards behind the two men. The argument was clearly about their kill count. Moshe smirked at the cringing and fuming

Akiba. "Wow, does that bring back memories. Do you want to go and…?" Akiba held up his finger and whispered, "I'm waiting for their sergeant to take control." Moshe slowly shook his head. "This guy's leadership skills are astounding. I could rule all of Egypt with troops like this," the old general mused. Yahweh made his usual throat-clearing sound in Moshe's gut. "Don't get any ideas. Besides, you're out of here in about three months, and you *will not* want any part of what you'll leave behind."

The little trio was in a heated dispute with five older boys. "I shot the first two; Yoshi shot the third one…" "I shot the three *and* four one," Little Yoshi protested. "Right," said Croc sarcastically. "I did, and I have a more better rank…" "Shut up, Yoshi," yelled Little Frog. "That doesn't mean you're silent and deadly as me and Croc." The oldest boy yelled, "All three of you little babies are wrong. We shot the first seven of them and our sergeant and squad leader got the rest. You three hit the horses or their saddles…." "Or their legs…" another boy chimed in. "…'cause you're too small to shoot any higher." The trio drew their little swords in unison. The older boys laughed and drew their full-sized Khopeshs. "Be careful, little babies. You might hurt yourselves with those little things…" The boys were so loud, they never heard their life-changing experience approaching.

Akiba heard the swords clank and had already turned to step in, then abruptly stopped. In the distance, the rapidly growing sound of a swearing haboob crashed through the stocks. When the growing storm was about fifty yards away, the sound suddenly went silent.

The trio would later swear to Sergeant Marasha, "When we were killing the older boys, a huge sha'dim with fiery eyes and a fiery sword and black wings dripping spit and blood rose out of the cornfield and flew in circles over our heads, and it screamed and screamed and screamed, then tried to kill us, but Yoshi pulled out his little knife sword and stabbed him between the legs, but he didn't die…and he…will…never…die; he'll just scream and fly and keep screaming and screaming and screaming until we die and kill him. "

Akiba smiled at Moshe, then whispered, "Here comes *my hammer*! You'll want to see this." Both men crept closer and watched as the stocks beside the carelessly yelling boys slowly parted. With his sword blade glinting in the bright moonlight, First Sergeant Abraham stepped toward the group. All eight yelling boys went silent. They swallowed hard in unison and simultaneously stepped back. The nearby troops who had stayed to watch the hilarious show quickly faded back into the dark field. But Moshe and Akiba silently crept closer.

The vicious-looking drill sergeant raised his sword like he was going to add the shocked little boys to the body count. Moonlight glinted off the stationary weapon. The highly polished blade was held straight over his head, then in an instant, it was a half inch from the oldest boy's upturned face. And no one even saw the sergeant move. Two terrifying seconds later, everyone heard the stream of urine gushing down the boy's leg, then splashing on the bent stalks' leaves. Even when the tightly wound First Sergeant took four four-count breaths, the sword hanging over the crying boy's nose never even quivered. He even straightened his tunic with the other hand, and still the sword never moved. But when Little Frog whispered, "Do it," the sword disappeared, and a long-jagged dagger suddenly materialized in the sixteen-year-old First Sergeant's hand. In a barely audible whisper, the sergeant ordered all eight boys to kneel, lace their fingers behind their heads, and stick out their chins. The scared boys complied. All eight boys were in tears after five eternal minutes of Mr. Abraham's infamous expletive-filled attitude adjustments. Then, to literally put a fine point on his lesson, the sergeant's dagger suddenly appeared embedded in Little Frog's sword handle. The handle stuck out of the boy's back scabbard. From the sergeant's point of view, the handle was less than four inches above and just behind the shoulder. The dagger barely wiggled right next to Little Frog's ear. Moshe later commented that he never saw the drill sergeant's hand move.

45

Three mornings after arriving in their "Eden," as Raisa had named it, they temporarily came up for air, so to speak. The bleary-eyed giant stepped out of his refuge. Compared to the typical Hebrew man his age, Kalev was at least fourteen inches taller and eighty pounds heavier.

The morning air was unusually cooler for this time of year. Kalev took a deep breath, held it for four counts, then blew it out. He'd never felt so alive, so content, and… *Happy?* That was an unknown concept, but he could get used to it.

The taut, stark-naked man stretched his back and received the satisfying pops. Which were followed by the usual groans as all the previously abused muscles and tendons painfully flared at the strain. For the last three days, he'd missed his brutal "wake up and sweat" strength and agility regimen. *But…* he happily chuckled to himself, *I have* significantly *increased my long-distance stamina and battle-breathing techniques.*

He yawned, then quickly headed around the corner to the rear of the tent. Once again, the son of Hezron was pleasantly surprised by his brother's ingenuity. Behind the large fifty-five-by-seventy-foot, six-room tent was a small, enclosed stall. Because they'd only slept, ate, and come out here when they absolutely *had to*, he'd never noticed the stall door. Probably because he'd been in too much of a hurry to get back inside.

So it was the first time he realized the door had pictures. The solid piece of black wood *had* to be previously carved and used as a table or something. The pictures had even more bunnies and horses dancing around a naked woman holding a bird. And right above her head, someone, probably Hoshe'a, had scratched the words "General Kalev's Royal Throne Room." Inside was an ornately carved box with a hole in it, and somehow this one also had flowing water. *Probably from the spring*, Kalev reasoned.

Kalev had just bathed his pleasantly exhausted body in the enclosed bubbling spring. He was returning to the tent to dry off when both of the front tent flaps flew open, and his overly energetic little wife raced out. Her arms were full of their bed blankets and the way-too-slippery, puffy mattress covers. The proud husband gawked at his bride. Her wild black hair streamed behind her head. *Like Boaz's tail at full gallop*, he innocently thought. And the sun caused her billowing full-length robe to shimmer as she ran. He realized it was actually *his discarded-forever*, see-through wedding tunic. The impromptu show was breathtaking.

His Raisa sprinted to the delivery basket, dropped the bedclothes, and started unloading the oversized crate. Again, because of their "hectic schedule," Kalev hadn't noticed the contraption hanging over the edge of the thirty-foot-high dune. A long wooden arm reached down to the grassy floor opposite their tent. Ropes and pullies were attached to the joints of the arm. The big man smiled. *Just like Hoshe'a's stringy muscles*, he thought. Kalev walked over and helped his frantic-looking wife unload the basket. "What's the rush?" he asked. Raisa didn't look up. "I was supposed to send these linens out the morning after our wedding night. I forgot, and your mother is probably wondering what happened." Kalev had stopped unloading and wordlessly looked at her quizzically. Raisa glanced up then went back to work. "I'll explain the tradition later." Kalev shrugged; they emptied the crate, Raisa yanked on the slack rope, and the arm began to rise. Kalev didn't think to ask how she knew how the mechanical marvel worked. He was too distracted with the amazing smells wafting up from the covered containers in his arms. After two more trips, the oversized dining table was filled. A five-gallon urn of wine sat next to a single-gallon urn. One burning sniff, and Kalev knew the smaller jar contained Yadin's very potent viper wine. It had to have been added to the basket without his ema knowing. Kalev was starving. He guessed he'd only eaten one loaf of bread and drank two cups of water a day since they got here. Raisa was looking down at the shiny tunic. "This thing smells, and we *accidentally* ripped my marriage robe in half that night." Kalev chuckled at the memory but didn't comment. "It just didn't seem right to bring my everyday robe for our wedding week, which, after careful consideration, I've decided will actually last fourteen days…I just sent a note on that basket, informing your ema of my decision. Any objections, General?" Kalev smiled, shook his head, and took a long drink. He could get used to following her orders. It was kind of exhilarating and dangerous at the same time. "So this is all I have to wear *if* I *have* to wear anything. Unlike my mouthwatering husband, I can't go outside in my birthday suit."

Kalev's eyes grew wide, and he choked on his wine. After he finished coughing and wiped away the burning wine dripping from the inside of his nose, he shot to his feet. "[illegible], I completely forgot! Okay, close your eyes and turn around. I have a surprise for you." She warily smiled, then shook her head in amazement. "Kalev, my love. I want to *experience* all of your surprises, but I really need to eat, drink something, then head to the 'ladybird seat' first." Kalev laughed. "Okay, but hurry." He handed her a cup and poured a couple swallows full of wine. "Here, drink this. I'll find you some ema bread before you get back." He hurried her out, then sprinted to the storage rooms in the rear of the tent. He opened all four of the front and room dividing curtains. Then jogged back to the dining space and twirled one of the shiny embroidered napkins into a blindfold. "Why does everything have to have pictures of bunnies on it?" he grumbled. Kalev stuffed his mouth with a quarter loaf of sweetbread and impatiently waited by the tent flap.

Two nights or days ago, he wasn't sure, Kalev watched his *exhausting* wife fall asleep. Out of curiosity, he slowly got up, grabbed the candle from the bedside table, and explored the amazing "rich man's" tent. The billowing material overhead curved up to two peaks that had to be over twenty-five feet above the padded floor. The sides had double layers of thick material, which kept the light out and the temperature cooler. The largest front area was turned into their elaborate bedroom and small eating spaces. A seven-foot-tall, shiny-blue-and-gold-embroidered curtain surrounded their twelve-by-twelve-foot, too-soft bed. A taller, white, shiny drape separated the front bed and dining areas from the rest of the tent. Four additional rooms spanned the entire rear section of the tent.

Kalev was very relieved when he pulled the first two room's curtains aside. Instead of the three trunks he'd asked Ema to fill with the best women's clothes she could find, i.e., Raisa's *Mattan*, both room's floors were covered with carefully folded and segregated stacks of "girl clothes," blankets, those embarrassing short bunches of folded material, and other girl things he didn't want to know about. And in the corner were three smaller stacks for him. He was relieved to see that two of the stacks were plain, unembroidered tunics and loincloths. The third stack consisted of folded robes he never thought he'd wear. And in front of the stacks were five pairs of plain, thick-leather sandals. The third and fourth rooms were crammed floor to ceiling with solid gold plates, cups, pitchers, basins, trays, weird-looking pokers, and other stuff *she'd* care about.

As he'd returned to their bed, Kalev noticed a pair of dangling ropes. They were connected to the canopy above their bed. He quietly pulled them apart, revealing a spectacular star-filled sky. He blew out the candle and literally slipped beneath their down-filled shiny blanket. Raisa's eyes popped open, and she smiled that amazingly mischievous smile again.

After a while, he lay there panting with her head on his chest. "I really like your version of wrestling better." Raisa started to sit up to get them a drink of water when she looked up and gasped. The full moon was peaking around the eastern edge of the open canopy. The wide-eyed General's jaw dropped. Breathlessly watching her upturned face in the bright moonlight almost scared him. "Raisa. How do you do that? Every time I look at you, I can't breathe." His innocent-sounding voice made her smile. "And *you* are my handsome husband. And I am so very proud to be your wife and wrestling partner. You are…" Raisa abruptly paused. In the bright moonlight, Kalev could see his wife's eyes widen. Then the daughter of the chief rabbi of the Yehudah tribe heard what her abba called "Yehovah's words" gush from her mouth.

"Son of Hezron, true to Yahweh, you are an Anshe man. Yehovah, your Elohim, chose *you* to lead those boys out there. You're *their* example, a larger-than-life champion, the gold standard for honorable character. You are *already* someone they point to and say, 'Someday I'm gonna be just like the General!'" Raisa's voice softened, and she tapped his hard chest four times. "Oh my love, everyone needs a hero…and you are ours."

But Kalev had already looked away out of embarrassment. Maybe it was because he felt safe with her. Maybe it was because he needed to talk it out for the 300th time. Or maybe it was simply because he hadn't slept two hours since the night before their wedding. Whatever the reason, Kalev's mental defenses disappeared, and the painfully familiar memories of his lifelong failures and inadequacies flooded his exhausted mind. "Raisa, I'm not a hero. I'm not really a general either. I've been making it up as I go along, and soon someone like Moshe is going to see I'm just a pretending wannabe. I don't deserve any honor, and I certainly don't deserve you." Raisa cupped his cheeks in her hands, smiled an innocent smile, and whispered, "I'll be right back." She jumped out of the huge bed and left the tent. Kalev lay back. His sad, bloodshot eyes stared at the enormous moon that was starting to fill the entire skylight. Raisa's brooding husband had just fallen asleep when she quietly snuck back into the room.

His dreamless sleep was violently interrupted by the overwhelming sense of drowning, his worst fear. The instant jolt of icy panic caused him to vault out of bed, hacking and gasping for air. Raisa stood on the bed with a single-gallon water jar under one arm and a devious smile. She pointed her finger at his face and proclaimed, "Kalev, son of Hezron, you are the General; you are a hero—you are and will always be *my* hero. And guess what, my mighty marked one! Just like this holy, soul-cleansing bath, you do not have a say in the matter." Raisa reached over and tapped the top of his head to accent each word. "Let. This. Be. Written."

Kalev growled and lunged for her. Raisa squealed, threw the urn at him, and leaped. She intended to escape out the front of the tent. But Kalev, in one fluid motion, dodged the urn, reflexively caught her in mid-air, and then the too-strong giant sent her spinning toward the glaring moon. Kalev's jaw dropped as he watched his naked little rotating wife pull her legs together, draw her arms in, and spin even faster. As Raisa reached her fourteen-foot apex, she threw her arms straight out, and the spinning slowed. She landed and disappeared into the large, soft pile of newly soaked blankets. Kalev roared and dove in. Then round twenty-seven of their wrestling match began.

So now, two days later, Raisa walked back into the tent. The nervous Kalev had stood there long enough to start second-guessing his ema's choices for Raisa's *Mattan. What if she doesn't like the clothes or the rest of the stuff? I hate the stupid bunnies, and they're all over everything. Of course*, he nervously chuckled to himself, *for the last couple of days, we have kind of acted like rabbits, sort of...* Raisa walked in. Kalev quickly blindfolded his wife and handed her half the loaf of his ema's special barley bread.

Raisa started voraciously eating, then pleaded, "Kalev, my stud, please let me sit down and eat first…" He chuckled, "Raisa, my single-minded fireball, there's more to life than wrestling. I'd just like to talk and get to know each other better. I mean, I have a lot of emotions and hopes and dreams to share…" She stopped walking, and he almost ran into her. With her last bite of bread in her cheek, she sadly asked, "Do you really mean that?" Kalev laughed. "Seriously, me? Of course not!" She smiled. "Good, 'cause I have a surprise for you too." Kalev held her shoulders so she couldn't turn around. "Okay, if you insist. But I want to show you something *else* first."

He'd already moved one of the heavy, padded thrones from the ugly furniture room and positioned it so he could sit and watch. Kalev stood her in front of the first room. That was when he realized he'd forgotten a candle, and this part of the tent was dark. "Just a second." Kalev rushed over and opened the closest pair of rear tent flaps. The bright sunlight streamed in and caused most of the four storage rooms' contents to sparkle. He bent down and whispered as he whipped the blindfold off her eyes. "Behold, wife of Kalev, your *Mattan*." Then he plopped back into the chair and anxiously watched.

Kalev watched from behind as she walked forward and bent down to examine the first stack of clothes. He swiftly rubbed his tired eyes, then stared at her, wide-eyed and slack-jawed. The sunlight caused his *very* see-through wedding tunic to shimmer. *Kalev, you idiot*, he wordlessly scolded himself, *you should have hidden the other clothes and given her gold coins or something. We are definitely keeping that shirt.*

Then, out of nowhere, his beautiful Raisa's taut back and smooth shoulders started shaking. Her sobs came in waves. Kalev grimaced. "[illegible]," he quietly groaned. He was instantly beside her, dropped to his knees so they could see eye to eye, then gently turned her toward him. She started sobbing even harder, and his heart sank.

"Raisa, I am soooo sorry. Ema picked out the clothes. I couldn't…I should have waited to see… We can burn all this stuff, and you can have the gold coins or a saddle or two saddles or a second horse or a Phoenician sword and shield or whatever you want. But please…I'm so sorry!" She threw her arms around his neck and cried into his bare shoulder. [illegible], he thought again. Kalev didn't know what to do. This girl crying thing was all new to him. Then the big man braced himself for the inevitable waterfall of unintelligible of words. *Maybe Nachshon could teach me how to interpret this female foreign language*, he silently hoped.

Kalev loved his wife. So for now, he'd concentrate and try to piece together this emotional word puzzle for himself. "…been poor…pretty things…since my ema…abba and Othniel…broken sandals… comb…never a mirror…ever…deserve you…Eden…wrestling and everything…*I love you so much it hurts!*" He understood the last line. But his frustration multiplied when she started crying even harder.

Kalev scowled at the closest stack of clothes as the tears and snot started to drip down his chest. He hated not knowing how to fix this. He wanted or needed to say something, anything, but his tired mind refused to work. So he wisely kept his mouth shut, picked her up, and sat on the stupid throne with her still clinging to his neck. As he sat for a while, the crying turned to whimpering and then went silent. Her arms fell from his neck, and her breathing deepened.

A faint rustling sound caused Kalev's eyes to flutter open. The tent was pitch black and silent. He looked up but didn't even see stars. He didn't remember carrying her back to bed, and he knew he hadn't closed the overhead skylight flaps. He'd told Raisa that unless there was a haboob, he wanted to always see the sky. It kept him from feeling shut in. That was the only drawback to his room in the Fortress. It always felt close. Oh, and there wasn't Raisa to wrestle with or the privacy to do it. So I guess that was at least three more deficits. Wow. He smiled to himself. If I had known about this version of wrestling… No. Hotep would have found out, and I'd have ended up killing him. Then I'd be murdered and leave Raisa a widow or, worse, leave her to marry Hoshe'a…so, for now, Kalev, the son of Hezron and Rachael, will be thankfully content to just lie here and revel in my wife and our Eden. His last thought was, *No, I'm sure I didn't close that curtain.*

Raisa suddenly bolted out of bed and ran out the front tent flap. Kalev sat up and lit the candle. His muscles felt stiff, and his neck felt kinked. The big man dropped to the floor and did push-ups until he heard her starting to open the tent flaps ten minutes later. Raisa stepped inside and Kalev flew past her. The Hebrew beauty hopped onto the bed and almost collapsed the tent trying to open the sky flaps. When she got them open as far as she could, she turned, and her husband was standing there with his own mischievous grin. "I don't suppose you could keep jumping and try to close them. I'm really enjoying the show." She smiled back. Round thirty-one.

Forty-five exhausting minutes later, the thirty-five-year-old wife and her forty-year-old husband lay back breathless and stared at the gray-blue sky. Kalev really didn't care, but when Raisa caught her breath, she whispered, "We slept about twenty-three straight hours." Kalev turned and stared at her. "And to me, that was wasted time. I think it would've been a much wiser use of at least twenty of those twenty-three hours watching you bounce on the bed." She hit him in the face with her pillow, then rolled the five feet to the other side of the bed. She stood, then looked up and pointed. "Did you close those flaps last night?" "No!" "Can they be closed from the outside? I hope." Kalev nodded. "Yeah, I saw other exterior ropes hanging from different parts of the canopy." Raisa relaxed a little. "Okay, that means someone was only…" Kalev was halfway to the tent flap before he remembered he was "without apparel." But he was too angry to stop. He exited, tore the boys' sign off the tent beside the main flaps, and knelt to write out a very precise directive. He quickly secured it to the lifting basket and almost brought Hoshe'a's arm device down with his first violent jerk of the signal rope. He jerked it a few more times to emphasize his seriousness. The basket rapidly ascended and then disappeared over the edge of the dune.

Kalev was fuming as he stomped back to the tent. He growled even louder when he realized that instead of having to unload the new load of food and wine containers from the delivery basket, they were already stacked on either side of the main entrance. Raisa stepped outside. In one quick glance, she deduced what had just happened. His stunning little wife patiently let Kalev relax before she asked, "Soooo, what did your note say?"

Kalev slowly exhaled. "Well, first of all, by the look of the tracks, only Ema and probably Ari were down here. It looks like they came over the dune next to the basket arm and left the same way… And since the torches have almost died out, it was probably sometime late last night." Raisa smiled but stayed silent. Kalev wasn't going to answer her question. But that smile…

"Okay. My official directive stated, '(1) For the next twelve days, if I even suspect someone is looking over the edge of the sand bowl, I will assume they're the enemy. I will hunt them down and hang them on the highest part of the basket arm. (2) They, friend or enemy, will be slowly scalped and skinned. (3) I'll throw their writhing and screaming body over the edge and leave it for the jackals to finish the job. (4) If that skinned, scalped, and eaten intruder somehow lives through it, I, General Kalev, will make it my life's mission to see that their ∟∿(ш)↓ᘓ ugly, scarred-up, mangled one-armed body is permanently assigned to tanning duty. (5) It will end much worse for the next person who steps on *my* dunes or green grass. And that includes *all* First Sergeants!'"

Raisa started snickering, "You added another day to the total." Kalev shrugged and smiled. "We slept through yesterday, so that one doesn't count." Raisa smiled. "I'm hungry."

They both ate for the first time in twenty-four hours. As they finished, Kalev grew serious. "Raisa, I have to admit something." She looked at the empty gallon urn on the table. Kalev smiled and slowly shook his head. "No…forget I said anything." Raisa read his brooding face. "Let's make a deal. You receive and seriously consider my accurate opinion of you, and I'll keep giving them. Otherwise, stay out of that dark place you always slid into. I love you, Kalev, more than I ever thought possible. It hurts me to see you hurt yourself, even if it's only in your head. And believe me, my love. Your thoughts and concerns are written on your face. How do you think Carni knew when to get the marriage feast in motion?" Kalev's eyebrows shot up. "Really?" Raisa smiled, then simply replied, "I love you."

Kalev thought about it. "Do you think my troops can read my face too?" Raisa shook her head. "Not the boys, no. But the girls, well…let's just say Carni has done a fantastic job teaching them about respect for their superiors. But you absolutely need her and her older girls to keep the younger ones in line. Not to mention those three boys." Kalev shook his head. "I'd never tell them this, but those three have helped me keep things in perspective more than once. That said, I'm really at a loss as how to keep them from killing each other and respect their chain of command. Their immediate superiors are just as frustrated." Raisa took a long drink of wine. And stared at her empty plate. "I assume you're talking about what they do in their off time behind the scenes, so to speak, versus what they do while they're on duty." Kalev was in the middle of chewing a thick piece of dried beef, so he just nodded. Raisa thought some more before she spoke again. Kalev loved that about her. But he was not ready for what was about to happen.

"Okay, so according to my abba, General Moshe, and your senior command staff, this army's immediate mission is to train for war. The ultimate objective being the recovery of our promised land by force. This army *will* shed a lot of blood and even some of their own. So the train up needs to be with that as its primary focus. Without question these 2000-plus troops need to train and fight as a single lethal unit.

"Thus, when the trio is on duty, it is an unequivocal necessity that they submit their individualisms to the proven concept of unwavering conformity to army training protocols."

Kalev had stopped chewing and stared at her wide-eyed. Raisa shrugged like this detailed "army terminology and stated mission plan" was common knowledge. She spoke like one of his senior officers. Raisa shrugged at his raised eyebrows. "I listen carefully. Plus your ema and I are always asking Colonel Yadin questions about army things."

Actually, Raisa and Carni had talked at length about themselves joining a new refugee platoon and submitting to the rigorous basic and advanced training. But by the look on Kalev's face, now *may not* be the best time to broach the subject. Still…

Kalev was scowling. "Raisa, the last couple of days here have taught me a lot of things. Oh, and you've taught me *many* more, but we'll put that one to bed for now." In unison, they glanced at the bed, then back at each other, and laughed. "The first thing I learned here in Eden is that I have a new appreciation for the exciting sport of wrestling, Raisa style.

"The second revelation is my newfound appreciation and growing need for privacy. Before you I'd never even thought about it. Well, except for the times in the Pit you saw me naked." Raisa grew a sly grin. "Appetizers."

Kalev grinned but continued. "Another important discovery is the critical necessity to keep my army and marriage life separate. I need the distance between the two. I *can't* talk with you about most of the army operations, And I think I like that. It'll be hard to do when we move back into my room in the Fortress. But I love you, and I know that together, we can make that complete separation between the two worlds work?" Kalev didn't mean this last statement to sound like a question.

Raisa tried and failed not to laugh. "Oh, *my* little one," she teased. "Let's look at this 'demarcation challenge' from a military point of view." Raisa reached beside her chair and opened an odd-shaped smaller trunk. She pulled out a blank scroll, a tiny sealed jar of ink, and the four sharpened quills. She had the forethought to request them from Colonel Yadin. The trunk was added to their first delivery.

Raisa narrated as she wrote.

MISSION PLAN A.

OPERATION: Army versus marriage differentiation and division

SITUATION

1. General Kalev's need for a balanced life
2. Location: Eden, Goshen
3. Approx. time for WORNO: 1000 hours
4. Major Raisa/Wife sends

MISSION

A. Separate and/or balance both objectives

1. Army versus marriage life
2. Marriage life and army combination
3. Weapons loadout
4. Ink, quills, planning parchment, and desire to achieve stated objectives

MISSION EXECUTION

A. Facts: Army

1. Fact: General Kalev is the Supreme Commanding General of Yisrael's Army
2. Fact: General Kalev has been marked by the Warrior King/Yahweh

A. Said General is commissioned to lead Yahweh's Army from the front

1. Fact: General Kalev exhibits a flagrant disregard for personal safety

A. To protect and defend those who cannot protect themselves

B. To protect and defend his troops

C. Mental/physical blind spots in need of exterior defense

1. Fact: General Kalev is strategically trained to lead/fight beside his troops

A. Over 1200 hours of weapons, tactical mission logistics, and troop support training completed

B. General Kalev *thinks and speaks* in army vernacular

1. Fact: General Kalev sleeps in the same outpost as his garrisoned troops
2. Fact: General Kalev eats both main meals with his garrisoned troops
3. Fact: General Kalev spends twelve-plus hours a day *every day* with his troops
4. Fact: General Kalev derives comic relief from said "difficult-to-control troops"
5. Fact: General Kalev and army life are one and the same, i.e., indivisible

C. Facts: Raisa/Marriage/Army

1. Fact: General Kalev is Raisa's newlywed husband
2. Fact: General Kalev and Raisa love to wrestle…a lot!
3. Fact: General Kalev loves, *needs*, and deeply respects Raisa's supportive opinions
4. Fact: Raisa deeply loves and respects General Kalev more every day
5. Fact: Raisa and General Kalev are indivisible
6. Fact: Immediate and long-term benefits of Raisa's formal basic through advanced weapons prep

a. Raisa achieves superior understanding of husband's military mindset

b. Raisa is qualified to protect General Kalev mentally and physically if injured

c. Raisa is equipped to defend herself and family

1. In General Kalev's absence
2. If, Yahweh forbid, General Kalev is KIA

a. Raisa and General Kalev can privately discuss concerns pertaining to

1. Troop discipline, assignments, off-duty obligations, and logistics
2. Ongoing operations
3. Possible advanced tactics and weapons training deficits
4. Troop loss

SUMMARY OF ACHIEVED MISSION OBJECTIVES

1. Fact: General Kalev and army life are indivisible
2. Fact: General Kalev and Raisa are indivisible
3. Fact: Army life and Raisa must be indivisible for marriage to solidify

Therefore, based on objectives, it is *mission-critical* that army life, General Kalev, and Raisa become a single, cohesive, army-minded unit. This will form one threefold marriage chord that is greater than any three separate entities. End mission plan 1015 Raisa sends.

By order of

____

Supreme Commanding General Kalev

Without looking up, Raisa started to slide the scroll, quill, and ink across the table toward Kalev. Then she thought better of it, blew the parchment dry, recovered the ink jar, dabbed the quill dry, and placed it all in the trunk. In the proceeding tense silence and still refusing to look at her husband, Raisa poured herself a large cup of wine. She gulped it down, stood, and headed toward the bed.

The disturbingly tense silence continued as she completely stripped the bed and delivered the linens to the lifting basket. Still in Kalev's wedding tunic, Raisa leaped into the cool spring water pool and bathed. Twenty minutes later she returned to the tent soaking wet with the tunic plastered to her body. But the stunned and very confused General hadn't moved.

46

Following the previous night's ambush and subsequent loud troop OPSEC fiasco, First Sergeant Abraham cleared the Pit's main deck and declared it off-limits until further notice. Seeing the too-familiar, sinister glint in the chief drill instructor's eyes, not even the officers dared to disagree.

The little trio were in a living Sha'al. According to their "fire breathing" First Sergeant Abraham, the preemptive ambush and its "[symbols]" aftermath was nothing more than "a total [symbols]-[symbols] [symbols]."

Little Frog would later report to Marasha that since the first attack by the "flying sha'dim with the black wings and fire sword and fire eyes who won't die" in the cornfield, the First Sergeant had screamed at them nonstop.

"What if that was only the first [symbols] wave of [symbols] Egyptian pigs headed your way?" he'd screamed into Yoshi's face. "These eight [symbols] idiots," Abraham repeatedly hissed to himself, "either had no idea, which would've been the fault of their superiors, or they simply didn't care.

"The fiery teen took the safety/security of this army personally. And these [symbols]-[symbols] idiots had threatened all their lives." Thus, had the boys and the sergeant sat down and calmly discussed it, Sergeant Abrahan would've *justifiably* killed them on the spot.

Their forced sprint back to the Pit gave the focused chief drill instructor time to think. Before they reached the Pit's ramp, he'd devised a *less-lethal* consequence for the "[symbols] deliberate [symbols] disregard for ongoing mission OPSEC."

The boys were ordered to unload and then wash out the twelve blood-and-[symbols]-caked wagons used to help disappear the ambush remains. "One [symbols] wagon at a time." The "first sha'dim," as the trio had labeled him, stood on each succeeding wagon seat and screamed at them to hurry or slow down or both. Then he'd repeat his sinister warning like he was relishing their eminent failure.

"And if I can find one [symbols] drop of [symbols] Egyptian [symbols] pig or [symbols] horse blood and/or [symbols], you [symbols] will fill each one of those [symbols] wagons with animal [symbols], push them a lap around the [symbols] drill floor, then empty each one onto that [symbols] drill floor. Then you [symbols] will clean it the right [symbols]-[symbols] way. Then guess what you [symbols] get to do?" Knowing he was about to reply to the question, Little Croc rammed his elbow into Frog's ribs and knocked the wind out of him. The first sha'dim's immediate screaming response to the [symbols] disrespect while standing at attention was far more severe than it would have been.

The exhausted troops finally finished the twelfth wagon and were pretty pleased with themselves… until the "black-winged, screaming first sha'dim from Sha'al's" formal inspection. First Sergeant Abraham took his time with the inspection, allowing the troops to literally sleep on their feet at parade rest. His immediate officers all agreed with the General's previous observation. There really *was* a hidden genius in the First Sergeant's supposed madness.

Abraham was also exhausted. But he never *ever* allowed it to show. He lived by and trained his troops to believe the motto, "You can sleep when you're dead." The officers joked to themselves that this was the primary reason for the First Sergeant's sunny disposition.

The sergeant completed his inspection, quietly jumped from the last wagon's bed, and snuck up in front of the barely standing sleeping squad. He reached into his tunic pocket, pulled out a small arrowhead caked with dried blood. He'd pulled the arrow out of a [non-Latin script] Egyptian's eye. Now he held it above his head. "Attention," he screamed at the top of his lungs.

"I have just inspected your *cleaned* wagons. And look what I found." True to his word, it took the eight [non-Latin script] troops eighteen more grueling hours. Every single boy had dry heaved at least once. The First Sergeant knew he could easily *invent* another infraction, but he'd been awake for almost four straight days. He needed to get to the delayed AAR, then eat, and get a few hours of sleep before he "welcomed" the newest group of [non-Latin script] recruits to army life.

Abraham glared at the delirious looking squad. They hadn't eaten or drank in forty-plus sleepless hours and looked it. "Attention," he hoarsely screamed. "I personally reserve the right to kill you if there is another breach of OPSEC… Now [non-Latin script] my [non-Latin script] AO." The squad just stood there deliriously confused. The "first sha'dim" took one step forward and screamed into the oldest boy's face. "That [non-Latin script] means *now*!" Abraham hit the kid in the gut so hard, the troop shot back almost five feet before he unconsciously landed, then rolled into a crumpled fetal position. When the grinning Abraham looked up, ready to choose his next target, the other seven had disappeared.

47

The combined shifts of officers sat in the Fortress' TOC either half asleep or half awake. Still, everyone knowingly smiled at First Sergeant Abraham when he tried to quietly enter the room. It was obvious he hated being there. He was infamous for his one-liners like, "I proudly respect my chain of command, but I just don't have time to sit around and gossip like a sweetbread eater." Or, "Don't [symbols] salute me, you [symbols] soldier wannabe. I *work* for a living."

The entire command staff had liked the guy from the beginning. Abraham had the gift of causing total compliance with a single, terrifying glance. They all enjoyed watching the master perform his troop-transforming magic. Yadin had already made seven attempts to give him a field commission to captain. First Sergeant Abraham had respectfully refused each attempt. Ari always knew what was happening with his troops. He knew that on top of hating to attend "officers' AARs" Abraham had to be exhausted from his two-day-long, "wayward troops' attitude adjustments." So he wanted to expedite this AAR. "Gentlemen. First of all I want to apologize for the delayed AAR. It was necessary. And along that line, I'd like to personally thank First Sergeant Abraham for being here." It surprised Ari when the room erupted in applause for the red-faced grumbling sergeant standing at attention.

Once the room settled, Ari cleared his throat. "Let's make this AAR fast but productive. First of all…" A loud pounding on the doors interrupted the instantly frustrated aleph-grade general. He hadn't slept much since the wedding. Nachshon wasn't doing well. Among all his other myriad responsibilities, he'd sit with the man a few hours every night and let Deborah get some sleep. So far, only a hand full of officers knew the man was obviously dying.

So Ari was too tired and overreacted to the intrusion. Ari yelled. "Make a hole," as he raced toward the door. The standing junior officers flattened themselves against the wall to get out of the fuming general's way. Ari felt like tearing whoever it was a new one.

The eighteen-year-old general flung both doors open so hard that they bounced off the walls. Without looking, he exploded, "*Whaaaat*!"

Ari's anger quickly morphed into red-faced, jaw-dropping embarrassment. A guilty-looking Moshe was frozen with his knocking hand in mid-air. He was flanked by his sneering brother Aharon and Major Hoshe'a. Ari cleared his throat, then rasped, "I'm sorry, General Moshe, Sir. I, um, thought you were one of my troops."

Moshe partly recovered and apologized. "No, I'm sorry, General. I know too well how important these briefings are. I, or we, were ordered to attend the AAR concerning the ambush action." Ari saw Hoshe'a lean back, point at Moshe, and shake his head while he mouthed the words, "Not my idea."

But it never occurred to Ari to ask where this man's orders came from. Ari stepped aside. "Please, Sir."

Moshe, angry at Yahweh for ordering him here, refused the offered seats and stood with his hard, muscled back stiff against the back wall. Next to him, Aharon looked around the room with a pompous smirk. Ari saw the arrogant  sneer and tried to ignore it. Less than five minutes after Nachshon had introduced him to Moshe's brother, Aharon, Ari knew this guy was a gutless, whining, and willfully foolish wannabe leader who couldn't hold a candle to his honorable brother.

Ari decided to ask Moshe for his tactically qualified observations first. Ari nodded at Moshe. "General Moshe, Sir, we'd appreciate your insights." To his credit, Moshe turned toward Ari, respectfully stiffened to attention, and began a well-thought-out and precise AAR about the one-sided battle. "Sirs, the three things that went right…"

After a few minutes, Moshe cleared his dry throat. "In conclusion, General Ari, I only have two more, um, concerns pertaining to future enemy contact." Moshe respectfully waited for Ari's nod to continue.

"(1) You had a forward LP (listening post) signal the opposition's approach?" Ari nodded. "And they were able to convey enemy weapons loadout, number of chariots versus mounted riders, or foot soldier troop strength?" Ari glanced at Akiba. The colonel half nodded. "Our standing order is to attack the incoming force if there were twelve or less. So the warning signal only conveyed a yes or no. We understand that by attacking more than two squads at a time, it would signal to their higher command that they had a capable enemy in the immediate AO. Which would necessitate them deploying a larger force to root out and crush the resistance. It may also permanently increase their troop strength for each troop movement. But we hadn't thought about our LP relaying details about the opposing force loadout." The very impressed Moshe nodded. "Those details have a direct correlation to how many casualties and KIAs you suffer… Fortunately these soldiers were probably pillaging their way back and had taken a lot longer to return. Plus, the garrisoned commanders already had their hands full with what's been happening here. But I wouldn't count on that in the future." Akiba was already whispering to Yadin what to write. Moshe patiently waited.

Akiba looked up. "Yes, Sir." Moshe continued, "Once the opposing force passed your LP's position, what was their secondary directive if any?" Akiba smiled. "They fell in behind and formed a rear blocking/assault force."

From the opposite rear corner First Sergeant Abraham loudly growled something that must have been in Egyptian. Yadin and two bilingual Captains groaned. Moshe smiled, nodded, and pointed toward Abraham. "He's absolutely right. If you moved your signal troops out of position, you completely severed your own early warning communications network. Your forward ambush teams were accurate shots, but if those Egyptian raiders were only a small advance team, for a larger block of flanking enemy troops…” He let that hang in the air. “Which, by the way, is a basic tactical strategy to force a lesser experienced opposition into signaling their position. So if they were only the first wave, your entire ambushing forces would’ve been caught out in the open with their  completely surprised and exposed.” The senior staffs’ eyebrows shot up, and they all stifled a laugh. “Thus, your original covert advantage would be nullified. And from what I saw, I would estimate your losses to be around 90 percent or worse. And that doesn’t account for their taking captives and torturing them to find out where your main force is located. Which they’ve been known to do just for fun.”

Moshe looked around the room. Everyone looked embarrassed except for Sergeant Abraham, who was shaking his head at the others like a disappointed parent. Moshe smiled to himself. “I really like that guy.” But Moshe knew exactly how the embarrassed senior staff was feeling about his observations. So he let them think about it for thirty seconds then he threw them a bone.

“That said. The advantage this army has over every opposing force out there is…” Moshe wisely paused until he was sure everyone was looking his way. “You have Yahweh watching your back. And He’s the best early warning system and rear guard any military force could ever have. Yahweh’s troops, these troops, will always have an advantage over every other opposing force, natural *or* spiritual. So be encouraged when Yahweh battles with you…well, let’s just say I *almost* pity the fool that stands against you…*almost*!” That seemed to encourage a few of the junior officers. “So let this be an experience that teaches, not defeats.”

Moshe was debating about dropping the other shoe when Yadin, the resident genius, spoke up. “General, Sir, your second point?” Moshe groaned to himself. There was always one literal thinker. Yahweh’s spokesman nodded thoughtfully. “Competition is inherent in our or, rather, your line of work, which is ‘kill them before they kill you.’ And it has the side effect of always pushing yourself to be the best. In a military setting, that should be encouraged and awarded.” Moshe grimly smiled. “But the usual comparative argument over body count should only happen when you’re absolutely positive the battle is over.

“Listen. I’ve lost a lot of men. And trust me, officers, it *will* happen to you. But too many were because of stupid mistakes, like not making sure the enemy you *thought* you killed was really dead. Or as in this case, they failed to stay concealed until given further orders.” Moshe sadly shook his head. “I’m eighty years old, and I still don’t understand why the most innocent mistakes cost the most.” Moshe looked down. “The pain from the loss under your watch and the accompanying second-guessing of your command decisions never really goes away. A painful truth your General Kalev can attest to.” Moshe shook himself out of that suffocating mental mudslide. “But that pain can be a positive force you can immediately use to fortify your prep for the next battle.

“Case in point. Based on my painful experience and the age of your soldiers, battlefield wisdom would dictate a pairing of your youngest troops with more seasoned and, in this case, your more mature soldiers. This is what's called a 'force multiplier.' It would facilitate the older ones learning how to 'ride herd,' so to speak, which is invaluable for future officers. It also teaches the younger troop patience and life-saving attention to detail. Both these benefits will be thankfully obvious in the future chaos that is the battlefield environment."

Moshe paused again, then added, "Sir, that said, I am very impressed with the detailed battlefield expertise I witnessed. Yahweh's chosen are extremely fortunate to have this army as their overwatch!" Moshe quickly cleared his throat to cover his brother's predictable condescending remark. "Sirs, this concludes my observations and after-action report. And I thank you for indulging this old warrior." Moshe crisply moved to a parade rest position. The pleasantly surprised Ari scowled at his officers and pointed at Moshe. "That, gentlemen, is how to deliver a proper AAR."

Ari had kept his eye on First Sergeant Abraham since the exhausted-looking teen walked in. The sergeant's face had grown redder by the second. The chief drill sergeant suddenly melted down. "I agree with General Moshe's assessment. It was a . We left our entire assault group exposed. Then there's those unbelievable little pukes who can't keep their mouths shut. !" he screamed. Then the teen wiped the spittle off his chin and continued his rant under his breath. Moshe, with his own stern expression, pointed at the fuming First Sergeant and declared, "Well said, Master Sergeant! And that, gentlemen, is how to deliver a proper AAR in the *Egyptian Army*!"

Sergeant Abraham took the rank assumption as the old man's ignorance. But Ari was looking right at Moshe when the old general winked at Akiba as if he knew Abraham wasn't but should be a Master Sergeant. The room erupted in laughter and war cries. Ari slumped back in his chair and rubbed his eyes.

The teen general whispered to the three colonels, who nodded their agreement. General Ari stood, causing everyone in the room except for the condescending Aharon to stiffen to attention. Ari marched over and crisply saluted Moshe. "Thank you, General Moshe." Moshe snapped off a perfect salute and nodded. The two generals shook hands. Aharon disdainfully snorted at his brother, "They're just a bunch of children playing army and you're just as diluted." The arrogant fool pushed his way past the troops standing at attention and rushed out the door.

Ari's jaw dropped and his fists clenched at the multilevel disrespect for and in front of his troops. Not to mention his public contempt for his brother. In the stunned silence, Moshe snapped to attention and addressed Ari, "General Ari, I want to sincerely apologize to you and your honorable leadership for my brother's insubordinate attitude and insolent comment. There's no excuse. Sometimes it's hard to remember that Yahweh has a purpose, even for the most mentally challenged among us. My brother's a shortsighted fool. Please disregard his incapacity to play nice with the other children. I'm pretty sure he was 'accidentally' dropped on his head when he was a baby and probably more than once." In the tense silence, Ari smiled and yelled, "At ease." The room erupted in laughter.

Ari motioned for Moshe to join them at the head of the table. "Please, Sir." General Moshe was given the throne between Akiba and Ari. But the teen general remained standing. And waited for others to calm down. General Ari leaned toward Yadin. "He finished his basic?" Yadin nodded. "And his advanced weapons training and helped revise the drill sergeant's training manual." Ari nodded. "Very well." Ari received the official-looking signed scroll from Yadin. And with a practiced flourish, general Ari stiffened to attention and yelled, "Attention to orders. Major Hoshe'a, report."

For most of the AAR, Hoshe'a was distractedly scowling at the table while his self-directed knee furiously bounced underneath. He'd heard very little of the AAR. His tired mind was firing off myriad concerns at the same time.

The night of the wedding feast, Hoshe'a had just left Nachshon's room and headed for the very loud dining area. By the look on his ema's face, he knew the prophet was in bad shape. And somehow Hoshe'a understood that the death of this seemingly obscure little man would change his brother's life forever.

As First Sergeant Carni's son slowly plodded out of the passageway, his mind had already raced toward his familiar world of structural design and analysis. In that mental land, there were only absolute numbers and angles.

It was a wonderful place where coefficients never changed, and they always brought a calming stability to his otherwise chaotic conscious mind. There, he could devise ways to improve his past projects to create a better mantrap as he did for most of his "pre-cave in" life. Now he used his superpowers for good. Kalev teased that it was both his brother's and Yadin's "happy places," which wasn't that far off.

Like Yadin, Hoshe'a's thoughts always seemed to default to his analytical refuge when things felt out of control or at least further out of control. Which was the case when Nachshon collapsed after the marriage blessing.

Hoshe'a was just about to mentally begin another underground storage design when *she* happened. The tall, slender woman carrying a large plate in each hand backed into him. She was talking to another serving girl as she turned to put the plates onto the table. The startled goddess dropped one of the plates, and the pile of mini sweetbread loaves fell to the floor. The trio of little boys laughed hysterically as the little loaves became "Shawmer the brave wolf's" appetizers.

The twenty-eight-year-old Jemimah angrily spun, and both their jaws dropped at the same time. The customary "I'm sorry" or "excuse me" or even "hi" would have been the *usual* response. But to Hoshe'a, the "usual" belonged in his happy place, not in his real life. It was too boring.

They spoke at the same time, like they had practiced it for hours. "Oooh 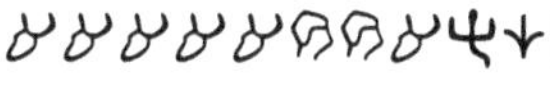!"

Both their minds worked at the same hyper speed. In fact, it was like Yahweh had built two distinctly different bodies yet duplicated the exact same brain. Their synonymous exclamation wasn't an "oh [illegible]-[illegible], it's you—what do *you* want!" kind of reaction. On the contrary, it was an instant recognition. More akin to an "oh [illegible], it's you—the soul mate I never knew I desperately needed." They both knew Carni couldn't see them together. Like they could read each other's mind, they'd escaped up two different ladders and ran laughing to Kalev's dune.

For the next eight wonderful hours, they finished each other's sentences and laughed at the same idiotic things. Halfway through their wonderfully exciting time together, they both realized they hadn't eaten.

Like a couple kids, they snuck into the darkened kitchen, sat on the floor, ate the morning meal's leftovers, and drank Yadin's latest batch of viper wine. The wine seemed to heighten the thrill and the speed they talked. Three loaves and an empty gallon urn later, they devised and wrote out a complicated series of subtle hand signals to silently communicate and places to hide and talk.

Now, in real time, Ari loudly cleared his throat and scowled at the dazed-looking Hoshe'a lost in thought. "*Again*, Major Hoshe'a, report." First Sergeant Othniel leaned over, jabbed his elbow into Hoshe'a's side, and whispered, "Sir, that means you're supposed to walk up there and come to attention in front of the General."

General Kalev's brother looked both surprised and guilty. Everyone watched as the red-faced Hoshe'a nodded his thanks to Othniel and then walked to the other end of the table. He sheepishly came to attention in front of the still-scowling Ari. The teen general held up the scroll and proclaimed:

"For outstanding service while operating as the Army of Yisrael's chief architect, Major Hoshe'a consistently performed his demanding duties in a highly professional manner. His leadership directly led to the successful accomplishment of all our missions. He has been an invaluable asset in aiding our survival. His excellence and insight have assisted in the advancement of our military strategies and execution. His efforts have made it possible for thousands of troops to be clothed, fed, and protected. He has been a vital part of this army from its inception. On his own, Major Hoshe'a volunteered to join and successfully complete First Sergeant Abraham's most vigorous recruit basic and weapons training class to date. Thus, Major Hoshe'a's outstanding leadership, tireless initiative, and total dedication to duty and protocol reflect great credit upon himself and are in keeping with the highest traditions of this, Yahweh's Army…" As Yadin tied the new medallion around Hoshe'a's neck, Ari continued, "Let it be known. By order of the Supreme Commanding General and his senior officer corps, Major Hoshe'a is hereby promoted to the rank of colonel in Yisrael's Army."

The war cries echoed throughout the entire Fortress. Ari called them all to attention again. "I assume the General's latest, um, communication is self-explanatory and has already circulated through your platoons. So moving on. Where are we with the war games expansion?"

Akiba was the organizer, yet even his eyes had shifted to Yadin, the keeper of all things logistics and scheduling. He nodded to his friend. "General Ari. If I may, I defer to Colonel Yadin for the details." Ari knowingly smiled and nodded. Yadin cleared his throat. His three friends groaned to themselves at the inevitable mind-numbing details to follow.

"Sir. Our inaugural competition consisted of six events. All platoons, ages, and ranks were combined. The official events lasted four and a half hours. The unofficial rivalries were finally quashed three days later…"

Ofek shot Akiba a questioning look and mouthed, "Quashed?" Akiba rolled his eyes and shook his head. He leaned behind Ari, covered his mouth, and whispered to his friend. "Their squad leaders threw gourds at the troops to keep them from killing each other… Try to keep up, Colonel!" Ari leaned back into the conversation covering his own mouth, hoping it looked like an official side conversation. "There was no gourd throwing, you geniuses." Ofek snickered. "Really. So what does quashed mean?" Ari looked at the ceiling like he had to think. "Oh, I remember. It means shut the  up." Then he leaned forward. Akiba shook his head at Ofek and silently mouthed, "They definitely threw squash gourds."

"…So, with the new competitions, there will be fourteen separate events. Each event has five separate categories, four- to twelve-year-olds, thirteen- to eighteen-year-olds, noncommissioned officers, oh and…"

Yadin glanced at his "inappropriately" smiling friend. "Colonel Ofek, this time, please '*strongly* invite' First Sergeant Abraham to register and participate in at least two events. Of his choosing, of course." Nervous chuckles rumbled through the room. The other officers were grateful they weren't the ones who had to deliver the "strong invitation." But only Ari knew that Yadin and the explosive sergeant had a mutually respectful friendship. Their off-duty alliance involved private combat weaponry training for Yadin and secret viper wine tasting" for both of them.

Yadin nodded at Ofek. "Don't worry. He'll gladly accept your invitation." Ofek nodded suspiciously but let it go. Colonel Ofek turned to General Ari, whose eyelids were drooping. "General Ari, are we letting those *girls* compete in one of the events? I guess we could invent a 'lethal' dough-throwing contest." The others laughed. Ari was startled but quickly recovered. He loudly growled at Ofek as he angrily locked eyes with every officer around the room. "Colonel Ofek. Are you referring to the people who went through the same basic, advanced combat weaponry and mounted assault training as the rest of us?" Ofek sheepishly shrugged. They'd never seen General Ari act so defensive before. "Then yes. They *should be* competing! In fact, they will be merged into each age group and category with *no* exceptions." Ofek, sufficiently corrected, nodded, and then continued. "Yes, Sir. All category finalists will compete against each other for that event's ultimate champion. And this time, the updated medallions will be announced and awarded sporadically throughout the competition. As this is considered a 'team and skills building' evolution, the war game will last for three consecutive nights, more or less. Company commanders, present your registration sheets to Colonel Yadin by 2100 tomorrow night. And this time, get someone who can actually write Hebrew to fill out your rosters.

The first events will start in three nights at 2100 hours." Yadin nodded to Ari. "Okay. Thank you, Colonel. If there's nothing else, I need to see Sergeant Othniel following this briefing." Ari nodded to Akiba, who called everyone to attention and then dismissed them. Othniel reported, and General Ari requested that he ask First Sergeant Carni and, um, Captain Deborah to please send in five morning meals. The First Sergeant knowingly grinned, saluted, and left.

Once they were alone, the previously silent Moshe stood and hesitantly addressed the row of senior officers. "Gentlemen, once again I apologize for my brother's disrespect." All eyes shifted to the scowling Ari. He opened his mouth to reply but paused as if listening to someone. And Moshe knew exactly who that someone was. Ari looked up and scowled at the decades-older general.

"General Moshe, Sir. You don't need to apologize for your brother's belligerence. He's an adult. He chooses his words, just like the rest of us. In addition, it's obvious he's chosen condescending self-importance over respect and honor. He may be your brother, but, Sir, *his* words and *his* actions are not your responsibility. That said, please convey a message to your brother from me. "The next time he enters my AO, he *will* show my troops, myself, and especially you, Sir, the respect we've earned. Oh, and there is no 'or else' inference in that order. Because he'll never see it coming. And according to Yahweh, one day soon one of these brave troops he clearly despises will save his [illegible] life. And Yahweh help him if he's brainless enough to do it in front of the General!"

Moshe winced, then grinned. In the last few minutes, his respect for this kid had grown exponentially. The eighty-year-old man stiffened to attention and nodded at the intense teen. "Consider it done, General. And thank you all for not killing him." Moshe meant that last line as a joke. But no one laughed. Ari exhaled a long four-count breath. "You're welcome, Sir… He's fortunate General Kalev wasn't here to see that." Moshe cringed and nodded. "Yes, he is…and so am I. I'd hate to make my sister dig the fool's grave." The others quietly chuckled, and the impromptu Q&A session with General Moshe began.

Soon, there was a soft knock on the door. Akiba snickered as he leaned over and whispered to Moshe, "Watch Ari." Yadin swung both doors wide. Deborah, with her braided hair under a sweaty scarf and a smudge of flower on her cheek, led eight little girls and First Sergeant into the TOC. Ari's and Deborah's eyes locked. He felt like he couldn't breathe. Lately, every time he saw her, it was like the first time.

The girls lined up behind the officers and began to serve them like First Sergeant Carni had instructed. The four grinning colonels and Moshe watched as Ari turned in his chair to keep eye contact. Deborah smiled as she stared back. She wasn't paying attention when she leaned in with Ari's mounded plate and sat it down in front of her glorious general. The wide-eyed Ari rasped, "Tha…um, tha…" but his mouth was so dry that he couldn't finish. Akiba quickly leaned past Moshe and loudly whispered, "Hey, buddy, breathe, then ask her if she has any friends." Neither Deborah nor Ari responded. So Akiba snapped his fingers loud enough to interrupt the couple's eternal staring match.

Ari glared at his friend. Akiba ignored Ari and smiled at the red-faced Deborah. "Hey, we were wondering if you had any friends we could meet. I mean, even our new colonel needs all the help he can get." Temporarily forgetting his ema was standing against the wall behind him, Hoshe'a blurted out, "Well, since you mentioned it, I'm looking for…" The new colonel proceeded to describe Jemimah in vivid detail. Deborah grinned. "I think I know just the right…" Carni's angry ema howl interrupted, "Captain Deborah! That's not *your* job. It's *mine*!" Hoshe'a winced, then thought to himself, *Oh,* [illegible] *you big-mouthed idiot. You know Ema will deduce Jemimah's description*. Deborah and Ari briefly locked eyes again, and Carni loudly cleared her throat. She barked, "Captain Deborah, I strongly recommend we leave. Now!"

In her fury, Carni had forgotten her last brutal conversation with Kalev. But Hoshe'a timed this one perfectly. The second his ema stepped behind him, Hoshe'a ducked and felt the breeze as her hand missed its target. She'd wound up and swung at the back of Hoshe'a's head so hard that when he ducked, she couldn't stop the swing. The loud slap on the side of the laughing Ofek's head surprised them all.

Yet, being the professional ema she was, Carni quickly recovered, pointed her finger, and scolded the surprised teen. "I'm sorry, but next time, you boys will ask me about my troops first." Ofek rubbed the side of his head and answered for all of them. "Yes, mam." Carni grabbed Deborah's arm, and they hurried out of the silent room. The stunned Yadin turned to Ari. "Ask her for *what*?"

The senior officers and Moshe ate, drank, and told embarrassing stories about each other for the next hour. A little after 0800, the laughter died down. As Ari started questioning the brilliant and experienced General Moshe, Yadin quickly produced several large parchments and pinned them to the wall. The four colonels took turns filling each parchment—first the question, then the answer. When he reached the bottom of the seventh papyrus, Hoshe'a held up his hand, interrupting the next question. "Okay, General Moshe, stop it. That's enough wisdom; no one is *that* smart." The shocked silence was followed by another round of belly laughter and more eating and drinking.

Ari paused, put his cup down, and grew very serious. "Sir, when are we leaving?" The others stopped chewing and stared at Moshe in stunned silence. The already-distracted man of Yahweh closed his eyes and groaned. "I've really hated this whole back-and-forth thing with that idiot Ramses. His arrogance, not unlike my brother's, has destroyed the only homeland I knew. I'm just glad my mother, Hatshepsut, wasn't around to see it.

"I'm not sure what the curses will be, but the pause between each of them will decrease. We'll leave after the tenth one, probably at sunup the next day. I estimate we'll [illegible] this AO in a little less than nine weeks from now. Again, it's only a rough estimate. I'll have a better idea by the end of the next disaster."

In the following stunned silence, Hoshe'a slammed his hand on the table. "[illegible], I'm sorry, General Moshe, that timeframe just won't work for me. I have a lot to do, but because it's you, I'll check my schedule and come up with a more convenient timeline you can pass on to Yahweh." The already-distracted Moshe looked confused, "Okay, I guess." Then they all erupted in howling laughter.

Suddenly, all five of them shot rapid-fire questions at Yahweh's spokesman. Moshe groaned, and Ari held up his hand to quiet the others. "Hey, give the General a break. You all need some sleep. Oh, and General Moshe, I hope you'll be our guest for the war games. I'd appreciate your critique." Ari glanced at their newest official senior staff member. "So, Colonel Hoshe'a, can you squeeze the war games into *your* too-busy schedule?"

They were all intrigued when the panicked-looking Hoshe'a didn't respond to the joke. But his mind had already returned to all the eventualities if Ema ever found out about him and Jemimah. Moshe knowingly smirked. "I know that look. He's already found his perfect woman, and his ema doesn't know." The others empathetically groaned.

48

Raisa pounded the table, causing all the plates, the two empty goblets, and all the utensils to loudly vibrate across its surface. "That's enough!" Kalev looked up wide-eyed. A serious Raisa pointed her finger in his smiling face. "Listen, my darling bottomless pit! I'm hungry. I've sat here and watched you loudly devour everything but the grass outside. I'm going to the Fortress to get some food."

Kalev had yet to respond to her outrageous written "mission plan." In fact he hadn't said a word or even slept in the last twenty-four hours. His silent debate with Yahweh was still in progress. But a few minutes ago, he'd finally forced himself to eat, temporarily tabling his mental dispute.

Raisa was afraid her audacity had pushed her husband too far. She feared that she'd damaged their still-vulnerable marriage and broken Kalev's already-loaded brain. So she decided to give him space. She'd fallen asleep late last night, and he was still silently staring at the table.

The sound of him stuffing his face woke her a few minutes ago. Raisa sat in the opposite chair intending to eat. But there was nothing left.

Kalev pushed the empty plates aside, reached over, picked her up, and sat her on the edge of the table in front of him. Raisa yelled, "No! No more wrestling, not until I've eaten, and that's final! If the basket's not here yet, I'm going to the Fortress." Kalev grinned. "Okay, but, um, are you going to wear that?" She looked down at his flimsy wedding tunic and grumbled something under her breath. Kalev chuckled. "I'll go check the basket."

Kalev returned with an even larger load of food. He smiled as she tore into the fresh barley bread. At one point he'd reached across to grab one of her pieces of dried beef. But she glared and growled at him. He jerked his hand back just in time to see a fork stab the table right where his hand had been a half second ago.

The big man laughed, headed to the "ladybird" stall, then washed in the "cool spring" pool. On his way back to the tent, he saw his three weapons leaning against one of the empty crates. *Ari*, he reasoned. It was the first time he'd been without them for more than a couple of conscious hours. *Wow*, he thought, *and I didn't even miss them*. Kalev honestly meant to leave the weapons outside. But just after he entered the tent, the General realized he'd automatically armed himself. It was like breathing; he didn't even think about it.

Raisa had finally finished eating and was slouching back into her chair. "I think I ate too much." Kalev smirked. "That's why we should always share. Just like I shared my wedding tunic. Oh, and I'd like it back now, please." It only took her a second to catch on. "I've created a wrestle maniac!" They both laughed.

"Raisa, um, we were pretty tired when I asked. Plus I guess I'm just not smart enough to understand the ancient language of girl-sob. So, um, do I burn your *Mattan* and start over or what?" Raisa sat up and silently burped into her hand. "Excuse me…are you serious? Why would you burn those things?"

Kalev shrugged. "Like I said, I didn't understand your answer the first time. Sooo?" She stood and walked to his side of the table. "Kalev, I was a little overwhelmed. Before the fire, I only had two robes, that beautiful wedding dress, two pairs of sandals, and a couple of other, um, girl things. I've never owned any jewelry or even my own mirror." She started to tear up again. Kalev shook his head. "Please don't. I can understand Hebrew. So please answer my question before you change languages."

She took a deep, shuddering breath and nodded. "I thought after our last conversation yesterday, you, um, you'd want it back, and, um, I'm sorry, and, and…" She started crying. Kalev rolled his eyes. "Listen, wife of Kalev. The *Matan* is yours, and I seriously want you to keep *that* tunic. We'll call it your wrestle wear."

Kalev thought she'd laughed, but the rest was literally lost in translation. The General gently picked her up and carried his beautiful, sobbing bride toward the store rooms. On the way Kalev brooded aloud. "So, General Kalev, how was your two weeks in paradise? Oh, um, I'm not really sure. First, we wrestled for a couple of days—then she almost drowned me, but I survived, so she threw an urn at my head. Then we wrestled again, and I presented her with my *Mattan*—then she really cried. We slept for twenty-four hours—then she wanted me to approve her training to become an expert killer. I don't respond, so she tries to stab me with a fork and take my food. Then we laughed, and she cried some more. So it kind of sounds like *she* was violently disappointed, and I'm *still* confused. Other than that, it was amazing, I think. So what's been happening with you?"

Kalev put his sniffing wife down in front of the third store room. She grabbed the closest, essentially useless gold-embroidered napkin and wiped her face. Raisa knew Kalev was exaggerating at least a little. Still, when he put it all in that order…it was just accurate enough to make her feel guilty. She was pulling his head down to kiss him and apologize when she suddenly froze. "Did you hear that?" she whispered. The tone of her voice was serious enough for him to nervously look around. And then he heard it too. He saw the folded shiny robe move.

Kalev drew his dagger. "It's probably a sand…" But Raisa had already stepped around him and picked up the writhing robe. "…Viper," he yelled in a panic.

"No, my fearless husband, in the Hebrew language, we call this a wolf cub." As she snuggled it against her cheek, she teased her man. "Then she stood and told me that wolf cubs were our friends and vipers aren't, and they don't look alike. Then she laughed at me."

"And there was that breathtaking smile again." Kalev lunged for her, but Raisa squealed, which caused the cub to bark as she danced away. "I need to get Shomer (guardian) something to drink and eat." "What about me?" Kalev asked. Raisa had already started to walk away. "Of course, my love, you may join us by the cool spring for a drink of water. Oh, and bring some beef for our fourth baby." Kalev yelled incredulously at her, receding back, "Join *us*? And why did you get to name the dog?" He grumbled to himself. But from outside of the tent he heard his sweet little wife yell, "Because *you* can't tell the difference between a guardian *wolf cub*, a dog, or a snake."

Raisa decided she wouldn't raise the basic training subject again. And she'd try to never cry in front of him. Or at least for the next twelve days. Once the cub was bathed, fed, and shown how to go through the rear tent flaps, Raisa and her "wrestle maniac" enjoyed another two rounds that day.

Four wonderful days later, the exhausted couple "celebrated" their first week together. An amazing beefsteak meal was followed by an impromptu plunge in the cool spring. Their day-long "celebration" ended with round fifty-three. Raisa had meticulously kept track of the positives and negatives of each round. One time she'd forgotten to put her cryptic accounting sheet away, and Kalev found it. She was gratefully relieved when he couldn't understand her coded "to-do" list. Round fifty-three ended in a split decision. So they decided that, due to the judges' bias, they'd have to redo the entire championship… starting tomorrow. Around four in the morning, the sweaty champions contentedly held each other and passed out under the open skylight.

At dawn, Shomer struggled to get out under the rear tent flap, dragging a shiny loincloth behind him. He suddenly started barking. The brightening sky was instantly blackened by a massive cloud of large grasshoppers. The loud hum drowned out the little cubs frightened howling, but Kalev and Raisa only stirred enough to roll closer together.

49

Ari and the four colonels were sitting on the edge of their dining table, which actually had expanded to two tables pushed together. From their *still-unobstructed* view, they could preside over the competition and eventual award ceremony. The senior officers were still oblivious of the unwritten rule amongst the enlisted troops that the further you stood from "General Kalev's viper pit," the better.

After a full night of sleep for Ari and a day's sleep for the other senior officers, they all were in very good spirits. Of course, the wine helped a little. As the others ate, laughed, and drank, Hoshe'a and Ari were trying hard not to look obvious as they scanned the crowd, looking for their special someones.

To his right, the teen general saw the crowd part as Moshe walked through. He was taking his time shaking hands and talking to the youngest troops. Ari asked Yadin if he had any viper wine left for Moshe. The colonel smiled, and much to the guilty disappointment of the other three colonels, he reached under the table and retrieved a three-gallon urn. Which now only contained two gallons. Ari thought it was hilarious that Yadin and Hoshe'a had sworn off drinking the nasty tasting concoction. Yadin had even assigned the "tasting duty" to one of his trusted first lieutenants who also hated the taste.

Moshe greeted the officers and then turned to the woman walking behind him. "Gentlemen. I'd like to introduce you to my sister Miriam." The eighty-year-old general turned away when he noticed the labeled urn of viper wine. He glanced over his shoulder at his distracted sister, then winked at Yadin.

Hoshe'a knew *of* Jemimah's aunt Miriam, but they'd never actually met. It wasn't tradition to shake a woman's hand, but Hoshe'a was an unconventional kind of guy. He stuck out his hand. "It's a pleasure to meet you." The woman may have been a couple of years older, but she looked half Moshe's age. And she had an unusually strong grip. In fact it reminded him of Kalev's.

Her penetrating stare took in his shiny new medallion, then bored into his brain through his eyes. *Why is she looking at me like that?* he wondered. Jemimah's *doda* (aunt) grinned. "So you're the one." Hoshe'a panicked and unconsciously scanned the crowd for his ema. Miriam smiled, winked, and shook her head. Hoshe'a's face went pale. Miriam just gave him and Jemimah his prearranged signal that meant that Carni was not in the immediate area. The stunning older woman shrugged like nothing had happened. "Since she was a little girl, I was her combination, ema, *doda*, and friend. We talked about everything. And since that shrew Zipporah left, thank Elohim, we're the only females in the same camp as my messy brothers. I'm happy she's found her place in this army. And just between the three of us. Aharon doesn't know she actually went through the basic and advanced weapon's training. He thinks she's just a cook for those 'poor lost orphans.' In fact I believe she's in the archery competition."

Miriam grew a concerned expression. "I'm really happy for you two. But you realize you both are walking a very fine line. You've got my always-looking-for-something-else-to-complain-about brother Aharon on one side and your formidable ema on the other. And though your ema and I have become friends, I've kept my promise to my niece to keep your secret." Miriam did her own scan of the crowd, then leaned closer. "By the way…" Thirty seconds later, when Carni walked up to greet her friend, Hoshe'a had already disappeared.

Moshe was feeling pretty good by the time the assault riding competition began. Fifty yards away, the melons atop the heads of the life-sized straw men were replaced with progressively smaller ones after each round. Thirty minutes later, the melon was the size of a lemon. The two finalists, surprisingly, were from Yadin's Aleph Company. They rode like they'd been born in the saddle. And they both severed their small melon at the same time. After the fourth, "final" round, Ofek decided to make it interesting.

He leaned over and explained the new challenge to Moshe. "Since the two riders always reached the target at the same time, the straw men were pushed closer together. The riders were told they had to ride between the two scarecrows. Only this time the melons would be tossed into the air in front of them at the same time. Which means they'll have to ride between the scarecrows with their legs touching in order to reach their airborne target in time."

Moshe looked doubtful. Yadin shrugged. "I'll bet another cup of wine that at least one of them hits their target. In fact I'll wager two cups that they both do." Moshe lifted his empty palms and frowned. "I don't have anything to bet. Zipporah took everything I had." A small pouch of gold coins suddenly materialized in his hand. The General spun to see who'd put it there, but the other two colonels were already standing on the table to get a better view.

Moshe grinned. "Okay, I'll take that bet." He poured the seventy-five silver coins into his hand and stared. He looked up at his smiling friend. "Colonel Yadin, when I lived here, Egyptian silver was worth more than thirty times the same amount of gold." He carefully slid the money back into the pouch. Yadin nodded then teased, "Wow, you're really *old.* My latest report stated that because of the devastation to the land and the lack of consistent manpower in the mines, one solid silver coin was worth 307 gold ones." Moshe's eyes went wide, and he fished five coins out of the bag and put them in his robe's pocket. He shrugged. "Just in case."

The loud *shofar* sounded, and the horses leaped forward in perfect step with each other. Moshe could barely believe his own eyes. The riders and horses looked like and achieved their objective as a single unit. The soon-to-be Aleph *Battalion* exploded with cheers and chants. Ofek smiled up at Yadin. "I told you they'd need to engrave two medallions." Moshe grew more astounded and maybe a little tipsier as the successive events unfolded.

Five plate-sized solid-blackwood targets were mounted on tripods and then slid into the center of the drill floor. The thirty-yard sword throw event was announced.

The onetime Supreme Commanding General of the Egyptian Army had joined the others on top of the table. He pointed at the targets and loudly slurred, "I used to be really good at this. Only it was usually a man's head at forty-plus yards." He started to laugh until he realized his other hand was holding the handle of a perfectly weighted Khopesh. Again he spun around. But the other two were already seated and pouring each other another cup of beer. Yadin laughed. "I'll bet you the rest of that special wine you can't hit that target from up…" But before Yadin could finish his challenge, Moshe had already dropped into a combat crouch, spun once, and let the sword fly.

The sound of the sword hitting, then splitting the impossibly hard wood caused two thousand rowdy troops to silence and look up at Colonel Yadin. He held the embarrassed but smiling General Moshe's hand in the air. The roaring applause morphed into the chant, "Lethal General Moshe, lethal General Moshe, lethal General Moshe!" Yadin smiled and winked at Ofek, who, in turn, ordered the closest troop to retrieve one of the three chunks of wood and Moshe's sword. Both items were taken to Major Dan.

The proud and tipsy Moshe plopped down onto the table's bench. Three large gold chalices were ceremoniously placed in front of him. All three were filled to the brim with the pungent-smelling viper wine. He'd almost finished the first cup when the world painlessly faded to black.

50

A hot, dirty breeze swirled around the inside of the sand bowl, i.e., Eden. By midafternoon Kalev had raised most of the front and rear tent sides. He thought it would allow the inside of the warming tent to "cool down." Bad idea. By the time he'd finished, Raisa was standing near the cool spring, frowning at the dog. In the last week and a half, he'd quickly learned that some wordless expressions actually yelled volumes. And now he could correctly interpret at least seven of them.

Her wonderful smile could turn her menacing-*looking* mountain of a man into a muddy pool of moldable clay. And strangely, he enjoyed that feeling. Her beautifully playful blue eyes combined with that smile were the exact opposite of or maybe the solution *for* the dark ooze he'd embraced for over thirty years.

In fact, last night in bed, when he started to turn over, he realized they'd left the single candle burning. But when he opened his eyes, Raisa was sitting on the bed smiling at him. Her face seemed to glow brighter than the candlelight. For over five minutes, they just wordlessly smiled at each other. He never wanted that glowing-smile moment to end.

Then there was his second favorite expression, a hungry glint in her eyes that transformed that same beaming smile into a pulse-pounding, wordless booming *shofar* signal, "Let's get ready to rumble!"

Since the first split-decision wrestling final, Raisa hadn't complained once—directly to him, that is. She'd just pick up Shomer and sweetly talk to the stupid dog about her loving husband's habits or self-destructive thinking. To Kalev this was as entertaining as listening to the trio talk about having to kiss one of those "not dangerous" girls.

The other night after the evening meal, Raisa was telling the dog a story about how her husband had ignored her "for over thirty long and very sad years." Adding to the storyteller's consternation, Kalev had shoved his chair back, propped his feet on the table, grabbed a beef stick, and enjoyed the show.

For her part, Raisa loved Kalev's tender heart. She knew it was her responsibility to protect and nourish it at all costs. She'd purposed to never become the typical emasculating, nagging wife and ema. She loved and respected her husband more than ever. But there were times…

Hoshe'a had built a four-foot-high wall around the spring, allowing the constantly flowing water to pool above the ground. At the far end, near the top, four holes allowed the water to flow into a trough that snaked its way around the back of the ladybird stall. Raisa made sure their drinking water was drawn out of the spring first thing in the morning or whenever they awoke. Hoshe'a had designed a thick wooden lattice deck at the bottom of the pool so the water could continue to flow and they could stand inside and bathe. Or, more importantly to Kalev, they could wrestle in the cool, clean water.

Raisa had Shomer standing on the edge of the wooden wall, and she was lecturing the fluffy, tan dog. "Then my big, strong general opened the tent so all the dust could blow inside and cover everything. That's why we both have to take a bath."

Kalev took a step toward the pool when the basket arm quickly swung over the top of the dune and lowered to bounce the basket off the grass. It looked empty. Raisa and Kalev traded quizzical glances, and then Kalev saw the parchment hanging on the side. Raisa dipped the dusty dog in the water and then joined him. Kalev read it aloud, "General Kalev and his wife are requested to *immediately* report to the Fortress for the evening muster." But there was no signature.

Kalev softly growled. "It's only been ten days." Raisa smiled. "Maybe we can get some hot sweet-bread after. We can bring it back, and I'll wrestle you for it." Before Kalev could open his mouth, Raisa ran and jumped into the spring. She leaped out and headed inside the tent. She yelled over her shoulder, "Kalev, my love, please wash that glorious body. Oh, and you may want to put some clothes on."

Eventually the newlywed couple reached the crest of the dune. And both newlyweds unconsciously looked back at their Eden. "I like it here," she said sadly. Kalev gave her a side hug. "We'll be back." At the base of the dune next to the road, both of the horses looked up and stamped a foot at the sound of their master's voices. The General and his wife started down the steep dune at a shallow angle. "Boaz and your mare almost look glad to see us." "Raisa. Her name is *Raisa the Prancing Pony*." Kalev's eyebrows shot up. "You named *your own* horse Raisa? I mean, don't get me wrong—I love your name." Raisa laughed. "Little Frog named her. He said it was the prettiest name he knew. And who am I to argue with that?" "So the prancing pony part," Kalev asked. Raisa shrugged. "I haven't figured that one out yet."

They'd just left the cornfield and were almost to the Fortress' ramp when Ari rode up beside Kalev. The General scowled at his second-in-command and wordlessly held up the parchment. In turn, Ari reached into his saddle bag and produced the same document addressed to him. "Yes, Sir. I received your order. I was inspecting our boulder listening post and road overwatch position when a runner…" "My order," Kalev boomed. And Raisa wisely dropped back a little. "My last order was the warning not to be disturbed." Now it was Ari's turn to scowl and growl. "Sir. I didn't do this."

At the top of the Fortress' ramp, Moshe walked up behind the three of them. He held up an identical parchment. "General Kalev, I thought you were still in seclusion. So why the urgency? And why so formal? You could have just asked." Kalev was fuming and didn't reply as he raced down the ramp.

Ari shrugged at Moshe. "Neither one of us called this muster, and I really pity the fool who did." Moshe curiously looked down the ramp then grimaced. "Oh [illegible]." General Moshe glanced at Raisa and lowered his voice. "He told me he needed a formal meeting. I thought he meant with your senior staff and I." He looked up at the scowling Ari and mouthed the name "Nachshon." Ari glanced down at his rapidly descending general. "Oh [illegible]."

Though they'd much rather wait at the top of the ramp, the three of them reflexively took their time descending. Ari whispered down to Moshe, "Any impromptu muster like this, especially in daylight, is inherently dangerous. My whole battalion was exposed when they crossed the river. It's at flood stage, so they had to take their time. This stunt has exponentially raised the risk of being discovered."

Before he'd reached the main deck, the Commanding General saw his troops standing at ease. For a split second, he was uncomfortably humbled at the sight of the now 4000-plus soldiers who called him their General. Then as he reached the deck behind the stage, his rage returned. Eleven civilians, Hoshe'a, and the other three colonels flanked an elevated bed of all things. Kalev raced Boaz around to the front of the stage, then reined in hard. The last time he was here, he was carefully carrying his bride down these same stairs.

He leaped off Boaz before the horse had time to recover from the slide. His foot had barely touched the top stair when Akiba yelled attention. The thunder from over 4000 sets of heels slapping together vibrated the stage.

Ari took his place behind and slightly to the right of his Commanding General, facing the bed. Moshe and a tearing Raisa stood next to the head of the bed, which was elevated so Nachshon could see to the entire army.

After his rush up the stairs, General Kalev's intended reprimand caught in his throat. Raisa's abba's deep-set eyes looked like two holes in a very colorless face. The old rabbi lay on top of his blankets. He wore a formal-looking, dark blue robe, and his gnarled staff lay beside his legs. Sensing the seriousness of the moment, Kalev locked sad eyes with his sobbing Raisa and mouthed, "I'm sorry."

With a trembling hand, the Prince of Yehudah raised an old-looking scroll close to his face. With the other, he pointed a shaking bony finger at Kalev. Belying his physical appearance, the high priest of Yehudah sternly yelled, "Son of Hezron, kneel before Yahweh." The man who was set apart as true to Yahweh obediently knelt, which automatically signaled his troops to do the same. Raisa sat on the bed next to her gaunt looking abba and silently wept as the civilian leaders stepped closer.

Belying his apparent grave condition, the old rabbi loudly declared the history of the Hebrew people. He included a very detailed genealogy of the tribe of Yehudah. Throughout his life, Kalev had heard these same stories repeated many times. But tonight, these threads of history seemed to weave into a single vivid tapestry. In his mind's eye, the almost tangible picture was alive with successive generations of the Hebrew people exuding fierce purpose and destiny. Kalev's eyes welled up when he saw an image of his abba standing tall and smiling proud. Then, for a fleeting moment, Kalev thought he saw the same picture of himself he'd seen that day he accidentally slugged the huge bull.

Nachshon started a wet hacking cough, jolting Kalev's attention back to the present. The old man loudly rasped for everyone to hear. "It's the purpose of every true leader to work with and train up his successor. This has always been Yahweh's way. It's right and good that the apprentice becomes like his master, then repeats the tradition." He started coughing again. Othniel suddenly appeared next to Raisa and handed her a goblet of wine. She, in turn, forced her obviously dying abba to take a drink. The rabbi drank, then coughed some more. He took a second drink, then resumed his proclamation.

"However, only Yahweh determines who will lead each of the twelve tribes." Kalev looked at the crowd of strangers. He innocently wondered who would be chosen as head of the almost forgotten tribe of Yehudah.

Suddenly, in a blur of miraculous agility, Nachshon sprang out of his bed, grabbed his staff, and walked in front of the kneeling Kalev. The prince of the Yehudah tribe clamped his right hand onto Kalev's arm and jerked it upward.

Thousands of people gawked in awe as Nachshon's other hand quickly raised his staff high. A white-hot bolt of fire pierced a fist-sized hole through one of the heavy beams overhead. It streaked down through Nachshon's staff, down his arm, and into Kalev. The shocked General went limp. The only thing holding him upright was Nachshon's supernatural iron grip on his arm. Unexpectedly, this was followed by complete silence. Without prompting, every man and beast had dropped prone with their face to the deck. The stillness lasted for a frightening forty-five seconds.

Then just as abruptly, the earsplitting audible voice of the Warrior King shattered the quiet. This caused a ripple of terror to spread through everyone who heard.

"Let it be written. The I AM that I AM, Creator of heaven and the *eretz*, your Warrior King, has chosen My faithful servant Kalev, the only son of Hezron. We have found him to be a trustworthy Kenezite in whom there is no guile. Because of his immovable devotion to your Elohim, he is forever marked as true to Yahweh…"

Once again, the brand on Kalev's upper chest burned. Only this time it felt like his whole being was on fire. "…and We have chosen him to lead both this army and the tribe of Yehudah. Through this tribe will come the lion of the tribe of Yehudah, Yeshua, the Deliverer of all nations. Let this be written; let it be done!"

For a moment it was silent again. Nachshon brought his staff down hard on Kalev's shoulder. "General Kalev, arise as the prince of Yehudah." He looked at the men around them. "Let all that the King of kings has spoken be written and obeyed."

A hundred *shofars* echoed off the walls. This was quickly followed by cheering, the usual chanting, and chaos. But Kalev didn't want to move. He knew it would be a long time before he could explain what he'd just experienced. The lingering sense of weightlessness and the sweet smell of flowers left him light-headed and wanting a lot more.

Eventually, Kalev reluctantly opened his eyes to see Nachshon staring right at him. Kalev and the old man shared a knowing smile. As Kalev stretched his shaky legs and began to stand, Nachshon closed his eyes and pitched forward into his new son's arms.

The din of *shofars* and two thousand boys cheering and chanting almost drowned out Raisa's scream, "Abba!" Kalev lifted the gaunt little man and gently put him on his bed. He quickly assisted the other tribal leaders in lifting then lowering the bed behind the stage. Kalev held his wife's trembling shoulders as she sobbed.

On the other side of the bed, Othniel held his abba's hand. The rabbi opened, then locked eyes with his son. In a barely audible voice, he croaked, "Othniel, my son, I have always been proud of you. I love you, boy." Nachshon coughed and wheezed. "Stay true to Yahweh. You're a mighty man of war in the army of *gibôr milchâmâh* (Yehovah strong and mighty in battle). We will see each other again, my son... but not yet." Then, with great effort, he turned his head toward Raisa and Kalev. His voice weakened, and the words came in short gasps. "Daughter...you've always...had my love...my heart...stay the course...you're a mighty warrior princess...skilled in...the art of war. Love...this man...unconditionally." Nachshon weakly coughed and smiled as he stared at the ceiling.

"Raisa, I...can see your ema...she's so proud of...the woman you've...become and the...ema you'll be... Remember us...both to your daughter...Aksa." Raisa gasped and glanced at Kalev, who looked innocently confused. Raisa continued to loudly sob as the head of the tribe of Yehudah grabbed Kalev's hand and weakly pulled him closer. The old rabbi rasped, "And you...my son Kalev...Nethaneel... knows and...respects you...trust his counsel." Nachshon wheezed. "Watch over my...children...bury... my bones...next to...the stream at...the mountain...of Yahweh." Then, with his last ounce of strength, the chief rabbi of the tribe of Yehudah thrust his staff into Kalev's hand and exhaled for the last time.

After a respectable ten minutes of loud wailing from Nachshon's children, Nethaneel signaled to the covered wagon at the top of the ramp and gently pulled Kalev aside. "Son, Prince Nachshon has already made arrangements to be placed in a plain sealed sarcophagus. We'll take him to your ema's house to prepare the body, then put him in the sarcophagus. You can decide where you want to keep the wagon before we leave Egypt...

"Did he tell you where to bury him? I assume it won't be here." A somber Kalev glanced at his ema now holding his wailing little wife, then nodded. "He said to bury his bones next to the stream at the foot of the mountain of Yahweh." Moshe looked puzzled as he stepped forward. "I know the place, but how did he...?" Moshe paused. "Yahweh must have shown him."

None of the adults realized that the cheering had ceased as word of the rabbi's death raced through the companies. Without waiting for an order, the troops quickly fell in, drew their swords, took a knee, and bowed their heads.

Kalev spoke quietly to Nethaneel as he sadly watched his Raisa's heartbroken sobbing. "Leave the wagon inside my ema's courtyard. When you're ready, I'll send his shadow troops to camouflage it and retrieve the oxen. It will remain there until we leave." Nethaneel and Moshe nodded their approval.

After another ten minutes in the eerily silent Fortress, the numb Kalev put his arms around Othniel and Raisa's shoulders and gently pulled them away from the bed. This allowed the other princes to lift the bed and slowly slide it into the wagon. Under Carni's direction, Raisa and Othniel lead the small procession of adults up the ramp toward the house.

Nethaneel glanced at Moshe. "Will he be able to handle all this *and* the massive Hebrew haboob headed his way?" Moshe watched Kalev put his arms around his heartbroken wife. The wise, old prince of Egypt nodded. "Yahweh thinks so! He's already a better leader than I am."

Kalev held the siblings to the side as the wagon barely made it through the courtyard gate. "Raisa and Othniel. Your abba gave me specific burial instructions. He requested to be buried by the stream at the foot of Yahweh's mountain. We'll have the burial prayer tomorrow after sunset." A teenage girl materialized behind Othniel. Kalev signaled the girl. "First Sergeant Othniel." The lost-looking boy stiffened reflexively. Kalev put his heavy hand on the boy's shoulder, leaned in, and whispered, "I'll take care of Raisa. Let…" Kalev looked at the sergeant standing behind him. "*Dana* (to judge), Sir. Sergeant, Aleph Company." Out of the corner of her eye, she saw Carni scowl. "…Uh, medical platoon." Kalev nodded. "Let Sergeant Dana help you back to your room. You are relieved of duty until sunset seven days from today." The lost-looking teen's tear-filled eyes stared at Kalev. "Sir, my abba just died." The General hugged his new brother. "I know, son. But, Othniel, it's very important that you never forget how proud he is of the great man and warrior you've become."

51

For the third morning in a row, Kalev awoke before dawn to the sound of his wife's soft crying. He knew *about* grief in theory. But his countless, horrendous experiences with death had mostly numbed him from the feeling of pain of losing someone close. He wasn't even sure he'd truly mourn his ema's death. Aware of this, Carni had instructed him to let Raisa mourn in her own way and in her own time. But Kalev grew more frustrated each time he saw her like this. He wanted—no, he needed to *fix* her grief immediately.

Raisa's loving husband turned toward her. And for the fiftieth time in three and a half days, he attempted to pull her to him. Raisa stiffened, but for the first time, she relented and allowed him to pull her close. And, for the moment, she stopped crying. Kalev looked at the top of Raisa's head and grinned. He was proud of himself; he'd defeated the problem. *You're actually good at this comforting thing—well done, Kalev*, he silently mouthed. Then he whispered to Raisa, "See? It's okay. You don't have to cry anymore; you'll get over it. When we leave Egypt, I'll tie his tomb wagon behind ours and..." Raisa bolted upright, shot him a disturbingly fierce look, then let out an ear-piercing wail, "*I can't believe you just said that*!" She rolled back to her side of the bed, screaming and yelling in the "girl-sob" language. Kalev panicked. "It's okay. I can add two more oxen to the front of our wagon and..." Her sobbing got even louder. Kalev watched the dog jump onto the bed for the first time. He waddled over to Raisa and started licking the tears on her face. Kalev cringed thinking she would scream at the dog and break its neck. But she didn't—in fact, she cuddled it close, and her sobbing quieted. G*reat*, he thought. *She chose a stupid dog over me*.

Kalev lay there for the next hour feeling extremely inept and maybe even a little afraid to move. Eventually, and without rolling over, Raisa asked what day it was. Kalev, glad to have one right answer, blurted out, "Well, your dad died three evenings ago, and they finished with his body. Then I gave the burial blessing two evenings ago. There was a half-moon last night, so that makes it the seventh day tonight at sundown...Raisa, um, since you're talking to me now, I, um, I'm sorry about your abba. He loved you very much. He called you his songbird." She turned over and stared at Kalev with bloodshot eyes. "He said that?" He nodded. "Yeah, it was when we were sitting at the table and watching you beat up that pile of dough. Do you remember?" Raisa sniffed, and he could feel her head nod against his chest. "That's when you knocked that urn of flour over and started yelling. Your father said that sometimes his songbird sounded more like a bird of prey." "He said that?" She sniffed again. "Yes, he did." Kalev paused and grinned. "I've been thinking about that mission plan you wrote. By the way, it was more of an evaluation report than a mission plan. But anyway, you did make a good point about having to train." Kalev smiled to himself. *Finally, she's over it*. "I can show you a few things in case I die and you have to defend the boys and Ema." Kalev smirked. "And you'd probably have to defend Hoshe'a too." Raisa tensed, but Kalev was lost in his own thoughts, staring out the sky light.

"You know, now that I think about it, I'm really glad we can't have kids. This place is Sha'al on *eretz*. Plus, there's probably a lot of killing to do before we can settle and farm our own land. It's going to be hard, and more kids…right, like we need more kids. Anyway I'm glad we won't have that problem. So do you want to wrestle?"

Only then did Kalev notice that Raisa had pulled away and was sitting up staring at him. "Do you mean that?" Kalev shrugged. "Sure, I always want to wrestle. But if you want, we could eat first." She howled again, but this time she shot out of bed, quickly dressed into a non-see-through robe, grabbed the *stupid* dog, and ran out of the tent. Kalev sat up and groaned.

"The Commanding General of Yisrael's Army," Kalev chided himself. "And you can't even fix your wife's problem." If he spent any more time here, he knew the black brooding ooze wasn't far off. He looked up. *Seventh-day command and staff in about an hour*, he thought.

It dawned on Kalev that the army *did* give him a sense of familiar purpose. "Raisa was right about that…I need to get cleaned up and get over there." Kalev glanced out the tent flap. His beautiful wife was talking to the stupid dog by the spring again.

Before Raisa realized what was happening, Kalev was already airborne. The splash temporarily emptied about a quarter of the pool. And when Kalev surfaced, it looked like his glaring wife and the dog caught the majority of that watery explosion. He hoped that Raisa's speechlessness was a good sign and she wanted to join him. Oh, was he so wrong!

Later in the TOC. Ari addressed his officers, "Gentlemen, according to Colonel Yadin, the girls outnumber the boys in Aleph Company. That wave of 219 refugees last night consisted of 198 girls that escaped from Queen Hatshepsut's temple. They used the locust invasion as a distraction and then commandeered a large temple's ceremonial solar bark. They rowed it down river…Akiba let out a low whistle. "That's over 300 miles." The other officers were obviously amazed. Yadin nodded. "We think they were left to sail by every city and army outpost because no one wanted anything to do with that particular sect of vile priests. And they did it without food and water." Ari soberly nodded. "They came ashore about ten miles north of here." "Gutsy move," commented Akiba. Ari continued, "As we all saw at the final archery competition, even girls can be lethal. Especially ones with nothing to lose." A low grumbling vibrated around the TOC.

Ari scowled. "All right, knock it off and suck it up! We have no idea the numbers we'll face in Caanan. General Moshe said the Canaanites, Hittites, and Phoenicians have always been formidable. We can expect heavy casualties from the first engagement on. We need every trained troop we can get.

Most of these girl refugees have survived a living Sha'al most of us have never known. So I expect you and your people to treat them with the same respect and honor as any accomplished male troop. Do you understand me!" "Yes, Sir."

"Plus consider this. What enemy would ever suspect a girl warrior? So, in a way, they have the potential to become this army's perfect secret weapon. Get used to the idea; it's going to happen. Over 90 percent of all the girls have completed basic and advanced weapons training." He glanced at Ofek who nodded back. "So far, there is a growing platoon of girl troops that have shown to be naturals at archery and close quarter fighting. Plus they're all trained medics. And according to General Moshe, we'll need every medic we can get.

"In the last two months, First Sergeant Carni took it upon herself to form support, medical, and assault platoons within her group. Gentlemen. They are organized and ready to go. Are your companies?" Ari let that hang. "Colonel Akiba and I are still ironing out the details. But for now we'll designate them as a detachment to Heh's expanding specialized company. Soon they'll need to be separated into their own self-sufficient company. They are that good. That said, expect their officers at the next command and staff meeting.

"However, Sergeant Carni has not completed any military training." Ofek smirked and interrupted, "Probably because there's only a 50 percent chance Sergeant Carni or First Sergeant Abraham survive that basic training class. And *if* she is approved to enter as a recruit, there will be no "official" betting pool as to who will survive." The room erupted in knowing laughter.

Ari scowled at his friend. "As I was saying. First Sergeant Carni cannot be promoted to an officer rank or assistant commander of the new girl company if she doesn't complete the training like the rest of us. But thankfully that's above my paygrade." They all laughed, as no one had ever been paid.

The teenage aleph-grade general slyly grinned at Hoshe'a. "Therefore, when the girls become their own company, which could happen within the next three weeks, Colonel Hoshe'a will be their new commanding officer." This took the startled Hoshe'a by surprise. All eyes shifted to the stunned colonel. Hoshe'a suddenly realized everyone was staring at him like they were waiting for an answer. He sheepishly looked up at the grinning Ari. "Colonel Hoshe'a, that would make your ema your subordinate." Hoshe'a was speechless, and then he grew a sly grin. "I'm sorry, General Ari. Would you repeat that, please?" Everyone else chuckled. Ari repeated himself, but all Hoshe'a's brain heard was, "Blah blah blah, you get to order your ema around, and she has to obey your every order. Blah blah blah and no more head slaps." Hoshe'a smiled. "I humbly accept that responsibility, and I hope I can live up to this army's high standard of leadership. I…"

From the floor in the back of the TOC, the General's laughter drowned out his brother's blustering acceptance speech. He knew exactly what Hoshe'a was thinking. Akiba's second-in-command yelled,

"Attention." Kalev stood and headed to his vacant seat at the head of the table. "As you were, people." Kalev eyed the five parchments on the wall. He didn't have to ask. "Nice work, General Yadin." Ari grinned at the senior staff. He hadn't gotten that far. The General nodded for Ari to continue. "The new battalions will need Commanding Generals for a myriad of reasons. Because of the massive influx of new recruits, the companies need to step up qualified troop promotions down the chain of command, starting with your field grade officers. People, your companies will become battalions in the very near future. Make your promotions happen in the next two days. Your colonels will be promoted as the companies are separated into battalions." "Correction," General Kalev interrupted. "In anticipation of this move to battalion status, I've made a unilateral decision. My entire senior staff will be promoted at the next muster." Kalev nodded. "I'm sorry, division commanding bet-grade General Ari. Please continue." Ari paused for a couple of seconds. That same old wave of inadequacy threatened to take his breath away. He swallowed hard and stowed the feeling in his mental vault.

"Gentlemen, every aspect of your new battalions will be mobile by the end of this month. Colonel Hoshe'a, the ovens and the forges must be mobile and operational at the same time." Hoshe'a glanced at the nodding Yadin. "Already on it, Sir. We'll be testing our first oven wagon tomorrow night." "Excellent, Colonel. People, you have two and a half weeks to prepare your companies to function as a complete mobile battalion.

"So"—Ari felt overwhelmed again and spoke a little quieter—"because of the General's announcement, from the next muster in three nights, the new battalions will be conducting their own command and staff meetings. So your, um, generals will need the appropriate updates on your progress." Ari swallowed hard.

"He will be delegating his current responsibilities to the new colonels. Your new aleph-grade Commanding General will be more concerned with the battalion's overall readiness and mobility. To that end, he will need detailed written reports to include a summary." Ari turned to Yadin and smiled. "Except for General Yadin—he will need far more detail than he's receiving now!" Yadin nodded his thanks. "Colonel—I mean, General Yadin. The battalions will use their appropriate TOC for their C&S (command and staff) meetings. Make sure they're scheduled on different days.

"People, until we deploy, *this* joint C&S meeting will be general staff only. And it will be extended to every other seventh day. General Kalev and I will be sitting in on your meetings, and they'd better be run as succinctly as this one. You have a lot to do in the next two days. And most importantly, remember the higher your rank, the more you allow your subordinates to do their jobs. If you've been a good leader, trust that your example will be duplicated. So let's get it done! And thank you!" Ari nodded to Akiba, who yelled, "Attention, you are dismissed."

By the time the doors shut, they were all anxiously smiling as they stared at their newlywed General. The same question was on all their minds. But Kalev turned to Ari as he spoke to his whole senior staff. "First, according to General Moshe, until we encounter the enemy, 80 percent of a general's job is meeting with his senior staff. Their job is to report their battalion's progress. You will make command decisions if and when they're appropriate. Gentlemen, take to heart what General Ari just advised the other officers. Trust your people.

"Now, in answer to your questions about marriage.

"(1) Yes, marriage is, was, is, um, *eretz*-shattering. I never knew it was possible to feel like this. She still takes my breath away, and the wrestling…" Kalev clamped his jaw shut. They were all staring at him quizzically, so he quickly pressed on.

"(2) Keep your wife's abba alive at all costs.

"(3) Yes, I recommend marriage to all of you. But learn the 'sobbing girl' language as soon as possible!" Ari interrupted with a shocked expression, "So I'm not the only one." "Yeah, that makes me feel better. I thought I was too stupid to understand." All eyes shot to the suddenly terrified-looking Hoshe'a. Who in turn read Kalev's obvious evil grin. *, you idiot*, he thought. *Now Kalev knows.* He cleared his throat. "Um, so I've heard."

Everyone knew about Jemimah, but Kalev let his hopeless-looking brother off the hook. "Anyway, the girl-sob language is very real. It can show its lethal head anywhere at any time. And you're expected to understand it completely and act accordingly! Good luck on that one."

"(4) From now on, I will be issuing all mohars to all troops as needed. There's more than enough. So don't hesitate to ask." Yadin chuckled as he wrote the General's list. "I'm glad I'm never getting married; I never saw the practical need." Kalev grinned. "General Yadin, you may want to consult Sergeant Marasha on that issue. I believe your current projection pertaining to your future marital status is woefully incorrect." The others teased their wide-eyed friend.

Kalev continued, "Okay. (5) Everything you thought you knew about women and what they want is 100 percent wrong. From day one you'll be blindsided by an extremely steep learning curve you are expected to scale immediately. There is no way to prepare for it, so don't worry about it.

"(6) That said, learn to appreciate privacy. Find some conscious time alone every day. Trust your people and this army as a whole to function just as well without you. *General Ari*, You'll be amazed at what happens when you let your brain think about non-army things. This discipline will make your transition to husband much smoother… Okay, rookie marriage wisdom time has now concluded. Which reminds me, I'll be right back."

Kalev checked the kitchen. Not seeing Raisa and the dog there. He headed through the meat butcher area into the hall and peeked around the corner of Carni's girls' area. In the center of the massive space, Raisa sat on a padded chair with hundreds of girls hanging on her every word. A circle of the littlest girls sat on the floor and took turns rolling a parchment ball at the dog, then shrieking when he bit it. Kalev couldn't exactly hear what Raisa was saying. But the ooohs and aaahs made him feel proud. He listened for a while and let his ego grow. *I must have done something right*, he mused.

Just before he decided to head back to the TOC, he heard laughing, then hundreds of collective gasps. Kalev was watching the stupid dog, but when he looked up, he saw them all glaring at him. He froze, and his mouth fell open. Raisa said something else; they all turned to look at her and responded in unison, "Ooooh." Then their heads whipped back around and stared at him, looking like they were going to cry.

Deborah was the first to act. "Attention," she yelled. Three hundred eighty-seven girls jumped to their feet and quickly formed up. Kalev swallowed hard, not sure what to expect. Yet too well acquainted with death, he stiffened and marched into a literal no-man's land. Kalev wasn't really sure what to do, and Raisa's sad stare didn't help. So he treated them like any other company. By the way they'd formed up, Kalev immediately recognized there had already been multiple promotions.

The General stood in front of the rank of new majors. The stupid dog barked and howled but actually shut up when Kalev scowled at it. He spoke to the majors, "I assume you've been told about you are about to become our newest battalion. It will be designated…" The General paused. "Zayin Battalion, your new commander is General Hoshe'a." Near the rear of the company, Jemimah proudly gasped and then covered her mouth. Major Deborah spoke up, "Sir, we've already promoted accordingly." She looked back, then hesitantly whispered, "Sir, can I speak with you privately?" Kalev warily nodded. Deborah yelled, "Zayin Battalion, as you were!" She motioned to a table out of ear shot. But the major didn't sit.

She seemed too scared to speak. Kalev faintly growled a little too sternly, "What, Major?" The look in the girl's eyes made the huge man cringe inside. *The last thing I need is more crying*, he thought. So he wisely softened his tone. "What did you need, Deborah?" She was partially shocked at the familiarity. But after what Raisa had just told them, she understood. "Yes, Sir, um, well, Sir, about general Hoshe'a? We thought First Sergeant Carni would be our battalion commander." Kalev nodded. "Tell me, Major. You were one of the first girls to complete basic through advanced?" Deborah proudly nodded. "Yes, Sir. Sergeant Abraham said I, um, was on my way to becoming a, um, master archer." Kalev knowingly smiled. "Excellent."

Turning so the rest of the battalion couldn't see, he raised his hands to waist level, palms up. "So, in one hand, we have First Sergeant Abraham. In the other we have an untrained First Sergeant Carni." When Kalev violently clapped his hands it echoed off the walls. Followed by a round of loud gasps, and the stupid dog started barking again. Kalev twisted around, snapped his fingers, and pointed at the dog. It stopped mid-howl. Deborah peaked around Kalev's other side and shook her head at the other majors.

There was a collective sigh.

Deborah thought about it. "I see what you mean, Sir… Okay, *if* First Sergeant Abraham is ordered to and *if* Major Carni decides to submit to the training *with no possible recourse*, there's a 50 percent chance only one of them comes out alive." Kalev's eyebrows shot up, and Deborah giggled. "Sir, we all live in the same hole. There are no secrets." Kalev smiled. "Yeah, I get that…so, Major, can I trust you to take our secure conversation to the grave?" She nodded her understanding. "I'm going to let you make a command-level decision. What would *you* do?" Wiseley, Zayin's future colonel, thought before she spoke.

"First, there *should* be a way for adults to join the army if they want to. Because some may be older, there should be an abbreviated version of basic and advanced. It has to cover the exact same evolutions but at a more rapid pace. That's how it can be presented to Sergeant Abraham. If he thinks he can do his worse to make them drop on request sooner, he'll jump at the challenge. Second, the arbitrary assigning a major rank to any support adult has to stop. Frankly, Sir, it's an insult to the rest of us who've paid our dues. So you're asking me what I'd do about my First Sergeant?" The extremely impressed General nodded. "I'd ask you to tell her that, um, (1) you need her to take command of this battalion she's built. (2) If she does not submit to and complete basic through advanced weapons training, she needs to step aside and allow the *trained* officers to take over. This is a military operation and should be driven by trained military leadership. So, as First Sergeant Abraham always says, 'Lead follow or get out of my ∟↘⑪✛ᘓ AO!'"

Kalev forced himself to keep a straight face. "Colonel Deborah"—she opened her mouth to correct him, then realized it was not a mistake—"again, this conversation is only between you and me." She nodded. "I agree with your observations and decision. With one correction. General Hoshe'a is her direct superior. He will be delivering your order. Of course, it will come down from me, and I'll be standing by to, um, back him up." They both knew he just wanted to watch his brother deliver the categorical ultimatum to their ema.

"And on a personal note. I love my Raisa with all my being. But I think she needs a friend more than a husband that keeps stepping on his own tongue." Deborah whispered, "She needs both of us, Sir." Kalev grinned. "I guess that goes for General Ari too." She blushed. "But thank you." "Um, Sir, if I may?" Kalev cautiously nodded. "Sir, women don't need men to fix them. They just want someone to silently love them. So when you feel the need to fix, close your eyes, grit your teeth, and just be there for her." Kalev nodded. "Good advice."

As they started back, Kalev smirked. "So when are you informing my second-in-command of his imminent betrothal?" Her shocked expression grew into a sly smile. "Soon." Kalev chuckled. "You do know that's not normal." "Sir, we're standing in a hole with 1247 armed and dangerous teens and child refugees. And that hole is in a land filled with an evil that wants to destroy us all… What is *normal*?"

Kalev returned to his seat in the TOC. Yadin was finishing up his summary. "…because of the locusts, the additional herd of *already-saddled* horses numbered 307. We now have one for every troop, including the girls nine years old and above. The horses will be assigned as needed. In addition, we've added seventy-five cattle, 128 goats, and one donkey *with attached cart.* Tonight we'll finish collecting the dead locusts."

Kalev's scowled. "First, what locusts? And second, why collect them?" Hoshe'a started laughing. "Wow, you missed the last plague entirely. You really *were* having an exciting time." Kalev grew a sinister grin, and Hoshe'a immediately shut up.

Yadin continued, "Sir. Two nights ago, our people found a stray horse eating the dead locusts off the ground as fast as he could. So we assigned the four basic training platoons to the collection detail. They returned with our largest wagon filled with the dead bugs. Master Sergeant Abraham reported that they barely made a dent in the numbers. And the bugs they left were even larger than the ones they'd collected." "I inspected the first load," added Yadin. "Those black bugs are at least eight inches long, but they're light and a little brittle, so they can be densely packed into crates or urns. They're already dried out, so they'll keep until we reach Cannan. If we can collect and store enough, they'll easily feed all our livestock through the first planting season up north." Kalev and Ari heard the Warrior King's voice at the same time. "And once again, it's Yahweh for the save; the crowd goes wild…" Kalev saw Ari's puzzled expression. "Don't worry. I don't understand *most* of His jokes."

Once they'd finished eating, Ari nodded to Akiba. "General, Sir. Um, we were waiting for you to get back. We need to discuss the trio…"

Kalev listened without interruption. By the time general Akiba finished his report, they'd all finished eating. Kalev asked, "So, General Akiba, are you telling me there've been two assaults?" "Yes, Sir, the second was last night. This time there were only six raiders, and they weren't Egyptian. Yet, during the cleanup, the trio's same loud argument ensued." Kalev shook his head. "So even after Sergeant Abraham threatened their lives, they still refused to follow procedures?" "Yes, Sir."

Though the trio was his much-needed comic relief, Kalev knew this couldn't be *his* decision. "So, General Akiba, what are you going to advise your subordinates to do about this flagrant disregard for our OPSEC?" The teen general and the rest of them smiled. "Sir, I've talked to First Sergeant Carni, who has more experience in this field." Kalev glanced at Hoshe'a, who scowled back. "Sooo, I think I have an unusual solution. For the next seven days, those three braying [symbols] will not speak one word." Kalev chuckled. "For them, that's a fate worse than death." Akiba grinned. "Worse than death from their point of view. To ensure their compliance, each of the three will be paired with a little girl their age. Each of those three pairs will have a female sergeant as their overwatch. If they disobey the silence order, the little girl will kiss them, and another day will be added to their personal 'little boy Sha'al.' This *will* tie up six extra troops for seven-plus days. However, if it's effective, it'll both keep them alive and serve as a warning to the other young boys."

Akiba smirked. "Of course, that would have the opposite effect for any boy over twelve. You know, like General Yadin." They all laughed when Yadin looked up from his parchment. "What? Oh, never! And you can write that on the wall out there." Ofek stole one of his friend's quills, a jar of ink, then ran into the hall and did just that. When he returned, he took his seat and took one of Yadin's clean parchments. "Okay. It'll cost you a coin to get into the 'when will General Yadin need a mohar' pool. I say four weeks…"

The General slid a coin down the table. "I have inside information. Put me down for six weeks. The other three slid their coins across the table and yelled, "Six weeks." Ofek smiled at his fuming friend Yadin. "We've got to open this up to Aleph Battalion's senior staff…oh, and all of Zayin."

Following the round of friendly goads, Akiba continued, "Anyhoo. Concerning the trio, the silence order is the stick. So I needed a carrot to add a little positive motivation. If they survive their silence evolution, they will be officially assigned to the General's shadow detail." Kalev's eyebrows shot up. Akiba frowned. "No, Sir, they were never *assigned* to your detail; it was their own idea, and it's driving First Sergeant Othniel crazy. He's the one who organizes the shadow troop assignments, Sir. We don't understand your point of view on those three haboobs." Akiba shook his head. "But the trio have a loyalty to you that is exemplary. Sir, when it comes to yours and Raisa's protection, those boys are dangerous. And that devotion can be used to everyone's benefit." "Not to mention," added Yadin, "Little Frog has a way of training a horse just by talking to it. But all three of them are excellent at assault riding, knife and spear throwing, and the bow. Their sword discipline still needs work, yet they can hide in plain sight. In fact, that would be a part of their assignment."

Akiba concluded, "So that is our recommendation, Sir." The teen general of Heh Battalion waited for the Commanding General's approval. Kalev was about to take a drink when he saw Akiba waiting. The General smirked while looking at the wine in his cup. "General Akiba, those three are soldiers first. They're responsible to their sergeant and so on up the chain of command. They're yours to deal with as you see fit, period.

"But on a personal note. When the weight of responsibility feels like it's crushing me, all I have to do is listen to one of their ongoing arguments. It puts things in perspective. And I highly recommend you people do the same.

"That said, General Hoshe'a, if General Akiba agrees, let's get the trio, their superiors, and their assigned Zayin counterparts in here now." Akiba smiled and nodded. "Again, this is General Akiba's battalion command decision." "I just wanted to watch." Hoshe'a left.

The smirking Ari shook his head and consulted his notes. "Okay, what's the latest on our night shift livestock-herding evolutions?" Akiba spoke up before Yadin had a chance. "Heh's newly formed 'scout platoon,' along with the 'cow troops platoon,' have ridden into the desert every night since Moshe gave us a time frame. So far, they've reconned and mapped out the route straight east for thirty miles.

"They know to stay away from any known Egyptian Army routes to the northeast and the southeastern route to the port at Mersa Gawisis on the *Yam Suph* (Red Sea)." Yadin added, "Which, by the way, is tonight's foraging target." Akiba nodded, then continued.

"Once we reach their thirty-mile marker, we'll turn straight north and parallel the coastal trade route east. According to General Moshe, the western border of our land is approximately 238 miles from here." Yadin blurted out, "Well, since you've already interrupted my report, I'll jump to that column." Akiba and Ofek smiled at each other.

"According to my calculations, the average man and burdened oxen wagon can travel at three miles per hour. But the sheep can only move in spurts. So they can travel an average of two miles per hour at best. The same with the goats." Kalev scowled. "All our people will be riding, so we're only limited to the distance an ox can travel before it needs food and water. But the freed slaves probably haven't walked fifteen miles at a time in their lives. There's still a lot we don't know, but I'm proud of you, gentlemen. I know we'll all adapt." Yadin looked sick, but he continued.

"Tonight's herding evolution jumps off in three hours. Once they get them across the river, they'll meet up with the Pit's troops and herd. The Fortress' cattle will remain on that side of the river. The Pit's extra corrals are large enough to accommodate the added cattle. It'll keep the river-crossing losses to a minimum. Eventually, we'll float the other herds across…"

Ari nodded. "Excellent, let's make sure they stay within their double perimeter. Our exposed livestock will attract every predator, man, *and* beast for miles around." Kalev added, "I'd like to see the cattle drive evolutions, but I don't want my presence to add to the chaos. And, General Yadin, why are you scowling more than usual?"

The frustrated genius rubbed his eyes and sighed. "Sir, you know I love a logistical challenge. But if General Moshe's projections are correct, there's going to be at least four million people in addition to the army making this trek northeast. Based on my refugee interviews and from my own observations, over 89 percent will be disabled in one form or another. Especially the ones from the Wadi Hammamat mines, if any have survived…"

The General's memory flashed back to the pits and each of the lifeless little faces of the children from the mines. He felt nauseated. Yet a powerful avenging rage welled up inside, and he yelled. "Excuse me, General Yadin. General Akiba, the moment we deploy from here, I want at least a company of troops, a medical wagon, and five *empty* wagons to execute an immediate evacuation and/or recovery of the captives in both the Hammamat mine and from the surrounding labor camps and caves. *If* there are survivors, they'll need water, food, clothes and blankets. And if we need to, we'll bury the bodies at our first stop east." "Yes, Sir, I'll add that mission planning." Kalev took a breath. The General's roared order was absolute, so no one dared to ask the obvious questions, and Kalev never explained his tormented outburst.

Eventually, the huge man took a long drink of regular wine and knew he'd need some of the viper wine to get the myriad faces out of his mind. "I'm sorry, General Yadin. Please continue." Yadin glanced at Ari and then back at his comforting numbers. "Yes, Sir, like I was saying. Most of the freed captives will have little more them the clothes on their back. And as you said, Sir, none of them are prepared for a 200-plus mile journey. Then there's the mind-bending problem of supplying food, water, and shelter. We've had time to prep, and we've been ready to deploy for the last two weeks. But…arghhhh."

Kalev pushed the faces to the back of his mind, and he felt Yahweh's hand gently rest on his shoulder. Kalev grew a smile he almost felt. "General Yadin, do you realize the beauty of following your superior's orders exactly?" The seemingly unrelated question caught the kid off guard, and he shook his head.

"Ultimately, this is the Warrior King's rescue mission. Don't you think He knew all this ahead of time? General Yadin, this will probably be hard to hear, but the Warrior King *may* even be a better quartermaster than *you* are. So our job is to follow His orders and do what we know to do. The rest is *His* problem, not yours…" The Warrior King groaned in Kalev's head, "Arghhhh, thanks for reminding Me." Kalev had to distract himself from the booming laughter.

"Yadin, son, you've done an excellent job, and I'm really proud of you. But you've *got* to relax that genius brain of yours. I'm afraid you're going to sprain it, or, worse, you'll end up like General Hoshe'a." They all laughed. "Yadin, your logistical priority is and will always be this army first, then the others if there's surplus. In addition, the inflow of new recruits will also swell before it levels off. But again, it's the Warrior King's job to provide, and as we've already seen, He's surprisingly good at it. So…"

The General was interrupted as the double doors flew open so hard that they boomed when they hit the walls. A scowling Hoshe'a stormed in, followed by a lengthy line of officers and troops. Everyone Kalev saw but the trio. The entire eastern half of the TOC was crowded with wary-looking troops. At the opposite end of the long map table, Hoshe'a pulled out six chairs and lifted the three little girls into every other chair and told them to stand up at attention. Akiba shot to his feet and yelled, "Attention."

Kalev was still seated as Hoshe'a marched up the side of the table to resume his seat. Just before he sat, his scowl disappeared, and he winked at Kalev. Who, in turn, covered his mouth, leaned toward Ari, and whispered, "Hoshe'a didn't tell them why they're here. They all think they're in trouble." Ari smirked and whispered back, "Yeah, everyone but Master Sergeant Abraham—he just looks annoyed."

Kalev smiled. "I think that scowl is permanently inked onto his face—, even Hotep can't swear with his eyes like that." Akiba yelled, "Little Croc, Little Frog, and Little Yoshiyah. Report!"

Five minutes later, and in case the trio thought he was bluffing, Akiba again called the three defeated and stunned boys to attention and added, "Don't you *dare* move a muscle." Then he nodded to the three sergeants from Zayin. They calmed and called the three ecstatic little girls to attention. All three sergeants leaned forward and whispered to the trio's new counterparts. All three little Zayin troops gasped at the same time. Once they stopped dancing and squealing, they leaned over and gave each stiff boy a kiss on the cheek. Kalev had to avert his eyes. All three boys looked like they were going to puke. And except for the little girls, everyone stayed at attention and/or silent.

With another stern warning, the crowd at the opposite end of the table was dismissed. Yadin called for Sergeant Abraham before he escaped. He handed him a copy of the order concerning Major Carni. No one said a word while the teen First Sergeant read and then reread the order.

During Akiba's attitude adjustment of the trio, Yadin had received whispered permission from both senior generals to add the last line.

"…is hereby promoted to Bet Battalion's *Rav Nagad Samal bakhír* (Master Sergeant)." Akiba hooked a thumb over his shoulder at the General's bedroom. "As the highest-ranking noncommissioned officer in the army, you'll move into that room behind us as soon as possible. Trust me, you'll need the peace and quiet when your initial adult training class begins. We're hoping you can rise to the accelerated challenge. And I wanted to reiterate the basic and advanced training companies are yours to grow and redesign as you see fit. The room is an example to the rest of the army. Hard work and self-sacrifice will always be rewarded." The entire general staff swallowed hard when the new Rav Nagad grew an evil grin and stiffened to attention. *Wow*, Kalev thought. He really *can* swear with his eyes. But to the teen's credit, his response was exactly as it should be. "Consider it done, Sirs." The red-faced and sweating Abraham saluted, did a perfect about-face, and practically ran out the four-inch thick double doors. The second they shut, expletives erupted in the outer hallway. Then all eyes shifted to the General.

Kalev wanted to wait long enough for the stunned trio and their overwatch to get to the drill deck. But after twelve excruciating seconds, his eyes started watering, and he exploded in belly laughter. They all laughed until they couldn't breathe. Akiba plopped back into his chair and laughed.

Yadin took out another clean sheet, wrote a title and "5 to 1" at the top, then made three long columns. Akiba glanced at the sheet, then slid three coins to his friend. "Little Yoshi seven, Little Croc fifteen, and Little Frog twenty days to complete their orders." Once they'd all made their predictions, Kalev turned to Akiba.

"And General Akiba. I am very impressed with your style of leadership. I've learned a few things from you tonight, so thank you. In fact, General Ofek, you may consider adding General Akiba's stick-

and-carrot approach to your new leadership advancement training."

Kalev slyly grinned at Ari. "When I left earlier, I inspected Zayin Battalion. At least the troops that were off duty. It's almost not fair to the rest of you. General Hoshe'a is inheriting a ready-made battalion of squared-away girls.

"Oh, and I wanted to inform you that for now. My wife and I will be staying in the sand bowl. The privacy protocol will remain in place. The delivery basket is to be used for any after-duty communication and/or specific invitations to enter the sand bowl. Due to her father's death, we have some, uh, catching up to do. Then I'll be here or wherever needed."

Ari nodded. "Sir, when you were with the girls, I mean, Zayin Battalion, we agreed that for now, our battalion observations need to be either very subtle or covert. Our subordinates know what we expect, and we need to give them some room, at least a little."

The General nodded, then reached into his pocket for a scrap of note parchment. "I agree. And that reminds me…gentlemen, I'm sure"—the sarcasm in his voice was obvious—"I'm the only one who thinks this army would implode if *I* weren't here to make things happen. I mean, where would Yahweh be without our help to run this army?" No one laughed. Which only confirmed the General's concern.

"General Yadin, I have a new directive." Kalev waited for his harried general to nod. "By order of General Kalev, supreme commander of Yisrael's Army, starting on the fourth day of this week, the following officers will take three uninterrupted days off from *all* army-related activities, including (1) all direct or indirect communication with any army personnel or support civilians, (2) no mission planning or AAR reports, (3) no meals in the dining area—meals will be delivered by an assigned troop to your room or at your campsite, (4) no observing any static or active operations. Disobeying this order the first time will result in an extension of three additional days and your immediate demotion to major. Second infraction: no additional days, as you'll be demoted to captain, and you'll wish you had a three-day leave.

"The three-day rotation roster is as follows: (1) General Yadin, (2) General Ofek, (3) General Akiba, (4) General Ari. I want each of your colonels to have a copy of this rotation list." True to form, Yadin looked up and waited. Kalev grinned. "*If* General Hoshe'a survives his second command directive as a general, he'll be busy learning about his battalion. Besides, you must work before you can take time off…"

The General saw everyone's panicked scowl. "People, following the burial and fire, how many days was I absent?" "Three and a half days, Sir," Yadin growled. Kalev smiled. "And the army continued to function without me"—Kalev let that hang in the air—"because my officers knew their job and performed it as admirably as usual. Gentlemen, the last time I checked, this was a covert insurgent force behind enemy lines. We have trained to kill. But so have all the enemies we'll face in the coming months.

We *will* lose people, maybe a lot of people. But what will happen if your battalion loses its Commanding General, or he's too mentally exhausted to execute his oversight?" Kalev didn't finish that statement. "The great leader raises up, then trusts his people. The key is to work yourself out of a job. I have *my* replacement ready to go, and so does he and so on."

Kalev tried to cover his own surprised expression. He had no idea where this wisdom was coming from. *Okay, I have* an *idea*, he thought. The laughing Warrior King's voice boomed in his head. "Thank you. Thank you very much. I'll be here all week, try the veal, and tip your waitress…"

Kalev took his last bite of bread and grinned around it. "Oh, and about that mohar pool. Each one of you is already betrothed; you just don't know it yet…so, General Yadin, please make a correction. General Ari's leave can be rescheduled and extended to seven days as dictated by Colonel Deborah.

"Therefore, General Ari, find First Sergeant Carni and ask her to help you with Colonel Deborah's *Matan*. You'd better do it now before General Hoshe'a delivers his ultimatum to his First Sergeant. Only Yahweh knows that result." Hoshe'a's eyebrows shot up.

Kalev was careful to frame Deborah's suggestions as his own order to be relayed to his ema through Hoshe'a. "And remember, once she begins, there is no escape contingency." Ofek smirked. "General Hoshe'a, *Mr.* Abraham will want this order in writing. To include the understanding that Recruit Carni will be treated like every other new adult recruit." Hoshe'a grew a sly grin and stared at Kalev as he spoke to Yadin. "General Yadin, I need another two copies of this 'ultimate attitude adjustment' within the hour." The grinning Yadin nodded. Kalev stared at Ari. "You'd better hurry." "Sir, I don't have time to…" Kalev's scowl stopped his protest. The scared-looking son of Adir nodded. "Yes, Sir." He took a deep breath, stood, and walked out.

52

The next four wonderful days in seclusion flew by. Raisa enjoyed the escape from the aching loss. She knew it was a temporary fix, but she'd purposed to enjoy their time together before the usual hard normalcy invaded their Eden. On the third day, they'd talked, laughed, and wrestled until they finally passed out an hour before dawn just as the twelve-hour guard shifts changed.

The newly fortified eastern listening post, or the "boulder watch duty," as the troops named it, flanked the road coming from the coastal trade route. The bleary-eyed teenage boys were suddenly energized when the three beautiful colonels from Zayin walked up. All three sergeants came to attention. The girls were too exhausted to even smile. Zilpah nodded, then ordered, "At ease." The boys deflated.

Colonel Zilpah rubbed her eyes and pointed back over her shoulder. "I'm sorry. We haven't slept much in the last four days." All three boys leaned sideways to see the six small children behind her. The oldest male sergeant nodded. "Yeah, we heard about that." The second oldest smirked. "I couldn't do it. After what they pulled, I would have disappeared them. They risked all our lives." The other two nodded. Zilpah sighed. "Believe me, we've thought about it. Master Sergeant Abraham stuck all of us in the same room. The one attached to the rear of the Fortress' TOC. I mean, it's big enough, and we all have a comfortable place to sleep..." She didn't need to finish. The senior male sergeant knowingly smiled. "Uh, so, *unofficially*, we're in the pool." The other two boys nodded sheepishly. "Can I ask what their penalty days are up to?"

It took Zilpah a few seconds before she caught on. "Wait, there's a betting pool?" The other two sergeants quickly looked away. The oldest one nodded. "I think the whole army's in on it. So far, the pot's up to 1200 coins. Of course, that'll be split three ways. But the side bets are where the real money is."

Zilpah rubbed her eyes again and shrugged resignedly. The newly promoted Colonel Marasha handed her the tally sheet. "Okay, *unofficially*, the totals are Little Croc and Frog are tied at twenty-eight days. Little Yoshi is up to seventy-one. I think he's unaffected by little Razili's kisses. They spent most of last night talking about which one of the trio is the smartest. And those numbers will probably rise another twelve by the end of this tour. I'm ready to strangle them myself!" She took a deep breath. "So anything to report?" He shook his head. "No, but we just started this thirty-day rotation. So it's been quiet for our first two days. We heard a platoon from Bet foraged a 200-camel caravan up the road toward the trade route last week. But nothing since... Hey, did you see the black wall?" he asked excitedly.

Zilpah yawned causing all six sergeants to yawn in response. "No, but frankly I'm too tired to care. Listen, we have another twelve mind-numbing hours before we can sleep again. So if there's nothing else..."

The exhausted colonels took up their high overwatch positions on both sides of the road. Little Croc and Little Frog were manning the two spider holes on either side next to the dusty road.

By the time it was two hours after sunrise, all three First Sergeants, Little Frog, and Little Croc had fallen asleep in their hidden positions. Little Yoshi and the three little girls were in a long game of parchment ball catching. None of them saw the distant cloud of dust.

The newlyweds were still asleep as the late morning sun threatened to crest the eastern dune. Kalev awoke because their bed was vibrating. The thick tent walls and the height of the encompassing sand dunes *almost* erased all sound from the other side of the dunes. Kalev was fully armed and halfway to the sand hill when he saw the large dust cloud roll over the top and down toward him. "It's probably just the front edge of a haboob," he warily reasoned. But his gut knew better.

He quickly changed directions and began to run up the northern dune. He remembered that the little boy's and girl's first assignment was to build a hidden, enclosed stall for the General's and Raisa's horses. And he needed to check on them.

Kalev reached the top of the dune and looked east. The dirty red cloud wasn't a haboob. The dirt cloud originated from the road to the east, then continued in front of the sand bowl, wound around to the west and over the canal. His tired mind didn't register the solid blackness beyond the canal. He heard something unintelligible pierce the cloud to the east, and his gut clenched.

For some reason Boaz was already saddled. Then Kalev heard the Warrior King's voice, "*East. Move now*!" The General shot out of the stall and raced up the road into the thinning cloud. In less than a minute, he was almost to the blind bend in the road. As he slowed, the chaotic screams and wails from the other side of the boulders grew louder.

Kalev leaped out of the saddle and quietly led Boaz between a set of boulders with a camouflage netting overhead. He silently climbed to the top and slowly raised his head just enough to peer over the edge. In a heartbeat, his mind switched off all emotion and slipped into a familiar numbness.

As if he was on the opposite side of the road, the Commanding General watched his deadened self sheath his two swords and leap from the top boulder. He landed in a crouch, straitened, and took in the whole grisly scene.

Kalev walked to where Little Croc and Little Frog were being attended to by Colonels Zilpah and Dana. The girls had already switched into their detached medic mode. Both boys' pale faces were streaked with blood. Colonel Dana was trying to wash and bandage a long, horizontal gash on the back of Frog's head. The little guy saw Kalev, raised his head, and began to cry. "We're…so sorry, Sir…we…" But his speech became incoherent, his head fell back onto her folded robe, and he was out.

"Colonel, report," the General roared. But Dana never looked up. Next to her, Zilpah briefly glanced at her trembling friend and then up at the General. She was trying to staunch the bleeding on Croc's right bicep. The senior medic continued her disciplined medical treatments as she reported. But her voice was as flat and emotionless as Kalev felt.

"The three of us colonels have not slept in three days. The sun was warm, and, um, I'd fallen asleep in my position before it happened." "We all did," added Dana, again without looking up. Zilpah nodded. "It appears that Little Frog and Little Croc had also fallen asleep in their spider holes.

"Little Yoshi and the three little…" Kalev saw Zilpah stop what she was doing and sat there motionless for seven long seconds. She resumed her bandaging and continued her detached-sounding report.

"They were playing catch in the road…Sir, the fifty-three chariots came on so fast, I didn't have time to order the children to clear the road. About five seconds before the front rank of frothing horses drew even with their spider holes, these two were out and running toward Yoshi and the girls. Of course, the hoofbeats drowned out their warnings. But they had their swords out, and right after the closest chariot ran over little Adva, both boys drove their swords into the lead chariots. The outside chariots sideswiped them at the same time. They both flew backward into boulders, then crumpled to the dirt." Still unconscious, Croc jerked his left arm. A deep medial laceration opened wider, and blood pulsed out. Zilpah expertly grabbed a large rolled-up bandage and pressed it hard into the cut. The colonel added, "It was like the Egyptian pigs never saw them, Sir."

Dana quickly glanced up with a severe scowl and shook her head. Her practiced hands were instinctively wrapping Frog's motionless head, so she used her chin to point up toward the top of the mound of boulders. "*No*. I was stationed up there on the other side of the road. When that first rank passed my position, I clearly saw their [illegible] platoon leader's face. That pig knew exactly what they'd just done. I'll never forget that [illegible] he was bald and had a wild-eyed grin. He has a scar below his right eye all the way back to his ear. Oh, and he had this large gold Khopesh sword hanging from a studded belt. I threw *my* sword at his head, but the trailing dust cloud seemed to swallow it. They didn't slow down or come back, so I guess I missed." She shook her head again then glanced back up at her General.

Even in his mind-numbed state, Kalev instantly felt the vengeful hatred burning in her eyes. Zayin Battalion's highly trained colonel growled. "No, Sir, I'll never forget that face because the next time I see it, I *won't* miss."

Colonel Dana would never learn that at the last split second, Hotep turned his head to look straight up at her. Dana's tumbling sword ripped Hotep's ear in half and then split the left side of the speeding chariot. The sha'dim-crazed man was so strung out on opium, he'd never remember how it happened.

Kalev expressionlessly nodded as if he'd received the report and was ready to move the meeting onto another subject. But neither Zilpah nor Dana said another word.

The General stood, then slowly walked the thirty yards up the road toward Colonel Marasha. With each step he lifted his knee a little higher than normal, like he was slogging through the mud pits again.

The wailing colonel was kneeling in a muddy puddle of blood. Yet she, too, never looked up at her General. Kalev's fogged mind refused to try and understand her rapid girl-sob dialect. The broken and bloody upper torso of Little Yoshi. The three little girls' remains were scattered in a wide circle around them. The numbed Kalev began to collect the body parts and put them in a pile.

When Carni turned her speeding horses into a hard left around the bend, her medical wagon slid sideways and bounced off a large flat boulder. Then she reined in hard. Once the dust cloud subsided, she gasped, then automatically shifted into her ema-in-charge mode. The two bandaged boys looked dead. Further up the road, Raisa was kneeling with her arm around Zilpah, Marisha, and Dana's shoulders. All four girls were in a tight circle with their bowed heads almost touching. They were obviously sobbing.

Ari and two squads from Heh's Aleph Company were the first ones to arrive behind Carni. Deborah quickly explained what had happened. "After three sleepless nights, we fell asleep on duty. This resulted in four killed and two severely injured…"

Carni realized that the three teenage girls were ordered, in essence, to become experienced emas of someone else's children overnight. She knew *she* couldn't have done it. Still, Carni understood that all adult emas were required to walk a fine line between comforting and ordering their children to suck it up. And this was definitely "suck it up time."

Ari walked up and yelled, "Report." And Zilpah repeated her report. Eventually Ari shook his head and walked away. The girls resumed their group sobbing and hugging. Carni's voice echoed of the surrounding rocks. "All right, that's enough, colonels! It's time to grow up and take care of these children!" They stopped crying, then stiffened to attention.

Carni walked over, hugged the shaking Raisa, and whispered, "You rode here?" Raisa sniffed and nodded. "Okay, you'll ride with me to the Pit then to the burial site." She hugged her trembling daughter again. Over Raisa's shoulder, Carni saw her blank-faced little one covered in blood, carrying most of Little Yoshi's mangled and oozing remains. And he was slowly headed their way. Carni sighed, "[illegible]. I know that stare." The chief ema squeezed her new daughter's arm and quickly pushed her up onto the wagon's seat. Carni stood in front of the three dazed teenage girls. She spoke in her usual menacing deep voice. "I want those two boys on my wagon now! And tie Raisa's horse to the back." Zilpah and Dana went back to gently lift and carry the two boys to the wagon. Without being asked, the blood-soaked Marasha grabbed a stack of blankets out of the wagon and ran back to the carnage.

Carni climbed onto the wagon seat. She watched them gently lift the brave little boys' limp bodies into the padded wagon bed. Then she growled. "General Ari. Would you please help Colonels Zilpah, Marasha, and Dana to carefully sort and wrap each girl's body? Then, General, if you would, use the other three horses to take them to the burial site." Ari nodded. "Of course." "Then you three resume your overwatch!"

Raisa turned in her seat when she heard the girls try to address their oblivious General as they ran by. The sight of the blood-drenched love of her life looking so vacant—it terrified her. She surrendered to a new wave of grief-filled sobbing. Carni followed Raisa's gaze. "[illegible]," she growled. The ema knew that vacant look too well. "[illegible] [illegible] [illegible] [illegible]," she yelled even louder. Carni silently scowled at the dusty sky and then reached over to take the reins off the hitch. "Kalev!" Raisa sobbed. But when Carni looked back, her son had disappeared around the bend in the road.

When he arrived at the first of the scattered body parts, Ari noticed his sullen troops looking lost as to what to do. The bet-grade general picked up a little sandaled foot and then pointed it at the new Master Sergeant. "Master Sergeant Abraham. Get your people over to the grave site where we buried Major Adir. Dig four graves and have the three troop's markers ready. We'll be there in about fifteen minutes. *Move*!"

The new Master Sergeant had anticipated this order. His basic training platoon already had shovels tied to their saddles and were headed to the grave site. A stack of nine wooden grave markers and wood engraving tools were tied behind his own saddle.

The teenage General Ari decided he'd do the grisly sorting. Each of the three small mud-and-blood-caked tunics was carefully emptied, folded, and laid in the center of a blanket. The corresponding arms and legs were respectfully placed beside each tunic. The remains were little more than pulpy skin filled with dripping pieces of pulverized bone and sinew. Little Yoshi's legs and arms were gently placed on the fourth blanket. Lastly, Ari insisted on collecting and placing the three remaining flattened heads. The hair lengths were the only distinguishable features, and Zilpah pointed to the appropriate blanket. The blankets were carefully bundled and labeled with the muddy blood. They secured them to Marasha's and Dana's horses and slowly rode away. Halfway to the gravesite, they passed the slower General. Out of respect, no one glanced at his lifeless face or the bloody remains he held in one arm. He wouldn't have noticed them anyway.

It wasn't until the AAR two evenings later that Kalev's mind cleared enough to piece it all together. Ari watched his General suddenly white-knuckle the edge of the table, and the huge man hissed, "It was Hotep."

The son of Hezron took four four-count breaths, and his hands relaxed. As if the General's tension relayed to his second-in-command, Ari's fists began to clench. He glanced at the General's oddly relaxed yet resolute expression and groaned to himself. He knew he couldn't stop the huge man if he wanted to. Then right in the middle of Colonel Zilpah's report, Kalev stood and excused himself. He told his staff he needed a few days to himself and quickly walked out of the TOC. Ari hung his head and silently pleaded, "Yahweh, please protect him…"

53

General Yadin stayed in "recruit" Carni's house for the duration of his three days of *forced* isolation. He used the new recruit's bedroom in the upper rear of the house. Yadin hung a thick blanket over the window and one over the doorway. He was satisfied that no candlelight could be seen from outside. Then he took out his secret accounting scrolls. General Ari had explicitly forbidden him from taking any parchment scrolls, ink, or even feathers into his exile. But they were comforting. Plus he did take his collection of knives and odd-looking Phoenician cloak pins. His days went fast because Captain Marasha was assigned to deliver his meals. Though she was never explicitly told how long she could stay. Thus she was glad to spend time with Yadin and his numbers. By the end of the second day, all four walls were covered ceiling to floor with accounting columns and numbers. So they spent time just talking about the logistical challenges ahead.

On the afternoon of the third day, Marasha awoke and was surprised and *slightly* embarrassed that they'd fallen asleep on the same bed. To Yadin it was simply the result of talking until dawn. But to Marasha it was both exciting and informative. Right then she decided it was "logical" to be married in three weeks. And now she knew exactly how *he'd* come to the same logical conclusion.

When Ari and Akiba saw Yadin after his three days, their friend seemed vague on the details. All he said was, "Well, I slept and ate a lot." Yet, Yadin had the same problem as the General. Their faces were easy to read. Ari, Ofek, and Akiba knew there was a lot more to the story. After all, they received the perimeter reports daily.

Still dreading his own time alone, Akiba mounted a thick wooden target on the wall of Carni's old bedroom. It was almost a year since he'd been in such a quiet place. He plopped down on the soft bed and fell into a deep sleep. Twelve hours later, something scared him awake. He was instantly crouching on top of the bed, knife in hand. After countless hours of training, he knew he could throw *two* knives simultaneously and hit a two-inch square target at thirty yards.

He heard feet shuffling behind the thick blanket covering the doorway. His arm had just started the downward arc when the most beautiful face he'd ever seen peeked around the side of the blanket. His brain automatically told his hand to roll outward a fraction of an inch. The movement resulted in the knife tip being buried into the wall, one foot from the passageway. *Captain* Zilpah never flinched, but her smile grew even wider. "Nice save."

Following that first day's evening meal, he and Zilpah had talked and thrown knives until dawn. He'd held her hand as she sobbed her way through the description of the "chariot murders," the subsequent burial, and resulting demotion. Much to his surprise, he understood about 25 percent of her girl-sob dialect. This allowed him to piece together most of the other 75 percent.

Eventually, they realized they had a lot in common. They were orphans, and even after her demotion, she still appreciated the dependable structure and safety of army life. By the evening of the second day, they discovered they *really* enjoyed kissing. Akiba knew that Recruit Carni had set the whole thing up, but by the morning of the third day of his "isolation," he never wanted to leave. He was sure the troops surrounding the house had reported the beautiful Zilpah's visits. But no one even mentioned it when he attended *his* battalion's first separate AAR.

During that AAR, General Akiba was informed that General Ari's three days would start that night. And they were not a part of his seven-day bridal week. His wedding feast was temporarily put on hold, as General Kalev had not been seen since he walked out of the Zayin AAR eight days ago.

General Akiba discussed the night's foraging mission with his two colonels. Back when the Pit was still being built, Heh's senior officers began the tradition of being armed and mounted during their briefings. It was another *unofficial* way to "set the elite apart from the typical "sweetbread eaters."

While Akiba was on his wonderful three-day leave, Ari had passed down the order that Zayin's assault troops would be a part of all future missions outside the AO. It seemed strange to the colonels that their battalion general looked pleased when he heard that the Zayin's common *girl* troops would be invading their finely tuned operation. The fact that the foraging missions were originally run by Aleph Battalion was irrelevant.

He handed out copies of the night's foraging mission objectives. "Here's the list of our primary and secondary target needs."

Right then, a squad of Heh's scouts came racing down the ramp and reined in behind the group of officers. The squad leader looked embarrassed when he realized he'd interrupted an officer's briefing. Red-faced, he stiffened in his saddle and saluted.

Akiba scowled but nodded. "Sirs, my squad and I spent the day observing two huge caravans on the road from the Red Sea. They're about eleven miles apart. The first one is made up of over two hundred camels and forty-plus wagons. The second is almost double that. We partially hid four huge skins of the special wine mixture where we thought they'd camp for the night.

"About an hour ahead of the first caravan, we set up our observation post behind an abandoned house. It was fifty yards from the road. We partially hid the first convoy's three large hogskins of wine two hundred yards further up the road past our OP. As usual, the caravan stopped for the night right where we wanted them to.

"But in the middle of the convoy was a squad of seven armed Egyptian soldiers. They were drunk and cussing at the camel herders. All their ranks were equivalent to our privates, yet their swords were pitted and heavily nicked like they'd just come from the war with the Canaanites…" Akiba scowled at the obviously beat-up sword tied to the sergeant's saddle. "They must have noticed our empty-looking house 'cause they started stumbling toward us. I guess they wanted to cover their feet or something.

"Because of our latest caravan protocols, I was about to order a cross-country retreat when this guy popped up from the dirt and stood between us and the soldiers. It was hard to see him because he wore all black. He had a heavy scimitar in each hand and actually ran *toward* the startled Egyptian pigs. The guy's swords flashed with the reflected moonlight, but we never saw his feet or arms move. It was like the swords attacked while we all watched." Another sergeant added, "He fought just like Master Sergeant Abraham." The scout squad leader continued, "We only heard a few grunts and moans before all seven pigs crumpled to the ground. We mounted up and raced to the spot, but the specter had already disappeared. The whole thing was over in less than ten seconds. We took the bodies behind the house. We started to bury them, but we heard a few wolf howls and decided against it. We stripped them naked and cut off any tattoos or brandings and left. I wanted to report before we headed back in an hour."

Akiba asked the squad leader, "Do you think this phantom is a threat to tonight's mission?" To the young scout's credit, he didn't answer right away. "Sir, we debated that all the way back here. Anyone who can fight like that would certainly have the situational awareness to know we were there. But we never saw him even look our way. Sir, he was defending us. So no, we don't see him as a threat. In fact, we'd like to meet him." Akiba scowled when he felt like grinning at the sergeant's comment. "Thank you, Sergeant. Take care of your horses and get some food."

Akiba turned to his senior officers. "The combined caravans will make this our largest foraging run yet. It sounds like there's a lot to scavenge in five short hours. Colonel Isaac and Colonel Ziff, your companies will take convoy two. Make sure the civilians are completely unconscious before you move in. It's important to General Yadin our Bedouin guests are completely 'satisfied' with our, um, hospitality. And this time, people, leave them fully clothed with money in their pockets and one sword each." The colonels chuckled. Ziff shook his head. "Wow, seriously? You stripped one group of smelly camel herders…" Akiba smirked. "Yeah, Colonel Yadin's mixture *is* known to cause one to, um, disrobe and dance into the night." They all laughed. "And tell your people to leave the dancers alone. They'll probably be jackal dung by morning anyway." Colonel Isaac nodded. "According to General Yadin, we have room for all the horses and oxen we can find. The General emphasized the need for more bull oxen. He said the General Kalev's ox needed a break."

Akiba glanced at the scowling Colonel Ziff and smiled to himself. Ziff was his first choice to replace him as battalion commander if needed. Colonel Ziff glanced at his general and got the half nod to take over. "Okay, the second convoy will also have a defensive security detachment, probably more [illegible] Egyptian pigs. Take care of their bodies the same way. Let's give our scouts a thirty-minute lead time to set up the AO's roving perimeter." He glanced at Colonel Isaac. "That means our scouts for the second caravan need to jump off in the next ten minutes. Inform First Sergeant Othniel. All forward observers will carry their bows and throwing knives. We don't know if that specter is an ally or not, and we don't need any more losses…"

Colonel Isaac silently lifted his fist over his head, raised his third and fourth fingers, then dropped his hand back to his saddle. Seemingly out of nowhere, First Sergeant Othniel appeared next to Isaac's left stirrup. While Ziff continued his part of the briefing, Isaac leaned down and relayed the orders.

Ziff glanced at Colonel Able. "We'll off-load half the camels in each convoy. Able, have your people drive those camels south a couple of miles before they set them free." The youngest colonel growled, "I hate those [illegible] things; they stink, bite, and are always complaining!"

Isaac punched his friend in the shoulder. "You just described the majority of Heh Battalion." Ziff smelled his arm pit and shrugged. Once the laughter died down, Ziff picked up the planning brief. "We'll hobble ten empty camels just outside of each convoy's campfire light. Make it look like they tried to run."

Akiba mistakenly believed he'd stayed very professional when Zilpah reported to their mission brief. "Captain Zilpah, you'll need to stage twenty-four empty wagons filled with enough of your troops to drive 150 more. Harness horses instead of oxen—we may need to get away from there quickly. Make sure the wheels are greased and quiet. The wagons we forage are probably already full, but don't take the time to do an inventory there. And don't wait for the rest of us. Immediately harness their oxen and head back to the rally point." Akiba winked at Zilpah. "Captain, split your people into two groups. Break off sixteen of your wagons to trail Aleph and Bet companies. You'll jump off in fifteen minutes. The other eight will follow Gimel Company. They'll jump off in thirty.

"Oh, and I think it'd be a good idea to get our two little heroes involved. *Recruit* Carni mentioned that the boys need a distraction." Zilpah nodded. "Even though it wasn't their responsibility, they blame themselves for not warning the others sooner." Akiba saw the pain in her eyes and felt useless to help. "Tell them, uh, tell them you need a silent and deadly security detachment to protect the most *important* wagon we forage tonight." She self-consciously glanced at the grinning colonels, traded salutes with Akiba, and then quickly rode away.

Akiba turned and saw Isaac and Ziff trading whispers and smiling at their general. Akiba scowled. "May I continue?" His two friends nodded. "Thank you! Initially I'll be with Gimel Company for the assault on the first caravan. Then I'll transition to Aleph and Bet's position. People, let's make this our cleanest foraging mission yet. No surprises and no trace left." "*Yes, Sir*!" The others stiffened to attention, and they traded salutes.

54

The caravan's campfires were so large that they could be seen a mile away. A hundred yards from the first camel herder's camp, Akiba silently ordered a halt. Then he and their newest colonel dismounted. He always wanted to keep the new ones close enough to guide and instruct. This was the twelve-year-old's first foraging mission. "Send your First Sergeant and Aleph Platoon forward to confirm the targets are asleep. Aleph is to surround the camel driver's camp. If any of them wake up, eliminate the threat. Then Split your company. Send each half in a wide arc on opposite sides. Approach from the rear of the caravan. Assess and eliminate any residual threat. The Zayin wagons should already be staged along the way. Offload the camels into our empty wagons. Zayin will take care of the caravans loaded wagons. Offload from the rear forward. Any questions?" "No, Sir." "Then move out." The young colonel began to raise his hand to his chest in salute, but Akiba grabbed his arm and hissed. "*Never* salute a superior officer in the field! You make them an easy target for the enemy." The chastised teen nodded. "Yes, Sir."

Twenty minutes later, Akiba and Colonel Ziff were observing from the second caravan, from the darkness thirty yards away. "…Yeah, the Egyptian guards were already dead before our scouts returned. So that drastically lowered the threat level.

"There are 132 camel herders. Our scouts count didn't include the additional 123 camels still in the dry creek bed when the herders stopped. And as for the herders," Ziff chuckled, "these herders completely emptied the two hundred-gallon hogskins we left under those little palms after the first line of camels past." Akiba shook his head. "They drank all 200 gallons?" Ziff shrugged. "I'm told it's pretty tasty. General Yadin said that his people grind five pounds of the dried black poppy tar and add it to the two gallons of the milky white juice from the cut poppy pod. Then it all goes into the huge skin before he adds the viper wine. He said it takes a while for the poppy mush to kick in. But the combination of the poppy mixture and wine makes them crave more. He said a half gallon of the stuff is more than enough to knock a big man out for at least eight hours. So a gallon-plus each…" Ziff stopped.

Both senior officers' swords were instantly drawn as a single dark figure sprung out of the dirt between them and the caravan. In the bright half-moon, they watched the black-hooded man slowly approach their position.

About ten yards from the two senior officers, the shadow man dropped his heavy pack with a very loud clang and drew the largest black-speckled sword Akiba had ever seen. The teen general growled in a low, ominous voice, "Nice sword…but you'd be wise to put it back in your sheath. Fifteen bows have already sighted you in." Only the whites of the man's eyes showed from under his odd-looking hood. The man rasped, "I'm really not in the mood to be held up by a bunch of thieves. I just wanted to borrow some of the herders' water." Akiba couldn't place the accent, but the voice was vaguely familiar. The teen general ignored the comment and slowly sheathed one of his swords. "Are you the one who defended my troops at sundown?" Akiba could sense this caught the stranger off guard. The man growled back, "All I saw were seven Egyptians headed my way. I hate Egyptians." Akiba smirked. "Apparently! Well, the enemy of my enemy is my friend. And we're not thieves. We're just accepting payment for our hundreds of years of slave labor." The dark man nodded but kept his eyes locked on Akiba's. The stranger planted his sword tip in the dirt, leaned heavily on the handle, and coughed. Ziff tossed him his waterskin. Then man looked surprised at the kindness. He nodded at Ziff.

Without drawing back his hood, he drained the skin and tossed it back. Akiba couldn't see them, but he knew the stranger's eyes had never left his. The man coughed, stood a little straighter, and then dryly growled. "What's your name, thief?" Akiba chuckled. "You kill Egyptians. We forage their stuff. What makes you any better than me?" The man didn't reply, so Akiba continued, "My name is Akiba. I am a general in the Army of Yisrael." The man's head cocked to one side. "Interesting. Just today, a Hebrew slave told me about this secret place that serves free beef and beer and is occupied by orphans who like to kill Egyptians. Have you heard of such a place?" Akiba cautiously nodded. "Maybe, but why should I trust you with such a secret?" The hooded man sheathed his sword, picked up his large bundle, and growled, "Wannabes." Then turned to walk away.

The arrogant hooded man hadn't taken a second step when a much larger black-robed figure rose in front of the belligerent invader. Akiba and Ziff were surprised at first, but then they both grew wide smiles. A huge black speckled knife was instantly at the shorter stranger's throat. The wraith was obviously not intimidated, but he froze in place anyway. The bigger one hissed. "My troops mean you no harm. My name is General Kalev. Who are you, stranger, and why would I allow you into my AO?" The hooded man hissed with a defiant rage that sent a chill down Akiba's back. "Never ever draw your knife on me again." Kalev felt a prick just above his groin. The hooded stranger was surprised when the much larger man withdrew his knife and sheathed it. "Nicely done… You speak Hebrew, so I guess that means you're not *that* stupid. But like my officer said, you are very fortunate our archers haven't used you for target practice." Instantly, the sound of thirty bow strings tightening, broke the tense silence. Under the blood-soaked hood, the warrior's eyes narrowed and he smirked. Kalev's hand was at his side, so the invader never saw the one-finger signal. Now fifty hidden bowmen drew their strings a little tighter. The subsequent stretching sound sobered the stranger. The man's shoulders slumped. "Well, I guess I won't be killing you tonight." Kalev laughed; for some reason he liked this guy. "What's your name, oh threatening one?" The man threw his hood back. "Listen, general or whoever you are, I'm tired, hurt, and hungry. I escaped from a cargo ship two days ago and haven't eaten or slept for three days. I think I'm from here, but I don't remember my Hebrew name. I've fought in too many countries for too many masters. They each gave me a new name. I…" Kalev interrupted. "We'll talk more later." The black-clad General looked up at Akiba. "Do you have any bread and wine?" Akiba chuckled. "Always, Sir." He threw the exhausted-looking man a loaf of bread, two sticks of beef, and a small skin of viper wine.

The General subtly flattened his hand, palm down. About half of the bow strings relaxed. "Troops, well done. Now mount up and bring my worthy opponent one of those Egyptian pigs' saddled horse."

The General sounded two high-pitch staccato whistles. A black-streaked Boaz bolted from behind a pile of boulders. "General Akiba. I don't suppose you have another loaf in that bottomless saddle bag of yours. I haven't eaten in…well, a long time." Akiba smiled. "Well, since it's you, Sir."

As their General devoured the large loaf of sweet bread, they watched the young warrior's knees almost buckle under the weight of his large bundle. "Can I carry that pack for you?" The nameless warrior didn't respond as he fell to his knees. By the time the offered horse arrived, he could barely stand. Without asking Kalev lifted him into the saddle. He handed him another waterskin. A very-foul-smelling Kalev walked over to Akiba and whispered. Akiba, in turn, whispered to Colonel Ziff. The colonel raced toward the closest filled wagon. The driver raced off toward the Pit.

A cool breeze suddenly blew out of the north. The light from the rising half-moon and brilliant stars made it easy to trail the last rank of the wagons fifty yards ahead. The General, General Akiba, and his three colonels flanking the dark warrior rode in silence.

Kalev's exhausted mind was still trying to sort through the last two weeks. He turned in his saddle to look at the stranger. The Warrior King's voice boomed in the General's gut. "This boy will lead My *kidon* (tip of the spear) one day. I led him here for such a time as this. Son of Hezron, in many ways this man is your equal. He too has suffered too many degrading and life-threatening assaults and monstrous abuses. Be careful with this gift I've brought you." Kalev nodded, then pulled back and fell in line next to the sick-looking kid. Akiba did the same and rode on the other side. He sent the colonels ahead. Akiba passed over another small skin of viper wine to the stranger.

The mottled-faced warrior drained the skin and nodded at Akiba. They rode in silence again for a few more minutes. Prompted by the Warrior King, Kalev asked, "What do you remember about Goshen?" Kalev guessed the man was eighteen going on sixty. The exhausted looking outsider looked at the others, then back at the huge, muscled man. "I keep having this dream. I was a young boy, and I was taken from the docks and…" Akiba sucked in a sharp breath. The stranger stopped his story, and all eyes shifted to Heh Battalion's general. Even in the moonlight, Akiba's shocked expression was evident. He knew this guy, or at least he thought he knew him.

"Excuse me, General." Kalev curiously nodded. Ignoring the overwhelming stench of blood and excrement, Akiba leaned closer to get a better look at the pain-filled, black-speckled face. He leaned back and groaned. "Okay. Let me tell you a story and see if it helps your memory. Our emas were friends from childhood. Both were present at my friend's and my birth. We grew up as best friends and neighbors. But…" Akiba paused, and his eyes began to glisten in the moonlight. He cleared his throat. "We liked to go to the docks near Ramses and watch the foreign ships come in. One day we hid behind a tall stack of stinking monkey cages and watched them unload that huge Minoan Galley. We'd dared each other to sneak on board and grab one sword out of a huge open crate. That's when we decided to run to the other side of the building to get closer to one of the mooring ropes. I got to the other side and thought my friend was behind me. I backtracked to the other side, but he wasn't there either. I searched for him until it got dark. I'd even sneaked onto two different ships, but he was gone. I ran home crying, and my abba and ema made me go with them to tell his ema. She'd been sick since his abba died in the quarry. I remember sobbing as I told his ema. She died three days later, and I've always blamed myself for her death and his disappearance. It really messed with my head. I grew up with an oozy darkness that seemed to get worse every year. I was in a really bad place when I met Ari…"

The stranger didn't respond. He rode on like he hadn't heard a word. They all silently rode for another mile. Kalev kept a close eye on the stranger's face. The kid looked like he could fall out of the saddle at any time. Then Yoshi'yah's eyes grew wide. Then his face suddenly aged decades and finally lost all expression. The very old teenager took a rattling deep breath. He grimaced and spoke in a pained, eerie growl.

"Akiba, when you first ran around the other side of that building, I started to follow. But a huge fat man jumped in front of me and clamped his hand over my mouth. He picked me up and…" He grew silent for a while. The two generals averted their eyes and rode in silence. Eventually the warrior took another ragged breath.

"For the next fifteen jaw-dropping minutes, Yoshi'yah relived most of his violent history. When he finished, he slumped in his saddle, looked at his hands, and mumbled. Kalev knew exactly what torment this gladiator was going through. He knew the best thing he could do right now was distract the kid. So he pointed at the large bundle tied to the back of the Yoshi'yah's saddle. "Are those all swords?" The teen distractedly nodded and responded in a flat monotone.

"I've been bought and sold too many times to remember. When I got older, I fought in arenas. Before each deathmatch, my masters would parade me and a wagon full of my 'victory' swords and axes through the streets. It was their way to increase the betting. *They* always got a percentage of the total take." The kid sourly smirked. "Never paid, rarely fed, and always dreaded my master's next beating. That was *my* life until two weeks ago."

The too-old looking teen shook his head. "Too many times I'd prayed for death, but at the same time, I refused to let someone kill me." Kalev glanced at the confused-looking Akiba. The General knew he was the only one that really understood the pain-filled meaning behind this dangerous teen's words. He felt a lump swell in his throat.

Yoshi'yah pointed over his shoulder. "These are a fraction of the swords and axes I've won in battle." In a blur of movement, he drew an enormous, black-speckled double-edged sword from his back sheath. Akiba cringed, but Yoshi'yah just stared at his lethal weapon. "But this one will always be my favorite." His voice grew ruff and ancient. "I think we were docked at Ugarit. My latest [illegible] chained me to a dock bollard while he went off to drink. Before dawn, he'd stumbled back to the docks. The pig woke me by jabbing my cheek with this sword's tip. Something in me broke. The rest is a little fuzzy. I don't remember attacking him with his own sword. I guess I severed his head because it rolled off his shoulders, bounced once, and then plopped into the water. His headless body lay at my feet quivering. I snatched the key to my shackles, grabbed his scabbard and money purse. I rolled his body off the dock, grabbed my weapon's bundle, and hid aboard an Egyptian cargo ship.

"Eventually, I heard Assyrian soldiers shouting about a headless and handless body floating in the water, but no one looked for me." He smiled at the huge sword. "Yeah, this one will always be my favorite." He sheathed it and looked at Akiba's tear-stained face. The General was nodding approvingly. "Did killing him make you feel better?" Yoshi'yah shook his head. "No. I can never kill enough people to feel better about my past. I wish I could forget most of it…" The exhausted-looking man slowly nodded. "These few swords and axes represent the only kills I want to remember."

Yoshi'yah glanced up at the tall man and recognized the indescribable stare. "Did your kills even the score?" The General didn't answer. He reined in hard; Boaz reared. This caused Akiba to do the same and draw his sword. Kalev stiffly adjusted himself in the saddle, then addressed Akiba. "Great job tonight. Ride ahead and get it all secured. I'll be there soon. Oh, and General Akiba. Have we ever observed what actually happens when the herders wake up the next morning?" The general chuckled. "No, Sir, but I'm sure General Yadin would like to know the results." Kalev nodded. "That's what I was thinking. Assign our most experienced day scouts to the detail. They're only to observe and report." "Yes, Sir." Akiba disappeared over the top of the hill. That was when Yoshi'yah noticed a similar large bundle on the back of the big guy's horse.

Kalev turned Boaz so he could see the teen's face. Yoshi'yah noticed that the huge warriors tunic looked sliced up, stiff, and solid black. Yoshi'yah carefully sized the man up. He'd faced many men this size. But this one was different. He saw the old scars and new cuts and bruises on his head, arms, and legs. Even in the stiff breeze, the too familiar smell of death exuded from the giant's tunic. To most others, he guessed, the stench was nauseating. But to the young fighter, it was the bitter smell of survival.

For a short while, they just stared at each other. Kalev wordlessly dismounted. The General unlashed the bundle from his saddle and rolled it out on the dry creek bed. Yoshi'yah counted thirty-three standard Egyptian-issue sickle swords and five gold officer's Khopesh swords, one gold-tipped composite bow, twenty-two arrows, and four Egyptian officer's leopard tails. The General emptied a small pouch of forty-five gold nose and earrings and five gold headbands. There was one other stiff black sack. The General mumbled something, grabbed the sack, and walked a few steps south. He used his heel to dig a wide hole in the sandy silt.

Kalev upended the bag, and a large clump of black-haired scalps, fingers, eyes, and tongues plopped into the hole. He filled in the hole and walked back. The silent giant refilled the oozing pouch with the rings and headbands. Without meeting Akiba's astonished gaze, the General handed him the pouch. He pointed at the cloth hanging out the end. "Is that a Kemet Chariot division guidon flag?" The General growled something under his breath but didn't answer the question. He stiffly bent down, rerolled the bundle, and tied it behind his saddle. The General's ragged voice quietly pierced the breeze. "No! I realized I could never kill enough Egyptian soldiers. Except for one. That one I'll take my time with." Yoshi'yah knowingly nodded yet remained silent. *Yeah, but I'm just getting started*, he thought.

The General mounted Boaz. "Yoshi'yah. If you want to continue your killing quest, we'll wait here for your supplies. The horse is yours, and you can go on your way. But if you want the freedom and security of your own warm bed, two hot meals a day, and a real purpose, you need to agree to our army protocols. And they are nonnegotiable." The old teen eyed the huge man warily. "I'm listening."

"First, complete secrecy. I take our OPSEC personally. If you choose to join us tonight, you'll never talk about what you see or hear to anyone outside of this army." Yoshi'yah smirked. "I don't know anybody, so…"

"Secondly, this is an army. We eat, sleep, train, and live as a single unit. We train to fight Egyptians, Nubians, Canaanites, etc. We have a chain of command you'll respect and obey. These conditions are not flexible." Kalev growled. "I'm very serious. This army is my family. Most of these boys and girls are orphans and refugees. It's my job to protect them. You're welcome to join us, but it's a one-way trip… We'll give you four days to heal up and make your decision." Kalev paused for the response.

That was when he saw the steady black trickles dripping from open wounds on Yoshi'yah's neck, shoulder, and legs. The dazed-looking kid's voice was faint and hard to hear. "You're giving me a horse? No one's ever given me anything. I…don't have anywhere to go… But I…need…"

The teen's head began to loll to the side. Kalev let out a series of loud ibis calls. In a few seconds, five horses leaped from the top of the berm behind them. Kalev watched one of Heh's largest sergeants jump behind Yoshi'yah's saddle and wrap his arm around the semiconscious teen's middle to keep him upright. "Take him to the medical room in the Pit. Inform General Akiba and Recruit Carni." The Sergeant nodded and raced up the bank.

Kalev rode Boaz into his stall and awkwardly fell off the horse. He barely made it to the top, then tumbled down the inside of the sand bowl. He stiffly stood and headed for the cool spring pool. The son of Hezron didn't see the two shocked women standing in the tent entrance as he limped by. The half-conscious Kalev made it to the spring's short wall and rolled into the dark water.

55

Two mornings later, Carni was sitting with Moshe and Ari outside Kalev's tent. They'd pulled four of the chairs outside to get some air. The ema, the prophet, and the teen general spoke quietly. They didn't know the exhausted Raisa was sitting right behind them on the other side of the tent wall. She listened as she laid her head on the table.

"...No, he's lost a lot of blood, but I've seen him in worse shape. Thankfully he's slept for the last two days. He'll wake up starving, and in another day he'll be back to his normal self."

Moshe slowly shook his head and scowled. "No, he won't." Yahweh's chosen leader spent the next fifteen minutes explaining why her son had vanished for two weeks. Carni silently wept. She was afraid she'd finally lost the little one she'd always known and loved. Moshe continued, and Ari had to cover his mouth to hide his proud and approving smile. Moshe shook his head. "They were brutal but warranted kills. He took down some of the best fighters in the Egyptian Army. And frankly I would have joined him if he'd asked. But no, Carni, I don't think he'll ever be normal again. Even justified killing changes a person. The carnage alone is almost unforgettable."

Carni dried her eyes and put her hand on the older man's muscular shoulder. "General Moshe, let me tell you about my son's usual day in the mud pits..." After ten minutes of graphic detail, Moshe groaned. "...then somehow he'd make it home, I'd piece him together, and he'd do it all again the next day."

The eighteen-year-old slowly shook his head. This was the first time he'd heard about the brick furnaces used for cremating the dead children's bodies. Ari sneered at the adults with fire in his eyes. He pointed at the two brief winks of light at the top of the southern dune. "You're not alone, Sir. The entire army is itching for the same opportunity to kill the pigs." Moshe looked up and another glint appeared. Bet-grade General Ari rolled his eyes, then looked at Carni. "They haven't left that overwatch in two days." Last night Little Croc told First Sergeant Othniel that the General is a hero, and they are the best hero overwatchers in the army." It was the first time in two weeks he'd heard either of them speak, so he let them stay. "On my way here this morning, I overheard Little Croc telling three perimeter guards that the General killed ninety-four L↘⦀✢ᘓtg Egyptian Army soldiers and fed half to the crocs, and then he gave us these army crowns and special swords 'cause we're heroes 'cause we tried to rescue Little Yoshi and those other girls like you, but the chariots already squished them, but we tried to save them, but they hit our heads on the rocks, and we almost died, especially Croc."

Moshe smiled. "Wait—he killed ninety-four? I only heard about forty-five." Ari shrugged. "Yadin determined that most of the axes and all the gold nose rings belonged to different soldiers. And those are the ones we know about."

Moshe pointed at the fluttering Egyptian Army standard. The pennant had a large blood-stained handprint obscuring the "all-seeing eye" on the Kemet battle standard. "That's a guidon flag for an, um"—he glanced at Carni—"overzealous and specialized Kemet unit. In fact, that was general Hotep's unit. Did he…?" "No," boomed the ragged voice from the open tent flap. "Not yet!"

The three turned to look. The silently weeping Raisa was already at the cool spring with an empty urn. Kalev stepped into the sun, stretched, and slightly winced. One of the wounds on his back opened up again and was starting to darken the back shoulder of his clean tunic. "Ema, I'm hungry." Carni winked at Moshe, then growled through her smile. "Arghhhh, you're also bleeding again. I just washed that." They both smiled at their too-familiar "morning after" routine. "Sit here and stop bleeding. I'll go get my basket."

Kalev nodded at the other two, plopped into the overly padded third chair, and sighed a ragged breath. "The Warrior King and I argued over killing Hotep for the entire two weeks. He said He had a more 'public' execution planned for Hotep. Still, I would've slowly filleted him like a butcher, but I never found him. I, um, *heard* he was at the Baranis docks. I was headed there when I ran into our foraging troops…" He looked toward the pool, but Raisa was already back in the tent.

Carni came out with her basket and bandages. She stood behind Kalev's chair, and as usual, she whipped off his short tunic and dropped it. Then she threw a clean one into his lap. They'd gone through this same multi-decade ritual so many times, he just shrugged at his friends' surprised smiles. "Yeah, it's kind of our thing." She leaned forward and whispered, "Little one, Raisa was there." Kalev turned his head and locked quizzical eyes with his ema. It took a moment, and then his foggy mind cleared. "Oh, [illegible]." "Kalev, she'd never seen carnage like that or you covered in blood. Plus you were in that dark place where…" Carni started to tear up. The General hissed loudly. "[illegible] [illegible] [illegible]." He leaped out of his chair and raced inside. Even Carni didn't follow or want to hear their discussion.

Fifteen minutes later he came out with a partially consoled Raisa. Ari quickly offered his chair. The pale-looking Kalev plopped back in his chair, and Raisa stood behind him with Carni.

Another glint at the top of the hill caught his eye. "General Ari, what day is this?" Ari told him. "I assume they've passed their test." "Yes, Sir, in fact they went eight days straight after the murders. But Colonel Carni assigned two other girls for the boys. She told the boys they were the most silent and deadly troops she knew, and the girls needed training in the deadly skills of war. Surprisingly they agreed. But they *told* the colonel that the girls were not allowed to kiss them, or they'd have to go to the tanning squad for the rest of their little girl lives."

Carni finished her expert bandaging, and both women went back inside.

The General raised his eyebrows and looked at Ari. "Colonel?" "Yes, Sir. Master Sergeant Abraham said, and I quote, 'That ∟∿(‖)↓ℓ୧ woman is the best ∟∿(‖)↓ℓ୧ troop I've ever trained. She'd be a ∟∿(‖)↓ℓ୧ fantastic drill instructor.' Then he added, 'I can't think of a better ∟∿(‖)↓ℓ୧ girls' battalion commander!'" Kalev smiled and shook his head. "Hoshe'a needs shadow troops now more than ever."

When Carni and Raisa returned, they were both giggling about something. But Kalev's nosy ema picked up the conversation like she'd never left. "Yes, the Master Sergeant and I sort of bonded over our similar approach to attitude adjustments. Plus, I really enjoyed the advanced weapons training." Kalev winced.

He looked at the top of the dune and tried to scowl. He raised his hand to shoulder height, then pointed two fingers at the ground in front of him. Four little kids stumbled and tumbled down the dune. The boys formed up in front of their General while the little girls stood at the foot of the dune.

Kalev opened his mouth, but his words caught in his throat. The boys' too-large gold swords protruded from their too-large belt scabbards and had dug a line in the grass from the dune to where they stood at attention. Their gleaming gold headbands had fallen around their necks. They both reeked like they hadn't bathed in weeks.

But before the General could speak, Little Croc, with a grand practiced flourish, raised his hand to shoulder height and pointed at the ground behind him. The little girls giggled and quickly shuffled behind the scowling boys. Little Frog, still trying to stand on his tiptoes, let out a high-pitched growl. "Arghh, we're sorry, Sir…they're still in training, and they aren't learning fast like me and Croc did!" Little Croc nodded and scowled.

Moshe almost bit his tongue off. Carni cleared her throat. Then Kalev felt her rest her trembling forehead on the back of his neck and cough a few times. Moshe started coughing, then quickly stood and walked toward the spring. But Ari just glared.

"At ease," Kalev halfheartedly growled. Little Croc whipped his head around to make sure their "recruits" had complied with the General's orders. Then he nodded for his General to continue. Carni finished treating another wound, and then she and Raisa quickly joined the others at the pool.

Ari grumbled something under his breath, then got in Little Croc's face. "First of all, *Corporal,* a squad leader can't keep an eye on his squad if they're standing behind him. Secondly, no one turns their head when standing at attention. If you have to, you can look out of the corner of your eye. Third and most important, the General doesn't need your approval or go-ahead to speak. When he speaks, you listen. Do you understand me, Corporal?" Little Croc yelled, "Yes, Sir, Sorry, Sir." Without turning his head, Little Croc made the same arm gestures and pointed to the other side of Frog. Ari growled, stiffened to attention, glanced at his General, and yelled, "Squad, about-face."

The little reproved troops complied. Ari nodded at his General, who mouthed thank you. Then General Ari headed for the pool. Kalev quickly dawned his too-tight tunic. Ari stopped and turned around, smiled, and yelled at the four little backs. "These troops are all yours, Sir. I can't take any more of this." He walked off smiling but not-so-softly swearing under his breath. The General yelled, "About-face! Now…"

The General talked with the little troops as the others stood at the cool spring. Carni had her arm around Raisa's trembling shoulder as she continued. "I know. It was…it was unreal. I mean…when I saw him covered in blood…and that vacant stare…it all seemed to get very real. We really *are* at war, aren't we?" She squeezed Carni's hand then shuddered a sigh. Moshe nodded. He understood, at least from Kalev's point of view, but remained silent.

Eventually, Raisa turned to see Kalev laughing. The four children were sitting on the grass in front of him. She smiled and unconsciously touched her flat stomach. Carni quietly gasped but kept her question to herself.

The five-foot Mrs. General turned to Ari and spoke quietly. "The next adult basic training class starts tomorrow night." Ari warily nodded. "Good. I'll be there." It was an emphatic statement, not a question.

Standing at the spring, Ari shot a worried glance at his General, then back at Raisa's fiery stare. "…And for my marriage's sake, he will *not* be told until I've graduated from the advanced course." Ari started to agree, but Colonel Carni shot daggers at him with *the look.*

Ari cleared his throat. "But I can't…I mean, it's you—um, the General needs to approve…" Raisa shook her head, and then she too shot him *the look.* The guilty-looking Ari glanced at his General and frowned. "Are you sure?" He went on to describe the basic and subsequent training agenda… "And then there's Master Sergeant Abraham… Mam, are you absolutely sure you want to submit yourself to that kind of, um, assault and…keep it a secret?"

The basket arm swung over the top of the dune. Raisa noticed but remained staring at Ari. "If you're sure, I'll have to notify General Akiba and Sergeant Abraham today…but please reconsider. I can privately show you how to…" But she interrupted him. "General Ari, as of one hour after sundown tomorrow night, I am a recruit in the second accelerated adult basic training class!" Ari glanced over at Kalev again, grimaced, then defeatedly nodded.

As the teenager watched the two women walk away, Moshe leaned over and whispered, "Son, that battle was over before it began. And from what I hear, you're about to marry your own female warrior. Even the Warrior King won't defend against this type of female attack. So you'd better get used to it." Ari defeatedly nodded. "I'm starting to see that, Sir." Moshe frowned, then spoke as the Warrior King prompted.

"Son, a wise warrior is strong, and knowledge makes him even stronger. For with guidance you wage your war, and with numerous advisers there is victory…and yes, this applies to marriage." Ari glanced at the General, who was smiling at him. He'd obviously heard Moshe and agreed.

Moshe slowly nodded. "My time has passed. Yet, even in this sha'dim-filled land, *you've* discovered a fantastic advantage I never had." This got Ari's attention. "You both are heading in the same purposeful direction. Son, cherish her as a gift from Yehovah… Oh, and no matter what, always remember 'happy wife, happy life'…because an unhappy wife makes the mud pits look appealing…"

Ari laughed and pointed at the two women disappearing into the tent. "General Moshe, I don't think Colonel Carni knows your time has passed. I saw your name on her list."

56

For the second morning in a row, Raisa was still asleep when Kalev awoke. He was starving, and for the first time in six weeks, there wasn't any food in the delivery basket. So he rode to the pit for the morning meal. He rode up to Moshe and his general staff at their usual dining table. They all stood when he dismounted. This caused a chain reaction of captains and First Sergeants loudly calling their troops to attention. The General still felt embarrassed when this happened, but he let it play out. Even the thousands of animals corralled in the Pit craned their necks to look his way. Kalev took a few seconds to look approvingly at the troops. The Commanding General yelled, "Good morning, Army of Yisrael?" The walls and deck shook as they all replied, "Good Morning, General, Sir!" "As you were troops!"

Kalev joined his general staff. Hoshe'a was nodding talking with his mouth full. "Well, welcome back, General." Kalev smirked. "Yeah, for some reason, killing the ∟∿⦀⍖ꝏ Egyptians got boring. Besides, I like my bread straight out of the oven." They guardedly laughed. Moshe's report about Kalev's one-man killing mission, both awed and made them a little all a little nervous. Kalev sensed this and spoke to his people in a low tone, "General Ofek, I can tell you for a fact the Warrior King's battle instructions work. And by the way He was with me the whole time." This really surprised Moshe. "The only drawback is it requires an upper-body endurance beyond what we've trained for. But I'm sure that can be remedied." Ofek nodded. "Yes, Sir. I'll see to it."

"Gentlemen, listen. I spent most of my life being tortured by an enemy that doesn't see us as people. Only a means to an end. The Warrior King and I talked about that often. He kept telling me that vengeance was His, and He was the one who'd balance the account. Of course, it took me a while to understand that. But He had my back and protected me the whole time. It wasn't pretty, but it *was* just."

The Commanding General climbed onto the table and faced his troops. They instantly went silent. The General could see in their eyes; they all knew what had happened. His words came out in a roar. "Army of Yisrael. They killed our troops, part of *our* family. We are the Warrior King's chosen. And that will *never* happen again. Yes, vengeance is our Warrior King's to deliver in His time frame. But we are His unforgiving sword to wield... People, we follow *His* orders; we train to fight *His* enemies. And we. Fight. To. *Kill*!"

The Fortress erupted in the expected war cries and chants. At that moment Yoshi'yah rode up and wordlessly stared at Kalev. The General grabbed two hot loaves of bread and yelled to Ari, "You and Akiba, walk with me. And General Ofek, have Sergeant Abraham join us."

Kalev motioned for the civilian warrior to follow. They all walked fifty yards toward the ramp, stopped in the center of the drill deck, and stood in a tight circle. Master Sergeant Abraham ran up and stood at attention. "At ease, First Sergeant." Four mornings prior, Abraham had immediately sized up the intruder and decided he didn't like the arrogant [illegible]tg wannabe.

By that time, just as Kalev had planned, a very large, silent circle had formed around the drill floor. The General nodded for Yoshi'yah to speak. The teen never intended to have an audience and briefly looked unsure—also a part of Kalev's plan. Yoshiyah cleared his throat and declared. "I've thought about your offer. But *if* I join, I have my own *nonnegotiable* condition."

Akiba winced, and Master Sergeant Abraham's face grew red at the intruder's insolence. But Kalev and Ari struggled to maintain their scowl. Both generals liked and respected this kid's fearless attitude. They saw what Yahweh saw. Kalev nodded for the audacious teen to continue.

"I get to kill Egyptians, Assyrians, or Minoans or Barbarians or Nubians or whoever *I* think is a threat…So, if you agree, I'll join your army." The General shot Ari a knowing glance. He acted like he was surprised at the confident stipulation, then scowled again. "No…I've changed my mind. You may think you're ready, but I'm not so sure anymore." In unison, Ari, Akiba, Kalev, and the Master Sergeant automatically took a half step back. "*I* now have another *nonnegotiable* requisite for you to join. You *cannot* kill Master Sergeant Abraham." The two generals took three more quick steps backward, and the duel began.

Amid a myriad of cheers, clanging sparks and expletives flew. Kalev and Ari ate their loaves with smiles plastered on their faces. Everyone was stunned at the flowing yet lethal dance. Ari gave a running description of each slash, thrust, and parry. Twenty-seven grueling minutes later, both bleeding warriors were gasping for air and could barely lift their swords. The cheering had morphed into a respectful admiration.

Kalev recognized and appreciated the familiar stubborn pride that refused to stop. He finally yelled, "Enough, drop your swords." Abraham obeyed immediately, but Yoshi'yah obviously struggled with the ridiculous order. The future leader of the Warrior King's kidon finally gave in, and his huge Khopesh dropped to the floor with a loud clang. "I declare a draw! Both exhausted, bleeding teens eyed each other with a newfound respect." Kalev paused to let them recover.

Ari dismissed the clapping and cheering troops. The two generals stepped closer to the two combatants. Kalev nodded approvingly. "Thank you both for the amazing exhibition. Yoshi'yah, *if* the Master Sergeant decides to admit you to his next basic training class, your greatest challenge will be learning the tactical skill of self-control and submission to an honorable authority. Your friend Akiba can prep you. The Warrior King thinks you have the skills and attitude to become an important part of this army. However, you'll have to adhere to Master Sergeant Abraham's training methods. So he has the final decision as to your future here."

Kalev nodded to the sneering Master Sergeant. Abraham and Yoshi'yah locked eyes. Then Abraham wearily growled. "*If* you think you're man enough, I can and will turn you into a soldier. But know this. At any point in your basic, advanced, and specialized training…" Kalev glanced at Ari curiously. His subordinate nodded toward Abraham and mouthed, "His idea." "…You're out of my L∿(‖)↓ɐ9 army." Yoshi'yah continued to wordlessly glare at Abraham. Then Yoshi'yah wordlessly nodded. Abraham came to attention and saluted his generals.

He reached down and picked up both badly nicked swords. Both hardened troops started back to the dining tables. The smiling generals watched Abraham deftly swing Yoshi'yah's large Khopesh. "It's not balanced, but we can fix that."

57

The two generals returned to their table. Hoshe'a chuckled, "I forgot." Kalev looked at him quizzically. "Brother, everywhere you go there's always food and a show…" He continued his conversation with Ofek and Akiba. "…As I was saying before the flamboyant interruption, the answer is yes. If you stood on our side of the canal, the blackness spanned north, south, and as high as you could see. And against his sergeant's direct orders, one of the new recruits walked across the canal bridge and stuck his hand in. He said it disappeared in the cold blackness. Then, right before his sergeant yanked him backward, the kid stuck his other arm in. He later swore that slimy hands were pawing at his arms."

Moshe grinned. "I don't know about that, but the darkness was complete. Even in the palace, it seemed to swallow the torchlight." Moshe shook his head in disgust. "As he obviously lied to me again, that  Ramses held the torch so close to his face, his headdress caught fire. It was the first time I'd laughed in the palace since my ema's death. Ramses refused to appreciate the irony. I told him about Yahweh's bright restorative presence. But his stubborn arrogance is the reason he keeps burning himself and all of Egypt to the ground. I told him Sha'al was much hotter."

Kalev shrugged. "I actually liked the heat. I even roasted a cob of corn over one of the burning Egyptian pigs' body." They all broke into a belly laugh. But the nearby troops were listening in awe of their conquering General. And soon, the legend of General Kalev's adventures grew even larger.

The General told his staff about the Warrior King's plans for Yoshi'yah. Akiba smiled at Ari, who nodded for him to go ahead. Akiba lowered his voice. "Kidon's the name we came up with last week for our new specialized company." Moshe smirked. "I guess Yahweh knew ahead of time." He looked at Kalev with a straight face. "I hope He didn't tell anyone else." But Moshe and Kalev were the only ones chuckling.

Akiba continued in a quieter, serious tone. "We used the Warrior King's diagrams to develop a more extensive training regimen. The Master Sergeant just demonstrated the basic techniques of kidon sword fighting. It was obvious he refused to use four of the most advanced methods. It would have ended that fight in the first minute. I guess he has a heart after all." They all laughed. Akiba continued the description.

"The Kidon's primary mission will be to infiltrate, kill, get out, and disappear the enemy before anyone knows they were there. Their bleached leopard skin banner is blank, except for the words 'Victory through deceptive strength' at the bottom." Kalev smiled around a bite of sweetbread.

"The candidates will be handpicked for their expert weaponry skills, concealment techniques, and wholehearted obedience to any and every order. Even during their secret training, they're expected to excel in their current Battalion responsibilities. And if their additional Kidon training becomes common knowledge, they are removed from the detachment without prejudice. Their training ground is about five miles straight east of here. All of them will slowly transition to day shift for the final two-week covert-survival evolution." Akiba smirked. "Their final go or no-go is a three-day, five-mile, camouflaged crawl to a set objective. If they're discovered, they'll be dismissed and given the option to repeat the training. Our first class starts in two weeks. Their graduation ceremony will also be on a need-to-know basis." Akiba locked eyes with each of the other aleph grade generals. "So unless it becomes vital to the army's survival, we will not discuss the Kidon's existence again." Kalev gravely nodded his agreement.

Moshe missed the significance of the *suggestion* and grinned. "Impressive. But if it's the first class, then who are your trainers?" Ari nodded soberly. "Sir, um, please don't ask. I could tell you, but then I'd have to kill you." Moshe's laugh caught in his throat when he saw the boy's grave expression.

Kalev quickly changed the subject. "How are the nightly herding maneuvers going?" Akiba shook his head. "Sir, you weren't kidding. The cattle seem to attract every jackal, leopard, cheetah, and wolf for twenty miles. So far, none have penetrated our outer perimeter. Last night, I overheard one of Zayin's sergeants talking about an unofficial contest. Each night a different predator is chosen. The company that kills the most of those specific animals wins a hundred silver coins. So far, Zayin Company has won every night." Akiba smirked. "And you can guess how the boys have taken that.

"Herding the cattle in front of the wagons followed by the four long files of camels was initially a good idea. Tonight, we'll load the wagons to determine what our normal pace will be." Ari nodded thoughtfully. "Remember most of the civilians will be walking. So the oxen will probably be a good gage. But stay flexible. You may want to use a few squads of dismounted troops to give you a better idea. Every troop has a horse?" Yadin grew his usual thinking scowl. "At this point, we have an extra 379 waiting to be assigned to new troops. And thanks to the two very gracious groups of drunk camel drivers, every two to four troops will be issued a tent, depending on the tent's size. Tonight we'll load the designated wagons with barrels of water, flour, beer, and the biggest skins of wine. Fifteen of the largest-covered six ox-drawn wagons are allocated for all the chests of gold and silver coins. Except to refresh the wagon water weekly, we won't unload the 'water wagons' before we leave. We have enough camel saddles for three hundred civilians to ride on the pack camels." Akiba grinned at his excited friend. "You really are having fun with all this." Yadin smiled. "It's a hard job, but someone has to do it. And you, Yadin, my friend, can't count to twenty with your shoes off." They all started laughing.

58

Five miles east of the Pit, Moshe and the generals sat horseback on the crest of a small hill. The new moon barely lit the surrounding desert. The light breeze carried the distant sound of wolf howls, a warning of an impending attack on the livestock. They watched two rings of perimeter guards pass below them followed by the first ranks of the heavy wagons.

Akiba whispered, "Two nights ago, the herd was in front of the wagons as usual. One of the calves broke from the herd and ran toward the hidden spring over there. Before our front 'cattlemen' could cut him off, a wolf pack sprung from the rocks surrounding the water. They hit the calf head-on. It was over in a couple of seconds… These aurochs are stubborn and sometimes redirect. So a sharp goad is used for the 'cattle attitude adjustment.' The herding company now call themselves 'the Fighting Cattlemen. Which prompted the tanning platoon to change their name to '*Qadosh*' (the ones set apart for a special purpose)." The others chuckled.

Suddenly, the bushes behind them began to rustle. The General, his staff, and Moshe drew their swords and spun their horses around. The scrub brush erupted with too-loud whispering. "I told you not to bring both your swords; besides you're not deadly enough to use two swords!" "I am deadlier than you, but you're not secret, just stupid…" Eventually the usual argument morphed into a swearing fight. Ofek grinned at the cringing General Ari. "They're baaaaaack!"

Hoshe'a reached into his saddle bag and pulled out two loaves of warm sweetbread. He offered one to Moshe, then quietly whispered, "I'm sorry. I should have offered this before the show started." Moshe's brow furrowed, and he whispered back, "How did you know there was going to be entertainment?" Hoshe'a grinned. "It's an unwritten rule when the General is around."

Eventually, Ari reprimanded the newly promoted corporals, and the bloodied boys raced away. The generals turned around to watch the maneuvers. Akiba continued his briefing. "We determined that when we put the wagons in front of the herds, the wagons set the pace and became a forward defensive blocking force. Tonight is the first time we have all the livestock and all wagons traveling in the same direction.

"When the terrain narrows our path forward, the appropriate number of outside wagon columns will halt long enough to fall to the rear and then fall in behind. Which means that the herders will also have to halt the menagerie until *they* can fall in behind the trailing wagons. It'll probably take a few nights to figure it all out. We have our path northeast mapped out and know what the topography looks like. We can train on similar types of terrain. By the time the wagons and livestock pass a certain point, the remaining path should be free of all smaller rocks. And the dried streambed banks will also be leveled out. This should make the road behind a lot wider and easier to walk on."

Yadin spoke up. "That's *my* primary concern, Sir. General Moshe, how many freed, um, captives are we talking about?" Moshe scowled. "That's a wise question, young man. The short answer is I don't know. According to Yahweh, and His math is usually pretty accurate…" Everyone, including the Warrior King, laughed. "…there are currently three million-plus Hebrew men in Egypt. I estimate each of those men have at least three additional family members." Moshe looked at his hands and frowned even deeper. "But Yahweh hasn't told me how many will leave with us."

Akiba leaned forward to see the old general. "Wait, what, Sir? I don't understand. They'll *all* want to leave, right?" Moshe shook his head. "Almost twelve months ago, Aharon and I sailed up the Nile. We visited multiple Hebrew hamlets and caves. We went as far as Abu Sembel, the southernmost city in the old upper Egypt. We talked with hundreds of our enslaved people. From what I've seen and heard, too many Hebrews believe they're doomed to live and die here. Most of the so-called Hebrew heads of clans scoffed when I reminded them of Yahweh's promise of freedom. At a village outside of Helwan, the leaders picked up rocks and threatened to kill us if we didn't leave. In another hamlet, the little kids were provoked by their parent's resentment. As we rode away, they *did* throw rocks at us. One hit Aharon in the side of the head, and he turned to point at the children. He *commanded* Yahweh to rain scorpions on that whole village. He didn't, of course, but that night my brother found a very large scorpion in his bed. I guess Serket (Egyptian goddess over venomous snakes and scorpions) was playing a practical joke." Akiba incredulously shook his head. "Still, Sir, I can't imagine why anyone would want to stay in this Sha'al; that's just stupid." The other teens quickly agreed. But Kalev shook his head and scowled.

"No, General Akiba, it's not stupid; it's just survival. I understand that attitude… If you've only known misery, submission becomes a way of life, a familiar evil. For hundreds of years, our people's only goal was to survive another day. Trust me, hope, especially in an absent Yahweh, never existed in the mud pits. There were too many days I just wanted to die, but I survived on hate-filled stubbornness *alone*." He paused in the silence to chase the shuddering memories away. "For a captive Hebrew in Egypt, optimism is actually painful and to be avoided at all costs. It robs you of the energy to survive. I hated the futile thought of a compassionate Yahweh almost as much as I hated Hotep. And, um, Prince Moshe. Sorry." Moshe smiled and nodded.

Hoshe'a grinned. "Listen to him, boys. Even as a kid, General Kalev hated to talk about Yahweh. Now he talks with and listens to the Warrior King Himself. My little brother's transformation is both miraculous and very rare." Kalev was embarrassed by the genuine compliment. So he did what he'd always done—he ignored it. "So yeah, the familiar captivity and the willful ignorance is much easier to survive without a baseless hope in a promised freedom."

Moshe knowingly nodded. "My own doubts keep me awake at nights. And since we're being honest,

I should admit that I still resent Yahweh for invading my quiet life in Midian. I certainly didn't volunteer for this nightmare. This whole mess has cost me my home and family. And I don't think I'll ever see either again. So I guess *I do* understand their rejection.

"Gentlemen, I still don't fully understand Yahweh's future plans for us. In fact, your troops can attest to the fact that Yahweh and I talk about it a lot. Or rather, He patiently listens while I yell at Him a lot."

Moshe suddenly felt the overwhelming power of Yahweh flow through his being. "You're right, General Kalev. To *really* believe in a rescuing Yahweh, which takes *emunah* (faith). Which is a learned certainty in a truth that transcends, rather than evades, our logic or experience. But *emunah* is an unseen yet tangible hope that is diametrically opposed to a Hebrew's life in Egypt.

"It's much easier for a child to trust the reality of a rescuing Yahweh than it is for a logical adult. But even for the most skeptical adult, true *emunah* is a *very* attainable skill. Much like your recruits train hundreds of hours to eventually become hardened warriors ready for battle. It takes painful practice to make trust in Yahweh a part of you. That's why we always end our prayers with '*emunah.*' It reminds us to stop trying to figure it all out and just believe. Still, He'd rather hear our arguments than our silence." Moshe paused to consider Yahweh's words. "So I guess, in a way, my arguing with the unseen Yahweh is my way of growing my *emunah* in Yahweh. Otherwise, I'm just insane, and none of this is really happening."

For a while, only the soft sound of the greased wagon wheels could be heard. Then Ari spoke up, "General Moshe, Sir, I've been wondering. In this army, we use military standards to maintain strict discipline. We drill into our troops their number one duty as a warrior is to respect and follow their superior's orders. But three million-plus captives set free for the first time in their lives…" Ari let out a low whistle. "I mean, well, it's a fact that Hebrews *live* to argue, and without an established chain of command…Sir, well, that's just mass chaos waiting to happen."

Moshe nodded, then looked at his hands again. "Son, all I can say is that these issues are, thankfully, way above all our pay grades. Still, it's hard for *me* to let go and let Yahweh be Yahweh. So, if this all disintegrates into chaos, well, it's His mess to clean up." Moshe chuckled. "It's a good thing *I'm not* Yahweh. I would have obliterated three-quarters of the Egyptian population and even a few dozen Hebrews by now."

Moshe quickly turned his horse so he could face the General's. He grinned at the two little boys scrambling for cover. Moshe silently locked eyes with each of the teens then Hoshe'a and Kalev. "Yahweh is especially fond and proud of each of you." He let that sink in. "His plan is to use this army as a model for the twelve tribes. But I believe General Ari is correct about the 'living to argue' mentality. I just hope some of them are smart enough to implement your example."

The other generals had started up a couple of spin-off conversations, but Kalev kept his eyes on the old general still facing them. He knew the Warrior King was still talking to His reluctant leader. In time, Moshe opened his eyes and moved his horse closer to Kalev's. He grinned, then pointed up. "Does the Warrior King ever speak to you at odd times?" Kalev grinned, leaned forward, and whispered, "The other day, when I was covering my feet, He started cracking jokes." Moshe nodded. "Been there, done that." Both men shared a laugh.

Moshe looked down the row at Yadin. "General Yadin, the Warrior King just asked me about your current inventory." There was silence for a couple of seconds. Everyone was asking themselves the same question. "Wouldn't an all-knowing Elohim already know the numbers?" Moshe knowingly shook his head. "Hey, I just ask His questions."

True to form, Yadin eagerly reached into one of his six saddle bags, produced a scroll, and handed it to General Moshe. "Sir. This is our current inventory: as of 1100 last night." Moshe glanced at Kalev, who was grinning like a proud abba. In Midian, Moshe had grown accustomed to reading by starlight.

The eighteen-year-old general grinned when Moshe looked impressed. He fidgeted as he watched the brilliant old general slide his finger across every line. Moshe's finger stopped and tapped on a line near the bottom.

"So, according to this, you have almost 4000 sheep? Are you sure?" Yadin scowled. "Yes, Sir, 3987." Moshe nodded. "And how many of these are lambs?" This took about five seconds for Yadin to calculate in his head. "Sir, at present, there are 907 yearlings." Moshe nodded again. "And how many troops total?" Yadin scowled, then guardedly answered. "Sir. As of 1100 hours yesterday, our total troop strength is 5597. That's not including the eighty-one that straggled in yesterday morning. That sum includes the 141 adult troops who've graduated or are currently in training. But so far only nineteen adults have requested accommodations."

Moshe smiled at the savant. "Son, this is an incredible accounting sheet. Every experienced general knows that an army is only as strong as its supply line." Yadin proudly sneered at Ofek. "And this army's logistical support is the best I've ever seen. General Yadin, I'm pretty sure I'm going to need your help. With Generals Kalev and Ari's permission, of course."

Moshe looked appreciatively at the generals. "Even this old general can see that Yahweh has chosen the best of the best for this army's leadership. Oh, and He just told me He's very proud of each of you."

Kalev cleared his throat. "General Ari. You're right about the initial mass chaos. That can and will result in large mistakes. We'll need to flesh out a few contingencies."

After a while, Moshe noticed the dazed look on Hoshe'a's face. The old general leaned over toward Kalev, slyly grinned, then whispered loud enough for the others to hear, "I've noticed he's been a little absent-minded lately." Kalev shook his head. "No more than usual. But I have been wondering if my ema's countless head slaps are finally showing their long-term effects. General Ari, please check him. I can't see from here. Is he drooling again?" The others belly laughed, but Hoshe'a never noticed. Moshe grinned at the others. "Watch this." Jemimah's protective uncle scowled at the deeply distracted Hoshe'a as he spoke to the others. "So I was talking with my niece Jemimah, you know Aharon's daughter? She said she'd been talking to your ema about moving our camp closer too…"

Hoshe'a reacted to Jemimah's name like he'd been slapped. He quickly shook his head and gawked at Moshe. And once again, Hoshe'a's mouth rapidly got ahead of his brain. "I'm sorry, Sir. You were saying something about me marrying your niece Jemimah?" The others bit their tongues as Zayin Battalion's commander dug the verbal hole deeper. "It was a secret. I mean, it is, but I guess it's not now, arghh." Moshe smiled. "You do realize my brother doesn't think anyone is good enough for her. Especially, um, how did he put it? Oh yeah, especially some 'boy-loving man who's playing war with little children all day.'" Kalev growled, "That pompous little [glyphs] coward. No one…" Moshe grinned, then hooked a thumb over his shoulder. "You mean *that* pompous little [glyphs] coward?"

When Aharon rode up, he forced his horse between Ari's and Moshe's. They all strained to ignore the intruder; he wasn't military, and he definitely hadn't earned the right to be here. The dangerously tense silence was ear-piercing.

Thankfully, one of the inner-perimeter troops rode between the last rank of wagons and the base of the hill. Kalev noticed the two very large dead wolves tied behind the troop's saddle.

Akiba pointed at the troop. "In the last three weeks, our perimeter troops have killed hundreds of attacking wolves, leopards, coyotes, and jackals. And, of course, it's become a competition. I think this week's prize for the most wolf pelts is a cushioned saddle." Akiba shrugged. "The animals are lethal; they've started attacking our mounted troops from the rear. Two days ago we had to put down a horse after a leopard leaped onto its back. So we encourage the competition, and it keeps them alert." The teenage general smirked. Ari knew that sneer; it was always a precursor to a practical joke. The problem was he was grinning at Aharon.

"Three troops have tied four weeks in a row." Kalev grinned and asked. "And who are our expert marksmen?" Aharon grumbled something under his breath. But after shooting Moshe a warning glance, Kalev let it go. Half to goad the intruder and half to tease Hoshe'a, Akiba's mischievous grin grew larger. "That would be Little Croc, Little Frog, and um." He paused for effect. Then quickly added, "General Hoshe'a's future wife, Jemimah."

Everyone but the shocked-looking Hoshe'a, the cringing Moshe, and the furious-looking Aharon started screaming with pressure-relieving laughter. While the others howled, Moshe poked his brother's bony shoulder to distract him from saying something he'd regret. "Why are you here!" Aharon foolishly yelled to be heard. "Miriam said *you* told her to move the camp to the rear of that little gossip Carni's house. Why do you want us any closer to that orphanage? You have to know those wannabe soldiers are just asking for the Egyptian Army to invade that whole area. We don't need the headache… No, I'm going to tell Miriam to stay put." The dimwit didn't realize the others had grown deathly silent and had drawn their swords. Moshe growled at him to shut up, but the fool was just getting started. "Moshe, we are Yahweh's true leaders. Why are you spending time with this imitation general and his little orphan children? At best, they'll be irrelevant entertainment for the freed adults and tribal leaders. But it's more likely they'll get us all killed. Yahweh's overall plans don't include these dirty little throwaways. That Midian sun must have fried your brain, you of all people should know what a real army looks like, and this isn't it!" Then Aharon abruptly turned toward the resigned looking Hoshe'a.

Colonel Carni's oldest son knew his brother too well. And he was 90 percent sure his belligerent future abba had just signed his own death warrant. Aharon disdainfully sneered at Hoshe'a, then yelled even louder, "And you, *boy lover*, don't even think…"

Moshe bowed his head and steeled himself for the inevitable. He even started rehearsing in his head what he'd tell Jemimah and Miriam. Then, in a split second, he and Kalev heard the Warrior King's voice. "The lips of a fool beg for a fight; they lay a snare for his life and invite a painfilled end. Yes, the mouth of a fool is his ruin. But don't forget I choose the foolish things of the world to confound the…"

But Kalev ignored the rest of Yahweh's declaration. Finely honed and brilliantly polished swords materialized in the hands of the blooded General. In a glint of starlight, the two swords shot out of the sky meteors. But they stopped two inches from the fool's neck. Moshe, Hoshe'a, and the teen generals recognized the lethal steadiness of the two blades. The unmoving tools of the warrior belied the fact that the General was on the verge of losing it. And everyone *but* the oblivious moron Aharon knew it.

In unrehearsed unison, Moshe and the others automatically moved their horses three steps back. From the base of the hill, these left shadows of the predator and his prey against the star-filled sky. It also gave the seventy gathering archers a clear line of sight from both ends of the hill.

The Commanding General's thunderous roar was heard a half mile away. And this served to alert all troops in earshot. Even as the General roared razor-sharp blades never moved. "Welcome to my *wannabe* world, you [illegible] waste of life!" Kalev's head pounded with a very dangerous fury he hadn't experienced in two weeks. The pompous Aharon didn't hear the softly running feet, the numerous bow strings slowly tightening, or the near-silent swish of hundreds of swords leaving their leather scabbards.

Hoshe'a's eyes darted between Aharon, Moshe, and his violent brother. Hoshe'a had never been ashamed of his brother. But Moshe's humiliation was very obvious. The old general took a deep breath and mouthed to Hoshe'a, "I'm sorry." Hoshe'a half nodded and mouthed back, "Was adopted?"

Then to everyone's astonishment, Moshe's older brother senselessly batted the two very sharp blades aside with his hand. Willfully ignorant of the viper pit he just talked himself into, Aharon leaned over and yelled into Kalev's sweating face.

"How dare you speak to me like that? I am Yahweh's chosen mouthpiece." Then he grew an evil grin. "Plus, I'm sure the pharaoh would be interested in where this whole child menagerie is hiding." A few of the nearby younger troops softly gasped, which caused Kalev to stiffen even taller in the saddle. But the idiot kept going. "I Am Yahweh's chosen spokesman. I'm the leader…!"

In a blur, Kalev had sheathed his swords, leaped, and landed between their two horses. Moshe's belligerent brother was brutally jerked out of his saddle and thrown twelve feet into the air. Even Moshe started to laugh. But before the screaming fool could reach his apex, the Commanding General leaped up, grabbed the back of Aharon's tunic, and violently threw him at the ground. The double-bounce landing forced all remaining air out of the fool's lungs. Instantly, the seething General's heel found the side of his enemy's neck, just below the jawline. He didn't press hard enough to pin Aharon's face to the dirt. Kalev wanted this belligerent piece of [symbols] to see what was coming. The General slowly drew his Khopesh sword, and the other generals' quiet laughter ceased. The son of Hezron slowly let the tip of his Khopesh sword lower and then gently come to rest straight down on the whimpering man's breastbone. He gradually let the weight of the sword continue the job. Had this [symbols] not been Moshe's brother, he'd already been butchered, then disappeared.

In the hazy moonlight, Kalev watched the small black blotch begin to grow around his slowly rotating sword tip. He'd only done this once before. Only that man was a soldier. "Still…maybe a quarter *pound* of flesh will be enough warning," he thought out loud. Right then, the Warrior King cleared His throat. "Um, General? I have plans for him too. And I need him in one piece. So please don't…"

But once again, Kalev refused to listen. He bent close to the whimpering man's ear and yelled, "I don't [symbols] care if you like me, my family, my troops, or even *your* brother. But your simpering insults end now. I swear to you if you mention this army to anyone, we'll know. And before the sun sets that day, you'll be jackal food that night and jackal [symbols] by the following morning." He dug the sword tip a fraction of an inch deeper for emphasis. Then lifted his heel, paused, then roared into the man's other ear. "Hey, you [symbols], did you hear me?" With a mindless fire still burning in his watering eyes, Aharon spit blood onto Kalev's tunic. Although he was barely moving, Kalev's palm shot out smashing Aharon's nose and splitting both lips.

"I'd like to gut you right here, but I can't 'cause Yahweh won't let me and Moshe's my friend. So this is your *only* reprieve. And from what my spies tell me, Ramses and I have one thing in this wretched world in common…we both hate you and would like to see your head on a pole." That was when Kalev realized his other sword had materialized in his hand again.

Unconsciously, Kalev had sliced a shallow groove down to the man's groin. The General lifted his foot. He needed this potential threat to remain conscious. Moshe read Kalev's face, then his brother started to sit up. He groaned to himself, *Stay down, you fool.*

The bleeding man defiantly sat up and pointed a shaking finger at Kalev. "You're the [illegible] idiot if you think the tribal princes will listen to my stuttering brother or you and *your* boy-loving brother. They'll kill you…" The General sent an expertly executed roundhouse kick into the man's chest. It was just hard enough to slam him back down and knock the air out of his lungs again. Kalev bent close to Aharon's ear and yelled, "I'm…not…finished." He waited until the gasping man could breathe again. Then he put his heavy foot down on the bloody chest. "You may *mimic* your brother's words, but he is the one who speaks for the Warrior King. You're only fooling yourself if you think that makes you a true prophet or honorable leader. Because *you*, my sad and hollow little friend, are the supreme example of a self-diluted *wannabe*. Look at you—you're nothing but a self-absorbed browbeater cowering in Moshe's shadow.

"Oh, and another thing, you don't have a clue about Yahweh's plans for this army. [illegible], our youngest recruits are better trained and have more respect, honor, integrity, and self-discipline than you or any other Hebrew slave you know. Tell me, you willfully ignorant [illegible]. Other than your honorable brother or General Hoshe'a, name one adult Hebrew you know that has the skill to fight with a sword, a spear, a knife, throwing stick, dart tube, bow, or even hand to hand. How about you, oh mighty judge of all things military? Surely *you* know how to use a blade. Kalev let him sit up, and he took three steps back.

"Here, show me." In a blur, Kalev drew his long knife and tossed it pommel first at Aharon's forehead. The surprised man clumsily reached to grab the handle but missed and grabbed the razor-sharp serrated blade. This allowed the pommel to hit the man right between his eyes. Moshe's brother yelped.

Kalev shook his head in disgust. He walked over, picked up the knife, then took a knee in front of the still-angry man. Holding his knife tip close to the man's eye, the General reached behind Aharon's head and grabbed a hand full of greasy hair to hold his head in place.

But Aharon started vomiting expletives at Kalev like they were arrows. Surprising everyone, Kalev shoved his four huge fingers into the blathering mouth, using his thumb to squeeze from below. He held the still-fuming man's lower jaw in an iron grip. Moshe's self-important brother squealed like a piglet when the General stood yanking the man to his knees. Kalev glanced at Moshe. "The same mother?" Moshe sheepishly shrugged. "Yahweh thinks so, but I'm not sure anymore." Everyone started coughing to hide their laughter.

With his fist still balled around the kneeling Aharon's chin, 1092 pairs of eyes watched the Supreme Commanding General start pacing back and forth. The sight was a source of campfire lore for decades to come. The General walked and stared at the stars like he'd forgotten about the frantically crawling man beside him. Kalev abruptly stopped, slowly drew his gleaming Khopesh, and silently mouthed something at the sliver of moon.

This time the Warrior King's grinning voice was audible for *everyone* to hear. "*Not today*!" Moshe and Hoshe'a traded wide-eyed glances. They both knew this wasn't the time to laugh. But…

Kalev reluctantly sheathed his sword and threw Aharon's head at the ground like it wasn't attached. He straddled the moaning man and yelled, "We are the army the Warrior King has chosen to fight for and defend His people, and I'm very sorry to say that includes you. We won't expect your thanks. But you *will* show every one of my troops the respect they've earned. And you will *not* speak of this army to anyone until we leave. In fact…" Kalev dropped to his knee, drew his knife, reached into Aharon's mouth, and forcefully pulled his tongue out about three inches. Then he loudly hissed into the whimpering man's ear. "Maybe I should just split your tongue to help you remember." Kalev readjusted his grip to pull it out even further.

Hoshe'a cleared his throat. "Uh, brother, um, I was wondering if, um, you'd let him keep his tongue intact until after he accepts my mohar. Besides, we both know you wouldn't stop with the tongue." This caught Kalev by surprise. He glanced between his pleading brother and the odd-sounding man in his grasp. "Arghh," he yelled at Hoshe'a. "Seriously, you too?" Hoshe'a shrugged. "Then you can cut it out. Normally I'd reason that your killing him would solve both our problems. But I love his daughter, and you know very well how the death of an abba can mess up your wedding week." Kalev slowly nodded and reluctantly let go. "Okay."

The General jerked Aharon off the ground and held him high enough so they were eye to eye. The bleeding coward had to balance on the tip of his toes. Carni's youngest son spoke just loud enough for Hoshe'a to hear. "You don't deserve to have my brother join your family. But for some reason, he's chosen to marry your daughter. [illegible], I hope their children are nothing like you." Now it was Kalev's turn to spit, only his splattered across Aharon's face. "So listen carefully, you [illegible] worm…" The experienced General barely moved his wrist, and Moshe's brother felt the burning sting of Kalev's knife tip pricking his groin. "You *will* accept his mohar, whatever it is, and as soon as it's offered. You will do it politely and thank him afterward. Now, if you understand and agree with what I've said, keep your [illegible] mouth shut and just nod." Tears ran down both sides of Aharon's face. He nodded and whimpered.

Kalev's growl seemed to vibrate the ground, "*My* wife, *my* ema, *my* brother, and this army are my family. And no one disrespects *my* family." Kalev's knife flicked forward a fraction of an inch then into its sheath before the groaning man hit the ground. The General wiped his bloody blade to Aharon's ripped sleeve. "Not today…pity." Then the Supreme Commanding General of Yisrael's Army ripped the awed silence with a maniacal war cry.

As Kalev began to walk away, the filthy bleeding fool actually laughed derisively and spit toward Hoshe'a again. "I'll take his mohar, but we all know he won't be able to consummate the marriage; he's a boy…"

The General backhanded him so hard that it broke both cheekbones. When Aharon's limp head bounced off the ground, his two front teeth went flying. Kalev grabbed the front of the man's split and bloody tunic and hauled Moshe's unconscious brother to his feet. That was when Aharon's very bloody loincloth fell to the ground in two pieces. Kalev held the rag doll of a man at arm's length. He laid the limp body across the horse's back behind his saddle. He tied the dangling hands with one end of a rope, ran the rope under the horse, and tied legs together. He held the excess rope and raised his eyebrows at Moshe. The man of Yahweh knowingly winced, then shrugged.

Kalev cinched the rope too tight and the horse started to buck. The second the hind legs hit the ground, Kalev grabbed the remains of Aharon's tunic, then slapped the horse's hindquarter hard. Everyone watched the empty-saddled horse with the bare-back man buck its way into the desert. Kalev smirked. "He may still end up jackal dung." Ari's hand slightly moved, and a lone rider slowly and reluctantly followed the bucking horse out of sight.

In the subsequent silence, Kalev walked back to Boaz. But before he could mount up, the awed silence was shattered by hundreds of screaming war cries. He unsheathed his sword and held it high as he mounted up.

He let the cheering and chanting continue as he rode back up the hill. Kalev turned Boaz toward the other smiling generals. The other generals formed up beside him. Moshe playfully slapped Kalev's shoulder. He had to yell to be heard.

"Thank you for not killing my idiot brother. I'd hate to make Miriam dig his grave while I engraved his marker." Hoshe'a smirked. "What would you have written?" Moshe shook his head. "One word. '*Stupid*.' In five different languages, of course."

59

For the last three weeks, Kalev and Raisa were on different schedules. To Kalev it felt like they were strangers. They'd sleep all day as usual, but that was all they did: sleep. Then she'd disappear an hour before sunset. She'd said Carni was helping her "Whatever that means," he'd grumble.

One evening before she ran out, Kalev tried to talk to her. "We haven't wrestled in three weeks…and why are your arms and cheek bruised?" But as always, she shrugged and laughed it off. Then she kissed him passionately. "I love you, General Kalev," she said, then ran out of the tent.

So now, as he'd done most of his life, the ex-captive Kalev silently sat atop his dune at sunset and ruminated. This was the only place in Egypt he'd miss. Hoshe'a quietly walked up and sat beside his brother. "Wow, does this bring back memories." He followed Kalev's intense stare down to the slow-moving river. Two unblinking pairs of big green croc eyes stared back from the water's surface. The slow movement of their long tales kept them stationary in the current.

When another set emerged, Hoshe'a smiled and whispered in the quietness, "They're going to miss you…especially that one on the left. He's massive. He *has* to be as old as we are… Hey do you think he's the one I fed you to? You know, when we were kids?" Hoshe'a chuckled, "You screamed like a little girl." Hoshe'a laughed even louder, shattering the remaining peacefulness. Kalev hid his smile at the memory but wasn't in the mood to be teased. He weakly protested. "That wasn't funny; he could have been out there." And, of course, this only fueled more of Hoshe'a's laughter.

Once Kalev's older brother shut up, the peacefulness returned. Carni's youngest son lay back and enjoyed the silent orange clouds above. This dune was the only part of Egypt he'd miss. But as usual Hoshe'a couldn't keep from talking. "You know, they really look hungry!" Then he started his stupid laugh again.

Kalev grew an evil grin, then growled. "Oh, why not?" Still on his back, Kalev slowly bent his knees, drawing back his feet. Hoshe'a was still laughing when Kalev yelled, "Then I guess I should feed them." Both feet shot straight toward Hoshe'a's back. Zayin Battalion's general was launched up and out toward the river. Now it was Kalev's turn to laugh. The two boys appeared at their General's side and watched General Hoshe'a fly. The tumbling pile of arms and legs ended its twenty-five-yard flight with a thud on the hard-packed, slimy mud. Both boys gawked at Kalev when they heard him sigh, "[illegible], I missed the water."

But Hoshe'a's journey hadn't ended yet. The momentum forward caused Carni's oldest to roll down the bank and halfway into the water. Through his laughing tears, Kalev watched the blurry scene below. Now four sets of unblinking croc eyes were picking up speed as they moved toward their dazed and half-submerged meal. The boys were already on their feet, and now there were six shadow troops beside the General. Out of nowhere, a bow and nocked arrow appeared in Little Frog's hands. But Little Croc kept him from letting it fly. They all looked at their general for the order to attack.

Hoshe'a lay with half his face in the mud as he waited for the dizziness to clear his head. He heard his brother's shrieking laughter abruptly stop. That was when Hoshe'a's blood-chilling, water-level view of the four open-mouthed crocs came into focus. They were less than five yards away and quickly converging on his position. Hoshe'a screamed like a little girl. But instead of standing and running back up the dune, he tried to reverse-roll his body back up the riverbank. The two largest crocs raced out of the water with their mouths wide open.

The screaming Hoshe'a never heard the two distinct thumps behind him as he'd finally made it to his feet and raced up the dune. It didn't even register in the big brother's terrified mind that his massive "little" brother had passed him, racing in the opposite direction. Kalev reached the shore at the same time his howling brother dove over the top and out of sight.

The General had instinctively drawn and thrown both swords. Now, both crocodiles lay three feet from the base of the dune. They looked like two prone Egyptian statues honoring their impotent, little-g god Sobek. Kalev guessed the one on the right spanned at least four feet wide and eighteen feet long. He smirked. The one on the left *was* massive. The end of both their tales was still in the water.

The protruding handle of Kalev's long Khopesh sword looked like an odd horn between the wide-set eyes of the left one. He guessed this one to be around twenty-one feet long. He gave the sword a half turn to confirm the unblinking animal was dead. Keeping a wary eye on both beached crocs. Kalev had to stand on the beast's head to free the Khopesh.

By then eleven boys lined the shoreline. They unleashed a barrage of arrows and knives at the two remaining crocs. Amidst the usual loud arguing over who killed which one, both of the smaller motionless crocs were eventually pulled ashore.

Kalev washed off his sword, then cautiously made his way back to the larger croc. He had to admit even dead the very large crocs were still intimidating. Kalev slowly circled the twenty-eight-foot monster twice. He didn't see a single puncture wound. He stopped short, then growled, "[illegible], where is my abba's sword?" The son of Hezron began to frantically search the shore and shallows.

Othniel and a squad of older teen troops suddenly appeared near the head of the largest croc. Kalev's new brother was impressed. "Those were amazing throws, Sir." The others nodded their agreement. Kalev scowled at the biggest croc. "I'm not sure I hit that one. I can't find my sword." While Kalev frantically looked for his abba's sword, Othniel ordered half the squad to start skinning and butchering the larger one. He and the others stood around its nose and looked for any puncture wounds or signs that the sword had penetrated the very dead animal. Othniel bent close to the croc's head and smirked. "Straddle its head and open its jaws." Othniel looked in and started laughing.

The croc's tongue was cleanly split down the middle. The First Sergeant drew his own sword and rammed it down the croc's foot-wide throat. They all heard the distinct clink of metal hitting metal. Othniel smiled and then raised his voice. "Uh, General, I found your sword."

It took four hours to skin and butcher the four crocs. The 510 pounds of usable croc meat would be served at the morning meal. They'd use the bones for various weapons and utensils. The rest went into the river, which attracted fish and more crocs.

The skins would be tanned and used for various coverings other things. But the largest skin, from chin to tail, would become the entire brigade's thirty-foot-high guidon banner mounted to the General's wagon. Large letters would be expertly bleached into the skin's smooth side.

Kalev
Son of Hezron
True to Yahweh
Prince of Yehudah
Supreme Commanding General of Yisrael's Army

Kalev watched the shore light up with tall torches as the skinning of the two crocs began. The General asked Othniel to take the smaller croc's largest tooth to Dan. "Once he finishes his advanced training evolutions tonight, ask if he can make it into a necklace for General Hoshe'a. Please have him engrave the words, 'Too tough to eat.'"

Ari joined Kalev on the top of his dune. They both silently watched the torch-lit butchering process on the beach and the ongoing teasing arguments. "Sir, um, about that *Mattan*? I wanted to have the wedding feast before we left, and General Moshe asked to address the army next week. He said the final plague will happen soon."

Kalev grinned. "I suppose Colonel Carni has every detail of your wedding already planned out." "Yes, Sir. She's been fixing up the Outpost for the last two weeks. We'll spend our wedding week in a tent in the Outpost's TOC." Kalev nodded. "I'm sure it will all be very extravagant." Ari grumbled something under his breath. Kalev laughed. "I felt the same way. But remember none of it is about you. Deborah is your main focus. Learn everything about her and make her happy.

"By the way, how is Colonel Carni's assault riding training going? Any deaths?" They both chuckled. "No, Sir. According to Master Sergeant Abraham, your little ema is one of the best assault riders in the army." Ari smirked. "And your little Raisa is..." He abruptly shut his mouth and cringed. The teenage bet-grade general mentally berated himself for almost divulging the secret. Kalev scowled at his second-in-command. “What about my wife, General?” Ari was very good at telling the truth carefully. He shrugged. “I guess she is helping Colonel Carni with decorating the Outpost. They actually climbed the trees. I’m told Raisa fell more than once and got a few bruises. She’s quickly learned how to land and roll.” Kalev nodded. “That explains the bruises. I guess that’s what she meant by helping my ema and training or something.” Ari shrugged, grateful for the offered save.

After a while, Kalev noticed Ari’s scowl but didn’t ask. “Sir, um, about the wedding night?” Kalev knew how the kid felt. “Son, you can relax. It’s nothing like killing Egyptians… Hey, I’m hungry.” Ari watched the General leap to his feet and walk away. The teen growled to himself, “What the [illegible] did that mean!”

60

The next morning, Kalev and his generals ate in the Fortress' dining area. They were almost finished when the Commanding General mounted the officer's table and waited for complete silence. When he had the attention of almost three thousand troops, Kalev quickly bent down, grabbed Hoshe'a's arm, and lifted him onto the table next to him. Ari handed the General the three-inch-wide, ten-inch-long gold-tipped croc tooth necklace. "Army of Yisrael, I'd like to personally award the Commanding General of the Zayin Battalion with this army's first-ever 'Golden Croc Hunter Award.' His expert and unique hunting skills were priceless in securing this morning's fine meal of fresh croc meat." Kalev forced a straight face as he tied the award around the scowling Hoshe'a's neck. Just before he lost it, Kalev scooped up his mug and held it high. "To general Hoshe'a, 'too tough to eat'!" Amidst the cheers and chants of, "Too tough to eat, too tough to eat, General Hoshe'a's too tough to eat, tougher than croc meat…" Hoshe'a swore at Kalev and made a hasty exit.

The General watched his older, grumbling brother walk toward the ramp. Hoshe'a checked the tooth twice but never took off his "award." The General dismissed the troops and sat back down.

Ofek, Yadin, and Akiba stood to excuse themselves when they all heard the familiar loud whispering come from under the next table. All three generals smiled to each other, then quickly sat, and grabbed another loaf of sweet bread. The General's table was silent as the inevitable comic show began. Hearing that the troops were dismissed, Little Croc didn't try to whisper to Little Frog.

"…No I have the best idea let's tie a rope around your waist and you can swim into that deep part of the river then when the biggest croc starts to eat you I'll pull you back and we can kill him and I can get a Golden Croc Killer award but you can get a regular croc food award." An unusual silence followed. The generals started coughing into their sleeves or choking on their beer. They knew the silence meant Little Frog was actually considering the proposition. It took another thirty seconds for Frog to speak. "I have a bester plan your name is Little Croc 'cause you killed that big croc and you can talk to crocs 'cause I seen you talk to crocs and they listen to you and I want to talk to crocs but I can't like you can so we'll tie the rope around your waist and you can swim out to the deep part and tie the rope around the bigger crocs nose then tell him he's your camel now and you can lead him back to shore and I can surprise him like Master Sergeant Abraham said to make a M bush then I can stab the croc dead 'cause I'm a better stabber than you." "No *I'm* the best stabber so stick out you hand and I'll stab it and show you I'm the bestess one." "No I am…ow stop it!" As the fight continued, Ofek and Akiba stood, saluted, and left the table.

Kalev glanced at the distracted Ari, then mouthed to Yadin, "Now." Yadin let out three ear-piercing staccato whistles. Which momentarily silenced the remaining troops. The First Sergeant from Zayin started driving an overly decorated two-oxen wagon down the ramp.

Facing the other way, Ari continued to eat. He watched Akiba talking to Colonels Zilpah and Deborah in the kitchen. Kalev slid closer to his adjutant. Ari subtly nodded toward Akiba. "When he was in his 'isolation,' he and Zilpah spent *a lot* of time together.

"While you were eliminating the Egyptian Army, we had another skills competition." Kalev growled at the memory but let it go. "Colonel Zilpah placed second in spear, knife, and sword throwing. And third in archery and blow darts…"

Ari wisely stopped himself before he mentioned that Raisa had placed first in all five events. He also failed to mention that halfway through her advanced weapons training, Akiba chose her to attend the second Kidon training class.

Kalev nodded his approval. "I take it she's redeemed herself for sleeping on duty?" Ari nodded. "After the massacre, she and the other two colonels were demoted and ordered to twenty-four seven boulder watch for two weeks. They wisely alternated eating and sleeping. I checked myself a couple of times."

Kalev nodded. "By the way, how's Yoshi'yah's training going?" Yadin glanced at Ari, then wordlessly went back to eating. Ari's face went blank before he carefully changed the subject and lowered his voice. "Sir, before I forget. The second class of Kidon troops graduates in five days. We'd like you to be there to award their medallions." Kalev nodded. "It will be an honor."

Ari continued watching Akiba's awkward interactions. He playfully teased Kalev. "Sir, it won't be long before giving the wedding blessing becomes your full-time job." Kalev grew a sly grin. "Well, no. My main spiritual responsibility is for my general staff. But as of today, you, *Rabbi* Ari, are responsible for the rest of the army."

Ari's laugh caught in his throat when he saw his General was serious. "Sir. I am *not* a rabbi." Kalev smirked. "Neither am I. But these are desperate times, and someone's gotta do it. I mean, look around, son. Do you see any other rabbi in our area of operation?" They both turned when the flowered wagon pulled up.

The identical thought struck them both at the same time, and they knowingly laughed. Kalev shook his head. "Yeah, she'd be perfect for the job. But no woman, including my ema, can be a rabbi." Then Kalev felt a surge of the Warrior King's forceful unction rise into his throat. "So let's make this official…"

Kalev stood and snapped his fingers over his head. The loud crack silenced the entire busy Fortress. And for some reason, every animal raised its head and also silently stared at the General. Even the oxen pulling the *Mattan* wagon raised their heads.

The General dipped a finger in the beer, took two steps back, and pointed at the deck in front of him. The embarrassed and skeptical-looking teen general followed the unspoken order. The other two flanked their General. Kalev placed one hand on Ari's shoulder and dipped his other in the mug Yadin was holding. Ari looked up and quietly pleaded. "Sir, please, I don't have the time to…" But Kalev's loud declaration drowned him out. "Attention to orders." Over 2000 troops jumped to attention.

"General Ari. By order of the Warrior King, this Supreme Commanding General of Yisrael's Army declares…" Kalev tapped the defeated-looking teen's forehead with his wet fingertip seven times. "You are now the Army of Yisrael's chief rabbi!" Then Yahweh clearly told him to place both hands on Ari's head. Something like fire shot from the ceiling. It surged through Kalev's hands and into the very surprised Ari. Kalev looked just as stunned as the teen.

The troops' cheers were silenced when the Warrior King's audible voice shook the ground. "I Am Yahweh! King of kings and pharaohs. And I approve this honor. Let it be written; let it be done." Yahweh paused to let the echo run its course. Then the Warrior King boomed with a smiling voice. "Army of Yisrael, as you were!" No one spoke, but all eyes stared at their dazed-looking General for further orders. Kalev distractedly nodded to Akiba, who yelled. "You heard the Warrior King. As you were."

The other teens gawked at their astonished-looking friend. But the stunned General Kalev was staring at his hands; they still burned. In his head, Kalev heard the Warrior King's smiling reply to his unasked question. "Yeah, be careful with those; they're loaded. And *yes*, that's how it's done. But next time please use olive oil; it's kind of a prophecy thing."

Kalev nodded in obedience. "Yes, Sir." They all looked at their General quizzically. Kalev didn't explain. "General Yadin, General Ari is now the Army's rabbi. Make sure his medallion is updated. And would you please give him a copy of Rabbi Nachshon's book?" Yadin and Ofek grinned at their confused-looking friend. "Right away, General, Sir."

As the garishly decorated wagon was expertly backed up near the General's table, Akiba signaled Deborah to move Zilpah out of sight. Kalev quietly spoke to his second in command, "Since her abba is gone, this is your *Mattan*." Ari looked at the wagon, swallowed hard, and whispered, "Sir. This marriage thing just got very real!" Kalev put his still-tingling hand on Ari's shoulder. Yadin quickly scrambled into the wagon and quietly read out loud the inventory list.

Two young oxen and tack

One large, covered wagon with attached guiden banner and very padded seat

One large chest of gold and silver coins plus ingots

One four-room shiny tent

Five interior hanging oil lamps

Two large Persian rugs

One combined wolf and leopard pelt rug

Two urns of Babylonian myrrh

Two sealed twenty-gallon urns of "special" wine

One gold scimitar, two daggers, one gold-tipped long bow, two quivers of arrows, a blow dart reed, and a belt of poison darts

Kalev was surprised by the last line and smirked. "A *Mattan* fit for an army general's wife." Ari groaned. "I wasn't expecting so much…" Kalev smiled. "This *Mattan* is perfect for a journey, then living in while you build your own home."

Kalev paused. "Okay. General Yadin please get with Colonel Carni about setting up the tent in the Outpost's TOC. Then place all this in the tent's smaller rooms." Yadin smirked. "There's already a, um, sort of tent set up in that TOC, Sir." Kalev nodded, then turned to his teering second-in-command.

"Sir. Deborah grew up abused with little more than food and one set of clothes. She was little more than a bruised and barefooted empty shell when she got here. She deserves this." Ari wiped his eyes. "Thank you, Sir." Kalev squeezed the teen's rock-hard shoulder and nodded. "She's very fortunate to have Major Adir's son for a husband."

Surprised and frustrated Raisa wasn't here, Kalev looked around the Fortress. He turned and asked the others, "Have any of you seen my wife?" In unison, the three aleph-grade generals replied, "No, Sir," then saluted and quickly walked away. Kalev turned back toward the receding *Mattan* wagon, but *Rabbi* Ari had vanished.

Hoshe'a suddenly appeared at his confused-looking brother's side. "Thanks for the ridiculous tooth. Oh, and nice inscription. I'll never forget flying and my *bravery* in the face of certain croc food. I can't believe you made this. It's really embarrassing!" Kalev grinned. "And yet you're still wearing it." Hoshe'a looked down. "It's a gift from my little brother. I *have* to wear it at least for a while. Besides, Jemimah was pretty impressed." Kalev laughed. "Brother, I ordered those troops that were present for your, um, encounter to keep it a secret." Kalev tried to gently punch is older brother in the arm. But Hoshe'a still stumbled back a couple of steps anyway. "Stop it, you big ox." Kalev laughed. "Too tough to eat? I think not." They both laughed.

Hoshe'a scowled then pointed at the heavy wagon halfway to the ramp. "Kalev, listen, I do not want any of the army's foraged money for my mohar. But do you remember what Aharon said about me being poor? You know, just before you permanently ruined his face?" Kalev scowled, "I remember it all, [illegible]." Hoshe'a winced. "Kalev, he's a small man with a very weak character. But he's my Jemimah's abba and will soon be mine." Kalev nodded. "Okay, okay. Like I won't cut his tongue out. Yet." Hoshe'a scowled. "Yeah, about that. If he insults my family, this army, and his brother again, I'll beat you to it." Kalev's eyebrows went up. He never pictured Hoshe'a as dangerous.

"Little brother, I appreciate your protectiveness. I truly do. But I *will* handle Aharon." Kalev heard the unusual strength in his brother's voice and smiled approvingly. "You're right, Hoshe'a. But it's hard for me to remember my brother's all grown up now." Hoshe'a smirked disgustedly. "Yeah, tell that to Ema." Kalev chuckled. "I will. And, Hoshe'a, I do trust you, but don't turn your back to that dishonorable [illegible]… He may stick a real knife in it."

Since his days with the pharaoh's chief architect, Hoshe'a had worn a loose robe down to his feet, and he looked completely unarmed. Suddenly, his hands caused the folds on each side to split. Hoshe'a whipped two swords down and out, then expertly spun them in opposite directions. Kalev smiled proudly. "Wow, my brother *is* a big boy now!" In another blur, Hoshe'a reversed the movement and sheathed the swords in his inverted back scabbard. "I will handle Aharon…"

They both headed toward the ramp. Hoshe'a noticed his brother's face lose all expression. "When I was *meeting* with a certain company of Egyptian chariot soldiers, one of them, um, told me a story. His company had pillaged their way south from the Northern Syrian border. He confessed they'd looted every port and fishing village along the 400-plus mile coastal trade route. But these pigs limited themselves to acquiring daily food and silver coins or ingots. The last one I, um, *met* with *insisted* I take the five large trunks of silver for your mohar. I guess he thought it was the right thing to do. Before he, um, died." Kalev shook his head to erase the memory. "I buried the crates in my stall. At the time I was too focused on other things to have to worry about the silver." "Meet me there after sundown; oh, and bring that donkey and cart. It should hold two of the trunks. You can use the others for your *Mattan*. We'll head for that [illegible] camp in the morning."

61

The Fortress was packed with all the troops not on duty. Plus all their previously vetted and cautioned families close enough to walk. The majority belonged to the Yehudah tribe. Seven vetted and warned tribal leaders and their rabbis, from the other closest tribes, were given a "place of honor" to the side of the front ranks.

Yadin would report at the next general's command and staff that there were exactly 777 civilian men, plus 1009 wives, savtas, emas, and children in attendance.

The fully armed general staff, Moshe, and the colonels from Zayin Battalion stood on the elevated platform and watched as a beaming Ari led his bride's armed and decorated horse down the Fortress' ramp. They were followed by the majority of Heh and the rest of Zayin Battalions.

Their entire long, indirect route from the sand bowl was lined shoulder to shoulder with troops from Heh and Zayin Battalions. The warriors had proudly stood at attention with their swords drawn in salute. As the marriage entourage passed by, the troops peeled off and marched behind their general and colonel. Seventy-five girls from Zayin led the way with their ceremonial lamps.

Kalev glanced down at *his* lovely bride. They'd spent the last two days just sleeping, eating, and wrestling. But mostly wrestling. Raisa's face glowed in the Fortress's additional torchlight. Even with the fading bruise under eye and the mysterious new red scar on her chin, she still took his breath away. Raisa, sensing her husband's gaze, looked up and grinned. She loved that lopsided smile. The General's gorgeous wife grew a sly smile and mouthed the word, "Later." Then she motioned for him to pay attention to Ari and Deborah. Kalev reluctantly looked away.

As the ramp boomed shut, more than 6000 troops were called to attention with swords presented. Ari and Deborah knelt before the General. Kalev had memorized the marriage blessing. Now, he closed his eyes and nervously raised his hands. As promised, the Warrior King was there to help him remember.

"... Hear, O Yisrael, Yahweh, your Elohim—the Yahweh is one. Praise be His name forever. Your kingdom will reign forever. We know Your Kingdom *will* reign forever.

"Blessed are You, Yahweh, our Elohim, Ruler of the universe, who creates the fruit of the vine. Blessed are You, Yahweh, our Elohim, Ruler of the universe, who created everything for His glory. Blessed are You, Yahweh, our Elohim, Ruler of the universe, who created humanity. May the barren one, the land You promised to our abba Abraham, rejoice greatly and delight in the ingathering of her children within her with great joy. Blessed are You, Yeshua, who causes us, *Your* chosen people, to rejoice in our promised inheritance. Blessed are You, Yahweh, our Elohim, Ruler of the universe, who created humanity in His image, in the image of the likeness of His form, and made for them an everlasting establishment. Blessed are you, Yahweh, our Elohim, Ruler of the universe, who created joy and gladness, groom and bride, mirth, song, delight and rejoicing, love, harmony, peace, and companionship. Soon, Yahweh, our Elohim, may there ever be heard throughout the tribe of Yehudah and from all the sons of Abraham voices of joy and gladness, voices of groom and bride, the jubilant voices of those joined in this 'taking of a wife,' the voices of young people feasting and singing. Blessed are You, I Am that I Am, our Yahweh, our Yeshua, who causes the groom to rejoice with his bride. Um, *emunah*!"

As the newlyweds stood, the Fortress erupted with ear-piercing war cries and loud animal noises. Kalev smiled at Ari and mouthed the words, "I'm proud of you, son. And have fun!" Ari smiled quizzically as his tears dripped onto *his* translucent tunic. Then the General turned to Deborah and yelled to be heard, "Colonel, I expect you to take care of this army's most important general and only rabbi."

Ari's eyes went wide, Deborah gasped, and Kalev grimaced. Apparently Ari had failed to mention to his new wife about his added responsibility and additional title. Surprising both men, Deborah cupped both of Ari's cheeks, yelled something to him, and jerked him forcefully forward. The surprised groom stumbled into a very passionate kiss.

Akiba's grin turned to a scowl as he purposefully walked to the front of the stage and called the chaotic throng to attention. Even the animals shut up. Then he yelled, "Salute!" In the ensuing silence, the ramp began to lower. But the couple didn't wait for it to reach the deck. In unison, they'd vaulted into their saddles and raced toward the ramp. Their horses jumped the still-descending four-foot gap. They were gone by the time the ramp boomed onto the deck. It immediately began to rise again. As soon as the ramp hissed closed, Akiba ordered the wedding feast to begin.

Kalev and Hoshe'a stood on the deck behind the stage. "So we're really doing this tomorrow morning?" Hoshe'a nervously nodded. "Okay. I'll follow at a distance. Raisa and Ema readied a two-ox wagon, a tent, bed, and bedding specifically for Moshe's sister Miriam. Raisa practically ordered me to deliver it at the same time, but I'm to stay out of the way or else!"

Hoshe'a laughed. "Oh, by the way, little brother, Jemimah wanted me to convey her thanks for not killing her abba the other night." Kalev was surprised. "You told her?" Hoshe'a shrugged. "We talk about everything. It just came up." Kalev playfully slugged his brother in the shoulder, knocking him back a step. "Hoshe'a, when it comes to women, and especially a wife, you need to practice a little thing called discretion. Trust me, knowing what *not* to say is just as important as talking about everything. I'm *still* learning that one."

Hoshe'a smirked, patted Kalev on the head, and spoke a little too loudly. "Oh, little one, that's the difference between you and me. With my superior intellect, I've already figured her out. I know exactly what to say, what she *needs* to hear, and what she'll say next. She's an open book to me…" Hoshe'a stopped cold when he saw Kalev glance past his shoulder and then grow a large grin. Hoshe'a cringed and whispered. "[illegible], Ema's standing right behind me, isn't she?" Kalev nodded, then started laughing.

Without turning to look, Hoshe'a started to hurry in the other direction but froze when he heard *two* women clear their throats simultaneously. Hoshe'a's shoulders visibly tensed, then slumped in resignation. He slowly turned to see his ema *and* his lovely future wife. Both had their hands on their hips and were giving him "*the look*." Kalev stopped laughing long enough to try to duck close behind his intimidated brother. He whispered, "Oh, wise big brother, if you want to see another day, repeat after me, 'Jemimah, my love'"—Hoshe'a haltingly repeated Kalev's words—"'I'm sorry. I was very wrong; I still have a lot to learn. Please, forgive me.'" Miraculously, this seemed to have the desired effect. Jemimah smiled and walked over to Hoshe'a; she cupped his face in her hands. "I forgive you, my love. And don't you worry, we have the rest of our lives for me to teach you." Hoshe'a swallowed hard. "I've just been outranked again, and this time it's for keeps," he mused. Hoshe'a forced himself to ignore his ema's still-fuming stare. He grabbed Jemimah's hand and led her up the ramp.

Kalev was still laughing when Carni walked up and futilely slugged him in his rock-hard chest. This caused a bolt of pain to shoot up her injured arm and she winced. Kalev examined her bruised knuckles and forearms. "Ema, have you been in a fight with my wife?" Carni expertly deflected the question. "No, well, sort of, we were sparring. But, Kalev, your brother doesn't need your help to get him out of the holes his mouth digs for him. Both of you still have a lot to learn." Kalev pulled his ema into a crushing hug. Carni stiffened as numerous parts of her body ignited with fresh pain. The General's experienced mind instantly registered the too-familiar groan and its cause. "Ema your advanced training was over five weeks ago. Why are you still in pain?" Carni gave him her practiced response. "I'm older than you, son. It takes my bones longer to heal. And I've been showing Raisa a few of the throws and moves I learned."

Carni noticed the two ever-watchful boys trying to hide under the stage. "That said, little one, I am so proud of you. You are a tender-hearted husband and an amazing abba. Kalev, your ema and abba would've been so proud to see all you've accomplished." She reached up and pulled his head down to kiss his cheek.

He smiled and hugged her gently. "Thank you, Ema." Then Kalev's grin grew into a look of practiced concern. "Ema, I think you should know something, but please keep it between us. Hoshe'a and I have been talking. No matter what my big brother says to you, Ema, he still wants your constant guidance, even after he's married. He said he'd be lost without it. Especially during his marriage week."

Carni scowled and shook her head. "Arghh, even with Jemimah's help, your brother is a full-time job." Kalev smirked. "I know he loves you and appreciates all your input." Carni smiled. "Of course he does. I'll always be his ema."

Colonel Carni glanced at the boys again, then nodded toward the stage. "Son, a good abba spends time with his children. He's both a teacher and an example. Those two need you. Especially after Little Yoshi's death." Kalev turned to see the two "not-so-silent" boys loudly scrambling further back under the stage.

Carni smiled. "Oh, and I wanted you to know, I ordered the Outpost's perimeter spider holes to be pushed out an additional fifteen yards. All of the Outpost's high overwatch positions were vacated. In their place, I have rotating archer squads from Zayin on my roof. The southern perimeter is actually on the opposite side of the river." Kalev smiled. "Excellent marriage week, defensive tactics major." Carni kissed his cheek again, smiled, took one step back, crisply saluted her son, then headed for the nearest ladder. The General watched in surprise as his fifty-three-year-old ema raced up the ladder like a much younger troop. "Pretty good for old bones."

Kalev snapped his fingers and pointed at the deck in front of him. The boys slowly crawled out and guiltily stood at attention in front of their general. Kalev put a reassuring hand on each boy's shoulder. "Thank you for doing such a great job at being my silent and deadly protectors. I feel very safe, and I'm proud of you both." Both boys' jaws dropped as their eyes welled up with tears. "Now, you two deserve a good meal. Go wash up, then have fun tonight. Mrs. General and I'll be here for a while." "Plus she can protect you more better now," declared Little Frog. Little Croc kicked his friend in the shin. "No, she can't, remember?" Little Frog's eyes went wide, and his hand flew to his mouth. Before Kalev could ask, both boys quickly saluted, then ran.

Right then, Akiba, Yadin, and two young troops walked up carrying a tall, padded chair, a tall side table, food, and wine. They saluted, then Akiba explained, "Sir, General Moshe said the prince of Judah needs to be fed and readied to hear his people. And, um," the commander of the lethal Heh Battalion grimaced, then spoke rapidly, "Sir, *he* said you're a tribal prince now, so just suck it up and do your job. Oh, and he said, 'Welcome to *my* world!'" Akiba motioned for the General to turn around.

Kalev groaned when he saw the growing line of people at the rear corner of the stage. And they were all looking his way. He scowled as he looked around. Yadin spoke up, "Sir, he gave us the instructions before he left." Kalev's eyebrows shot up. "Left! Where did he go?" "We don't know, Sir. He said he and Yahweh had some things to talk about. He left the instructions to set you up for receiving your people, then ordered his shadow troops to stand down and wait for him at his camp." Kalev didn't have time to ask before Akiba answered, "Yes, Sir. He *and* his horse were impressively kitted-up." Kalev glanced at the growing line of people and groaned. Not for the last time.

Kalev looked at the throne, dismissed the other troops, and whispered to his two generals, "First of all, bring me my undecorated chair from the TOC. Secondly, I was wondering if either of you would like to be promoted to prince of Judah." Both smiling generals' eyes went wide, and their jaws dropped in unison. Kalev heard the Warrior King loudly clear His throat and boom, "I don't think that's how it works, General." Instantly, Akiba repeated, "I don't think that's how it works, General." Kalev sighed. "Okay, but please bring that other chair now. I'm not some pharaoh holding court." The General felt exhausted already. While he waited for the other chair, he downed the pitcher of new wine and ate the whole loaf of sweetbread.

Soon the Commanding General of Yisrael's Army took a deep breath and signaled for the first person in line. The first was Ari's aunt. "I had no idea. I mean, this place, this army of boys, you are a hero to us all…" Kalev held up his hand and interrupted. "Mam, this all came from the mind and heart of your nephew. Without General Ari, most, if not all, of these young troops would be dead, banished to the mud pits, or worse." They talked a little more, then she thanked him and left.

As the second person was allowed to approach the General, Kalev noticed Prince Nethaneel and a circle of officers gathered at the head of the line.

Later, as the grumbling man walked away, Kalev grabbed the third pitcher of wine that had materialized during his last conversation. He looked at his feet and hissed under his breath. "This was your idea, not mine. So respectfully, Sir, I expect more help!" Kalev heard the Warrior King chuckle.

"Son, leading these people is very much like being a good abba to a couple of strong-willed boys and a fireball of a daughter named Aksa." The specific reference to a daughter was lost on the still-brooding general. "Kalev, sometimes they'll need an unyielding hand to bring swift, um, guidance." Yahweh laughed. "And sometimes they'll really need your help but are too stubborn to ask. Sound familiar? Then, there will be those times when they cry out for help and your heart will melt. Those are the ones you'll fight for.

"Yeah, when it comes to your own, their contented laughter will warm your heart, and their tears will break it. Still, you wouldn't trade any of it because they're yours. You'd die to save them from destruction. That's who My chosen people are and will always be to Me. My heart beats for them.

"Always remember, General, you've willingly agreed to be marked as true to your Warrior King, your Yeshua. And the I AM will always be true to you. I AM permanently by your side to help and guide you. It's not easy to lead, but you were created and equipped for such a time as this." The Warrior King started to laugh. "So suck it up, General, and get to work."

For the next long hour, the new prince of Judah listened to his people. He was surprised at how exhausting it was. Near the end of the hour, he noticed Othniel refusing to let other people line up and was grateful.

Before he joined Raisa for the feast that had predictably evolved into another war game competition, Kalev turned down the hall toward the Fortress' TOC. He wanted to briefly study the large map table. Lately, he'd become curious and concerned over their possible routes out of Egypt. He'd just opened the TOC door when he heard a familiar squeal reverberating down the hall. He barely turned in time to see a slightly tipsy Raisa flying through the air in his direction. She thumped against his chest and wrapped her arms around his neck. Her forward momentum caused the big man to stumble back through the TOC's double doors. Kalev held his laughing little wife close as they tumbled into the TOC. She sat on his chest and peeled off her tunic while he viciously kicked the door shut.

For forty-five minutes, the boys sat on the deck with their backs to the TOC door. "We're missing the party," complained Little Frog. "How long can they wrestle in there before they need a drink of water?" "The General doesn't need a drink; besides you don't know how to wrestle like me very good." "I don't need no water when *I* wrestle," boasted Little Croc. "My camel can wrestle better than you," chided Little Frog. "But I'm hungry. I want some more beer, beef, onions, and sweetbread." Croc nodded. "One of us should go. Then when I get back, you can go and get you a plate and bring me some more sweetbread and beer. That way if they need water, me or you can go get it."

62

Kalev drove the huge six-wheeled covered wagon and stopped about fifteen yards from Moshe's camp. Hoshe'a had driven the purposely rickety, high-sided, single-donkey wagon to the front of Aharon's tent. The donkey cart had a goat tethered to the back. When Miriam opened her tent flap, Kalev caught a glimpse of Carni scrambling to stay out of sight. He growled under his breath. He'd specifically instructed her to stay away from Hoshe'a's presentation of the mohar. It was important that his older brother present himself in public as the decision-maker instead of looking like his overbearing ema's puppet.

Kalev jumped down from the wagon and waved Miriam over. He quietly spoke to her as they watched and waited for the mohar transaction to begin. "My wife, Raisa, told me you didn't have a wagon. The oxen, this wagon, and everything in it is yours. But *only* yours." Aharon hadn't emerged yet, so Kalev led her around the back and unfolded the built-in sturdy steps. Miriam stood there and gasped. She gasped a couple more times as she inspected the contents. She opened a trunk and carefully pulled out a large gold mirror. Moshe's eighty-three-year-old sister looked up at Kalev and shook her head as tears flowed down her cheeks. "I can't accept these beautiful things. I'm just a poor slave. I don't deserve any of this. I..." Kalev interrupted her. "Pardon me, Miss Miriam, but from what I've seen, you deserve a hundred times this for putting up with those two brothers of yours." She laughed. "Besides, have you met my sweet little lioness of a wife? I'm not about to take this back and face her wrath." She smiled uncomfortably. "I've never had a real bed before. And these clothes and combs and this mirror. I... um"—she swallowed hard—"thank you, General." Kalev lowered his voice. "Up front, under the seat, I secured three scabbards. They carry a couple of large knives and a Khopesh sword. Just in case you've had enough of your brother Aharon. And don't worry, I'd be glad to help hide the body." Her chuckle caught in her throat when she saw Kalev's too-serious expression. She tried to shrug it off. "My brother's an acquired taste. Kind of like old vinegar." Kalev nodded. "Well, the knives are sharpened and ready when you are." He helped her down. "When we leave, I'll assign one of my troops to drive the wagon. The rest of your protection detail will help set up and take down your tent." Her eyebrows went up. "I have a detail?" Kalev finally smiled. "Yes, mam. You've had a personal three-shift overwatch for the last four months." She blushed at a memory. "They've been watching for four months?" Kalev nodded and chuckled. "Sooo...they saw me dump the water on my drunk brother Aharon?" Kalev laughed. "Yes, mam. Personally, I would have done the same thing. Of course, I would have let it come to a boil first." Neither one of them laughed. "General, I wanted to apologize for Aharon's disrespectful words and attitude toward you and your soldiers. Moshe told me about the other night. We've both warned him to keep his short-sighted opinions to himself." She grew a sly grin. "So thank you for leaving *me* the option to feed the jackals." They both laughed.

As if on cue, Aharon walked out of his tent and froze. He wordlessly gaped at the nervous Hoshe'a standing beside the cart. The very tense silence was broken by the bleating goat tied to the back.

Aharon's swollen and dark face looked like it would pop. At any other time, his odd-sounding screams would have been hilarious. "This is what you think my daughter is worth? A broken-down cart, a sad old donkey, and a goat?" Kalev knew his brother too well. The General looked at his feet and quietly mumbled, "Please don't say something stupid. Please don't say something stupid. Please don't say something stupid." But, as usual, Hoshe'a stood tall, smiled, and cleared his throat. "Actually, Sir, this *incredibly happy* donkey is only a year old and has never been worked or ridden. And this happy goat is only a year old. I don't know how to milk it, but I'm sure my ema would be glad to teach you…" Kalev groaned. At that moment, a board fell off the side of the cart. Kalev heard Yahweh deadpan, "Oops, too soon?" Miriam covered her mouth, bolted for the other side of her wagon, and exploded with muffled squeals of laughter.

Aharon burst out into a long list of a jumbled mix of almost intelligible obscenities. He cursed Hoshe'a, the donkey, and the goat. But he saved his best expletives for Kalev, his troops, and Carni. That was when Jemimah, Raisa, and Carni popped their heads out of Miriam's tent. Carni instantly saw Kalev scowling in her direction, so she quickly pulled the other two back inside.

When he heard the same insults, Kalev's swords appeared in his hand, but he forced himself to remain still. So far, the loud-mouthed fool hadn't seen him. *Hoshe'a needs to manage this*, he reminded himself. Miriam appeared at Kalev's side. She glanced between the swords, Kalev, and her foolish brother. And to Kalev's big brother's credit, Hoshe'a's silent smile never wavered as he patiently let the man finish his spitting tirade.

In the subsequent silence, Carni's oldest son wordlessly turned and purposely marched to the back of the cart. He flipped open the lid to the larger of the two trunks, pointed, and angrily yelled at the man. "This is a fraction of what I know your daughter is worth."

As the still-cursing Aharon walked toward the rear of the cart, Kalev's jaw dropped. Hoshe'a subtly drew a long knife from a slit in the side of his robe. The General cringed when he heard the quiet sound of bow strings tightening in the nine spider holes surrounding the camp. He silently signaled for his troops to hold.

When Aharon rounded the back of the cart, Hoshe'a viciously grabbed the back of the man's head and shoved his broken face into the chest filled of silver coins and one silver brick. Kalev saw his brother put the knife behind the man's ear and then whisper into it.

Hoshe'a would tell Kalev later that he'd growled into Aharon's ear, "You sorry excuse of a man. If I ever hear of you disrespecting that fine donkey, the goat, my family, or the army again, I'll slice you into little pieces and feed them to this excellent goat. You'll be [illegible] before sunup. The only reason you're not dead already is because I don't want to cause Jemimah any heartache. But don't doubt me…*I know where you sleep*."

The General watched with pride as Hoshe'a sheathed his knife and pulled Aharon's face out of the chest. The man's previously smashed nose was gushing with fresh blood. Kalev heard Little Frog's voice come from under the wagon.

"General Hoshe'a made his nose break again." "No, that's *your* fault," corrected Little Croc. "I told you not to put the shiny brick in there. Now look what you did; he looks like an ugly, bleeding, smashed watermelon." "No, you do…" The General quietly snapped his fingers, and the boy's building argument softened to harsh whispers. Kalev heard Miriam's muffled laughter again.

He watched his older brother smile at him and mouth, "I told you." Kalev proudly nodded and sheathed his swords. Hoshe'a roared. "The other two are filled with silver as well." Then he thrust out his hand. "Do we have an agreement?" That was when Aharon saw Kalev, and Kalev saw that the bloody-faced fool had pee running down his shaky legs. Aharon hung his head, gurgled an apology, and then limply shook Hoshe'a's hand. As Moshe's brother turned and headed back to his tent, Hoshe'a yelled at the man's back, "And this goat better remain a virgin." Hoshe'a winked at Kalev, then walked away whistling. The General joined the familiar belly laugh erupting from Moshe's tent.

A laughing Miriam returned to Kalev's side of the wagon. "That was the most fun I've had in years. Thank you for everything." Then she slyly winked at Kalev, turned, and addressed the wagon. "General, I have too many loaves of warm sweetbread by my fire. But both my brothers seem to have lost their appetite, and there's no one to eat them." Two gasps came from under the wagon. "It's really too bad. I guess I could feed them to my brother's new livestock. But I just don't know if I should." In a chaotic cloud of dust, both boys tumbled from under the wagon. They came to attention in front of Kalev. Croc coughed, then spoke up, "Sir, I, um, we would like your permission to help Miss Miriam with her sweetbread problem, Sir." Frog frantically nodded his agreement. Kalev bit his tongue and scowled. He turned to Miriam. "It's up to you, mam, but I've seen these two successfully complete this type of perilous mission before. They have my total confidence." To her credit, Miriam scowled at the boys, then slowly circled them. "They'll have to wash up first, but I'd appreciate their help." Kalev nodded seriously. "Very well, mam, send them back when they complete their mission." The General scowled at the two anxious boys. "I want a detailed AAR later today." Both boys nodded, saluted, then obediently followed her back to the campfire. Kalev nodded to a grinning Moshe, then ran to catch up to Hoshe'a.

63

Kalev had looked for Raisa and/or her protective detail since that morning. As the day wore on, his concern increased. Not one of his other troops claimed to know where she was. At the evening meal, Akiba found his worried general. "Sir, I think she and a squad from Zayin Company rode into the desert for target practice. I'm sure you'll see her soon. I'll send out a squad after they eat. She has our best overwatch troops with her." Yadin ran up, winked at Akiba, and saluted. "Sir, um, the adult and special graduation is about to start. We need to be there." Akiba added, "You'll probably pass her on your way, Sir." Kalev had forgotten all about the ceremony.

The previous graduations were always held in the Outpost. But by order of Colonel Carni, the Outpost and its vacated fifty-yard perimeter was a no man's land for the next few days. So the graduation ceremony was moved five miles east into a wide depression on the far side of a line of small hills. The two generals and Kalev didn't see the dusty glow from the huge torch-ringed area until they reached the hilly perimeter. Master Sergeant Abraham's adult graduating class was already formed up and silently waiting in front of the stage.

The generals mounted the reviewing stand. Akiba and Ofek were already on stage. Once the General took his place between Ofek and Yadin, Akiba nodded, and the procession began.

The proud graduates stiffly marched by in perfect step. Kalev was surprised by the size of this graduating class. Yadin smiled at the General's expression. He covered his mouth and explained. "Originally, the required basic and advanced training was limited to the adult men already supporting the army. Almost from the beginning, many of the troops' abbas asked to join or at least train. Then, about two months ago, the emas found out about the Zayin Battalion." Kalev whispered back, "Armed emas… that's a terrifying thought to any son." Yadin smiled. "Moshe said the same thing. In fact out of this class, Master Sergeant Abraham referred more women than men for additional special training. So these 105 are not the entire adult graduating class." Kalev quickly scanned the ranks, then scowled at Ofek. "Where is my ema?" Ofek shrugged. "She said she was too occupied to attend her class's graduation." Then, to distract from any further questions, the Bet Battalion's commander suggested the other generals have a seat in the chairs that had just appeared behind them.

Moshe shuffled past the other two to sit next to Kalev. Ofek quickly stepped to the medallion-covered table and gave the graduation address. Kalev had become exceptionally good at looking interested while his mind was somewhere else. Or at least *he* thought so.

The experienced Egyptian ex-general leaned close and whispered, "I used to try to memorize the name with the face to stay awake. I was successful most of the time." Kalev smiled. Then Moshe intensely scanned the ranks. "I thought your ema was in this class." Kalev nodded. "Yeah, so did I. Apparently, she was too occupied to make it." Moshe nodded. "And your wife?" Kalev scowled and quietly growled. "What about my wife…? Have you seen her today?"

But before the surprised old prophet could pull his foot out of his mouth and answer, Ofek introduced Kalev. "…to introduce the Supreme Commanding General of Yisrael's Army." Everyone in earshot came to a stiff attention.

Still eyeing Moshe suspiciously, Kalev grew his customary scowl, then turned and walked to the edge of the stage. He made a point to glare at each troop individually, starting with the rear rank. But as he'd expected, their eyes were glued to the back of the head in front of them. Kalev half-smiled when he saw Dan carrying the guidon banner. He had a carefully written speech scroll in his pocket. But he left it there and spoke from the heart.

"Today you officially become a warrior in Yahweh's Army. This is a unique honor. It will become a source of pride for your following generations. Always remember the power you feel at this moment. You are no longer defenseless captives in this Egyptian Sha'al. Let that secret, life-sustaining pride carry you through your remaining days here and each battle *we will* face… Let me sum up by giving you some advice.

"(1) This reserve unit is as expertly trained and ready as any other active-duty unit in the army…" The General automatically glanced at the proud Master Sergeant Abraham, who gave a half nod. "So keep your minds and swords sharp. Even before your day begins, hone your bodies and fighting techniques just like I do.

"(2) This is only the beginning of your training. As we learn more about the people and armies temporarily occupying *our* land in the east, your training will be updated. Adapt, adjust, and overcome.

"(3) And most importantly, all our lives depend on your strict adherence to your *signed* commitment concerning this army's OPSEC. That means until we leave this L↘Ш+ᘓ Sha'al called Egypt, this army, and especially your part in it, does not exist and is *not* to be discussed with any civilian. Do you understand me, recruits?" "Yes, Sir," came the thunderous reply.

The generals were glad Ofek chose this area. The loud response was deadened by the surrounding hills of loose sandstone and the dried streambed silt. It was also fortunate that a haboob had overlaid the area two days prior. The remaining dust-filled air aided in muffling the sound.

"(4) Trust the Warrior King, trust your superiors, and trust your training. And this army will be victorious!" Kalev's war cry was echoed by the rest.

The award ceremony went quickly. Instead of calling each one to the stage, the generals moved through the ranks to award each new troop their rank medallion and congratulate them. Eventually the seven generals made it back to the stage, and General Ofek dismissed the troops. Once all but the rear rank disappeared over the hill, the remaining troops were ordered to extinguish all but the tall torches at the rear of the stage. The generals' flickering shadows eerily stretched across the ground to the low-rising hills eighty yards away.

Forgetting about the second ceremony, Kalev talked with Moshe as they started to follow Hoshe'a and Yadin off the stage. Ofek got the General's attention by loudly clearing his throat. When Kalev turned, the other three generals continued to their horses as planned.

Kalev scowled at Akiba questioningly. The teen general mouthed, "Please, Sir." Kalev assumed the three generals needed to speak with him away from the others. He walked over and heard Akiba whispering, "…Yeah, 321 started three weeks ago. These are the only ones left standing. They're the best of the best."

Ofek quietly dragged a small table from the opposite end of the stage. On it was a shiny blue covering and a small silver-inlaid box. He opened it, and Kalev saw a row of seven slightly smaller gold medallions.

As they'd practiced, the two teenage generals faced the empty riverbed and stiffened to attention. Intrigued, Kalev followed suit. Five yards in front of the stage, seven ghostlike figures slowly and silently rose out of the dirt. Because the torches were behind them, the generals' dancing shadows stretched across the open expanse. It made it extremely hard to distinguish the camouflage troops from their surroundings.

Each had a full-length, dirt-colored mesh draped over their heads. Ari nodded and the guidon troop mounted the stage. The senior teenage general reached into the box, and the troop removed his covering. The sand-colored camo paint on the troop's face seemed to absorb the torchlight. Othniel stared straight ahead as Ari began to tie the leather medallion cord around his neck.

General Akiba spoke quietly, "You are the razor-sharp tip of the Warrior King's spear. You are the unseen breath of Yahweh's wrath. You own the night yet were never there. By way of deception you are invincible. You are and will always be…kidon."

Kalev was looking right at the seven wraiths when one disappeared and then instantly materialized in front of Akiba. The camouflaged troop pulled his head netting up. Kalev was surprised. It was Othniel, Raisa's brother. Akiba paused to pick up the new medallion. "Kidon. Your leadership and expertise as this class's leader have made you the example for the classes that follow. Well done, Lieutenant Othniel." Raisa's brother crisply saluted, nodded to the General, pulled the netting back over his head, turned, and leaped off the stage. And Kalev's jaw dropped. The boy seemed to *literally* fly up and away.

At first, the second apparition in line didn't move. At least in the dusty, flickering torchlight it looked that way. Kalev suddenly sensed the silent movement of air on his left arm as the figure walked past him and took his place in front of the generals. The specter flipped his netting back. The battle-wisened eighteen-year-old Yoshi'yah locked knowing eyes with Kalev and then stared straight ahead. His medallion was tied around his neck.

Following the salute, the new lieutenant recovered his head and stood there. Kalev blinked and Yoshi'yah's netting seemed to drop a foot. But when the netting was flipped back again, it was someone else. Only it wasn't Yoshi'yah. Kalev remembered the face. This was one of the original boys who'd plowed his field. *His name is Bibi*, Kalev silently reminded himself.

This time Akiba handed the next medallion to the surprised General. "Repeat after Me…" the Warrior King boomed in his gut. Kalev repeated, "You are the tip of the Warrior King's spear. You are the unseen breath of Yahweh. You own the night yet were never there. By way of deception you are invincible. You are and will always be…kidon." Kalev paused. "I'm proud of you, Lieutenant Bibi." Without showing it, the extremely dangerous eleven-year-old was surprised and very humbled that the General remembered his name. He quickly redonned his netting to hide his grateful tears. Then the boy simply fell backward off the stage, but no one saw him land.

The next one seemed to fall out of the sky. His name was Abijah. Kalev was shocked. This eleven-year-old boy was Yadin's unrelated twin. They both had the same obsession with numbers. And just like his mentor, Abijah had pockets added to his tunics so he could carry extra scrolls.

But something was dramatically different about the boy receiving this medallion. Kalev's gut instantly identified the personally familiar fire in the boy's eyes. *Somehow, this one has killed many enemies*, Kalev mused. *And he's dangerously hungry to kill many more*. The Commanding General glanced at Akiba, who glanced back. The aleph-grade general's flat expression verified Kalev's silent recognition. The General wondered if Yadin knew. As if he could read his general's thoughts, Akiba quietly coughed the word "no." Abijah pulled his net over his head. Then, in a blur, an extraordinarily long stiletto appeared and was flipped high in the air.

Out of a sense of self-preservation, the three generals watched the lethal weapon sparkle as it spun upward, quickly blending with the stars. The trio of generals nervously searched the night sky. But the foot-long blade never returned. In unison the trio looked back at the boy, but he, too, had disappeared. They looked down to where seven Kidon had once stood. But only one remained.

Kalev glanced at the box and confirmed that there were two remaining medallions. Had it not been for the blast of horse breath hitting the side of his face, none of them would have looked that way. The netted and riderless horse was almost see-through in the torchlight. All three generals' heads turned at the same time when they heard a soft scratching on the table. The shrouded figure stood motionless on the other side. Ofek half-smiled when he reached for the medallion and handed it to the General.

As he made his way around the table, Kalev looked at the back of the solid gold identification medal. In the middle of the mirror-like finish was a single long, thin knife. Just before he stepped behind the "soon-to-be officer," the kidon lifted her head covering. The generals watched as their stunned commander distractedly looked down and flipped the medallion over to confirm. "Colonel Carni, Zayin Battalion, lethal." The General continued walking behind her. But as he tied the leather thong behind her neck, Kalev not so quietly growled in her ear. "Ema, what have you done?" To her credit, Colonel Carni never lost her expert military bearing. "General, Sir. I obeyed your order, or was it an ultimatum? Either way I submitted to all military training as ordered. And that mission has been accomplished..." Kalev's head pulsed with the Warrior King's smiling voice. "Hey, even I can't argue with that... And, Kalev, too soon she'll need these skills."

The General hated being outmaneuvered. But he knew she was correct. There were no specified limitations in his order. *Still...my ema, the assassin*, he thought. *I have to warn Hoshe'a*. Again, Akiba quietly coughed the word "no."

Kalev felt for his unwitting brother, but he understood the added OPSEC. He glanced at his little, now-very-lethal ema. She was actually giving him a slightly new and improved "look."

The Commanding General took a deep breath and quietly snarled, "You are the tip of the Warrior King's spear. You are the unseen breath of Yahweh. You own the night yet were never there. By way of deception you are invincible. You are and will always be...kidon." Kalev paused. "I'm proud of you, Colonel Carni, but we will discuss this later."

Carni crisply saluted and pulled the net back over her head. Kalev was still standing behind his deadly ema when she slammed both palms on the table. The three generals watched the remaining medallion leap three feet off the table. Both Carni *and* the cloaked horse were gone before it landed perfectly in the box.

Kalev had just made his way back around the table when he noticed the three generals staring at the empty desert beyond the stage. Then the other two generals closed their eyes at the same time. Kalev could hear Akiba faintly groan under his breath. But the final figure had not appeared yet.

Then, in a soft voice that was meant to both calm and explain, the Warrior King spoke to the proud son of Hezron. "Kalev, son, you need to take a deep breath and relax. This was My idea. She was only following My..." But Kalev's attention had already turned to the table. No one heard or saw where the long-serrated knife came from. The twelve-inch stiletto had replaced the box in the center of the table. It slowly rotated while balancing on its pommel. The flickering light of the single torch behind them projected the illusion that the knife was floating three inches off the table. The killing blade began to spin faster, then suddenly shot into the air like an arrow. This, too, made all three generals nervous. When they looked back, the table covering was gone, and the cloaked figure was standing *on* the table. Without even bending his knees, the troop backflipped and silently landed alongside of the tabletop. The box seemingly emerged out of the center of the table. Kalev noticed the teen generals were grimacing with their eyes closed again. Forgetting about using his turn to award Carni, Kalev started to make his way around the table to do the honors. *This kid is really talented*, he thought. The General glanced at the table, but the gold identification disk was gone. Kalev stopped and looked questioningly at Akiba. But he and Ofek still had their eyes screwed shut.

Only then did the huge General notice that the medallion was already in his thickly callused palm. Kalev smiled approvingly. He inadvertently glanced down at the polished gold disk. But it took one more step before his brain registered what he'd just read. The General sucked in a sharp breath, held it, and froze in place. The troop sheepishly lifted the netting off her face. In unison, the teenage generals quietly sighed, "Oh [illegible]."

Knowing he had to do something, Akiba quickly made his way around the opposite side of the table and stopped behind the new Kidon. Heh Battalion's Commanding General tentatively held out his hand in a silent request for the necklace. But the General shot him a glance that made the hairs on the back of his neck tingle with fear.

General Akiba took a half step back. He'd known all along that keeping this a secret from his commander was an unbelievably bad idea. But it wasn't his decision; he, too, was just following orders. So now what am I supposed to do? he silently intreated Yahweh.

Kalev stood there silently staring for another thirty seconds. His next words were barely audible and carried a tone filled with hurt and genuine confusion. "Raisa, what have you done…?"

Three weeks ago, the General's wife was thrilled to have finished her advanced weapons training evolutions. She hated keeping secrets from her gentle giant but knew this training was important for the near future journey. On their very last day of weapons training, which she'd excelled at, Master Sergeant Abraham pulled her aside. He told her about the first "additional training" class that would be starting the next night. She intended to say absolutely not. But the same "Yahweh promptings" took over, and she feebly agreed. For the next three grueling weeks, Kalev's little wife continued to excel in the deadly arts. All the while, she knew her loving husband began to question her love for him.

The "Night of the March" was one of the three most brutal challenges she'd ever endured. With forty-pound packs, she and Carni had teamed up to encourage each other on the thirty-two-mile hike/jog for time. By the last mile marker, neither of them had spoken for a half hour. Out of breath and willpower, she'd stopped running and wheezed at Carni's back, "Why does obeying Yahweh always seem to cost more than I can pay?" Carni had continued stumbling forward until she realized her daughter had started walking and was on the verge of dropping on request. The fierce older ema stumbled back and began to push Raisa forward from behind. "I don't understand Him either, but I won't let your little daughter's mom fail, so move it, girl, before you have to carry me!"

Now, as she stood in the shimmering low light, her tears began to trace little streaks down her muddy cheeks. Kalev couldn't seem to breathe. His numbed mind was a jumble of extreme and incongruent thoughts. *Even with that muddy face, she's the most stunning woman I've ever seen. Why did she lie to me? Did she lie to me? How did she make that knife do that? How am I going to kill those two kids who kept this from me?*

The whole time she'd been in training, she had practiced her response to every potential angry outburst Kalev could muster. But she wasn't prepared for the pain she saw in his eyes. Raisa glanced at General Akiba for help, but he *looked* as out of his depth as she felt.

The newest kidon took a deep breath and broke protocol. Raisa walked over and cupped Kalev's cheek in one hand as she deftly lifted the medallion out of his palm and tossed it to Akiba without her husband even noticing. Raisa stared up into his eyes. It took her a couple of deep breaths before she could speak.

"Kalev, my love, I've become the best warrior I could because that is what Yahweh wanted. And the last time I checked, He still outranks you. But it was also something I needed to do for our future. When you're away from us, you'll never have to worry about anyone harming me or our daughter. We can talk later if you want…but please be proud of me and our daughter." Still stunned, the General watched as Raisa's hand dropped to her stomach. Kalev stared at her hand and then at her smiling face. Two questions crashed into his foggy brain at the same time.

She did this pregnant with our *child? But I can't have children; is this mine? She did this* pregnant with our child*!* He opened his mouth to scream in frustration, but his mind and mouth disconnected. What came out sounded more like a lost little kid.

"But ema said because of what Hotep did to me I can't have children, so how are you pregnant?" The teens glanced at each other wide-eyed, but they never moved or made a sound.

Raisa smiled. "First of all, my love, your ema said you *probably* couldn't have children. But it seems that our Yahweh enjoys creating blessings out of impossibilities. I mean, I'd almost given up on becoming your wife. And now…" Raisa started to choke up. "I just hope you still see me as the one you wanted to marry. Do you…still love me?"

Forgetting her arm was mud-caked, Raisa wiped her snotty, tear-stained face with the back of her hand. Her face paint took on an even more abstract shape. But the little killer half-smiled. "My abba knew it before I did. So I guess he was the first one to name her…" Having remembered Nachshon's words, Kalev finished Raisa's statement. "…Akhsah…" Raisa's tears began to flow again as she nodded. "Your ema said you will be a wonderful abba…so please be proud of me…I know Akhsah is."

Raisa waited, then realized her silent husband needed time to think before he could coherently talk about any of this. Yahweh…help my husband, and please do it now, she silently prayed/ordered.

Raisa waited a beat. But Kalev remained silently tongue-tied. Thus, she did what she'd done for the last three weeks. Captain Raisa took charge of the situation. "So, General, Sir. If there's nothing else… I'd like to accomplish this mission. Your daughter and I have earned it. Plus, I'm dirty, sweaty, and this thing itches, so I need to get cleaned up. And I need to eat something that doesn't slither or crawl. Then I will sleep for the next two days. Oh, and I'm on leave for the next two weeks, so we have plenty of time to talk when you're ready." Raisa stood on her tip toes and kissed her stunned husband passionately.

The General's little assassin walked back to her place on the other side of the table. Akiba averted his eyes from the General's deadly glare. He cautiously tied the leather thong around her neck. The polished gold reflected the torchlight long enough for Kalev to read it.

Raisa, Captain, Zayin Battalion
Most Lethal Sword
Most Dangerous Knife
Most Deadly Spear
Extremely Dangerous

General Akiba stepped back then repeated the charge loudly. "You are the unseen breath of Yahweh. You own the night yet were never there. By way of deception you are invincible. You are and will always be…Kidon. Congratulations, Captain Raisa." Raisa half hoped that Kalev would say something encouraging, but she didn't wait. She quickly pulled the netting back over her head. With Akiba still standing behind and Kalev staring right at his cloaked wife. The empty camouflaged netting simply dropped to the floor.

As the astonished Akiba bent forward to pick up the shroud, the knife fell from the stars and landed five inches from Akiba's face. The stiletto's tip plunged into the suddenly covered tabletop with such force, it completely split the thick slab of wood in half. Then it, too, faded away.

Akiba looked up and cringed. Ofek had conveniently used the distraction to perform his own vanishing act. So he was the only target available for the General to sight in on. Kalev controlled his rage long enough to ask, "Without my knowledge! Did you know my wife was pregnant!" The kid's expression said it all. The Commanding General of Yisrael's Army hissed bitterly. "Yahweh…"

The deep blue, star-filled sky was starting to lighten as an exhausted Kalev sat on his dune. For the first four hours after the kidon ceremony, Kalev had yelled at the "silent" Warrior King. Then the ex-captive descended into a confused and wounded grumbling for another hour.

The one marked as "true to Yahweh" watched the still black river. The oddly cool breeze began to push whirls of the morning river fog up the side of the dune. It swirled around the General like a soft and silent gray veil.

“Okay, son, but let me ask you this. Do your troops trust you?” Kalev rolled his eyes. The Warrior King always seemed to ask more questions than He answered, and the General’s mind was tired. “Yes, they do,” the exasperated Kalev groaned. “Yet, most of them don’t really know you. So why do your troops trust you?” Kalev silently thought about that. “I don’t know most of them, but they do trust me.” The big General shrugged and then answered.

“I guess they trust me because they’ve entrusted their lives to the army’s higher authority. In basic training, they’re taught to believe in themselves, each other, and their chain of command. Then every sergeant on up is required to know that true command authority over others can only happen when *they* entrust *themselves* to their higher authority and so on up the chain. And for better or worse, I’m at the top of that chain of command. So I guess trust in *my* leadership is implied. Plus, they know I’d sacrifice myself to protect them from the enemy.” The Warrior King sounded pleased with that answer.

“So let me see if I got this straight. This army’s confidence in you as their leader, the one who would kill and die to protect them, is based on their trust in their superior. So, General Kalev, who is *your* higher authority? Who do you trust to lay down *His* life for you?” Kalev’s upper left chest burned at the instant he answered emphatically, “You are, Sir. I trust you, Sir.”

Yahweh chuckled then paused to give Kalev’s thoughts time to catch up. “Consequently, General, am I, as *your* superior authority, required to get your approval before I make a command decision?” Kalev bowed his head and yielded. “No, Sir…it’s just that, I thought it was my responsibility to protect my wife and…family.” The Warrior King’s voice reminded Kalev of his father’s. “It is, son, but your ability to truly protect her is in direct proportion to your trust in Me. Kalev I have complete authority over any and every threat. Your enemies are My enemies. Look what I have already done to your enemies in Egypt. And you can *trust* that I will protect My people and especially you and yours in the years to come… After all, where do you think that need to defend those who can’t defend themselves came from? I just do it on a much larger scale…

Kalev, My people can only know real peace and protection when they, too, have submitted to My highest authority. Sadly, this simple truth will probably be their biggest challenge…but as for you, son, your troops and your loving wife trust you to trust Me. Now get back to your tent and get some sleep. Oh, and before I forget”—Yahweh laughed—“in less than thirty days, you *will* encounter Hotep, and he *will* subsequently lose his head…”

The swirling cloud dissipated, and the General saw Moshe sitting right next to him. “I assume you heard that.” Moshe shook his head. “Yeah, we’ve had that same conversation more than once. And no matter how many times I think I have a sound argument, it always ends up the same…He’s right and I’m wrong.” Kalev laughed. Moshe stood and then pointed at the river. “More friends of yours?” Kalev saw the six crocs staring up at them. But before he could answer, all six suddenly raced out of the water and charged the dune. Moshe was surprised when swarms of arrows hit the charging beasts from all directions.

In the blink of an eye, the six huge creatures lay motionless with a garden of arrows sprouting from their backs. Kalev turned, and they both started walking toward the sand bowl. “Yeah, I don’t get that,” Kalev said with a forced scowl. “Every other animal seems to like me.” Moshe grinned. “General, it’s not that they don’t like you; they’re just skeptical Hebrew crocs. They want a little taste before they make up their minds…”

64

Following six wonderful hours of eating and wrestling, Kalev was able to fall asleep for an hour before a "bored and *hungry*" Raisa woke him. She was softly tapping his forehead. "Hey, mister, hey, mister, hey, mister, hey, mister…" Kalev opened one bloodshot eye, grinned, and whispered, "How do you get more beautiful every time I see you?" Raisa smiled and kissed his nose. Then her smile converted into a mischievous sneer. "Don't change the subject, mister. If I was keeping score, I'd say you've lost the last three rounds. What's wrong? Are you not *up* to the challenge?" Kalev's little wife grabbed a pillow, covered her husband's face, and sat on it.

A few exhausting yet victorious hours later, Kalev mounted the Fortress' stage as the ramp closed shut. At the rear of the stage, Kalev stood beside the table where Yadin, his dangerous assistant Abijah, and Captain Marasha sat. In front of them were three neat stacks of blank parchments.

Yadin looked up at his General. "We moved the remaining livestock to the Pit." Yadin nodded to the front of the stage." Kalev looked out at the mass of people and let out a low whistle; the sight was staggering. Yadin continued his impromptu report. "As of last night, our total troop strength is up to 6777. This evening, we vetted 1414 civilians before they approached the top of the ramp. Most are family and friends of the troops. There are also five other tribal princes and/or chief rabbis."

The General saw that the troops were as skillfully formed up as usual. But the spaces between the ranks and files were filled with men, women, and restless little kids. There were hundreds of emas with squirming little babies. And Kalev's face went pale. Out of nowhere, the realization that he, too, would soon be an abba hit him like a roundhouse kick to the gut. Yadin saw the General's dazed and panicked expression. He quickly got Ari's attention and nodded toward Kalev. Ari and Akiba walked back to their General and snapped to attention in front of him.

Kalev's expression was very unnerving and absolutely *not* what the other troops needed to see. Ari growled to get Kalev's attention. "Reporting as ordered, Sir." Still stunned, Kalev looked at Ari and mumbled, "I'm going to be an abba…I don't know how to be an abba. How did this happen?" Ari glanced at the grinning Akiba, then down at the confused-looking Yadin. The bet-grade general coughed twice before he could suppress his laughter. "Well, Sir, as far as I know, when a man takes a wife and they…" Kalev suddenly shook his head. "What? No! I know that part; I meant I don't…arghh, never mind. Are we ready?" Ari could only nod for fear of exploding in laughter.

Still dazed, the Commanding General of Yisrael's Army grew his practiced scowl and walked to the front of the stage. Ari roared, "Attention!" Six thousand seven hundred seventy-seven pairs of heels slapped together as the troops "stood tall." At the same time, almost 2000 civilians cut loose with deafening cheers and applause. The troops nervously glanced between their general and their "embarrassing civilian" parents. Kalev was so used to the army's obedient silence that he didn't understand what was happening. He looked back at Ari, who shrugged. Moshe grinned at his naively confused-looking friend. He stepped forward and yelled into Kalev's ear, "These are your troops' families. They're cheering the man who's kept their children alive." Kalev was instantly embarrassed. Instinctively, his eyes looked for Raisa. She, too, stood at attention with the other officers in Zayin Battalion. Kalev saw her glistening cheeks and proud smile. She wasn't looking at him, but he read her lips. "I am so proud of you… It is an honor to be your wife… I want to rip off…"

Kalev's scowl almost slipped when he guessed the rest of her statement and quickly looked away. At that split second, the Warrior King's laughter boomed in his head. "And that's how the abba thing happens…any other questions?"

Before the applause ended, Kalev turned and signaled for his general staff to stand beside him and Moshe. Ari and the four battalion commanders stepped forward and flanked their general. The cheering grew impossibly louder as five-thousand-plus war cries were added to the mix.

After two humbling minutes, Kalev held up his hand. Ari's deafening command was echoed by every First Sergeant. "Troops, ten-hut!" The soldiers obediently resumed their silent military baring. But it took a while for the families to quiet down.

The faces of Kalev and his fidgeting senior staff were a bright crimson, and Kalev's voice sounded hoarse. "I'm humbled by your appreciation. But these soldiers beside me deserve all the honor. They are the true guardians." Before the cheering began again, Kalev held up his hands. "Please thank them after the muster.

"But for now…" He paused to gather his thoughts. Then spoke like a caring abba, "Parents, a couple of things about these, um, your soldiers. Nothing in Yahweh's Army is easy or without personal sacrifice. That medallion around your soldier's neck was not given; it was earned. It designates their rank and battalion assignment. They're not just your children, they are now your overwatch, your protectors. These are Yehovah's skilled warfighters, and they're experts…"

Thankfully, Kalev didn't hear Aharon quietly snort in derision, but Hoshe'a and Moshe did, and they both glared at him. Kalev's brother covered his mouth and quietly growled at Moshe. "Does he have a death wish?" Moshe shook his head and groaned, "Could you make it look like an accident?" "Really?" Hoshe'a asked, then licked his lips like a hungry predator. "*No*, not really," the Warrior King roared in their heads, "at least not today." They both averted their eyes back to Kalev and strained not to laugh. But true to form, Hoshe'a whispered to Moshe, "So I'll put that on my to-do list for tomorrow." Moshe almost bit his tongue off.

"…Your troop is trained to obey orders without hesitation. Your children are experts in the use of lethal weaponry. They're Yahweh's precision weapon against our enemies. Our primary mission is to safeguard Yehovah's chosen people and eliminate their enemies with extreme prejudice." Kalev paused a few seconds to let that sink in. "We have all sworn to protect you and your families with our lives... As we journey to the land promised to our abba Abraham, listen and follow Yahweh's troops' directions. They'll keep your family alive and safe. Encourage and honor your troops." Kalev smiled. "And on a personal note, I'd like to encourage you to welcome those soldiers without parents into your family. They, too, *need* a caring savta's guidance." Both Moshe and the Warrior King chuckled. "...Emas, please spoil Yahweh's troops with a favorite meal every chance you get."

Kalev cleared his throat and resumed in his Supreme Commanding General's voice. "General Yadin's officers will be manning designated information tables around the eating area. Please make your way to one of these tables. If you have elders who are ill or injured or have a hard time walking, we will do our best to issue you a horse or camel or a wagon with oxen. We will only move as fast as our slowest person. Oh, and that issue is also for single emas with babies and/or children too young to walk a full day. These people will have top priority when we issue our surplus tents and supplies. The officers also have copies of the order of march for your tribe..." Kalev paused. Everyone watched the giant general nod affirmingly. His voice took on a tone of comforting certainty.

"People, for most of us, freedom from this land of *misri* (Egypt) will be both exhilarating and terrifying." Kalev suddenly felt Yahweh's breath rise in his throat. "But know this...even now, the Warrior King's foot is on the neck of our enemies, and *His* lethal sword *never* misses! So remember you can trust Him and your troops. We, His chosen, will see with our own eyes Yahweh's miraculous rescue. For the Egyptians you see today, you will never see again. *Never again, never again, never again*!" The General paused.

"People of Yisrael. Trust your very capable army as we trust the Warrior King"—Kalev's scowl broke into a reassuring grin—"and let's go home!" The Supreme Commanding General of Yisrael's Army cut loose with an ear-piercing war cry that was echoed by thousands, troops and civilians alike. Moshe turned to Hoshe'a and yelled over the din, "Wanna swap brothers?" Hoshe'a forced a frown and thoughtfully shook his head. "Not today!"

Kalev turned and curtly nodded to Moshe, then he and his senior staff took two steps back, while Moshe stepped forward and held up his hands. The sudden silence was followed by a cool breeze that came from the ceiling and swirled around the inside of the massive Fortress. Moshe closed his eyes and the Prophet's words echoed with the power of the Warrior Kings voice.

"Attention to orders. Yahweh has decreed..." The entire army, minus the three scribes on stage, automatically dropped to their knees and then put their face to the ground. The civilians quickly followed suit. Only a handful knew that the prophet used to have a stuttering problem. But no more. "...

This month is to be your beginning of months; it will be your first month of the year. In the tenth day of this month you will take a lamb for your whole family, a lamb for each household (7–9 people). If any household is too small for a lamb, the man and his next-door neighbor are to take a lamb according to the number of people. You will make your count for the lamb according to how much each one can eat.

"Your one-year-old male lamb must be spotless and without defect. You may take it from the sheep or from the goats. You must take it into your home (a monstrous insult to the Egyptians and especially to their lamb god Khnum) and care for it until the fourteenth day of this month, which is in four days. Then My elect will kill their lamb between noon and sundown. This will be to you the *zebah pesach* (sacrifice of exemption). You will take some of the blood and put it on the two side posts and top of the doorframe of your house where the lamb was eaten.

"You will eat all the meat that same night; you will eat it roasted over the fire with bread, made without yeast and with bitter herbs (chicory, bitter cress plants, hawkweeds, sow-thistles and wild lettuces/Romain). Do not eat it raw or boiled in water but roast it whole and unbroken over the fire with its head, its legs, and its entrails. You must leave nothing until morning, but you must burn with fire whatever remains.[2]

"You are to eat it—dressed to travel, your sandals on your feet, and your staff in your hand. You are to eat it quickly. It is Yahweh's Pesach (Passover).[3] For He will unleash and direct the destroyer in the land of the Egyptians that same night, and Yahweh will slay all the firstborn in the land, both of humans and animals. And He will expose the fake and powerless gods of Egypt. Abaddon will execute the Warrior King's judgment. For I AM that I AM has ordered this.

"In the days to come, the blood of the Most High's Lamb will be a banner for *you* on your house, a mark to distinguish you as Yahweh's chosen and redeemed people. And when the Warrior King sees the blood, He will cause the destroyer to pass over you, and this plague *will not* be allowed to destroy you as He moves on to exact His vengeance on the land and peoples of Egypt. For He is Yeshua Hamashiach, your deliverer. The blood of Yahweh's Lamb shall be to you a memorial on your house, the place where you dwell. When He sees the saving blood of the Lamb, the wrath of Yahweh will pass over you, and you will live!

"This day will become a reminder for you, and you will celebrate it as a holy day to Yahweh—you will celebrate it with feasting and procession as a lasting ordinance. In the first month, from the fourteenth day of the month, in the evening, you will eat bread made without yeast (*matzah*) until the twenty-first day of the month in the evening.

"On the first day you *will* remove all yeast from your house. Because anyone who eats bread made with yeast from the first day to the seventh day will be cut off from My chosen people Yisrael, as *their* mildewed hearts refused to leave Egypt. On the first and seventh days, there will be holy assemblies. For those seven days, you will not work, no work of any kind. You will prepare only what every person will eat and nothing else.

"You will keep the Feast of Matza, because on this very day, I brought My battalions out from the land of Egypt. You will keep this fourteenth day of the first month continuously as a lasting ordinance. For seven days, yeast must not be found in your houses, for whoever eats what is made with yeast, that person will be expelled from the community of Yisrael, whether a foreigner or one born in the land. You will not eat anything made with yeast; in all the places where you live you must eat bread made without yeast."[4]

Moshe's arms fell to his side and the breeze ceased. But the Fortress remained silent and bowed. The only sound in the massive bunker was the hurried scratching noise coming from Yadin and his two assistants as they carefully documented Yahweh's decrees. Eventually Moshe opened his eyes. He turned and whispered to Kalev, "That's all for now." The General grinned. "That's enough."

Ari dismissed the troops and civilians for the evening meal. Kalev whispered to Akiba, and soon a table and chairs were brought onto the stage for the General's meal. Moshe turned to Kalev. "General, I'll need twenty-four copies of General Yadin's record. I'll sign every one and affix my seal to the scroll. And if you can spare them, I'll need twenty-four fast riders to take them to specific villages and caves upriver. Word of Yahweh's directives will travel from those main districts outward." Kalev turned to look at Yadin. The teen general never looked up but replied to the request. "We're on it, Sir. Give us three and a half hours for all twenty-four copies." Moshe looked around the Fortress and smiled. "General Yadin, would you include a map and directions to our staging area?"

Yadin's head snapped up and scowled at General Kalev quizzically. The generals struggled not to laugh. They all knew Yadin hated surprises. But the General and Ari had prepared for this probability two months prior. Kalev nodded. "It's the expanse exactly sixteen miles straight east of the Pit, near that natural spring. I believe it's at waypoint Vav." Ari nodded and addressed Kalev and Moshe, "The army will set camp in that wide riverbed on the eastern side of those low hills. The low line of hills will give us cover, and the taller eastern bank will be perfect for overwatch. The front rank will halt at the waypoint facing north. Heh Battalion will split to form a point and rear guard. We assume any Egyptian assault will be from the northern trade route or the road west from the Red Sea docks. Then our course will take us north to the trade route, then northeast to Beersheba." Yadin chimed in. "Yeah, but there's still too many unknown factors." Moshe smiled. "Are you referring to the Egyptian Army?" General Yadin scowled. "Yes, Sir, that and the exact number of civilians, their physical conditions, how fast and how far we can move in a day. The army could easily make the 183 miles in five days, but…"

Moshe soberly nodded. "Three nights ago I kitted up and did my own recon in the opposite direction. I thought we needed a firsthand battlefield assessment." Everyone stopped chewing or writing and stared speechless at Yahweh's prophet. Moshe was eating, so he didn't notice his stunned audience. He shrugged. "I guess old habits die hard…I'd heard rumblings about troop ships returning from Gaza. The bulk of the Egyptian Army has redeployed back to Ramses, Memphis, and Thebes. The Ramses brigade landed at the docks three nights ago. And from what I saw and heard, the majority of those are looking to muster out. I heard two livid brigade generals grumbling about the pharaoh's politics. The Ramses brigade general stated they were ordered to pull out of Tyre at the height of their battle. The Thebes brigade commander actually cursed the pharaoh's name. He said his forward battalions had already taken Joppa and were digging in when they received the order to retreat to the sea." Moshe looked at the ground and sadly smirked. "Some things never change. The politicians *never* know the first thing about winning a war. Especially that idiot Ramses. I doubt he knows which end of the sword to hold…" Moshe grinned at Kalev. "It seems my brother and the pharaoh have that in common." Moshe was unaware that the teen general's respect for the ex-Egyptian soldier had just increased exponentially.

The old general paused to watch the receding troops. "You're fortunate, General Kalev. You only have to answer to Yahweh, and He knows exactly what it will take to win our land back…however, at least four battalions of infantry and the sixth armored chariot battalion were split between the border outposts at Tjel and Al-Arish. Those are the ones we'll have to contend with…but I'm sure they're just as disgusted and miserable as the ones I saw at the docks. They may let us pass unharmed out of pure spite for the throne."

After a while, Moshe saw the other boys staring at Yadin. The teens always tried not to watch, but they couldn't help themselves. Watching their friend's genius mind play out across his face was *way* too much fun. Moshe saw that Yadin was drawing a very accurate map, including the Egyptian border outposts along the proposed route. The guy was smiling ear to ear while he quietly cajoled, berated, then flattered himself.

Moshe chuckled and whispered to Kalev, "Your General Yadin really enjoys the details, doesn't he?" Kalev grinned and whispered back, "I'm glad *he* does; my mind would melt." Moshe shook his head and whispered back, "Does he understand this mass exodus, journey, and assault will be the first of this size in history? It's a logistical nightmare." Kalev grinned and nodded to oblivious teen general. "Why do you think he's smiling?"

65

Eventually Kalev, Raisa, and Moshe moved the assembled mass to the General's table at the other end of the Fortress. Following the abundant evening meal, the skills demonstration was *supposed* to show the troops' families and local tribal leaders some of the "lesser violent" army combat skills. It only took five minutes before the "civilian friendly" demonstration transformed into the inevitable competition. The adults at the table laughed when a swarm of scowling emas started yelling at their trash-talking sons and daughters.

It didn't take long for the all-out war games to become aggressive. Yadin and Ofek were supposed to be the senior officers in charge. Instead of ordering the competition to stay "civil," they were persuaded by their junior officers to compete. Soon the competition threatened to get out of hand. All the General had to do was draw his sword, walk out onto the drill deck, and glare at his troops. Order was immediately restored.

Just before sunset, Kalev opened his bloodshot eyes and smiled at the sound of his Raisa's heavy breathing. He slowly got out of their fluffy bed. Forgetting he was stark naked, Kalev stepped outside the tent. He looked around the sand bowl and sighed. This was the day they'd leave their newlywed oasis. He'd miss the privacy, but he reasoned they'd reach Beersheba by the end of the lunar month, and then he'd have his own land to build a huge house and farm. But in prep for leaving Egypt, they'd spend their last couple of nights in the Fortress.

Suddenly, two loud gasps came from the pair of camouflaged heads at the top of the dune he was facing. Little Frog loudly whispered, "He forgot to wear his knife and swords. What if he has to kill something? Should we tell him? Oww, stop it." Both heads disappeared from sight. Embarrassed, Kalev returned to the tent. Raisa was just getting out of bed and laughed when she saw Kalev's red cheeks. "I could hear that boy's 'whisper' from in here." She gawked at her husband's rock-hard body like it was the first time. She forced herself to look away. But her voice was suddenly husky. "Well, um, if you have to, I guess you'd better, um, arm yourself. I mean, put on your other swords—I mean…"

66

An hour before sunup, Kalev, Ari, Yadin, and Ofek stood off to the side of the almost empty dining area. They continued to eat the fluffy sweetbread and drink the thick beer like they were starving. General Kalev noticed that Ari, Akiba, and Ofek looked as exhausted as he felt. But Yadin looked well rested and more energetic than usual. Kalev shook his head in amazement and silently asked Yahweh if He needed any help organizing *His* supply chain. "Maybe I'll let you know," the Warrior King chuckled. Moshe had warned them last night that the next twenty-four hours would be the most terrible and exciting yet. Kalev hoped so, then yawned.

The Commanding General's usual "Hotep nightmare" had grown much more intense in the previous four days. And if that wasn't bad enough, it was a new extended version. Now the pig's face glowed with a ring of fire around it. Hotep would violently scream and curse at him with an intensity Kalev had never experienced before. Next the pig's face would morph into a pale yet darker version. The new expression seemed frozen on his sightless and surprised face. Then just before the whole violent dream started over, the face of Kalev's mortal enemy slowly sank into darkness. For the last four days, no matter how many times he told himself it wasn't real, the dream repeated at least once every night. And he continued to wake up drenched in sweat.

Then two days ago, three little girls left Carni's courtyard and headed toward the Outpost. They were dropped off at Carni's house by relatives who'd attended Moshe's "night of the instruction."

The little ones had run ahead of their troop escort, who was still talking to Carni in the courtyard. The little refugees hadn't made it ten yards up the road when an Egyptian Army platoon road up. The three lead pigs halted long enough to capture all three shrieking girls and race away. They were gone before Kalev's armed ema made it out of the gate. The General found out about it ten minutes too late.

The high overwatch squad leaders AAR stated:

"(1) Following his notification of the kidnapping, the General spent the next two hours destroying the bridge over the canal.

"(a) He only used his swords and hands.

"(b) He scared off anyone offering to help, including Colonel Carni.

"(2) The General took one of the thick broken bridge planks and carved a sign.

"(a) It read, 'Hotep, you worthless murdering [illegible] coward, Ox is still alive. *Find me* here at sunrise on [illegible] (the fifteenth day of the first Hebrew month), you motherless [illegible] pig!'

"(3) The General buried the signpost on the other side of the canal facing up the road to Ramses.

"(4) The General relieved himself on and at the base of the sign.

"(5) End of AAR."

By the time the General made it back to his room in the Pit, the Kidon already had a mission plan in place. At sunrise on the fifteenth day of the first Hebrew month, all seven of the Kidon would infiltrate the Egyptian barracks and eliminate Hotep. But neither the elite assassins nor their general would ever get the chance. Yahweh would keep that kill for himself.

Ofek wiped his mouth. "What is yeast anyway?" Kalev glanced at the resident mastermind. "It's fermented wheat, rye, or barley. First, you take a one-gallon urn and mix…" Ofek rolled his eyes. "Okay, Yadin, stop. Not this morning. Just…how long does it take?" His frustrated friend growled. "For bread, it takes two weeks." Yadin looked at Ari. "So, rabbi, why doesn't the Warrior King like yeast?"

Ari cringed and the other tired teens laughed. They knew their friend still couldn't figure out what a rabbi actually did, and General Ari hated uncertainty. But he took on an "all-knowing" attitude just for the entertainment value.

"Well, according to my vast understanding of all things spiritual…and because I asked Moshe the same question yesterday"—they all laughed—"the answer to your question, my son, is yeast starts out as a mold that eats the wheat flour its fed. You can tell it's alive because it bubbles and stinks." *Just like Hoshe'a*, Kalev thought. The teens laughed, and Kalev blinked hard. "Wait, did I just say that out loud?" This fueled more stress-relieving laughter.

Eventually Ari resumed his scowl, just like every other contrary teaching rabbi he'd ever met. All two of them. "Those same nasty bubbles make our bread loaves fluffy. It's also what turns Yadin's grape juice into that vile stuff they started using to tan the cowhides." "Wait, *seriously*?" the surprised genius yelled. Ari ignored his frustrated friend. "So for the next seven days, Yahweh is using yeast as a physical example of Egypt's putrid influence on our lives. In summary, my children, we remove it from where we live, apply the blood, and we live to leave. So there you go! Let my wisdom be written and obeyed."

So this morning they greedily ate with a loaf of hot, puffy yeast bread in each hand. Yadin swallowed and turned toward Kalev. "Sir, late last night, the riders we sent out with General Moshe's decree returned." Yadin quickly took a long drink of beer to hide his disgust. Kalev saw the flash of disdain in the teen's eyes and patiently waited. "Sir, only half of the village leaders were grateful and promised to spread the message to everyone they could." Yadin scowled. "The other half, our riders reported, laughed and ridiculed our troops. Three of our riders reported they had rocks, bricks, and/or spears thrown at them. Those three returned with serious head and back wounds.

"The AAR stated that the Hebrew leaders near Memphis and Thinis didn't even open the scroll. They just tore them up. One threw it in a fire pit, then cursed out our troops in Egyptian." Yadin shook his head. "These people are tortured slaves, and Yahweh is offering them freedom for the first time in

400-plus years…" Ari nodded. "Well, look on the bright side. In a way, the fools are doing us a favor. Every first born that rejects Yahweh's warning is one less rebel we'll eventually have to kill." "I guess that means more bread for us. Sir, do you want another?" "Of course, thank you."

Raisa sat at the closest table with a cup of water. She was trying to wipe flour off her cheeks. Kalev smiled as he plopped down beside her. "So does everyone have to bathe in flour to make bread, or is it just your secret recipe?" Kalev started laughing. Raisa didn't even smile. She'd slept less than her husband. Raisa simply sprinkled water on her floured cheeks, jumped into Kalev's lap, and rubbed her gooey face all over his.

The Fortress' ramp began to lower. The night's herding maneuvers had ended about an hour ago. And the tired wagon drivers from Zayin began their slow descent. Even from 300 yards away, Kalev's acute vision could make out Zayin's unique-looking guidon banner. Hoshe'a had previously described it, but it was the first time Kalev had seen it.

It was embroidered on the largest framed auroch hide he'd ever seen. In the center was a huge black Khopesh sword pointing up to the large blood-red letters "ZAYIN BATTALION." Raisa snickered. "Even you, my kestrel-eyed husband, can't see the Zayin motto from here." "Motto? You mean like 'Zayin Battalion: we bake killer bread,'" Kalev chuckled.

In a flash, the General's four-foot-eleven assassin wife spun from his lap to his back and had his thick neck in a stranglehold, or at least the best one her too-short arms could accomplish. Kalev had never experienced the move before, and it actually hurt. She leaned in close to his ear. "No, General, it reads, '' (WE *NEVER* MISS)." He smiled and croaked, "I'm impressed. But, Captain Raisa, you probably shouldn't attack the Supreme Commanding General of Yisrael's Army in front of the troops." Kalev pointed down at the table. "Besides, my silent and deadly overwatch might have to subdue you." Raisa immediately let go and whispered, "You're right. I'm sorry." Then just as fast, Kalev reached back, grabbed his wife, and flipped her over his head, and she landed back in his lap. In midair, Raisa started to counter the move but stopped herself. Instead, she landed, stood on his thighs, and passionately kissed him. She went nose to nose and whispered, "The boys haven't been your official overwatch for almost three weeks; they've been temporarily reassigned…" "On whose order?" Kalev quietly growled. Raisa looked around to make sure no one could hear their muted tones. "General, does the kidon mission operate outside the army's usual chain of command or not?" Kalev paused, then nodded. "Yes, of course, but the boys?"

Raisa nodded soberly. "As captain, I have the added duty of managing the selection of the next class's two hundred candidates. The boys were my first choice. Their special warfare training started three weeks ago. They train all day, then run to assume your overwatch. So far, they're in the final fifteen candidates. But please, my love, don't ask me about my unofficial duties again. I'd like to have many more children with you." Kalev saw her serious expression but smiled anyway. "Be careful, my little captain. I am your *very* superior officer. There's only one place on *eretz* where you outrank me!"

Hoshe'a joined them at the table, Heh Battalion followed Zayin down the ramp with Colonel Carni in the lead. The General was surprised to see the front ranks driving a small herd of aurochs in front of them. Lieutenant Othniel held Heh Battalion's new guidon banner. It had a single deep blue letter colorfully dyed on the back of a stiff leopard skin. Akiba raced ahead and reined in hard in front of his seated general. They traded salutes. "So, General Akiba, did you find more cattle?" "No, Sir. They're ours.

"I spoke with General Moshe last week. We discussed the most logical route that will hopefully bypass the two Egyptian garrisons. For the last week, we've pushed north ten miles from the rendezvous point at marker Vav (6). Yadin and I agreed that the more we run that same route, the easier it will be to walk it.

"The very first night, our scouts and perimeter troops reported seeing numerous leopards, large packs of wolves, hyenas, and jackals along that route." Kalev nodded approvingly. "And you used the cattle as bait?" Akiba tensed and hesitantly nodded. "Two nights ago, a pair of sickly cows died *en route*, and we used them as added bait." "I'm impressed with your initiative, General Akiba…" The dirty-faced teen relaxed. "Sooo how many kills did you end up with?" Raisa asked. Akiba pulled a parchment out of his saddle bag. "During last night's evolution, we killed and field-dressed eighty-seven leopards, thirty-two huge sand vipers, eighteen Egyptian cobras and 107 jackals. We bagged six packs of wolves but heard a lot more all along the route. Oh, and we also killed 177 of those plate-sized camel spiders. The predators will be a threat to the unarmed civilians, especially the children. Our perimeter guards have done an excellent job. We moved the inner layer of roving troops closer to the livestock. Still, the preds are smart, so we've had to change our tactics every night."

Akiba consulted his list, then continued his unplanned AAR. "Let's see…this month's mission-related injuries are…Oh yeah, 229. They were mostly minor cuts, scrapes, and bites. There were seven serious injuries, four sprained ankles, one broken leg, and one cobra bite." Akiba grimaced. "I don't think private Ahava is going to make it." Kalev noticed the surprised and pained look on Raisa's flour-smeared face. He asked Akiba, "How was she that close to a live snake?" Akiba sighed. "The snake was an eleven-footer and must have weighed twenty-five pounds. It was pinned to the dirt with five arrows and a spear. The private didn't wait for the snake to stop writhing before she cut its head off. The jaws were still moving, and one extended fang grazed the top of her big toe.

"By the time I got there, the medic had already made a cut on top of the toe. But the foot had swollen to the size of a small wineskin. It happened a few hours ago. I was headed there after we stowed the cattle and our gear." Kalev could tell the tired-looking teen was taking the loss personally. "General Akiba," Kalev growled. The boy stiffened to attention, and Kalev softened his tone.

"At ease, Akiba, and have a seat... Did you know the private?" Akiba was rubbing off the flecks of dried blood from the back of his hands. He looked up and shook his head. "No, Sir, she was one of Colonel Zilpah's." "Listen, son, I know better than most that this cursed land wants to devour everyone."

Kalev stood so he could see the others. "I hate it too, but we *will* lose many more before this thing is over. That's just an army reality. Personally speaking, I don't think it's possible for a leader of men to prepare for the loss of his troops. The best we can do is expect it and be there for his or her remaining squad and platoon. You don't need to give them some pre-planned speech; just be present and let them talk. Kalev looked down at his wife specifically. But she'd disappeared right in front of him. Akiba's face was blank when Kalev looked back at him.

"That said." Kalev eyed Ofek. "I know our troops are trained how and when to handle a dead animal." The training commander nodded. Kalev turned to Ari. Let's reiterate those cautions at the end of every mission brief down range. It's the best we can do." Ari nodded. "Yes, Sir."

Kalev glanced back at Akiba. "The cobra heads are kept and boiled, right?" General Akiba nodded. "Yes, Sir. Then the snake skull is presented to the troop as a trophy, who will paint it. They're always hunting for the largest snake they can find so they can eventually paint the larger skull with their company's crest. For the last four months, there's been a weekly 'Best Pred Killer' competition." "So who has the most animal kills overall?" Kalev asked. Akiba smirked. "Well, since Little Croc and Frog were reassigned for 'extra training,' Lieutenant Abijah has taken over first place."

Yadin choked on a mouthful of bread and had to take a drink before he yelled, "So that's where he's been. I've needed him." Akiba forced a surprised expression. "Oh, I thought Captain Marasha had taken his place. You two seem to be spending a lot of *organizational management* time together." The others laughed and teasingly punched their friend's shoulder. Yadin scowled. "I don't see what's so funny; she's even more focused on my numbers than Abijah." The others howled. Kalev paused for the laughing to slow down.

"Gentlemen, you and your people need to grab as much extra food and sleep as you can in the next five hours. It might be the last for a couple of days. General Yadin, are the lambs ready?" Yadin nodded.

"Yes, Sir. Captain Marasha and I personally delivered 136 of our pristine lambs and the same number of wineskins to the local civilians. All are our troops' families, friends, and tribal leaders.

"I took an unofficial inventory of each home we visited. Colonel Marasha estimates, and I whole heartedly agree with her figure—I mean, figures...." The other teens started belly laughing again. Yadin's voice rose an octave higher when he yelled above the screaming laughter. "I, um, we estimate that only 7 percent of these civilians can sustain themselves and/or their families for a two-week journey. And most of them were crippled by the Egyptians to one extent or another." He turned to Akiba. "That means our pace will need to slow by 3.9 percent."

Yadin turned back to face Kalev and Ari. "There are exactly 900 lambs for the army's use. They've been secured here and are ready to go for this afternoon. But…"

Yadin sighed and shook his head. "Sir. Those civilians are barely surviving day to day. And too many own little more than the clothes on their back and a couple of pots and eating utensils. For most of them, these lambs will be the first good meal they've had in months." Kalev scowled.

"Once we're on the road, covertly determine who's the most needy. Then quietly supply them with the surplus clothes and tents from our supplies. Oh, and by the way General Yadin. I, for one, am pleased that you're keeping Colonel Marasha so close. I mean, keeping an eye on her figure—I mean, figures." Everyone but the blushing Yadin started screaming with laughter."

When the others cleared out, it was just Kalev and Ari at the table. He followed Ari's gaze. A blood-soaked Deborah rode to her new stall beside Ari's. She dismounted and pulled something fury out of a shallow saddlebag. "So how is married life?" Kalev knowingly chuckled. "Are you getting to know each other?"

Ari groaned, "Well, yes and no, Sir. I thought I had this whole marriage thing figured out." "Really!" Kalev said in mock surprise. "Yes Sir. Everything was really great, right up to the moment I told her she *absolutely* couldn't have a pet until we got there and I built our house. And maybe not even then." Kalev winced. "And did she obey her husband's *order*? After all, you are her general." Ari nodded seriously. "I told her that too." "That seems like a very direct, clear order to me." "So, General Ari, has Colonel Deborah obeyed your command thus far?" Ari looked at the floor and shook his head and pointed at the approaching Deborah. "Sir, what is an army general/husband supposed to do when his subordinate officer/wife refuses to obey a direct order?" Kalev put a reassuring hand on the confused kid's shoulder. "General, I'll let you know if I ever figure that one out. For some reason, my captain and your colonel seem to outrank us." "But it shouldn't be that way, Sir." Kalev spoke faster as Deborah got closer. "Ari, I'm going to pass along some wise, um, advice our Warrior King gave to me." The teen bet-grade general looked up hopefully. "He said 'suck it up, General; apologize. And that's an order!'" Ari growled incredulously. "Apologize for what, Sir?" "For everything, I guess. Like I said, I'll let you know if I ever figure it out." "Oh, and, General Ari, let's keep this conversation to ourselves." "Yes, Sir."

Deborah walked up, crisply saluted Kalev, and frowned at Ari. The boy groaned under his breath. Deborah looked like she'd bathed in blood. Her short hair stood straight out from her ears. The four-legged furball in her arms let out a high-pitched screaming howl. "We found Shomer a sister. Her name is Rayah. I guess her pack left her to die alone in the desert. She was barely moving when we rescued her."

Kalev didn't see or hear Raisa walk up behind him. While Ari silently stared at his hands, Kalev cleared his throat and spoke to Deborah with his best Commanding General's voice.

"Tell me, Colonel Deborah, when you give an order, do you expect it to be carried out every time?" She stiffened back to attention. "Yes, Sir. I expect them to be followed exactly as ordered every time." Kalev nodded. "As you should. Strict adherence to our chain of command is the main reason these 6977 troops are still alive and thriving." She nodded and then instantly understood where this was headed. She swallowed hard. "Did General Ari give you permission to bring home a wild wolf cub? An animal that will one day grow to be a man-eater?"

Kalev felt a small thumb stab his left kidney. It hurt, but he ignored Raisa's not-so-subtle hint to stay out of the private matter. Deborah hugged the cub a little tighter and glanced at her embarrassed husband pleadingly. Her shoulders momentarily slumped, then she shook her head. "No, Sir. In fact General Ari specifically ordered me not to…and I, um, disobeyed his direct order." Now Raisa drove her thumbs into both kidneys. Kalev stood to change Raisa's angle of attack and hopefully relieve the pain. The General nudged his second-in-command. And Raisa relented. The obviously lost teen cleared his throat. But his frustrated words came out weaker and grittier than he intended. "Her general gives his permission, and um, he apologizes for pulling rank on a private matter." Deborah nodded. "And?" Kalev looked surprised. Ari groaned again. "And I apologize for the other two things. *Which* we will never mention again outside our tent." Deborah glanced at Kalev, who weakly scowled, then nodded his approval of the apology. "The colonel accepts her General's apology." She almost ordered him to kiss the pup, but she'd wait on that one.

Kalev looked at the dog and got an idea. He opened his mouth, but, for whatever reason, Raisa started on her husband's right kidney again. Kalev's hand shot behind him and grabbed Raisa's thumb mid-jab. He whipped her around in front of him. And she was holding Shomer. By now, they had an audience of over a hundred giggling little girls. Apparently, the dogs were a big attraction.

At the same time Kalev spun his wife around to face Deborah, the General saw two little girls make their way to the front of the crowd. They, too, had wriggling fur balls in their arms. But little Evee actually had a whining leopard cub in her arms. Kalev sternly looked at the growing crowd of troops. "Who else found a pet?" Twelve more Zayin troops sheepishly made their way to the front, each with a leopard cub.

Kalev nodded. "All of you, stand by." That was when Hoshe'a walked up with a quizzical smile. Kalev grabbed Ari's shoulder, and the three of them headed toward the kitchen. Following a few whispered comments and chuckles, the three generals returned and mounted the table.

Ari yelled, "Attention to orders." Over two hundred girls stiffened to attention, and over half tried to stand on their tiptoes. By then, a good portion of Heh Battalion and the rest of Zayin had surrounded the original crowd of little girls.

Kalev tried to scowl. "Generals Ari, Hoshe'a, and I have agreed that now is the perfect time to reveal the Army of Yisrael's newest secret platoon. Zayin Battalion and especially its littlest troops are the first to be assigned this especially important mission."

Every single little girl gasped. "In three days, we will reveal the new Predator Assault Platoon to the rest of the army." Another round of gasps. "This platoon will take care of and train *all* dog, I mean, wolf and leopard cub recruits. And just like you, all new cubs will be required to train if they want to stay in this army. Once grown, these secret weapons' primary mission will be to attack our enemies on command." Kalev grinned at his frowning wife, who'd already figured out what was coming. The General looked at the growing mass of tired-looking troops. "This specialized 'Predator Assault Platoon' will be commanded by Colonel Deborah and her second-in-command, Captain Raisa. They will decide which cubs are smart enough to train. And their word is final. This platoon will initially be limited to only fifty-five troops. Each will be promoted and awarded their own cub recruit to train. To volunteer for this platoon, you must already be a graduate of advanced weapons training. This honor is exclusively for troops within Zayin Battalion. This platoon will have its own banner, and its troops will be awarded a special designation on their medallions." Kalev briefly glanced down at the two frowning wives. "When you're dismissed, the two commanders will begin accepting volunteers. So congratulations, Predator Assault Platoon, and make us proud."

Hundreds of high-pitched cheers and chanting were joined by miniature wolf screeches and leopard cub screaming sounds. Kalev grabbed Ari's arm, and the three generals quickly headed toward the other end of the tables. Behind them, the high-pitched cheers had morphed into hundreds of little girls pushing forward and desperately yelling, "Pick me, pick me, pick me…" The two wives stared daggers into the backs of their laughing husbands. Kalev, Ari, and Hoshe'a sat with their back to the farthest table. They were served more bread and beer. The trio ate and laughed as they watched Raisa and Deborah try to bring order to the chaos. Kalev playfully sneered at Hoshe'a, "It looks like their general needs to get over there and sort that mess out."

Hoshe'a smirked, then shook his head. "With respect, *General*, I don't want to interrupt my perfectly executed command training evolution." Right then Carni ran by and shot Hoshe'a the "don't move—I'm coming back" look. But Hoshe'a nodded as if this was his plan all along. "See, *I* have everything under control." Kalev winked at Ari. "It looks to me like Ema is getting it all under control."

Colonel Carni climbed atop a table and waited. At first nothing happened. Then a shocked and silencing wave flowed from the front of the crowd to the rear. Heh Battalion melted away. The archetypal Hebrew ema silently assaulted her 1247 troops with her too-familiar "I'm the supreme commanding ema; shut up or die" glare. The shocked silence morphed into terrified gasps as they scurried to form up. Ari saw the General's and General Hoshe'a's shoulders tense. The brothers remembered that look all too well.

Colonel Carni's expletive-laced reprimands were barely audible, but no one mistook their meaning. Hoshe'a quietly groaned to Kalev, "Better them than me." Kalev nodded. "I was just thinking the same thing." Ari thought that was hilarious. But he was the only one quietly laughing into his sleeve.

In the crackling silence that followed the rebuke, Colonel Carni was brought up to speed by her two subordinates. In unison, all three women turned and scowled "*the look*" at the wide-eyed generals. Kalev smirked and whispered at his brother, "Guess who Ema's glaring at."

Once Carni expertly cleared the drill deck, Kalev slightly turned toward Ari so his back was to Hoshe'a. "General Ari, I think we just witnessed an expert battalion commander at work." Kalev heard Hoshe'a chuckle behind him and then proudly declare, "Yes, it was a perfectly planned training evolution. I…" But Ari interrupted, "She *is* a model commander. We need that kind of leader on our general staff." Kalev ignored his brother's panicked protest. "Yeah, her ability to silence a whole battalion with just a look. She is definitely general material." Ari nodded. "Yes, Sir. I agree." Hoshe'a stood and stepped in front of the two scheming generals. "Wait—you're not serious…" The Commanding General and his second-in-command seemingly ignored Kalev's frantic older brother and nodded at each other. Ari sounded very official when he again interrupted Hoshe'a's desperate pleas. "He nodded toward the four-foot-eleven haboob baring down on their position. "Should we tell her right now? We'll have time for the formal promotion ceremony when we reach the rendezvous point." Kalev's eyes began to water as he strained to keep from laughing. "It kind of rolls off the tongue…bet-grade General Carni." Hoshe'a sucked in a panicked breath. "*Nooo*!"

67

That afternoon, all dining tables were removed from the Pit and the Fortress. Once all the livestock was herded into the Pit, Kalev oversaw the application of gallons of lamb blood to the underside of the ramp's frame. And just to make sure, the barely perceptible seam of the closed ramp was outlined with twice as much blood.

Two hours before sundown the army was assembled on the Fortress' drill deck. Ari stepped to the front of the stage and yelled. "Attention. Battalion roll calls sound off!" All companies' First Sergeants began yelling at the same time. Each of their troops' names was called and followed by that troop yelling, "Present, First Sergeant!" To the civilians it sounded like very loud chaos, but the six proud generals on stage only heard a finely tuned instrument of war preparing for battle.

It surprised Kalev when Yahweh's prophet and his siblings quickly descended the ramp. Moshe walked up the stage steps, stiffened to attention in front of the General, and saluted. "Permission to join Yisrael's finest tonight." The relieved Kalev smiled as he returned the salute.

Over Moshe's shoulder a smiling Miriam and a nervously fidgeting Aharon—his entire face was swollen—stood at the bottom of the stairs. Kalev winked toward Aharon as he slyly grinned at Moshe and whispered, "He's a firstborn?" Moshe smiled back. "Yeah, I brought him along so we'd know if the lambs' blood was applied correctly." Hoshe'a and the other generals heard Moshe, and they all had to turn and laugh into their sleeves. That is until Hoshe'a abruptly sobered. "Hey, I'm a firstborn too. And so are you guys." The four laughing teens went silent, and they nervously avoided looking at each other.

Kalev put his huge paw on Moshe's solid shoulder. "I'm really glad you're here. I don't know what to do next." Moshe nodded reassuringly. "Well, I've learned the hard way that prayer is always the easiest place to start."

The General took one step forward, and Yahweh's Chosen Army stiffened even straighter. The Fortress's ramp began its slow ascent, and a palpable tension quickly spread through the massive crowd of 9000-plus bodies. Even the small children and babies sensed the seriousness of the moment and remained subdued.

Moshe stepped to the front of the stage and raised his hands. The Fortress boomed when 7777 pairs of knees hit the deck. This was quickly followed by the civilians. Moshe paused in the ensuing silence. Then he sang in a voice that sounded timeless and very powerful.

*"Baruch atah Adonai, Eloheinu melech haolam, borei p'ri hagafen (*blessed are You, Adonai, our Elohim, Ruler of the universe, who creates the fruit of the vine). *Baruch atah Adonai, Eloheinu melech haolam, shehecheyanu v'kiy'manu v'higiyanu laz'man hazeh* (blessed are You, Adonai, our Elohim,

Ruler of the universe, who has kept us alive, sustained us, and brought us to this day). *Baruch atah Adonai, Eloheinu melech haolam, borei p'ri ha'adamah* (blessed are You, Adonai, our Elohim, Ruler of the universe, who creates the fruit of the earth). *Baruch atah, Adonai Eloheinu melech haolam hamotzi lechem min haaretz (blessed are You, Adonai, our Elohim, absolute king of all, who brings forth bread from the earth)."*

Moshe dropped his hands at the same time the huge ramp boomed shut. He turned to the prostrated Kalev, touched his back, and whispered, "Let's eat." Kalev and the others stood. Ari dismissed the troops, and the majority of the crowd headed toward the dining area. Moshe looked up at the closed ramp.

"I'll eat with you, then I need to get back to my tent. When this thing hits, it won't be long before the idiot sends for me. I'll get back here to let you know what happened as soon as I can break camp and head..." Moshe noticed the General's sly grin. "[illegible], you'll know before I leave the palace. I'll probably have to run to catch up." Kalev winked. "Sir, we'll take care of your camp. I assume you won't be under guard when you leave Ramses." Moshe nodded. "Your saddled horse will be waiting for you a hundred yards east of the city gate. So let your horse run to catch up; he's faster anyway." In the middle of their relieved laughter, Moshe stopped and then led Kalev and Akiba to the far side of the stage. The eighty-year-old ex-Egyptian general looked around to make sure they were alone. Moshe tried and failed not to smile. "I saw Hotep's invitation..." Kalev's face turned to stone. "That little pile of gifts was a nice touch." The General snarled under his breath.

Moshe stiffened to his full height and stared at the General, then caught Akiba's attention. He led the pair behind the curtain at the rear of the stage.

"Now don't kill the messenger." Kalev glanced at Akiba, then smirked at Moshe. "Okay, not today..." Moshe grimaced, took a deep breath, and pushed through his weary dread... "Yahweh has two questions for you both." Moshe didn't wait for any comment. "Are you or are you not men under authority?" Kalev swore under his breath, but they both nodded. "Is Yahweh at the top of this or, rather, *His* army's chain of command?" Akiba nodded while staring at his General. The Supreme Commander groaned as he rubbed his tired eyes. He knew this was another painful test of his trust in and loyalty to the Warrior King. "Yes, Sir. The Warrior King is our ultimate Commander." the surrendering General growled. Moshe swallowed hard. "The Warrior King decrees that Hotep and his minions are *His* to eliminate. And you, His subordinates, are ordered to stand down...immediately!"

Moshe shrugged apologetically and quickly left the stage. Both Kalev and Akiba swore under their collective breath. Akiba's hand slowly dropped to his side. And with two subtle finger movements, seven assassins stood down, and Hotep's violent death was delayed.

Eventually, a sullen Kalev, Hoshe'a, and the four other generals joined over 500 anxious-looking troops on the deck behind the stage. All of the troops knew or guessed they were a firstborn. Some grabbed the urns of blood and scampered up the access ladders. They used almost three hundred gallons of lamb blood to soak the Fortress ramp and its previously hidden above-ground seam. And just to make sure, they painted the trees and other hidden access hatches and ladders. Even the hot vents were thickly coated. The subsurface "Blood Spillers," as they proudly called themselves, split into twelve squads. These troops used Hoshe'a's ingenious rope and pulley hoist to send twenty of the smaller troops racing toward the ceiling.

In less than fifteen minutes, the Fortress' ramp seams and accesses were thickly painted with four coats of lamb blood. For another twenty minutes, the dark red ooze rained down to the deck. By the time they'd finished, everyone even close to the ramp was soaked in blood. And boys being boys, the blood-stained face became a badge of honor. Soon every remaining troop, including the majority of the civilian teens and children, raced to the other end of the drill deck to get their share of the "honor of the Lamb's blood."

Soon the generals were back on stage standing and eating their "exemption" meal. Moshe had previously told them that tonight was the night of nights. This day would be a pivotal point for every true Hebrew life that would ever live. That the next generations would be proud to trace their lineage back to the night their *sabas* and/or savtas were saved from the doomed land of Egypt.

Exactly five hours after sunset, on the fourteenth day of the first month, history was written in eternal stone.

Merely sensing the slight change in the air, Kalev cut loose with a long shrill whistle. The troops sprinted from every direction to form up. In fifty-five seconds, the General called the Army of Yisrael to attention. As the deck began to vibrate, Ari gave the signal, and four squads of *shofars* screamed four quick blasts.

In three perfectly choreographed movements, the three center battalions split down the middle and the halves rushed toward both walls. Zayin Battalion ran to the gap in the middle and quickly reassembled in reverse order (officers and First Sergeants in the rear four ranks). This would allow the female officers and First Sergeants to help the parents comfort their children if needed.

Colonel Carni had already prepped the civilians about what to do if they heard the *shofars*. But this did little more than cause the emas and children to start screaming and crying. A secretly scared but proud Colonel Carni watched as Zayin's officers took charge and quickly herded the panicked civilian throng to the rear of their battalion. The muffled yet terrifying high-pitched howl above the Fortress grew louder. With another two blasts, the other battalions completely surrounded Zayin and then came to attention facing outward. As one, the two columns of the oldest perimeter troops drew their weapons. The front row of spearman took a knee as the second row nocked their arrows.

Kalev and Raisa were also prepared. When their eyes met and Kalev nodded, she raced from the rear of Zayin toward the stage. The other generals waited for Raisa, Little Frog, Little Croc, and the disobedient but scared little Evee to reach the bottom of the stage stairs. Then the generals leaped off the stage and form their own armed cordon around the General's "family." Which included the squirming and howling Shomer in little Evee's arms.

When they'd planned and practiced this maneuver, the boys were offended and uselessly protested that they should be a part of the outer protection detail. But now, as the four unrelated members of Kalev's family clung to each other, the boys looked scared *and* relieved.

The screeching wail and deep rumbling under the floor beneath them grew deafening. The troops tracked with their eyes as the sound reached its horrifying crescendo over the top of the ramp. Every eye watched the Commanding General of Yisrael's Army. They needed him to confidently alleviate their fears like he always had. But all the General wanted to do was leap to the floor and comfort Raisa.

Before Kalev could take one step toward his wife, the Warrior King boomed in his gut. "General. About-face! Raise…your…hands!" He obeyed the King of kings and pharaoh's order. Out of sheer muscle memory, both his swords appeared in his up-raised hands, and he widened his stance with one foot slightly forward. He was ready to fight. At that very moment, the ear-piercing wail then thunderous rumble came to a literal "screeching halt."

In the fierce silence, a violent, overwhelming wave of anger engulfed every part of Kalev's being. The "locked away and forgotten," seemingly real-time memories came flooding back with breathtaking vengeance. The thousands of lifeless little faces of dead children. The wails of the dying savtas and *sabas*. And, of course, the ever-present Hotep's venomous grin and high-pitched maniacal laughter. And if that wasn't bad enough, the too-vivid myriad memories of the daily unbearable pain. It all hit him at the same time, and his white-knuckled hands gripped the sword handles impossibly tighter. In fact they went numb.

And now, as he stood there in a head-throbbing rage, he realized that whatever that thing was, it was threatening *his* family. Which included his 7777 troops and his brave little wife.

Suddenly, all the civilians and many of his younger troops shrieked in terror and pointed at the closed ramp. Kalev opened his mouth to challenge the blackness seeping through the ramp's seams.

Then, out of nowhere, the Warrior King's brilliant light suddenly appeared and enveloped the General. It was warm and comforting like his ema Rachael's hug. The huge warrior was immediately lost in the timeless life-giving swirl of Yahweh's presence. The proud son of Hezron would never remember roaring at the still-leashed "destroyer." He was told that Yahweh's ultimate promise of protection, a prayer that wouldn't even be written for another 431 years, thundered at the black presence like a verbal spear.

“*Yoshev beseter elyovn betzel dai yitlovnan* (we are Yahweh’s chosen, *His* firstborn! We are the preferred who live in the covert place of Elyon and reside in the protective defense of the Almighty Shaddai. Tell your generations. Say this about your Yahweh, ‘El-Gibhor is my refuge, my Fortress, my Elohim. In Him is my security, my hope. It was in that dark night that Yahweh rescued me from the mouth of the destroyer and exempted me from its destructive plague’)…”

From the drill deck below, the terrified thousands watched the ramp in the ceiling disappear. It was swallowed by a blackness that absorbed all light around it and dulled the other torches in the entire Fortress. Then, in the center of the darkness, a pair of burning, hate-filled eyes glowered down at the thundering General. It opened its fire-ringed bottomless mouth, ready to vomit its earsplitting, hate-filled mocking laughter. That was when it heard Sha’al’s third-most-hated man of this age, the “marked one of Elohim,” continue to proclaim Yahweh’s words.

Suddenly, the terrifying face looked stunned, like the General’s verbal assault had wounded it. The black face quickly drew back into its own darkness like a frightened turtle into its shell. Immediately the surrounding blackness evaporated. The closed ramp reappeared, and the torchlight grew brighter.

Yet the screeching and rumbling resumed even louder. It didn’t cease until the Commanding General defiantly proclaimed Yahweh’s final words. “*…orech yamim asbi’ehu ve’ar’ehu bishu’ati* (…and your Yahweh Jireh will satisfy your hunger with a long length of days. You will see *His* Lamb, *your* Yeshua, and you…will live!).”

The rumbling instantly ceased, and the screaming howl faded into the distance. Then Yahweh’s soothing breeze blew around and threw everyone in the Fortress. It felt wonderful. In fact every infant and toddler began their high-pitched laughter. But everyone else silently stared in slacked-jawed awe at the victorious sha’dim fighter on the stage.

Kalev blinked hard, like he’d just awakened from a deep and wonderful night’s sleep. That was when he realized that he was pointing his swords at the closed ramp and the rumbling howl was gone.

Um, what are you doing? he quietly asked himself. As the warrior lowered his swords, the swirling breeze continued to sprinkle drops of lamb blood from the ramp seams above.

The General curiously watched a single drop of blood slowly dance on the breeze and then land on the flat of his blade. The drop ran in a thick, dark red line down to the hilt. Kalev swiped his finger across the line to wipe the blade clean. But the blood remained as if etched into the metal, except for the finger smear, which formed a perfect letter ✕ (T). Another curiously warm drop splatted on his forehead, and he swiped it away with the back of his hand. Not realizing he’d drawn the same letter right between his eyes. He sheathed his abba’s sword, but for some reason, he kept the Khopesh in his hand. Only then did it hit him he was standing at the front of the stage with his back to the troops. And the Fortress was completely silent.

Still not sure what had just happened, Kalev did what he'd always done in times of uncertainty. He sucked it up, forced his usual general scowl, and squared his shoulders. At the same time he did a perfect about-face, then opened his mouth to call the troops to attention. But a gust of wind blew down his throat, and the Warrior King's words rushed from his mouth. They supernaturally thundered off the cedar-planked walls and ceiling.

"People of Yahweh, kneel!" Then, 7000-plus overwhelmed people dropped to their knees and automatically put their foreheads to the deck. "Tonight, the night of nights. Remember where you are right now. Remember the blood of Yeshua's Lamb saved you from the destroyer. Let that memory burn into your soul. The Warrior King conquers the darkness every time. And by *His* sword our enemies fall. Army of Yahweh…you are that sword… What you've just seen and heard is only a foretaste of the mighty victories to come. Never forget when we kneel our lives before the Elohim, not even the worst of Sha'al can stand against us. Army of Yisrael, tonight we secretly knelt as captives. "But *now*, by the all-powerful hand of Yahweh and the always-protecting blood of His Lamb, we rise and leave this Egyptian Sha'al as proud, free men and women." Kalev smirked inwardly as he added his *own* summary of the Warrior King's words. "'Cause no one messes with our Yeshua!"

The ferocious-looking general cleared his throat. "Army of Yisrael…attention to orders." As four very full battalions got to their feet and reassembled, Kalev briefly smiled at Raisa and looked at the stage beside him. His stunning and very dangerous little wife, the boys, Evee, and Shomer raced up the stairs and proudly stood beside their sha'dim-vanquishing hero.

The Warrior King's chosen General subtly signaled the *shofar* squad leader. Fifty rams' horns sounded the order to draw swords. Kalev paused as the glittering brilliance of 7777 swords sparkled on the walls and ceiling like a moonless night's sky.

He raised both of his blood-speckled swords and boomed, "By the blood and the sword!" The Warrior King's very audible war cry melded with Kalev's. The ear-piercing combination was awe inspiring. The troops quickly joined in and the ground shook. The emotionally spent civilians cheered.

The usual thunderous chants and cheering were a needed release. But the usual company chants morphed into words that made Kalev cringe. "By the blood of the Lamb and the sha'dim-conquering swords of our General, we…are…free! By the blood of the Lamb and the sha'dim-conquering swords of our General, we…are…free…"

Kalev noticed the weary but smiling ex-Egyptian general descend the closest ladder. Moshe dropped the last eight feet like someone sixty years younger. Yahweh's faithful prophet hit the deck, rolled once, and then leaped onto the stage. He stood there wordlessly grinning. And with a single wink, Kalev sheathed his swords and signaled for the ramp to open. The chanting and cheering abruptly ceased, and fear-filled, wary silence returned.

Before the ramp boomed onto the deck for the very last time, Kalev whispered to Raisa, then turned and leaped off the stage. He splashed through the ankle-deep pool of lamb blood that ran the entire width of the open portal. Days later, Moshe would add a line to Yadin's record, "No one in Yahweh's Army could leave Egypt behind except through the blood of Yeshua's Lamb."

In the days to come, Colonel Marasha would use six sheets of parchment to describe the terrible and victorious night. "By the blood of the Lamb and the sha'dim-conquering swords of our General, we were freed to leave!"

Thousands watched the General splash through the "river of blood" vault over the descending edge of the ramp and race up the incline. At the top of the ramp, Kalev unintentionally spun twice as he drew his swords. He stopped and glared down at the brightly lit bunker. With a giant moon at his back, the General's shadow cut loose with his loudest war cry yet. Many of the civilians and children shrieked in fear. But no one else spoke or moved a muscle.

The General forgot that even with the brilliant moonlight blood looked black at night. And he was soaked in it. Only his eyes reflected back the bright torchlight from below.

Moshe stared up at Kalev and then started laughing. He knew what the others were thinking—he'd faced the sha'dim at his campsite. And from below Kalev looked like a miniature version of the destroyer. Moshe nodded at the slack-jawed generals at the bottom of the stage, then raced up the ramp. And still, no one moved.

After Moshe told Kalev what he looked like from below, they both started laughing. It was exactly midnight when the General roared down to his troops. "If this army is not moving in the next five seconds, you're staying here! Now move your 𓆛𓆛𓆛♉!" The troops' training kicked in, and the usual controlled chaos ensued.

Thirty minutes later, the exhausted Kalev and Moshe sat atop their nervous horses enjoying the abnormally fresh air. Both generals, old and new, appreciated the expertly choreographed staging below. Then 2010 ox-drawn wagons descended the ramp in perfectly spaced ranks of twelve.

After a while, Moshe looked at Kalev and smirked. "So let me see if I heard this right. The Lamb's blood only slowed the destroyer's assault, but *you're* the defiant one who scared it off." Kalev grimaced and shook his head. "Not my idea, and just between you and me…I never even saw the thing." Then both laughing men heard the Warrior King's comforting chuckle. "But the other version *will* make for a fantastic campfire story. Or rather thousands of campfire stories in the decades to come."

Kalev didn't see the deep lines on Moshe's face bunch into a fleeting grimace as he despairingly shook his head once. "Not now!" the eighty-one-year-old prophet silently mouthed.

Once Moshe, Kalev, and Ari followed the last rank of wagons across the deeply rutted sand bar. The other four teens and Hoshe'a brought up the rear. The teens kept up a running joke at Hoshe'a's expense.

"So, General Ari, when Colonel Carni is promoted, will General Hoshe'a be promoted too?" Kalev wanted to reply, but Ari spoke up. "The General and I are still discussing it, but unless he gets married soon…well, let's just say he'd better start practicing his 'yes, mam,' 'no, mams.'" The others howled as Hoshe'a became more agitated. Moshe looked surprised. "You'd promote your ema over your brother?"

Kalev winked, then ignored the entertaining pleas from the rank behind them. "General Moshe. Do you think the Warrior King would mind if we broke out some beer? And maybe just a little very good *regular* wine for us generals?" Moshe flashed a tired grin. "I could use *a lot* of that very good regular wine right now."

Four months prior, Yadin, or "General Brew Master," as his secret "brew squad" named him, had discovered a way to make wine out of corn. Or rather a partially clear watery something they could drink. It was made from water, freshly picked then smashed corn and yeast. The first trial run had cost him both eyelashes, both eyebrows, and the front half of his curly tresses.

At the end of one of the more *eternal* command and staff meetings, the proud kid presented Kalev with a small cup of the fairly clear liquid. The General politely smiled and raised the cup to his lips. But before Yadin could yell, "Take a breath first," the son of Hezron had downed the cup in a gulp. Kalev's reaction would be repeated to Captain Marasha by all five other generals. It'd taken the sweating, bug-eyed general five minutes to stop coughing and cursing. By the time he was done, there wasn't a dry eye in the room. Needless to say, the 305 forty-gallon urns were banished to the Outpost, and no one was to open them by order of General Kalev. But in the process of making the vile drink, Yadin inadvertently discovered a very dangerous weapon. But now, they were leaving all that behind, as far as the General knew. Kalev had left the destruction of the Fortress and the Pit up to Yadin. The teen general just smiled and said he'd think of something.

The little band of generals were clear of the river and headed toward the Pit; the General caught Yadin's attention and raised an eyebrow. The teen general nodded. "I took care of it, Sir. In twenty minutes the Fortress will be…" Yadin was cut off by the loudest ground-shaking boom and whoosh sound any of them had ever heard. This was immediately followed by the Outpost's above-ground explosions, which were even louder. The bright, white explosion temporarily blinded them. Once they got their rearing horses under control and their eyes adjusted, they all stared across the river. The army's first home and the remainder of the dead palm grove was completely erased. The only evidence anything had ever been there was the charred and glowing palm fronds and ash that fell from the sky like rain.

Moshe stared at Kalev quizzically. The General opened his mouth to reply, but the Warrior King's audible voice stepped in. "Ugh, firewater…*always* leave home without it!"

68

The Commanding General was the last one to inspect the Pit. Twelve campfires lined both of the drill decks walls, but they were over two hundred yards away. So the TOC end of the Pit was eerily dark and quiet. Kalev was just mounting Boaz when he remembered Yadin's *mistimed* explosion on the other side of the river.

The General kicked Boaz's flanks hard and gave him his head. Halfway to the ramp, Kalev realized that each growing fire was closely ringed by ten five-foot tall, forty-gallon urns. Only these urns looked sealed and glistened like they'd been dipped in gold.

Boaz leaped over the bank and landed in the dry creek bed fifty yards from the Pit's ramp. Suddenly, a violent whooshing boom seemed to suck the air out of Kalev's lungs. The full moon instantly disappeared behind the thick red dust cloud. The gagging General had to hold onto the saddle horn and practically fall forward when the stallion leaped straight up and screamed. It wasn't until he'd calmed the horse that Kalev heard what sounded like a raging river. He crawled up the bank and hesitantly peered over the edge. It took another fifteen minutes for the man-made haboob over the Pit to settle. By then the other generals were standing on the bank beside him. Kalev scowled at Yadin. The cowed teen refused to look at his General. Kalev coughed a few more times before he could rasp. "General Yadin, killing me would probably make Colonel-general Carni really angry. And she knows where you sleep." Kalev glanced at Hoshe'a, who was silently staring at what used to be the home of the lethal Heh Battalion. Kalev wiped the dust out of his eyes and followed Hoshe'a's stare. The dust was blowing away, revealing a glistening black lake or, rather, a massive inlet from the river. The stunned Hoshe'a looked at his brother. "Sometimes I amaze myself. Do you realize what we would have done with that stuff as kids?" Kalev grinned. "Yeah, you would have tricked me into drinking it first. Then two drunk kids would have blown up ema's house, and she would have killed you." Hoshe'a nodded. "Or we could have sold it to the Egyptian Army and made a fortune. We could have left thirty years ago." Moshe suddenly materialized next to Kalev. "Yeah, but look at all the fun you would've missed."

No matter the age of a man, some things never change. It started out as the generals giving their nervous horses a chance to run out their tension. But boys will be boys, and the casual horse's exercise period quickly morphed into a heated two-mile race east over the uneven ground.

The victorious Kalev reined in the frothing Boaz and leaped out of the saddle. He'd just begun leading the horse when the others showed up. Kalev looked completely surprised to see them. "Nice night for a peaceful stroll, don't you think?" The grumbling losers rode ahead.

About a mile from the rendezvous point, Little Croc finally caught up to his walking General. His horse and Boaz looked like identical twins in the moonlight. Kalev smirked; he didn't know how that small boy stayed in that silver-studded, man-sized saddle.

"Sir, we're silent and deadly, but we can't keep up with Boaz the Lightening Horse." Kalev raised an eyebrow at the boy. "Boaz the lightening horse?" Little Croc nodded. "Frog named him that 'cause he's faster than lightening; mine's called Thunder 'cause his farts sound like thunder, so he's slower, but he's louder…" "We?" Kalev looked around. "Where's Little Frog?" Croc turned in his saddle and pointed west. "He's on that stupid camel he won shooting targets but I should have won but he split my arrow and it fell out of the target but I hate camels anyways 'cause they bite and stink and are slow and stupid Frog said he trained it to fight and bite me but I never seen it fight I think he's lying so Mrs. General should tell him to stop lying and ride a horse." Kalev was constantly amazed at how children could say so much in a single breath. Still, he always enjoyed the entertainment.

Eventually, a very large loping camel was reined in beside the General. A tall, enclosed canopy sat askew on the single hump. The gleaming strands of gold interlaced the tightly twisted rope/reins. They disappeared into the canopy's shiny sheer curtains. A swearing Little Frog threw the curtains aside. His too-large, brass Phoenician war helmet fell off when the boy leaned forward and awkwardly cartwheeled to the ground. The gold embroidered robe fluttered down over his prone and puking head. But Little Croc couldn't help himself.

"I told you camels were stupid I never get horse sick like you get camel sick and you shouldn't have drunk so much of General Yadin's viper wine you're not supposed to drink anyway 'cause you don't know how to drink viper wine like me. You should've gave your stupid camel the stinky wine then he'd run in circles and it would be funny but you'd probably puke your guts out too but that would be funny too but it would probably be worse too so get a horse Frog!" Kalev knew he shouldn't laugh. Because this one had just confessed to getting into Yadin's vile viper wine. But between the "camel sick" kid and his chiding friend…

After a while, the grinning General wiped his tear-stained cheeks, knelt, and gave the dry-heaving boy his waterskin. The blurry-eyed Little Frog sat up and sipped some water. Kalev watched the boy take a deep breath, draw, and point his evil-looking sixteen-inch feather knife at Croc. The General knew he should stop this before it escalated, but…

"It wasn't the viper wine…" yelled Little Frog. "…It was the secret corn water that burns my nose and my camel isn't stupid 'cause I know you wanted him but I'm a better archeryer than you are Croc but General I think I need a horse 'cause Boaz the Lightening Horse is too fast and my very smart camel is too slow so Mrs. General can ride in the camel house if she wants to but I'll ask her later but she has to be careful 'cause I trained Ramses to fight and bite Croc but she can let him bite Croc because he's smarter than that stinky Thunder who stinks so you should stop feeding him sweetbread and beer like

Colonel Carni said so shut up Croc your horse is stupid." Croc drew his sword. "He's not stupid you're stupid and camels can't fight but horses…" Kalev choked down a laugh, shook his head, and stood. "Mount up, troops!"

The boys immediately forgot about killing each other. Little Frog found his helmet in a pile of fresh camel dung, and to Kalev's surprise, the oblivious boy put it back on his head. Little Frog reached up, grabbed the camel's bridle, and yanked the long face down to his eye level. The little guy actually yelled at the large snout in Phoenician. After receiving a punch in the nose for trying to bite Frog's face, the camel lowered to its knees. "He can bite, but he can't fight," chided Croc.

Little Frog vaulted into the canopy, and the camel stood. The camel walked to the side of the mounted Croc. Kalev adjusted his tired and sore backside in the saddle. Then, just before he turned Boaz toward the camp, he saw a long and too-heavy, jewel-encrusted scimitar thrust out of the canopy curtain and swing down toward Croc. "This is his sword so he can fight can your stupid horse…?"

But instead of intimidating his friend, Frog accidentally nicked the back of the camel's ear. The beast spit and loudly bellowed. It bent its neck around to bite its rider. But Frog's canopy was too high for the camel to reach, so it did the next best thing. It angrily reared up on two legs to throw the whole annoying thing off its back. When that didn't work, it took off at a loping run.

Little Frog screamed in Phoenician, Egyptian, and Hebrew at the uncontrollable beast. All the while, his opulent shelter rocked wildly from side to side. As the screaming canopy swung to each side, its long tassels would drag in the dirt. The royal ropes almost tripped the animal twice, which, in turn, made it canter even faster. Little Croc smirked. "That's not silent, and camels are stupid!" Kalev groaned, "Go get your bother before he ends up in Nubia."

69

Half-asleep General crested the final low hill and peered down at his brightly lit tent and campfire. "Home," the General sighed. Kalev slept for the next twenty-four hours. Kalev awoke an hour before sunrise on the fifteenth day of the first month. Raisa was already up. Kalev followed the less-than-mouth-watering scent of the baked *unleavened* bread. He pulled the tent flap aside and saw Raisa, Carni, and Deborah busily preparing the morning meal. Deborah looked up from their camp oven, and her mouth fell open; then she put her hand over her mouth to cover her stunned smile. Ari's new wife quickly jabbed Carni with her elbow. The General's ema did the same to Raisa before she went back to work. Raisa stood, turned around, and proudly smiled. "My darling General Kalev, you forgot your other swords again." It took the half-awake, hard-muscled man a couple of seconds too long before he looked down. The tent flap was thrown shut as *seven* women laughed and whispered.

Kalev spent that entire day seated on his usual, very out-of-place throne. AARs, status reports, twice daily inventory summaries, lists of wagon placement changes, northern scouting and clearing reports, and on and on… By the time the stars came out, Kalev's backside was sore, and his head felt ready to explode. Raisa had just started warming their frying pan over the fire. An eighteen-inch stack of thick beef steaks sat on a large gold plate near the edge of the low table beside the fire. Kalev's mouth watered.

Still embarrassed at the memory, Kalev apologized for the ninth time that day. "Raisa, I really am sorry about my early morning, um, show." Raisa wordlessly stood and uselessly wiped her hands on her apron. The little assassin straddled his lap and took Kalev's cheeks in her hands. Her smile still took his breath away. "Oh, Kalev, my stud, I am so proud to be your wife." Then she kissed him hard and headed into the tent. The confused General stood there for a full minute. But his overworked brain couldn't figure out whether she'd accepted his apology or not. Finally, the big man shrugged then started up the hill next to their tent.

At the top, he walked up beside Moshe. The sight of a couple thousand campfires spread across the desert below them was dazzling. The boys and the teen generals materialized beside the two men. Yet no one spoke for a while. The giant moon, the canopy of shimmering stars, and the tiny twinkling orange fires made up a mosaic none of them would ever forget. In unison they all silently sat and just watched.

But, as usual, it wasn't long before the always calculating Yadin interrupted the peaceful scene. "At sunset, we counted 200031 civilian men. I estimate only 10 percent of them and/or their families look healthy enough to travel north. And only a few…" But Ofek and Ari shooshed him silent again. Soon the amazing smell of fried beef steaks and garlic wafted up the hill. The boys were the first to evaporate, and then the four generals nodded to Kalev and raced each other down the backside of the hill. But Kalev relished the soft, peaceful breeze and the view. At one point, Kalev heard something and turned to see Moshe's lips silently moving. The scowl on his face answered Kalev's suspicion. Then General smiled at his haggard-looking friend. "So He still won't let you play Yahweh for a day?"

Moshe blinked away the silent, one-sided argument and shook his head. "He can have the job. And I wish He'd tell you, um, the people Himself…arghh." Kalev was puzzled by the expression on the prophet's face. He sounded frustrated, but his eyes conveyed a sense of guilt and regret. The General didn't ask, and Moshe changed the subject. "My sister is a great cook, but even *she* can't make unleavened bread tasteful." Kalev nodded. "I told Raisa she only needed to make enough for the others. But what's your opinion of garlic beef steak—oh and aged wine?" Moshe leaped to his feet. "What took you so long to ask!" Both men laughed, then vaulted over the backside of the hill.

For Kalev, the accuracy of his internal hourglass was a given. He'd simply choose when to wake, and it just happened. The night before their third morning in the desert, Kalev had decided to get up an hour and a half before daybreak. He wanted to tour the army's line of encampments before sunup. That was why he awoke so confused. According to the bright glow of light under the tent walls, the sun was already up, and it had risen in the south. Plus, there weren't the usual sounds of troops eating and laughing before their workday began. Except for Raisa's light snoring, it was eerily silent.

The General carefully got out of bed to allow his stunning little wife a few more minutes of sleep. This time he remembered to dress before leaving the tent. When he opened the tent flap, he was temporarily blinded. A brilliant white light blazed from the other side of the hill.

Kalev rubbed his eyes and rapidly blinked a few times. He could barely make out the familiar shadow of the single back-lit man sitting at the top of the hill. The General wearily climbed the hill and froze.

The brilliant vertical column of undulating fire was at least a hundred yards tall and ten yards wide and stood less than fifteen yards away. It gave off a subtle warmth that belied its size and intensity. Plus, the surprisingly silent flames seemed to be cloud-wrapped. Kalev looked up and couldn't figure out why the smoke didn't rise straight up and blow away on the breeze. The smokey clouds would rise to the top of the fire column, then roll outward horizontally in all directions. A bright yet soft orange glow reflected off the bottom of the clouds. The huge moon and expanse of stars were still visible in the night sky, just beyond the cloud cover. And by the position of the moon, Kalev figured it was only three in the morning. He wordlessly sat next to Moshe and stared, mesmerized.

Suddenly, the familiar warm breeze of the Warrior King's life-giving breath inflated his lungs. Kalev closed his eyes and gulped the air like it was the first time he'd ever taken a breath. The thrill caused hot tears to stream down his cheeks. "Thank You, Yahweh. I, um…" But before he could finish his sentence, he felt the Warrior King gently lift his hands into the air, and Kalev greedily sucked in another exhilarating breath.

The words that began to surge from his throat seemed to originate from his core and bypass his logical mind. He didn't even try to understand the strange-sounding language. But the son of Hezron instinctively knew the words were a kind of personal worship. A secret communication between him and the Warrior King. Every time he allowed Yahweh to fill his lungs, the words flowed out as he exhaled. Kalev stood there breathing in and praying out for over an hour.

Eventually, he dropped his arms, opened his eyes, and dried his tear-stained cheeks. Kalev self-consciously glanced at Moshe. The man's face glowed, and his hands were raised. Moshe looked half his age. No sound passed his rapidly moving lips. Out of respect, Kalev quickly looked away to give Yahweh's chosen leader some privacy. He was very content to sit there and enjoy the comfortable exhilaration of the Warrior King's presence. In fact, the ever-changing column of white-hot-looking fire seemed to exude that same life-giving breath.

Moshe's whisper startled Kalev when it broke the stillness, "I was up here, um, *discussing* the direction of our march, um, south." Moshe instinctively cringed. Then he saw that Kalev was so enjoying the Warrior King's breeze that he missed that last statement. Yahweh's reluctant mouthpiece shrugged and mouthed the words, "You tell him." Yahweh's chuckle spoke volumes. It also infuriated the old general. Kalev smiled. "I'm sorry. What did you say?"

Moshe shook his head. "I said I was up here enjoying the view and arguing with you-know-who when that thing fell out of the sky. I always expected Him to lead *His* people into His promised land. I just didn't think it would be with so much flare." Kalev smirked at the pun. "Nice one." Moshe chuckled. "Did you notice it's not even touching the ground?"

That was when Kalev saw the boys standing directly beneath the pillar of fire. The base of the fire was barely two feet above their heads. Kalev leaped to his feet, but before he could yell, Moshe stood and grabbed his arm. "Wait, it's not like the fire we use. It's not hot, and apparently it hasn't consumed them yet." Both boys craned their necks to look straight up. It was so quiet that Kalev and Moshe could hear the boys' conversation.

"It looks hot like an oven. Do you think it would burn my hand if I touched it?" Frog started to raise his arm, but Croc stopped him. "Don't you'll probably burn your arm off and then you can't eat or ride your stupid camel or shoot arrows anymore then Mrs. General will be mad then sad that you don't have two arms and you'll have to pick up cow ΨȣϦȣΨ↓ forever till you get old like General Moshe and die and stink like cow ΨȣϦȣΨ↓ I'm bigger so let me teach you the smart way to not burn your arm off."

Before Kalev could yell, "Stop!" Croc bent down, picked up a gnarled stick, and threw it straight up into the fire. Both Kalev and Moshe cringed. The General moved to race down the hill but froze when the Warrior King's voice roared and rippled through the entire hundred-yard-high column. "Oww, that hurt!"

Kalev and Moshe looked at each other wide-eyed, then started laughing. For a few seconds, nothing happened. Then the same stick dropped out of the fire column and hit Croc on the head. "Oww, that's not funny." As the older boy complained and rubbed his head, Little Frog, Kalev, Moshe, and even Yahweh howled with laughter. Kalev loved Yahweh's sense of humor; it reminded him of his own.

The two men watched the two boys throw the stick up and then try to dodge it when it decided to drop. After a while the snickering General glanced at Moshe. Tears streamed down the man's face. But they definitely *weren't* from laughing. Kalev had seen that same oddly apologetic expression on Moshe's face before. The General didn't ask, but Moshe knew he'd run out of excuses. The prophet relented.

"Kalev, my son, I'm so sorry. Please forgive me; I should have told you before now. Trust me—this wasn't my idea, but…"

The Warrior King boomed in Kalev's gut. "Son of Hezron, sit still and take a deep breath." That too-familiar warning caused Kalev's mind to panic. Nothing good ever followed that kind of caveat. After everything that'd happened this last year, good and horrible, they were finally free to head north and build a life. One without fear of being discovered and/or hunted. One outside of this cursed and oppressive Sha'al called Egypt. That was the life he'd survived to live with his beautiful Raisa. That life was only a couple of weeks northeast of there.

So just when his new life was about to begin, the Warrior King used that "you're *really* not going to like this" tone of voice and told him to take a deep breath. His tired mind went into overload mode, and he started to sweat in the cool air. He could feel his heart racing as it loudly throbbed in his ears. Kalev watched Moshe's lips move, but he only caught small snippets between each head-pounding heartbeat.

"Egyptian army…Philistines…can't go north…people will run…Yahweh said…follow…cloud…southeast…Etham…Egyptian Army…will corner us at…we can't fight them…so sorry…told you before…" Moshe pointed a trembling finger south. Kalev sat there very confused. He took another ragged breath and repeated in his mind the few words he understood. Then repeated them again.

Interrupting another of his friend's apologies, the Commanding General of Yahweh's Army exploded. His panic turned into the fierce rage of a mother bear protecting her cubs. "WAIT! NO! We're headed WHERE!"

ENDNOTES

1 Matthew 11

2 Exodus 12:2–10

3 Exodus 12:11

4 Exodus 12:14–20

Milton Keynes UK
Ingram Content Group UK Ltd.
UKHW010842290724
446181UK00011B/403

9 798890 410238